OBSERVER'S
HANDBOOK
2002

EDITOR
RAJIV GUPTA

NINETY-FOURTH YEAR OF PUBLICATION

© THE ROYAL ASTRONOMICAL SOCIETY OF CANADA
136 DUPONT STREET, TORONTO, ONTARIO M5R 1V2
2001

ISSN 0080-4193
ISBN 0-9689141-0-1

PRINTED IN CANADA
BY THE UNIVERSITY OF TORONTO PRESS

CANADIAN PUBLICATIONS MAIL REGISTRATION NO. 09818
CANADA POST PUBLICATION AGREEMENT NO. 40069313
U.S. PERIODICALS REGISTRATION NO. 010-751

CONTENTS

Key to Marginal Chapter Symbols

Basic Data

Time

Optics and Observing

The Sky Month by Month

The Sun

The Moon

Planets and Satellites

Asteroids

Meteors, Comets, and Dust

Stars

Nebulae and Galaxies

THE OBSERVER'S HANDBOOK

The *Observer's Handbook* is one of Canada's oldest scientific publications. Created by C.A. Chant, Professor of Astronomy at the University of Toronto, it first appeared nearly a century ago as *The Canadian Astronomical Handbook for 1907*, a small (13 × 17 cm), 108-page publication. A second edition covered the year 1908, but for the following two years most of the information that would have appeared was published instead in installments in the *Journal of the RASC*. The Council of the Society decided to return to a separate publication for 1911 with a new name—the *Observer's Handbook*—and it has been published annually ever since.

Each year some 12 000 copies of the Handbook are distributed to many countries throughout the world, to amateur and professional astronomers, to educators at school and university levels, and to many observatories, planetaria, and libraries. The Handbook is the main source of income for The Royal Astronomical Society of Canada. Since the first edition in 1907, the various editors, assistant editors, editorial assistants (see p. 7), and contributors (see the inside front cover) have voluntarily contributed their time and expertise to produce this unique book.

EDITORS OF THE OBSERVER'S HANDBOOK

		Position	Editions	President RASC
C.A. Chant	(1865–1956)	Editor	1907–1957	1903–1907
Frank Hogg	(1904–1951)	Assistant Editor	1939–1951	1940–1942
Ruth Northcott	(1913–1969)	Assistant Editor	1952–1957	1962–1964
		Editor	1958–1970	
John Percy	(1941–	Editor	1971–1981	1978–1980
Roy Bishop	(1939–	Editor	1982–2000	1984–1986
Rajiv Gupta	(1958–	Editor	2001–	

The *Observer's Handbook* is intended to be "a companion which the observer would wish always to have in his pocket or on the table before him."

C.A. Chant, Toronto, 1906

"We believe that the *Observer's Handbook* is a truly significant contribution that Canadian astronomy in general and our Society in particular has been making to the dissemination of astronomical knowledge for half a century. I trust that it will still occupy the same position of respect after the first hundred years."

Ruth Northcott, Ottawa, 1964

"The more one knows, the more one can benefit from the Handbook. It inspires all who leaf through its pages to learn and question what the tables, graphs and data mean, perhaps to speculate on the mysteries of the Universe, and above all, to get out and look beyond our world. You have in your hands a key to the Universe—a key which will fit many doors. Please use it well and treasure it."

Peter Broughton, Toronto, 1992
Author of *Looking Up, A History of the RASC*

"The *Observer's Handbook* is the single most useful publication for the observational astronomer. Its combination of authoritative data, informative diagrams, and concise text is unique. Anyone interested in astronomy, beginner or expert, amateur or professional, student or teacher, will find the *Observer's Handbook* indispensable. Its international reputation for quality is a credit both to its many contributors and to Canadian astronomy."

Roy Bishop, Halifax, 2000

HOW TO USE THIS HANDBOOK

This Handbook is a concise, high-density compilation of information that is of interest to observers. By reading the following points, you will allow yourself to reap maximum benefit from it.

(1) The Handbook is composed of various *sections*. Related sections are grouped into chapters, as listed in the CONTENTS. Chapter titles are given in large dark-grey boxes and section titles against light background shades, both of which extend to the edge of the page. The section title and chapter title are given in headers at the top of the pages. In addition, staggered marginal symbols (see p. iii for a key) mark the right-hand edges of the pages in each chapter. These various identifiers are meant to facilitate the quick location of desired material.

(2) References to other sections are given in SMALL CAPITAL TYPE, and this type is generally reserved for this purpose. Internet email addresses and websites are also given in a **distinctive font**.

(3) The INDEX at the back contains a short listing of keywords.

(4) Long tables are broken into blocks, usually with the shading of blocks of rows, to make the location of entries easier. Every table has a shaded header with the titles of the various columns given in bold type. Detailed explanation of the meaning of the columns is usually given in accompanying text.

(5) SI symbols and abbreviations are used throughout. See pp. 28 and 31 in the section SOME ASTRONOMICAL AND PHYSICAL DATA for the most common abbreviations. The letter "m" is used to denote both minutes of right ascension and metres; the meaning will be clear from the context. Minutes of time are usually abbreviated "min."

(6) The time scale Universal Time is generally used. Times of day are usually given in the 24-hour clock, using numerals separated by colons. The section TIME AND TIME SCALES on pp. 34–38 explains the various time scales used in astronomy.

(7) The section TERMINOLOGY AND SYMBOLS on p. 19 lists Greek letters (and other symbols) and defines some basic terms.

(8) The section TEACHING AND THE OBSERVER'S HANDBOOK on pp. 16–18 gives an overview of the contents of this Handbook.

(9) The website of the Handbook is **www.rasc.ca/handbook**. Resources related to the Handbook are given at this site, and any updates and corrections will also be posted there.

Cover photo

Most wide-angle images of our galaxy feature the galactic centre in Sagittarius and Scorpius or the rich star fields of Cygnus. This deep, 65°-high-image of the fainter Winter Milky Way captures a wide array of nebulae including the bright Orion Nebula (M42), the Rosette Nebula (NGC 2237 in Monoceros, just below and to the left of centre), and the expansive but visually elusive Barnard's Loop (Sh 2-276 in eastern Orion). Also captured in the bottom half of the photo are 4 of the 10 brightest stars in the sky: Sirius, Rigel, Betelgeuse, and Procyon.

The photo was taken by Alan Dyer using a 28-mm camera lens, a 15-minute exposure on Ektachrome 200 slide film with the lens at f/3.5. For information on the many deep-sky objects depicted in the photo, see Dyer's articles on pp. 258–266 in this Handbook.

EDITOR'S COMMENTS

Work on this edition of the *Observer's Handbook* was made especially enjoyable by the creation of a formal editorial team, the composition of which is listed at the right. Members of this team exchanged close to 400 Word files, sometimes as many as 15 revisions per article. We had several lively discussions on many fine points of grammar and style, but each of us derived great satisfaction and pleasure from our extensive interaction.

I welcome the following new contributors: Kerriann H. Malatesta, Paul Markov, Peter Jedicke, and Toomas Karmo. The following additions appear in this edition:

(1) Marginal symbol guides have been reinserted.

(2) The listing of websites in the previous edition has been expanded to include sites not mentioned specifically in another section.

(3) Mean orbital elements have been replaced by more accurate osculating elements for the year, with some accompanying explanatory text, and elements for the largest 30 asteroids have been added.

(4) The FILTERS section has been revised and now includes an illustrative diagram.

(5) The former Sky Transparency section has been retitled LIMITING MAGNITUDES and now treats both limiting visual and telescopic magnitudes.

(6) The FREQUENCY OF CLEAR NIGHT SKIES section now has two maps.

(7) A new section, THE OBSERVING LOGBOOK, has been added.

(8) The PLANETS FOR 2002 section now includes a table of daily central meridians for Jupiter.

(9) The STAR CLUSTERS section now has two authors and an expanded table of globular clusters.

Many of these enhancements would not have occurred without the urging of the Handbook users listed at the right. Suggestions for further improvement are, as always, welcome.

Dr. Rajiv Gupta
Department of Mathematics
University of British Columbia
Vancouver BC V6T 1Z2, Canada
gupta@interchange.ubc.ca

Vancouver, 2001 Aug. 19

THE OBSERVER'S HANDBOOK

EDITOR
Rajiv Gupta
COPY EDITOR
Betty Robinson
PROOFREADER
James Edgar

In addition to the 39 contributors listed on the inside front cover, several other individuals and organizations played a role in the production of this Handbook.

Much of the data contained in this Handbook comes from the publications *Astronomical Phenomena for the Year 2002* and *The Astronomical Almanac 2002*, both prepared jointly by the U.S. Naval Observatory's Nautical Almanac Office and Her Majesty's Nautical Almanac Office. Also, the Institut de Mécanique Céleste et de Calcul des Ephémérides in Paris provided ephemerides for Jupiter's Galilean satellites.

The following individuals provided suggestions that led to major enhancements in this edition: Marc Bernstein (orbital elements for asteroids), Geoff Gaherty (daily central meridians for Jupiter), Andrew Livingston (limiting telescopic magnitudes diagram), Paul Markov (expanded article on filters), and Douglas Pitcairn (explanation of orbital elements).

In addition, corrections and suggestions for improvement were received from Roy Bishop, Randall Brooks, James Edgar, Dave Hare, Lee Johnson, Dave Lane, Richard Langley, Brian Marsden, Robert Richards, Jeremy Tatum, Bruce Thompson, Mary Lou Whitehorne, and Alan Whitman.

AN INVITATION FOR MEMBERSHIP IN
THE ROYAL ASTRONOMICAL SOCIETY OF CANADA

The beginnings of the Royal Astronomical Society of Canada go back to the middle of the 19th century. The Society was incorporated within the province of Ontario in 1890, received its Royal Charter from King Edward VII in 1903, and was federally incorporated in 1968. The National Office of the Society (containing the business office and library) is located at 136 Dupont Street, Toronto ON M5R 1V2; telephone: (416) 924-7973 or (888) 924-7272 from within Canada; email: rasc@rasc.ca; website: www.rasc.ca.

The RASC consists of two employees, Executive Secretary Bonnie Bird and Membership and Publications Coordinator Isaac McGillis, plus more than 4500 members. RASC members are from many countries and from all walks of life. Members receive the *Observer's Handbook* (published in September for the next calendar year) and the bimonthly *Journal of the RASC*, which contains review articles, research papers on historical and contemporary topics, education notes, general notes of astronomical interest, book reviews, news items concerning the Society and its Centres, informal articles, and letters. Also included in a membership is Canada's popular bimonthly astronomy magazine *SkyNews*.

Membership fees are $44 per year, or $27.50 for persons under 21 years of age. Life membership is $880. (To cover higher mailing costs, these figures are to be read as U.S. dollars for members outside of Canada.) An applicant may affiliate with one of the Centres of the Society across Canada or join the Society directly as an unattached member (some Centres levy a surcharge above the regular membership fee).

Mailing addresses, telephone numbers, and email addresses of the 26 RASC Centres, listed in the order that the stars rise, are given below. Each Centre's website may be accessed by appending the Centre's name, with punctuation marks and spaces omitted, to the base URL www.rasc.ca—for example, www.rasc.ca/stjohns—or by clicking a link at this base URL (for the Centre Francophone de Montréal, append montrealf).

St. John's: c/o 206 Frecker Drive, St John's NF A1E 5H9; (709) 364-4953; randy@morgan.ucs.mun.ca

Charlottetown: 38 Mt Edward Road, Charlottetown PE C1A 5S2; (902) 894-9613; cperryphoto@pei.sympatico.ca

Halifax: P.O. Box 31011, Halifax NS B3K 5T9; (902) 420-5633; halifax@rasc.ca

Moncton: c/o Dr. Francis LeBlanc, Département de physique et d'astronomie, Université de Moncton, Moncton NB E1A 3E9; (506) 858-3781; leblanfn@umoncton.ca

Québec: 2000 boul. Montmorency, Québec QC G1J 5E7; (418) 661-3098; srac_quebec@hotmail.com

Montréal: (Centre Francophone) C.P. 206, Station St-Michel, Montréal QC H2A 3L9; (514) 728-4422; sam@cam.org

Montreal: P.O. Box 1752, Station B, Montreal QC H3B 3L3; (514) 845-2612; rascmtl@altavista.net

Ottawa: P.O. Box 33012, 1974 Baseline Rd., Nepean ON K2C 0E0; (613) 830-3381; contact@ottawa.rasc.ca

Kingston: P.O. Box 1793, Kingston ON K7L 5J6; (613) 353-7910; rascexec@cliff.path.queensu.ca

Niagara: P.O. Box 4040, St. Catharines ON L2R 7S3; (905) 935-9355; rascniag@vaxxine.com

Toronto: c/o Ontario Science Centre, 770 Don Mills Road, Don Mills ON M3C 1T3; (416) 724-7827; nason@tvo.org

Hamilton: P.O. Box 1223, Waterdown ON L0R 2H0; (905) 689-0266; mark.kaye@sympatico.ca

Kitchener-Waterloo: c/o Peter Daniel, 36 Talbot Street, Apt 101, Kitchener ON N2M 2A9; (519) 579-1651; burns@mjburns.net

London: P.O. Box 842, Station B, London ON N6A 4Z3; (519) 474-5899; pjedicke@fanshawec.on.ca

Sarnia: c/o Jim Selinger, 160 George St., Sarnia ON N7T 7V4; (519) 337-6815; jselinge@mnsi.net

Windsor: c/o Frank J. Shepley, 671 Inman Sideroad, RR #2, Ruthven ON N0P 2G0; (519) 839-5934; fshepley@wincom.net

Thunder Bay: 286 Trinity Crescent, Thunder Bay ON P7C 5V6; (807) 475-3406; bronsont@air.on.ca

Winnipeg: P.O. Box 2694, Winnipeg MB R3C 4B3; (204) 988-0627; Scott_Young@ManitobaMuseum.MB.ca

Regina: P.O. Box 20014, Cornwall Centre, Regina SK S4P 4J7; (306) 751-0128; info@ras.sk.ca

Saskatoon: P.O. Box 317, RPO University, Saskatoon SK S7N 4J8; (306) 249-1091; dickson@sk.sympatico.ca

Edmonton: c/o Edmonton Space & Sciences Centre, 11211-142 St., Edmonton AB T5M 4A1; president@edmontonrasc.com

Calgary: c/o Calgary Science Centre, P.O. Box 2100, Station M, Loc.#73, Calgary AB T2P 2M5; (403) 255-3811; dechesne@telusplanet.net

Okanagan: P.O. Box 20119 TCM, Kelowna BC V1Y 9H2; (250) 861-3074; guy.m@home.com

Prince George: c/o Bob Nelson, College of New Caledonia, 3330-22nd Ave., Prince George BC V2N 1P8; (250) 563-6928; bnelson@netbistro.com

Vancouver: c/o Gordon Southam Observatory, 1100 Chestnut St., Vancouver BC V6J 3J9; (604) 437-3103; cbrecken@home.com

Victoria: 764 Mapleton Place, Victoria BC V8Z 6W2; (250) 479-5187; David_Lee@telus.net

REPORTING OF ASTRONOMICAL DISCOVERIES

To report a possible significant discovery (e.g. a new comet, nova, or supernova), a message should be sent to the International Astronomical Union's Central Bureau for Astronomical Telegrams. Send electronic mail to **cbat@cfa.harvard.edu**. Messages are monitored at all times. If this preferred method of communication is unavailable, a telephone call may be made to (617) 495-7244 or -7440 or -7444, but telephone calls are discouraged and these numbers will not be answered at all times. Also, a follow-up letter should be sent to the Central Bureau at 60 Garden St., Cambridge, MA 02138, U.S.A. Inexperienced observers should have their observation checked before contacting the Central Bureau.

For any new object, specify the date and time of observation, RA and Dec (with epoch), magnitude, and some physical description. For photographic discoveries, confirmation with a second image is highly desirable. In the case of a new comet, the rate of motion in RA and Dec should also be indicated.

Reports may instead be filled out at **cfa-www.harvard.edu/iau/cbat.html**. Recent IAU circulars and subscription information are also available at this web address.

VISITING HOURS AT SOME CANADIAN OBSERVATORIES AND PLANETARIA

BY MARY LOU WHITEHORNE

OBSERVATORIES

Burke-Gaffney Observatory, Saint Mary's University, Halifax NS B3H 3C3. Public tours are held on many Saturday evenings, weather permitting. General: (902) 496-8257; Monday evening or daytime group tours: (902) 420-5633; bgo@ap.stmarys.ca; apwww.stmarys.ca/bgo

Canada-France-Hawaii Telescope (CFHT), Mauna Kea, Hawaii, U.S.A. RASC members visiting the "Big Island" of Hawaii may arrange daytime group tours of the CFHT installations by contacting, at least one month in advance, the Canada-France-Hawaii Telescope Corporation, either by letter (CFHT Corp., P.O. Box 1597, Kamuela HI 96743, U.S.A.) or by telephone: (808) 885-7944. www.cfht.hawaii.edu

Climenhaga Observatory, Dept. of Physics and Astronomy, University of Victoria, Victoria BC V8W 3P6. Public viewing for groups from April until August. Appointments: (250) 721-7750

David Dunlap Observatory (DDO), P.O. Box 360, Richmond Hill ON L4C 4Y6. Thursday mornings October–April, 10 a.m. Saturday evenings, April–September; Friday evenings, July–August. Call or visit website for information on tour times and dates: (905) 884-2112; ddo.astro.utoronto.ca

Dominion Radio Astrophysical Observatory, Penticton BC V2A 6K3. Conducted tours: Sundays, July and August only, 2 to 5 p.m. Visitors' Centre: Open every day April 1 to October 15, 10 a.m. to 5 p.m. Open weekdays only October 16 to March 14. (250) 490-4355; www.drao.nrc.ca

Gordon MacMillan Southam Observatory, 1100 Chestnut St., Vancouver BC V6J 3J9. Open Fri. and Sat., 7 to 11 p.m., weather and volunteer staff permitting. Extended hours during school holidays. 150-mm refractor for hydrogen-alpha solar views, 500-mm reflector. (604) 738-STAR; ddodge@hrmacmillanspacecentre.com; www.hrmacmillanspacecentre.com

Helen Sawyer Hogg Observatory, Canada Science & Technology Museum, P.O. Box 9724, Stn. T, 1867 St. Laurent Blvd., Ottawa ON K1G 5A3. 380-mm refractor (from the Dominion Observatory) and Starlab Planetarium. "Discover the Universe" public visits by appointment only and group tours Monday to Thursday from October to May, rain or shine. Reservations: (613) 991-9219; www.science-tech.nmstc.ca

Herzberg Institute of Astrophysics (National Research Council of Canada), 5071 West Saanich Road, Victoria BC V8X 4M6. Includes the Dominion Astrophysical Observatory and Interpretive Centre. Open daily 10 a.m. to 4:30 p.m. Closed Mondays, Thanksgiving through Easter. Information and program bookings: (250) 363-8262; www.hia.nrc.ca

Hume Cronyn Observatory, Department of Physics and Astronomy, The University of Western Ontario, London ON N6A 3K7. Summer Open Houses (slide show and viewing with a 250-mm refractor) are held Saturdays in June, July, and August 8:30 to 11 p.m. A winter public program is available to groups and individuals by appointment. (519) 661-3183; phobos.astro.uwo.ca

Ken Odaisky Memorial Observatory, Sudbury Astronomy Club, Suite M250, 800 Lasalle Blvd., Sudbury ON P3A 4V4. Free private and group tours through the observatory, housing a 150-mm refractor, April through October. Reservations: Karen or Garry Lalonde, (705) 858-4343; hhealy@sympatico.ca; ww2.isys.ca/astroclub

Observatoire astronomique du mont Mégantic, Notre-Dame-des-Bois QC J0B 2E0. An interpretation centre, ASTROLab du Parc du mont Mégantic, with an exhibition hall, a multimedia show, observing nights with 350-mm and 600-mm telescopes, is open daily to the public during the summer (May–September) and on weekends during spring and fall. Inquire for updates about the schedule and for reservations (required for observations). Information: (514) 343-6718; observatory: (819) 888-2941; fax: (819) 888-2943; astrolab@interlinx.qc.ca; astrolab.qc.ca

Prince George Astronomical Society Observatory, c/o 3330 22nd Ave., Prince George BC V2N 1P8. 610-mm Cassegrain telescope. Public viewing Fridays 8 p.m. to midnight from March–May and August–October. Group tours available. (250) 964-3600; nelson@cnc.bc.ca; www.pgweb.com/~astronomical

University of British Columbia Observatory, 2219 Main Mall, Vancouver BC V6T 1Z4. Free public observing on clear Saturday evenings: (604) 822-6186; tours: (604) 822-2267; fax: (604) 822-6047; www.astro.ubc.ca

University of Saskatchewan Observatory, c/o Dept. of Physics & Engineering Physics, 116 Science Place, Saskatoon SK S7N 5E2. Public viewing on Saturday evenings. (306) 966-6429

York University Observatory, Dept. of Physics and Astronomy, 4700 Keele St., Toronto ON M3J 1P3. Tours run all year, daytime or evening, by appointment. Wednesday evening is Public Viewing, rain or shine, no appointment necessary. Use Steeles Ave. entrance; observatory is in the Petrie Science Building. Hours vary, depending on the season. (416) 736-2100, ext. 77773; www.astro.yorku.ca/observatory/

PLANETARIA

Calgary Science Centre, 701-11 Street SW. Mailing address: P.O. Box 2100, Station M, Calgary AB T2P 2M5. Features Discovery Dome, with Canada's only Digistar projector and Super-70-mm dome movies. Program and sky information: (403) 221-3700; fax: (403) 237-0186; discover@home.com; www.calgaryscience.ca

Doran Planetarium, Laurentian University, Ramsey Lake Road, Sudbury ON P3E 2C6. Shows in English and French. Information: (705) 675-1151; group reservations: ext. 2227; fax: (705) 675-4868; plegault@nickel.laurentian.ca; www.laurentian.ca/physics/planetarium/planetarium.html

Gemini Space Exploration, 43 Dauphin Ave., Kingston ON K7K 6B2. Offers Starlab portable planetarium presentations. Information: Theodore Micholias, (613) 547-2317; theo@geminispace.com; www.geminispace.com

H.R. MacMillan Space Centre, 1100 Chestnut St., Vancouver BC V6J 3J9. Open daily July and August; otherwise open Tues.–Sun. and holidays (except Christmas). Star theatre, motion simulator, exhibit gallery, multimedia theatre. (604) 738-STAR (738-7827); fax: (604) 736-5665; lkomori@hrmacmillanspacecentre.com; www.hrmacmillanspacecentre.com

Herzberg Institute of Astrophysics (National Research Council of Canada) Centre of the Universe, 5071 West Saanich Road, Victoria BC V8X 4M6. Exhibits, theatre, Starlab planetarium, programs, tours of 1.8-m Plaskett telescope, 16-inch telescope with CCD. Public observing 7–11 p.m. Saturdays, April through October. Open 10 a.m. to 4:30 p.m. daily. Closed Mondays, Thanksgiving through Easter. Information and program bookings: (250) 363-8262; www.hia.nrc.ca,

The Lockhart Planetarium, 394 University College, 220 Dysart Road, The University of Manitoba, Winnipeg MB R3T 2M8. Group reservations and public show schedule: (204) 474-9785

Manitoba Planetarium, 190 Rupert Ave. at Main St., Winnipeg MB R3B 0N2. Victoria Day to Labour Day: shows daily; rest of year: Tuesday to Sunday and holidays, closed Mondays. The Planetarium is part of the Manitoba Museum of Man and Nature, which includes a Science Centre as well as a Starlab mobile planetarium program. The Museum Shop carries science books for all ages. Reception: (204) 956-2830; planetarium show times: (204) 943-3139; gift shop: (204) 988-0615; fax: (204) 942-3679; info@manitobamuseum.mb.ca; www.manitobamuseum.mb.ca

Odyssium, Coronation Park, 11211-142 Street, Edmonton AB T5M 4A1. Features Margaret Zeidler Star Theatre, IMAX® Theatre, public observatory and exhibit galleries, Science Magic gift shop featuring telescopes. Advance ticket sales and program information: (780) 451-3344; recorded astronomy information: (780) 493-9000/4254; gift shop: (780) 452-9100; info@odyssium.com; www.odyssium.com

Ontario Science Centre, 770 Don Mills Road, Toronto ON M3C 1T3. Open every day except Dec. 25. Live planetarium shows daily. (416) 696-3127; www.osc.on.ca

Planétarium de Montréal, 1000 St. Jacques St. W., Montreal QC H3C 1G7. Multimedia presentations in French and in English every open day. (514) 872-4530; fax: (514) 872-8102; info@planetarium.montreal.qc.ca; www.planetarium.montreal.qc.ca

Royal Ontario Museum, Education Department, 100 Queen's Park, Toronto ON M5S 2C6. Operates three mobile planetariums for "Travelling Stars" educational programs both at the Museum and in the community. Topics from grades K–13 cover basic astronomy to the astronomy of ancient civilizations, complementing the Ontario school curriculum, and are presented by trained astronomy teachers. (416) 586-5801; fax: (416) 586-5807; schoolv@rom.on.ca; www.rom.on.ca/schools

Solar Wind Portable Planetarium, Toronto ON. Offers curriculum-based presentations. For information: Kathy McWatters, (416) 221-7375; solar.wind@pathcom.com

W. J. McCallion Planetarium, Department of Physics and Astronomy, McMaster University, 1280 Main Street West, Hamilton ON L8S 4M1. (905) 525-9140, ext. 27777; fax: (905) 546-1252; physun.physics.mcmaster.ca/Grad_Matthews/planetarium

The Night Sky with its beautiful stars
and its message of our place in the Universe
is a precious treasure of all humanity,
on which we rely for our knowledge and understanding
of our origins and destiny.†

†The International Astronomical Union, Exposition on Adverse Environmental Impacts on Astronomy, Paris, 1992 [I.A.U. Information Bulletin 69, January 1993, p. 10].

RECOMMENDED READING AND ATLASES

Astronomy, a popular, nontechnical, monthly magazine for amateur astronomers (phone: (800) 446-5489, fax: (414) 796-0126).

The Backyard Astronomer's Guide, by Terence Dickinson and Alan Dyer. Firefly Books (Canada: (800) 387-6192, United States: (800) 387-5085), 1991. The best guide to equipment and techniques for amateur astronomers, by two experienced observers.

Catalogue of the Astronomical Society of the Pacific (A.S.P., 390 Ashton Ave., San Francisco CA 94112, U.S.A., (415) 337-2624), an excellent source of astronomical educational resources such as books, slides, videos, globes, posters, software, teacher's classroom activity guides and more.

Catalogue of Sky Publishing Corporation, a good source of astronomical books, atlases, globes, slide sets, software, and posters.

Exploring the Night Sky, by Terence Dickinson. Firefly Books (see above), 1987. A guide to stargazing, recommended for children.

The Guide To Amateur Astronomy (2nd edition), by Jack Newton and Philip Teece. Cambridge University Press, Cambridge, 1995. A valuable introduction to many diverse aspects of amateur astronomy.

Nightwatch (3rd ed.), by Terence Dickinson. Firefly Books (see above), 1998. An excellent, introductory observing guide.

SkyNews, the (bimonthly) Canadian magazine of astronomy & stargazing. Send $24 Cdn ($24 U.S. for U.S. addresses) to: SkyNews, RR 1, Cedar Valley ON L0G 1E0; by credit card call (866) 759-0005 (preferred).

Starlight Nights, by Leslie Peltier (1900–1980), 1965. Sky Publishing Corporation. Anyone who enjoys the night sky should read this book.

Sky & Telescope, a monthly magazine widely read by both amateur and professional astronomers (phone: (800) 253-0245, fax: (617) 864-6117).

Atlas of the Moon, by Antonín Rükl. Kalmbach Books, Waukesha, 1992, or Hamlyn Publishing, London, 1991. A first-rate lunar atlas for amateur astronomers.

Bright Star Atlas 2000.0, by Wil Tirion. Contains 9000 stars to magnitude 6.5 and 600 clusters, nebulae and galaxies on 10 charts.

Sky Atlas 2000.0 (2nd ed.), by Wil Tirion and Roger Sinnott, 1998. Large format and well done. Contains 81 000 stars to magnitude 8.5 and 2700 clusters, nebulae and galaxies on 26 charts.

Uranometria 2000.0, by Wil Tirion, Barry Rappaport, and George Lovi. A comprehensive star atlas. Volume 1 covers the northern sky to declination −6°. Volume 2 covers the southern sky to declination +6°. Contains 332 000 stars to magnitude 9.5 and more than 10 000 clusters, nebulae and galaxies on 473 charts.

Millennium Star Atlas, by Roger Sinnott and Michael Perryman. A recent sky atlas based on data from the European Space Agency's HIPPARCOS satellite. Three volumes, each covering 8 hours in RA. Contains more than 1 000 000 stars to magnitude 11 and more than 10 000 clusters, nebulae and galaxies on 1548 charts.

Computer-based Planetarium Programs: Several are available, for example, *ECU* (Earth Centered Universe), *Redshift 3*, *TheSky*, *Voyager II*, *Starry Night*. For information on the last four, see the two catalogues listed above; for *ECU* visit www.nova-astro.com.

Visit www.rasc.ca/handbook/books.html for links to booksellers who carry these books and atlases. Many of these items are also available from Sky Publishing Corp., 49 Bay State Rd., Cambridge MA 02138-1200, U.S.A.; (800) 253-0245, www.skypub.com.

SELECTED LISTING OF WEB RESOURCES

Increasingly, the World Wide Web is becoming an important source of astronomical information. A selection of websites together with a reference to a page number in this Handbook (if any) is given below. A listing of all websites mentioned in this Handbook, with URL links to the various sites, is available at:

www.rasc.ca/handbook/websites.html

URL	Description
www.aavso.org	American Association of Variable Star Observers (p. 242)
www.amsmeteors.org	American Meteor Society (pp. 205, 208)
adc.gsfc.nasa.gov	Astronomical Data Center (ADC), maintained by NASA
www.astrosociety.org	Astronomical Society of the Pacific
www.astronomy.com	*Astronomy* magazine
www.astronomynow.com	*Astronomy Now*, Britain's "Sky & Telescope"
www.cfht.hawaii.edu	Canada-France-Hawaii Telescope (p. 10)
www.cmc.ec.gc.ca/cmc/htmls/astro_e.html	Canadian Meteorological Centre site that provides cloud forecasts for astronomers
www.space.gc.ca	Canadian Space Agency
www.spacedaily.com	Clipping service related to space news
physics.nist.gov/constants	CODATA recommended constants (p. 28)
ddo.astro.utoronto.ca	David Dunlap Observatory (p. 10)
www.drao.nrc.ca	Dominion Radio Astrophysical Observatory (p. 10)
www.mreclipse.com	Eclipse photography and safety (p. 132)
www.hia.nrc.ca	Herzberg Institute of Astrophysics (p. 10)
heritage.stsci.edu	Hubble Heritage Site, emphasizing compelling HST images distilled from scientific data
gdcinfo.agg.nrcan.gc.ca	Impact craters information (p. 211)
cfa-www.harvard.edu/iau/cbat.html	International Astronomical Union Central Bureau (p. 9)
www.darksky.org	International Dark-Sky Association (p. 62)
www.amsmeteors.org/imo-mirror	International Meteor Organization (pp. 204–208)
www.lunar-occultations.com/iota	International Occultation Timing Association (pp. 150, 201)
www.jpl.nasa.gov	Jet Propulsion Laboratory site, many activities for adults and kids
www.kennedyspacecenter.com	Kennedy Space Centre
leonid.arc.nasa.gov	Leonid meteor shower information (p. 204)
miac.uqac.uquebec.ca	Meteorites and Impacts Advisory Committee, Canadian Space Agency (p. 208)
gdcinfo.agg.nrcan.gc.ca	Meteorite impact craters (p. 211)
umbra.nascom.nasa.gov/eclipse	NASA eclipse bulletins (p. 131)

URL	Description
sunearth.gsfc.nasa.gov/eclipse	NASA eclipse site (pp. 126–131)
nedwww.ipac.caltech.edu	NASA/IPAC Database, an extensive listing of extragalactic data (p. 269)
spaceflight.nasa.gov	NASA space flight site giving current information on Space Shuttle missions and ISS activities
www.namnmeteors.org	North American Meteor Network (pp. 205, 208)
astrolab.qc.ca	Observatoire astronomique du mont Mégantic (p. 11)
www.rasc.ca/handbook	*Observer's Handbook* website (p. 6)
planetary.org	Planetary Society—contains over 2000 pages of information about space exploration
www.starlab.com	Project STAR (p. 18)
www.odxa.on.ca/meteor.html	Radio detection of meteors (p. 207)
www.rasc.ca	Royal Astronomical Society of Canada (p. 8)
occsec.wellington.net.nz	Royal Astronomical Society of New Zealand occultations section (p. 151)
www.saguaroastro.org	Saguaro Astronomy Club, includes observing list database (p. 65)
www.heavens-above.com	Satellite tracking information, including International Space Station and Space Shuttle
simbad.u-strasbg.fr/Simbad	SIMBAD database—an extensive listing
www.skypub.com	Sky Publishing Corporation, including *Sky & Telescope* (p. 13)
www.skynewsmagazine.com	*SkyNews*—Canada's astronomy magazine (p. 18)
oposite.stsci.edu/pubinfo	Space Telescope Science Institute
www.seds.org	Students for the Exploration and Development of Space—includes much useful data

To make suggestions for additions to this listing, please contact the editor (see. p. 7 for contact information).

TEACHING AND THE OBSERVER'S HANDBOOK
By John R. Percy

You are holding in your hand a valuable resource for teaching astronomy. Every user of this Handbook, whether amateur or professional astronomer or teacher in any setting, at any level, can contribute to education in astronomy. Partnerships and coalitions between scientists and educators are especially effective and enjoyable.

As a result of curriculum renewal in Canada, the United States, and other countries, astronomy is now taught in many elementary and secondary schools; see *JRASC*, *92*, 38, February 1998. The Canadian astronomical community, including the RASC, has now embarked on a major education and public outreach initiative; see www.casca.ca/ecass/issues/winter2000.

The Night Sky

Teachers should make sure that their students are aware of what can be seen in the night sky, even though "the stars come out at night, but the students don't." THE SKY MONTH BY MONTH section of this Handbook (pp. 66–91) provides an excellent guide. Star charts can be found in many books and magazines (see p. 13) as well as in the section MAPS OF THE NIGHT SKY (pp. 276–283). (Study the first page of this section to get the most out of these maps.) Make sketches, including the horizon and compass points, to record the appearance and changes of the sky.

Night and Day, Seasons, and the Phases of the Moon

These basic astronomical concepts are misunderstood by most people, as many surveys have found. One of the common misconceptions about the seasons is that it is hottest in the summer because of the shape of Earth's orbit—we are closest to the Sun in the summer. But does this explain why the seasons are reversed in the Southern Hemisphere? Even those who "know" that the seasons are due to "the tilt of Earth's axis" may think that, because of the tilt, the hemispheres are closer to the Sun during their respective summers.

Other misconceptions relate to a lack of understanding of the scale of the solar system. Assuming a high speed that we are familiar with, say that of a commercial jet plane, how long would it take to travel to the Moon? To the Sun? If a beach ball represents the Sun, the solar system fits in your town, but the next nearest star is another beach ball on the opposite side of Earth! The sections BASIC DATA (pp. 20–33), THE BRIGHTEST STARS (pp. 224–233), and THE NEAREST STARS (pp. 234–238) are useful references for constructing such models.

Here is a useful hands-on activity: Choose a day when the Sun and Moon are both visible in the sky (in the afternoon when the Moon is near first quarter or in the morning when the Moon is near last quarter; see THE SKY MONTH BY MONTH section). Hold a ball in your hand so that the Sun shines on it, and extend it toward the Moon. You will see the ball and the Moon illuminated by the Sun in the *same* way—a clear demonstration that the Moon is a spherical, nonluminous body floating in space.

These concepts are so basic that it is worth teaching them correctly, that is, monitoring the students' preconceptions through interviews and discussions, and being absolutely sure that they understand the concepts and can explain them from their understanding—not just from memorization.

The Sun

(1) Track the path of the Sun in the sky during one day and over successive days and weeks. This may be done safely and simply by using the shadow of a pole (or a

student). Sunrise/sunset data and the changing position of the Sun in the heavens are given in THE SUN section of this Handbook (pp. 100–102 and p. 93, respectively).

(2) Project an image of the Sun on a sheet of white cardboard, using binoculars or a small telescope. Observe sunspots, and watch the Sun rotate from day to day. Practise setting up such a demonstration ahead of time. Once you get the hang of it, it can be set up very quickly. **Warning:** Never observe the Sun directly, especially not by looking through binoculars or a telescope. Permanent eye damage could result. When projecting a solar image, use a barrier to prevent anyone from looking directly into the light beam. See the sections FILTERS (pp. 52–55) and VIEWING A SOLAR ECLIPSE—A WARNING (p. 149) in this Handbook.

The Moon

(1) Keep a "Moon journal" as a class project: Observe and record where the Moon is, what shape it is, and when it rises and sets. Note how these variables change over several days and weeks. (Don't forget that the Moon is often visible in daytime.)

(2) Draw the general appearance of the Moon's surface as seen with your naked eye. Many features, including the regions of the Apollo landing sites, can be identified using the MAP OF MOON on pp. 106–107. A film or video of one of the Apollo missions is worth showing to a class.

(3) Eclipses: a three-dimensional model, to the correct scale, is a great aid in explaining eclipses and why there is not an eclipse every two weeks. See the ECLIPSES DURING 2002 section in this Handbook (pp. 125–145) for information on eclipses that may be visible from your locality this year.

(4) If ocean tides occur in your area, correlate the times and the range of the tide with the Moon's position in your sky, its phases, and distances. Lunar phases, perigees, and apogees are tabulated in THE SKY MONTH BY MONTH section, and an overview of tides appears in the TIDES AND THE EARTH–MOON SYSTEM article in this Handbook (pp. 165–167).

The Planets

(1) Nothing can stimulate student interest like direct experience, so observe the planets when they are visible. See THE SKY MONTH BY MONTH and PLANETS sections (pp. 168–185 for the latter) for the visibility of the planets during the year.

(2) Develop an awareness of Earth as a planet. Study photographs of Earth from space. For a hands-on experience, place an Earth globe in sunlight with its north pole oriented northward. Then rotate and tilt the globe so your locality is at the "top" of the globe (the globe will then be oriented the same way in space as is planet Earth). The regions on Earth where the Sun is rising or setting at that moment will be apparent. Note which pole is experiencing 24 hours of daylight. Slowly turn the globe eastward about its axis to show a sped-up day/night progression.

(3) Use slides, films, videos, and posters to capture the excitement of planetary exploration (see the catalogues in RECOMMENDED READING AND ATLASES on p. 13).

Comets and Asteroids

These are interesting topics, especially as it now appears that collisions between these objects and Earth may explain the extinctions of species such as dinosaurs. Use the section METEORITE IMPACT CRATERS OF NORTH AMERICA (pp. 211–214) to have students locate nearby impact craters on geographical maps. See THE BRIGHTEST ASTEROIDS (p. 197) for a finder chart to locate a bright asteroid in the night sky (only binoculars are needed). There is a classic demonstration of "Creating a Comet" (out of dry ice and sand) described at www.noao.edu/education/crecipe.html.

Is a Telescope Necessary?

Binoculars and telescopes can be useful but are not essential; much interesting astronomy can be done with the unaided eye. However, binoculars are often available and should be used when helpful. See the section BINOCULARS (pp. 48–51) for a guide to their selection and use. The inexpensive, make-it-yourself *Project STAR* telescopes are highly recommended. See TELESCOPE PARAMETERS (p. 43) and TELESCOPE EXIT PUPILS (pp. 44–47) for a summary of some quantitative aspects of telescopes.

Resources

In addition to the list of reading material below, you may be able to make use of the following:

(1) See the VISITING HOURS AT SOME CANADIAN OBSERVATORIES AND PLANE-TARIA article in this Handbook (pp. 10–12). Take your students to visit one of these.

(2) The Royal Astronomical Society of Canada is the largest organization of amateur astronomers in Canada. Their 25 centres across Canada (see the section AN INVITATION FOR MEMBERSHIP IN THE ROYAL ASTRONOMICAL SOCIETY OF CANADA on pp. 8–9) present a wide variety of activities that might be interesting to you and your students. A member of the RASC might be willing to visit your class and demonstrate a telescope. The Astronomical Society of the Pacific's *Project ASTRO Manual* can facilitate such visits. See www.aspsky.org/project_astro.html.

Astro Adventures: An Activity-Based Astronomy Curriculum, by Dennis Schatz and D. Cooper. Pacific Science Center, 200 2nd Ave. N., Seattle WA 93109-4895, U.S.A.

Astronomical Society of the Pacific, 390 Ashton Ave., San Francisco CA 94112, U.S.A. In addition to their excellent astronomical slides and other such material (send for their catalogue), the ASP publishes a free quarterly teachers' newsletter; to order it, write on your school letterhead, or download current and back issues from www.aspsky.org/education/tnl.html.

Astronomy Adventures (Ranger Rick's NatureScope). National Wildlife Federation, 1412 16th St. NW, Washington DC, U.S.A. Excellent, fun activities for younger children in schools and youth groups.

Project SPICA: A Teacher Resource to Enhance Astronomy Education, edited by N. Butcher Ball et al. Kendall/Hunt Publishing Co. 1994. An excellent compilation of activities and resources for teaching grades 3–12.

Project STAR Textbook. Kendall/Hunt Publishing Co. 1993. See also www.learner.org/teacherslab/pup.

Project STAR Hands-on Science Materials: Learning Technologies, Inc., 40 Cameron Ave., Somerville MA 02144, U.S.A.; (800) 537-8703; www.starlab.com. Unique, high-quality, low-cost materials for introducing students (and teachers) to astronomy.

SkyNews, RR 1, Cedar Valley ON L0G 1E0; (866) 759-0005; www.skynewsmagazine.com. Bimonthly. General astronomy from a Canadian perspective. Free with membership to the RASC.

The Universe at Your Fingertips, and *More Universe at Your Fingertips*, edited by Andrew Fraknoi et al. Astronomical Society of the Pacific, 390 Ashton Ave., San Francisco CA 94112, U.S.A. Another excellent collection of teaching activities and resources for grades 3–12. See also www.aspsky.org/education/astroacts.html.

TERMINOLOGY AND SYMBOLS

COORDINATE SYSTEMS

Astronomical positions are usually measured in a system based on the *celestial poles* and *celestial equator*, the intersections of Earth's rotation axis and equatorial plane, respectively, and the infinite sphere of the sky. *Right ascension* (RA or α) is measured in hours (h), minutes (m), and seconds (s) of time, eastward along the celestial equator from the vernal equinox (see below). *Declination* (Dec or δ) is measured in degrees (°), minutes ('), and seconds (") of arc, northward (N or +) or southward (S or –) from the celestial equator toward the north or south celestial pole.

Positions can also be measured in a system based on the *ecliptic*, the intersection of Earth's orbital plane and the infinite sphere of the sky. The Sun appears to move eastward along the ecliptic during the year. *Longitude* is measured eastward along the ecliptic from the vernal equinox; *latitude* is measured at right angles to the ecliptic, northward or southward toward the north or south ecliptic pole. The *vernal equinox* is one of the two intersections of the ecliptic and the celestial equator; it is the one at which the Sun crosses the celestial equator moving from south to north.

An object is *in conjunction* if it has the same longitude as the Sun and *at opposition* if its longitude differs from that of the Sun by 180°. Mercury and Venus are at *superior* conjunction when they are more distant than the Sun and at *inferior* conjunction when they are nearer than the Sun (see the diagram on p. 169).

Two *nonsolar* objects are in conjunction if they have the same RA. Generally, but not always, close mutual approaches correspond to conjunctions. Following Jean Meeus, we use the term "quasi-conjunction" to denote separations less than 5° that do not correspond to a conjunction.

If an object crosses the ecliptic moving northward, it is at the *ascending node* of its orbit; if it crosses the ecliptic moving southward, it is at the *descending node*.

Elongation is the geocentric angle between a planet and the Sun, or between a satellite and its primary, measured in the plane formed by Earth and the other two bodies.

SYMBOLS

Sun, Moon, and Planets

⊙	Sun	☽	Last Quarter	⊕	Earth	⛢	Uranus
🌑	New Moon	☾	Moon generally	♂	Mars	♆	Neptune
☺	Full Moon	☿	Mercury	♃	Jupiter	♇	Pluto
☽	First Quarter	♀	Venus	♄	Saturn		

Signs of the Zodiac

♈	Aries	0°	♌	Leo	120°	♐	Sagittarius	240°
♉	Taurus	30°	♍	Virgo	150°	♑	Capricornus	270°
♊	Gemini	60°	♎	Libra	180°	♒	Aquarius	300°
♋	Cancer	90°	♏	Scorpius	210°	♓	Pisces	330°

The Greek Alphabet

A, α	alpha	H, η	eta	N, ν	nu	T, τ	tau
B, β	beta	Θ, θ, ϑ	theta	Ξ, ξ	xi	Y, υ	upsilon
Γ, γ	gamma	I, ι	iota	O, o	omicron	Φ, ϕ	phi
Δ, δ	delta	K, κ	kappa	Π, π	pi	X, χ	chi
E, ε	epsilon	Λ, λ	lambda	P, ρ	rho	Ψ, ψ	psi
Z, ζ	zeta	M, μ	mu	Σ, σ	sigma	Ω, ω	omega

BASIC DATA

PRINCIPAL ELEMENTS OF THE SOLAR SYSTEM

PHYSICAL ELEMENTS

Object	Equat. Diam. km	Oblate- ness	Mass Earth=1	Den- sity t/m³	Grav- ity Earth=1	Escape Speed km/s	Rot'n. Period d	Incl. °	Albedo
Sun	1 392 000	0	332 946.0	1.41	27.9	617.5	25–35*	—	—
Mercury	4 879	0	0.055 274	5.43	0.38	4.2	58.646	0.0	0.11
Venus	12 104	0	0.815 005	5.24	0.90	10.4	243.019	177.4	0.65
Earth	12 756	1/298	1.000 000	5.52	1.00	11.2	0.9973	23.4	0.37
Moon	3 475	0	0.012 300	3.34	0.17	2.4	27.3217	6.7	0.12
Mars	6 794	1/154	0.107 447	3.94	0.38	5.0	1.0260	25.2	0.15
Jupiter	142 980†	1/15.4	317.833	1.33	2.53	59.5	0.4101‡	3.1	0.52
Saturn	120 540†	1/10.2	95.159	0.70	1.06	35.5	0.4440	25.3	0.47
Uranus	51 120†	1/43.6	14.500	1.30	0.90	21.3	0.7183	97.9	0.51
Neptune	49 530†	1/58.5	17.204	1.76	1.14	23.5	0.6712	28.3	0.41
Pluto	2 300	0?	0.002 5	1.1	0.08	1.3	6.3872	123.	0.3

The table gives the mean density, the gravity and escape speed *at the equator*, and the inclination of the equator *to the orbital plane.*
*Depending on latitude. †At 1 bar (101.325 kPa).
‡For the most rapidly rotating part of Jupiter, the equatorial region.

OSCULATING ORBITAL ELEMENTS, 2002

The tables at the right give the orbital elements of the planets and 30 largest main-belt asteroids, the latter provided by Dr. Brian Marsden. At any given time or "epoch," 6 basic quantities determine each body's elliptical orbit, for example:

(1) the mean distance from the Sun, a, equal to the semimajor axis of the ellipse;
(2) the eccentricity e of the ellipse;
(3) the inclination i of the orbital plane to the ecliptic;
(4) the longitude Ω of the ascending node of the orbital plane on the ecliptic;
(5) the longitude $\tilde{\omega}$ of perihelion;
(6) the body's mean longitude L at the given epoch.

The date of the ecliptic and equinox used to measure the last 4 quantities must also be specified, and may be different from the given epoch. Other, equivalent parameters may be substituted: the distance q of perihelion in place of a; the argument of perihelion, $\omega = \tilde{\omega} - \Omega$, in place of $\tilde{\omega}$; or the mean anomaly, $M = L - \tilde{\omega}$, or time T of perihelion in place of L. Once 6 fundamental quantities are known, all other attributes of the orbit of the body, such as the sidereal period P and synodic period S, can be derived.

If the body followed a perfectly elliptical orbit as predicted by classical orbital mechanics, then for a fixed ecliptic and equinox the first 5 quantities above would be constant over time. However, because of perturbations caused by the gravitational influence of other bodies, the orbits are not perfectly elliptical; hence the orbital elements depend on the epoch. The given *osculating* elements can be used to determine an elliptical orbit that is a close approximation to the actual path of the body for times near the given epoch. Two epochs, corresponding to Jan. 6 and Jul. 25, are provided for the planets; the elements for these epochs can be linearly interpolated to other epochs in 2002 for precision of a few arcseconds (typically 1″ or 2″). For the asteroids one epoch, corresponding to May 6, is given, with resulting precision of about 1′.

HELIOCENTRIC OSCULATING ORBITAL ELEMENTS, 2002
REFERRED TO THE MEAN ECLIPTIC AND EQUINOX OF J2000.0

Planet	Epoch Julian Date 245	Mean Distance a AU	Eccentricity e	Inclination i °	Long. of Asc. Node Ω °	Long. of Perihelion $\tilde{\omega}$ °	Long. at Epoch L °	Sidereal Period P a	Synodic Period* S a
Mercury	2280.5	0.387 097	0.205 641	7.0048	48.3286	77.4627	22.1630	0.2409	0.3173
	2480.5	0.387 098	0.205 640	7.0048	48.3280	77.4624	120.6336	0.2409	0.3173
Venus	2280.5	0.723 334	0.006 797	3.3946	76.6739	131.5370	280.3467	0.6152	1.5987
	2480.5	0.723 326	0.006 792	3.3946	76.6734	131.4900	240.7739	0.6152	1.5986
Earth†	2280.5	1.000 002	0.016 693	0.0003	183.9	102.9230	105.3783	1.0000	—
	2480.5	1.000 015	0.016 656	0.0003	179.6	102.9377	302.4999	1.0001	—
Mars	2280.5	1.523 650	0.093 346	1.8495	49.5580	335.9814	20.8821	1.8808	2.1355
	2480.5	1.523 785	0.093 409	1.8493	49.5514	336.0634	125.6751	1.8811	2.1352
Jupiter	2280.5	5.203 242	0.048 904	1.3039	100.5127	15.1000	95.4350	11.8637	1.0921
	2480.5	5.202 592	0.048 916	1.3038	100.5120	14.9540	112.0520	11.8615	1.0921
Saturn	2280.5	9.585 696	0.057 633	2.4857	113.6268	92.3452	74.8039	29.6750	1.0349
	2480.5	9.585 004	0.057 720	2.4857	113.6266	92.9410	81.5134	29.6718	1.0349
Uranus	2280.5	19.154 83	0.048 160	0.7719	73.8812	168.5975	322.0454	83.8350	1.0121
	2480.5	19.142 41	0.048 966	0.7718	73.8649	168.7381	324.3460	83.7535	1.0121
Neptune	2280.5	29.967 17	0.010 985	1.7701	131.7880	61.851	309.4651	164.0495	1.0062
	2480.5	29.951 85	0.010 599	1.7706	131.7871	65.730	310.5921	163.9237	1.0062
Pluto	2280.5	39.278 30	0.245 747	17.1713	110.2315	223.4389	241.7393	246.1765	1.0041
	2480.5	39.330 50	0.246 870	17.1716	110.2307	223.4089	242.4790	246.6674	1.0041

Elements are for epochs 2002 Jan. 6 and 2002 Jul. 25 respectively.

*Synodic period = (product of Ps of two planets) ÷ (difference of the Ps). Tabular values are relative to Earth.
†Values are actually for the Earth-Moon barycentre.

Asteroid	Diameter km	Mean Distance a AU	Eccentricity e	Inclination i °	Long. of Asc. Node Ω °	Long. of Perihelion $\tilde{\omega}$ °	Long. at Epoch L °	Sidereal Period P a	Synodic Period* S a
(1) Ceres	1003	2.766 412	0.079 116	10.5835	80.4863	154.4707	343.7459	4.6014	1.2777
(2) Pallas	608	2.773 483	0.229 937	34.8425	173.1716	123.5661	298.9804	4.6191	1.2763
(4) Vesta	538	2.362 648	0.088 878	7.1349	103.9471	253.6260	106.9194	3.6318	1.3800
(10) Hygiea	450	3.135 867	0.119 356	3.8439	283.6576	237.6158	8.9581	5.5533	1.2196
(31) Euphrosyne	370	3.147 116	0.227 131	26.3250	31.2652	93.2790	167.9119	5.5832	1.2182
(704) Interamnia	350	3.062 753	0.146 046	17.3277	280.6560	15.5006	55.0790	5.3603	1.2293
(511) Davida	323	3.167 368	0.183 718	15.9479	107.7674	86.8761	54.2153	5.6372	1.2156
(65) Cybele	309	3.437 326	0.103 853	3.5468	155.8210	261.7529	278.1488	6.3731	1.1861
(52) Europa	289	3.100 155	0.101 344	7.4687	129.0224	111.7622	308.4432	5.4587	1.2243
(451) Patientia	276	3.063 922	0.077 338	15.2308	89.4602	71.7549	108.5206	5.3633	1.2292
(15) Eunomia	272	2.644 616	0.185 590	11.7479	293.4919	30.5950	333.6571	4.3009	1.3029
(16) Psyche	250	2.919 211	0.139 655	3.0954	150.3563	18.6980	163.9395	4.9879	1.2508
(3) Juno	247	2.667 458	0.258 898	12.9711	170.1326	58.1262	131.9595	4.3568	1.2979
(324) Bamberga	246	2.682 432	0.338 287	11.1069	328.0571	12.2329	152.3177	4.3935	1.2947
(24) Themis	234	3.132 259	0.134 206	0.7601	36.0100	144.1453	116.3322	5.5438	1.2201
(95) Arethusa	230	3.069 691	0.145 081	12.9873	243.4409	38.1362	53.6979	5.3785	1.2284
(45) Eugenia	226	2.719 925	0.083 185	6.6119	147.9621	233.9581	352.7996	4.4859	1.2869
(13) Egeria	224	2.576 741	0.084 598	16.5379	43.3216	124.3784	273.8427	4.1364	1.3188
(19) Fortuna	215	2.442 405	0.158 216	1.5719	211.4846	33.6855	69.4495	3.8172	1.3550
(107) Camilla	211	3.476 440	0.079 569	10.0465	173.1683	122.4047	226.5278	6.4822	1.1824
(88) Thisbe	210	2.772 489	0.162 284	5.2232	276.8613	312.9566	115.1388	4.6166	1.2765
(7) Iris	209	2.386 307	0.229 900	5.5240	259.8647	45.0661	327.1063	3.6864	1.3722
(747) Winchester	205	2.991 584	0.345 146	18.1789	130.2132	45.8588	196.8751	5.1745	1.2395
(41) Daphne	204	2.764 942	0.272 713	15.7551	178.2599	224.3204	107.6703	4.5978	1.2780
(6) Hebe	201	2.425 562	0.201 452	14.7667	138.8477	17.7720	287.1951	3.7778	1.3600
(241) Germania	200	3.049 966	0.096 623	5.5187	271.0635	346.1589	28.2321	5.3267	1.2311
(29) Amphitrite	195	2.555 135	0.071 607	6.1012	356.5486	58.8598	287.6756	4.0845	1.3242
(145) Adeona	195	2.674 122	0.143 275	12.6278	77.5127	122.2419	262.5236	4.3731	1.2965
(194) Prokne	191	2.616 286	0.236 889	18.4968	159.5505	322.6553	234.4062	4.2320	1.3094
(386) Siegena	191	2.895 094	0.172 625	20.2494	166.9516	27.5420	132.6189	4.9262	1.2547

Elements are for epoch Julian Date 245 2400.5 (2002 May 6).

SATELLITES OF THE PLANETS
BY JOSEPH VEVERKA

Name	Diam. km	Density t/m³	Mass^A Pt	Visual Mag.	Visual Albedo	Mean Dist. from Planet 10³ km	"	Orbital Period d	Eccentricity	Orbit Incl.† °	Discovery
Satellite of Earth											
Moon*	3476.	3.34	73 490. (70)	-12.7	0.11	384.5	—	27.322	0.0549	18.–29.	—
Satellites of Mars											
I Phobos*	21.	≈2.	0.013 (0.002)	11.6	0.07	9.4	25.	0.319	0.015	1.1	A. Hall, 1877
II Deimos*	12.	≈2.	0.0018 (0.0002)	12.7	0.07	23.5	63.	1.263	0.0005	1.8v	A. Hall, 1877
Satellites of Jupiter											
XVI Metis	43.		—	17.5	≈0.05	128.	42.	0.294	0.	0.	S. Synnott, 1979
XV Adrastea*	16.		—	18.7	≈0.05	129.	42.	0.297	0.	—	D. Jewitt et al., 1979
V Amalthea*	167.		—	14.1	0.05	180.	59.	0.498	0.003	0.4	E. Barnard, 1892
XIV Thebe**	99.		—	16.	≈0.05	222.	73.	0.674	0.013	—	S. Synnott, 1979
I Io*^B	3630.	3.55	89 200. (400)	5.	0.6	422.	138.	1.769	0.004	0.	Galileo, 1610
II Europa*^B	3140.	3.04	48 700. (500)	5.3	0.6	671.	220.	3.551	0.01	0.5	Galileo, 1610
III Ganymede*^B	5260.	1.93	149 000. (600)	4.6	0.4	1070.	351.	7.155	0.001	0.2	Galileo, 1610
IV Callisto*	4800.	1.83	107 500. (400)	5.6	0.2	1885.	618.	16.689	0.007	0.2	Galileo, 1610
1975J1^C	≈4.			20.0	—	7507.	2462.	130.	0.24	43.	C. Kowal, 1975‡
XIII Leda	≈15.		—	20.	—	11 110.	3640.	240.	0.147	27.	C. Kowal, 1974
VI Himalia***	185.		—	14.8	0.03	11 470.	3760.	251.	0.158	28.	C. Perrine, 1904
X Lysithea***	≈35.		—	18.4	—	11 710.	3840.	260.	0.107	29.	S. Nicholson, 1938
VII Elara	75.		—	16.8	0.03	11 740.	3850.	260.	0.207	28.	C. Perrine, 1905
2000J11^C	≈3.		—	20.5	—	12 557.	4119.	287.	0.25	28.	S. Sheppard et al., 2000
2000J3^C	≈4.		—	20.1	—	20 210.	6629.	585.	0.22	150.	S. Sheppard et al., 2000
2000J7^C	≈5.		—	19.8	—	20 929.	6865.	616.	0.22	149.	S. Sheppard et al., 2000

Pronunciations of the names of the satellites are given on p. 170.

Visual Magnitude and angular Mean Distance from Planet are at mean opposition distance.

†Inclinations of inner satellites (those closer than 100 planetary radii) are relative to the planet's *equator*. As customary, inclinations for outer satellites (those beyond Jupiter IV, Saturn VIII, Uranus IV, and Neptune I) are relative to the planet's *orbital plane*. Outer satellite inclinations relative to a planet's equator vary due to precession effects. For our Moon, the inclination relative to Earth's orbital plane is 5°; relative to Earth's equator it varies between 18° and 29° in an 18.61-year cycle. A value >90° indicates retrograde motion.

*synchronous motion; **probably synchronous; ***nonsynchronous; ****chaotic motion; (no asterisk) rotation unknown

^AThe numbers in parentheses are possible errors.

^BLaplace resonance. Longitudes satisfy: L(Io) – 3L(Europa) + 2L(Ganymede) ≈ 180°. Also, the mean motions are such that the three periods are nearly 1:2:4.

^CDiameters assume an albedo of 0.06.

‡Initially detected in 1975 and then lost; recovered in 2000 by S. Sheppard and D. Jewitt.

SATELLITES OF THE PLANETS (continued)

Name	Diam. km	Mass[A] Pt	Density t/m³	Visual Mag.	Visual Albedo	Mean Dist. from Planet 10³ km	Orbital Period d	Eccentricity	Orbit Incl.† °	Discovery
Satellites of Jupiter (continued)										
2000J5[C]	≈3.	—	—	20.2	—	21 132.	6931.	624.	0.23	149.	S. Sheppard et al., 2000
XII Ananke***	≈30.	—	—	18.9	—	21 200.	6954.	631.	0.17	147.	S. Nicholson 1951
XI Carme	≈40.	—	—	18.	—	22 350.	7330.	692.	0.21	164.	S. Nicholson 1938
2000J10[C]	≈3.	—	—	20.3	—	22 988.	7540.	716.	0.16	166.	S. Sheppard et al., 2000
2000J6[C]	≈3.	—	—	20.5	—	23 074.	7568.	719.	0.26	165.	S. Sheppard et al., 2000
2000J9[C]	≈4.	—	—	20.1	—	23 140.	7590.	723.	0.25	165.	S. Sheppard et al., 2000
2000J4[C]	≈3.	—	—	20.4	—	23 169.	7599.	723.	0.27	165.	S. Sheppard et al., 2000
VIII Pasiphae	≈50.	—	—	17.1	—	23 330.	7650.	735.	0.38	148.	P. Melotte, 1908
IX Sinope***	≈35.	—	—	18.3	—	23 370.	7660.	758.	0.28	153.	S. Nicholson, 1914
2000J2[C]	≈4.	—	—	20.1	—	23 746.	7789.	751.	0.24	165.	S. Sheppard et al., 2000
2000J8[C]	≈4.	—	—	20.0	—	23 913.	7843.	758.	0.43	153.	S. Sheppard et al., 2000
1999J1[C]	≈7.	—	—	19.4	—	24 103.	7906.	759.	0.28	147.	J. Scotti & T. Spahr, 1999
Satellites of Saturn										
XVIII Pan[D]	≈20.	—	—	≈19.	≈0.5	134.	22.	0.577	≈0.	≈0.	M. Showalter, 1990
XV Atlas	30.	—	—	≈18.	0.4	137.	23.	0.601	0.002	0.3	R. Terrile, 1980
XVI Prometheus**[E]	100.	—	—	≈15.	0.6	139.	23.	0.613	0.002	0.	S. Collins, D. Carlson, 1980
XVII Pandora**[E]	90.	—	—	≈16.	0.5	142.	24.	0.628	0.004	0.1	S. Collins, D. Carlson, 1980
X Janus*[F]	190.	—	—	≈14.	0.6	151.	25.	0.695	0.009	0.3	A. Dollfus, 1966
XI Epimetheus*[F]	120.	—	—	≈15.	0.5	151.	25.	0.695	0.007	0.1	J. Fountain, S. Larson, 1966
I Mimas*	390.	38. (1)	1.2	12.5	0.8	187.	30.	0.942	0.02	1.5	W. Herschel, 1789
II Enceladus*	500.	80. (30)	1.1	11.8	1.0	238.	38.	1.37	0.004	0.02	W. Herschel, 1789
III Tethys*	1060.	760. (90)	1.2	10.3	0.8	295.	48.	1.888	0.	1.1	G. Cassini, 1684
XIII Telesto	25.	—	—	≈18.	0.7	295.	48.	1.888[G]	≈0.	≈0.	B. Smith et al., 1980
XIV Calypso**	25.	—	—	≈18.	1.0	295.	48.	1.888[H]	≈0.	≈0.	D. Pascu et al., 1980
IV Dione*	1120.	1050. (30)	1.4	10.4	0.6	378.	61.	2.737	0.002	0.02	G. Cassini, 1684
XII Helene	30.	—	—	≈18	0.6	378.	61.	2.737[I]	0.005	0.2	P. Laques, J. Lecacheux, 1980
V Rhea*	1530.	2 490. (150)	1.3	9.7	0.6	526.	85.	4.517	0.001	0.4	G. Cassini, 1672
VI Titan**	5550.[J]	134 570. (30)	1.88	8.4	0.2	1 221.	197.	15.945	0.029	0.3	C. Huygens, 1655
VII Hyperion****	255.	—	—	14.2	0.3	1 481.	239.	21.276	0.104	0.4	W. Bond, G. Bond, W. Lassell, 1848

[D] Orbits within the Encke gap.
[E] Prometheus and Pandora are shepherds of the F-ring.
[F] Co-orbital satellites.
[G] Telesto librates about the leading (#4) Lagrangian point of Tethys' orbit.
[H] Calypso librates about the trailing (#5) Lagrangian point of Tethys' orbit.
[I] Helene librates about the leading (#4) Lagrangian point of Dione's orbit with a period of ≈ 790 d.
[J] Titan's cloud-top diameter. Solid-body diameter equals 5150 km.

1₂3

SATELLITES OF THE PLANETS (continued)

Name	Diam. km	Mass[A] Pt	Density t/m³	Visual Mag.	Visual Albedo	Mean Dist. from Planet 10³ km	"	Orbital Period d	Eccentricity	Orbit Incl.† °	Discovery
Satellites of Saturn (continued)											
VIII Iapetus*	1460.	1880. (120)	1.2	11.0v	0.08–0.4	3 561.	575.	79.331	0.028	14.7	G. Cassini, 1671
2000S5[C]	14.	—	—	21.9	—	11 300.	1827.	449.	0.33	46.	B. Gladman et al., 2000
2000S6[C]	10.	—	—	22.5	—	11 400.	1843.	453.	0.32	47.	B. Gladman et al., 2000
IX Phoebe***	220.	—	—	16.5	0.05	12 960.	2096.	550.46	0.163	150.	W. Pickering, 1898
2000S2[C]	20.	—	—	21.2	—	15 200.	2458.	687.	0.36	45.	B. Gladman et al., 2000
2000S8[C]	6.	—	—	23.5	—	15 500.	2506.	720.	0.27	153.	B. Gladman et al., 2000
2000S3[C]	32.	—	—	20.0	—	16 800.	2717.	796.	0.26	45.	B. Gladman et al., 2000
2000S12[C]	6.	—	—	23.8	—	17 600.	2846.	877.	0.12	176.	B. Gladman et al., 2000
2000S11[C]	26.	—	—	20.4	—	17 900.	2894.	888.	0.38	33.	M. Holman et al. 2000
2000S10[C]	8.	—	—	22.9	—	18 200.	2943.	913.	0.48	34.	B. Gladman et al., 2000
2000S4[C]	14.	—	—	22.0	—	18 250.	2951.	924.	0.54	34.	B. Gladman et al., 2000
2000S9[C]	6.	—	—	23.7	—	18 400.	2975.	935.	0.23	167.	B. Gladman et al., 2000
2000S7[C]	6.	—	—	23.8	—	20 100.	3250.	1067.	0.44	176.	B. Gladman et al., 2000
2000S1[C]	16.	—	—	21.6	—	23 100.	3735.	1311.	0.34	173.	B. Gladman et al., 2000
Satellites of Uranus											
VI Cordelia[K]	25.[L]	—	—	24.2	<0.1	49.8	3.7	0.333	≈0.	≈0.	Voyager 2, 1986
VII Ophelia[K]	30.[L]	—	—	23.9	<0.1	53.8	4.0	0.375	≈0.	≈0.	Voyager 2, 1986
VIII Bianca	45.[L]	—	—	23.1	<0.1	59.2	4.4	0.433	≈0.	≈0.	Voyager 2, 1986
IX Cressida	65.[L]	—	—	22.3	<0.1	61.8	4.6	0.463	≈0.	≈0.	Voyager 2, 1986
X Desdemona	60.[L]	—	—	22.5	<0.1	62.6	4.7	0.475	≈0.	≈0.	Voyager 2, 1986
XI Juliet	85.[L]	—	—	21.7	<0.1	64.4	4.9	0.492	≈0.	≈0.	Voyager 2, 1986
XII Portia	110.[L]	—	—	21.1	<0.1	66.1	5.0	0.513	≈0.	≈0.	Voyager 2, 1986
XIII Rosalind	60.[L]	—	—	22.5	<0.1	70.0	5.2	0.558	≈0.	≈0.	Voyager 2, 1986
XIV Belinda	68.[L]	—	—	22.1	<0.1	75.3	5.6	0.621	≈0.	≈0.	Voyager 2, 1986
1986U10	40.[L]	—	—	23.6	<0.1	76.4	5.8	0.638	≈0.	≈0.	E. Karkoschka, 1999††
XV Puck	155.	—	—	20.4	0.07	86.0	6.5	0.763	≈0.	≈0.	Voyager 2, 1985
V Miranda*[M]	485.	75. (22)	1.3	16.5	0.34	129.9	9.7	1.413	0.017	3.4	G. Kuiper, 1948
I Ariel*[M]	1160.	1340. (240)	1.6	14.	0.4	190.9	14.3	2.521	0.0028	0.	W. Lassell, 1851
II Umbriel*[M]	1190.	1270. (240)	1.4	14.9	0.19	266.0	20.0	4.146	0.0035	0.	W. Lassell, 1851

[K] Cordelia and Ophelia are shepherds of the ε-ring.
[L] Diameter assuming the same albedo (0.07) as Puck.
†† In Voyager 2 (January 1986) images.
[M] Near resonance(?). L(Miranda) – 3L(Ariel) + 2L(Umbriel) drifts slowly (period ≈ 12.5 a).

SATELLITES OF THE PLANETS (continued)

Name	Diam. km	Mass[A] Pt	Density t/m³	Visual Mag.	Visual Albedo	Mean Dist. from Planet 10³ km	Mean Dist. from Planet "	Orbital Period d	Eccentricity	Orbit Incl.† °	Discovery
Satellites of Uranus (continued)											
III Titania*	1610.	3470. (180)	1.6	13.9	0.28	436.3	32.7	8.704	0.0024	0.	W. Herschel, 1787
IV Oberon*	1550.	2920. (160)	1.5	14.1	0.24	583.4	43.8	13.463	0.0007	0.	W. Herschel, 1787
XVI Caliban	60.	—	—	≈22.5	<0.1	7169.	538.	580.	0.082	140.	B. Gladman et al., 1997
XX Stephano	30.	—	—	≈25.	<0.1	7920.	584.	674.	0.146	142.	B. Gladman et al., 1999
XVII Sycorax	120.	—	—	≈21.	<0.1	12214.	900.	1290.	0.509	153.	P. Nicholson et al., 1997
XVIII Prospero	30.	—	—	≈24.	<0.1	16670.	1229.	2057.	0.323	146.	M. Holman et al., 1999
XIX Setebos	30.	—	—	≈24.	<0.1	17810.	1313.	2271.	0.528	148.	J. Kavelaars, 2000
Satellites of Neptune											
III Naiad	60.	—	—	24.6	≈0.06	48.0	2.3	0.3	≈0.	4.5	*Voyager 2*, 1989
IV Thalassa	80.	—	—	23.9	≈0.06	50.0	2.4	0.31	≈0.	0.4	*Voyager 2*, 1989
V Despina	150.	—	—	22.5	0.06	52.5	2.5	0.33	≈0.	<1.	*Voyager 2*, 1989
VI Galatea	160.	—	—	22.4	≈0.06	62.0	2.9	0.43	≈0.	<1.	*Voyager 2*, 1989
VII Larissa**	190.	—	—	22.	0.06	73.6	3.5	0.55	≈0.	<1.	*Voyager 2*, 1989
VIII Proteus**	420.	—	—	20.3	0.06	117.6	5.5	1.12	≈0.	<1.	*Voyager 2*, 1989
I Triton*	2700.	21400. (200)	2.07	13.6	0.8	354.	17.	5.877	<0.0005	160.	W. Lassell, 1846
II Nereid***	340.	—	—	19.7	0.16	5510.	260.	365.21	0.76	27.6	G. Kuiper, 1949
Satellite of Pluto											
Charon*	1200.	—	—	17.	—	19.1	0.9	6.387	≈0.	≈0.	J. Christy, 1978

ORBITAL MOTION
By Roy Bishop

An understanding of orbital motion is central to an appreciation of the heavens. Whether you are observing a distant galaxy, the stars in a globular cluster, the waltz of Jupiter's Galilean satellites, the drift of the Moon during an occultation, or merely uttering an expletive as an artificial satellite passes through the field of your camera, an understanding of orbital motion adds a deep insight to all of these views.

Among early cosmologies were those of **Aristotle** (340 BC) and **Ptolemy** (140 AD), and the superior heliocentric one proposed by **Copernicus** (1543). These attempts at modelling the heavens used complex systems of circles upon circles, of epicycles, eccentrics, and deferents. John Milton, a contemporary of Galileo, wrote the following lines in his epic poem "Paradise Lost" (1674), possibly expressing his discontent with the Ptolemaic and Copernican systems of compounded circles:

> *To ask or search I blame thee not, for Heav'n*
> *Is as the Book of God before thee set,*
> *Wherein to read his wond'rous Works, and learn*
> *His Seasons, Hours, or Days, or Months, or Years:*
> *This to attain, whether Heav'n move or Earth,*
> *Imports not, if thou reck'n right; the rest*
> *From Man or Angel the great Architect*
> *Did wisely to conceal, and not divulge*
> *His secrets to be scann'd by them who ought*
> *Rather admire; or if they list to try*
> *Conjecture, he his Fabric of the Heav'ns*
> *Hath left to thir disputes, perhaps to move*
> *His laughter at thir quaint Opinions wide*
> *Hereafter, when they come to model Heav'n*
> *And calculate the Stars, how they will wield*
> *The mighty frame, how build, unbuild, contrive*
> *To save appearances, how gird the Sphere*
> *With Centric and Eccentric scribbl'd o'er,*
> *Cycle and Epicycle, Orb in Orb.*

Kepler (1609), using observations accumulated by Tycho, broke with the 2000-year preoccupation with circles when he discovered that the planets move in an elegantly simple way along elliptical paths. Although he had discovered *how* the planets move, Kepler was unable to explain quantitatively *why* they move in this way. **Galileo** (1632) achieved brilliant insights concerning the motion of objects; however, he ignored Kepler's ellipses and did not apply his mechanics to the sky.

Newton united the heavens and Earth by showing that the laws governing motions on Earth also apply to the heavens. In his *Principia* (1687), the greatest book in the physical sciences, Newton presented his three laws of motion and the first ever physical force law, his law of gravitation. He used these to explain the motions not only of bodies on Earth, but also of the planets, comets, stars, equinoxes, tides, etc. Newton was the first to realize that the Moon is falling toward Earth just as freely as does an apple, and that the elliptical orbit of the centre of mass of the Earth–Moon system is the path that results (as he described it) as these two bodies free-fall under the action of the Sun's gravitational force.

A common misconception concerning orbits is that the inward gravitational force is balanced by an outward "centrifugal force." Newton's view is simpler: there is only one force, the inward pull of gravity. There is *no physical agent* to cause an outward force, and if there *were* an outward supporting force, the two forces would cancel and, as Galileo realized, the body would then move along a straight line. If you choose a rotating reference frame and then ignore the rotation (mistake no. 1), you have to pretend there is a "centrifugal force" (mistake no. 2) in order to make sense of motions occurring within this frame. The two mistakes effectively cancel, but understanding is compromised.

Einstein's General Theory of Relativity (GTR) of 1915 superseded Newton's description of gravity. The arbiter of which is a good theory and which theory is wrong is nature. Newton's laws are accurate enough for most of NASA's calculations, but they do not work exactly. In the case of strong gravitation and/or speeds approaching the speed of light, Newton's laws fail dramatically. The GTR may be wrong too, but so far it has passed all experimental tests.

According to Einstein's GTR, gravitation is not a mysterious force that one mass exerts upon a distant mass; gravitation is the geometry (non-Euclidean) of the 4-dimensional space-time within which we and the stars exist. Golf balls (if air friction is ignored), satellites, planets and stars follow *geodesics*, the straightest possible, force-free paths through a space-time whose geometry is shaped by mass-energy. The difficulty in intellectually grasping a non-Euclidean space-time originates with us. Common sense is inadequate. This is not surprising, given that our common sense is based on the Euclidean, 3-dimensional geometry of straight lines, rectangles, and spheres we learned in the crib by age 2.

Gravitation is geometry. This is why no one has ever felt a force of gravity. Like the centrifugal force, it never did exist. A force of gravity was the glue Newton invented to make his naive Euclidean model of space-time approximate the real universe. (Newton himself was well aware of the unsatisfactory nature of several of his assumptions, far more so than most people who came after him.) When you release a coin from your hand, you see the coin "fall" because the contact force of the ground on your feet (the *only* force you feel) accelerates you the other way. An orbiting astronaut experiences no such force, so he remains beside a released coin. Orbital motion could not be simpler—*no* forces are involved.

What would Milton have written had he been familiar with the conjectures of Newton and Einstein?

SOME ASTRONOMICAL AND PHYSICAL DATA
BY ROY BISHOP

Many of the numbers listed below are based on measurement. Exceptions include defined quantities (indicated by ≡), quantities calculated from defined quantities (e.g. m/ly, AU/pc), and numbers of mathematical origin such as π and conversion factors in angular measure. Of those based on measurement, some are known to only approximate precision and the equal sign is reduced to ≈. Many others are known to quite high precision (the uncertainties occur after the last digit given) and several are from "the 1998 CODATA recommended values of the fundamental physical constants" (see physics.nist.gov/constants). The units (*Système International* (SI) where possible), symbols and nomenclature are based on recommendations of the *International Astronomical Union* and the *International Union of Pure and Applied Physics*.

LENGTH

1 metre (m) = the distance travelled by light in a vacuum in $(299\,792\,458)^{-1}$ s
1 astronomical unit (AU) $= 1.495\,978\,707 \times 10^{11}$ m = 499.004 784 light-s
1 light-year (ly) $= 9.460\,536 \times 10^{15}$ m (based on avg. Gregorian year)
$\qquad\qquad\qquad = 63\,239.8$ AU
1 parsec (pc) $\qquad = 3.085\,678 \times 10^{16}$ m
$\qquad\qquad\qquad = 206\,264.8$ AU $= 3.261\,631$ ly
1 mile* $\qquad\qquad ≡ 1.609\,344$ km
1 micron* $\qquad\quad ≡ 1$ μm $\qquad\qquad\qquad$ *Indicates deprecated unit;
1 Angstrom* $\qquad ≡ 0.1$ nm $\qquad\qquad\qquad$ unit on right is preferred

TIME

1 second (s) ≡ 9 192 631 770 periods of the radiation involved in the transition between the two hyperfine levels of the ground state of the ^{133}Cs atom at mean sea level

Day: Mean sidereal (equinox to equinox) $= 86\,164.092$ s
$\qquad$ Mean rotation (fixed star to fixed star) $= 86\,164.100$ s
$\qquad$ Day (d) $\qquad\qquad\qquad\qquad\qquad\quad ≡ 86\,400.$ s
$\qquad$ Mean solar $\qquad\qquad\qquad\qquad\qquad = 86\,400.001$ s

Month: Draconic (node to node) $\qquad\qquad = 27.212\,221$ d
$\qquad$ Tropical (equinox to equinox) $\qquad = 27.321\,582$ d
$\qquad$ Sidereal (fixed star to fixed star) $\quad = 27.321\,662$ d
$\qquad$ Anomalistic (perigee to perigee) $\quad = 27.554\,550$ d
$\qquad$ Synodic (New Moon to New Moon) $= 29.530\,589$ d

Year: Eclipse (lunar node to lunar node) $\quad = 346.620\,075$ d
$\qquad$ Tropical (equinox to equinox) (a) $\quad = 365.242\,190$ d
$\qquad$ Average Gregorian $\qquad\qquad\qquad ≡ 365.242\,5$ d
$\qquad$ Average Julian $\qquad\qquad\qquad\qquad ≡ 365.25$ d
$\qquad$ Sidereal (fixed star to fixed star) $\quad = 365.256\,363$ d
$\qquad$ Anomalistic (perihelion to perihelion) $= 365.259\,635$ d

EARTH

Mass $= 5.974 \times 10^{24}$ kg $\qquad$ Age ≈ 4.6 Ga $\qquad$ Central T ≈ 5000 to 6000 K
Radius: Equatorial, $a = 6378.140$ km $\qquad$ Polar, $b = 6356.755$ km
$\qquad\qquad$ Mean $= (a^2 b)^{1/3} = 6371.004$ km $\quad$ Of metallic core = 3475 km
Solar parallax = 8.794 148″ (Earth equatorial radius ÷ 1 AU)
1° of latitude $= 111.132\,95 - 0.559\,82 \cos 2\phi + 0.001\,17 \cos 4\phi$ km (at latitude ϕ)
1° of longitude $= 111.412\,88 \cos \phi - 0.093\,50 \cos 3\phi + 0.000\,12 \cos 5\phi$ km

1 knot = 1 nautical mile (1′ of latitude) per hour = 0.5148 m/s = 1.853 km/h
Distance of sea horizon for eye h metres above sea level
   (allowing for refraction) $\approx 3.9h^{1/2}$ km
Standard atmospheric pressure (1 atm) ≡ 101.325 kPa ($\approx$ 1 kg above 1 cm^2)
Values of atmospheric refraction for various elevations (assuming 1 atm, 10°C):
   90°: 0′; 44°: 1′; 26°: 2′; 18°: 3′; 11°: 5′; 6°: 8′; 4°: 12′; 2°: 18′; 0°: 34′
Speed of sound in standard atmosphere = 331 m/s $\approx$ 1 km/3 s $\approx 10^{-6} c$
Magnetic field at surface $\approx 5 \times 10^{-5}$ T (**B** field comes out of a N-seeking pole)
Magnetic poles: 76°N, 101°W; 66°S, 140°E
Standard acceleration of gravity ≡ 9.806 65 m/s^2
Meteoritic flux $\approx 1 \times 10^{-15}$ kg/(m^{2}s) $\approx 10^4$ t/a over entire Earth
Obliquity of ecliptic = 23.4393° (2000.0)   Constant of aberration = 20.495 52″
Annual general precession = 50.29″ (2000.0); Precession period $\approx$ 25 800 a
Escape speed from Earth = 11.2 km/s   Mean orbital speed = 29.786 km/s
Escape speed at 1 AU from Sun = 42.1 km/s (= $\sqrt{2}$ × orbital speed)

SUN
Mass = 1.9891 × 10^{30} kg   Radius = 696 265 km   Eff. Temp. $\approx$ 5780 K
Output: Power = 3.85 × 10^{26} W, M_{bol} = 4.79
     Luminous intensity = 2.84 × 10^{27} cd, M_v = 4.82
At 1 AU outside Earth's atmosphere:
   Energy flux = 1.37 kW/m^2, m_{bol} = −26.82
   Illuminance = 1.27 × 10^5 lx, m_v = −26.75
Inclination of the solar equator on the ecliptic of date = 7.25°
Longitude of ascending node of the solar equator on the ecliptic of date = 76°
Period of rotation at equator = 25.38 d (sidereal), 27.275 d (mean synodic)
Solar wind speed near Earth $\approx$ 450 km/s (travel time, Sun to Earth $\approx$ 4 d)
Solar velocity = 19.4 km/s toward α = 18.07h, δ = +30° (solar apex)
Location in Milky Way Galaxy: $\approx$ 25 kly from centre, $\approx$ 50 ly N of galactic
   plane, on the inner edge of the Orion arm

MILKY WAY GALAXY
Mass $\approx 10^{12}$ solar masses   Diameter $\approx$ 300 kly (including the galactic halo)
Centre: α = 17h 45.7m, δ = −29°00′; N pole: α = 12h 51m, δ = 27°08′ (2000.0)
Rotation speed at Sun $\approx$ 230 km/s, period $\approx$ 200 Ma
Velocity relative to 3 K background radiation $\approx$ 600 km/s toward $\alpha \approx$ 10h, $\delta \approx$ −20°

CONSTANTS
Speed of light, $c \equiv$ 299 792 458 m/s (This, in effect, defines the metre.)
Planck's constant, h = 6.626 07 × 10^{-34} J·s = 4.135 667 × 10^{-15} eV·s
Gravitational constant, G = 6.674 × 10^{-11} N·m^2/kg^2
Elementary charge, e = 1.602 176 × 10^{-19} C
Constant in Coulomb's law ≡ 10^{-7} c^2 (SI units) (This defines the Coulomb.)
Avogadro constant, N_A = 6.022 142 × 10^{26} kmol^{-1}
Boltzmann constant, k = 1.380 65 × 10^{-23} J/K = 8.617 × 10^{-5} eV/K $\approx$ 1 eV/10^{4}K
Stefan-Boltzmann constant, σ = 5.6704 × 10^{-8} W/(m^{2}K^4)
Wien's Law: $\lambda_m T$ = 2.8978 × 10^{-3} m·K (per dλ)
Hubble constant, $H \approx$ 60 to 80 km/(s Mpc)
−273.15°C (degree Celsius) = 0 K (kelvin) (lowest thermodynamic temperature)
Volume of ideal gas at 0°C, 101.325 kPa = 22.4140 m^3/kmol
Water: fusion at 0°C: 0.333 MJ/kg   vaporization at 100°C: 2.26 MJ/kg
    specific heat & density (near 20°C): 4.18 kJ/(kg·C°) & 1.00 t/m^3

MASS AND ENERGY

Mass is a measure of sluggishness of response to a net force. (SI unit: kg)
Weight ($\neq$ mass) is the force required to support a body. (SI unit: N)

1 kilogram (kg) $\equiv$ mass of a platinum-iridium cylinder stored in Paris, France
1 atomic mass unit (u) $\equiv 1/12^{th}$ of the mass of an atom of ^{12}C
$$= 1.660\,539 \times 10^{-27} \text{ kg} = N_A^{-1} = 931.4940 \text{ MeV}$$
1 joule (J) $\equiv$ work done by a force of 1 N acting through a distance of 1 m
$\approx$ the kinetic energy gained by this Handbook in falling freely 0.4 m
1 electron-volt (eV) $\equiv$ the kinetic energy gained by a particle carrying one unit
of elementary electrical charge (e) in falling through an
electrical potential difference of one volt (V)
$$= 1.602\,176 \times 10^{-19} \text{ J}$$

Electron mass $= 9.109\,38 \times 10^{-31}$ kg $= 548.579\,91$ μu $= 0.510\,998\,9$ MeV
Proton mass $= 1.672\,622 \times 10^{-27}$ kg $= 1.007\,276\,467$ u $= 938.2720$ MeV
Neutron mass $= 1.674\,927 \times 10^{-27}$ kg $= 1.008\,664\,92$ u $= 939.565$ MeV

Some atomic masses:
$^1H = 1.007\,825$ u	$^5Li = 5.0125$ u	$^{16}O = 15.994\,915$ u
$^2H = 2.014\,102$ u	$^8Be = 8.005\,305$ u	$^{56}Fe = 55.934\,940$ u
$^4He = 4.002\,603$ u	$^{12}C \equiv 12.000\,000$ u	$^{235}U = 235.043\,928$ u

Thermochemical calorie* (cal) = 4.184 J
1 erg*/s = 10^{-7} J/s = 10^{-7} W
1 BTU*/h = 0.2930 W   *Indicates deprecated unit;
1 horsepower* = 745.7 W   unit on right is preferred
1 eV per event = 23 060 cal/mol
$C + O_2 \rightarrow CO_2 + 4.1$ eV $4\,^1H \rightarrow {}^4He + 26.73$ MeV

Highest cosmic ray energy (carried by protons) $\approx 10^{20}$ eV
Power output (average) of an adult human $\approx$ 100 W
1 kg of TNT or milkshake releases 4.20 MJ $\approx$ 1 kWh

Relation between rest mass (m), linear momentum (p), total energy (E), kinetic
energy (KE), and $\gamma \equiv (1 - v^2/c^2)^{-0.5}$ where c is the speed of light and v is the
speed of the object: $E = \gamma mc^2 = mc^2 + \text{KE} = [(mc^2)^2 + (pc)^2]^{0.5}$

MAGNITUDE RELATIONS

Log of light intensity ratio $\equiv 0.4$ times magnitude difference
Distance Modulus (D) $\equiv$ apparent magnitude (m) – absolute magnitude (M)
Log of distance in ly = $0.2D + 1.513\,435$ (neglecting absorption)
Magnitude of sum of magnitudes $m_i = -2.5 \log \Sigma_i\, 10^{-0.4\,m_i}$

DOPPLER RELATIONS FOR LIGHT

$\alpha \equiv$ angle between velocity of source and line from source to observer
$\beta \equiv v/c$
$\gamma \equiv (1 - \beta^2)^{-0.5}$
Frequency: $\nu = \nu_0\, \gamma^{-1}(1 - \beta \cos \alpha)^{-1}$
$z \equiv (\lambda - \lambda_0)/\lambda_0 = \gamma (1 - \beta \cos \alpha) - 1$
For $\alpha = \pi$ radians: $z = (1 + \beta)^{0.5}(1 - \beta)^{-0.5} - 1$ ($\approx \beta$ if $\beta \ll 1$)
$\beta = [(1 + z)^2 - 1][(1 + z)^2 + 1]^{-1}$

OPTICAL WAVELENGTH DATA

Bright-adapted (photopic) visible range ≈ 400 – 750 nm
Dark-adapted (scotopic) visible range ≈ 400 – 620 nm
Wavelength of peak sensitivity of human eye: ≈ 555 nm (photopic)
                                               ≈ 510 nm (scotopic)
Mechanical equivalent of light: 1 lm ≡ 1/683 W at 540 THz (λ ≈ 555 nm)
i.e. 1.46 W/klm (A 60 W incandescent light bulb emits about 1 klm = 1000 lm.
Compared to an optimum light source that delivers all its energy as light
at 540 THz, a 60 W incandescent light bulb is 1.46/60 ≈ 2.4% efficient.)
Colours (representative wavelength, nm):
violet (420), blue (470), green (530), yellow (580), orange (610), red (660)

Some useful wavelengths (element, spectral designation or colour and/or
(Fraunhofer line)):

H Lyman α	121.6 nm	N_2^+ blue†	465.2	Hg yellow	579.1
Ca (K solar)	393.4	Hβ (F solar)*	486.1	Na (D_2 solar)	589.0
Ca (H solar)	396.8	O^{++} green*	495.9	Na (D_1 solar)	589.6
Hg violet	404.7	O^{++} green*	500.7	O red†	630.0
Hδ (h solar)	410.2	Hg green	546.1	He-Ne laser	632.8
Hγ (g solar)	434.0	O yel.-green†	557.7	O red†	636.4
Hg deep blue	435.8	Hg yellow	577.0	Hα (C solar)	656.3

*Strong contributor to the visual light of gaseous nebulae
†Strong auroral lines

ANGULAR RELATIONS

2π radians = 360° π = 3.141 592 653 589 793 2... ≈ $(113 \div 355)^{-1}$
Number of square degrees on a sphere = 41 253

For 360° = 24 h, 15° = 1 h, 15′ = 1 min, 15″ = 1 s

Relations between sidereal time t, right ascension α, hour angle h, declination δ,
azimuth A (measured east of north), altitude a, and latitude ϕ:

$h = t - \alpha$
$\sin a = \sin \delta \sin \phi + \cos h \cos \delta \cos \phi$
$\cos \delta \sin h = -\cos a \sin A$
$\sin \delta = \sin a \sin \phi + \cos a \cos A \cos \phi$
Annual precession in α ≈ 3.0750 + 1.3362 sin α tan δ seconds   (α must be
Annual precession in δ ≈ 20.043″ cos α in degrees)

SOME SI SYMBOLS AND PREFIXES

m	metre	N	newton (kg·m/s^2)	f	femto 10^{-15}
kg	kilogram	J	joule (N·m)	p	pico 10^{-12}
s	second	W	watt (J/s)	n	nano 10^{-9}
min	minute	Pa	pascal (N/m^2)	μ	micro 10^{-6}
h	hour	t	tonne (10^3 kg)	m	milli 10^{-3}
d	day	Hz	hertz (s^{-1})	c	centi 10^{-2}
a	year	C	coulomb (A·s)	k	kilo 10^3
A	ampere	V	volt (J/C)	M	mega 10^6
rad	radian	T	tesla (J·A^{-1}m^{-2})	G	giga 10^9
sr	steradian	lm	lumen	T	tera 10^{12}
K	kelvin (temperature)	cd	candela (lm/sr)	P	peta 10^{15}
ha	hectare (10^4 m^2)	lx	lux (lm/m^2)	E	exa 10^{18}

VOYAGES IN OUR PLANETARY SYSTEM
By Roy Bishop

A topic of considerable interest is the remarkable series of spacecraft that have explored our Moon and all but one of the other planets during the past half century. These explorations are significant for what they have revealed of our solar system, for the technological progress they represent, and for the broad awareness they have generated of humanity's place in the heavens. A knowledge of these achievements provides an invaluable historical perspective of this unique era.

The following chronological list should be a useful reference. No attempt has been made to record all space missions, nor even all space "firsts." Missions were carried out by the former Soviet Union (*), by the U.S.A. (no mark), by the European Space Agency (†), and jointly by the U.S.A. and European Space Agency (‡).

Year	Name	Significance
1957	*Sputnik 1**	First artificial satellite of Earth (October 4)
1957	*Sputnik 2**	First living being in space (a dog named Laika)
1959	*Luna 1**	First spacecraft to escape Earth's gravity
1959	*Luna 2**	First spacecraft to impact on the Moon
1961	*Vostok 1**	First human in space (Yuri Gagarin) (April 12)
1962	*Mariner 2*	First successful flyby of another planet (Venus)
1965	*Mariner 4*	First successful flyby of Mars
1966	*Luna 9**	First soft landing on the Moon
1966	*Venera 3**	First spacecraft to impact on another planet (Venus)
1966	*Luna 10**	First spacecraft to orbit the Moon
1968	*Apollo 8*	First human voyage to the Moon (and orbit, without landing) (Frank Borman, James Lovell, William Anders) (Dec. 24)
1969	*Apollo 11*	First humans on the Moon (Neil Armstrong, Edwin Aldrin) (July 20)
1970	*Venera 7**	First soft landing on another planet (Venus)
1971	*Mariner 9*	First spacecraft to orbit another planet (Mars)
1971	*Mariner 9*	First close views of other satellites (Phobos, Deimos)
1972	*Apollo 17*	Last human visit to the Moon (Dec. 14)
1973	*Pioneer 10*	First flyby of Jupiter
1973	*Pioneer 10*	First spacecraft to achieve escape speed from the Sun
1974	*Mariner 10*	First flyby of Mercury
1976	*Viking 1*	First successful Mars landing
1979	*Voyager 1*	First close-up study of Jupiter and its satellites
1979	*Pioneer 11*	First flyby of Saturn
1980	*Voyager 1*	First close-up study of Saturn and its satellites
1981	*STS-1*	First reusable spacecraft for humans (Space Shuttle, Columbia)
1985	*ICE*	First cometary encounter (Comet Giacobini-Zinner)
1986	*Giotto†*	First good image of a cometary nucleus (Comet Halley)
1986	*Voyager 2*	First flyby of Uranus
1989	*Voyager 2*	First flyby of Neptune
1991	*Galileo*	First flyby of an asteroid (951 Gaspra)
1994	*Galileo*	First satellite of an asteroid (243 Ida) discovered
1994/5	*Ulysses‡*	First flyby above the Sun's south/north poles
1995	*Galileo*	First probe into Jupiter's atmosphere
1997	*Pathfinder*	First roving vehicle on another planet (Mars)
2000	*Shoemaker*	First spacecraft to orbit an asteroid (Eros)

TABLE OF PRECESSION FOR ADVANCING 50 YEARS

RA for Dec–	RA for Dec+	Prec in Dec	Precession in right ascension for declination in row immediately below											Prec in Dec	RA for Dec+	RA for Dec–
			85°	80°	75°	70°	60°	50°	40°	30°	20°	10°	0°			
h m	h m	′	m	m	m	m	m	m	m	m	m	m	m	′	h m	h m
12 00	0 00	16.7	2.56	2.56	2.56	2.56	2.56	2.56	2.56	2.56	2.56	2.56	2.56	−16.7	12 00	24 00
12 30	0 30	16.6	4.22	3.39	3.10	2.96	2.81	2.73	2.68	2.64	2.61	2.59	2.56	−16.6	11 30	23 30
13 00	1 00	16.1	5.85	4.20	3.64	3.35	3.06	2.90	2.80	2.73	2.67	2.61	2.56	−16.1	11 00	23 00
13 30	1 30	15.4	7.43	4.98	4.15	3.73	3.30	3.07	2.92	2.81	2.72	2.64	2.56	−15.4	10 30	22 30
14 00	2 00	14.5	8.92	5.72	4.64	4.09	3.53	3.22	3.03	2.88	2.76	2.66	2.56	−14.5	10 00	22 00
14 30	2 30	13.3	10.31	6.41	5.09	4.42	3.73	3.37	3.13	2.95	2.81	2.68	2.56	−13.3	9 30	21 30
15 00	3 00	11.8	11.56	7.03	5.50	4.72	3.92	3.50	3.22	3.02	2.85	2.70	2.56	−11.8	9 00	21 00
15 30	3 30	10.2	12.66	7.57	5.86	4.99	4.09	3.61	3.30	3.07	2.88	2.72	2.56	−10.2	8 30	20 30
16 00	4 00	8.4	13.58	8.03	6.16	5.21	4.23	3.71	3.37	3.12	2.91	2.73	2.56	−8.4	8 00	20 00
16 30	4 30	6.4	14.32	8.40	6.40	5.39	4.34	3.79	3.42	3.15	2.94	2.74	2.56	−6.4	7 30	19 30
17 00	5 00	4.3	14.85	8.66	6.57	5.52	4.42	3.84	3.46	3.18	2.95	2.75	2.56	−4.3	7 00	19 00
17 30	5 30	2.2	15.18	8.82	6.68	5.59	4.47	3.88	3.49	3.20	2.96	2.76	2.56	−2.2	6 30	18 30
18 00	6 00	0.0	15.29	8.88	6.72	5.62	4.49	3.89	3.50	3.20	2.97	2.76	2.56	0.0	6 00	18 00
0 00	12 00	−16.7	2.56	2.56	2.56	2.56	2.56	2.56	2.56	2.56	2.56	2.56	2.56	16.7	24 00	12 00
0 30	12 30	−16.6	0.90	1.74	2.02	2.16	2.31	2.39	2.44	2.48	2.51	2.54	2.56	16.6	23 30	11 30
1 00	13 00	−16.1	−0.73	0.93	1.49	1.77	2.06	2.22	2.32	2.39	2.46	2.51	2.56	16.1	23 00	11 00
1 30	13 30	−15.4	−2.31	0.14	0.97	1.39	1.82	2.05	2.20	2.31	2.41	2.49	2.56	15.4	22 30	10 30
2 00	14 00	−14.5	−3.80	−0.60	0.48	1.03	1.60	1.90	2.09	2.24	2.36	2.46	2.56	14.5	22 00	10 00
2 30	14 30	−13.3	−5.19	−1.28	0.03	0.70	1.39	1.75	1.99	2.17	2.31	2.44	2.56	13.3	21 30	9 30
3 00	15 00	−11.8	−6.44	−1.90	−0.38	0.40	1.20	1.62	1.90	2.11	2.27	2.42	2.56	11.8	21 00	9 00
3 30	15 30	−10.2	−7.54	−2.45	−0.74	0.13	1.03	1.51	1.82	2.05	2.24	2.41	2.56	10.2	20 30	8 30
4 00	16 00	−8.4	−8.46	−2.91	−1.04	−0.09	0.89	1.41	1.75	2.00	2.21	2.39	2.56	8.4	20 00	8 00
4 30	16 30	−6.4	−9.20	−3.27	−1.28	−0.27	0.78	1.33	1.70	1.97	2.19	2.38	2.56	6.4	19 30	7 30
5 00	17 00	−4.3	−9.73	−3.54	−1.45	−0.39	0.70	1.28	1.66	1.94	2.17	2.37	2.56	4.3	19 00	7 00
5 30	17 30	−2.2	−10.06	−3.70	−1.56	−0.47	0.65	1.25	1.63	1.92	2.16	2.37	2.56	2.2	18 30	6 30
6 00	18 00	0.0	−10.17	−3.75	−1.59	−0.50	0.63	1.23	1.63	1.92	2.16	2.36	2.56	0.0	18 00	6 00

If declination is positive, use inner RA scale; if declination is negative, use outer RA scale and reverse the sign of the precession in declination.
To avoid interpolation in this table, which becomes increasingly inaccurate for large |Dec|, precession formulae may be used (see p. 31).

TIME

TIME AND TIME SCALES
By Roy Bishop

Time has been said to be nature's way of keeping everything from happening at once. Isaac Newton (1687) perceived time as being separate from and more fundamental than the spinning of changeable planets or the oily mechanisms of clocks: "Absolute, true, and mathematical time, of itself, and from its own nature flows equably without regard to anything external." This is the common sense or intuitive view most people have of time.

Albert Einstein was the first to understand that time is but an abstraction that does not exist independently of clocks. In his special theory of relativity (1905), Einstein predicted that clocks moving relative to an observer tick slower (time dilation). A decade later in his theory of gravitation, the general theory of relativity, Einstein predicted that clocks lower or higher than the observer in a gravitational field run slower or faster, respectively, than the observer's clock. In the case of a lower clock, this is called the gravitational redshift. These counterintuitive effects are not only real, but in recent years they have found their way into the consumer marketplace in the form of GPS (Global Positioning System) receivers. These handheld units receive signals from orbiting atomic clocks and rely on programs that allow for time dilation and gravitational redshift.

As to understanding time, Lord Kelvin said that you know a physical quantity if you can measure it. Time can indeed be measured, with mind-boggling precision. For those who feel compelled to state "We still don't know what time actually is," perhaps the mystery resides merely in the meaning of this statement.

The essence of time is that isolated material changes occur in invariant ratios one with respect to another. That is, as Sir Hermann Bondi has put it: "Time is that which is manufactured by clocks." Thus, to deal with time, clocks must be devised and units established.

Periodic Time Intervals and Clocks

There are three obvious, natural, periodic time intervals on Earth: the seasonal cycle (year); the cycle of lunar phases (month); and the day–night cycle (day). The cycle of the seasons is called the *tropical year* and contains 365.242 190 days. The cycle of lunar phases is known as the *synodic month* and equals 29.530 589 days. The average day–night (diurnal) cycle is the *mean solar day* and presently contains approximately 86 400.001 s. Other types of year, month, and day have been defined and are listed along with brief definitions and durations on p. 28.

The problem of accurately subdividing these natural intervals to make time locally available at any moment (i.e. timekeeping) was satisfactorily solved in 1657 by Christiaan Huygens, who invented the first practical pendulum clock. Through successive refinements the pendulum clock reigned supreme for nearly three centuries, until it was surpassed in precision by the quartz oscillator in the 1940s. Within another 20 years the quartz clock was, in turn, superseded by the cesium atomic clock which today has a precision near 2 in 10^{15} (one second in 16 million years) using the technique of *laser cooling* of atomic beams (see *Physics Today*, December 1997, p. 17, February 1998, p. 21, and March 2001, p. 37).

Earth's Rotation and Time Scales

Of the three obvious, natural, periodic time intervals on Earth (year, month, and day), the day dominates our lives and determines the various time scales we have created. The day is caused primarily by Earth's rotation on its axis. To count rotations a reference or fiducial point is required. Four such points are of interest, and three of these are the basis of five time scales:

(1) Earth's rotation relative to the distant stars: Although the distant stars (or better, extragalactic sources) provide a reference frame to determine the "true" period of Earth's rotation (presently about 86 164.100 s), because of Earth's orbital motion and its rotational precession, this true period is not that of either the solar day or the RA/Dec coordinate grid used to specify astronomical positions. Hence no time scales are based on Earth's true rotational period.

(2) Earth's rotation relative to the equinox: The equator and poles of the RA/Dec celestial coordinate grid are aligned with Earth's mean equator and poles. ("Mean" denotes that small, periodic variations caused by the nutation of Earth's axis have been averaged out. Nutation involves the true pole moving relative to the mean pole with an amplitude of about 9″ and a variety of short periods up to 18.6 years.) Hence the RA/Dec grid slowly shifts relative to the distant stars as Earth's rotation axis precesses—a motion caused primarily by the torques exerted by the Moon and Sun on Earth's equatorial bulge. The gravitational influence of the other planets causes the plane of the ecliptic also to precess, although this *planetary precession* is far smaller than the *lunisolar precession* of the mean equator. The sum of these two precessions is called *general precession*. General precession causes the zero point of right ascension (the "Greenwich of the skies," the vernal equinox, or "first point of Aries") to drift westward along the ecliptic about 50″ per year. As a result, Earth's rotation period relative to the equinox (called the *mean sidereal day*, currently 86 164.092 s) is about 8.4 ms shorter than the time for one rotation. At any longitude on Earth, the RA of a star on the meridian (corrected for nutation) is the **Local Mean Sidereal Time (LMST)** at that instant. At the Greenwich meridian (0° longitude) this is called **Greenwich Mean Sidereal Time (GMST)**. LMST may be used to set a telescope on an object of known right ascension. The hour angle of the object equals the sidereal time less the right ascension. LMST may be available from a sidereal clock, or it can be calculated as explained in the middle of p. 39. Because Earth makes one more rotation with respect to the other stars than it does with respect to the Sun during a year, sidereal time gains relative to time scales linked to the Sun (see below) by about 3 min 56 s per day, or 2 hours per month.

(3) Earth's rotation relative to the real Sun: It is a common misconception that the Sun is highest in the sky and lies on the local north–south meridian at 12:00 noon. However, time based on the position of the Sun in the sky, known as local *apparent solar time* or *sundial time*, can differ by up to an hour or more from civil time (the time that we normally use). There are two reasons for this discrepancy. One reason is that the Sun's eastward annual apparent motion around the sky is far from uniform both because of Earth's elliptical orbit and because of the inclination of the celestial equator to the ecliptic. Thus apparent solar time does not have a uniform rate (see the next paragraph). The second reason for the difference between sundial time and civil time is addressed in the penultimate paragraph of this section.

(4) Earth's rotation relative to the mean Sun: If the Sun is replaced by a fictitious mean sun moving uniformly along the celestial equator, Earth's rotation relative to this mean sun defines **Local Mean (solar) Time (LMT)**. Apparent solar time can differ by up to 16 min from LMT depending upon the time of year (see Sundial Correction on p. 92). Small, periodic shifts of Earth's crust relative to the axis of rotation (*polar motion*) affect astronomical time determinations through the resulting east–west shift in the meridian at latitudes away from the equator. LMT at the Greenwich meridian (0° longitude) when corrected for this polar motion is called *Universal Time* (**UT1**, or often simply **UT**). UT1 is determined using very long baseline interferometry, satellite laser-ranging, lunar laser-ranging data, and GPS data (via the International GPS Service).

All of the above mean time scales (LMST, GMST, LMT, and UT1), being based upon Earth's rotation, are only as uniform as this rotation. By the mid-19th century, discrepancies between theory and the observed motion of the Moon indicated that, over the long term, Earth's rotation is slowing down. However, not until clocks became better timekeepers than the spinning Earth (c. 1940 when crystal-controlled clocks exceeded precisions of 1 in 10^{10}) was it realized how complex is the variable rotation of our planet. There are (i) long-, (ii) medium-, and (iii) short-term accelerations:

(i) Over many centuries there is a *secular* slowing caused by tidal friction of about 8 parts in 10^{13} per day (i.e. the day becomes one second longer about every 40 000 years).

(ii) Over a few decades there are *random* accelerations (positive and negative), apparently caused by core–mantle interactions. These are about 10 times larger than the tidal deceleration and thus completely obscure the latter effect over time intervals of less than a century or so.

(iii) The largest accelerations in Earth's rotation rate are short-term ones: *periodic components* are associated mainly with lunar-induced tides (over two-week and monthly intervals) and seasonal meteorological factors (over semiannual and annual intervals); *nonperiodic* (chaotic) high-frequency variations are associated mainly with the global atmospheric wind and pressure distributions. These short-term accelerations are typically one or two orders of magnitude larger again than the random, decade fluctuations on which they are superimposed (see the article by John Wahr in the June 1986 issue of *Sky & Telescope*, p. 545).

Uniform Time Scales

(1) Based on orbital motion: Although Earth's axial rotation is not sufficiently predictable to serve as a precise clock, the orbital motions of our Moon, Earth, and the other planets are predictable to high accuracy. Through the dynamical equations describing these motions plus extended astronomical observations, a uniform time scale can be derived. Such a scale, known as *Ephemeris Time* (ET), was for several years (1952–1984) the basis of astronomical ephemerides. Early in the 20th century the UT1 and ET scales coincided, but since Earth's rotation rate has been generally slower than the ET rate, by 1970 UT1 was 40 s behind ET and was losing more than one second per year. During the next 15 years, Earth's rotation rate increased (part of the random decade fluctuations). During the 1990s UT1 lost about 0.7 s per year relative to ET (actually TT, see two paragraphs ahead).

(2) Based on atomic motion: Atoms display a permanence and stability that planets, quartz crystals, and pendulums cannot. The idea of an atomic clock was proposed by the American physicist Isidor Rabi in 1945. In 1967, *the second became the basic unit of time* when it was given an atomic definition: 9 192 631 770 periods of the radiation involved in the transition between the two hyperfine levels of the ground state of the cesium 133 atom at mean sea level. This is known as the SI (for Système International) second (abbreviation s, *not* sec). The number 9 192 631 770 was chosen so that the SI second is identical to the older ET second to within the precision of measurement.

Because of several difficulties surrounding both the original concept of ET and its determination, and because atomic clocks had become readily available, in 1984 ET was abandoned in favour of *Terrestrial Dynamical Time* (TDT). The unit of TDT is the SI second, and its scale was chosen to agree with the 1984 ET scale. In 1991, when the general theory of relativity was explicitly adopted as the theoretical background for defining space-time reference frames, TDT was renamed simply **Terrestrial Time (TT).** The unit of TT is the SI second on the geoid (i.e. as would be produced by a perfect SI clock located at mean sea level on Earth). TT is the time reference for apparent geocentric ephemerides, and it is realized via TAI (see below).

International Atomic Time (**TAI** = Temps Atomique International) is based on a weighted average of atomic clocks in many countries and is the most precise *achievable* time scale. Because not even atomic clocks are perfect timekeepers, TAI shifts unpredictably relative to the ideal SI rate (the TT rate) by a few microseconds over several years. TAI was arbitrarily set to agree with UT1 at the beginning of 1958, which led to the definition that TT be exactly 32.184 s ahead of TAI on 1977 January 1.0 TAI. This ensured continuity of TT with ET.

Two other SI-based time scales are in use: *Geocentric Coordinate Time* (**TCG**) and *Barycentric Coordinate Time* (**TCB**) for nonrotating coordinate grids located at the centres of mass of Earth and of the solar system, respectively. Both use the SI second but, because of the gravitational redshift, relative to an observer at sea level on Earth both have rates slower than TT (TCG and TCB lose about 22 ms per year and 489 ms per year, respectively, relative to TT). TCG and TCB were arbitrarily set to agree with TT at Earth's centre at the beginning of 1977. Like TT, TCG and TCB are realized via TAI.

(3) Based on pulsars: Millisecond radio pulsars (old, rapidly spinning neutron stars) display extraordinary stability in their periods of rotation, comparable with the best atomic clocks. However, given the elaborate equipment needed to observe pulsars and the data analysis required, it is unlikely that, as the basis for a uniform time scale, a laboratory-based reproducible physical phenomenon like the cesium atomic transition will be abandoned in favour of a pulsar.

Uniform Time Scales with Steps (to track the mean Sun)

Closely related to UT1 (which follows Earth's variable rotation relative to the mean Sun) is *Coordinated Universal Time* (**UTC),** introduced in its present form in 1972 as the basis of the world system of civil time. UTC runs at the SI rate and is offset an integral number of seconds from TAI so that it approximates UT1. When required (at the end of June 30 or December 31), "leap seconds" are inserted into (or, if necessary, deleted from) UTC so that the difference UT1 − UTC = ΔUT1 does not exceed ±0.9 s. UTC now lags TAI, and as of 1999 January 1, 0h UT (when a leap second was last inserted) TAI − UTC = ΔAT = 32 s. Thus as this edition of the *Observer's Handbook* goes to press (summer 2001), TT − UTC = 32 s + 32.184 s = 64.184 s exactly (see the diagram on the next page). In late 1998 Earth's rotation sped up slightly; as a consequence another leap second will not be needed until at least the end of June 2002. UTC is readily available via radio time signals or GPS receivers. (Note: The term *Greenwich Mean Time* (GMT) over the years has had three different meanings: the same as UT1, UTC, or mean solar time at the Greenwich meridian with 0 hours corresponding to noon. To avoid confusion, the term Greenwich Mean Time should not be used.)

Anyone in North America can keep track of Earth's varying rotation by listening to the CHU or WWV radio time signals in which is coded the difference $\Delta UT1 =$ (UT1 − UTC) (see TIME SIGNALS at the right). It is interesting to record $\Delta UT1$ about once a month and use these data to make a graphical display of (TT − UT1) as a function of time over several years. Note that at least until the end of June 2002, TT − UT1 = 64.184 − (UT1 − UTC).

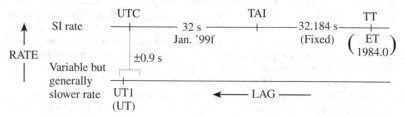

This diagram displays the rate and scale relations between time scales that run at or near the SI rate and which are not longitude dependent.

Local Mean (solar) Time (LMT) would suffice for the inhabitants of an isolated village, but with the advent in the 19th century of rapid travel and communication (railways, steamships, and the telegraph), it became essential that clocks over a range of longitudes indicate the same time. To keep these clocks reasonably in phase with the day–night cycle and yet to avoid the inconvenience to travellers of a local time that varies continuously with longitude, in 1884 Earth was divided into 24 **Standard Time** zones, adjacent zones generally differing by one hour and each ideally 15 degrees wide (see the time zone map on p. 41). All clocks within the same zone read the same time. The Canadian railway surveyor and construction engineer Sir Sandford Fleming (1827–1915) was instrumental in establishing this system of standard time zones. The zero zone is centred on the Greenwich meridian (longitude 0°), and, since 1972, standard time in that zone is UTC. Thus the world system of civil time is based on UTC and includes the "leap seconds," which keep UTC near UT1. Depending upon an observer's location within his or her standard time zone, standard time may differ by up to an hour or so from LMT (see the third paragraph on p. 99). This is the second reason why the Sun seldom, if ever, is on the observer's meridian at 12:00 noon, standard time.

Some countries observe *Daylight Saving Time* during the summer months. In Canada and the United States, clocks are generally* set one hour ahead of standard time at 2 a.m. local time on the first Sunday in April, and return to standard time at 2 a.m. local time on the last Sunday in October: "spring ahead, fall back."

---

*Saskatchewan, Arizona, Indiana, and Hawaii do *not* observe daylight saving time.

TIME SIGNALS

National time services distribute Coordinated Universal Time (UTC). UTC is coordinated through the Bureau International des Poids et Mesures (BIPM) in Sèvres, France so that most time services are synchronized to a tenth of a millisecond. Radio time signals available in North America include:

CHU Ottawa, Ontario, Canada 3.330, 7.335, 14.670 MHz
WWV Fort Collins, Colorado, U.S.A. 2.5, 5, 10, 15, 20 MHz

For CHU, each minute starts at the *beginning* of the tone following the voice announcement, the tone for the 29th second is omitted, and the tones for seconds 31 through 39 have a different sound from the others.

The difference $\Delta UT1 = UT1 - UTC$ to the nearest tenth of a second is coded in the signals. If UT1 is ahead of UTC, second markers beginning at the 1-second mark of each minute are doubled, the number of doubled markers indicating the number of tenths of a second UT1 is ahead of UTC. If UT1 is behind UTC, the doubled markers begin at the 9-second point.

Time signals are also available by telephone from the National Research Council in Ottawa, Canada. Call (613) 745-1576 (English) or (613) 745-9426 (French).

MEAN SIDEREAL TIME, 2002

The following is the Greenwich Mean Sidereal Time (GMST) in hours on day 0 at 0h UT of each month ("day 0" is the last day of the previous month):

Jan. 6.6327	Apr. 12.5466	Jul. 18.5262	Oct. 0.5715
Feb. 8.6697	May 14.5179	Aug. 20.5632	Nov. 2.6085
Mar. 10.5096	Jun. 16.5549	Sep. 22.6002	Dec. 4.5798

GMST (in hours) at hour t UT on day d of the month =
GMST at 0h UT on day $0 + 0.065710d + 1.002738t$
LMST (Local Mean Sidereal Time) = GMST − west longitude (or + east longitude)

LMST calculated by this method will be accurate to ±0.2 s provided t is stated to ±0.1 s or better and the observer's longitude is known to ±1″. (Note that t must be expressed in decimal hours UT. Also, to achieve ±0.1 s accuracy in t, the correction $\Delta UT1$ must be applied to UTC. See the TIME SIGNALS section above.)

JULIAN DATE (JD), 2002

The Julian Date (JD) is commonly used by astronomers to refer to the time of astronomical events, because it avoids some of the annoying complexities of the civil calendar. Julian Date 0.0 was the instant of Greenwich mean noon on January 1, 4713 BC (see: "The Origin of the Julian Day System" by G. Moyer in *Sky & Telescope*, April 1981).

The Julian day **commences at noon** (12h) UT. To find the Julian Date at any time during 2002, determine the day of the month and time at the Greenwich meridian, convert this to a decimal day, and add it to one of the following numbers according to the month (these numbers are the Julian Dates for 0h UT on the 0th day of each month):

Jan. ...245 2274.5	Apr. ...245 2364.5	Jul. 245 2455.5	Oct. ...245 2547.5
Feb. ...245 2305.5	May ..245 2394.5	Aug. ..245 2486.5	Nov. ..245 2578.5
Mar. ..245 2333.5	Jun. ...245 2425.5	Sep. ...245 2517.5	Dec. ..245 2608.5

For example, 21:36 EDT on May 18 = 1:36 UT on May 19 = May 19.07 UT = 245 2394.5 + 19.07 = JD 245 2413.57.

The Julian Dates for 0h UT January 0 for the three previous years are 245 0000.5 plus: 1178 (1999), 1543 (2000), 1909 (2001).

STANDARD TIME ZONES

The map at the right shows the world system of standard time zones. It was prepared and provided by Her Majesty's Nautical Almanac Office. Over the open oceans, the time zones are uniformly spaced and are bounded by lines of longitude 15° apart. In populated regions, political and other considerations have considerably modified the ideal geometry.

As Earth rotates with sunlight shining from one side, at some line of longitude the day of the week must jump discontinuously ahead by one day (otherwise, Monday would be followed by Monday!). The line chosen for this jump is in the relatively unpopulated central part of the Pacific Ocean and approximates longitude 180°. It is called the International Date Line. A person travelling westward across this line has to advance the calendar date by one day, while an eastward-bound traveller moves back one day on the calendar.

The standard time zones are generally designated by letters of the alphabet. The zero time zone, centred on the longitude 0° meridian passing through the Airy Transit Circle at the Old Royal Observatory in Greenwich, England, is denoted Z. Standard time within this zone is Coordinated Universal Time (UTC). Zones A, B, C, ..., M (J excluded), run eastward at one-hour intervals to the International Date Line, while zones N, O, P, ..., Y run westward to the same boundary. Zones M and Y are only one-half hour wide. Also, as indicated on the map, there are several partial zones that are one-half hour different from the adjacent main zones.

In North America there are seven standard time zones. In terms of their name (and letter designation, hours behind the Greenwich zone, and the west longitude of the reference or standard meridian), these are:

(1) Newfoundland (P*, 3 h 30 min, 52.5°)
(2) Atlantic (Q, 4 h, 60°)
(3) Eastern (R, 5 h, 75°)
(4) Central (S, 6 h, 90°)
(5) Mountain (T, 7 h, 105°)
(6) Pacific (U, 8 h, 120°)
(7) Alaska (V, 9 h, 135°)

Note: Caution is advised when relying on the time-zone information given in this map. The zones are drawn based on the best information available as of July 2001 and are subject to change. Also, local jurisdictions, especially those near depicted zone boundaries, often adopt a a different time. For current official Canadian time zones visit **www.nrc.ca/inms/time/tze.html**. Current U.S. and world time zones can easily be found by doing an Internet search using the key words "time zones."

WORLD MAP OF TIME ZONES

International Date Line

Standard Time = Universal Time + value from table

	h m		h m		h m		h m		h m
Z	0	E*	+5 30	K	+10	N	−1	T	−7
A	+1	F	+6	K*	+10 30	O	−2	U	−8
B	+2	F*	+6 30	L	+11	P	−3	U*	−8 30
C*	+3 30	G	+7	L*	+11 30	P*	−3 30	V	−9
D	+4	H	+8	M	+12	Q	−4	V*	−9 30
D*	+4 30	I*	+9	M*	+13	R	−5	W	−10
E	+5			M†	+14	S	−6	X	−11
								Y	−12

‡ No Standard Time legally adopted

STANDARD TIME ZONES

Corrected to July 2001
Zone boundaries are approximate
Daylight Saving Time (*Summer Time*), usually one hour in advance of Standard Time, is kept in some places
Map outline © *Mountain High Maps*
Compiled by HM Nautical Almanac Office

International Date Line

ASTRONOMICAL TWILIGHT AND SIDEREAL TIME
BY RANDALL BROOKS

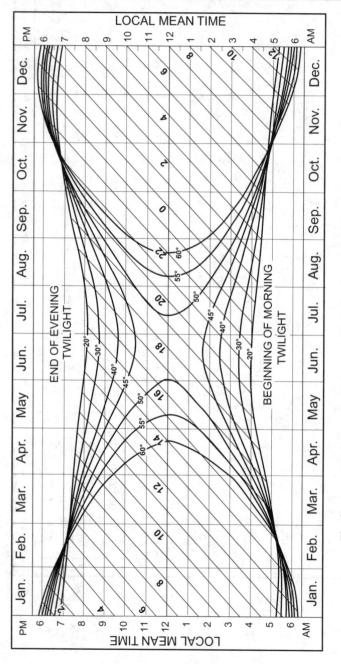

The diagram gives for any day of the year: (1) the local mean time (LMT) of the end and beginning of astronomical twilight at seven specified northern latitudes (curved lines); (2) the local mean sidereal time (LMST = right ascension at the observer's meridian) as a function of LMT (diagonal lines).

OPTICS AND OBSERVING

TELESCOPE PARAMETERS

Equations

Objective: f_o = focal length   *Eyepiece*: f_e = focal length
D = diameter d_f = diameter of field stop
FR = focal ratio θ_p = apparent angular field

Whole Instrument: M = angular magnification
d_p = diameter of exit pupil
θ_c = actual angular field

$$M = f_o/f_e = D/d_p \approx \theta_p/\theta_c \qquad FR = f_o/D \qquad d_f* = f_o\theta_c \approx f_e\theta_p$$

   (θ_c and θ_p must be expressed in radians.)

Performance

D is assumed to be expressed in millimetres.

Light Grasp (LG) is the ratio of the light flux intercepted by a telescope's objective lens or mirror to that intercepted by a human eye having a 7-mm-diameter entrance pupil.

Limiting Visual Magnitude $m \approx 2.7 + 5 \log D$, assuming transparent, dark-sky conditions and magnification $M \geq 1D$. (See *Sky & Telescope*, *45*, 401, 1973; *77*, 332, 1989; *78*, 522, 1989).

Smallest Resolvable Angle $\alpha \approx 120/D$ seconds of arc. However, atmospheric conditions seldom permit values less than 0.5″.

Useful Magnification Range $\approx 0.2D$ to $2D$. The lower limit ($0.2D$) guarantees that, for most observers, all the light exiting a telescope can reach the retina. (The reciprocal of the coefficient to D is the diameter (in mm) of the telescope's exit pupil. Also, see the next section concerning exit pupils and magnification.) The upper limit ($2D$) is determined by the wave nature of light and the optical limitations of the eye, although atmospheric turbulence usually limits the maximum magnification to 400× or less. For examination of double stars, detection of faint stars, and studying structure in bright nebulae, magnifications of up to $3D$ are sometimes useful.

Values for some common apertures are:

D (mm):	60	100	125	150	200	250	330	444
LG:	73	200	320	460	820	1300	2200	4000
m:	11.6	12.7	13.2	13.6	14.2	14.7	15.3	15.9
α:	2.0″	1.2″	1.0″	0.80″	0.60″	0.48″	0.36″	0.27″
$0.2D$:	12×	20×	25×	30×	40×	50×	66×	89×
$2D$:	120×	200×	250×	300×	400×	500×	660×	890×

TELESCOPE EXIT PUPILS
By Roy Bishop

The performance of a visual telescope is constrained by Earth's atmosphere, the wave aspect of light, the design of the telescope, imperfections in its optical system, and the properties of the human visual system. Telescope and eye meet at the *exit pupil* of the telescope, which is the image of the telescope's objective lens or mirror formed by its eyepiece. When a telescope is pointed at a bright area, such as the daytime sky, the exit pupil appears as a small disk of light hovering in the space just behind the eyepiece. (Insert a small piece of paper in this vicinity to demonstrate that this disk of light *really is* located behind the eyepiece.) Since the exit pupil is the narrowest point in the beam of light emerging from the telescope, it is here that the observer's eye must be located to make optimum use of the light passing through the telescope.

The diagram on p. 47 may be used to display the relation between the diameter of the exit pupil (d_p) of a telescope and the focal lengths (f_e) of various eyepieces. Both d_p and f_e are expressed in millimetres. The numbered scale around the upper right-hand corner of the diagram indicates the focal ratio (FR) of the objective lens or mirror of the telescope. (The FR equals the focal length of the objective divided by its diameter; see the previous page.) To prepare the diagram for a particular telescope, locate the FR of the telescope's objective on the FR scale, and draw a straight diagonal line from there to the origin (the lower left-hand corner). The diagram provides a visual display of the standard relation $d_p = f_e/\text{FR}$.

To determine, for example, the eyepiece focal length required to give an exit pupil of 3 mm on a certain telescope, locate $d_p = 3$ on the ordinate, run horizontally across to the diagonal line corresponding to the FR of that telescope, and from there drop vertically downward to the abscissa to find f_e. This procedure may, of course, be reversed: for a given f_e, find the corresponding d_p.

Magnification Ranges

The ranges H, M, L, and RFT blocked off along the ordinate of the diagram break the d_p scale into four sections, starting at 0.5 mm and increasing by factors of 2. Although this sectioning is somewhat arbitrary, it does correspond closely to what are usually considered to be the high (H), medium (M), low (L), and "richest-field telescope" (RFT) magnification ranges of any visual telescope—and the associated d_p ranges are easy to remember.

High Magnifications: In the case of the Moon, the planets, and all but the dimmest stars, the highest useful magnification is the point at which blurring due to diffraction (caused by the wave nature of light) becomes noticeable. This corresponds approximately to $d_p = 0.5$ mm, assuming good optics and negligible atmospheric turbulence (i.e. excellent "seeing"). Higher magnifications will not reveal any more detail in these images and will cause reductions in four desirable features: sharpness, brightness, field of view, and eye relief (the space between the eye and eyepiece). Also, as d_p is made progressively smaller, imperfections and debris in the interior of the eye (in the vitreous humour in front of the retina) become more noticeable and interfere with clear vision. However, for objects requiring the use of averted vision (e.g. faint stars, nebulae, and galaxies), the acuity of the eye is much reduced and very high magnifications ($d_p < 0.5$ mm) can sometimes be used to advantage (although only the brightest areas of nebulae and galaxies will still be visible at such magnifications).

Very Low Magnifications: Magnifications in the RFT range are useful because they yield wide fields of view, the brightest (highest luminance) images of extended objects, and for common telescope apertures, the most stars visible in one view (hence the term "richest field"). The lowest magnification that still makes use of the full aperture of a telescope is determined by the point at which the diameter of the telescope's exit pupil matches the diameter of the *entrance pupil* of the observer's eye.

For the dark-adapted eye, the entrance-pupil diameter seldom equals the often-quoted figure of 7 mm, but depends, among other things, upon the age of the observer as indicated by the scale in the upper left portion of the diagram (see Kadlecová et al., *Nature*, *182*, 1520, 1958; *Sky & Telescope*, May 1992, 502). Note that this scale indicates *average* values; the maximum diameter of the entrance pupil of the eye of any *one* individual may differ by up to a millimetre from these values. A horizontal line should be drawn across the diagram corresponding to the maximum diameter of one's own entrance pupil. This line will be an upper bound on d_p in the same sense that the line at $d_p = 0.5$ mm is a lower bound. Note that in daylight, the entrance pupil of the eye has a diameter in the range of 2 mm to 4 mm. Thus for daylight use of telescopes, the upper bound on d_p will be correspondingly reduced.

Ultra-Low Magnifications: If a d_p value larger than the entrance pupil of the eye is used, the iris of the observer's eye will cut off some of the light passing through the telescope to the retina; that is, the iris will have become the light-limiting aperture (*aperture stop*) of the system rather than the edge of the telescope's objective. In this case, the cornea of the eye together with the lenses of the telescope's eyepiece form an image of the observer's iris at the objective of the telescope; to the incoming starlight, a highly magnified image of the iris hovers as an annular skirt covering the outer region of the objective of the telescope! A telescope can be used at such "ultra-low" magnifications, but obviously a telescope of smaller aperture would perform as well. However, ultra-low magnifications on any telescope *do* have two advantages:

(1) A wider actual field of view, assuming the field stop of the eyepiece will permit this (an eyepiece requiring a 2-inch-diameter focuser is usually necessary).

(2) Ease of alignment of the entrance pupil of the eye with the exit pupil of the telescope, an aspect of viewing that is usually troublesome when these two pupils are nearly the same size. An oversize exit pupil provides "slop," making alignment less critical. This is particularly helpful when using binoculars during activities involving motion, such as boating or bird-watching. This is one advantage of using 7×50 (= $M \times D$) binoculars rather than 7×35 binoculars for daytime activities, although less than half of the light entering the larger binoculars can reach the observer's retinas.

Optimum Low Magnification: A value of d_p a millimetre or two *smaller* than the entrance pupil of the eye has several advantages:

(1) Viewing is more comfortable, since the observer can move a bit (move the head and/or scan the field) without cutting into the light beam and dimming the image. As mentioned above, ultra-low magnifications have the same advantage, but light is wasted.

(2) Light entering near the edge of the pupil of the dark-adapted eye is not as effective in stimulating the rod cells in the retina—the "scotopic Stiles-Crawford effect" (see VanLoo and Enoch, *Vision Research*, *15*, 1005, 1975). Thus the smaller d_p will result in more effective use of the light.

(3) Aberrations in the cornea and lens of the eye are usually greatest in the peripheral regions and can distort star images. The smaller d_p will avoid the worst of these regions and produce sharper star images.

(4) With the higher magnification, structure in dim, extended objects, such as galaxies and bright and dark nebulae, will be more easily seen. (Our ability to see detail is greatly reduced in dim light, since the retina organizes its cells into larger units, thereby sacrificing resolution in order to improve signal-to-noise in the sparse patter of photons.)

(5) The background sky glow will be darker, producing views that some observers consider to be aesthetically more pleasing.

(The only disadvantage of having d_p a millimetre or two smaller than the entrance pupil of the eye is a somewhat reduced field of view, but this will be minimal if an eyepiece having a larger apparent angular field is available at this higher magnification.)

Using the Diagram

Once the diagonal line corresponding to a telescope's focal ratio has been drawn and the upper bound on d_p is established, the diagram at the right gives a concise and convenient display of the eyepiece/exit pupil/magnification range relations for a particular telescope and observer. One can see at a glance what range of eyepiece focal lengths is suitable.

Some examples:

(1) Consider the common 8-inch Schmidt-Cassegrain telescopes. These have $D = 200$ mm and (usually) FR = 10. The diagram indicates that eyepieces with focal lengths from 5 mm to 55 mm are usable for most observers. With a 32-mm eyepiece, the diagram gives $d_p = 3.2$ mm, in the L magnification range, and the magnification $M = D/d_p = 200/3.2 = 62\times$.

(2) If an observer wishes to use the full aperture of an FR = 4.5 telescope, a 40-mm eyepiece is ruled out. Similarly, a 70-year-old observer should probably not use even a 27-mm eyepiece on such a telescope and should not bother with 7×50 or 11×80 binoculars, unless ease of eye/exit pupil alignment is the main consideration.

(3) With ordinary eyepieces ($f_e \leq 55$ mm), a telescope with FR = 15 cannot be operated in the RFT range, unless a compressor lens is added to reduce its FR.

(4) There is no point in using extremely short focal length eyepieces and Barlow lenses on telescopes having large FRs. This is a common fault (among many others!) with camera/department store "junk telescopes."

(5) Exit-pupil diameters of about 1 mm and smaller cause "floaters" (mobile debris within the eye) to interfere with vision. This problem increases with age. To avoid the distraction of floaters, an observer might choose to keep exit-pupil diameters larger than 1.5 mm. For this lower limit the diagram indicates a minimum eyepiece focal length of, for example, 7 mm for a FR = 4.5 telescope and 24 mm for a FR = 16 telescope. With this restriction, to achieve a magnification of 250× for observing planets, a telescope would need an aperture of at least $D = M \times d_p = 250 \times 1.5 = 375$ mm. Hence, in addition to providing more light and greater resolution, a large-aperture telescope makes floaters less noticeable.

EXIT PUPILS DIAGRAM

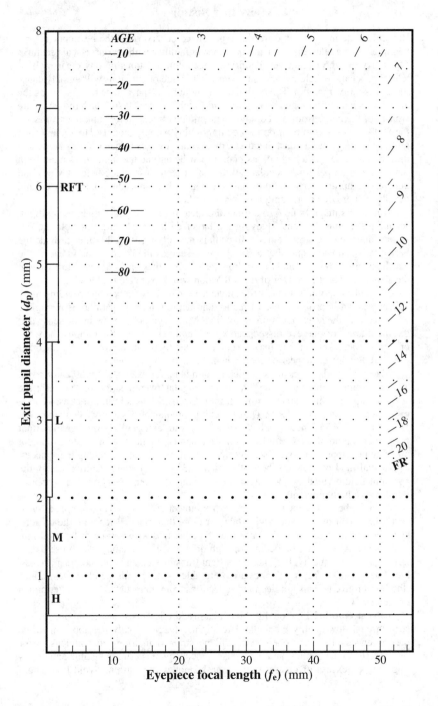

BINOCULARS
BY ROY BISHOP

Binoculars are indispensable for the experienced observer and the best choice for a beginner over a telescope. For the beginner unfamiliar with the large-scale features of the sky or who cannot yet identify a dozen constellations on any clear night, a telescope's narrow field of view and confusing image orientations will quickly cause more frustration than fun. The beginner is at a double disadvantage because he or she also does not know enough about astronomical telescopes to distinguish those that are worthy of the name from the common camera/department store "junk telescopes"— the $299 wonders with poor optics and impossibly wobbly mounts. How many such telescopes are gathering dust in closets, their young owners turned off astronomy and their parents a few hundred dollars poorer? Far better had the same investment been made in a good pair of binoculars. With their ease of use, wide field of view, and unreversed, upright images, binoculars are a great help in finding one's way around the sky, and provide many unique views of the heavens.

Binoculars magnifying 6 to 8 times are ideal for locating planets in the twilight, scanning the constellations, studying the larger dark nebulae and star fields of our galaxy, and viewing large comets. Binoculars magnifying 10 to 20 times provide the best views of objects spanning a few degrees, such as the Hyades, the Pleiades, the North American Nebula, and the Andromeda Galaxy; they also give the finest view of the slender crescent Moon, or of the full Moon with broken clouds blowing by.

Binoculars permit us to view the universe with both eyes, thereby providing more advantages: an improved sense of reality and depth (although parallax is negligible when viewing the heavens); more relaxed viewing; a complete view in the sense that the blind areas of one eye (associated with blood vessels and the region where the optic nerve attaches to the retina) are compensated by the field provided by the other eye; and dim objects appear brighter when viewed with two eyes.

Sizes: Binocular sizes are specified by numbers, for example, 7×50 and 8×30. The first number, including the "$\times$," is the angular magnification or "power"; the second number is the diameter of the front (objective) lenses in millimetres. That is, in the notation on p. 43: $M \times D$. Thus the exit pupil diameter is easily calculated from $D \div M$ (e.g. 7×35 binoculars have $35 \div 7 = 5$ mm exit pupils). Another important parameter is field of view. Binoculars have apparent angular field diameters of about $50°$ when equipped with standard eyepieces, to near $70°$ with wide-angle eyepieces. The actual field of view on the sky (typically $3°$ to $10°$) equals approximately the apparent field divided by the magnification. Thus the area of sky visible decreases rapidly with higher magnifications.

What is the best binocular size for astronomical use? There is no simple answer. Almost *any* pair of binoculars will show far more than can be seen with the unaided eyes; however, for astronomical use the objective lenses should be at least 30 mm in diameter. Also, small binoculars of high quality are more enjoyable to use than a large pair of low quality. For maximum light transmission and high-contrast images, binoculars with *multicoated* optics are preferable to those with merely *coated* optics (the former give greenish or deep red reflections from their surfaces, the latter bluish or violet).

Caveat emptor! Low-quality binoculars (and telescopes) are common. Images seen through low-quality binoculars are slightly fuzzy (usually not apparent to the inexperienced observer), one's eyes will be strained in trying to compensate for imperfectly aligned optics, and the focusing mechanism is usually flexible and crackling with an excess of grease used to mask poor workmanship. Avoid both zoom (variable magnification) binoculars and binoculars that do not have an adjustable focus—invariably these are of low quality.

Considering that binoculars contain at least 14 pieces of glass with 36 optical surfaces, antireflection coatings on (hopefully) all air-to-glass surfaces, plus two focusing mechanisms and an interpupillary adjustment, it is not surprising that top-quality instruments are in the same price range as video cameras. Such prices buy crisp, high-contrast images, accurately aligned optics, precise, rugged, dust- and moisture-proof construction, and pleasurable service for a lifetime. Nevertheless, there is a big market for $99 binoculars and $299 telescopes, and manufacturers are happy to satisfy the demand. When it comes to optical equipment, quality usually matches price.

Stability: One aspect of binocular use not often appreciated is how much more can be seen if the binoculars are mounted on a stable support, such as a camera tripod. This eliminates the constant jiggling associated with hand-holding. Adapters for attaching binoculars to a tripod are available, although usually it is not difficult to make your own. A recent major advance in binocular design is "image-stabilization," an active optical system built into binoculars that compensates for the tremor associated with hand-holding. For example, the Canon company has introduced microprocessor-controlled binocular image stabilization, which gives near tripod-like stability with the convenience of hand-holding. Canon has produced 10×30, 12×36, 15×45, 15×50, and 18×50 models, the latter three being particularly impressive for astronomy (see *SkyNews*, July/August 1998, p. 12; and *Sky & Telescope*, July 2000, p. 59).

Rating Binoculars

A frequently cited figure for binocular performance is "Relative Brightness," which equals the square of the diameter (in millimetres) of the instrument's exit pupils. For example, for 7×50 binoculars this figure is $(50 \div 7)^2 = 51$. Although this is a measure of the surface brightness *(luminance)* of an extended object seen through the binoculars under nighttime conditions, it is a totally inadequate measure of binocular performance on the night sky. For instance, using this figure of merit, large 14×100 binoculars have practically the same rating as the unaided eyes (which, when young and in dim light, are effectively 1×7 binoculars)!

Since seeing depends upon light, and the amount of light passing through a pair of binoculars depends primarily upon the *area* of its objective lenses (diameter D), a D^2 dependence appears reasonable. However, although the amount of light going into the point images of stars increases as D^2, assuming constant magnification the increase in the luminance of the background sky as D increases leads to a somewhat slower improvement in the visibility of these stars. A similar muted improvement occurs for dim extended images, resulting in an approximately D^1 dependence, rather than D^2.

Also, for constant D the detail that can be seen in the night sky increases with the magnification M. The resulting lower luminance of the background sky allows fainter stars to be seen, and the visibility of structure in extended images improves as M increases because the image is larger and of fixed contrast relative to the sky background.

The simplest figure of merit for the performance of binoculars in low-light conditions that combines both variables is the mathematical product $M \times D$ (which looks the same as the binocular size specification!). In the case of two pairs of binoculars, one having twice the M and twice the D of the other, $M \times D$ indicates that "four times as much" should be visible in the larger instrument (e.g. 16×60 versus 8×30 binoculars). This is to be expected since in the larger instrument stars will be four times brighter and extended images will have four times the area from which the eyes can glean information, with luminances being the same in both instruments.

For many decades the venerable Carl Zeiss optical company has cited $\sqrt{(M \times D)}$ as a "Twilight Performance Factor" for binoculars, its value said to be proportional to the distance at which various binoculars will show the same detail. This is equivalent to $M \times D$ being proportional to *the amount of detail that can be seen at the same distance.* The latter situation is relevant for astronomy since, unlike a bird or other object on Earth, a star or a galaxy is always at essentially the *same distance* from the observer. $M \times D$ could be called the *visibility factor.*

Binocular Performance Diagram

The diagram at the right enables one to quickly compare binoculars in terms of their ability to reveal detail in the night sky. The vertical axis is magnification M; the horizontal axis is aperture D. The uniform grid of small dots is a guide to reading the diagram. The five straight lines indicate constant exit pupil diameters of 3, 4, 5, 6, and 7 mm, as indicated both by numbers and by circles of these diameters near the top ends of the lines. The five curved arcs indicate constant values of $M \times D$ (the visibility factor), increasing by successive powers of 2 toward the upper right (100, 200, 400, 800, and 1600). Each large dot represents a common size of binoculars. The arrows in the lower right corner indicate the directions on the diagram in which various quantities increase most rapidly.

Each straight line (constant exit pupil diameter) also corresponds to constant luminance of extended areas, such as the Orion Nebula or the background sky glow, with the luminance being proportional to the square of the exit pupil diameter (provided the entrance pupils of the observer's eyes are large enough to accommodate the exit pupils of the binoculars). However, exit pupils of 3 to 5 mm ensure (1) that all the light transmitted by the binoculars can enter the dark-adapted eyes no matter what the observer's age, (2) that alignment of exit pupils with dark-adapted eye pupils is relatively easy to achieve, (3) that the background sky glow will be subdued, and (4) that star images will be less distorted by aberrations in the observer's eyes (see the previous section).

Examples: Some examples apparent from the diagram: for viewing the night sky 10×50 binoculars will show about twice as much detail as 7×35s; 11×80 and 15×60 binoculars are equally capable, as are 8×30s and 6×42s (assuming one's eye pupils can accommodate the exit pupils of the instrument with the larger D); 10×50 binoculars are appreciably better than 7×50s for visibility (although, assuming equal apparent angular fields, 7×50s will show about twice as much sky area as will 10×50s). Canon's image-stabilized 15×45 binoculars are nearly equivalent to tripod-mounted 10×70s, with the *triple* advantage of smaller size, accommodating observers whose pupils will not open to 7 mm, and not requiring a tripod!

The visibility factor ($M \times D$) is applicable to the usual range of binocular sizes (exit pupils between about 3 mm and 7 mm), but should not be extrapolated indefinitely. For instance, as the magnification is increased on a telescope and the exit pupil approaches 1 mm or less, a point will be reached (dependent upon the darkness of the sky) where the background sky glow is imperceptible. A further increase in M will not cause a noticeable improvement in the visibility of stars, and the perceived contrast between an extended object and the sky will decrease. Also, the angular size of an extended object must be kept in mind. Once M is increased to the point at which the object fills the field of view of the instrument, the object may not be visible at all! For example, a large, dim comet coma may be visible in 15×60 binoculars ($M \times D = 900$) but be *invisible* in a 45×200 telescope ($M \times D = 9000$).

BINOCULAR PERFORMANCE DIAGRAM

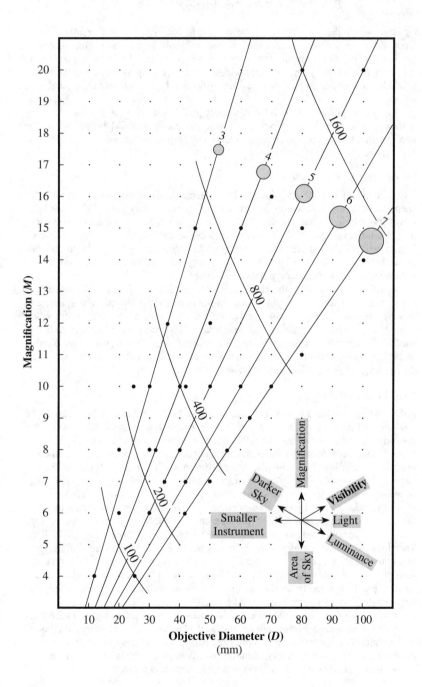

FILTERS
BY ROY BISHOP

Optical filters reflect and absorb some portion of the incident light. *Neutral-density filters* reflect and absorb light more or less uniformly across the visible spectrum. *Coloured (dye) filters* typically pass only one or two moderately broad portions of the spectrum. *Interference filters* are more selective and typically pass only one or two well-defined, narrow segments of the spectrum. All three types of filter are invaluable in astronomy.

In addition to categorization by physical type, filters may be categorized according to their intended use: for the Moon and planets (neutral-density and dye filters), for the Sun (neutral-density and interference filters), and for interstellar plasmas or emission nebulae (interference filters).

Lunar and Planetary Filters

As viewed in a telescope, the Moon and the planets Venus, Mars, and Jupiter are often uncomfortably bright. A neutral-density filter, which passes only 5% to 20% of the light, solves this problem while avoiding the loss in resolution that would accompany stopping down the aperture of the telescope to decrease the brightness to the same level. With a less-glaring image, light scattering in the observer's eye is reduced and fine details are easier to see. A neutral-density filter is typically about 26 mm in diameter and is attached to the forward-facing end of an eyepiece.

Dye filters can enhance the visibility of various planetary features. For instance, a red or yellow filter will absorb bluish light scattered by the Martian atmosphere and thereby improve the contrast of features on the surface of Mars. A green filter will increase the visibility of pale red and blue areas in the atmosphere of Jupiter (although the entire image will then appear green). Also, since they absorb an appreciable fraction of the light, dye filters or polarizing filters have the same advantage as a weak neutral-density filter when viewing bright objects.

Solar Filters

For observing the Sun a filter is essential and must be designed not only to reduce the brightness of the solar surface to a comfortable level but to block out the invisible but damaging infrared and ultraviolet radiation. Just because a filter makes the Sun dim enough to view comfortably is no guarantee that it is not transmitting damaging amounts of invisible radiation! This is no place to experiment with do-it-yourself filter designs—use only a proper solar filter from a reputable manufacturer. *Failure to use a proper filter when observing the Sun can cause immediate and irreversible damage to vision.*

A *special warning*: Heavy atmospheric haze near sunrise or sunset often dims the Sun so that it appears as a dull red disk, not uncomfortably bright to the eye. At such times resist the temptation to view the Sun with a telescope without using a solar filter. The atmosphere at such times is still relatively transparent in the invisible infrared portion of the spectrum, and the great light grasp of a telescope can result in thermal retinal damage! With the unaided eyes the retinal solar image, although just as bright, is much smaller and the eye can better dissipate the heat. Also, with unaided vision, one is less apt to fixate on the Sun for a prolonged period.

For white-light views of the Sun, a dark, broad-spectrum, neutral-density solar filter is needed. Aluminized Mylar and metal-coated glass are common designs, although they usually do not attenuate light uniformly across the visible spectrum (i.e. they are not perfect neutral-density filters). Aluminized Mylar gives a bluish colour to the solar image, while metal-coated glass filters usually give an orange colour.

The filter should be 50 mm or more in diameter and must be positioned to cover the *front* of the telescope. Ensure that the filter is *securely attached* so that a gust of wind or a bump cannot dislodge it. (Some small telescopes are sold with a "sun filter" designed to attach to the eyepiece, just before the observer's eye. Sunlight concentrated by the telescope can overheat and shatter a filter of this design. Such filters should be thrown in the garbage!)

For direct viewing of the Sun (not using binoculars or a telescope) shade #14 (no other shade) rectangular welder's glass may be used; this is available for a few dollars at welding supplies shops. These filters are not suitable for attaching to the front of binoculars or a telescope simply because their poor optical quality results in a fuzzy image.

Red, flame-like prominences at the Sun's limb and much structure in its chromosphere across the solar disk can be seen in hydrogen-alpha (Hα) light, a strong spectral line emitted by atomic hydrogen. This light is totally overwhelmed by the rest of the solar spectrum, so a neutral-density filter will not work. Advances in vacuum thin-film technology have made possible interference filters, filters that operate on the same principle as Fabry-Perot interferometers, involving the interference of multiply reflected beams of light. These filters can be constructed so they are transparent only to light having an extremely narrow range of wavelengths, typically 0.15 to 0.05 nm for solar viewing, although band-passes of up to 1 nm are used in solar prominence viewers that are designed to occult the solar disk. If this band-pass is centred on the Hα wavelength (656.3 nm), nearly all of the Sun's light will be blocked, leaving an image in Hα light.

Hα filters are expensive, particularly for band-passes near 0.05 nm that are needed for high-contrast images of the solar disk. Because Hα filters usually are mounted near the back end of a telescope, and because the wavelength of the centre of their narrow band-pass varies with the angle at which light rays enter the filter (a characteristic of interference filters), the focal ratio of the imaging telescope must be near f/20 for 0.15-nm band-pass filters and f/30 or higher for filters with narrower band-passes. Temperature control is usually required to keep the band-pass centred on the Hα wavelength, although some Hα filters are designed to be tilted in order to tune them to the Hα wavelength (the wavelength of peak transmittance is shifted toward shorter wavelengths when the filter is tilted away from 90° incidence).

Hα filters are usually mounted just ahead of the eyepiece (or film holder, if photography is planned). Also, Hα filters require a broadband "energy rejection prefilter," located at the front of the telescope. The prefilter has a band-pass of about 100 nm in the red part of the spectrum and blocks essentially all of the infrared, ultraviolet, and much of the visible part of the solar radiation from entering the telescope.

Nebula Filters

From the surface of Earth, the night sky is not completely dark. Even in the absence of light pollution (human-made and lunar), the air itself emits a feeble light called airglow. In higher latitudes, aurorae can also contribute to the glow of the atmosphere. Two other components of the light of the night sky are the zodiacal light and background starlight. The diffuse glow from all three sources reduces the contrast of celestial objects and, in the case of dim galaxies and nebulae, the object may be completely obscured by the brightness of the sky.

Filters transmit only a fraction of the incident light. Thus, employing them to see faint objects may seem counterproductive. However, there are objects in the heavens that emit light only at certain wavelengths. This behaviour is characteristic of plasmas— excited gases, matter composed of separate atoms that are energized either by ultraviolet radiation from nearby hot stars or by collisions such as occur in supernova explosion shock fronts. Such regions are called emission nebulae and include star-forming regions, planetary nebulae, and some supernova remnants. A filter that selectively blocks most of the background sky glow but is transparent to the wavelengths at which such objects emit most of their visible light will darken the sky background without appreciably dimming the object of interest. With narrow band-pass interference-type filters the effect can be dramatic, improving contrast and revealing details that otherwise are completely invisible. It is the next best thing to observing these objects from above Earth's atmosphere!

Dark-adapted (scotopic) human vision responds to light having wavelengths from approximately 400 to 620 nm. In bright light (photopic vision) the spectral range extends to somewhat longer wavelengths, about 750 nm. For both types of vision the response curve (sensitivity versus wavelength) is "bell-shaped," the wavelength of maximum sensitivity being in the middle of the visible range—near 510 nm for scotopic vision and 555 nm for photopic vision (see the figure "Nebular Filter Transmission" on the next page). The photopic sensation produced by 555-nm light is green; for scotopic vision colour is not produced, but at photopic levels 510-nm light appears blue-green.

Hydrogen is the predominant element in the universe. Atomic hydrogen, when excited by ultraviolet radiation from a nearby hot star, emits light in the visible spectrum at only four discrete wavelengths: 656, 486, 434, and 410 nm (designated as Hα, Hβ, Hγ, and Hδ, respectively, part of the "Balmer spectrum" of hydrogen). Scotopic vision is blind to 656-nm (Hα) light and relatively insensitive to the less intense 434- and 410-nm light. However, 486 nm (Hβ) lies near the 510-nm peak sensitivity of scotopic vision, and an Hβ ("H-beta") filter that has a narrow band-pass at this wavelength will greatly reduce the surrounding sky brightness and reveal Hβ-emitting nebulae.

The classic example is the Horsehead Nebula, a dark, silhouetted column of dust just southeast of the east end of Orion's belt. The surrounding hydrogen gas, excited probably by the nearby hot star ζ Orionis, fluoresces dimly with Hβ light. If the obscuring airglow is blocked by an Hβ filter, the dark Horsehead can distinctly be seen in a telescope having an aperture of 400 mm or greater. However, the number of objects that can be viewed advantageously with an Hβ filter is very limited, apparently because few nebulae emit strongly in Hβ light.

Two other strong nebular emission lines lie at 496 and 501 nm, nearly at the peak sensitivity of scotopic vision. Originally detected in 1864 by the British astronomer William Huggins, the origin of these lines was unknown at that time, and they were attributed to a hypothetical new element, "nebulium." In 1927, the American astrophysicist Ira Bowen identified the lines as due to doubly ionized oxygen (O^{++} or OIII), which glows brightly when very low-density nebular gas is strongly excited (high temperature). A filter that has a narrow band-pass spanning these two wavelengths gives striking views of highly excited nebulae. A good example is the Veil Nebula, a supernova remnant in eastern Cygnus. Through an OIII filter on a dark, transparent night, the direct view of the Veil in a large amateur telescope is more spectacular than any photograph or CCD image. Planetary nebulae (fluorescing, low-density shells of gas surrounding hot central stars) also show up well with an OIII filter; examples include the Helix Nebula, the Owl Nebula (M97), the Dumbbell Nebula (M27), and the Ring Nebula (M57).

Because of their narrow band-passes, Hβ and OIII filters are sometimes called "line filters," although their band-passes are much wider than that of an Hα filter. Filters encompassing both the Hβ and OIII lines, such as the Lumicon Ultra High Contrast (UHC) filter, are termed "narrowband filters." These filters also enhance views of many emission nebulae, although with the wider band-pass the sky background is brighter. With a large telescope under dark skies I find that the single most useful filter is the OIII line filter. With smaller apertures (less than about 200 mm), the narrowband Lumicon UHC filter (or equivalent filter from other manufacturers) may be preferable since it dims the stars less.

Some other nebulae that are greatly enhanced by OIII and narrowband filters include the Omega or Loon Nebula (M17), the Trifid Nebula (M20), the Lagoon Nebula (M8), the Rosette Nebula, the Eagle Nebula (M16), the North American Nebula, and the Eta Carina Nebula.

Nebular Filter Transmission

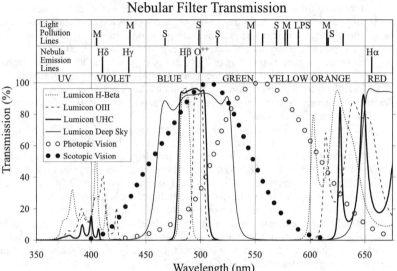

The dotted, dashed, and continuous curves show the transmission versus wavelength characteristic of four interference filters (in descending order in the legend): two line filters, a narrowband filter, and a broadband filter. The bell-shaped curves composed of small open and solid circles show the relative response of bright-adapted (photopic) vision and dark-adapted (scotopic) vision. In ascending sequence above the curves are spectral colours, nebula emission lines, and light pollution lines (M = mercury, S = high-pressure sodium, and LPS = low-pressure sodium). High-pressure sodium light sources emit an additional broad continuum spectrum that is not shown. The two unlabeled light pollution lines are strong airglow/auroral lines produced by atomic oxygen. (David Lane used a "Varian Model Cory 50 Conc. UV-Visible Spectrophotometer" owned by the Chemistry Department at Saint Mary's University to obtain the filter curves, and he also prepared the diagram.)

Stars emit light across the entire visible spectrum. Thus line filters and narrowband filters impair views of single stars, reflection nebulae, star clusters, and galaxies. Filters with wide band-passes extending from about 450 to 530 nm are called "broadband filters." Examples are the Lumicon Deep Sky filter, the Orion SkyGlow filter and the Meade Broadband filter. These decrease the airglow somewhat and block several of the brighter wavelengths emitted by sodium- and mercury-vapour streetlights, without dimming stars and galaxies too much. Thus they provide a modest improvement in the visibility of some objects from light-polluted sites. Because of their wide band-pass and high transmission at the Hα line, they are also useful for photography of emission nebulae. However, under dark skies an unfiltered view is preferable to that through a broadband filter.

LIMITING MAGNITUDES
By Douglas Pitcairn

Limiting Visual Magnitudes

One of the many difficulties with visual observing from the surface of our planet is the variability of the atmosphere. In any record of observations it is important to note the condition of the sky. Parameters such as brightness and contrast are greatly affected by the transparency of the sky and the presence of light pollution or aurorae.

One of the simplest ways to quantify local sky conditions is to note the magnitude of the faintest star visible with the unaided eye—the *limiting visual magnitude* (LVM). Although individuals differ in their ability to detect faint stars, these differences are generally small, and for any one observer such observations provide a consistent measure of sky quality.

The chart below shows a 12°-wide field in the vicinity of Polaris (the brightest star on the chart) and is useful for observers at latitude 20°N or higher. For orientation, the solid lines mark the beginning of the handle of the Little Dipper, as in the ALL-SKY MAPS on pp. 277–282. Several stars have their visual magnitudes indicated (with decimal points omitted). Using this field to determine your LVM has several advantages: it is always above the horizon in midnorthern latitudes; its altitude does not change with the time of night or year, so the variation of atmospheric extinction with altitude is not a consideration; there are no bright stars or planets in the field to dazzle the eye; the faint stars are quite well spaced and therefore easy to identify; and being a simple field, it can be memorized. Especially note the dashed spiral of descending magnitudes labelled "A" through "F."

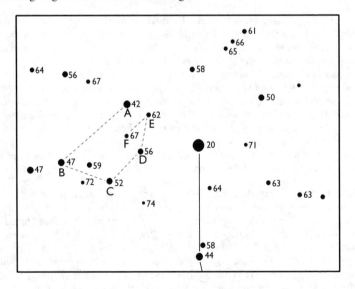

Limiting Telescopic Magnitudes

Aperture, telescope design, eyepiece design, magnification, and the quality of optical surfaces are a few of the many variables that will determine the faintest stars visible through a given telescope and eyepiece. By determining an instrument's limiting magnitude—the *limiting telescopic magnitude* (LTM)—you can effectively assess the effect of these variables. The quality of the night sky will also affect the LTM. Therefore, changes in the LVM should be taken into account when determining the LTM. (The relationship between LTM and LVM is complex; readers may explore it using the excellent web-based calculator at **www.go.ednet.ns.ca/~larry/astro/maglimit.html**.) The LTM is a useful guide when attempting faint targets (Pluto in a 150-mm scope?), comparing the performance of different instruments ("Can my scope see as faint as yours?"), or determining whether a mirror or lens needs cleaning (many people clean their optics too often, assuming that dust degrades optical performance more than it actually does).

To help determine the LTM of your instrument, use the chart below, which shows an 8′-wide section of the northwest quadrant of M67 centred at RA 8h 50.4m and Dec +11°49′. This old open cluster lies 8° south-southeast of M44, Cancer's famous Beehive cluster. The accompanying table lists the visual magnitudes and the $B - V$ colour indices of the labelled stars. The diagram was constructed from a photograph taken by René Racine of the University of Montreal, who exposed a 103a-D plate at the f/3.67 focus of the Hale Reflector. The magnitudes are based on work by Racine and Ronald Gilliland of the Space Telescope Science Institute.

STAR	VISUAL	$B - V$
A	10.60	1.10
B	11.19	0.43
C	11.59	0.42
D	12.01	0.57
E	12.26	0.68
F	12.57	0.59
G	13.04	0.85
H	13.35	0.59
I	13.61	0.59
J	13.96	0.62
K	14.34	0.56
L	14.66	0.67
M	14.96	0.69
N	15.30	0.79
O	15.58	0.84
P	16.06	0.74
Q	16.31	0.99
R	16.62	0.81
S	17.05	1.26
T	17.38	1.17
U	17.64	1.31
V	18.04	1.27
W	18.38	0.76
X	18.69	1.17
Y	19.07	1.56
Z	19.29	0.61
a	19.42	1.34
b	20.10	0.00
c	20.35	0.83
d	20.61	1.55
e	21.03	0.32

Correction for Atmospheric Extinction

Atmospheric extinction varies with altitude above the horizon. To normalize observations to the zenith (altitude 90°), the following values should be added to estimates of faintest visible magnitude obtained using the charts (format: altitude range/ **correction**):

18° – 20°/**0.5**; 20° – 24°/**0.4**; 24° – 29°/**0.3**; 29° – 36°/**0.2**; 36° – 52°/**0.1**; 52° – 90°/**0.0**

These corrections are for near sea level and would be reduced at higher elevations. Also, excellent sky conditions are assumed; under less than ideal conditions the corrections are generally larger and can be quite uncertain, especially when the target area is closer to the horizon.

FREQUENCY OF CLEAR NIGHT SKIES
By Jay Anderson

APRIL–MAY CLEAR SKY FREQUENCY

The above maps are constructed from observations taken from over 750 stations in North America over a 7- to 12-year period. The isochrones indicate the percent frequency of three-tenths or less cloud and visibilities greater than 3 miles (4.8 km) for the midnight-to-dawn interval. This corresponds to skies with clear or scattered cloud conditions and no heavy fog or mist. Since fog is relatively uncommon in most areas, the contours mostly represent the cloud cover over nighttime North America.

The chart at left is an average of April and May observations; that on the right is for July and August. The data are collected by the U.S. Air Force and published in an extensive collection of airfield summaries. Data for Canada are grouped mostly near the international border, and the short period of record of some stations limits the utility of the data north of the 49th parallel.

The earlier chart shows that the clearest skies are found in the southwestern United States, stretching northwestward through Mexico into southern California, where frequencies peak above 80%. Parts of Arizona and Nevada share in these favourable skies. Cloudiness increases north and eastward, peaking along the northern Appalachians and over the Atlantic coasts of Nova Scotia and Newfoundland. In western Canada the cloud climatology is highly variable in the spring months (and

JULY–AUGUST CLEAR SKY FREQUENCY

not entirely believable), but the best conditions tend to be found in more westerly loca-
tions. In British Columbia, the Okanagan Valley exhibits a small advantage over sites
along the West Coast, a reflection of the retreat of the endemic cloudiness that plagues
the mountain valleys in winter.

In July and August the clear springtime skies of the southwestern deserts of the
United States give way to an equally dramatic cloudiness as the "monsoon season"
brings moisture and frequent thunderstorms into Arizona, New Mexico, and Colo-
rado. California's interior retains its reputation as the sunniest location, but clearer
skies return to the midwestern plains, extending northward into Manitoba and
Saskatchewan and eastward into Ontario. Almost all regions are clearer than in the
April–May chart, although the Appalachians and the Atlantic Provinces continue to
be among the cloudiest locations. Nighttime cloud cover decreases significantly in
Central Florida.

The maps may be used for planning travel to star parties and sunnier climates
or to special astronomical events. Cloud conditions change rapidly in North America
in the spring months—cloud increases in the far north and decreases elsewhere—and
the April–May chart depicts a time when the patterns depicted in the July–August
chart are developing rapidly. Cloudiness at the end of May most likely resembles that
of the later chart, although with values that are not quite so favourable.

LIGHT POLLUTION
By David L. Crawford

A Lost Heritage: During this and the 20th century, most people have lost the spectacular view of the universe that our ancestors enjoyed on clear nights. The development of electrical lighting technology and the increase in urban population have caused a rapid increase in sky glow above towns and cities. Few members of the general public have ever seen a prime dark sky. For urban dwellers, star-studded nights are limited to simulations at planetaria. Comets Hyakutake and Hale-Bopp, the most spectacular comets of our time, were for many people merely dim fuzz-balls because of the glare of light pollution. Even in rural areas, poorly designed yard lights often obscure the splendour of the night sky. As Leslie Peltier, one of the most famous amateur astronomers of the twentieth century, stated eloquently in his autobiography *Starlight Nights:*

> *"The moon and the stars no longer come to the farm. The farmer has exchanged his birthright in them for the wattage of his all-night sun. His children will never know the blessed dark of night."*

A nighttime satellite view of central North America

The increased sky glow that adversely affects the environment is called "light pollution," for it originates mainly from excess light that does nothing to increase useful nighttime illumination. It is light that sprays horizontally and upward into the sky from poorly designed lighting fixtures. It is light that glares into the eyes of motorists and homeowners, compromising visibility, safety, and security. It is light that depresses property values by reducing the aesthetic quality of a neighbourhood. In the United States and Canada over a billion dollars plus large amounts of energy are lost annually in generating this wasted light.

A Threat to Astronomy: Light pollution poses special perils to astronomy. Many observations, including most of those of cosmological interest, can be made only from prime observing sites, far removed from centres of population. Some older observatories, such as the David Dunlap in Ontario and Mount Wilson in California, are severely affected by light pollution from nearby urban centres. New observatories usually are located at remote sites, and amateur astronomers routinely drive large distances to escape the glare of towns and cities. The argument that all astronomy can be done from space is incorrect because it does not make sense to do in space, at much higher costs, what can be done from the ground. There are observations that can only be done from space, but more than three decades of space astronomy have greatly increased the need for ground-based observatories.

Solutions: There are solutions to the problem of light pollution; outdoor lighting ordinances have been instituted in a number of communities near large observatories, such as Tucson, Arizona, and San Diego, California. *The main solution is the use of full-cutoff lighting fixtures that direct all their light below the horizontal, such that the light source itself is not directly visible from the side—an almost universal fault with street and yard lights. Since this places the light where it is needed, less total light and thus less electrical energy is required.*

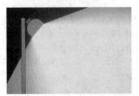

Inefficient street lighting

Additional major cost savings are realized by switching to light sources that are more efficient, that require less power to produce a given amount of light. The table below shows the efficiency of common types of outdoor lights; the comparative numbers indicate the approximate amount of electrical power (watts) required to produce the same amount of visible light (1000 lm). In addition to providing light at the lowest cost, low-pressure sodium (LPS) lights are nearly monochromatic, with the result that much of their glare can be filtered out by astronomers. Low-pressure sodium lights are especially good for street lighting, parking lot lighting, security lighting, and any application where colour rendering is not important.

Common Types of Outdoor Lights
(in increasing order of efficiency)

Type	Power (W/klm)
incandescent (ordinary bulbs)	60
mercury vapour (violet-white light)	24
metal halide (white)	17
high-pressure sodium (orange-gold)	12
low-pressure sodium (yellow)	8

A full-cutoff, efficient light fixture

Although full-cutoff, efficient light fixtures generally have a higher capital cost than polluting fixtures, this cost is quickly recovered through the much lower operating costs. In California, the cities of Long Beach, San Diego, and San Jose are each realizing substantial savings each year through extensive use of LPS street lighting. For example, one can usually replace a 175-W mercury vapour lighting fixture with a full-cutoff, 35-W LPS fixture and get the same amount of useful light, with none of the glare and light trespass. The energy saving is remarkable, as is the better visibility.

Even less light pollution and more savings can be realized by using *no more light than is required*. In particular, too much light and/or poorly shielded lights can ruin adaptation to night lighting, blinding us just when we need to see. When we go from too bright to too dark or vice versa, "transient adaptation" is impaired and we have poor visibility for awhile. Do not exceed IESNA (Illuminating Engineering Society of North America) recommended lighting levels. Overkill never helps; it usually just adds glare and it always wastes energy. In addition, lights should be used only when necessary (timers are useful for controlling lights).

Increased lighting generally gives a perception of greater security, yet there is no statistically significant evidence that more lighting results in less crime. Criminals need light. "Security lights" provide this, may draw attention to a house or business that would otherwise not be noticed, and mask any additional light that criminals may need to do their work. Our cities and towns are far more brightly lit than ever, yet the crime rate soars. Security can best be provided by shielded, motion-activated lights that come on only when triggered by movement nearby. These serve to frighten criminals, alert others that there is a potential problem, and provide glare-free visibility (when properly installed so they are glare-free); they also use insignificant amounts of energy.

Lack of Awareness: The biggest problem in controlling light pollution is lack of awareness rather than resistance. After all, it costs money to light pollute! Unlike the case with many other forms of pollution, simple solutions are available; moreover, *everyone benefits* in applying these solutions. Most people are not yet conscious of the expense, the waste, and the harm associated with excess lighting. They put up with distant lights that shine directly into their eyes, not realizing that not only does this do *nothing* to illuminate the area near the light but that it also produces a veiling glare. The pollution usually involves not only the light itself but also other forms of environmental pollution associated with the production of the wasted light: the extraction, transportation, and burning of coal and oil. This general lack of awareness has been summarized nicely by Doug Pitcairn, an astronomy teacher in Nova Scotia:

"It surprises me how someone who would never think of leaving a plastic bottle on the ground at a picnic site will pay extra money each month to illuminate half the neighbourhood with unnecessary, distracting light."

Education: Educating the public, government officials, lighting professionals, and astronomers is a major thrust of current programs. These efforts have helped. Most committees in the IESNA have been addressing these issues, and upcoming Recommended Practices and other documents are fully reflecting these concerns. As they are issued, one will expect to see them implemented, albeit on a slow time schedule. Astronomers and environmentalists should do all they can to help publicize these documents when they come out to help get them into existing practices in our communities.

The International Dark-Sky Association: The International Dark-Sky Association (IDA) is a tax-exempt, nonprofit, membership organization dedicated to overcoming this awareness problem. Its goal is to preserve dark skies while at the same time maximizing the quality and efficiency of nighttime outdoor lighting. The IDA needs your help. Memberships begin at $30 (U.S.) per year. To join this effort or to obtain further information on any aspects of the issue, write to the International Dark-Sky Association, 3225 N. First Avenue, Tucson, AZ 85719, U.S.A. (phone: (520) 293-3198; fax: (520) 293-3192; email: ida@darksky.org; website: www.darksky.org). Plenty of useful information is on the website, including images, and content is added regularly. The IDA has many information sheets available to assist you in educating others—in several languages in addition to English and French—and can provide examples of lighting ordinances that have been enacted in many communities to enforce high-quality, effective nighttime lighting. For more information, see the July 1990 (p. 23) and September 1998 issues of *Sky & Telescope*.

Within Canada, the Royal Astronomical Society of Canada has an active Light Pollution Abatement Committee under the chairmanship of Robert Dick (his address: P.O. Box 79, Rideau Ferry, ON K0G 1W0, email: rdick@ccs.carleton.ca); or you may contact the RASC directly (see p. 8). Also, some local centres of the RASC have taken action to address poor lighting practices in their areas.

Editor's Note: An indication that the IDA is making its message heard where it counts is the election of its (volunteer) executive director, David Crawford, as a Fellow of the Illuminating Engineering Society of North America in 1997. The IDA has members in 70 countries, and its total membership as of July 2001 was about 7600 (with 170 from Canada). Despite the almost 70% growth in membership over the previous July, this is still less than 10% of the community of amateur and professional astronomers. As Daniel Green of the Smithsonian Astrophysical Observatory has put it (see *Sky & Telescope*, May 1998, p. 10): "Where are all the astronomers?" Anyone who values the night sky should support this unique and deserving organization.

DEEP-SKY OBSERVING HINTS
BY ALAN DYER

In the 1960s and 1970s, few observers owned telescopes larger than 200-mm aperture. Today, 250-mm to 600-mm Dobsonian-mounted reflectors are commonplace. Using computerized telescopes, observers can now find thousands of objects at the push of a button. As a result, deep-sky observing has soared in popularity.

However, owners of less sophisticated, small-aperture instruments shouldn't think they are shut out of deep-sky viewing. In a dark sky an 80-mm to 100-mm telescope will show all the Messier objects and reveal hundreds of brighter NGC (New General Catalogue) objects. In fact, many large objects are best seen in fast (f/4 to f/6), small-aperture telescopes or in giant 70-mm and 80-mm binoculars. Contrary to popular belief, even slow f-ratio instruments (f/11 to f/16) are useful; their only disadvantage is the difficulty of achieving a low-power wide field. No matter what telescope you use, follow these techniques to get the most out of a night's deep-sky viewing:

- Always plan each night's observing: Prepare a list of a dozen or so objects for the night. Hunt them down on star charts or with computer programs first during the day to become familiar with their location.
- Seek out dark skies; a black sky improves contrast and makes up for lack of aperture.
- To preserve night vision, always use a dim red flashlight for reading charts.
- Avoid prolonged exposure to bright sunlight earlier in the day (such as a day at the beach); it will reduce your ability to dark adapt and make for tired eyes at night.
- Use averted vision; looking to one side of an object places it on a more sensitive part of the retina.
- Another technique for picking out faint objects is to jiggle the telescope (and the image) slightly.
- Don't be afraid to use high power; it often brings out small, faint objects such as planetary nebulae and galaxies and resolves detail in globulars, in small, rich open clusters, and in bright galaxies.
- Use a nebula filter on emission and planetary nebulae (see the section FILTERS on pp. 52–55); even in a dark sky, filters can dramatically enhance the view of these kinds of objects, often making obvious an otherwise elusive nebula.
- Be comfortable; sit down while at the eyepiece and be sure to dress warmly.
- Collimate and clean your optics; a poorly maintained telescope will produce distorted star images, reduce image contrast, and make it more difficult to see faint stars and other threshold objects.
- Don't expect to use analog setting circles; in a portable telescope "dial-type" circles will rarely be accurate.
- Digital setting circles and Go To telescopes can find objects precisely. While they are wonderful observing aids, they can overwhelm observers with thousands of targets, often supplying scant information about each one. When making a list for a night's viewing, books such as the three-volume *Burnham's Celestial Handbook* and the two-volume *Night Sky Observer's Guide* by Kepple and Sanner are still the best guides.
- Don't be in a rush to check off targets; take time to examine each object, and take notes or make drawings. Both will help train your eye to see subtle detail; you'll learn to see the most through your telescope.
- Consider keeping a logbook or journal of your nightly tours of the sky; including eyepiece impressions and drawings provides a record of your improving observing skills that is fun to look back upon in future years. See the section THE OBSERVING LOGBOOK (immediately following) for suggestions on organizing a journal.

THE OBSERVING LOGBOOK
By Paul Markov

There are many good reasons for maintaining an observing logbook: A logbook is useful for recalling the details of previous observations and comparing past observations with current ones; maintaining one will make your observing organized and methodical; and having to describe an object forces you to *look* for more details, thus sharpening your observing skills. Finally, if you are planning to apply for an observing certificate (e.g. the RASC's Explore the Universe, Messier, or Finest NGC Certificate; see p. 258), then a logbook with your observations may be required when submitting your application.

Logbooks can be chronological or sectional. In a chronological logbook all observations are listed sequentially by date, regardless of object type. In a sectional logbook observations are grouped by object type, such as open clusters and galaxies. With either format, you may want to keep a master index of objects for cross referencing to the correct page in your logbook.

What about the book itself? Typical choices are the simple three-ring binder with standard lined paper, spiral bound notebooks, and hardcover record/accounting books. In my opinion, the most practical is the three-ring binder because it allows you to insert auxiliary materials into your logbook with the help of a three-hole punch. With this choice, entering observations out of sequence is never an issue because you can easily rearrange the sheets. Also, should you wish to make a copy of your logbook for safekeeping, it's much easier with loose sheets.

For recording observations, using a preprinted observing form offers these advantages: the fill-in-the-blank fields remind you to record the relevant data; many of these forms have a space for making a drawing of the observed object; and they give your book a neat and organized look. An example of an observing form can be found at **www.rasc.ca/handbook/obsform.pdf**; you may prefer to design your own observing form by using the fields suggested below. However, you can also use plain lined paper: you will never have to worry about running out of forms, and you will not need different forms for different types of objects.

There are two choices for recording your observations: using full sentences and using acronyms and abbreviations. Using full sentences is the preferred method if you enjoy re-reading your observations from past years, or if you want others to be able to easily read your logbook. But if your intent is to keep a data book for reference purposes only, then acronyms and abbreviations are the recommended choices.

It is useful to record the following information for each observing session: date; time of arrival and departure (if you have travelled somewhere to observe); location; names of other people at the observing site; sky transparency (i.e. clarity of the atmosphere, which is generally noted by faintest visible stellar magnitude; see pp. 56–57); seeing (i.e. the steadiness of the atmosphere: if stars and planets appear to shimmer, that indicates poor seeing; if they appear sharp and steady, that indicates good seeing), and environmental conditions (e.g. temperature, dew, wind, sources of light pollution, snow cover, and mosquitoes). You can also number each observing session sequentially for easy referencing within your logbook.

Be sure to standardize your time/date format. For recording time, choose either the military time or a.m./p.m. format. In addition, use alpha characters to specify the month rather than numbers. For example, use Aug. 5, 2002 instead of 8/5/2002; this will avoid ambiguity in reading the date.

For each object observed, record the following information as a minimum: date and time of observation, object name or designation, type of object, constellation, telescope and magnification used, type of filter (if any), and visual description. Making drawings is highly recommended and adds substantially to the appearance of your logbook. It is also important to record failed observations because these entries will remind you to try again in your next observing session.

If you are able to write neatly while observing, it is best to enter observations directly into your logbook. However, if this proves too difficult given the environmental circumstances, you can record your observations in a temporary notebook and transcribe them into your logbook the next day. A tape recorder can also be used if you are careful to ensure its mechanical integrity while in the field and if you are diligent enough to transcribe the recorded observations into your observing logbook regularly. Below are some suggestions on what to look for when observing deep sky objects.

All Object Types: What is the shape of the object? What is its size (based on the field of view of your eyepiece)? Is averted vision required to see the object? Does averted vision allow you to see more detail? (If yes, describe the extra detail.) Is the object near (or in the same field of view as) other deep sky objects or bright stars? What magnification gives the best view of the object? Does a filter improve the view? (See the section FILTERS on pp. 52–55.)

Open Cluster: Is there a greater concentration of stars in a specific part of the cluster? Is it fully resolved into its component stars, or are there any unresolved stars causing the cluster to appear nebulous? How many stars can you see (only if reasonable to count them)? Are there any bright stars within the cluster? Are there any coloured stars? (If so, describe their tints and locations within the cluster.) Does the cluster stand out from the background star field?

Globular Cluster: What is the degree of star concentration (high, medium, low)? How much can be resolved to component stars (none, outer edges, middle, to the core)?

Galaxy: Is it uniform in brightness, or does it have a brighter nucleus? Is it diffuse or stellar? Can any detail or mottling be seen in the arms? Are there any stars visible within the arms?

Emission or Reflection Nebula: Is the brightness even, or are there brighter/darker areas? Are the edges of the nebula well defined? Are there any stars within the nebula? Is there a hint of any colour?

Planetary Nebula: Is it stellar in appearance, or can a disk be seen? Are the edges well defined or diffuse? Are there any brighter/darker areas? Can a central star be seen? Is there a hint of any colour?

Dark Nebula: Is it easy or difficult to discern the dark nebula from the background sky? Are there any stars within the nebula?

Logbooks and Databases

If you enjoy using computers, an electronic database can be a helpful complement to an observing logbook. You can obtain commercially available deep sky databases that allow you to enter your own observations for any object. These databases are also useful for creating observing lists and planning observing sessions. A highly recommended database, which also happens to be freeware, is the Saguaro Astronomy Club (SAC) database, available at **www.saguaroastro.org**. With minimal tweaking, the SAC database can be formatted to accept your own observations.

You can transcribe complete observations from your logbook into the database or simply enter four valuable pieces of information for each observed object: seen (Y/N), date, telescope used, and location. With these fields filled in, in a matter of seconds you can determine which and how many objects you have observed, and the date field for any object will direct you to the correct page in your observing logbook. You can also determine interesting facts such as from which observing location you observed the most objects or which telescope produced the most observations.

THE SKY MONTH BY MONTH

LEFT-HAND PAGES BY DAVID LANE

INTRODUCTION

In the descriptions on the next 24 pages (two pages for each month), the right ascension (RA), declination (Dec) (both for epoch J2000.0), distance from Earth's centre in AU (Dist), visual magnitude (Mag), and equatorial angular diameter (Size) are tabulated for seven planets for 0h UT on the 1st, 11th, and 21st day of each month. For positional reference, the RA and Dec of the Sun are also given. Unless noted otherwise, the descriptive comments about the planets apply to the middle of the month. Any stated planet visibility times are in local standard time. "Northern observers" and "southern observers" are assumed to be at latitudes 45°N and 30°S, respectively. Descriptions are given first for northern observers and then for southern observers. Events of special interest are in **boldface**.

Sun—Data concerning the position, transit, orientation, rotation, and activity of the Sun plus times of sunrise and sunset appear on pp. 92–102. For detailed information on solar eclipses during the year, see ECLIPSES DURING 2002 on pp. 125–145.

Moon

The phases, perigee and apogee times and distances of the Moon (distances from *Astronomical Tables of the Sun, Moon, and Planets* by Jean Meeus, 2nd ed., Willmann-Bell, 1995), and its conjunctions with the planets are given in the monthly tables. For times of moonrise and moonset, see pp. 108–121.

Elongation, age, and phase of the Moon—The elongation is the angular distance of the Moon from the Sun counted eastward around the sky. Thus elongations of 0°, 90°, 180°, and 270° correspond to the phases new, first quarter, full, and last quarter, respectively. The age of the Moon is the time since the new phase. Because the Moon's orbital motion is not uniform, age does not accurately specify phase. The Moon's elongation increases on average 12.2° per day, first quarter, full, and last quarter phases corresponding approximately to 7.4, 14.8, and 22.1 days, respectively.

The Sun's selenographic colongitude (SSC) indicates the position of the sunrise terminator as it moves across the face of the Moon, and provides an accurate method of ascertaining the angle of illumination of features on the Moon's surface. The SSC is the angle of the sunrise terminator measured toward the observer's east (i.e. westward on the Moon) starting from the lunar meridian which passes through the mean centre of the apparent disk. Its value increases by nearly 12.2° per day, or about 0.5° per hour, and is approximately 0°, 90°, 180°, and 270° at the first quarter, full, last quarter, and new phases, respectively. Values of the SSC are given on the following pages for the beginning of each month.

Selenographic longitude (λ) is measured toward the observer's west (i.e. eastward on the Moon) from the mean central lunar meridian. Thus sunrise will occur at a given point on the Moon when SSC = (360° – λ), values of which for several lunar features are listed in the MAP OF MOON on pp. 106–107. The longitude of the sunset terminator differs by 180° from that of the sunrise terminator.

Libration is the apparent rocking motion of the Moon as it orbits Earth. As a consequence, over time, about 59% of the lunar surface can be viewed from Earth (see *Sky*

& *Telescope*, July 1987, p. 60). Libration in longitude (up to ±8°) results from the nearly uniform axial rotation of the Moon combined with its varying orbital speed along its elliptical orbit, while libration in latitude (±7°) is caused by the tilt of the Moon's equator to its orbital plane. A smaller contribution (up to ±1°), called *diurnal libration*, is associated with the shifting of the observer due to Earth's rotation.

When the libration in longitude is positive, more of the Moon's east limb, the limb near Mare Crisium, is exposed to view (in reference to the lunar limbs, *east* and *west* are used in this lunar sense; see also the "E" and "W" labels on the MAP OF MOON). When the libration in latitude is positive, more of the Moon's north limb is exposed to view. The monthly dates of the greatest positive and negative values of the libration in longitude and latitude are given in the following pages, as are the dates of greatest northern and southern declination.

The Moon's orbit is inclined at 5°09′ to the ecliptic. The gravitational influences of Earth and the Sun cause (1) the orbital plane to wobble and (2) the major axis of the orbit to precess. (1) The wobble shifts the line of nodes westward (retrograde) along the ecliptic with a period of 18.61 years. During 2002 the ascending node regresses from longitude 86.4° to 67.0°, and remains in Taurus. Thus the ascending node is yet further from the autumnal equinox (at longitude 180°), and the monthly range of the Moon's declination increases from its 1997 minimum of ±18° to ±26° by the end of 2002. (2) The precession shifts the perigee point eastward (direct) with a period of 8.85 years, although the positions of successive perigees fluctuate considerably from the mean motion. The Moon's mean equatorial plane, its mean orbital plane, and the plane of the ecliptic intersect along a common line of nodes, the equator being inclined at 1°32′ to the ecliptic and at 1°32′ + 5°09′ = 6°41′ to the orbit (i.e. the ascending node of the equator on the ecliptic coincides with the descending node of the orbit).

Planets—See CONTENTS or the INDEX for the location of more information on each of the planets.

Jupiter's Satellites—The configurations of Jupiter's Galilean satellites, provided by Larry Bogan, are given on the right side of the monthly pages. In these diagrams the central, vertical, straight, double line represents the equatorial diameter of the disk of Jupiter. Time is shown on the vertical scale, successive horizontal lines indicating 0h UT on the various days of the month. The relative east–west positions of the four satellites with respect to the disk of Jupiter are given by the four curves, where I = Io, II = Europa (dashed curve), III = Ganymede, and IV = Callisto. Note the "West–East" orientation given at the top of each diagram; these directions are those of the observer's sky, not Jupiter's limbs, and correspond to the view in an inverting telescope. For the various transits, occultations, and eclipses of Jupiter's Galilean satellites, see PHENOMENA OF THE GALILEAN SATELLITES on pp. 186–192. (Diagrams are also given for the five brightest satellites of Saturn. See CONFIGURATIONS OF SATURN'S BRIGHTEST SATELLITES on pp. 193–196.)

Minima of Algol—Predicted times of mideclipse are based on the formula heliocentric minimum = 244 1598.608 + 2.867315E, and are expressed as geocentric times for comparison with observations (the first number is the Julian date for the minimum of 1972 October 8.108, and the second is the period of Algol in days; E is an integer).

Occultations Involving the Moon, Stars, Planets, and Asteroids—The footnotes give areas of visibility; see "Occultations" in the INDEX for more details.

THE SKY FOR 2002 JANUARY

		Mercury	Venus	Mars	Jupiter	Saturn	Uranus	Neptune	Sun
RA	1	$19^h 52^m$	$18^h 31^m$	$23^h 13^m$	$6^h 46^m$	$4^h 32^m$	$21^h 40^m$	$20^h 39^m$	$18^h 45^m$
	11	$20^h 49^m$	$19^h 26^m$	$23^h 39^m$	$6^h 40^m$	$4^h 29^m$	$21^h 42^m$	$20^h 41^m$	$19^h 29^m$
	21	$21^h 04^m$	$20^h 19^m$	$0^h 06^m$	$6^h 35^m$	$4^h 27^m$	$21^h 44^m$	$20^h 42^m$	$20^h 12^m$
Dec	1	$-23° 03'$	$-23° 39'$	$-5° 50'$	$+23° 01'$	$+20° 04'$	$-14° 42'$	$-18° 19'$	$-23° 02'$
	11	$-18° 43'$	$-22° 45'$	$-2° 47'$	$+23° 08'$	$+20° 00'$	$-14° 32'$	$-18° 13'$	$-21° 52'$
	21	$-14° 54'$	$-20° 41'$	$+0° 17'$	$+23° 15'$	$+19° 59'$	$-14° 22'$	$-18° 08'$	$-19° 59'$
Dist	1	1.23	1.71	1.50	4.19	8.21	20.71	30.97	
	11	1.01	1.71	1.57	4.21	8.31	20.81	31.03	
	21	0.75	1.71	1.65	4.26	8.43	20.89	31.07	
Mag	1	−0.8	−3.9	0.8	−2.7	−0.3	5.9	8.0	
	11	−0.6	−3.9	0.9	−2.7	−0.2	5.9	8.0	
	21	1.3	−3.9	0.9	−2.7	−0.1	5.9	8.0	
Size	1	5.5″	9.8″	6.3″	47.0″	20.2″	3.4″	2.2″	
	11	6.7″	9.7″	6.0″	46.8″	19.9″	3.4″	2.2″	
	21	9.0″	9.7″	5.7″	46.3″	19.6″	3.4″	2.2″	

Moon—On Jan. 1.0 UT, the age of the Moon is 17.1 d. The Sun's selenographic colongitude is 113.25° and increases by 12.2° each day thereafter. The libration in longitude is maximum (east limb exposed) on Jan. 9 (+6°) and minimum (west limb exposed) on Jan. 24 (−7°). (See the paragraph concerning libration two pages earlier.) The libration in latitude is maximum (north limb exposed) on Jan. 18 (+7°) and minimum (south limb exposed) on Jan. 4 (−7°). The Moon reaches its greatest northern declination on Jan. 27 (+24°) and its greatest southern declination on Jan. 12 (−24°).

Mercury reaches greatest elongation east (19°) on Jan. 11. It can be seen low in the west-southwest after sunset before being lost in evening twilight after midmonth. Less favoured southern observers can see it with difficulty very low in the west-southwest after sunset in the first half of the month. Mercury is in inferior conjunction with the Sun on Jan. 27.

Venus is in superior conjunction with the Sun on Jan. 14 and is not observable this month.

Mars moves from Aquarius to Pisces early in the month. Mars is not at opposition with the Sun this year and therefore this is a poor year to observe Mars. It stands about 35° high in the southwest at the end of evening twilight and sets in late evening. Southern observers will find Mars low in the west after dark and setting in late evening.

Jupiter, in Gemini, is at opposition with the Sun on Jan. 1. It rises about 1 h before sunset for both northern and southern observers, transits in late evening, and sets during morning twilight. **Jupiter is occulted by the Moon on Jan. 26**.

Saturn, in Taurus, is high in the southeast at the end of evening twilight and sets near 4 a.m. For southern observers, Saturn is near the meridian after the end of evening twilight and sets near 2 a.m. The south side of its ring system faces Earth for the next 7 years (the rings were last edge-on in 1996 February). During 2002, the tilt of the rings increases from 25.8° in January to 26.8° in late June, closes slightly to 26.3° in October, then increases slightly to 26.7° by late December. **Saturn is occulted by the Moon on Jan. 24**.

Time (UT)			JANUARY EVENTS
d	h	m	
Tue. 1			
	6		**Jupiter at opposition**
	23	40	Algol at minimum
Wed. 2	7		Moon at perigee (365 406 km)
	14		**Earth at perihelion** (147 098 Mm)
Thu. 3	18		**Quadrantid meteors peak**
Fri. 4	20	29	Algol at minimum
Sat. 5			
Sun. 6	3	55	**Last Quarter**
Mon. 7	17	18	Algol at minimum
Tue. 8	22		Pallas in conjunction with Sun
Wed. 9	5		Mercury 1.3° S of Neptune
Thu. 10	14	07	Algol at minimum
Fri. 11	23		**Mercury greatest elongation E (19°)**
Sat. 12			
Sun. 13	10	57	Algol at minimum
	13	29	**New Moon**
Mon. 14			Mercury at ascending node
	12		Venus in superior conjunction
Tue. 15	2		Mercury 4° N of Moon
	22		Uranus 4° N of Moon
Wed. 16	7	46	Algol at minimum
	17		Vesta stationary
Thu. 17			
Fri. 18	9		Mercury stationary
	9		Moon at apogee (405 505 km)
	22		Mars 5° N of Moon
Sat. 19			Mercury at perihelion
	4	35	Algol at minimum
Sun. 20			
Mon. 21	17	46	**First Quarter**
Tue. 22	1	24	Algol at minimum
Thu. 24	16		**Saturn 0.08° S of Moon, Occultation†**
	22	14	Algol at minimum
Fri. 25			Venus at aphelion
Sat. 26	19		**Jupiter 0.9° S of Moon, Occultation‡**
Sun. 27	19		Mercury in inferior conjunction
	19	03	Algol at minimum
Mon. 28	14		Neptune in conjunction with Sun
	22	50	**Full Moon**
Tue. 29			Mercury at greatest heliocentric latitude N
Wed. 30	9		Moon at perigee (359 996 km)
	15	52	Algol at minimum
Thu. 31			

Configuration of Jupiter's Satellites

†Central Africa, Saudi Arabia, S Asia except S tip of India, Philippines, S Japan
‡N Atlantic Ocean, British Isles, Scandinavia, Greenland, Arctic Ocean, N Alaska, N Canada, NE Asia

THE SKY FOR 2002 FEBRUARY

		Mercury	Venus	Mars	Jupiter	Saturn	Uranus	Neptune	Sun
RA	1	20ʰ 16ᵐ	21ʰ 16ᵐ	0ʰ 35ᵐ	6ʰ 30ᵐ	4ʰ 26ᵐ	21ʰ 46ᵐ	20ʰ 44ᵐ	20ʰ 58ᵐ
	11	20ʰ 02ᵐ	22ʰ 05ᵐ	1ʰ 01ᵐ	6ʰ 27ᵐ	4ʰ 26ᵐ	21ʰ 49ᵐ	20ʰ 45ᵐ	21ʰ 38ᵐ
	21	20ʰ 32ᵐ	22ʰ 53ᵐ	1ʰ 28ᵐ	6ʰ 25ᵐ	4ʰ 27ᵐ	21ʰ 51ᵐ	20ʰ 47ᵐ	22ʰ 17ᵐ
Dec	1	−16° 04′	−17° 16′	+3° 37′	+23° 20′	+19° 59′	−14° 09′	−18° 01′	−17° 13′
	11	−18° 19′	−13° 17′	+6° 33′	+23° 23′	+20° 01′	−13° 58′	−17° 56′	−14° 09′
	21	−18° 41′	−8° 43′	+9° 23′	+23° 26′	+20° 05′	−13° 46′	−17° 50′	−10° 42′
Dist	1	0.67	1.71	1.73	4.34	8.58	20.95	31.08	
	11	0.79	1.70	1.80	4.45	8.74	20.98	31.05	
	21	0.96	1.69	1.88	4.58	8.90	20.97	31.00	
Mag	1	2.8	−3.9	1.0	−2.6	−0.1	5.9	8.0	
	11	0.5	−3.9	1.1	−2.6	0.0	5.9	8.0	
	21	0.1	−3.9	1.2	−2.5	0.0	5.9	8.0	
Size	1	10.1″	9.8″	5.4″	45.3″	19.3″	3.3″	2.2″	
	11	8.5″	9.8″	5.2″	44.2″	18.9″	3.3″	2.2″	
	21	7.0″	9.9″	5.0″	43.0″	18.6″	3.3″	2.2″	

Moon—On Feb. 1.0 UT, the age of the Moon is 18.4 d. The Sun's selenographic colongitude is 130.14° and increases by 12.2° each day thereafter. The libration in longitude is maximum (east limb exposed) on Feb. 5 (+7°) and minimum (west limb exposed) on Feb. 22 (−8°). The libration in latitude is maximum (north limb exposed) on Feb. 14 (+7°) and minimum (south limb exposed) on Feb. 1 (−7°) and Feb. 28 (−7°). The Moon reaches its greatest northern declination on Feb. 23 (+24°) and its greatest southern declination on Feb. 8 (−24°).

On Feb. 27 the Moon reaches its closest perigee distance of the year (356 897 km). With a Full Moon occurring less than half a day earlier, extra large tides will occur (see the section TIDES AND THE EARTH–MOON SYSTEM on pp. 165–167).

Mercury reaches greatest elongation west (27°) on Feb. 21. It is not easily observed until midmonth after it has risen in the morning twilight and become brighter. In this poor morning apparition for northern observers, Mercury rises only about an hour before the Sun and is visible only with difficulty very low in the east-southeast near midmonth; it is lost in twilight before month's end. For more favoured southern observers, Mercury rises about 2 h before the Sun and can be observed low in the east-southeast before sunrise for about the last 3 weeks of the month.

Venus is not easily observable this month. It was in superior conjunction with the Sun on Jan. 14.

Mars moves from Pisces to Aries late in the month. It stands about 30° high in the west-southwest at the end of evening twilight and sets in late evening. Less favoured southern observers will find Mars very low in the west-northwest after dark and setting in midevening.

Jupiter, in Gemini, stands about 60° high in the southeast at the end of evening twilight and sets in the northwest about 1 h before the beginning of morning twilight. Southern observers will find Jupiter about 35° high near the meridian at the end of evening twilight and setting in the west-northwest in early morning. **Jupiter is occulted by the Moon on Feb. 23**.

Saturn, in Taurus, is stationary on Feb. 8 and returns to direct (eastward) motion. For northern observers, it is near the meridian at the end of evening twilight and sets near 2 a.m. For southern observers, Saturn is in the north-northwest at the end of evening twilight and sets near midnight. **Saturn is occulted by the Moon on Feb. 21**.

Time (UT)			FEBRUARY EVENTS	Configuration of
d	h	m		Jupiter's Satellites

Fri.	1			
Sat.	2	12 42	Algol at minimum	
Sun.	3			
Mon.	4	13 33	**Last Quarter**	
Tue.	5	9 31	Algol at minimum	
Wed.	6			
Thu.	7			
Fri.	8	6 20	Algol at minimum	
		10	Mercury stationary	
		10	Saturn stationary	
Sat.	9			
Sun.	10	5	Mercury 5° N of Moon	
			Mars at ascending node	
Mon.	11	1	Juno at opposition	
		3 09	Algol at minimum	
Tue.	12	7 41	**New Moon**	
Wed.	13	17	Uranus in conjunction with Sun	
		23 59	Algol at minimum	
Thu.	14	22	Moon at apogee (406 363 km)	
Fri.	15			
Sat.	16		Venus at greatest heliocentric latitude S	
		13	Ceres in conjunction with Sun	
		20 48	Algol at minimum	
Sun.	17	0	Mars 5° N of Moon	
Mon.	18			
Tue.	19	17 37	Algol at minimum	
Wed.	20	12 02	**First Quarter**	
		13	Vesta 0.6° S of Moon, Occultation†	
Thu.	21	0	**Saturn 0.2° S of Moon, Occultation‡**	
		16	**Mercury greatest elongation W (27°)**	
Fri.	22		Mercury at descending node	
		14 27	Algol at minimum	
Sat.	23	2	**Jupiter 0.9° S of Moon, Occultation††**	
Sun.	24	13	**Mercury 0.5° S of Neptune**	
Mon.	25	11 16	Algol at minimum	
Tue.	26			
Wed.	27	9 17	**Full Moon (Largest of 2002)**	
		20	Moon at perigee (**356 897 km**) (Large tides)	
Thu.	28	8 05	Algol at minimum	

West   East

†N Africa, Europe including British Isles, N Saudi Arabia, N Asia, Arctic Ocean, N Japan, N Alaska
‡Central Pacific Ocean, U.S.A., Mexico, N Caribbean, SE Canada, central Atlantic Ocean, far NW Africa.
††Alaska, N Canada, N Russia, Arctic Ocean, Greenland, W Europe including British Isles

THE SKY FOR 2002 MARCH

		Mercury	Venus	Mars	Jupiter	Saturn	Uranus	Neptune	Sun
RA	1	21^h 10^m	23^h 30^m	1^h 49^m	6^h 24^m	4^h 28^m	21^h 53^m	20^h 48^m	22^h 47^m
	11	22^h 05^m	0^h 15^m	2^h 17^m	6^h 25^m	4^h 30^m	21^h 55^m	20^h 49^m	23^h 24^m
	21	23^h 06^m	1^h 01^m	2^h 44^m	6^h 27^m	4^h 32^m	21^h 57^m	20^h 50^m	0^h 01^m
Dec	1	−17° 24′	−4° 47′	+11° 33′	+23° 27′	+20° 10′	−13° 37′	−17° 46′	−7° 45′
	11	−13° 51′	+0° 20′	+14° 04′	+23° 27′	+20° 16′	−13° 26′	−17° 40′	−3° 53′
	21	−8° 12′	+5° 27′	+16° 23′	+23° 27′	+20° 25′	−13° 15′	−17° 36′	+0° 04′
Dist	1	1.08	1.67	1.94	4.69	9.03	20.95	30.94	
	11	1.20	1.65	2.01	4.84	9.20	20.90	30.84	
	21	1.29	1.63	2.08	5.00	9.36	20.82	30.72	
Mag	1	−0.0	−3.9	1.3	−2.5	0.0	5.9	8.0	
	11	−0.2	−3.9	1.3	−2.4	0.1	5.9	8.0	
	21	−0.5	−3.9	1.4	−2.3	0.1	5.9	8.0	
Size	1	6.2″	10.0″	4.8″	42.0″	18.3″	3.3″	2.2″	
	11	5.6″	10.1″	4.7″	40.7″	18.0″	3.4″	2.2″	
	21	5.2″	10.2″	4.5″	39.4″	17.7″	3.4″	2.2″	

Moon—On Mar. 1.0 UT, the age of the Moon is 16.7 d. The Sun's selenographic colongitude is 110.84° and increases by 12.2° each day thereafter. The libration in longitude is maximum (east limb exposed) on Mar. 5 (+8°) and minimum (west limb exposed) on Mar. 22 (−8°). The libration in latitude is maximum (north limb exposed) on Mar. 14 (+7°) and minimum (south limb exposed) on Mar. 27 (−7°). The Moon reaches its greatest northern declination on Mar. 22 (+25°) and its greatest southern declination on Mar. 8 (−25°).

Mercury is not observable by northern observers until mid-April. For southern observers, Mercury continues a favourable morning apparition this month. It continues to brighten, but at the same time it slowly descends further into the eastern morning twilight, becoming lost in the glare of the Sun late in the month.

Venus begins to emerge in the western evening twilight sky early in the month in what will be a very poor evening apparition for northern observers. By month's end, it sets about 1.5 h after the Sun. Southern observers will have to wait until the second half of the month before Venus begins to emerge very low in the west during evening twilight.

Mars, in Aries, is low in the west after dark and sets about 4 h after the Sun. Less favoured southern observers will find Mars very low in the west-northwest after dark and setting about 2.5 h after the Sun.

Jupiter, in Gemini, is stationary on Mar. 1 and returns to direct (eastward) motion. For northern observers, it stands over 60° high in the southwest at the end of evening twilight and sets in the west-northwest in early morning. Less favoured southern observers will find Jupiter about 35° above the north-northwestern horizon at the end of evening twilight and setting near midnight. **Jupiter is occulted by the Moon on Mar. 22**.

Saturn, in Taurus, stands about 45° high in the west-southwest at the end of evening twilight and sets after midnight. For less favoured southern observers, Saturn stands about 25° above the western horizon at the end of evening twilight and sets in late evening. **Saturn is occulted by the Moon on Mar. 20**.

Time (UT) d h m	MARCH EVENTS	Configuration of Jupiter's Satellites
Fri. 1 15	Jupiter stationary	West East
Sat. 2	**Zodiacal Light** vis. in N latitudes in W after end of evening twilight for next two weeks	
Sun. 3 4 54	Algol at minimum	
Mon. 4	Mercury at aphelion	
Wed. 6 1 24	**Last Quarter**	
1 44	Algol at minimum	
Thu. 7		
Fri. 8 22 33	Algol at minimum	
Sat. 9 3	Mercury 1.2° S of Uranus	
Sun. 10 9	Neptune 4° N of Moon	
Mon. 11 17	Uranus 4° N of Moon	
19 22	Algol at minimum	
Tue. 12	Jupiter at maximum northern declination (+23°27′24″)	
1	Mercury 3° N of Moon	
Wed. 13		
Thu. 14 1	Moon at apogee (**406 707 km**)	
2 02	**New Moon**	
5 13	**Double shadow transit on Jupiter**	
16 11	Algol at minimum	
Fri. 15		
Sun. 17 13 01	Algol at minimum	
Mon. 18 1	Mars 4° N of Moon	
Wed. 20 9 50	Algol at minimum	
10	**Saturn 0.5° S of Moon, Occultation†**	
10	Vesta 0.5° S of Moon, Occultation‡	
19 16	**Equinox**	
Thu. 21 6	Pluto stationary	
7 08	**Double shadow transit on Jupiter**	
Fri. 22 2 28	**First Quarter**	
12	**Jupiter 1.1° S of Moon, Occultation††** (last of a series)	
Sat. 23 6 39	Algol at minimum	
12	Juno stationary	
Sun. 24	Mercury at greatest heliocentric latitude S	
Tue. 26 3 28	Algol at minimum	
Wed. 27		
Thu. 28 8	Moon at perigee (357 010 km) (Large tides)	
10 14	**Double shadow transit on Jupiter**	
18 25	**Full Moon**	
Fri. 29 0 17	Algol at minimum	
Sat. 30		
Sun. 31	**Zodiacal Light** vis. in N latitudes in W after end of evening twilight for next two weeks	
16	Saturn 4° N of Aldebaran	
21 06	Algol at minimum	

†NE Africa, Saudi Arabia, NW India, Central Asia, Japan except S, Siberia, W Alaska
‡NE Africa, Saudi Arabia, NW India, Central Asia, Japan except S, NE Russia, W Alaska
††Greenland except S, Arctic Ocean, NW Canada

THE SKY FOR 2002 APRIL

		Mercury	Venus	Mars	Jupiter	Saturn	Uranus	Neptune	Sun
RA	1	0ʰ 19ᵐ	1ʰ 51ᵐ	3ʰ 15ᵐ	6ʰ 31ᵐ	4ʰ 36ᵐ	21ʰ 59ᵐ	20ʰ 52ᵐ	0ʰ 41ᵐ
	11	1ʰ 33ᵐ	2ʰ 38ᵐ	3ʰ 43ᵐ	6ʰ 35ᵐ	4ʰ 40ᵐ	22ʰ 01ᵐ	20ʰ 52ᵐ	1ʰ 17ᵐ
	21	2ʰ 49ᵐ	3ʰ 27ᵐ	4ʰ 11ᵐ	6ʰ 41ᵐ	4ʰ 44ᵐ	22ʰ 02ᵐ	20ʰ 53ᵐ	1ʰ 54ᵐ
Dec	1	+0° 15′	+10° 50′	+18° 38′	+23° 25′	+20° 34′	−13° 05′	−17° 32′	+4° 23′
	11	+9° 20′	+15° 18′	+20° 24′	+23° 23′	+20° 44′	−12° 56′	−17° 28′	+8° 10′
	21	+17° 48′	+19° 07′	+21° 52′	+23° 18′	+20° 54′	−12° 49′	−17° 26′	+11° 43′
Dist	1	1.35	1.60	2.16	5.18	9.52	20.70	30.57	
	11	1.31	1.56	2.22	5.34	9.66	20.58	30.42	
	21	1.15	1.52	2.29	5.49	9.78	20.44	30.25	
Mag	1	−1.3	−3.9	1.5	−2.2	0.1	5.9	7.9	
	11	−1.9	−3.9	1.5	−2.2	0.1	5.9	7.9	
	21	−1.1	−3.9	1.6	−2.1	0.1	5.9	7.9	
Size	1	5.0″	10.5″	4.3″	38.0″	17.4″	3.4″	2.2″	
	11	5.1″	10.7″	4.2″	36.9″	17.1″	3.4″	2.2″	
	21	5.8″	11.0″	4.1″	35.9″	16.9″	3.4″	2.2″	

Moon—On Apr. 1.0 UT, the age of the Moon is 17.9 d. The Sun's selenographic colongitude is 128.39° and increases by 12.2° each day thereafter. The libration in longitude is maximum (east limb exposed) on Apr. 3 (+8°) and minimum (west limb exposed) on Apr. 19 (−7°). The libration in latitude is maximum (north limb exposed) on Apr. 10 (+7°) and minimum (south limb exposed) on Apr. 23 (−7°). The Moon reaches its greatest northern declination on Apr. 19 (+25°) and its greatest southern declination on Apr. 4 (−25°).

Mercury is in superior conjunction with the Sun on Apr. 7 following which, the **best evening apparition of the year begins for northern observers**. It emerges in the west-northwestern evening twilight during the last half of the month, and at month's end it sets nearly 2 h after the Sun and stands nearly 20° above the horizon at sunset. For less favoured southern observers, in the last week of the month Mercury rises just high enough in west-northwestern evening twilight to be observed with difficulty.

Venus improves in visibility during the month; however, it still remains low in the west-northwest during evening twilight for both northern and southern observers. From about Apr. 18 and continuing until about May 18, Venus is the lead participant in a one-month grouping of **all five naked-eye planets** in the western evening sky.

Mars moves from Aries to Taurus early in the month. It is very low in the west-northwest after dark and sets about 3 h after the Sun. Less favoured southern observers will find Mars very low in the west-northwest after dark and setting less than 2 h after the Sun.

Jupiter, in Gemini, stands about 40° high in the west after the end of evening twilight and sets in the northwest after midnight. For less favoured southern observers, Jupiter stands about 30° high in the west at the end of evening twilight and sets in the west-northwest in late evening.

Saturn, in Taurus, is visible low in the west after sunset and sets about 4 h after the Sun. For less favoured southern observers, Saturn is very low in the northwest after sunset and sets about 2.5 h after the Sun. **Saturn is occulted by the Moon on Apr. 16**.

Time (UT) d h m	APRIL EVENTS	Configuration of Jupiter's Satellites

		West East
Mon. 1		
Tue. 2		
Wed. 3 17 56	Algol at minimum	
Thu. 4 15 29	**Last Quarter**	
Fri. 5		
Sat. 6 14 45	Algol at minimum	
16	Neptune 4° N of Moon	
Sun. 7 2	**Daylight Saving Time begins**	
9	Mercury in superior conjunction	
23 57	**Double shadow transit on Jupiter**	
Mon. 8 1	Uranus 4° N of Moon	
Tue. 9 11 34	Algol at minimum	
Wed. 10 5	Moon at apogee (406 408 km)	
Thu. 11		
Fri. 12	Mercury at ascending node	
8 23	Algol at minimum	
19 21	**New Moon**	
Sat. 13	Venus at ascending node	
Sun. 14 17	Venus 3° N of Moon	
Mon. 15 5 12	Algol at minimum	
23	**Mars 2° N of Moon**	
Tue. 16 20	**Saturn 0.8° S of Moon, Occultation†**	
Wed. 17	Mercury at perihelion	
10	Vesta 0.7° S of Moon, Occultation‡	
Thu. 18 2 01	Algol at minimum	
23	**Jupiter 1.6° S of Moon**	
Fri. 19		
Sat. 20 12 48	**First Quarter**	
22 50	Algol at minimum	
Sun. 21		
Mon. 22 11	Lyrid meteors peak	
Tue. 23 19 39	Algol at minimum	
Wed. 24		
Thu. 25 16	Moon at perigee (360 085 km)	
Fri. 26 16 28	Algol at minimum	
Sat. 27	Mercury at greatest heliocentric latitude N	
3 00	**Full Moon**	
Sun. 28		
Mon. 29 13	Mars 6° N of Aldebaran	
13 17	Algol at minimum	
Tue. 30		

†NW of North America, Arctic Ocean, Greenland, N Russia, N Europe including British Isles
‡N Africa, Europe including British Isles, Russia, Arctic Ocean, Greenland, Alaska, NW Canada, N Japan

THE SKY FOR 2002 MAY

		Mercury	Venus	Mars	Jupiter	Saturn	Uranus	Neptune	Sun
RA	1	$3^h 52^m$	$4^h 17^m$	$4^h 40^m$	$6^h 48^m$	$4^h 49^m$	$22^h 03^m$	$20^h 53^m$	$2^h 32^m$
	11	$4^h 28^m$	$5^h 09^m$	$5^h 09^m$	$6^h 55^m$	$4^h 54^m$	$22^h 04^m$	$20^h 54^m$	$3^h 11^m$
	21	$4^h 29^m$	$6^h 02^m$	$5^h 38^m$	$7^h 03^m$	$4^h 59^m$	$22^h 05^m$	$20^h 53^m$	$3^h 50^m$
Dec	1	+22° 51′	+22° 08′	+23° 00′	+23° 12′	+21° 04′	−12° 43′	−17° 25′	+14° 57′
	11	+23° 57′	+24° 07′	+23° 49′	+23° 04′	+21° 14′	−12° 39′	−17° 24′	+17° 46′
	21	+21° 49′	+24° 59′	+24° 17′	+22° 54′	+21° 23′	−12° 36′	−17° 24′	+20° 06′
Dist	1	0.92	1.47	2.34	5.64	9.88	20.28	30.08	
	11	0.71	1.42	2.40	5.77	9.96	20.12	29.91	
	21	0.58	1.37	2.45	5.89	10.02	19.95	29.75	
Mag	1	−0.0	−3.9	1.6	−2.1	0.1	5.9	7.9	
	11	1.4	−3.9	1.7	−2.0	0.1	5.8	7.9	
	21	3.8	−4.0	1.7	−2.0	0.1	5.8	7.9	
Size	1	7.3″	11.3″	4.0″	34.9″	16.7″	3.5″	2.2″	
	11	9.5″	11.7″	3.9″	34.1″	16.6″	3.5″	2.2″	
	21	11.6″	12.2″	3.8″	33.4″	16.5″	3.5″	2.3″	

Moon—On May 1.0 UT, the age of the Moon is 18.2 d. The Sun's selenographic colongitude is 134.30° and increases by 12.2° each day thereafter. The libration in longitude is maximum (east limb exposed) on May 1 (+7°) and on May 29 (+6°) and minimum (west limb exposed) on May 16 (−6°). The libration in latitude is maximum (north limb exposed) on May 7 (+7°) and minimum (south limb exposed) on May 21 (−7°). The Moon reaches its greatest northern declination on May 16 (+25°) and its greatest southern declinations on May 1 (−25°) and May 29 (−25°).

There is a **penumbral lunar eclipse** on May 26 (see p. 125 in ECLIPSES DURING 2002).

Mercury reaches greatest elongation east (21°) on May 4. It can be observed low in the west-northwest after sunset early in the month by both northern and southern observers. It fades rapidly as it descends into the evening twilight and is lost in the glare of the Sun near midmonth. Mercury is in inferior conjunction with the Sun on May 27.

Venus continues to improve in visibility this month low in the northwest after dark. At month's end, it sets over 2.5 h after the Sun, but because of the shallow angle of the ecliptic it lies low during evening twilight. More favoured southern observers will find that Venus has climbed to nearly 10° above the horizon at the end of evening twilight at month's end. Until about May 18, Venus continues to lead a grouping of **all five naked-eye planets** in the western evening sky. **Venus is in a close grouping with Saturn and Mars on May 6** (see Mars below). **Venus is occulted by the Moon on May 14**.

Mars moves from Taurus to Gemini late in the month. It is visible only with difficulty very low in the west-northwest after dark. By month's end it sets less than 2 h after the Sun. Southern observers can observe Mars with difficulty very low in the west-northwest after dark; by month's end it sets about 1.5 h after the Sun. **Mars is in a close grouping with brighter Saturn and Venus on May 6**. On May 10, **Venus is in conjunction with Mars** (~0.3°), and the crescent Moon enters the scene on May 14 causing an occultation.

Jupiter, in Gemini, is visible low in the northwest at the end of evening twilight for both northern and southern observers. It sets about 3 h after the Sun in the west-northwest.

Saturn can be observed with difficulty very low in the west-northwest after sunset, before being lost in the glare of the Sun by midmonth. It is in conjunction with the Sun on Jun. 9. **Saturn is in conjunction with Mars on May 4 and with Venus on May 7** (see Venus and Mars above). **Saturn is occulted by the Moon on May 14**.

Time (UT) d h m	MAY EVENTS	Configuration of Jupiter's Satellites
Wed. 1		West East
Thu. 2 10 06	Algol at minimum	
Fri. 3		
Sat. 4 0	Neptune 4° N of Moon	
4	**Mercury greatest elongation E (21°)**	
7 16	**Last Quarter**	
14	Venus 6° N of Aldebaran	
17	**Mars 2° N of Saturn**	
Sun. 5 4	η-Aquarid meteors peak	
6 55	Algol at minimum	
10	Uranus 4° N of Moon	
Mon. 6		
Tue. 7 18	**Venus 2° N of Saturn**	
19	Moon at apogee (405 483 km)	
Wed. 8 3 44	Algol at minimum	
Fri. 10 21	**Venus 0.3° N of Mars**	
Sat. 11 0 33	Algol at minimum	
Sun. 12 10 45	**New Moon**	
Mon. 13 14	Neptune stationary	
21	Mercury 3° N of Moon	
21 22	Algol at minimum	
Tue. 14 8	**Saturn 1.1° S of Moon, Occultation†**	
	(last of a series)	
	three **occultations on this day**	
19	**Mars 0.6° N of Moon, Occultation‡**	
23	**Venus 0.8° N of Moon, Occultation††**	
Wed. 15 12	Vesta 1.1° S of Moon, Occultation‡‡	
Thu. 16 5	Mercury stationary	
12	**Jupiter 2° S of Moon**	
18 11	Algol at minimum	
Fri. 17	Venus at perihelion	
Sat. 18		
Sun. 19 15 00	Algol at minimum	
19 42	**First Quarter**	
Tue. 21	Mercury at descending node	
Wed. 22 11 49	Algol at minimum	
Thu. 23 16	Moon at perigee (364 984 km)	
Fri. 24 20 30	**Double shadow transit on Jupiter**	
Sat. 25 8 37	Algol at minimum	
Sun. 26 11 51	**Full Moon, Penumbral Eclipse**	
Mon. 27 7	Mercury in inferior conjunction	
Tue. 28 5 26	Algol at minimum	
Wed. 29		
Fri. 31	Mercury at aphelion	
2 15	Algol at minimum	
8	Neptune 4° N of Moon	
23 05	**Double shadow transit on Jupiter**	

†British Isles, W Scandinavia, Greenland, Arctic Ocean, N Canada, NE Asia
‡SE Pacific Ocean, South America except far N and S, SW Atlantic Ocean
††S Pacific Ocean   ‡‡N Canada, Arctic Ocean, N Alaska, NE Siberia

THE SKY FOR 2002 JUNE

		Mercury	Venus	Mars	Jupiter	Saturn	Uranus	Neptune	Sun
RA	1	$4^h 07^m$	$7^h 00^m$	$6^h 10^m$	$7^h 12^m$	$5^h 05^m$	$22^h 05^m$	$20^h 53^m$	$4^h 35^m$
	11	$4^h 01^m$	$7^h 51^m$	$6^h 39^m$	$7^h 21^m$	$5^h 11^m$	$22^h 05^m$	$20^h 53^m$	$5^h 16^m$
	21	$4^h 23^m$	$8^h 40^m$	$7^h 07^m$	$7^h 30^m$	$5^h 17^m$	$22^h 04^m$	$20^h 52^m$	$5^h 58^m$
Dec	1	+17° 54′	+24° 34′	+24° 25′	+22° 40′	+21° 33′	−12° 35′	−17° 26′	+22° 00′
	11	+16° 24′	+22° 59′	+24° 10′	+22° 24′	+21° 40′	−12° 36′	−17° 28′	+23° 03′
	21	+18° 00′	+20° 23′	+23° 37′	+22° 07′	+21° 47′	−12° 39′	−17° 31′	+23° 26′
Dist	1	0.56	1.30	2.50	6.01	10.05	19.77	29.58	
	11	0.65	1.24	2.54	6.10	10.06	19.61	29.44	
	21	0.82	1.17	2.58	6.17	10.05	19.46	29.32	
Mag	1	4.3	−4.0	1.7	−1.9	0.0	5.8	7.9	
	11	1.9	−4.0	1.7	−1.9	0.0	5.8	7.9	
	21	0.6	−4.0	1.7	−1.9	0.0	5.8	7.9	
Size	1	12.0″	12.8″	3.7″	32.8″	16.5″	3.5″	2.3″	
	11	10.3″	13.5″	3.7″	32.3″	16.4″	3.6″	2.3″	
	21	8.2″	14.3″	3.6″	31.9″	16.5″	3.6″	2.3″	

Moon—On Jun. 1.0 UT, the age of the Moon is 19.5 d. The Sun's selenographic colongitude is 152.86° and increases by 12.2° each day thereafter. The libration in longitude is maximum (east limb exposed) on Jun. 25 (+5°) and minimum (west limb exposed) on Jun. 11 (−5°). The libration in latitude is maximum (north limb exposed) on Jun. 3 (+7°) and Jun. 30 (+7°) and minimum (south limb exposed) on Jun. 17 (−7°). The Moon reaches its greatest northern declination on Jun. 12 (+25°) and its greatest southern declination on Jun. 25 (−25°).

There is an **annular solar eclipse** on Jun. 10–11 whose path completely crosses the northern Pacific Ocean and ends at sunset at the western coast of Mexico. Partial phases are visible in parts of the far east, northern Australia and Asia, and most of North America (except for the extreme eastern parts) (see pp. 125–126 in ECLIPSES DURING 2002). There is also a **penumbral lunar eclipse** on Jun. 24 (see p. 126 in ECLIPSES DURING 2002).

Mercury reaches greatest elongation west (23°) on Jun. 21. For southern observers, it emerges in the east-northeastern morning twilight early in the month; however, due to its faint magnitude, it is difficult to observe until it brightens sufficiently late in the month. Northern observers can glimpse Mercury in the last few days of the month very low in the east-northeast before sunrise.

Venus is becoming slightly more difficult to observe this month for northern observers when compared to last month due to the unfavourable tipping of the ecliptic. It is visible low in the west-northwest during evening twilight. More favoured southern observers will find Venus nearly 15° high in the northwest at the end of evening twilight. **Venus is in conjunction with Jupiter** on Jun. 3.

Mars, in Gemini, is visible with difficulty low in the west-northwest during evening twilight. It is lost in the glare of the Sun early in the month for northern observers and late in the month for southern observers. **Mars is occulted by the Moon on Jun. 12**.

Jupiter, in Gemini, is visible very low in the west-northwest after sunset early in the month. By month's end, it is lost in the glare of the Sun. **Jupiter is in conjunction with Venus** on Jun. 3.

Saturn is in conjunction with the Sun on Jun. 9. It cannot be observed by northern observers this month; however, for more favoured southern observers, it emerges late in the month in the east-northeast during morning twilight.

Pluto, in Ophiuchus, is at opposition with the Sun on Jun. 7. See the finder chart for Pluto on p. 185.

Time (UT) d h m	JUNE EVENTS	Configuration of Jupiter's Satellites
Sat. 1 18	Uranus 4° N of Moon	
Sun. 2 23 04	Algol at minimum	
Mon. 3 0 05	**Last Quarter**	
7	Uranus stationary	
18	**Venus 1.6° N of Jupiter**	
Tue. 4 13	Moon at apogee (404 522 km)	
Wed. 5 19 53	Algol at minimum	
Thu. 6		
Fri. 7 5	**Pluto at opposition**	
Sat. 8	Venus at greatest heliocentric latitude N	
2 16	Double shadow transit on Jupiter	
11	Mercury stationary	
16 41	Algol at minimum	
23	Pallas stationary	
Sun. 9 11	Saturn in conjunction with Sun	
14	Mercury 3° S of Moon	
20	Venus 5° S of Pollux	
Mon. 10 23 46	**New Moon, Annular Solar Eclipse†**	
Tue. 11 13 30	Algol at minimum	
Wed. 12 12	**Mars 0.9° S of Moon, Occultation‡**	
Thu. 13 4	**Jupiter 2° S of Moon**	
21	**Venus 1.5° S of Moon**	
Fri. 14 10 19	Algol at minimum	
Sat. 15 6 15	Double shadow transit on Jupiter	
Sun. 16		
Mon. 17 7 08	Algol at minimum	
Tue. 18 0 29	**First Quarter**	
Wed. 19 7	Moon at perigee (369 309 km)	
Thu. 20	Mercury at greatest heliocentric latitude S	
3 56	Algol at minimum	
Fri. 21 13 24	**Solstice**	
15	**Mercury greatest elongation W (23°)**	
Sat. 22		
Sun. 23 0 45	Algol at minimum	
Mon. 24 4	**Mercury 2° N of Aldebaran**	
21 42	**Full Moon, Penumbral Eclipse**	
Tue. 25 21 34	Algol at minimum	
Wed. 26		
Thu. 27 16	Neptune 4° N of Moon	
Fri. 28 18 22	Algol at minimum	
Sat. 29 2	Uranus 4° N of Moon	
Sun. 30		

†E Asia, Japan, Indonesia, N Australia, Pacific Ocean, N Mexico, U.S.A., Canada except far NE—see pp. 125–126 for further details
‡NE Canada, Greenland, Arctic Ocean, NE Asia

THE SKY FOR 2002 JULY

		Mercury	Venus	Mars	Jupiter	Saturn	Uranus	Neptune	Sun
RA	1	$5^h 13^m$	$9^h 27^m$	$7^h 35^m$	$7^h 39^m$	$5^h 22^m$	$22^h 04^m$	$20^h 51^m$	$6^h 39^m$
	11	$6^h 30^m$	$10^h 11^m$	$8^h 02^m$	$7^h 49^m$	$5^h 27^m$	$22^h 03^m$	$20^h 50^m$	$7^h 20^m$
	21	$8^h 02^m$	$10^h 52^m$	$8^h 29^m$	$7^h 58^m$	$5^h 32^m$	$22^h 02^m$	$20^h 49^m$	$8^h 01^m$
Dec	1	+21° 12′	+16° 56′	+22° 45′	+21° 46′	+21° 53′	−12° 43′	−17° 34′	+23° 08′
	11	+23° 29′	+12° 48′	+21° 36′	+21° 24′	+21° 58′	−12° 48′	−17° 38′	+22° 10′
	21	+22° 06′	+8° 13′	+20° 11′	+21° 00′	+22° 01′	−12° 55′	−17° 42′	+20° 33′
Dist	1	1.03	1.09	2.61	6.22	10.01	19.33	29.22	
	11	1.23	1.02	2.63	6.25	9.95	19.21	29.14	
	21	1.33	0.94	2.65	6.26	9.86	19.12	29.09	
Mag	1	−0.3	−4.0	1.8	−1.8	0.1	5.7	7.9	
	11	−1.3	−4.1	1.8	−1.8	0.1	5.7	7.8	
	21	−2.1	−4.1	1.7	−1.8	0.1	5.7	7.8	
Size	1	6.5″	15.2″	3.6″	31.7″	16.5″	3.6″	2.3″	
	11	5.5″	16.4″	3.6″	31.5″	16.6″	3.6″	2.3″	
	21	5.0″	17.7″	3.5″	31.4″	16.8″	3.7″	2.3″	

Moon—On Jul. 1.0 UT, the age of the Moon is 20.0 d. The Sun's selenographic colongitude is 159.48° and increases by 12.2° each day thereafter. The libration in longitude is maximum (east limb exposed) on Jul. 22 (+5°) and minimum (west limb exposed) on Jul. 8 (−6°). The libration in latitude is maximum (north limb exposed) on Jul. 28 (+7°) and minimum (south limb exposed) on Jul. 14 (−7°). The Moon reaches its greatest northern declination on Jul. 9 (+25°) and its greatest southern declination on Jul. 22 (−25°).

Mercury can be observed with difficulty by both northern and southern observers low in the east-northeast before sunrise in the first week of the month, following which it becomes lost in the glare of the Sun. **Mercury is in conjunction with Saturn on Jul. 2 (~0.2°).** It is in superior conjunction with the Sun on Jul. 21.

Venus's visibility continues to degrade this month for northern observers when compared to last month. It is visible with difficulty very low in the west during evening twilight, setting only 2 h after the Sun. More favoured southern observers will find Venus high in the west-northwest at the end of evening twilight.

Mars cannot be observed this month. It is in conjunction with the Sun on Aug. 10.

Jupiter is in conjunction with the Sun on Jul. 20 and cannot be observed this month.

Saturn, in Taurus, emerges in the east-northeast morning twilight in the second half of the month. By month's end it stands about 10° above the horizon at the beginning of morning twilight. For more favoured southern observers, Saturn is over 15° above the northeastern horizon at month's end as morning twilight begins. **Saturn is in conjunction with Mercury on Jul. 2 (~0.2°).**

Time (UT) d h m	JULY EVENTS	Configuration of Jupiter's Satellites

West   East

Mon.	1	15 11	Algol at minimum	
Tue.	2	8	Moon at apogee (404 210 km)	
		11	**Mercury 0.2° S of Saturn**	
		17 19	**Last Quarter**	
Wed.	3	6	**Mars 0.8° N of Jupiter**	
Thu.	4	12 00	Algol at minimum	
		17	Mars 6° S of Pollux	
Fri.	5			
Sat.	6	4	**Earth at aphelion** (152 094 Mm)	
Sun.	7	8 48	Algol at minimum	
Mon.	8	13	**Saturn 1.7° S of Moon**	
Tue.	9		Mercury at ascending node	
Wed.	10	5 37	Algol at minimum	
		10	**Venus 1.1° N of Regulus**	
		10 26	**New Moon**	
Thu.	11			
Fri.	12			
Sat.	13	2 25	Algol at minimum	
		12	Venus 4° S of Moon	
Sun.	14		Mercury at perihelion	
		13	Moon at perigee (367 847 km)	
Mon.	15	23 14	Algol at minimum	
Tue.	16			
Wed.	17	4 47	**First Quarter**	
Thu.	18	20 03	Algol at minimum	
Fri.	19			
Sat.	20	1	Jupiter in conjunction with Sun	
Sun.	21	2	Mercury in superior conjunction	
		16 51	Algol at minimum	
Mon.	22			
Tue.	23	8	Vesta in conjunction with Sun	
Wed.	24		Mercury at greatest heliocentric latitude N	
		9 07	**Full Moon**	
		13 40	Algol at minimum	
		23	Neptune 4° N of Moon	
Thu.	25			
Fri.	26	9	Uranus 4° N of Moon	
Sat.	27	10 28	Algol at minimum	
Sun.	28			
Mon.	29	0	S δ-Aquarid meteors peak	
Tue.	30	2	Moon at apogee (404 743 km)	
		7 17	Algol at minimum	
Wed.	31			

THE SKY FOR 2002 AUGUST

		Mercury	Venus	Mars	Jupiter	Saturn	Uranus	Neptune	Sun
RA	1	9ʰ 33ᵐ	11ʰ 35ᵐ	8ʰ 58ᵐ	8ʰ 08ᵐ	5ʰ 38ᵐ	22ʰ 00ᵐ	20ʰ 48ᵐ	8ʰ 44ᵐ
	11	10ʰ 39ᵐ	12ʰ 13ᵐ	9ʰ 24ᵐ	8ʰ 17ᵐ	5ʰ 42ᵐ	21ʰ 59ᵐ	20ʰ 47ᵐ	9ʰ 22ᵐ
	21	11ʰ 32ᵐ	12ʰ 48ᵐ	9ʰ 49ᵐ	8ʰ 26ᵐ	5ʰ 46ᵐ	21ʰ 57ᵐ	20ʰ 46ᵐ	10ʰ 00ᵐ
Dec	1	+16° 20′	+2° 52′	+18° 22′	+20° 31′	+22° 05′	−13° 03′	−17° 47′	+18° 07′
	11	+9° 26′	−2° 05′	+16° 29′	+20° 03′	+22° 06′	−13° 11′	−17° 52′	+15° 24′
	21	+2° 26′	−6° 56′	+14° 26′	+19° 34′	+22° 08′	−13° 19′	−17° 56′	+12° 15′
Dist	1	1.31	0.86	2.67	6.25	9.75	19.04	29.07	
	11	1.22	0.78	2.67	6.22	9.63	19.00	29.09	
	21	1.10	0.70	2.67	6.17	9.49	18.99	29.13	
Mag	1	−0.9	−4.2	1.7	−1.8	0.1	5.7	7.8	
	11	−0.3	−4.2	1.7	−1.8	0.1	5.7	7.8	
	21	0.0	−4.3	1.7	−1.8	0.1	5.7	7.8	
Size	1	5.1″	19.5″	3.5″	31.5″	17.0″	3.7″	2.3″	
	11	5.5″	21.5″	3.5″	31.7″	17.2″	3.7″	2.3″	
	21	6.1″	24.0″	3.5″	31.9″	17.4″	3.7″	2.3″	

Moon—On Aug. 1.0 UT, the age of the Moon is 21.6 d. The Sun's selenographic colongitude is 178.35° and increases by 12.2° each day thereafter. The libration in longitude is maximum (east limb exposed) on Aug. 17 (+6°) and minimum (west limb exposed) on Aug. 5 (−6°). The libration in latitude is maximum (north limb exposed) on Aug. 24 (+7°) and minimum (south limb exposed) on Aug. 10 (−7°). The Moon reaches its greatest northern declination on Aug. 6 (+25°) and its greatest southern declination on Aug. 19 (−25°).

Mercury cannot be observed by northern observers until early October; however, the **best evening apparition of the year begins for southern observers**. It emerges rapidly in the western evening twilight early in the month. It remains visible all month; however, during the month it fades by about 2 magnitudes. At month's end, Mercury sets more than 2 h after the Sun and stands nearly 5° above the horizon at the end of evening twilight.

Venus is at greatest elongation east (46°) on Aug. 22. It is visible only with difficulty very low in the west-southwest after sunset and sets about 1.5 h after the Sun. Conversely, for more favoured southern observers (where the ecliptic is nearly vertical with respect to the horizon), Venus stands over 25° above the west-northwestern horizon at the end of evening twilight.

Mars cannot be observed this month. It is in conjunction with the Sun on Aug. 10.

Jupiter, in Cancer, emerges in the dawn twilight during the month. By month's end, it stands about 10° above the east-northern horizon at the beginning of morning twilight.

Saturn, in Taurus, rises after midnight in the east-northeast and stands about 25° above the eastern horizon at the beginning of morning twilight. For southern observers, it rises about 3.5 h before the Sun in the east-northeast and stands less than 25° above the northeastern horizon as morning twilight begins.

Uranus is near the border of Capricornus and Aquarius this year; it is at opposition with the Sun on Aug. 20 and was in conjunction with the Sun on Feb. 13. Its southerly declination in 2002 makes it low in the sky for northern observers. See the finder chart for Uranus on p. 183.

Neptune, in Capricornus, is at opposition with the Sun on Aug. 2 and was in conjunction with the Sun on Jan. 28. Its southerly declination in 2002 makes it low in the sky for northern observers. See the finder chart for Neptune on p. 184.

Time (UT) d h m	AUGUST EVENTS	Configuration of Jupiter's Satellites
Thu. 1 10 22	**Last Quarter**	
Fri. 2 1	**Neptune at opposition**	
4 06	Algol at minimum	
Sat. 3	Venus at descending node	
Sun. 4		
Mon. 5 0 54	Algol at minimum	
4	**Saturn 2° S of Moon**	
Tue. 6 4	**Mercury 0.9° N of Regulus**	
Wed. 7 21 43	Algol at minimum	
Thu. 8 19 15	**New Moon**	
Sat. 10 1	Mercury 4° S of Moon	
18 31	Algol at minimum	
22	Mars in conjunction with Sun	
23	Moon at perigee (362 927 km)	
Sun. 11 15 59	Double shadow transit on Jupiter	
22	Venus 6° S of Moon	
Mon. 12 12	Pallas at opposition	
22	**Perseid meteors peak**	
Tue. 13 15 20	Algol at minimum	
Wed. 14	Mars at greatest heliocentric latitude N	
Thu. 15 10 12	**First Quarter**	
Fri. 16 12 08	Algol at minimum	
Sat. 17	Mercury at descending node	
15	Ceres stationary	
Sun. 18 18 07	Double shadow transit on Jupiter	
Mon. 19 8 57	Algol at minimum	
Tue. 20 1	**Uranus at opposition**	
Wed. 21 4	Neptune 4° N of Moon	
Thu. 22 5 46	Algol at minimum	
13	**Venus greatest elongation E (46°)**	
14	Uranus 4° N of Moon	
22 29	**Full Moon**	
Fri. 23		
Sat. 24		
Sun. 25 2 34	Algol at minimum	
Mon. 26 18	Moon at apogee (405 695 km)	
Tue. 27	Mercury at aphelion	
20	Pluto stationary	
23 23	Algol at minimum	
Wed. 28		
Thu. 29		
Fri. 30 20 11	Algol at minimum	
Sat. 31 2 31	**Last Quarter**	

THE SKY FOR 2002 SEPTEMBER

		Mercury	Venus	Mars	Jupiter	Saturn	Uranus	Neptune	Sun
RA	1	12^{h}17^m	13^{h}24^m	10^{h}16^m	8^{h}36^m	5^{h}50^m	21^{h}55^m	20^{h}45^m	10^{h}40^m
	11	12^{h}40^m	13^{h}54^m	10^{h}40^m	8^{h}44^m	5^{h}52^m	21^{h}54^m	20^{h}44^m	11^{h}16^m
	21	12^{h}35^m	14^{h}20^m	11^{h}04^m	8^{h}52^m	5^{h}54^m	21^{h}53^m	20^{h}43^m	11^{h}52^m
Dec	1	−4° 17′	−11° 58′	+12° 01′	+19° 02′	+22° 08′	−13° 28′	−18° 00′	+8° 26′
	11	−8° 18′	−16° 04′	+9° 41′	+18° 32′	+22° 08′	−13° 36′	−18° 04′	+4° 43′
	21	−7° 58′	−19° 30′	+7° 15′	+18° 04′	+22° 08′	−13° 42′	−18° 06′	+0° 52′
Dist	1	0.94	0.61	2.66	6.09	9.32	19.02	29.21	
	11	0.79	0.53	2.65	6.00	9.16	19.07	29.30	
	21	0.67	0.46	2.62	5.89	9.00	19.15	29.42	
Mag	1	0.2	−4.4	1.8	−1.9	0.1	5.7	7.8	
	11	0.6	−4.5	1.8	−1.9	0.1	5.7	7.9	
	21	2.3	−4.5	1.8	−1.9	0.0	5.7	7.9	
Size	1	7.1″	27.4″	3.5″	32.3″	17.7″	3.7″	2.3″	
	11	8.5″	31.4″	3.5″	32.8″	18.1″	3.7″	2.3″	
	21	10.0″	36.4″	3.6″	33.4″	18.4″	3.7″	2.3″	

Moon—On Sep. 1.0 UT, the age of the Moon is 23.2 d. The Sun's selenographic colongitude is 197.00° and increases by 12.2° each day thereafter. The libration in longitude is maximum (east limb exposed) on Sep. 14 (+7°) and minimum (west limb exposed) on Sep. 2 (−7°) and Sep. 30 (−8°). The libration in latitude is maximum (north limb exposed) on Sep. 20 (+7°) and minimum (south limb exposed) on Sep. 7 (−6°). The Moon reaches its greatest northern declinations on Sep. 2 (+25°) and Sep. 30 (+26°) and its greatest southern declination on Sep. 15 (−25°).

Mercury reaches greatest elongation east (27°) on Sep. 1; however, northern observers cannot observe this apparition. Southern observers continue their **best evening apparition of the year**; however, Mercury fades rapidly as it descends into the western evening twilight, becoming lost in the glare of the Sun about midmonth. It is in inferior conjunction with the Sun on Sep. 27.

Venus reaches greatest brilliancy on Sep. 26; however, northern observers can only glimpse it early in the month very low in the west-southwest after sunset. It is lost in the glare of the Sun late in the month. For more favoured southern observers, Venus remains a striking object high in the west-northwest well after evening twilight ends.

Mars cannot be observed this month by southern observers. It emerges in the eastern morning twilight late in the month for northern observers and rises only about 1.5 h before the Sun at month's end.

Jupiter, in Cancer, improves in visibility this month in the predawn sky. By month's end, Jupiter stands more than 20° above the eastern horizon at the beginning of morning twilight. Less favoured southern observers will find Jupiter less than 10° high in the east-northeast at the beginning of twilight.

Saturn moves into Orion on Sep. 1. For northern observers, it rises in late evening and is high in the southeast during morning twilight. For southern observers, it rises near 2 a.m. and stands nearly 35° high in the east-northeast at the beginning of morning twilight.

Time (UT) d h m	SEPTEMBER EVENTS	Configuration of Jupiter's Satellites
Sun. 1 6	**Venus 0.9° S of Spica**	
10	**Mercury greatest elongation E (27°)**	
17	**Saturn 2° S of Moon**	
Mon. 2 17 00	Algol at minimum	
Tue. 3		
Wed. 4 13	Jupiter 4° S of Moon	
Thu. 5 13 49	Algol at minimum	
Fri. 6	**Zodiacal Light** vis. in N latitudes in E before start of morning twilight for next two weeks	
Sat. 7	Venus at aphelion	
3 10	**New Moon**	
Sun. 8 3	Moon at perigee (358 746 km) (Large tides)	
10 37	Algol at minimum	
17	Mercury 9° S of Moon	
Mon. 9		
Tue. 10 2	Venus 8° S of Moon	
Wed. 11 7 26	Algol at minimum	
Thu. 12		
Fri. 13 18 08	**First Quarter**	
Sat. 14 4 15	Algol at minimum	
14	Mercury stationary	
Sun. 15		
Mon. 16	Mercury at greatest heliocentric latitude S	
Tue. 17 1 03	Algol at minimum	
9	Neptune 4° N of Moon	
Wed. 18 18	Uranus 4° N of Moon	
Thu. 19 21 52	Algol at minimum	
Fri. 20		
Sat. 21	Mars at aphelion	
13 59	**Full Moon** (the *Harvest Moon*)	
Sun. 22 18 41	Algol at minimum	
Mon. 23 3	Moon at apogee (406 352 km)	
4 55	**Equinox**	
Tue. 24		
Wed. 25 15 29	Algol at minimum	
Thu. 26 11	**Venus greatest brilliancy**	
Fri. 27 19	Mercury in inferior conjunction	
Sat. 28 12 18	Algol at minimum	
Sun. 29	Venus at greatest heliocentric latitude S	
3	Saturn 3° S of Moon	
17 03	**Last Quarter**	
Mon. 30 0	Pallas stationary	

THE SKY FOR 2002 OCTOBER

		Mercury	Venus	Mars	Jupiter	Saturn	Uranus	Neptune	Sun
RA	1	$12^h 02^m$	$14^h 37^m$	$11^h 27^m$	$8^h 59^m$	$5^h 55^m$	$21^h 52^m$	$20^h 43^m$	$12^h 28^m$
	11	$12^h 01^m$	$14^h 44^m$	$11^h 51^m$	$9^h 05^m$	$5^h 56^m$	$21^h 51^m$	$20^h 42^m$	$13^h 04^m$
	21	$12^h 47^m$	$14^h 35^m$	$12^h 14^m$	$9^h 11^m$	$5^h 56^m$	$21^h 50^m$	$20^h 42^m$	$13^h 42^m$
Dec	1	$-1° 53'$	$-22° 02'$	$+4° 45'$	$+17° 36'$	$+22° 08'$	$-13° 48'$	$-18° 09'$	$-3° 01'$
	11	$+1° 16'$	$-23° 16'$	$+2° 13'$	$+17° 11'$	$+22° 07'$	$-13° 52'$	$-18° 10'$	$-6° 52'$
	21	$-2° 53'$	$-22° 35'$	$-0° 21'$	$+16° 49'$	$+22° 06'$	$-13° 55'$	$-18° 10'$	$-10° 33'$
Dist	1	0.68	0.39	2.60	5.77	8.83	19.26	29.56	
	11	0.90	0.33	2.56	5.64	8.67	19.38	29.72	
	21	1.17	0.29	2.52	5.49	8.52	19.53	29.88	
Mag	1	3.6	−4.6	1.8	−2.0	0.0	5.7	7.9	
	11	−0.2	−4.5	1.8	−2.0	−0.1	5.8	7.9	
	21	−0.9	−4.3	1.8	−2.1	−0.1	5.8	7.9	
Size	1	9.8″	42.8″	3.6″	34.1″	18.7″	3.6″	2.3″	
	11	7.4″	50.3″	3.7″	34.9″	19.1″	3.6″	2.3″	
	21	5.8″	57.7″	3.7″	35.8″	19.4″	3.6″	2.2″	

Moon—On Oct. 1.0 UT, the age of the Moon is 23.9 d. The Sun's selenographic colongitude is 203.04° and increases by 12.2° each day thereafter. The libration in longitude is maximum (east limb exposed) on Oct. 12 (+8°) and minimum (west limb exposed) on Oct. 28 (−7°). The libration in latitude is maximum (north limb exposed) on Oct. 17 (+7°) and minimum (south limb exposed) on Oct. 4 (−7°) and Oct. 31 (−7°). The Moon reaches its greatest northern declination on Oct. 27 (+26°) and its greatest southern declination on Oct. 12 (−26°).

On Oct. 6 the Moon reaches its second closest perigee distance of the year (356 918 km). With a New Moon occurring at nearly the same time, extra large tides will occur (see the section TIDES AND THE EARTH–MOON SYSTEM on pp. 165-167).

Mercury reaches greatest elongation west (18°) on Oct. 13. Northern observers can observe it low in the east during morning twilight after about Oct. 8. The geometry is poor for southern observers; as a result, this morning apparition is not easily observed. Mercury is in quasi-conjunction (see. p. 19) with Mars on Oct. 10.

Venus cannot be observed this month by northern observers. For southern observers, Venus descends rapidly into the west-southwestern evening twilight as the month progresses. It is lost in the glare of the Sun by about Oct. 24. Venus is at inferior conjunction with the Sun on Oct. 31.

Mars moves from Leo to Virgo early in the month. Its visibility improves this month for northern observers. By month's end, it is nearly 10° above the east-southeastern horizon at the beginning of morning twilight. For less favoured southern observers, Mars emerges in the eastern dawn sky late in the month; however, it is still a difficult observation at month's end when still embedded in twilight. Mars is in quasi-conjunction with Mercury on Oct. 10.

Jupiter, in Cancer, rises near midnight in the east-northeast and stands about 45° high in the east-southeast at the beginning of morning twilight. For southern observers, Jupiter rises near 2 a.m. and stands about 20° high in the northeast at the beginning of morning twilight.

Saturn, in Orion, is stationary on Oct. 11 and begins retrograde (westward) motion. It rises in the east-northeast in midevening for northern observers and late evening for southern observers and is visible for the remainder of the night.

Time (UT) d h m	OCTOBER EVENTS	Configuration of Jupiter's Satellites
Tue. 1 9 07	Algol at minimum	West East
Wed. 2 7	Jupiter 4° S of Moon	
Thu. 3 22	Juno in conjunction with Sun	
Fri. 4 5 55	Algol at minimum	
8	Ceres at opposition	
Sat. 5	**Zodiacal Light** vis. in N latitudes in E before start of morning twilight for next two weeks	
	Mercury at ascending node	
1	Mars 4° S of Moon	
Sun. 6 2	Mercury stationary	
11 18	**New Moon**	
13	Moon at perigee (356 918 km) (Large tides)	
Mon. 7 2 44	Algol at minimum	
Tue. 8 10	Venus 10° S of Moon	
Wed. 9 23 33	Algol at minimum	
Thu. 10	Mercury at perihelion	
9	Venus stationary	
13	Mercury–Mars quasi-conjunction (2°50′)	
Fri. 11 13	Saturn stationary	
Sat. 12 20 22	Algol at minimum	
Sun. 13 5 33	**First Quarter**	
8	**Mercury greatest elongation W (18°)**	
Mon. 14 14	Neptune 5° N of Moon	
Tue. 15 17 10	Algol at minimum	
22	Uranus 4° N of Moon	
Wed. 16		
Thu. 17		
Fri. 18 13 59	Algol at minimum	
Sat. 19		
Sun. 20	Mercury at greatest heliocentric latitude N	
5	Moon at apogee (406 360 km)	
11	Neptune stationary	
Mon. 21 7 20	**Full Moon** (the *Hunter's Moon*)	
10 48	Algol at minimum	
Tue. 22 8	Orionid meteors peak	
Wed. 23		
Thu. 24 7 37	Algol at minimum	
Fri. 25		
Sat. 26 9	Saturn 3° S of Moon	
Sun. 27 2	**Daylight Saving Time ends**	
4 26	Algol at minimum	
9	Mercury 4° N of Spica	
Mon. 28		
Tue. 29 5 28	**Last Quarter**	
22	Jupiter 4° S of Moon	
Wed. 30 1 15	Algol at minimum	
Thu. 31 12	Venus in inferior conjunction	

THE SKY FOR 2002 NOVEMBER

		Mercury	Venus	Mars	Jupiter	Saturn	Uranus	Neptune	Sun
RA	1	13^h 54^m	14^h 13^m	12^h 40^m	9^h 16^m	5^h 54^m	21^h 50^m	20^h 42^m	14^h 24^m
	11	14^h 56^m	13^h 55^m	13^h 03^m	9^h 19^m	5^h 52^m	21^h 50^m	20^h 43^m	15^h 04^m
	21	16^h 00^m	13^h 51^m	13^h 27^m	9^h 22^m	5^h 50^m	21^h 50^m	20^h 43^m	15^h 45^m
Dec	1	−10° 16′	−19° 19′	−3° 09′	+16° 28′	+22° 06′	−13° 56′	−18° 10′	−14° 17′
	11	−16° 32′	−15° 16′	−5° 40′	+16° 14′	+22° 05′	−13° 56′	−18° 09′	−17° 18′
	21	−21° 29′	−12° 13′	−8° 08′	+16° 06′	+22° 05′	−13° 53′	−18° 06′	−19° 49′
Dist	1	1.36	0.27	2.47	5.33	8.37	19.71	30.07	
	11	1.43	0.28	2.41	5.17	8.25	19.87	30.24	
	21	1.45	0.32	2.35	5.01	8.16	20.05	30.41	
Mag	1	−1.0	−4.0	1.8	−2.1	−0.2	5.8	7.9	
	11	−1.2	−4.3	1.8	−2.2	−0.2	5.8	7.9	
	21	−1.0	−4.6	1.7	−2.3	−0.3	5.8	7.9	
Size	1	5.0″	61.6″	3.8″	37.0″	19.8″	3.6″	2.2″	
	11	4.7″	58.7″	3.9″	38.1″	20.0″	3.5″	2.2″	
	21	4.6″	51.7″	4.0″	39.3″	20.3″	3.5″	2.2″	

Moon—On Nov. 1.0 UT, the age of the Moon is 25.5 d. The Sun's selenographic colongitude is 220.79° and increases by 12.2° each day thereafter. The libration in longitude is maximum (east limb exposed) on Nov. 9 (+7°) and minimum (west limb exposed) on Nov. 25 (−6°). The libration in latitude is maximum (north limb exposed) on Nov. 13 (+7°) and minimum (south limb exposed) on Nov. 27 (−7°). The Moon reaches its greatest northern declination on Nov. 23 (+26°) and its greatest southern declination on Nov. 8 (−26°).

There is a **penumbral lunar eclipse** on Nov 19–20 (see p. 126 in ECLIPSES DURING 2002).

Mercury is in superior conjunction with the Sun on Nov. 14 and cannot be observed this month.

Venus was in inferior conjunction with the Sun on Oct. 31. Early in the month, it ascends rapidly into view in the east-southeastern morning twilight, by month's end standing nearly 15° above the horizon at the beginning of morning twilight. This begins a favourable morning apparition of Venus for northern observers. For less favoured southern observers, Venus also ascends in the eastern morning sky reaching only about 5° above the horizon at the beginning of morning twilight at month's end.

Mars, in Virgo, continues to improve in visibility in the morning sky this month; however, it remains very low in the east-southeast at the beginning of morning twilight, rising only 2 h before the Sun. For less favoured southern observers, Mars is visible with difficulty very low in the eastern morning twilight sky.

Jupiter moves from Gemini to Leo on Nov. 23. It rises in late evening in the east-northeast and is visible for the remainder of the night. Southern observers will have to wait until after midnight for Jupiter to rise, also in the east-northeast.

Saturn moves from Orion to Taurus on Nov. 21. It rises in the east-northeast during evening twilight and is visible for the remainder of the night. For southern observers, Saturn rises about 3.5 h after sunset in the east-northeast and is visible for the remainder of the night.

Time (UT) d h m	NOVEMBER EVENTS	Configuration of Jupiter's Satellites
Fri. 1 0	Vesta 1.3° S of Moon, Occultation†	
22 04	Algol at minimum	
Sat. 2 18	Mars 4° S of Moon	
Sun. 3 8	S Taurid meteors peak	
12	Juno 0.6° N of Moon, Occultation‡	
Mon. 4 1	Moon at perigee (358 154 km) (Large tides)	
12	Uranus stationary	
18 52	Algol at minimum	
20 34	**New Moon**	
Tue. 5		
Thu. 7 15 41	Algol at minimum	
Fri. 8		
Sat. 9		
Sun. 10 12 30	Algol at minimum	
22	Neptune 5° N of Moon	
Mon. 11 17 13	**Double shadow transit on Jupiter**	
20 52	**First Quarter**	
Tue. 12 5	Uranus 5° N of Moon	
Wed. 13	Mercury at descending node	
7	N Taurid meteors peak	
9 19	Algol at minimum	
Thu. 14 5	Mercury in superior conjunction (Sun occults Mercury)	
Fri. 15		
Sat. 16 6 08	Algol at minimum	
11	Moon at apogee (405 796 km)	
Sun. 17		
Mon. 18		
Tue. 19 2 57	Algol at minimum	
4	Venus stationary	
4	**Leonid a meteors peak**	
11	**Leonid b meteors peak**	
Wed. 20 1 34	**Full Moon, Penumbral Eclipse**	
5	Mars 3° N of Spica	
Thu. 21 23 46	Algol at minimum	
Fri. 22 12	Saturn 3° S of Moon	
Sat. 23	Mercury at aphelion	
Sun. 24	Venus at ascending node	
20 35	Algol at minimum	
Mon. 25		
Tue. 26 7	Jupiter 4° S of Moon	
Wed. 27 15 46	**Last Quarter**	
17 24	Algol at minimum	
Thu. 28		
Fri. 29 3	Vesta 0.04° N of Moon, Occultation††	
18	Ceres stationary	
Sat. 30 14 13	Algol at minimum	

†E Siberia, Alaska, Arctic Ocean
‡South America except S, South Atlantic Ocean, E Antarctica
††N Africa except W, Saudi Arabia, S tip of India, Indian Ocean, W Australia

THE SKY FOR 2002 DECEMBER

		Mercury	Venus	Mars	Jupiter	Saturn	Uranus	Neptune	Sun
RA	1	17^{h}07^m	14^{h}00^m	13^{h}51^m	9^{h}23^m	5^{h}47^m	21^{h}51^m	20^{h}44^m	16^{h}27^m
	11	18^{h}14^m	14^{h}21^m	14^{h}16^m	9^{h}23^m	5^{h}43^m	21^{h}52^m	20^{h}45^m	17^{h}11^m
	21	19^{h}18^m	14^{h}50^m	14^{h}41^m	9^{h}21^m	5^{h}40^m	21^{h}53^m	20^{h}46^m	17^{h}55^m
Dec	1	−24° 38′	−11° 02′	−10° 29′	+16° 03′	+22° 04′	−13° 49′	−18° 03′	−21° 44′
	11	−25° 40′	−11° 28′	−12° 44′	+16° 06′	+22° 04′	−13° 44′	−18° 00′	−22° 58′
	21	−24° 17′	−12° 58′	−14° 50′	+16° 15′	+22° 03′	−13° 36′	−17° 55′	−23° 26′
Dist	1	1.40	0.38	2.29	4.86	8.10	20.22	30.57	
	11	1.30	0.44	2.21	4.72	8.06	20.38	30.71	
	21	1.12	0.52	2.14	4.60	8.05	20.53	30.83	
Mag	1	−0.7	−4.7	1.7	−2.3	−0.4	5.8	7.9	
	11	−0.6	−4.6	1.7	−2.4	−0.5	5.9	8.0	
	21	−0.6	−4.6	1.6	−2.5	−0.5	5.9	8.0	
Size	1	4.8″	44.1″	4.1″	40.5″	20.4″	3.5″	2.2″	
	11	5.2″	37.6″	4.2″	41.7″	20.5″	3.4″	2.2″	
	21	6.0″	32.4″	4.4″	42.8″	20.5″	3.4″	2.2″	

Moon—On Dec. 1.0 UT, the age of the Moon is 26.1 d. The Sun's selenographic colongitude is 225.89° and increases by 12.2° each day thereafter. The libration in longitude is maximum (east limb exposed) on Dec. 8 (+6°) and minimum (west limb exposed) on Dec. 21 (−5°). The libration in latitude is maximum (north limb exposed) on Dec. 10 (+7°) and minimum (south limb exposed) on Dec. 25 (−7°). The Moon reaches its greatest northern declination on Dec. 20 (+26°) and its greatest southern declination on Dec. 6 (−26°).

There is a **total solar eclipse** on Dec. 4 visible from southern Africa, the Indian Ocean, and near sunset in southeastern Australia (see pp. 127–128 in ECLIPSES DURING 2002).

Mercury reaches greatest elongation east (20°) on Dec. 26. It emerges low in the west-southwest evening twilight early in the month for southern observers. Northern observers will have to wait until the second half of the month to glimpse Mercury very low in the southwest during evening twilight.

Venus stands about 20° above the southeastern horizon at the beginning of morning twilight. Less favoured southern observers will find Venus about 10° high in the east at the beginning of morning twilight. **Venus is in quasi-conjunction** (see p. 19) **with Mars on Dec. 6** (see Mars below).

Mars moves from Virgo to Libra at midmonth. It continues to improve in visibility in the morning sky this month. By month's end, it rises about 4 h before the Sun and stands nearly 20° above the southeastern horizon at the beginning of morning twilight. Mars's visibility improves considerably this month for southern observers—by month's end it stands over 20° above the eastern horizon at the beginning of morning twilight. **Mars is in quasi-conjunction with brighter Venus** to the east on Dec. 6, and the two planets remain close to each other for most of December. **Mars is occulted by the Moon on Dec. 30.**

Jupiter, in Leo, is stationary on the Dec. 4, following which it begins retrograde (westward) motion. It rises in the east-northeast in midevening for northern observers and late evening for southern observers. It is visible for the remainder of the night.

Saturn, in Taurus, rises near sunset and sets near sunrise. It is at opposition with the Sun on the Dec. 17.

Time (UT) d h m	DECEMBER EVENTS	Configuration of Jupiter's Satellites

Time (UT) d h m	DECEMBER EVENTS
Sun. 1 10	Mars 3° S of Moon
13	**Venus 2° S of Moon**
Mon. 2 9	Moon at perigee (362 289 km)
Tue. 3 11 02	Algol at minimum
Wed. 4 7 34	**New Moon, Total Solar Eclipse†**
21	Jupiter stationary
Thu. 5	
Fri. 6 7 52	Algol at minimum
12	**Venus–Mars quasi-conjunction (1°33′)**
Sat. 7 1	**Venus greatest brilliancy**
Sun. 8 8	Neptune 5° N of Moon
Mon. 9 4 41	Algol at minimum
14	Uranus 5° N of Moon
17	Pluto in conjunction with Sun
Tue. 10	
Wed. 11 15 49	**First Quarter**
Thu. 12 1 30	Algol at minimum
Fri. 13	Mercury at greatest heliocentric latitude S
Sat. 14 4	Moon at apogee (404 914 km)
9	**Geminid meteors peak**
22 19	Algol at minimum
Sun. 15 7 33	**Double shadow transit on Jupiter**
Mon. 16	
Tue. 17 2 02	**Double shadow transit on Jupiter**
17	**Saturn at opposition**
19 08	Algol at minimum
Wed. 18	
Thu. 19 15	Saturn 3° S of Moon
19 10	**Full Moon**
Fri. 20 14 58	**Double shadow transit on Jupiter**
15 57	Algol at minimum
Sun. 22 1 14	**Solstice**
18	Ursid meteors peak
Mon. 23 12	Jupiter 4° S of Moon
12 46	Algol at minimum
Tue. 24 3 55	**Double shadow transit on Jupiter**
Wed. 25	
Thu. 26 5	**Mercury greatest elongation E (20°)**
9 36	Algol at minimum
Fri. 27 0 31	**Last Quarter**
16 51	**Double shadow transit on Jupiter**
Sat. 28	
Sun. 29 6 25	Algol at minimum
Mon. 30 1	**Mars 1.2° S of Moon, Occultation‡**
1	Moon at perigee (367 902 km)
9	**Venus 2° N of Moon**
Tue. 31 5 48	**Double shadow transit on Jupiter**

†Africa except N, SE Atlantic Ocean, central Indian Ocean, part of Antartica, Indonesia, Australia, South Island of New Zealand—see pp. 127–128 for further details
‡NE Asia except NE Siberia, Japan except S tip

THE SUN

EPHEMERIS FOR THE SUN

Sundial Correction

The **Greenwich Transit** time in the table at the right may be used to calculate the sundial correction at the observer's position. For example, to find the correction at Winnipeg on August 16, 2002: At Greenwich the Sun transits at 12:04:52 on August 13 and at 12:04:05 on August 17. Thus, to the nearest minute, on August 16 at both Greenwich and Winnipeg the Sun will transit at 12:04 local mean solar time (LMT), or 12:33 CST (Central Standard Time) since Winnipeg has a longitude correction of +29 min (see the 3rd paragraph on p. 99). Thus a 4 minute correction must be added to the reading of a simple sundial to obtain LMT, and an additional 29 minutes must be added to obtain CST.

A figure accurate to a second or two can be obtained by interpolating for longitude. The interpolated transit time at Greenwich for August 16 is 12:04:17, the daily change in time being −11.8 s. Adjusting this for the longitude of Winnipeg: 12 h 4 min 17 s − (11.8 s × 6 h 29 min ÷ 24 h) = 12 h 4 min 14 s. Thus the sundial correction is 4 min 14 s. To find the standard time of the Sun's transit to the nearest second or two, the observer's longitude must be known to 10″ or better. For example, suppose an observer in Winnipeg is at longitude 97°13′50″W, or 6 h 28 min 55 s W of Greenwich. The time of transit will be 12:04:14 + 28 min 55 s = 12:33:09 CST (13:33:09 CDT).

Orientation of the Sun

The table at the right gives three angles that specify the orientation of the Sun.

P is the position angle of the axis of rotation, measured eastward in the observer's sky from the north point on the disk. Note that P varies between +26° (solar north pole tilted eastward) and −26° (tilted westward) during the year. This tilt is associated mainly with the inclination of the ecliptic in the observer's sky, with a smaller contribution from the Sun's 7.2° inclination to the ecliptic (the longitude of the ascending node of the solar equator on the ecliptic is 76°).

B_0 is the heliographic latitude of the centre of the disk, and is the result of the Sun's 7.2° inclination to the ecliptic. Note that positive values of B_0 correspond to the solar equator passing south of the centre of the disk, with the solar north pole being tipped toward the observer.

L_0 is the heliographic longitude of the centre of the disk measured from Carrington's solar prime meridian in the direction of rotation. L_0 decreases about 13° per day. The dates during the year when $L_0 = 0°$ are given in the table below. The rotation period of the Sun depends upon heliographic latitude. The synodic and sidereal periods of rotation at the solar equator are 27.275 days and 25.38 days, respectively.

Commencement (UT) of Numbered Synodic Solar Rotations

No*	Commences	No	Commences	No	Commences	No	Commences
1984	'01 Dec. 10.73	1988	Mar. 30.04	1992	Jul. 16.94	1996	Nov. 2.98
1985	Jan. 7.06	1989	Apr. 26.31	1993	Aug 13.16	1997	Nov. 30.29
1986	Feb. 3.40	1990	May 23.54	1994	Sep. 9.41	1998	Dec. 27.61
1987	Mar. 2.73	1991	Jun. 19.74	1995	Oct. 6.68		

*Based on R.C. Carrington's Greenwich photoheliocentric series in which rotation number 1 commenced 1853 November 9.

EPHEMERIS FOR THE SUN, 2002

Date 0h UT	Apparent RA (2002) Dec	Greenwich Transit UT	Orientation P	B₀	L₀

Jan.–Apr.

Date 0h UT	Apparent RA (2002)	Dec	Transit UT	P	B₀	L₀
Jan. 1	18 45.2	−23 02	12:03:31	+2.1	−3.0	79.7
5	19 02.8	−22 39	12:05:21	+0.2	−3.5	27.0
9	19 20.3	−22 09	12:07:05	−1.7	−3.9	334.4
13	19 37.7	−21 33	12:08:40	−3.7	−4.3	281.7
17	19 54.9	−20 49	12:10:04	−5.5	−4.7	229.0
21	20 11.9	−19 59	12:11:18	−7.4	−5.1	176.4
25	20 28.7	−19 03	12:12:19	−9.1	−5.5	123.7
29	20 45.3	−18 02	12:13:06	−10.9	−5.8	71.0
Feb. 2	21 01.7	−16 56	12:13:41	−12.5	−6.1	18.4
6	21 17.8	−15 44	12:14:03	−14.1	−6.4	325.7
10	21 33.8	−14 29	12:14:13	−15.6	−6.6	273.0
14	21 49.6	−13 09	12:14:10	−17.0	−6.8	220.4
18	22 05.1	−11 46	12:13:56	−18.3	−7.0	167.0
22	22 20.5	−10 20	12:13:30	−19.6	−7.1	115.0
26	22 35.7	−8 52	12:12:54	−20.7	−7.2	62.3
Mar. 2	22 50.7	−7 21	12:12:09	−21.7	−7.2	9.6
6	23 05.6	−5 49	12:11:17	−22.7	−7.3	316.9
10	23 20.4	−4 16	12:10:18	−23.5	−7.2	264.2
14	23 35.1	−2 41	12:09:14	−24.2	−7.2	211.5
18	23 49.8	−1 07	12:08:06	−24.9	−7.1	158.8
22	00 04.4	+0 28	12:06:55	−25.4	−7.0	106.1
26	0 18.9	+2 03	12:05:42	−25.8	−6.8	53.3
30	0 33.5	+3 37	12:04:29	−26.1	−6.7	0.6
Apr. 3	0 48.0	+5 09	12:03:18	−26.2	−6.4	307.8
7	1 02.7	+6 41	12:02:09	−26.3	−6.2	255.0
11	1 17.3	+8 10	12:01:04	−26.2	−5.9	202.2
15	1 32.1	+9 37	12:00:03	−26.1	−5.6	149.4
19	1 46.9	+11 02	11:59:08	−25.8	−5.3	96.6
23	2 01.9	+12 24	11:58:19	−25.4	−5.0	43.8
27	2 16.9	+13 42	11:57:38	−24.8	−4.6	350.9

May–Aug.

Date 0h UT	Apparent RA (2002)	Dec	Transit UT	P	B₀	L₀
May 1	2 32.1	+14 57	11:57:04	−24.2	−4.2	298.1
5	2 47.5	+16 08	11:56:40	−23.4	−3.8	245.2
9	3 03.0	+17 15	11:56:24	−22.6	−3.4	192.3
13	3 18.6	+18 17	11:56:18	−21.6	−2.9	139.4
17	3 34.4	+19 14	11:56:21	−20.5	−2.5	86.5
21	3 50.4	+20 06	11:56:32	−19.3	−2.0	33.6
25	4 06.4	+20 53	11:56:52	−18.0	−1.5	340.7
29	4 22.7	+21 33	11:57:20	−16.6	−1.1	287.8
Jun. 2	4 39.0	+22 08	11:57:55	−15.1	−0.6	234.8
6	4 55.4	+22 37	11:58:36	−13.6	−0.1	181.9
10	5 12.0	+22 59	11:59:22	−12.0	+0.4	128.9
14	5 28.6	+23 15	12:00:12	−10.3	+0.9	76.0
18	5 45.2	+23 24	12:01:04	−8.6	+1.4	23.1
22	6 01.8	+23 26	12:01:56	−6.8	+1.8	330.1
26	6 18.5	+23 22	12:02:47	−5.1	+2.3	277.2
30	6 35.0	+23 12	12:03:36	−3.2	+2.7	224.2
Jul. 4	6 51.6	+22 55	12:04:21	−1.4	+3.2	171.3
8	7 08.0	+22 31	12:05:01	+0.4	+3.6	118.3
12	7 24.4	+22 01	12:05:36	+2.2	+4.0	65.4
16	7 40.6	+21 26	12:06:02	+4.0	+4.4	12.5
20	7 56.7	+20 44	12:06:20	+5.7	+4.8	319.5
24	8 12.7	+19 57	12:06:29	+7.4	+5.1	266.6
28	8 28.4	+19 04	12:06:29	+9.1	+5.5	213.7
Aug. 1	8 44.1	+18 07	12:06:19	+10.7	+5.8	160.8
5	8 59.5	+17 05	12:05:59	+12.3	+6.1	107.9
9	9 14.8	+15 58	12:05:31	+13.8	+6.3	55.0
13	9 30.0	+14 47	12:04:52	+15.2	+6.5	2.1
17	9 45.0	+13 33	12:04:05	+16.6	+6.7	309.2
21	9 59.9	+12 15	12:03:10	+17.9	+6.9	256.4
25	10 14.6	+10 54	12:02:07	+19.1	+7.0	203.5
29	10 29.2	+9 30	12:00:57	+20.2	+7.1	150.7

Sep.–Dec.

Date 0h UT	Apparent RA (2002)	Dec	Transit UT	P	B₀	L₀
Sep. 2	10 43.8	+8 04	11:59:43	+21.3	+7.2	97.8
6	10 58.2	+6 35	11:58:24	+22.2	+7.2	45.0
10	11 12.6	+5 05	11:57:02	+23.1	+7.3	352.2
14	11 27.0	+3 34	11:55:37	+23.9	+7.2	299.4
18	11 41.3	+2 01	11:54:11	+24.5	+7.2	246.6
22	11 55.7	+0 28	11:52:46	+25.1	+7.1	193.7
26	12 10.0	−1 05	11:51:22	+25.5	+6.9	141.0
30	12 24.5	−2 39	11:50:02	+25.9	+6.8	88.2
Oct. 4	12 39.0	−4 12	11:48:46	+26.1	+6.6	35.4
8	12 53.5	−5 44	11:47:36	+26.3	+6.4	342.6
12	13 08.2	−7 15	11:46:32	+26.3	+6.1	289.8
16	13 23.1	−8 44	11:45:36	+26.2	+5.8	237.1
20	13 38.0	−10 12	11:44:50	+26	+5.5	184.3
24	13 53.2	−11 37	11:44:13	+25.6	+5.2	131.6
28	14 08.5	−12 59	11:43:48	+25.1	+4.8	78.8
Nov. 1	14 24.0	−14 18	11:43:36	+24.5	+4.4	26.1
5	14 39.8	−15 33	11:43:36	+23.8	+4.0	333.3
9	14 55.8	−16 45	11:43:50	+23	+3.6	280.6
13	15 12.0	−17 51	11:44:16	+22	+3.1	227.8
17	15 28.4	−18 53	11:44:57	+20.9	+2.6	175.1
21	15 45.0	−19 49	11:45:50	+19.7	+2.2	122.4
25	16 01.8	−20 40	11:46:56	+18.4	+1.7	69.7
29	16 18.9	−21 24	11:48:15	+16.9	+1.2	16.9
Dec. 3	16 36.1	−22 02	11:49:45	+15.4	+0.7	324.2
7	16 53.6	−22 34	11:51:24	+13.8	+0.1	271.5
11	17 11.1	−22 58	11:53:11	+12.1	−0.4	218.8
15	17 28.7	−23 15	11:55:04	+10.3	−0.9	166.1
19	17 46.5	−23 24	11:57:01	+8.5	−1.4	113.4
23	18 04.2	−23 26	11:59:00	+6.6	−1.9	60.7
27	18 22.0	−23 21	12:00:59	+4.7	−2.4	8.0
31	18 39.7	−23 08	12:02:56	+2.7	−2.9	315.3

SOLAR ACTIVITY
By Ken Tapping

It looks as though the peak of Solar Activity Cycle 23* is now past. Although we can expect plenty of activity for the next two years or so, it appears likely that this maximum will be the second lowest since 1946, when Canada started monitoring solar activity using the 10.7-cm solar flux. Most predictions for this activity maximum suggested this would be a high one, following a trend of increasing amplitude since 1970. It's clear that we still have a lot to learn about causes of solar activity.

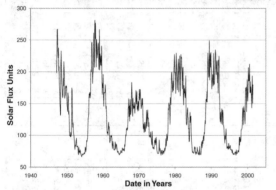

The figure shows solar activity as represented by the adjusted 10.7-cm solar microwave flux activity index (see p. 98) from 1947 to the present. The plotted values are averaged values of the index over each solar (≈27-day) rotation; the horizontal scale shows the time in years. The ≈11-year activity cycle is clearly evident.

The term "solar activity" comprises all the Sun's variable aspects, such as the occurrence of sunspots and active regions, the variable emissions in soft X-rays, spectral lines such as CaII K and MgII K, emissions at radio wavelengths, and flares, a particularly dramatic form of solar activity. The Sun's brightness is also variable; measurements made using space-borne radiometers show that as the level of solar activity increases, the Sun becomes slightly brighter. All manifestations of solar activity are driven by an underlying engine: the varying spatial and temporal distribution of magnetic flux in the photosphere, chromosphere, and corona.

Deep below the photosphere the density is high enough for the solar material to drag the magnetic fields; differential rotation and convection give rise to electrical currents, which in turn produce magnetic fields. These fields form complex networks of twisted "magnetic flux ropes," containing enormous amounts of stored energy. The penetration of sections of these flux ropes through the photosphere and into the chromosphere and corona gives rise to the many observed forms of solar activity. Above the photosphere the situation is strikingly different. The density is much lower, and the distribution and movement of the magnetic fields trap and confine the ionized gas of the solar atmosphere, supporting loops and filaments and forming the diverse menagerie of photospheric, chromospheric, and coronal structures we are familiar with in the Sun.

Most activity occurs in active regions: bipolar magnetic structures form when magnetic loops emerge through the photosphere into the overlying chromosphere and corona. The formation of a new region, called an emerging flux region, is heralded by the formation of small pores (about 1000 km across). These pores coalesce into a patch a few thousand kilometres across and eventually spread to form a patch of magnetic flux that may exceed 50 000 km in length. The average magnetic field strength in the patch is of the order of 0.01 T (100 gauss). The emergence of these magnetic fields modifies the spatial and density structure of the chromosphere, giving rise to enhanced emission

---

*The numbering system for solar activity cycles was started by Rudolph Wolf, who arbitrarily designated the activity maximum of 1750 as that of Cycle 1.

in the calcium and magnesium II K spectral lines. These bright patches (called plage), which stand out prominently in filtergrams, are the most conspicuous aspect of active regions.

Concentrations of magnetic flux having strengths of the order of 0.1 T locally impede the transfer of energy from deeper within the Sun; therefore, the concentrations are about 3000 K cooler than the surrounding (6000 K) photosphere. Although actually quite hot and shining quite brightly, in contrast with their hotter surroundings these flux concentrations appear as dark spots: sunspots. The first direct manifestation of solar activity to be observed, sunspots are present in most active regions. As a region grows, one or more large spots form at the leading end, and a scattering of smaller ones form at the trailing end.

Repeated episodes of magnetic flux emergence occur during the growth phase of the active region. The size the region reaches is directly related to how much magnetic flux it accumulates. As flux emergence slows and stops, so does the growth of the region. Fragmentation sets in, the spots disappear, and the remains are left as a large area of magnetic flux arranged in a network pattern, blending in slowly with the remains of other decayed active regions.

The redistribution of magnetic flux during the evolution of active regions leads to distortion and stressing of magnetic structures in the chromosphere and corona. Energy from below the photosphere is propagated into the chromospheric and coronal magnetic fields through twisting and motions of "footpoints," which are photospheric anchors of chromospheric or coronal magnetic loops. This is stored as magnetic energy in stressed loops and flux tubes. Evolution of the host active region requires that this energy be dissipated. This occurs noncatastrophically through slow reconnection and heating or explosively in mass ejections and flares.

The organization of the subphotospheric magnetic fields gives rise to a consistent pattern in the magnetic configuration of active regions. Each region is magnetically bipolar, with the bipoles arranged east–west on the disk. All bipoles lying in the same hemisphere are arranged with the same magnetic polarity leading (facing in the direction in which the region appears to move as it is carried across the disk by solar rotation—westward in the observer's sky). In the other hemisphere the leading and following magnetic polarities are reversed.

Exceptions do occur. Regions are sometimes formed that have a magnetic orientation perpendicular to or even the reverse of the norm for that hemisphere. Such regions usually try to move into the conventional orientation but are impeded by the magnetic linkages they have formed with their surroundings. These regions tend to produce flares as potential energy builds up in their magnetic structures and is subsequently released catastrophically.

The "conventional" magnetic configurations for active regions reverse on alternate activity cycles. For example, during Cycle 22, active regions in the northern solar hemisphere were oriented with their "negative" (i.e. south-seeking) magnetic polarity ends leading and "positive" (north-seeking) ends following, with the reverse situation in the southern hemisphere. In Cycle 23 this arrangement is reversed. A *magnetic* activity cycle, which is probably a more realistic description of the rhythms of solar activity, is equal to two of Wolf's activity cycles and takes about 22 years to complete.

Active regions are not isolated phenomena; they occur in complexes, comprising several active regions at various stages of development, together with the network elements remaining from decayed regions. This localization of activity gives rise to a rotational modulation of the 10.7-cm flux as active region clusters are carried across the disk and disappear around the west limb. To smooth out this modulation in long-term studies of solar activity, the data are averaged over solar rotations rather than by month. Active regions can persist for one or more solar rotations and the complexes for a dozen or so.

The large-scale organization of solar magnetic activity is also apparent in the spatial distribution of active regions during the solar cycle. The first activity of the new cycle is marked by the formation of active regions at high latitudes. As activity builds toward the maximum of the cycle, the number of active regions increases, and they tend to form at lower latitudes. As the activity wanes toward the next minimum, the number of regions decreases, but the average latitude continues to decrease until the last activity of the cycle is located near the equator. Then, as the new cycle starts, new active regions form at high latitudes.

The Solar Wind and Aurorae: The solar atmosphere is not stable. It is constantly flowing outward as a stream of particles and magnetic fields—the *solar wind.* The flow is strongest where the magnetic loops are very large and impose the least drag on the outwardly flowing particles. Because of their lower coronal densities, these regions produce a lower flux of X-rays and appear as dark patches in X-ray images, called coronal holes. The solar wind is not homogeneous or steady; its speed, density, and direction can change according to the positions of coronal holes and the nature of current solar activity.

The flow of the solar wind past Earth produces profound changes in Earth's magnetic field. The pressure of the solar wind pushes Earth's magnetic field out of its dipole shape into a long teardrop. The magnetic geometry in this tail makes it the site of many plasma instabilities. The flow of the solar wind over the interface between it and Earth's magnetic field (the magnetopause) excites many types of waves, which move along Earth's magnetic field lines and which can be detected on the ground at high magnetic latitudes. Increases in the density or velocity of the solar wind change the pressure equilibrium between the solar wind and the magnetosphere, producing fluctuations in the strength and direction of the magnetic field lines at ground level. If the fluctuations are strong enough, the events are referred to as magnetic storms and substorms. These can disrupt any human activity that involves connected metal networks covering large geographical areas, especially at high magnetic latitudes.

Complex interactions between the solar wind and Earth's magnetic field lead to an accumulation of trapped particles in the magnetosphere. During magnetic storms, instabilities and waves excited in the magnetosphere by the solar wind accelerate some of the trapped particles downward along Earth's magnetic field into increasingly dense atmosphere, where they collide with the atmospheric constituents, exciting them with sufficient energy to produce light. These displays are called aurorae, or the northern and southern lights: *aurora borealis* and *aurora australis*, respectively. Views from space show that aurorae fall in a rough circle (the auroral oval), centred around the magnetic pole, that is, in a definite band of magnetic latitudes. As activity increases, the auroral oval expands, covering lower and lower magnetic latitudes. It also becomes increasingly distorted. During the period of very high activity in March 1989, auroral displays were seen as far south as the Caribbean.

Aurorae occur in many forms and can be steady, moving, or rapidly pulsating, depending upon the nature of the particle streams causing them. Aurorae can appear green or red, although if they are faint, the eye cannot respond in colour and they appear grey. The greenish colour is due to spectral lines from oxygen (558 nm) and a range of lines from nitrogen covering the band 391 nm to 470 nm. Under highly disturbed conditions, red spectral line emissions at 630 nm and 636 nm and in a series of bands between 650 nm and 680 nm can also be seen. The green emissions are produced at a height of about 110 km; the red, 630-nm and 636-nm emissions, due to atomic oxygen, originate at heights between 200 km and 400 km; the 650-nm to 680-nm emissions are produced at about 90 km.   *(text continued on p. 98)*

AURORAL FORMS

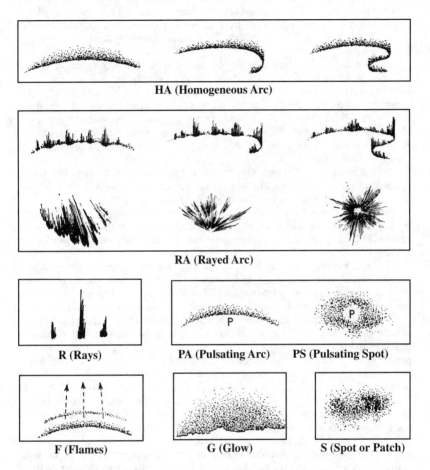

The above sketches illustrate standard auroral forms. This simplified classification was devised for visual observers during the International Geophysical Year over four decades ago (1957–58). Although there is great variety in auroral patterns, the sketches emphasize fundamental features and minimize variations that depend on the location of the observer. The light of the aurora is emitted by the upper fringes of Earth's atmosphere (heights of 100 to 400 km) as it is bombarded by electrons of the solar wind (solar wind protons contribute a smaller amount of energy). The modification of the trajectories of these particles by Earth's magnetic field restricts activity to high latitudes, producing the "aurora borealis" in the Northern Hemisphere and the "aurora australis" in the Southern Hemisphere. The wavelengths of four atmospheric molecular and atomic emission lines that can contribute strongly to auroral light are included in the list on p. 31. Whether aurorae appear coloured depends on their luminance—light that is too faint will not activate colour vision and appears white. When the luminance is sufficiently great, the relative contributions of blue, green, and red emission lines can result in a variety of auroral hues.

The Impact and Measurement of Solar Activity: Solar activity has had profound effects upon Earth extending as far back in time as we have been able to look. The solar activity cycle is reflected in the growth rates of trees (determined from the study of tree rings) in recently living timber, wood from medieval buildings, and fossilized trees; it is also evident in the changes in the thickness of annual sedimentary deposits in lakes that dry up in summer.

There is extensive evidence of the dramatic effects solar activity has upon our activities. Magnetic storms due to solar activity induce currents in communications and power transmission systems having long distance wires, disrupting their operation for hours. The power blackouts in Quebec and Scandinavia produced by a large flare on 1989 March 10 are a particularly outstanding example. Railway signalling systems can also be affected. Increased X-ray emissions from flares cause enhanced ionization of Earth's atmosphere at D region heights (about 90 km), producing blackouts of short-wave communications.

Solar activity heats the upper atmosphere, causing it to expand further into space, increasing the drag experienced by artificial satellites in low orbits. It is ironic that the lifetime of the Solar Max satellite was dramatically shortened in this way.

Above the atmosphere, satellites have no protection from high-energy particle fluxes produced by the Sun. Their electronic systems can be damaged, leading to cata-strophic failures in some cases, as occurred with two Anik communications satellites in January 1994.

The oldest index of solar activity is the sunspot number. A number of techniques, many empirical, have been developed to combine observations from various observato-ries and observers to form the *International Sunspot Number.* This is a rather poor index; however, it has given us a database extending back to at least the 17th century.

Probably the best available index of solar activity, at least covering the last 50 years or so, is the *10.7-cm flux*, or $F_{10.7}$. This index is an objective measurement of the inte-grated emission at the 10.7-cm wavelength (a frequency of 2.8 GHz) from all sources present on the solar disk. It has been measured daily by the National Research Council of Canada for nearly 50 years and is now used worldwide as a primary index of solar activity. It is expressed in solar flux units (1 sfu = 10^{-22} W·m^{-2}Hz^{-1}). The 10.7-cm flux has the great advantage that it can be measured in any weather and requires no human involvement or "interpretation." When quiet, the Sun produces a 10.7-cm flux of 64 sfu, due to free-free thermal emission from the quiet solar corona. This index is expressed in two main forms: the *observed* and *adjusted* flux values.

The *observed* value is what is measured, and since this represents the impact of solar activity on Earth, it is useful in studying the consequences of solar activity here on Earth and our near-Earth space environment. The *adjusted* value is what we would observe at a constant distance from the Sun of one astronomical unit. This version of the index describes the activity of the Sun as a star, with the effect of the changing Earth–Sun distance taken out.

The 10.7-cm flux can be used as an objective proxy for other activity-related quanti-ties. For example, the *adjusted* 10.7-cm flux can be used as a proxy for sunspot number through the relation *sunspot number* = 1.14 × (*adjusted solar flux*) − 73.21, and the total *photospheric magnetic flux*, in units of 10^{22} Maxwells, equals (*adjusted flux*)/2 − 10.

We are a long way from understanding the nature and the extent of the effects solar activity has upon Earth. Some correlations, like that between the length of miniskirts and solar activity, are probably spurious; others might not be. As we exploit our environ-ment more fully, we become increasingly sensitive to things that might affect it, even slightly.

TIMES OF SUNRISE AND SUNSET

The tables on the next three pages give the times of sunrise and sunset at four-day intervals for locations ranging from 20° to 62° north latitude. "Rise" and "set" correspond to the upper limb of the Sun appearing at the horizon for an observer at sea level. The times are local mean time (LMT) for the Greenwich meridian (i.e. UT at 0° longitude), although for North American observers the stated values may be read directly as LMT at the observer's position with an error less than 1 minute. The tables may be interpolated linearly for both nontabular latitudes and dates, and can be extrapolated beyond the 20° and 62° latitude limits a few degrees without significant loss of accuracy.

It is a common misconception that extreme values for sunrise and sunset times occur on the shortest and the longest days of the year. This is not the case and is due to the tilt of Earth's spin axis to the axis of its orbit and to Earth's varying speed along its elliptical orbit (as Kepler described in his second law). At midnorthern latitudes, the earliest sunset occurs early in December and the latest sunrise in early January whereas the shortest day (in the sense of hours of daylight) is December 21 or 22. For more information see *Sky & Telescope*, December 1988, p. 674 and July 1972, p. 20, and an article by Terence Hicks in *JRASC*, *88*, p. 86, February 1994.

The standard time of an event at a particular location must take account of the observer's longitude relative to his or her standard meridian (see STANDARD TIME ZONES on pp. 40–41). The **table below** lists the latitude and the longitude correction (in minutes of time) for a number of cities in Canada and the United States. For example, to find the time of sunrise at Toronto on February 15, 2002: the latitude is 44°, and from the table the time of sunrise at 0° longitude is 6:59 UT (after interpolating for latitude). Thus, at Toronto, the time of sunrise will be approximately 6:59 LMT. Toronto is in the Eastern time zone (E) and is 18 minutes of time west of the standard meridian for this zone (75°W). Thus, sunrise in Toronto will occur at 7:17 EST (Eastern Standard Time). The longitude correction for any location may be found by converting the difference between the longitude of the place and that of its standard meridian to time (1° = 4 minutes of time), the correction being + if the place is west of its standard meridian, − if east. **Note**: Due to a difference in height between the observer and the actual horizon, the observed time may differ by several minutes from the predicted time.

Canadian Cities				American Cities	
Brandon	50°+40C	Québec	47°−15E	Atlanta	34°+37E
Calgary	51°+36M	Regina	50°+58C	Boston	42°−16E
Charlottetown	46°+12A	Resolute	75°+20C	Chicago	42°−10C
Corner Brook	49°+22N	Rimouski	48°−26E	Cincinnati	39°+38E
Edmonton	54°+34M	Saint John	45°+24A	Denver	40° 00M
Halifax	45°+14A	St. John's	48°+01N	Fairbanks	65°+50A
Hamilton	43°+20E	Sarnia	43°+29E	Flagstaff	35°+27M
Kelowna	50°−03P	Saskatoon	52°+67C	Kansas City	39°+18C
Kingston	44°+06E	Sudbury	47°+24E	Los Angeles	34°−07P
Kitchener	43°+22E	Thunder Bay	48°+57E	Miami	26°+21E
London	43°+25E	Toronto	44°+18E	Minneapolis	45°+13C
Moncton	46°+19A	Vancouver	49°+12P	New Orleans	30° 00C
Montreal	46°−06E	Victoria	48°+13P	New York	41°−04E
Niagara Falls	43°+16E	Whitehorse	61°+60P	San Francisco	38°+10P
Ottawa	45°+03E	Windsor ON	42°+32E	Seattle	48°+09P
Pangnirtung	66°+23A	Winnipeg	50°+29C	Tucson	32°+24M
Prince George	54°+11P	Yellowknife	62°+38M	Washington	39°+08E

SUNRISE AND SUNSET, 2002 JANUARY–APRIL
UNIVERSAL TIME AT GREENWICH MERIDIAN

Latitude: Event:	+20°		+30°		+35°		+40°		+45°		+50°		+54°		+58°		+62°	
	RISE	SET	RISE	SET	RISE	SET	RISE	SET	RISE	SET	RISE	SET	RISE	SET	RISE	SET	RISE	SET
Jan. −2	6:34	17:30	6:55	17:09	7:07	16:57	7:21	16:43	7:38	16:26	7:58	16:06	8:19	15:45	8:46	15:18	9:24	14:40
2	6:35	17:33	6:56	17:12	7:08	17:00	7:22	16:46	7:38	16:30	7:58	16:10	8:19	15:49	8:45	15:23	9:22	14:46
6	6:37	17:35	6:57	17:15	7:09	17:03	7:22	16:50	7:38	16:34	7:58	16:14	8:17	15:55	8:43	15:29	9:18	14:54
10	6:37	17:38	6:57	17:18	7:08	17:07	7:22	16:54	7:37	16:38	7:56	16:19	8:15	16:00	8:39	15:36	9:13	15:02
14	6:38	17:40	6:57	17:21	7:08	17:10	7:20	16:58	7:35	16:43	7:54	16:25	8:12	16:07	8:35	15:44	9:07	15:12
18	6:38	17:43	6:56	17:25	7:07	17:14	7:19	17:02	7:33	16:48	7:50	16:31	8:08	16:14	8:29	15:52	8:59	15:22
22	6:38	17:46	6:55	17:28	7:05	17:18	7:17	17:07	7:30	16:54	7:46	16:37	8:03	16:21	8:23	16:01	8:51	15:33
26	6:37	17:48	6:54	17:32	7:03	17:22	7:14	17:12	7:26	16:59	7:42	16:44	7:57	16:29	8:16	16:10	8:41	15:45
30	6:36	17:51	6:52	17:35	7:00	17:26	7:11	17:16	7:22	17:05	7:37	16:50	7:51	16:36	8:08	16:19	8:31	15:56
Feb. 3	6:35	17:53	6:49	17:39	6:57	17:31	7:07	17:21	7:18	17:10	7:31	16:57	7:44	16:44	8:00	16:29	8:21	16:08
7	6:33	17:55	6:47	17:42	6:54	17:35	7:03	17:26	7:13	17:16	7:25	17:04	7:36	16:53	7:51	16:38	8:10	16:20
11	6:31	17:57	6:43	17:45	6:50	17:39	6:58	17:31	7:07	17:22	7:18	17:11	7:29	17:01	7:42	16:48	7:58	16:31
15	6:29	17:59	6:40	17:49	6:46	17:42	6:53	17:36	7:01	17:28	7:11	17:18	7:20	17:09	7:32	16:57	7:46	16:43
19	6:27	18:01	6:36	17:52	6:42	17:46	6:48	17:40	6:55	17:33	7:04	17:25	7:12	17:17	7:22	17:07	7:34	16:54
23	6:24	18:03	6:33	17:55	6:37	17:50	6:43	17:45	6:49	17:39	6:56	17:32	7:03	17:25	7:11	17:16	7:22	17:06
27	6:21	18:04	6:28	17:57	6:32	17:54	6:37	17:49	6:42	17:44	6:48	17:38	6:54	17:33	7:01	17:26	7:10	17:17
Mar. 3	6:18	18:06	6:24	18:00	6:27	17:57	6:31	17:54	6:35	17:50	6:40	17:45	6:44	17:40	6:50	17:35	6:57	17:28
7	6:15	18:07	6:20	18:03	6:22	18:01	6:25	17:58	6:28	17:55	6:31	17:52	6:35	17:48	6:39	17:44	6:44	17:39
11	6:12	18:08	6:15	18:06	6:17	18:04	6:18	18:02	6:20	18:00	6:23	17:58	6:25	17:56	6:28	17:56	6:31	17:50
15	6:09	18:10	6:10	18:08	6:11	18:07	6:12	18:07	6:13	18:06	6:14	18:05	6:15	18:04	6:17	18:02	6:18	18:01
19	6:05	18:11	6:05	18:11	6:06	18:11	6:06	18:11	6:06	18:11	6:06	18:11	6:06	18:11	6:06	18:11	6:05	18:12
23	6:02	18:12	6:01	18:13	6:00	18:14	5:59	18:15	5:58	18:16	5:57	18:17	5:56	18:19	5:54	18:20	5:52	18:22
27	5:58	18:13	5:56	18:16	5:54	18:17	5:53	18:19	5:51	18:21	5:48	18:24	5:46	18:26	5:43	18:29	5:39	18:33
31	5:55	18:14	5:51	18:18	5:49	18:20	5:46	18:23	5:43	18:26	5:40	18:30	5:36	18:34	5:32	18:38	5:26	18:44
Apr. 4	5:51	18:15	5:46	18:20	5:43	18:23	5:40	18:27	5:36	18:31	5:31	18:36	5:26	18:41	5:20	18:47	5:13	18:55
8	5:48	18:16	5:41	18:23	5:38	18:27	5:33	18:31	5:28	18:36	5:22	18:42	5:16	18:48	5:09	18:56	5:00	19:05
12	5:45	18:17	5:37	18:25	5:32	18:30	5:27	18:35	5:21	18:41	5:14	18:49	5:07	18:56	4:58	19:05	4:47	19:16
16	5:41	18:18	5:32	18:28	5:27	18:33	5:21	18:39	5:14	18:46	5:06	18:55	4:57	19:03	4:47	19:14	4:34	19:27
20	5:38	18:20	5:28	18:30	5:22	18:36	5:15	18:43	5:07	18:51	4:58	19:01	4:48	19:11	4:37	19:23	4:22	19:38
24	5:36	18:21	5:24	18:33	5:17	18:39	5:10	18:47	5:01	18:56	4:50	19:07	4:39	19:18	4:26	19:32	4:09	19:49
28	5:33	18:22	5:20	18:35	5:13	18:43	5:04	18:51	4:54	19:01	4:42	19:14	4:30	19:26	4:16	19:41	3:57	20:00

SUNRISE AND SUNSET, 2002 MAY–AUGUST
UNIVERSAL TIME AT GREENWICH MERIDIAN

Latitude: / Event:	+62°		+58°		+54°		+50°		+45°		+40°		+35°		+30°		+20°	
	RISE	SET	RISE	SET	RISE	SET	RISE	SET	RISE	SET	RISE	SET	RISE	SET	RISE	SET	RISE	SET
May 2	3:44	20:11	4:06	19:50	4:22	19:33	4:35	19:20	4:48	19:06	4:59	18:55	5:08	18:46	5:17	18:38	5:30	18:24
6	3:33	20:23	3:56	19:58	4:14	19:40	4:28	19:26	4:43	19:11	4:54	18:59	5:04	18:49	5:13	18:40	5:28	18:25
10	3:21	20:34	3:47	20:07	4:06	19:47	4:22	19:32	4:37	19:16	4:50	19:03	5:01	18:52	5:10	18:43	5:26	18:27
14	3:10	20:45	3:38	20:16	3:59	19:54	4:16	19:38	4:32	19:21	4:46	19:07	4:57	18:56	5:07	18:46	5:24	18:28
18	2:59	20:56	3:30	20:24	3:53	20:01	4:10	19:43	4:28	19:25	4:42	19:11	4:54	18:59	5:05	18:48	5:23	18:30
22	2:49	21:06	3:23	20:32	3:47	20:07	4:06	19:48	4:24	19:30	4:39	19:14	4:52	19:02	5:03	18:51	5:22	18:32
26	2:40	21:16	3:16	20:39	3:42	20:13	4:01	19:53	4:21	19:34	4:37	19:18	4:50	19:05	5:01	18:53	5:21	18:33
30	2:31	21:25	3:10	20:46	3:37	20:19	3:58	19:58	4:18	19:38	4:34	19:21	4:48	19:07	5:00	18:55	5:20	18:35
Jun. 3	2:24	21:34	3:05	20:52	3:33	20:24	3:55	20:02	4:16	19:41	4:33	19:24	4:47	19:10	4:59	18:57	5:20	18:36
7	2:18	21:41	3:01	20:57	3:30	20:28	3:52	20:06	4:14	19:44	4:31	19:26	4:46	19:12	4:58	18:59	5:20	18:38
11	2:13	21:47	2:58	21:01	3:28	20:31	3:51	20:08	4:13	19:46	4:31	19:29	4:45	19:14	4:58	19:01	5:20	18:39
15	2:10	21:51	2:57	21:05	3:27	20:34	3:50	20:11	4:13	19:48	4:31	19:30	4:46	19:15	4:58	19:02	5:20	18:40
19	2:09	21:54	2:56	21:07	3:27	20:36	3:50	20:12	4:13	19:50	4:31	19:32	4:46	19:17	4:59	19:04	5:21	18:42
23	2:10	21:54	2:57	21:07	3:28	20:36	3:51	20:13	4:14	19:51	4:32	19:33	4:47	19:17	5:00	19:04	5:22	18:42
27	2:12	21:53	2:59	21:07	3:30	20:36	3:53	20:13	4:15	19:51	4:33	19:33	4:48	19:18	5:01	19:05	5:23	18:43
Jul. 1	2:17	21:50	3:02	21:05	3:32	20:35	3:55	20:12	4:17	19:50	4:35	19:33	4:50	19:18	5:02	19:05	5:24	18:43
5	2:22	21:46	3:06	21:02	3:35	20:33	3:58	20:11	4:19	19:49	4:37	19:32	4:51	19:17	5:04	19:05	5:25	18:44
9	2:29	21:39	3:11	20:58	3:40	20:30	4:01	20:09	4:22	19:48	4:39	19:31	4:54	19:15	5:06	19:04	5:27	18:43
13	2:38	21:32	3:17	20:53	3:44	20:26	4:05	20:06	4:26	19:45	4:42	19:29	4:56	19:13	5:08	19:03	5:28	18:43
17	2:47	21:24	3:24	20:47	3:50	20:22	4:09	20:02	4:29	19:43	4:45	19:27	4:58	19:11	5:10	19:02	5:30	18:42
21	2:57	21:14	3:31	20:41	3:55	20:16	4:14	19:58	4:33	19:39	4:48	19:24	5:01	19:09	5:12	19:00	5:31	18:41
25	3:07	21:04	3:38	20:33	4:01	20:10	4:19	19:53	4:37	19:35	4:52	19:21	5:04	19:06	5:15	18:58	5:33	18:40
29	3:17	20:54	3:46	20:25	4:08	20:04	4:25	19:47	4:42	19:31	4:55	19:17	5:07	19:02	5:17	18:56	5:34	18:38
Aug. 2	3:28	20:43	3:55	20:16	4:15	19:57	4:30	19:41	4:46	19:26	4:59	19:13	5:10	19:02	5:19	18:53	5:36	18:37
6	3:39	20:31	4:03	20:07	4:21	19:49	4:36	19:35	4:51	19:20	5:03	19:08	5:13	18:58	5:22	18:50	5:37	18:34
10	3:50	20:19	4:12	19:57	4:28	19:41	4:42	19:28	4:55	19:15	5:07	19:04	5:16	18:54	5:24	18:46	5:38	18:32
14	4:01	20:07	4:20	19:47	4:36	19:33	4:48	19:21	5:00	19:08	5:10	18:58	5:19	18:50	5:27	18:42	5:40	18:30
18	4:11	19:54	4:29	19:37	4:43	19:24	4:54	19:13	5:05	19:02	5:14	18:53	5:22	18:45	5:29	18:38	5:41	18:27
22	4:22	19:42	4:38	19:27	4:50	19:15	5:00	19:05	5:10	18:55	5:18	18:47	5:25	18:40	5:31	18:34	5:42	18:24
26	4:33	19:29	4:46	19:16	4:57	19:05	5:06	18:57	5:14	18:48	5:22	18:41	5:28	18:35	5:34	18:30	5:43	18:20
30	4:43	19:16	4:55	19:05	5:04	18:56	5:12	18:49	5:19	18:41	5:26	18:35	5:31	18:30	5:36	18:25	5:44	18:17

SUNRISE AND SUNSET, 2002 SEPTEMBER–DECEMBER
UNIVERSAL TIME AT GREENWICH MERIDIAN

←───

Latitude / Event	+62° RISE	SET	+58° RISE	SET	+54° RISE	SET	+50° RISE	SET	+45° RISE	SET	+40° RISE	SET	+35° RISE	SET	+30° RISE	SET	+20° RISE	SET
Sep. 3	4:54	19:03	5:04	18:54	5:11	18:46	5:18	18:40	5:24	18:34	5:29	18:29	5:34	18:24	5:38	18:20	5:45	18:14
7	5:04	18:50	5:12	18:43	5:18	18:37	5:24	18:32	5:29	18:27	5:33	18:22	5:37	18:19	5:40	18:16	5:46	18:10
11	5:15	18:37	5:21	18:31	5:26	18:27	5:29	18:23	5:34	18:19	5:37	18:16	5:40	18:13	5:42	18:11	5:46	18:07
15	5:25	18:24	5:29	18:20	5:33	18:17	5:35	18:14	5:38	18:11	5:41	18:09	5:43	18:07	5:44	18:06	5:47	18:03
19	5:35	18:11	5:38	18:09	5:40	18:07	5:41	18:05	5:43	18:04	5:44	18:03	5:46	18:02	5:47	18:01	5:48	17:59
23	5:46	17:58	5:46	17:57	5:47	17:57	5:47	17:56	5:48	17:56	5:48	17:56	5:48	17:56	5:49	17:56	5:49	17:56
27	5:56	17:45	5:55	17:46	5:54	17:47	5:53	17:48	5:53	17:49	5:52	17:49	5:51	17:50	5:51	17:51	5:50	17:52
Oct. 1	6:06	17:32	6:04	17:35	6:01	17:37	6:00	17:39	5:58	17:41	5:56	17:43	5:54	17:44	5:53	17:46	5:51	17:48
5	6:17	17:19	6:12	17:23	6:09	17:27	6:06	17:30	6:03	17:34	6:00	17:36	5:58	17:39	5:56	17:41	5:52	17:45
9	6:27	17:06	6:21	17:12	6:16	17:18	6:12	17:22	6:08	17:26	6:04	17:30	6:01	17:33	5:58	17:36	5:53	17:41
13	6:38	16:53	6:30	17:01	6:24	17:08	6:18	17:13	6:13	17:19	6:08	17:24	6:04	17:28	6:00	17:32	5:54	17:38
17	6:49	16:41	6:39	16:51	6:31	16:59	6:25	17:05	6:18	17:12	6:12	17:18	6:07	17:23	6:03	17:27	5:55	17:35
21	7:00	16:28	6:48	16:40	6:39	16:50	6:31	16:57	6:23	17:05	6:17	17:12	6:11	17:18	6:06	17:23	5:57	17:32
25	7:11	16:16	6:57	16:30	6:46	16:41	6:38	16:50	6:29	16:59	6:21	17:07	6:14	17:13	6:08	17:19	5:58	17:30
29	7:22	16:04	7:07	16:20	6:54	16:32	6:44	16:43	6:34	16:53	6:25	17:02	6:18	17:09	6:11	17:16	6:00	17:27
Nov. 2	7:34	15:52	7:16	16:10	7:02	16:24	6:51	16:36	6:39	16:47	6:30	16:57	6:22	17:05	6:14	17:12	6:02	17:25
6	7:45	15:41	7:25	16:01	7:10	16:17	6:58	16:29	6:45	16:42	6:34	16:52	6:25	17:01	6:18	17:09	6:04	17:23
10	7:57	15:30	7:35	15:53	7:18	16:09	7:04	16:23	6:50	16:37	6:39	16:48	6:29	16:58	6:21	17:07	6:06	17:22
14	8:08	15:20	7:44	15:44	7:25	16:03	7:11	16:18	6:56	16:32	6:44	16:45	6:33	16:55	6:24	17:05	6:08	17:21
18	8:19	15:10	7:53	15:37	7:33	15:57	7:17	16:13	7:01	16:29	6:48	16:42	6:37	16:53	6:27	17:03	6:10	17:20
22	8:30	15:01	8:01	15:30	7:40	15:51	7:23	16:08	7:07	16:25	6:53	16:39	6:41	16:51	6:31	17:01	6:13	17:19
26	8:41	14:53	8:10	15:24	7:47	15:47	7:29	16:05	7:12	16:23	6:57	16:37	6:45	16:49	6:34	17:00	6:15	17:19
30	8:50	14:46	8:18	15:19	7:54	15:43	7:35	16:02	7:16	16:20	7:01	16:36	6:48	16:49	6:37	17:00	6:18	17:19
Dec. 4	8:59	14:40	8:25	15:15	8:00	15:40	7:40	16:00	7:21	16:19	7:05	16:35	6:52	16:48	6:40	17:00	6:20	17:20
8	9:07	14:36	8:31	15:12	8:05	15:38	7:45	15:58	7:25	16:18	7:09	16:35	6:55	16:48	6:43	17:00	6:23	17:21
12	9:14	14:33	8:36	15:11	8:10	15:38	7:49	15:58	7:29	16:18	7:12	16:35	6:58	16:49	6:46	17:01	6:25	17:22
16	9:19	14:32	8:41	15:10	8:13	15:38	7:53	15:58	7:32	16:19	7:15	16:36	7:01	16:50	6:49	17:02	6:28	17:23
20	9:23	14:32	8:44	15:11	8:16	15:39	7:55	16:00	7:34	16:21	7:18	16:37	7:03	16:52	6:51	17:04	6:30	17:25
24	9:25	14:34	8:46	15:13	8:18	15:41	7:57	16:02	7:36	16:23	7:20	16:39	7:05	16:54	6:53	17:06	6:32	17:27
28	9:25	14:38	8:46	15:17	8:19	15:44	7:58	16:05	7:38	16:25	7:21	16:42	7:07	16:56	6:55	17:08	6:34	17:29
32	9:23	14:44	8:46	15:21	8:19	15:48	7:59	16:08	7:38	16:29	7:22	16:45	7:08	16:59	6:56	17:11	6:35	17:32

TWILIGHT

There are three definitions for the beginning of morning and ending of evening twilight: (1) *Civil twilight*—centre of the Sun 6° below the horizon, brightest stars visible, artificial illumination required for most outdoor activities, marks the ending or beginning of night for aviation purposes; (2) *Nautical twilight*—centre of the Sun 12° below the horizon, horizon no longer visible; (3) *Astronomical twilight*—centre of the Sun 18° below the horizon, amount of sunlight scattered by the atmosphere is negligible.

The table below gives the beginning of morning and ending of evening astronomical twilight in UT at 0° longitude. For observers in North America the times may be handled in the same way as those of sunrise and sunset (see p. 99).

Latitude M=E:	+20°		+30°		+35°		+40°		+45°		+50°		+54°		+58°		+62°	
	MORN	EVE	MORN	EVE	MORN	EVE	MORN	EVE	MORN	EVE	MORN	EVE	MORN	EVE	MORN	EVE	MORN	EVE
Jan. 0	5:16	18:50	5:30	18:36	5:37	18:29	5:44	18:22	5:52	18:14	6:00	18:07	6:06	18:00	6:14	17:52	6:23	17:44
10	5:19	18:56	5:32	18:43	5:39	18:36	5:45	18:30	5:52	18:23	5:59	18:17	6:05	18:11	6:11	18:04	6:19	17:57
20	5:21	19:01	5:32	18:50	5:38	18:45	5:43	18:39	5:48	18:34	5:54	18:29	5:58	18:24	6:03	18:20	6:08	18:14
30	5:20	19:06	5:29	18:58	5:34	18:53	5:37	18:50	5:41	18:46	5:45	18:43	5:47	18:40	5:50	18:38	5:52	18:35
Feb. 9	5:18	19:11	5:24	19:05	5:27	19:02	5:29	19:00	5:31	18:58	5:32	18:57	5:32	18:57	5:32	18:57	5:31	18:58
19	5:13	19:15	5:16	19:12	5:17	19:11	5:18	19:11	5:17	19:11	5:16	19:13	5:14	19:15	5:10	19:19	5:05	19:24
Mar. 1	5:07	19:18	5:07	19:18	5:06	19:20	5:04	19:21	5:01	19:25	4:57	19:29	4:52	19:34	4:45	19:41	4:35	19:51
11	4:59	19:21	4:56	19:25	4:53	19:28	4:49	19:32	4:43	19:38	4:35	19:46	4:27	19:55	4:16	20:06	4:01	20:22
21	4:50	19:25	4:43	19:32	4:38	19:37	4:32	19:44	4:23	19:53	4:12	20:04	4:00	20:17	3:44	20:33	3:21	20:56
31	4:41	19:28	4:30	19:39	4:23	19:46	4:14	19:56	4:02	20:08	3:46	20:24	3:30	20:41	3:07	21:04	2:35	21:38
Apr. 10	4:32	19:32	4:17	19:46	4:07	19:56	3:55	20:08	3:40	20:24	3:19	20:45	2:57	21:08	2:26	21:41	1:32	22:38
20	4:22	19:36	4:04	19:55	3:52	20:07	3:37	20:22	3:17	20:42	2:51	21:09	2:21	21:40	1:33	22:31		
30	4:14	19:41	3:52	20:03	3:37	20:18	3:19	20:37	2:55	21:01	2:21	21:36	1:39	22:20				
May 10	4:07	19:46	3:41	20:12	3:24	20:30	3:02	20:52	2:33	21:21	1:49	22:06	0:35	23:30				
20	4:01	19:52	3:32	20:21	3:13	20:41	2:48	21:06	2:13	21:41	1:14	22:42						
30	3:58	19:58	3:26	20:30	3:04	20:51	2:37	21:19	1:56	22:00	0:26	23:37						
Jun. 9	3:56	20:02	3:23	20:36	3:00	20:59	2:29	21:29	1:44	22:15								
19	3:57	20:06	3:22	20:40	2:59	21:04	2:28	21:35	1:40	22:23								
29	4:00	20:07	3:25	20:41	3:02	21:05	2:31	21:35	1:44	22:22								
Jul. 9	4:04	20:06	3:31	20:39	3:09	21:01	2:39	21:30	1:56	22:13								
19	4:09	20:04	3:38	20:34	3:18	20:54	2:51	21:20	2:14	21:57	1:03	23:06						
29	4:14	19:59	3:46	20:26	3:28	20:44	3:05	21:07	2:33	21:38	1:42	22:28						
Aug. 8	4:19	19:52	3:55	20:15	3:39	20:31	3:19	20:51	2:53	21:17	2:14	21:55	1:20	22:46				
18	4:24	19:43	4:04	20:04	3:50	20:17	3:33	20:33	3:12	20:55	2:41	21:24	2:06	21:59	0:56	23:03		
28	4:28	19:34	4:11	19:50	4:00	20:01	3:47	20:15	3:29	20:32	3:06	20:55	2:39	21:21	2:03	21:58	0:26	23:18
Sep. 7	4:31	19:24	4:19	19:37	4:10	19:45	3:59	19:56	3:45	20:09	3:27	20:27	3:08	20:46	2:40	21:13	1:58	21:53
17	4:34	19:15	4:25	19:23	4:19	19:30	4:11	19:37	4:00	19:48	3:47	20:01	3:32	20:15	3:13	20:34	2:45	21:01
27	4:37	19:05	4:31	19:10	4:27	19:14	4:22	19:19	4:14	19:25	4:04	19:36	3:54	19:46	3:40	20:00	3:21	20:18
Oct. 7	4:39	18:56	4:37	18:58	4:35	19:00	4:32	19:03	4:27	19:07	4:21	19:13	4:14	19:20	4:05	19:29	3:52	19:41
17	4:42	18:49	4:43	18:47	4:43	18:47	4:42	18:48	4:40	18:50	4:37	18:53	4:33	18:56	4:28	19:01	4:20	19:09
27	4:45	18:43	4:49	18:38	4:51	18:37	4:52	18:35	4:53	18:34	4:52	18:35	4:51	18:36	4:49	18:37	4:46	18:40
Nov. 6	4:49	18:39	4:56	18:31	4:59	18:28	5:02	18:25	5:05	18:22	5:07	18:20	5:08	18:18	5:09	18:17	5:10	18:16
16	4:53	18:36	5:03	18:26	5:08	18:22	5:12	18:17	5:16	18:13	5:21	18:08	5:24	18:05	5:28	18:01	5:31	17:57
26	4:58	18:36	5:10	18:24	5:16	18:18	5:22	18:11	5:27	18:07	5:34	18:00	5:39	17:55	5:44	17:50	5:50	17:43
Dec. 6	5:03	18:38	5:17	18:25	5:24	18:21	5:30	18:11	5:37	18:04	5:45	17:57	5:51	17:51	5:58	17:44	6:06	17:36
16	5:09	18:42	5:23	18:28	5:30	18:26	5:38	18:13	5:45	18:06	5:53	17:58	6:00	17:51	6:08	17:43	6:17	17:34
26	5:14	18:47	5:28	18:33	5:35	18:32	5:43	18:18	5:50	18:11	5:58	18:03	6:05	17:56	6:13	17:48	6:22	17:39
Jan. 5	5:18	18:53	5:32	18:39	5:38	18:32	5:45	18:25	5:52	18:18	6:00	18:11	6:06	18:05	6:13	17:57	6:22	17:49

MIDNIGHT TWILIGHT AND MIDNIGHT SUN
By Roy Bishop

Astronomers generally desire dark skies, free of moonlight and man-made light pollution. As mentioned on the previous page, the beginning or end of *astronomical twilight* corresponds to the centre of the Sun being 18° below the horizon. At that point the amount of sunlight scattered by the upper layers of Earth's atmosphere is negligible; that is, it is less than the combined illuminance (about 2×10^{-3} lux) from starlight, airglow, and zodiacal light, the three main contributors to the light of the "dark" night sky.

For observers in countries at high latitudes (e.g. the United Kingdom, Norway, southern Argentina and Chile, and most of Canada), around the time of the summer solstice the Sun always lies less than 18° below the horizon, and the sky does not get dark at night. This "midnight twilight" phenomenon can be displayed in a graph as a function of latitude and time of year.

The **diagram** at the right indicates the brightness of the sky at local midnight at any time of the year for any latitude north of 45°N or south of 45°S. Below the lower curve the natural sky is dark. Between the two curves twilight prevails. Above the upper curve the Sun is in the sky. Place names in roman type (left-hand side) are in the Northern Hemisphere; place names in *italic* type (right-hand side) are in the *Southern Hemisphere*. On the horizontal axis use the roman-type months for the former, *italic*-type months for the latter. The diagram is simplified slightly in that the months are assumed to be of equal duration, and the seasonal pattern of months and summer solstices for Earth's two hemispheres are assumed to be identical except for a six-month phase shift.

The latitude of the Arctic and Antarctic Circles (90° subtract the obliquity of the ecliptic = 66°34′) is indicated by the dashed line. This line is *not* tangent to the Midnight Sun curve because at midnight on the summer solstice at either the Arctic or the Antarctic Circle the Sun is above the horizon. Atmospheric refraction raises the apparent Sun about 34′ above the true Sun. Also, rise/set is defined as the top limb of the Sun at a sea level horizon; thus the 16′ semidiameter of the Sun must also be taken into account. To see the top limb of the Sun on the horizon at local midnight on the summer solstice, an observer must be 34′ + 16′ = 50′ south of the Arctic Circle (or north of the Antarctic Circle), at latitude 65°44′.

By running a horizontal line across the chart at a selected latitude, the reader can determine the approximate dates when midnight twilight and, possibly, midnight sun begin and end for any locality at north or south latitudes above 48.6°, the lower limit for midnight twilight on the summer solstice. (Remarkably, when rounded to the nearest degree, the latter figure is the latitude of the longest east-west international border: the 2000-km-long 49th parallel between the United States and western Canada.)

Some examples: The diagram shows that at Grise Fiord (a hamlet on the stunning south coast of Ellesmere Island, and Canada's most northerly community) the sky is never dark from about March 10 until early October, and the midnight sun lasts from late April until mid-August. Note that Cape Horn at midnight is bathed in dim Antarctic twilight from early November until early February. Even at the latitude of Vancouver there is a period of almost a month each year when the sky never gets astronomically dark—although the natural night sky is obliterated *every* night near any town or city unless there is an electrical power failure! Finally, note that Earth's poles are astronomically dark for less than 3 months of the year.

MIDNIGHT TWILIGHT AND MIDNIGHT SUN DIAGRAM

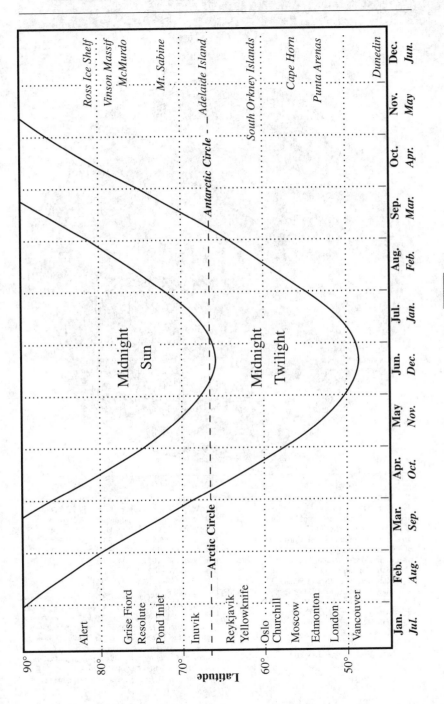

THE MOON

MAP OF MOON

BY ROY BISHOP

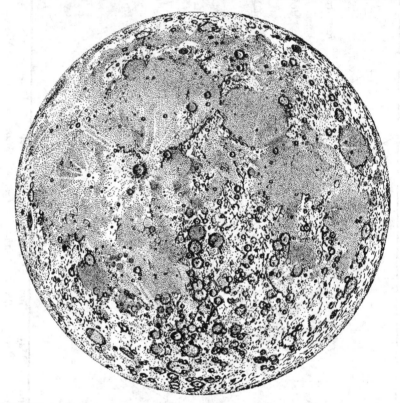

Maria

LS   Lacus Somniorum (Lake of Dreams) (330°)
MC   Mare Crisium (Sea of Crises) (300°)
MFe Mare Fecunditatis (Sea of Fertility) (310°)
MFr Mare Frigoris (Sea of Cold) (0°)
MH   Mare Humorum (Sea of Moisture) (40°)
MI   Mare Imbrium (Sea of Rains) (20°)
MNe Mare Nectaris (Sea of Nectar) (325°)
MNu Mare Nubium (Sea of Clouds) (15°)
MS   Mare Serenitatis (Sea of Serenity) (340°)
MT   Mare Tranquillitatis (Sea of Tranquillity) (330°)
MV   Mare Vaporum (Sea of Vapors) (355°)
OP   Oceanus Procellarum (Ocean of Storms) (50°)
SA   Sinus Aestuum (Seething Bay) (8°)
SI   Sinus Iridum (Bay of Rainbows) (32°)
SM   Sinus Medii (Central Bay) (0°)
SR   Sinus Roris (Bay of Dew) (60°)

Lunar Probes

2 *Luna 2*, First to reach Moon (1959.9.13) (0°)
7 *Ranger 7*, First close pictures (1964.7.31) (21°)
9 *Luna 9*, First soft landing (1966.2.3) (64°)
11 *Apollo 11*, First men on Moon (1969.7.20) (337°)
12 *Apollo 12* (1969.11.19) (23°)
14 *Apollo 14* (1971.2.5) (17°)
15 *Apollo 15* (1971.7.30) (356°)
16 *Apollo 16* (1972.4.21) (344°)
17 *Apollo 17* (1972.12.11) (329°)

Angles in parentheses equal $(360° - \lambda)$, where λ is the selenographic longitude of the centre of the feature. 0° marks the mean centre of the lunar disk and the angles increase toward the observer's east (i.e. westward on the Moon). These angles facilitate locating the feature on the accompanying map, and may be correlated with the Sun's selenographic colongitude (see THE SKY MONTH BY MONTH (pp. 66–91)) to determine the optimum times for viewing the feature.

MAP OF MOON (continued)

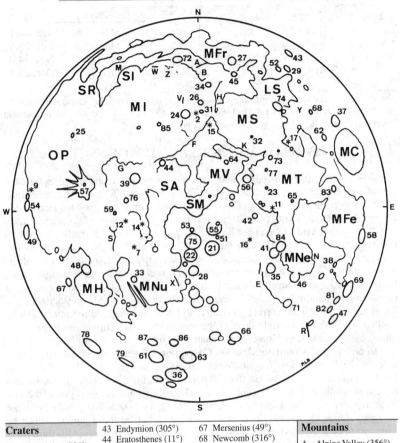

Craters				Mountains

Craters

21 Albategnius (356°)
22 Alphonsus (3°)
23 Arago (338°)
24 Archimedes (4°)
25 Aristarchus (47°)
26 Aristillus (358°)
27 Aristoteles (342°)
28 Arzachel (2°)
29 Atlas (315°)
31 Autolycus (358°)
32 Bessel (342°)
33 Bullialdus (22°)
34 Cassini (355°)
35 Catharina (336°)
36 Clavius (15°)
37 Cleomedes (304°)
38 Cook (311°)
39 Copernicus (20°)
41 Cyrillus (336°)
42 Delambre (342°)

43 Endymion (305°)
44 Eratosthenes (11°)
45 Eudoxus (343°)
46 Fracastorius (326°)
47 Furnerius (299°)
48 Gassendi (40°)
49 Grimaldi (68°)
51 Halley (354°)
52 Hercules (321°)
53 Herschel (2°)
54 Hevelius (66°)
55 Hipparchus (354°)
56 Julius Caesar (345°)
57 Kepler (38°)
58 Langrenus (299°)
59 Lansberg (27°)
61 Longomontanus (21°)
62 Macrobius (314°)
63 Maginus (6°)
64 Manilius (351°)
65 Maskelyne (330°)
66 Maurolycus (345°)

67 Mersenius (49°)
68 Newcomb (316°)
69 Petavius (298°)
71 Piccolomini (327°)
72 Plato (10°)
73 Plinius (336°)
74 Posidonius (330°)
75 Ptolemaeus (2°)
76 Reinhold (23°)
77 Ross (338°)
78 Schickard (55°)
79 Schiller (40°)
81 Snellius (304°)
82 Stevinus (305°)
83 Taruntius (313°)
84 Theophilus (333°)
85 Timocharis (13°)
86 Tycho (11°)
87 Wilhelm (20°)

Mountains

A Alpine Valley (356°)
B Alps Mts. (359°)
E Altai Mts. (336°)
F Apennine Mts. (2°)
G Carpathian Mts. (24°)
H Caucasus Mts. (352°)
K Haemus Mts. (349°)
M Jura Mts. (34°)
N Pyrenees Mts. (319°)
R Rheita Valley (312°)
S Riphaeus Mts. (27°)
V Spitzbergen (5°)
W Straight Range (20°)
X Straight Wall (8°)
Y Taurus Mts. (319°)
Z Teneriffe Mts. (13°)

UNIVERSAL TIME OF NEW MOON DATES

2002			2003		
Jan. 13.6	May 12.4	Sep. 7.1	Jan. 2.8	May 1.5	Sep. 26.1
Feb. 12.3	Jun. 11.0	Oct. 6.5	Feb. 1.4	May 31.2	Oct. 25.5
Mar. 14.1	Jul. 10.4	Nov. 4.9	Mar. 3.1	Jun. 29.8	Nov. 24.0
Apr. 12.8	Aug. 8.8	Dec. 4.3	Apr. 1.8	Jul. 29.3	Dec. 23.4
				Aug. 27.7	

These dates will be useful for planning observing sessions, determining favourable dates for observing very thin lunar crescents, and setting moon dials on clocks. The dates are indicated to lower precision in the calendar on the inside back cover.

TIMES OF MOONRISE AND MOONSET

The following 12 pages of tables give the times of moonrise and moonset for each day of the year for locations ranging from 20° to 62° north latitude. The tables may be interpolated linearly for nontabular latitudes and can be extrapolated beyond the 20° and 62° latitude limits a few degrees without significant loss of accuracy. "Rise" and "Set" correspond to the upper limb of the Moon appearing at the horizon for an observer at sea level. The times are local mean time (LMT) for the Greenwich meridian (i.e. UT at 0° longitude). Because of the relatively rapid eastward motion of the Moon, unlike the sunrise and sunset tables, for observers not near 0° longitude the times cannot be read directly as LMT; the table must be interpolated according to the observer's longitude. Also, to convert from the observer's LMT to standard time, the observer's longitude correction relative to his or her standard meridian must be applied. The chart at the right enables the sum of these two corrections to be determined easily in one step. However, the chart must first be set for your longitude.

To prepare the **Moonrise/Moonset Correction Diagram**, first mark your longitude on the *West or East Longitude* scale. Using a straight-edge, draw a diagonal line from this mark to the origin (the 0,0 point). Next, the *Correction in minutes* axis (which is subdivided at two-minute intervals) must be labelled. As a guide, the first three divisions have been tentatively labelled 0, ±2, ±4 (*use + if you are west of the prime meridian in Greenwich, England, – if east*); but, to these numbers must be added your longitude correction relative to your standard meridian (see the third paragraph on p. 99.) As an aid both for labelling and for reading the chart, the vertical lines at 10-minute intervals are wider. **Examples:** For Toronto, which is 4.5°W of its standard meridian of 75°, the longitude correction is +18 minutes, so an observer in Toronto would label the Correction axis divisions 18, 20, 22, 24,...; an observer in Boston (longitude correction –16) would label the axis –16, –14, –12,...; an observer in Hong Kong (east longitude, longitude correction +24) would label the axis: 24, 22, 20,...; an observer in Vienna (longitude correction –6) would label the axis: –6, –8, –10,....

The chart is now ready for use on any day from your position. Interpolating for nontabular latitudes, from the table obtain today's time for the event (moonrise, or moonset) and tomorrow's time if you are west of Greenwich, yesterday's time if east, enter the difference on the Tabular Delay axis, and run horizontally across to meet the diagonal line. The correction, to the nearest minute, can then be read directly below off the Correction axis. This correction is applied to the tabular "today's time" and results in the standard time of the event for your position. **Note:** Due to a difference in height between the observer and the actual horizon, the observed time may differ by several minutes from the predicted time.

MOONRISE/MOONSET CORRECTION DIAGRAM

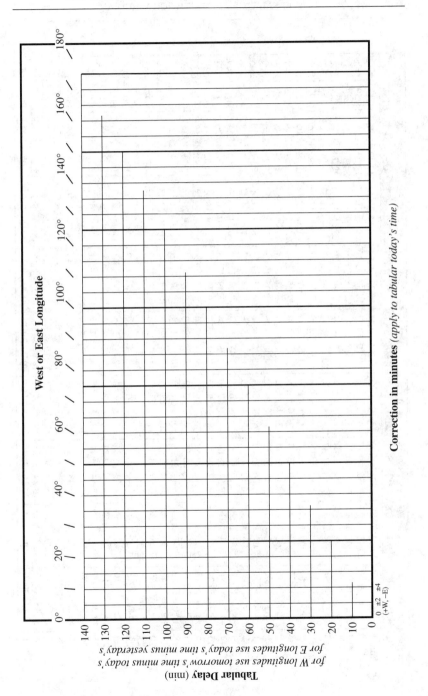

MOONRISE AND MOONSET, 2002 JANUARY
UNIVERSAL TIME AT GREENWICH MERIDIAN

Latitude: Event:	+20° RISE	+20° SET	+30° RISE	+30° SET	+35° RISE	+35° SET	+40° RISE	+40° SET	+45° RISE	+45° SET	+50° RISE	+50° SET	+54° RISE	+54° SET	+58° RISE	+58° SET	+62° RISE	+62° SET
Jan. 1	19:51	8:28	19:32	8:48	19:21	9:00	19:08	9:14	18:52	9:31	18:33	9:51	18:14	10:11	17:49	10:36	17:15	11:12
2	20:56	9:20	20:41	9:37	20:32	9:47	20:22	9:58	20:10	10:11	19:56	10:27	19:41	10:43	19:23	11:02	18:59	11:28
3	21:58	10:08	21:48	10:21	21:42	10:28	21:36	10:36	21:28	10:45	21:18	10:56	21:09	11:07	20:58	11:20	20:43	11:37
4	22:58	10:52	22:54	11:00	22:51	11:04	22:48	11:08	22:44	11:14	22:40	11:20	22:36	11:26	22:30	11:34	22:24	11:43
5	23:57	11:34	23:57	11:36	23:58	11:37	23:58	11:38	23:59	11:40	23:59	11:41	—	11:43	—	11:45	—	11:47
6	—	12:14	—	12:10	—	12:09	—	12:07	—	12:04	—	12:01	0:00	11:59	0:00	11:55	0:01	11:51
7	0:54	12:54	1:00	12:46	1:04	12:41	1:07	12:36	1:12	12:29	1:17	12:22	1:23	12:15	1:29	12:06	1:37	11:56
8	1:52	13:35	2:02	13:22	2:09	13:15	2:16	13:06	2:24	12:57	2:35	12:45	2:45	12:33	2:57	12:19	3:13	12:01
9	2:49	14:19	3:05	14:02	3:14	13:52	3:24	13:41	3:36	13:27	3:51	13:11	4:06	12:55	4:24	12:35	4:49	12:09
10	3:47	15:06	4:06	14:45	4:18	14:33	4:31	14:20	4:46	14:03	5:05	13:43	5:24	13:24	5:49	12:58	6:24	12:22
11	4:45	15:56	5:07	15:33	5:20	15:20	5:35	15:04	5:52	14:44	6:15	14:23	6:37	14:00	7:07	13:30	7:51	12:45
12	5:41	16:48	6:04	16:25	6:18	16:11	6:34	15:55	6:53	15:36	7:16	15:12	7:41	14:48	8:13	14:15	9:02	13:26
13	6:34	17:42	6:57	17:20	7:10	17:06	7:26	16:51	7:45	16:33	8:08	16:10	8:31	15:46	9:03	15:15	9:50	14:29
14	7:23	18:36	7:44	18:16	7:57	18:04	8:11	17:50	8:28	17:34	8:49	17:13	9:10	16:53	9:38	16:26	10:17	15:47
15	8:07	19:29	8:26	19:12	8:37	19:02	8:49	18:50	9:04	18:37	9:21	18:20	9:39	18:03	10:02	17:41	10:32	17:12
16	8:48	20:21	9:03	20:07	9:12	19:59	9:22	19:50	9:33	19:40	9:47	19:27	10:01	19:14	10:18	18:58	10:41	18:37
17	9:25	21:10	9:36	21:01	9:43	20:55	9:50	20:49	9:58	20:42	10:09	20:33	10:19	20:25	10:31	20:14	10:46	20:01
18	10:00	21:59	10:07	21:54	10:11	21:51	10:15	21:47	10:21	21:44	10:27	21:39	10:33	21:34	10:41	21:29	10:50	21:22
19	10:33	22:47	10:36	22:46	10:37	22:46	10:39	22:45	10:41	22:45	10:44	22:44	10:46	22:43	10:49	22:43	10:53	22:42
20	11:06	23:35	11:05	23:39	11:04	23:41	11:03	23:43	11:01	23:46	11:00	23:50	10:59	23:53	10:57	23:57	10:55	—
21	11:40	—	11:34	—	11:31	—	11:27	—	11:22	—	11:17	—	11:12	—	11:06	—	10:58	0:03
22	12:16	0:24	12:05	0:33	11:59	0:38	11:53	0:43	11:45	0:49	11:36	0:57	11:27	1:05	11:16	1:14	11:02	1:25
23	12:55	1:16	12:40	1:29	12:32	1:36	12:22	1:45	12:11	1:55	11:58	2:07	11:45	2:18	11:29	2:33	11:08	2:52
24	13:38	2:11	13:20	2:28	13:09	2:38	12:57	2:49	12:43	3:02	12:25	3:18	12:08	3:35	11:47	3:55	11:18	4:23
25	14:28	3:09	14:06	3:29	13:54	3:41	13:39	3:55	13:22	4:11	13:01	4:31	12:40	4:52	12:13	5:18	11:35	5:56
26	15:23	4:09	15:00	4:32	14:47	4:46	14:31	5:01	14:12	5:19	13:49	5:42	13:25	6:06	12:54	6:37	12:07	7:23
27	16:25	5:11	16:02	5:34	15:48	5:48	15:33	6:04	15:14	6:23	14:51	6:46	14:27	7:10	13:55	7:42	13:07	8:30
28	17:31	6:11	17:10	6:33	16:57	6:46	16:43	7:01	16:26	7:18	16:05	7:40	15:44	8:02	15:16	8:30	14:37	9:11
29	18:38	7:07	18:20	7:26	18:10	7:37	17:59	7:50	17:45	8:04	17:28	8:22	17:12	8:40	16:51	9:02	16:22	9:32
30	19:43	7:59	19:31	8:13	19:24	8:22	19:16	8:31	19:06	8:42	18:55	8:55	18:43	9:08	18:29	9:24	18:11	9:44
31	20:47	8:46	20:40	8:56	20:36	9:01	20:32	9:07	20:26	9:14	20:20	9:22	20:14	9:30	20:07	9:40	19:57	9:52

MOONRISE AND MOONSET, 2002 FEBRUARY
UNIVERSAL TIME AT GREENWICH MERIDIAN

Latitude: Event: Feb.	+62° RISE	+62° SET	+58° RISE	+58° SET	+54° RISE	+54° SET	+50° RISE	+50° SET	+45° RISE	+45° SET	+40° RISE	+40° SET	+35° RISE	+35° SET	+30° RISE	+30° SET	+20° RISE	+20° SET
1	21:40	9:57	21:41	9:52	21:42	9:48	21:44	9:45	21:45	9:42	21:46	9:39	21:46	9:36	21:47	9:34	21:48	9:30
2	23:19	10:01	23:13	10:03	23:09	10:05	23:05	10:06	23:01	10:07	22:57	10:09	22:55	10:09	22:52	10:10	22:48	10:12
3	—	10:05	—	10:14	—	10:21	—	10:27	—	10:33	—	10:38	—	10:42	23:56	10:46	23:46	10:53
4	0:57	10:10	0:43	10:26	0:33	10:39	0:24	10:49	0:15	11:00	0:08	11:09	0:01	11:16	—	11:23	—	11:34
5	2:34	10:17	2:12	10:41	1:55	11:00	1:42	11:14	1:28	11:29	1:17	11:42	1:07	11:52	0:59	12:02	0:45	12:18
6	4:10	10:29	3:38	11:02	3:15	11:26	2:57	11:45	2:39	12:04	2:24	12:19	2:12	12:32	2:01	12:44	1:43	13:03
7	5:40	10:48	4:58	11:30	4:29	11:59	4:07	12:22	3:46	12:44	3:28	13:02	3:14	13:17	3:01	13:30	2:40	13:52
8	6:56	11:22	6:07	12:11	5:35	12:43	5:11	13:08	4:47	13:31	4:28	13:50	4:13	14:06	3:59	14:20	3:36	14:43
9	7:50	12:17	7:01	13:05	6:29	13:38	6:05	14:02	5:41	14:25	5:22	14:44	5:06	15:00	4:52	15:13	4:29	15:36
10	8:22	13:31	7:40	14:13	7:11	14:41	6:48	15:03	6:26	15:24	6:09	15:42	5:54	15:56	5:41	16:09	5:19	16:30
11	8:40	14:55	8:06	15:27	7:42	15:50	7:23	16:08	7:04	16:26	6:49	16:41	6:35	16:54	6:24	17:04	6:04	17:23
12	8:50	16:20	8:25	16:43	8:06	17:01	7:51	17:15	7:35	17:30	7:23	17:41	7:12	17:51	7:02	18:00	6:46	18:15
13	8:56	17:44	8:38	18:00	8:24	18:12	8:13	18:22	8:02	18:32	7:52	18:41	7:44	18:48	7:37	18:54	7:24	19:05
14	9:00	19:06	8:49	19:15	8:40	19:22	8:32	19:28	8:25	19:34	8:18	19:39	8:13	19:44	8:08	19:47	7:59	19:54
15	9:03	20:26	8:57	20:32	8:53	20:32	8:49	20:33	8:46	20:35	8:42	20:37	8:40	20:38	8:37	20:40	8:33	20:42
16	9:05	21:47	9:05	21:43	9:05	21:41	9:06	21:39	9:06	21:37	9:06	21:35	9:06	21:33	9:06	21:32	9:06	21:30
17	9:08	23:08	9:14	22:58	9:18	22:51	9:22	22:45	9:26	22:39	9:29	22:33	9:32	22:29	9:35	22:25	9:39	22:18
18	9:11	—	9:23	—	9:32	—	9:39	23:52	9:47	23:42	9:54	23:33	9:59	23:26	10:05	23:19	10:13	23:08
19	9:15	0:32	9:34	0:15	9:48	0:03	9:59	—	10:11	—	10:21	—	10:30	—	10:37	—	10:50	—
20	9:23	1:59	9:48	1:35	10:08	1:16	10:24	1:02	10:39	0:47	10:53	0:35	11:04	0:25	11:14	0:16	11:30	0:00
21	9:35	3:29	10:10	2:56	10:35	2:31	10:54	2:12	11:14	1:54	11:30	1:38	11:44	1:26	11:55	1:14	12:16	0:55
22	9:58	4:58	10:42	4:15	11:12	3:45	11:35	3:22	11:57	3:00	12:16	2:43	12:31	2:28	12:44	2:15	13:07	1:53
23	10:42	6:14	11:31	5:25	12:04	4:53	12:28	4:28	12:52	4:04	13:11	3:45	13:27	3:30	13:41	3:16	14:04	2:52
24	11:56	7:06	12:41	6:20	13:12	5:49	13:35	5:26	13:58	5:03	14:16	4:44	14:31	4:28	14:44	4:15	15:07	3:52
25	13:35	7:35	14:10	6:59	14:35	6:33	14:54	6:13	15:13	5:53	15:29	5:36	15:42	5:22	15:53	5:10	16:13	4:49
26	15:24	7:51	15:48	7:25	16:06	7:06	16:20	6:50	16:34	6:34	16:46	6:21	16:56	6:10	17:05	6:00	17:20	5:43
27	17:14	7:59	17:28	7:43	17:39	7:30	17:48	7:20	17:57	7:09	18:04	7:00	18:11	6:52	18:16	6:45	18:26	6:33
28	19:02	8:05	19:08	7:57	19:12	7:50	19:15	7:45	19:19	7:39	19:22	7:34	19:24	7:30	19:26	7:26	19:30	7:20

MOONRISE AND MOONSET, 2002 MARCH
UNIVERSAL TIME AT GREENWICH MERIDIAN

Latitude: Event:	+62° RISE	+62° SET	+58° RISE	+58° SET	+54° RISE	+54° SET	+50° RISE	+50° SET	+45° RISE	+45° SET	+40° RISE	+40° SET	+35° RISE	+35° SET	+30° RISE	+30° SET	+20° RISE	+20° SET
Mar. 1	20:47	8:10	20:45	8:09	20:42	8:08	20:41	8:07	20:39	8:06	20:37	8:06	20:36	8:05	20:35	8:05	20:33	8:04
2	22:31	8:14	22:20	8:20	22:11	8:25	22:04	8:29	21:57	8:33	21:51	8:36	21:46	8:39	21:42	8:42	21:34	8:46
3	—	8:18	23:53	8:32	23:38	8:42	23:26	8:51	23:14	9:00	23:04	9:07	22:55	9:14	22:48	9:19	22:35	9:29
4	0:13	8:24	—	8:46	—	9:02	—	9:16	—	9:29	—	9:40	—	9:50	23:53	9:59	23:35	10:14
5	1:53	8:33	1:23	9:04	1:02	9:27	0:45	9:45	0:28	10:03	0:14	10:17	0:03	10:30	—	10:41	—	11:00
6	3:28	8:49	2:48	9:30	2:20	9:58	1:59	10:20	1:38	10:42	1:22	10:59	1:07	11:14	0:55	11:27	0:34	11:48
7	4:51	9:18	4:02	10:07	3:30	10:39	3:06	11:04	2:43	11:27	2:24	11:46	2:08	12:02	1:55	12:16	1:32	12:40
8	5:52	10:07	5:01	10:58	4:28	11:31	4:03	11:56	3:39	12:20	3:20	12:39	3:04	12:55	2:50	13:09	2:26	13:32
9	6:29	11:17	5:44	12:02	5:13	12:32	4:50	12:55	4:27	13:17	4:08	13:35	3:53	13:50	3:40	14:04	3:17	14:26
10	6:49	12:39	6:13	13:14	5:47	13:40	5:27	13:59	5:06	14:19	4:50	14:34	4:36	14:48	4:24	14:59	4:03	15:19
11	7:00	14:04	6:33	14:31	6:12	14:50	5:56	15:06	5:39	15:21	5:25	15:34	5:14	15:45	5:03	15:55	4:46	16:11
12	7:07	15:29	6:47	15:47	6:32	16:01	6:19	16:13	6:06	16:24	5:56	16:34	5:46	16:42	5:38	16:49	5:24	17:01
13	7:11	16:52	6:58	17:03	6:47	17:12	6:39	17:19	6:30	17:26	6:22	17:33	6:16	17:38	6:10	17:42	6:00	17:50
14	7:14	18:13	7:07	18:18	7:01	18:22	6:56	18:25	6:51	18:28	6:47	18:31	6:43	18:33	6:40	18:35	6:34	18:39
15	7:16	19:34	7:14	19:32	7:13	19:31	7:12	19:30	7:11	19:29	7:10	19:29	7:09	19:28	7:09	19:27	7:07	19:26
16	7:18	20:55	7:22	20:47	7:25	20:41	7:28	20:36	7:31	20:31	7:33	20:27	7:35	20:23	7:37	20:20	7:40	20:15
17	7:21	22:18	7:30	22:00	7:38	21:52	7:45	21:43	7:51	21:34	7:57	21:26	8:02	21:20	8:06	21:14	8:14	21:04
18	7:24	23:44	7:40	23:22	7:53	23:05	8:03	22:52	8:14	22:38	8:23	22:27	8:31	22:18	8:38	22:09	8:49	21:55
19	7:29	—	7:53	—	8:11	—	8:25	—	8:40	23:44	8:52	23:29	9:03	23:17	9:12	23:07	9:28	22:48
20	7:39	1:13	8:11	0:42	8:34	0:19	8:53	0:01	9:12	—	9:27	—	9:40	—	9:51	—	10:11	23:44
21	7:55	2:42	8:37	2:01	9:06	1:32	9:28	1:11	9:50	0:49	10:08	0:32	10:23	0:18	10:36	0:05	10:58	—
22	8:28	4:03	9:17	3:14	9:50	2:41	10:15	2:17	10:38	1:53	10:58	1:34	11:14	1:18	11:28	1:04	11:51	0:41
23	9:27	5:03	10:16	4:13	10:49	3:40	11:14	3:16	11:38	2:52	11:57	2:33	12:13	2:16	12:26	2:02	12:50	1:39
24	10:54	5:39	11:35	4:57	12:04	4:28	12:25	4:05	12:47	3:43	13:04	3:26	13:18	3:10	13:31	2:57	13:52	2:35
25	12:37	5:58	13:07	5:27	13:29	5:04	13:46	4:45	14:03	4:27	14:17	4:12	14:29	3:59	14:39	3:48	14:57	3:29
26	14:26	6:08	14:45	5:47	15:00	5:31	15:12	5:17	15:24	5:04	15:34	4:52	15:42	4:43	15:50	4:34	16:02	4:19
27	16:15	6:14	16:25	6:02	16:33	5:52	16:39	5:44	16:46	5:35	16:51	5:28	16:56	5:22	17:00	5:16	17:07	5:07
28	18:03	6:19	18:04	6:14	18:06	6:10	18:07	6:07	18:08	6:03	18:08	6:00	18:09	5:58	18:09	5:55	18:11	5:51
29	19:50	6:22	19:43	6:25	19:37	6:27	19:33	6:28	19:29	6:30	19:25	6:31	19:22	6:32	19:19	6:33	19:14	6:35
30	21:36	6:26	21:20	6:36	21:08	6:44	20:59	6:50	20:49	6:57	20:41	7:02	20:34	7:07	20:28	7:11	20:17	7:19
31	23:22	6:31	22:56	6:49	22:38	7:02	22:23	7:14	22:07	7:25	21:55	7:35	21:45	7:43	21:36	7:51	21:20	8:04

MOONRISE AND MOONSET, 2002 APRIL
UNIVERSAL TIME AT GREENWICH MERIDIAN

Latitude:	+20°		+30°		+35°		+40°		+45°		+50°		+54°		+58°		+62°	
Event: Apr.	RISE	SET	RISE	SET	RISE	SET	RISE	SET	RISE	SET	RISE	SET	RISE	SET	RISE	SET	RISE	SET
1	22:22	8:50	22:42	8:33	22:54	8:23	23:07	8:11	23:23	7:58	23:43	7:41	—	7:25	—	7:05	—	6:38
2	23:22	9:40	23:45	9:19	23:59	9:07	—	8:52	—	8:36	—	8:15	0:02	7:54	0:28	7:28	1:05	6:50
3	—	10:32	—	10:09	—	9:55	0:14	9:39	0:32	9:20	0:56	8:57	1:19	8:32	1:51	8:00	2:38	7:13
4	0:20	11:26	0:44	11:02	0:58	10:47	1:14	10:31	1:34	10:12	1:58	9:47	2:24	9:22	2:58	8:47	3:51	7:54
5	1:13	12:20	1:37	11:57	1:51	11:43	2:07	11:28	2:26	11:09	2:50	10:45	3:14	10:21	3:47	9:49	4:36	9:00
6	2:02	13:14	2:23	12:53	2:36	12:41	2:51	12:27	3:08	12:10	3:30	11:49	3:51	11:28	4:20	11:01	5:00	10:21
7	2:45	14:07	3:04	13:49	3:15	13:39	3:28	13:27	3:43	13:13	4:01	12:56	4:19	12:39	4:42	12:17	5:13	11:47
8	3:25	14:57	3:41	14:44	3:49	14:36	4:00	14:27	4:11	14:16	4:26	14:03	4:39	13:50	4:57	13:34	5:19	13:13
9	4:02	15:47	4:13	15:37	4:20	15:32	4:27	15:26	4:36	15:18	4:46	15:10	4:56	15:01	5:08	14:50	5:24	14:37
10	4:36	16:35	4:43	16:30	4:47	16:27	4:52	16:24	4:57	16:20	5:03	16:16	5:10	16:11	5:17	16:06	5:26	15:59
11	5:09	17:23	5:12	17:23	5:13	17:23	5:15	17:22	5:17	17:22	5:20	17:21	5:22	17:21	5:25	17:20	5:28	17:20
12	5:42	18:12	5:40	18:16	5:39	18:18	5:38	18:21	5:37	18:24	5:35	18:28	5:34	18:31	5:32	18:36	5:30	18:41
13	6:15	19:01	6:09	19:09	6:05	19:14	6:01	19:20	5:57	19:27	5:51	19:35	5:46	19:43	5:40	19:52	5:32	20:04
14	6:50	19:52	6:40	20:05	6:33	20:12	6:27	20:21	6:19	20:31	6:09	20:44	6:00	20:56	5:49	21:11	5:34	21:31
15	7:28	20:45	7:13	21:02	7:04	21:12	6:55	21:23	6:43	21:37	6:30	21:53	6:16	22:10	6:00	22:31	5:38	23:00
16	8:09	21:39	7:50	22:00	7:40	22:12	7:27	22:26	7:13	22:43	6:55	23:03	6:37	23:24	6:15	23:51	5:45	—
17	8:55	22:36	8:33	22:59	8:20	23:13	8:06	23:28	7:49	23:47	7:27	—	7:06	—	6:38	—	5:58	0:30
18	9:46	23:33	9:22	23:57	9:08	—	8:52	—	8:33	—	8:09	0:11	7:45	0:35	7:12	1:07	6:23	1:55
19	10:41	—	10:17	—	10:03	0:11	9:47	0:27	9:27	0:47	9:03	1:11	8:38	1:37	8:04	2:11	7:11	3:03
20	11:41	0:28	11:18	0:52	11:05	1:05	10:50	1:21	10:31	1:40	10:09	2:03	9:45	2:27	9:14	2:58	8:28	3:45
21	12:43	1:21	12:23	1:42	12:12	1:54	11:59	2:08	11:43	2:25	11:24	2:45	11:05	3:05	10:39	3:31	10:05	4:07
22	13:46	2:11	13:30	2:28	13:22	2:38	13:12	2:49	13:00	3:02	12:45	3:18	12:31	3:34	12:13	3:53	11:49	4:19
23	14:48	2:58	14:38	3:10	14:33	3:17	14:26	3:25	14:18	3:34	14:09	3:45	14:00	3:56	13:49	4:09	13:35	4:26
24	15:51	3:42	15:46	3:49	15:44	3:53	15:41	3:57	15:38	4:02	15:34	4:08	15:31	4:14	15:26	4:21	15:20	4:30
25	16:53	4:25	16:55	4:26	16:56	4:27	16:57	4:27	16:58	4:28	17:00	4:29	17:01	4:30	17:03	4:32	17:06	4:33
26	17:56	5:07	18:03	5:03	18:08	5:00	18:13	4:57	18:18	4:54	18:25	4:50	18:32	4:46	18:41	4:42	18:52	4:36
27	18:59	5:51	19:12	5:41	19:20	5:35	19:28	5:29	19:39	5:21	19:51	5:12	20:04	5:04	20:19	4:53	20:39	4:39
28	20:03	6:37	20:21	6:22	20:31	6:13	20:43	6:03	20:58	5:52	21:15	5:38	21:33	5:24	21:56	5:07	22:27	4:45
29	21:06	7:27	21:28	7:07	21:40	6:56	21:55	6:42	22:13	6:27	22:35	6:08	22:57	5:50	23:27	5:26	—	4:53
30	22:07	8:19	22:31	7:56	22:45	7:43	23:01	7:27	23:21	7:09	23:45	6:47	—	6:24	—	5:53	0:10	5:09

MOONRISE AND MOONSET, 2002 MAY
UNIVERSAL TIME AT GREENWICH MERIDIAN

Latitude: Event:	+62° RISE	SET	+58° RISE	SET	+54° RISE	SET	+50° RISE	SET	+45° RISE	SET	+40° RISE	SET	+35° RISE	SET	+30° RISE	SET	+20° RISE	SET
May 1	1:38	5:41	0:45	6:34	0:10	7:09	—	7:34	—	7:59	23:59	8:19	23:42	8:35	23:28	8:50	23:04	9:14
2	2:37	6:38	1:43	7:32	1:09	8:06	0:43	8:31	0:19	8:56	—	9:15	—	9:32	—	9:46	23:56	10:10
3	3:08	7:57	2:23	8:42	1:52	9:12	1:29	9:35	1:06	9:57	0:48	10:15	0:32	10:30	0:19	10:43	—	11:05
4	3:24	9:25	2:49	9:59	2:24	10:24	2:04	10:43	1:44	11:01	1:28	11:17	1:15	11:29	1:03	11:41	0:42	12:00
5	3:32	10:53	3:06	11:18	2:47	11:36	2:31	11:51	2:15	12:05	2:02	12:17	1:51	12:28	1:41	12:36	1:24	12:52
6	3:36	12:19	3:18	12:35	3:04	12:48	2:53	12:58	2:41	13:08	2:31	13:17	2:22	13:24	2:15	13:31	2:02	13:42
7	3:39	13:42	3:28	13:51	3:18	13:58	3:11	14:04	3:03	14:11	2:56	14:16	2:51	14:20	2:46	14:24	2:37	14:31
8	3:41	15:03	3:35	15:06	3:31	15:08	3:27	15:10	3:23	15:12	3:20	15:14	3:17	15:15	3:15	15:17	3:10	15:19
9	3:42	16:24	3:42	16:21	3:42	16:18	3:43	16:16	3:43	16:14	3:43	16:12	3:43	16:11	3:43	16:09	3:43	16:07
10	3:44	17:47	3:50	17:37	3:54	17:30	3:58	17:23	4:02	17:17	4:06	17:12	4:09	17:07	4:11	17:03	4:16	16:56
11	3:46	19:13	3:58	18:56	4:07	18:43	4:15	18:32	4:23	18:21	4:30	18:12	4:36	18:05	4:41	17:58	4:50	17:46
12	3:49	20:43	4:08	20:17	4:23	19:58	4:35	19:43	4:47	19:27	4:57	19:15	5:06	19:04	5:14	18:55	5:27	18:39
13	3:55	22:15	4:22	21:39	4:42	21:14	4:58	20:54	5:15	20:35	5:28	20:19	5:40	20:05	5:50	19:54	6:07	19:34
14	4:05	23:44	4:41	22:58	5:08	22:27	5:28	22:03	5:49	21:41	6:05	21:22	6:19	21:07	6:31	20:54	6:52	20:31
15	4:24	—	5:11	—	5:43	23:33	6:07	23:07	6:30	22:43	6:49	22:23	7:05	22:07	7:19	21:53	7:42	21:28
16	5:04	1:00	5:57	0:07	6:32	—	6:57	—	7:22	23:38	7:42	23:19	7:58	23:03	8:12	22:49	8:37	22:25
17	6:12	1:50	7:02	1:00	7:35	0:27	7:59	0:02	8:23	—	8:42	—	8:58	23:53	9:12	23:40	9:35	23:18
18	7:44	2:17	8:23	1:37	8:50	1:08	9:11	0:47	9:32	0:25	9:49	0:08	10:03	—	10:15	—	10:36	—
19	9:25	2:30	9:53	2:01	10:14	1:39	10:30	1:22	10:46	1:04	10:59	0:50	11:10	0:38	11:20	0:27	11:37	0:08
20	11:08	2:38	11:26	2:18	11:40	2:02	11:51	1:50	12:02	1:37	12:11	1:26	12:19	1:17	12:26	1:09	12:38	0:55
21	12:51	2:42	13:00	2:30	13:07	2:21	13:13	2:13	13:19	2:05	13:24	1:58	13:28	1:53	13:32	1:47	13:39	1:38
22	14:32	2:45	14:33	2:40	14:34	2:37	14:35	2:34	14:36	2:31	14:37	2:28	14:37	2:26	14:38	2:24	14:39	2:20
23	16:15	2:47	16:08	2:50	16:02	2:52	15:58	2:54	15:54	2:55	15:50	2:57	15:47	2:58	15:44	2:59	15:39	3:01
24	17:59	2:50	17:44	3:00	17:32	3:08	17:22	3:14	17:12	3:21	17:04	3:26	16:57	3:31	16:51	3:35	16:40	3:43
25	19:46	2:54	19:20	3:12	19:01	3:25	18:46	3:37	18:31	3:48	18:18	3:58	18:08	4:06	17:59	4:14	17:43	4:27
26	21:32	3:00	20:55	3:27	20:28	3:48	20:08	4:04	19:48	4:21	19:32	4:34	19:18	4:46	19:07	4:56	18:47	5:14
27	23:11	3:11	22:21	3:50	21:49	4:17	21:24	4:38	21:01	4:59	20:42	5:16	20:26	5:30	20:12	5:43	19:49	6:04
28	—	3:33	23:31	4:24	22:56	4:57	22:30	5:21	22:05	5:45	21:45	6:05	21:28	6:21	21:14	6:35	20:49	6:59
29	0:27	4:18	—	5:14	23:47	5:49	23:22	6:15	22:58	6:40	22:39	7:00	22:23	7:17	22:09	7:31	21:45	7:55
30	1:11	5:30	0:20	6:20	—	6:53	—	7:17	23:41	7:41	23:24	8:00	23:10	8:16	22:57	8:29	22:35	8:53
31	1:32	6:58	0:52	7:37	0:24	8:04	0:03	8:25	—	8:46	—	9:02	23:49	9:16	23:38	9:28	23:20	9:49

MOONRISE AND MOONSET, 2002 JUNE
UNIVERSAL TIME AT GREENWICH MERIDIAN

Latitude:	+20°		+30°		+35°		+40°		+45°		+50°		+54°		+58°		+62°	
Event:	RISE	SET	RISE	SET	RISE	SET	RISE	SET	RISE	SET	RISE	SET	RISE	SET	RISE	SET	RISE	SET
Jun. 1	—	10:43	—	10:26	—	10:16	0:01	10:04	0:16	9:51	0:33	9:34	0:51	9:18	1:13	8:57	1:43	8:29
2	0:00	11:35	0:14	11:22	0:23	11:14	0:33	11:06	0:44	10:56	0:57	10:43	1:11	10:31	1:27	10:16	1:48	9:57
3	0:36	12:24	0:47	12:16	0:53	12:11	1:00	12:05	1:07	11:59	1:17	11:51	1:26	11:43	1:37	11:33	1:51	11:21
4	1:10	13:13	1:16	13:09	1:20	13:06	1:24	13:04	1:28	13:01	1:34	12:57	1:39	12:53	1:45	12:49	1:53	12:43
5	1:43	14:00	1:45	14:01	1:46	14:01	1:47	14:02	1:48	14:02	1:49	14:03	1:51	14:03	1:52	14:04	1:55	14:05
6	2:15	14:49	2:13	14:54	2:11	14:57	2:09	15:01	2:07	15:04	2:05	15:09	2:02	15:14	1:59	15:20	1:56	15:27
7	2:49	15:39	2:42	15:49	2:38	15:54	2:33	16:01	2:27	16:08	2:21	16:17	2:15	16:26	2:07	16:37	1:58	16:51
8	3:25	16:31	3:13	16:45	3:06	16:53	2:59	17:03	2:50	17:14	2:39	17:27	2:29	17:41	2:16	17:58	2:00	18:20
9	4:04	17:25	3:48	17:44	3:39	17:54	3:28	18:07	3:16	18:21	3:01	18:39	2:46	18:57	2:28	19:20	2:05	19:52
10	4:47	18:22	4:27	18:44	4:16	18:57	4:03	19:11	3:47	19:29	3:28	19:51	3:10	20:13	2:45	20:42	2:13	21:25
11	5:36	19:21	5:13	19:44	5:00	19:58	4:45	20:15	4:27	20:34	4:04	20:58	3:41	21:23	3:11	21:57	2:28	22:49
12	6:30	20:19	6:06	20:43	5:51	20:57	5:35	21:14	5:15	21:33	4:51	21:58	4:26	22:23	3:52	22:57	3:00	23:50
13	7:28	21:14	7:04	21:37	6:50	21:50	6:34	22:06	6:14	22:24	5:50	22:47	5:25	23:09	4:51	23:40	3:59	—
14	8:29	22:06	8:08	22:26	7:55	22:37	7:40	22:51	7:22	23:06	7:01	23:25	6:38	23:44	6:09	—	5:26	0:23
15	9:31	22:54	9:13	23:10	9:03	23:19	8:50	23:29	8:36	23:41	8:18	23:55	8:01	—	7:38	0:08	7:07	0:40
16	10:33	23:38	10:19	23:49	10:11	23:55	10:02	—	9:52	—	9:39	—	9:26	0:09	9:11	0:26	8:50	0:49
17	11:33	—	11:24	—	11:20	—	11:14	0:02	11:08	0:10	11:00	0:19	10:53	0:28	10:44	0:40	10:32	0:54
18	12:32	0:20	12:29	0:25	12:27	0:28	12:25	0:32	12:23	0:35	12:21	0:40	12:18	0:45	12:16	0:50	12:12	0:57
19	13:30	1:00	13:33	1:00	13:35	1:00	13:37	1:00	13:39	1:00	13:41	1:00	13:44	0:59	13:47	0:59	13:51	0:59
20	14:30	1:40	14:38	1:34	14:43	1:31	14:48	1:28	14:55	1:24	15:03	1:19	15:10	1:14	15:20	1:09	15:32	1:02
21	15:30	2:21	15:44	2:11	15:51	2:05	16:01	1:58	16:11	1:50	16:24	1:40	16:37	1:31	16:53	1:19	17:14	1:05
22	16:31	3:06	16:50	2:50	17:01	2:41	17:13	2:31	17:27	2:19	17:45	2:04	18:04	1:50	18:27	1:32	18:59	1:09
23	17:34	3:54	17:56	3:34	18:08	3:22	18:23	3:09	18:41	2:54	19:03	2:34	19:26	2:15	19:56	1:51	20:40	1:18
24	18:34	4:46	18:59	4:23	19:13	4:09	19:29	3:54	19:49	3:36	20:13	3:13	20:39	2:49	21:14	2:19	22:08	1:34
25	19:32	5:41	19:57	5:17	20:11	5:03	20:27	4:46	20:47	4:26	21:12	4:01	21:38	3:36	22:12	3:01	23:06	2:06
26	20:25	6:39	20:48	6:15	21:01	6:01	21:17	5:44	21:35	5:25	21:58	5:00	22:21	4:35	22:52	4:00	23:36	3:07
27	21:13	7:36	21:33	7:14	21:44	7:01	21:58	6:46	22:14	6:29	22:33	6:06	22:52	5:44	23:17	5:14	23:51	4:30
28	21:55	8:32	22:12	8:13	22:21	8:02	22:32	7:50	22:44	7:35	23:00	7:16	23:15	6:58	23:33	6:34	23:58	6:02
29	22:34	9:25	22:46	9:10	22:53	9:02	23:01	8:52	23:10	8:41	23:21	8:27	23:32	8:13	23:45	7:55	—	7:32
30	23:09	10:16	23:16	10:06	23:21	10:00	23:26	9:53	23:32	9:45	23:39	9:35	23:46	9:26	23:54	9:14	0:02	8:59

MOONRISE AND MOONSET, 2002 JULY
UNIVERSAL TIME AT GREENWICH MERIDIAN

Latitude:	+20°		+30°		+35°		+40°		+45°		+50°		+54°		+58°		+62°	
Event:	RISE	SET	RISE	SET	RISE	SET	RISE	SET	RISE	SET	RISE	SET	RISE	SET	RISE	SET	RISE	SET
Jul. 1	23:42	11:05	23:45	10:59	23:47	10:56	23:49	10:52	23:52	10:48	23:55	10:42	23:58	10:37	—	10:31	0:04	10:23
2	—	11:53	—	11:52	—	11:51	—	11:50	—	11:49	—	11:48	—	11:47	0:02	11:46	0:06	11:44
3	0:14	12:41	0:13	12:44	0:13	12:46	0:12	12:49	0:11	12:51	0:10	12:54	0:10	12:57	0:09	13:01	0:07	13:05
4	0:47	13:30	0:42	13:38	0:38	13:42	0:35	13:48	0:31	13:54	0:26	14:01	0:21	14:08	0:16	14:17	0:09	14:28
5	1:22	14:21	1:12	14:33	1:06	14:40	0:59	14:48	0:52	14:58	0:43	15:10	0:34	15:21	0:24	15:36	0:11	15:54
6	1:59	15:14	1:45	15:30	1:36	15:40	1:27	15:51	1:16	16:04	1:03	16:21	0:50	16:37	0:35	16:57	0:14	17:24
7	2:40	16:10	2:22	16:30	2:11	16:42	1:59	16:56	1:45	17:12	1:28	17:32	1:11	17:53	0:49	18:20	0:20	18:57
8	3:26	17:08	3:05	17:31	2:52	17:45	2:38	18:00	2:21	18:19	2:00	18:42	1:38	19:06	1:11	19:39	0:32	20:27
9	4:19	18:07	3:55	18:31	3:41	18:45	3:25	19:02	3:06	19:22	2:42	19:46	2:17	20:12	1:45	20:46	0:56	21:40
10	5:16	19:05	4:52	19:28	4:38	19:42	4:21	19:58	4:02	20:17	3:37	20:41	3:11	21:05	2:37	21:37	1:43	22:24
11	6:18	20:00	5:55	20:21	5:42	20:33	5:26	20:47	5:08	21:03	4:45	21:24	4:21	21:44	3:50	22:10	3:03	22:47
12	7:21	20:50	7:02	21:07	6:50	21:17	6:37	21:28	6:21	21:41	6:02	21:57	5:43	22:13	5:18	22:32	4:42	22:58
13	8:25	21:36	8:09	21:49	8:01	21:56	7:51	22:04	7:39	22:13	7:24	22:24	7:10	22:34	6:52	22:47	6:28	23:04
14	9:26	22:19	9:16	22:26	9:11	22:30	9:04	22:35	8:57	22:40	8:47	22:46	8:38	22:52	8:27	22:59	8:13	23:08
15	10:26	23:00	10:22	23:02	10:20	23:03	10:17	23:03	10:13	23:05	10:09	23:06	10:06	23:07	10:01	23:09	9:55	23:10
16	11:25	23:40	11:27	23:36	11:27	23:34	11:28	23:31	11:29	23:29	11:30	23:25	11:32	23:22	11:33	23:18	11:35	23:13
17	12:24	—	12:31	—	12:35	—	12:39	—	12:45	23:53	12:51	23:45	12:57	23:37	13:05	23:28	13:14	23:15
18	13:23	0:21	13:35	0:12	13:42	0:06	13:50	0:00	14:00	—	14:11	—	14:22	23:55	14:36	23:40	14:55	23:19
19	14:23	1:03	14:40	0:49	14:50	0:41	15:01	0:32	15:15	0:21	15:31	0:08	15:48	—	16:08	23:56	16:37	23:26
20	15:24	1:49	15:45	1:31	15:57	1:20	16:11	1:07	16:28	0:53	16:49	0:35	17:10	0:18	17:38	—	18:18	23:38
21	16:24	2:39	16:48	2:17	17:01	2:04	17:17	1:49	17:37	1:31	18:01	1:10	18:25	0:48	18:59	0:19	19:50	—
22	17:22	3:32	17:47	3:08	18:01	2:54	18:18	2:37	18:38	2:18	19:03	1:53	19:29	1:28	20:04	0:55	20:59	0:03
23	18:16	4:28	18:40	4:03	18:54	3:49	19:10	3:33	19:29	3:13	19:53	2:48	20:17	2:22	20:50	1:47	21:38	0:52
24	19:06	5:25	19:27	5:02	19:40	4:48	19:54	4:33	20:11	4:14	20:31	3:51	20:52	3:27	21:19	2:55	21:57	2:07
25	19:50	6:21	20:08	6:01	20:18	5:49	20:30	5:36	20:44	5:20	21:01	5:00	21:18	4:40	21:39	4:13	22:07	3:36
26	20:30	7:16	20:44	6:59	20:52	6:50	21:01	6:39	21:12	6:26	21:24	6:10	21:37	5:55	21:52	5:35	22:12	5:08
27	21:07	8:08	21:16	7:56	21:22	7:49	21:28	7:41	21:35	7:31	21:44	7:20	21:52	7:09	22:02	6:55	22:15	6:37
28	21:40	8:58	21:46	8:50	21:49	8:46	21:52	8:41	21:56	8:35	22:00	8:28	22:05	8:21	22:10	8:13	22:16	8:02
29	22:13	9:46	22:14	9:43	22:14	9:42	22:15	9:40	22:15	9:37	22:16	9:35	22:16	9:32	22:17	9:29	22:18	9:25
30	22:46	10:34	22:42	10:36	22:40	10:37	22:37	10:38	22:34	10:39	22:31	10:40	22:28	10:42	22:24	10:44	22:19	10:46
31	23:19	11:22	23:11	11:28	23:06	11:32	23:01	11:36	22:54	11:41	22:47	11:46	22:40	11:52	22:31	11:59	22:21	12:07

MOONRISE AND MOONSET, 2002 AUGUST
UNIVERSAL TIME AT GREENWICH MERIDIAN

Latitude: Event:	+20° RISE	SET	+30° RISE	SET	+35° RISE	SET	+40° RISE	SET	+45° RISE	SET	+50° RISE	SET	+54° RISE	SET	+58° RISE	SET	+62° RISE	SET
Aug. 1	23:54	12:11	23:42	12:22	23:34	12:28	23:26	12:35	23:17	12:44	23:05	12:54	22:54	13:03	22:41	13:16	22:23	13:31
2	—	13:03	—	13:18	—	13:26	23:56	13:36	23:43	13:48	23:27	14:03	23:12	14:17	22:53	14:35	22:28	14:58
3	0:33	13:57	0:16	14:16	0:07	14:27	—	14:39	—	14:54	23:55	15:13	23:36	15:32	23:11	15:56	22:36	16:29
4	1:16	14:53	0:56	15:15	0:44	15:28	0:31	15:43	0:15	16:01	—	16:23	—	16:46	23:38	17:16	22:53	18:01
5	2:05	15:51	1:42	16:15	1:29	16:30	1:13	16:46	0:55	17:06	0:32	17:30	0:09	17:55	—	18:30	23:28	19:23
6	3:00	16:50	2:36	17:14	2:22	17:28	2:05	17:45	1:46	18:04	1:21	18:29	0:55	18:54	0:21	19:28	—	20:20
7	4:01	17:47	3:37	18:09	3:23	18:22	3:07	18:37	2:47	18:55	2:23	19:17	1:58	19:39	1:25	20:09	0:33	20:50
8	5:04	18:40	4:43	18:59	4:31	19:10	4:16	19:22	3:59	19:37	3:38	19:55	3:16	20:13	2:48	20:35	2:07	21:05
9	6:09	19:29	5:52	19:43	5:42	19:52	5:31	20:01	5:17	20:12	5:01	20:25	4:44	20:37	4:23	20:53	3:54	21:13
10	7:14	20:15	7:02	20:24	6:55	20:29	6:47	20:35	6:37	20:41	6:26	20:49	6:15	20:57	6:01	21:06	5:43	21:18
11	8:16	20:57	8:10	21:01	8:06	21:03	8:02	21:05	7:57	21:07	7:51	21:10	7:46	21:13	7:39	21:16	7:30	21:21
12	9:17	21:39	9:17	21:36	9:17	21:35	9:16	21:34	9:16	21:32	9:15	21:30	9:15	21:28	9:14	21:26	9:14	21:23
13	10:18	22:20	10:23	22:12	10:26	22:08	10:29	22:03	10:33	21:57	10:38	21:50	10:43	21:43	10:48	21:35	10:56	21:25
14	11:18	23:02	11:28	22:49	11:35	22:42	11:42	22:34	11:50	22:24	12:00	22:12	12:10	22:01	12:22	21:47	12:38	21:29
15	12:18	23:47	12:34	23:30	12:43	23:20	12:53	23:08	13:06	22:54	13:21	22:38	13:36	22:22	13:55	22:01	14:21	21:34
16	13:18	—	13:38	—	13:50	—	14:04	23:47	14:20	23:31	14:40	23:10	15:00	22:49	15:26	22:22	16:03	21:44
17	14:18	0:35	14:41	0:14	14:55	0:02	15:11	—	15:29	—	15:53	23:50	16:17	23:26	16:49	22:53	17:38	22:03
18	15:17	1:27	15:41	1:03	15:55	0:49	16:12	0:33	16:32	0:14	16:57	—	17:23	—	17:59	23:39	18:55	22:43
19	16:11	2:22	16:35	1:57	16:50	1:43	17:06	1:26	17:26	1:06	17:50	0:41	18:15	0:14	18:49	—	19:42	23:50
20	17:02	3:18	17:24	2:54	17:37	2:40	17:52	2:24	18:10	2:05	18:32	1:41	18:54	1:16	19:23	0:42	20:05	—
21	17:47	4:14	18:06	3:52	18:17	3:40	18:30	3:26	18:45	3:08	19:03	2:47	19:22	2:26	19:45	1:57	20:16	1:16
22	18:28	5:08	18:43	4:51	18:52	4:40	19:02	4:28	19:14	4:14	19:28	3:57	19:42	3:40	20:00	3:18	20:22	2:47
23	19:05	6:01	19:17	5:47	19:23	5:40	19:30	5:30	19:39	5:20	19:49	5:07	19:58	4:54	20:10	4:38	20:25	4:17
24	19:40	6:52	19:47	6:43	19:50	6:37	19:55	6:31	20:00	6:24	20:06	6:16	20:11	6:07	20:18	5:57	20:27	5:44
25	20:13	7:41	20:15	7:36	20:16	7:34	20:18	7:31	20:19	7:27	20:21	7:23	20:23	7:19	20:25	7:14	20:28	7:07
26	20:45	8:29	20:43	8:29	20:42	8:29	20:40	8:29	20:38	8:29	20:36	8:29	20:34	8:29	20:32	8:29	20:29	8:29
27	21:18	9:16	21:11	9:21	21:07	9:24	21:03	9:27	20:58	9:30	20:52	9:35	20:46	9:39	20:39	9:44	20:30	9:50
28	21:52	10:05	21:41	10:14	21:34	10:19	21:27	10:25	21:19	10:33	21:09	10:41	20:59	10:49	20:47	11:00	20:32	11:13
29	22:29	10:55	22:13	11:08	22:05	11:16	21:55	11:25	21:43	11:36	21:29	11:49	21:15	12:01	20:58	12:17	20:35	12:38
30	23:09	11:47	22:50	12:04	22:39	12:15	22:26	12:27	22:12	12:41	21:53	12:58	21:35	13:15	21:12	13:37	20:41	14:07
31	23:55	12:41	23:33	13:02	23:20	13:15	23:05	13:29	22:47	13:46	22:25	14:07	22:03	14:28	21:34	14:57	20:53	15:37

MOONRISE AND MOONSET, 2002 SEPTEMBER
UNIVERSAL TIME AT GREENWICH MERIDIAN

| Latitude: | +20° | | +30° | | +35° | | +40° | | +45° | | +50° | | +54° | | +58° | | +62° | |
Event:	RISE	SET	RISE	SET	RISE	SET	RISE	SET	RISE	SET	RISE	SET	RISE	SET	RISE	SET	RISE	SET
Sep. 1	—	13:37	—	14:01	—	14:15	23:51	14:31	23:32	14:50	23:07	15:14	22:42	15:39	22:08	16:12	21:17	17:04
2	0:46	14:35	0:22	14:59	0:08	15:14	—	15:30	—	15:50	—	16:16	23:36	16:41	23:01	17:17	22:06	18:12
3	1:43	15:31	1:18	15:55	1:04	16:09	0:47	16:25	0:27	16:44	0:02	17:08	—	17:32	—	18:04	23:28	18:52
4	2:44	16:26	2:21	16:47	2:08	16:59	1:52	17:13	1:34	17:29	1:11	17:50	0:47	18:10	0:15	18:36	—	19:12
5	3:48	17:17	3:29	17:34	3:18	17:43	3:04	17:54	2:49	18:07	2:30	18:23	2:10	18:38	1:46	18:57	1:11	19:22
6	4:53	18:04	4:39	18:16	4:30	18:23	4:20	18:30	4:09	18:39	3:55	18:49	3:41	18:59	3:24	19:12	3:01	19:27
7	5:58	18:49	5:49	18:55	5:44	18:58	5:38	19:02	5:31	19:07	5:22	19:12	5:14	19:17	5:04	19:23	4:51	19:30
8	7:02	19:32	6:58	19:32	6:57	19:32	6:55	19:32	6:52	19:32	6:49	19:32	6:47	19:32	6:43	19:32	6:39	19:33
9	8:04	20:14	8:07	20:09	8:09	20:06	8:11	20:02	8:13	19:58	8:16	19:53	8:18	19:48	8:21	19:42	8:26	19:35
10	9:06	20:58	9:15	20:47	9:20	20:40	9:26	20:33	9:33	20:24	9:41	20:14	9:49	20:04	9:59	19:52	10:12	19:37
11	10:09	21:43	10:23	21:27	10:31	21:17	10:41	21:07	10:52	20:54	11:06	20:39	11:19	20:24	11:36	20:06	11:59	19:41
12	11:11	22:31	11:30	22:11	11:41	21:59	11:54	21:45	12:09	21:29	12:28	21:09	12:47	20:50	13:11	20:24	13:45	19:49
13	12:13	23:23	12:35	22:59	12:48	22:46	13:04	22:30	13:22	22:11	13:45	21:47	14:08	21:23	14:40	20:52	15:26	20:04
14	13:12	—	13:37	23:52	13:51	23:38	14:08	23:21	14:28	23:01	14:53	22:35	15:19	22:09	15:55	21:33	16:52	20:36
15	14:08	0:17	14:33	—	14:47	—	15:04	—	15:24	23:58	15:50	23:33	16:16	23:07	16:51	22:32	17:48	21:36
16	15:00	1:13	15:23	0:49	15:36	0:34	15:52	0:18	16:11	—	16:34	—	16:58	—	17:29	23:44	18:15	22:58
17	15:46	2:09	16:07	1:46	16:18	1:33	16:32	1:18	16:48	1:00	17:08	0:38	17:28	0:15	17:53	—	18:28	—
18	16:28	3:04	16:45	2:44	16:54	2:33	17:05	2:21	17:18	2:05	17:34	1:47	17:49	1:28	18:09	1:03	18:34	0:30
19	17:06	3:56	17:19	3:41	17:26	3:33	17:34	3:23	17:44	3:11	17:55	2:56	18:06	2:42	18:20	2:24	18:37	2:00
20	17:41	4:47	17:49	4:37	17:54	4:31	17:59	4:24	18:05	4:15	18:13	4:05	18:20	3:55	18:28	3:43	18:39	3:28
21	18:14	5:37	18:18	5:31	18:20	5:27	18:22	5:23	18:25	5:18	18:28	5:13	18:31	5:07	18:35	5:01	18:40	4:52
22	18:46	6:25	18:45	6:23	18:45	6:23	18:44	6:22	18:44	6:21	18:43	6:19	18:42	6:18	18:41	6:16	18:40	6:14
23	19:19	7:13	19:13	7:16	19:10	7:18	19:07	7:20	19:03	7:22	18:58	7:25	18:53	7:28	18:48	7:32	18:41	7:36
24	19:52	8:01	19:42	8:09	19:37	8:13	19:30	8:18	19:23	8:24	19:14	8:32	19:05	8:39	18:55	8:47	18:42	8:58
25	20:28	8:50	20:13	9:02	20:05	9:09	19:56	9:18	19:45	9:27	19:32	9:39	19:20	9:50	19:04	10:04	18:44	10:23
26	21:06	9:41	20:48	9:57	20:38	10:07	20:26	10:18	20:12	10:31	19:55	10:47	19:38	11:03	19:16	11:23	18:48	11:50
27	21:49	10:34	21:28	10:54	21:15	11:06	21:01	11:20	20:44	11:36	20:23	11:56	20:02	12:16	19:34	12:43	18:56	13:20
28	22:37	11:28	22:13	11:52	21:59	12:05	21:43	12:21	21:24	12:40	21:00	13:03	20:35	13:27	20:02	14:00	19:13	14:48
29	23:30	12:24	23:05	12:49	22:51	13:03	22:34	13:20	22:13	13:43	21:48	14:06	21:22	14:32	20:46	15:08	19:48	16:05
30	—	13:20	—	13:44	23:50	13:59	23:33	14:15	23:14	14:35	22:49	15:00	22:23	15:26	21:49	16:01	20:55	16:55

MOONRISE AND MOONSET, 2002 OCTOBER
UNIVERSAL TIME AT GREENWICH MERIDIAN

Latitude:	+20°		+30°		+35°		+40°		+45°		+50°		+54°		+58°		+62°	
Event:	RISE	SET	RISE	SET	RISE	SET	RISE	SET	RISE	SET	RISE	SET	RISE	SET	RISE	SET	RISE	SET
Oct. 1	0:28	14:13	0:04	14:36	—	14:49	—	15:04	—	15:22	—	15:45	23:40	16:07	23:11	16:37	22:29	17:20
2	1:29	15:04	1:08	15:24	0:55	15:35	0:40	15:47	0:23	16:02	0:02	16:20	—	16:38	—	17:01	—	17:32
3	2:32	15:52	2:15	16:07	2:05	16:15	1:53	16:25	1:39	16:36	1:23	16:49	1:06	17:02	0:44	17:17	0:15	17:38
4	3:36	16:38	3:24	16:47	3:17	16:52	3:09	16:58	2:59	17:04	2:48	17:12	2:37	17:20	2:23	17:29	2:04	17:41
5	4:40	17:21	4:33	17:24	4:30	17:26	4:26	17:28	4:21	17:31	4:15	17:33	4:09	17:36	4:02	17:39	3:53	17:43
6	5:43	18:04	5:43	18:01	5:43	18:00	5:43	17:58	5:43	17:56	5:42	17:53	5:42	17:51	5:42	17:48	5:42	17:45
7	6:47	18:48	6:53	18:39	6:56	18:34	7:00	18:29	7:05	18:22	7:10	18:14	7:16	18:07	7:22	17:58	7:31	17:46
8	7:51	19:33	8:03	19:19	8:10	19:11	8:18	19:02	8:27	18:51	8:38	18:38	8:49	18:25	9:03	18:09	9:21	17:49
9	8:56	20:22	9:13	20:03	9:23	19:52	9:35	19:39	9:49	19:24	10:05	19:06	10:22	18:48	10:44	18:25	11:13	17:55
10	10:00	21:14	10:22	20:51	10:35	20:38	10:49	20:23	11:07	20:05	11:29	19:42	11:51	19:19	12:20	18:49	13:03	18:05
11	11:03	22:09	11:28	21:44	11:42	21:30	11:58	21:13	12:18	20:53	12:43	20:27	13:09	20:01	13:45	19:25	14:41	18:29
12	12:02	23:06	12:28	22:41	12:42	22:26	13:00	22:09	13:20	21:49	13:46	21:23	14:13	20:56	14:50	20:19	15:50	19:19
13	12:57	—	13:21	23:40	13:35	23:26	13:51	23:10	14:11	22:51	14:35	22:27	15:00	22:03	15:34	21:30	16:25	20:39
14	13:45	0:03	14:07	—	14:19	—	14:34	—	14:51	23:56	15:12	23:36	15:34	23:16	16:01	22:49	16:40	22:11
15	14:28	0:59	14:47	0:39	14:57	0:27	15:09	0:13	15:23	—	15:40	—	15:57	—	16:19	—	16:47	23:43
16	15:07	1:53	15:21	1:36	15:29	1:26	15:39	1:15	15:49	1:02	16:02	0:46	16:15	0:30	16:31	0:10	16:51	—
17	15:43	2:44	15:53	2:32	15:58	2:25	16:04	2:17	16:12	2:07	16:20	1:56	16:29	1:44	16:39	1:30	16:52	1:12
18	16:16	3:33	16:21	3:26	16:24	3:21	16:28	3:16	16:32	3:10	16:36	3:03	16:41	2:56	16:46	2:48	16:53	2:37
19	16:48	4:22	16:49	4:19	16:49	4:17	16:50	4:15	16:50	4:13	16:51	4:10	16:51	4:07	16:52	4:04	16:53	4:00
20	17:20	5:09	17:17	5:11	17:14	5:12	17:12	5:13	17:09	5:15	17:05	5:16	17:02	5:18	16:58	5:19	16:53	5:22
21	17:53	5:58	17:45	6:04	17:40	6:08	17:35	6:12	17:28	6:17	17:21	6:22	17:13	6:28	17:05	6:35	16:54	6:44
22	18:28	6:47	18:15	6:57	18:08	7:04	18:00	7:11	17:50	7:20	17:38	7:30	17:27	7:40	17:13	7:52	16:55	8:08
23	19:06	7:37	18:49	7:52	18:39	8:01	18:28	8:12	18:15	8:24	17:59	8:38	17:43	8:53	17:23	9:11	16:58	9:36
24	19:47	8:29	19:27	8:49	19:14	9:00	19:01	9:13	18:44	9:28	18:25	9:47	18:05	10:07	17:39	10:31	17:03	11:06
25	20:33	9:24	20:10	9:46	19:56	9:59	19:40	10:15	19:21	10:33	18:58	10:56	18:34	11:19	18:02	11:50	17:15	12:36
26	21:24	10:19	20:59	10:43	20:44	10:58	20:27	11:14	20:07	11:34	19:41	12:00	19:15	12:26	18:39	13:02	17:42	13:59
27	22:19	11:13	21:54	11:38	21:39	11:53	21:22	12:10	21:02	12:31	20:37	12:56	20:10	13:23	19:34	13:59	18:36	14:58
28	23:17	12:07	22:54	12:30	22:41	12:44	22:25	13:00	22:07	13:19	21:44	13:43	21:20	14:08	20:48	14:40	20:00	15:29
29	—	12:57	23:58	13:18	23:47	13:30	23:34	13:44	23:18	14:00	22:59	14:21	22:40	14:41	22:15	15:07	21:40	15:43
30	0:18	13:44	—	14:01	—	14:11	—	14:22	—	14:35	—	14:50	—	15:06	23:49	15:25	23:25	15:50
31	1:19	14:29	1:04	14:41	0:56	14:47	0:46	14:55	0:34	15:04	0:20	15:15	0:06	15:25	—	15:37	—	15:53

MOONRISE AND MOONSET, 2002 NOVEMBER
UNIVERSAL TIME AT GREENWICH MERIDIAN

Latitude:	+62°		+58°		+54°		+50°		+45°		+40°		+35°		+30°		+20°	
Event:	RISE	SET	RISE	SET	RISE	SET	RISE	SET	RISE	SET	RISE	SET	RISE	SET	RISE	SET	RISE	SET
Nov. 1	1:11	15:55	1:25	15:47	1:35	15:41	1:44	15:35	1:52	15:30	1:59	15:25	2:06	15:21	2:11	15:18	2:20	15:12
2	2:57	15:56	3:02	15:56	3:05	15:55	3:08	15:55	3:12	15:55	3:14	15:54	3:17	15:54	3:19	15:54	3:22	15:53
3	4:44	15:57	4:40	16:04	4:37	16:10	4:35	16:15	4:32	16:19	4:30	16:24	4:28	16:27	4:27	16:30	4:24	16:36
4	6:33	15:59	6:20	16:14	6:10	16:26	6:02	16:36	5:54	16:46	5:47	16:55	5:42	17:02	5:37	17:09	5:28	17:20
5	8:26	16:02	8:03	16:27	7:45	16:46	7:31	17:02	7:17	17:17	7:06	17:30	6:56	17:41	6:48	17:51	6:33	18:08
6	10:21	16:09	9:44	16:46	9:19	17:13	8:59	17:34	8:40	17:55	8:24	18:11	8:11	18:26	7:59	18:38	7:39	18:59
7	12:11	16:24	11:20	17:16	10:46	17:50	10:22	18:16	9:58	18:40	9:38	19:00	9:23	19:16	9:09	19:30	8:45	19:55
8	13:40	17:01	12:38	18:03	12:00	18:41	11:33	19:08	11:07	19:35	10:46	19:55	10:29	20:13	10:14	20:28	9:49	20:53
9	14:30	18:13	13:33	19:10	12:56	19:45	12:30	20:12	12:04	20:37	11:44	20:57	11:27	21:13	11:12	21:28	10:47	21:52
10	14:51	19:45	14:07	20:29	13:36	20:59	13:13	21:21	12:50	21:43	12:32	22:01	12:16	22:16	12:03	22:29	11:40	22:50
11	15:00	21:21	14:27	21:52	14:03	22:15	13:45	22:33	13:26	22:51	13:10	23:05	12:57	23:17	12:46	23:28	12:26	23:46
12	15:04	22:53	14:41	23:14	14:23	23:31	14:09	23:44	13:54	23:57	13:42	—	13:32	—	13:23	—	13:07	—
13	15:05	—	14:50	—	14:38	—	14:28	—	14:18	—	14:09	0:08	14:02	0:17	13:55	0:25	13:44	0:39
14	15:06	0:20	14:57	0:33	14:50	0:44	14:44	0:52	14:38	1:01	14:33	1:08	14:29	1:15	14:25	1:20	14:18	1:29
15	15:06	1:44	15:03	1:50	15:01	1:55	14:59	2:00	14:57	2:04	14:55	2:07	14:54	2:11	14:52	2:13	14:50	2:18
16	15:06	3:06	15:09	3:06	15:11	3:06	15:13	3:06	15:15	3:06	15:17	3:06	15:18	3:06	15:20	3:06	15:22	3:06
17	15:06	4:28	15:15	4:21	15:22	4:16	15:28	4:12	15:34	4:08	15:39	4:04	15:44	4:01	15:48	3:58	15:55	3:53
18	15:07	5:51	15:22	5:38	15:35	5:28	15:44	5:19	15:55	5:10	16:03	5:03	16:11	4:57	16:17	4:51	16:29	4:42
19	15:09	7:18	15:32	6:57	15:50	6:41	16:04	6:28	16:18	6:14	16:30	6:04	16:41	5:54	16:50	5:46	17:05	5:32
20	15:13	8:49	15:45	8:18	16:09	7:55	16:28	7:37	16:46	7:20	17:02	7:05	17:15	6:53	17:26	6:43	17:46	6:25
21	15:22	10:21	16:06	9:38	16:36	9:09	16:59	8:47	17:21	8:25	17:39	8:08	17:54	7:53	18:08	7:40	18:30	7:19
22	15:43	11:49	16:38	10:54	17:13	10:19	17:39	9:53	18:04	9:29	18:24	9:09	18:41	8:53	18:55	8:38	19:20	8:14
23	16:27	12:57	17:27	11:57	18:04	11:20	18:31	10:53	18:56	10:27	19:17	10:07	19:34	9:50	19:49	9:35	20:14	9:10
24	17:43	13:36	18:35	12:43	19:09	12:09	19:34	11:43	19:58	11:18	20:17	10:59	20:34	10:42	20:48	10:28	21:11	10:03
25	19:19	13:53	19:58	13:13	20:25	12:45	20:46	12:23	21:07	12:01	21:24	11:44	21:38	11:29	21:50	11:16	22:10	10:54
26	21:01	14:02	21:28	13:33	21:48	13:11	22:04	12:54	22:20	12:37	22:33	12:23	22:44	12:11	22:54	12:00	23:10	11:42
27	22:43	14:05	23:00	13:46	23:13	13:31	23:24	13:19	23:35	13:07	23:44	12:56	23:51	12:47	23:58	12:40	—	12:26
28	—	14:07	—	13:56	—	13:48	—	13:40	—	13:33	—	13:26	—	13:21	—	13:16	0:10	13:07
29	0:25	14:08	0:33	14:05	0:40	14:02	0:45	13:59	0:51	13:57	0:55	13:54	0:59	13:52	1:03	13:51	1:09	13:48
30	2:07	14:09	2:07	14:13	2:07	14:15	2:07	14:18	2:08	14:20	2:08	14:22	2:08	14:24	2:08	14:25	2:08	14:28

MOONRISE AND MOONSET, 2002 DECEMBER
UNIVERSAL TIME AT GREENWICH MERIDIAN

●   ◑   ○   ◐

Latitude:	+62°		+58°		+54°		+50°		+45°		+40°		+35°		+30°		+20°	
Event: Dec.	RISE	SET	RISE	SET	RISE	SET	RISE	SET	RISE	SET	RISE	SET	RISE	SET	RISE	SET	RISE	SET
1	3:51	14:10	3:43	14:21	3:36	14:30	3:31	14:37	3:26	14:45	3:22	14:51	3:18	14:56	3:14	15:01	3:09	15:10
2	5:39	14:12	5:21	14:32	5:08	14:47	4:57	15:00	4:46	15:12	4:37	15:23	4:30	15:32	4:23	15:40	4:11	15:54
3	7:31	14:16	7:03	14:47	6:41	15:10	6:25	15:28	6:08	15:46	5:54	16:00	5:43	16:13	5:33	16:24	5:16	16:43
4	9:25	14:26	8:42	15:10	8:13	15:41	7:51	16:04	7:29	16:27	7:11	16:45	6:57	17:00	6:44	17:14	6:22	17:37
5	11:10	14:49	10:12	15:48	9:36	16:24	9:09	16:51	8:44	17:17	8:24	17:38	8:07	17:55	7:52	18:09	7:28	18:35
6	12:23	15:44	11:21	16:46	10:43	17:24	10:15	17:51	9:49	18:17	9:28	18:38	9:11	18:55	8:56	19:10	8:31	19:35
7	12:56	17:12	12:05	18:02	11:31	18:35	11:06	19:00	10:42	19:24	10:22	19:43	10:06	19:59	9:52	20:12	9:28	20:35
8	13:10	18:51	12:32	19:27	12:05	19:53	11:44	20:13	11:23	20:33	11:06	20:49	10:52	21:02	10:39	21:14	10:18	21:34
9	13:15	20:27	12:48	21:11	12:28	21:11	12:12	21:27	11:55	21:42	11:42	21:54	11:30	22:05	11:20	22:14	11:03	22:29
10	13:18	21:58	12:59	22:15	12:45	22:27	12:33	22:38	12:21	22:48	12:11	22:57	12:02	23:04	11:55	23:11	11:42	23:22
11	13:18	23:24	13:07	23:33	12:58	23:40	12:51	23:46	12:43	23:52	12:36	23:57	12:31	—	12:26	—	12:17	—
12	13:19	—	13:13	—	13:09	—	13:06	—	13:02	—	12:59	—	12:57	0:01	12:54	0:05	12:50	0:12
13	13:19	0:47	13:19	0:49	13:20	0:51	13:20	0:53	13:21	0:55	13:21	0:56	13:22	0:57	13:22	0:58	13:22	1:00
14	13:19	2:09	13:25	2:05	13:32	2:02	13:35	1:59	13:39	1:56	13:43	1:54	13:46	1:52	13:49	1:51	13:54	1:48
15	13:19	3:32	13:32	3:21	13:42	3:12	13:50	3:06	13:59	2:59	14:06	2:53	14:12	2:48	14:18	2:43	14:28	2:36
16	13:20	4:57	13:40	4:39	13:56	4:25	14:08	4:14	14:21	4:02	14:32	3:53	14:41	3:45	14:49	3:37	15:03	3:25
17	13:24	6:26	13:52	5:59	14:13	5:39	14:30	5:23	14:48	5:07	15:02	4:54	15:14	4:43	15:24	4:33	15:42	4:17
18	13:31	7:59	14:10	7:21	14:37	6:54	14:59	6:33	15:20	6:13	15:37	5:57	15:51	5:43	16:04	5:31	16:26	5:11
19	13:46	9:30	14:37	8:40	15:11	8:07	15:36	7:42	16:00	7:18	16:20	6:59	16:36	6:43	16:50	6:30	17:14	6:06
20	14:21	10:49	15:21	9:49	15:57	9:12	16:24	8:46	16:50	8:20	17:11	7:59	17:28	7:42	17:43	7:28	18:08	7:03
21	15:28	11:38	16:24	10:42	16:59	10:06	17:25	9:40	17:50	9:15	18:10	8:55	18:26	8:38	18:41	8:23	19:05	7:58
22	17:01	12:01	17:44	11:17	18:14	10:47	18:36	10:24	18:58	10:01	19:15	9:43	19:30	9:27	19:43	9:14	20:05	8:51
23	18:43	12:12	19:13	11:40	19:36	11:16	19:53	10:58	20:10	10:39	20:25	10:24	20:37	10:11	20:47	10:00	21:05	9:40
24	20:26	12:17	20:45	11:55	21:01	11:38	21:13	11:25	21:25	11:11	21:35	10:59	21:44	10:49	21:51	10:41	22:04	10:25
25	22:06	12:19	22:17	12:06	22:26	11:55	22:33	11:46	22:40	11:37	22:46	11:30	22:51	11:23	22:55	11:18	23:03	11:07
26	23:46	12:20	23:49	12:14	23:51	12:09	23:53	12:05	23:55	12:01	23:56	11:58	23:58	11:55	23:59	11:52	—	11:47
27	—	12:21	—	12:22	—	12:23	—	12:23	—	12:24	—	12:25	—	12:25	—	12:26	0:01	12:26
28	1:26	12:22	1:21	12:30	1:17	12:36	1:13	12:42	1:10	12:47	1:07	12:52	1:05	12:56	1:03	13:00	0:59	13:06
29	3:08	12:23	2:55	12:39	2:44	12:52	2:35	13:02	2:27	13:13	2:19	13:21	2:13	13:29	2:08	13:36	1:59	13:48
30	4:55	12:26	4:31	12:51	4:13	13:11	3:59	13:26	3:45	13:42	3:33	13:55	3:23	14:06	3:15	14:16	3:00	14:33
31	6:45	12:32	6:09	13:10	5:43	13:37	5:23	13:57	5:04	14:18	4:48	14:35	4:35	14:49	4:23	15:01	4:04	15:23

☽

ECLIPSE PATTERNS
By Roy Bishop

Eclipse Seasons

The plane of the Moon's orbit is tilted about 5° to the plane of Earth's orbit, the ecliptic. Since 5° is considerably larger than the angular sizes of the Sun and Moon ($\approx$0.5°), eclipses can occur only when the Sun is near (within about ±15° to ±18° for solar eclipses) one of the two points (nodes) at which the Moon's orbit crosses the ecliptic. The *ascending* node is the one at which the Moon crosses to the *north* side of the ecliptic.

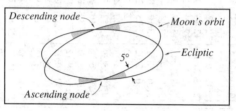

The Sun moves eastward along the ecliptic about 1° per day; thus the interval during which an eclipse can occur is at most about $(2 \times 18°) \div 1°/d = 36$ d, an *eclipse season*. Since the interval between new moons (29.5 days) is somewhat less, one or two solar eclipses will occur in each eclipse season. Six months later, when the Sun is near the other node, another eclipse season occurs. However, the plane of the Moon's orbit wobbles, making the nodes regress slowly westward along the ecliptic with a period of 18.61 years; thus the two eclipse seasons drift backward through the year, occurring about 19 days earlier each year.

The eclipse seasons of 2002 occur in May/June and November/December.

In a calendar year there can be as many as seven eclipses (solar and lunar combined, as last occurred in 1982) and as few as four (the usual number, as in 1999). In a calendar year there can be as many as five solar or lunar eclipses, and as few as two. The number of total or annular solar eclipses in a calendar year can range from zero to two, the number of total lunar eclipses from zero to three. *In 2002 there are five eclipses: three lunar (all penumbral) and two solar (one annular and one total).*

The Saros

Eclipses of the Sun and Moon recur with various periodicities that are more or less approximate. These periodicities are interesting both as numerical curiosities and because they may be used to predict eclipses. The most famous periodicity, the *Saros*, has been known since ancient times. It is a consequence of a remarkable commensurability among three lunar average periods:

Synodic month (S) (new to new) $= 29.530\,589$ d, $223S = 6585.3213$ d
Draconic month (N) (node to node) $= 27.212\,221$ d, $242N = 6585.3575$ d
Anomalistic month (P) (perigee to perigee) $= 27.554\,550$ d, $239P = 6585.5375$ d

Several aspects of this arithmetic are relevant to the pattern of eclipses (for brevity, the following comments are restricted primarily to the case of solar eclipses):

(1) An integer number of Ss (223) ensures a new Moon and hence the possibility of a second solar eclipse.

(2) $242N \approx 223S$ means that the new Moon will be almost at the same position relative to a node, ensuring that an eclipse *will* occur again and that it will occur somewhere near the same geographic latitude.

(3) The Saros (223S) = 6585.3213 d = 18 years + *only* 10.3213 d or 11.3213 d (depending on the number of intervening leap years). Thus one Saros later Earth will be at almost the same point in its elliptical orbit and hence at nearly the same distance from the Sun. Moreover, the inclination of Earth toward the Sun (season) will be nearly the same; thus the same latitude region of Earth will be exposed to the eclipse.

(4) 239P ≈ 223S means that one Saros later the new Moon will be at almost the same point in its elliptical orbit and thus at the same distance from Earth. With the same lunar and solar distances, the type of eclipse (total or annular) will be the same. Since the eclipse will occur near the same geographic latitude (see (2) and (3)), the duration of totality or annularity, or the magnitude of partial eclipse if the eclipse is not central, will be almost the same as it was one Saros earlier.

(5) 242N – 223S = 0.0361 d = 0.87 h. This, together with the 0.55°/h eastward speed of the Moon in its orbit, means that after one Saros, the Moon will be about 0.5° west of its former position relative to its node. Thus a Saros series does not last forever; there will be about 36°/0.5° ≈ 72 eclipses in a Saros series (the number ranges from 69 to 86). Furthermore, any one Saros series will last for about 72 × 18 ≈ 1300 years (the range is 1226 to 1532 years).

A Saros series begins with about 10 partial eclipses of increasing magnitude in the north or south polar region, depending upon whether the eclipses are occurring near the ascending or descending lunar node, respectively. These are followed by about 50 central eclipses (either total or annular), which over many centuries progressively shift southward or northward across Earth (about 300-km shift in latitude with each successive eclipse). The series ends with 10 or so partial eclipses of decreasing magnitude in the opposite polar region.

Currently, for solar eclipses 39 Saros series are running simultaneously, numbers 117 through 155 (for lunar eclipses, 41 Saros series are running, numbers 109 through 149). That is, in any 18-year 11-day interval, one eclipse from each of these 39 (and 41) series takes place, after which the whole pattern repeats. Those series occurring at the lunar ascending node are given odd numbers; those at the descending node, even numbers (vice versa for lunar eclipses).

The eclipse sequence of the year 2002 is similar to that of the five-eclipse year 1984.

(6) The Saros = 223S = 6585.3213 d, and the fractional 0.3213 d ≈ one-third of a day. Thus each successive solar eclipse in a Saros series will be shifted one-third of the way westward (120° in longitude) around Earth. After three Saros periods (54 years and 33 days, a cycle known as the *Exeligmos*), the eclipse will be back at approximately the same geographic longitude, although shifted about 1000 km in latitude. Two examples follow.

(a) Two total lunar eclipses will be visible from much of North America in 2003, on the nights of May 15/16 (Saros 121) and November 8/9 (Saros 126). One Saros earlier, nearly identical eclipses occurred on 1985 May 4 (Saros 121) and 1985 October 28 (Saros 126), except they were visible about 120° further east, from Europe and Asia, not from North America.

(b) The total solar eclipse of 2024 April 8 (no. 30 of Saros 139), which sweeps northeastward across eastern North America, will be geographically similar to that of 1970 March 7 (no. 27 of Saros 139), which followed the eastern seaboard of North America one Exeligmos earlier.

The Metonic Cycle

The sequence of lunar phases and the year repeat their relative pattern at 19-year intervals, a cycle known to astronomers in ancient Babylon and which was discovered independently around 430 BC by a Greek astronomer, Meton. We have

$235S = 235 \times 29.530\,589 = 6939.6884$ d;

19 years $= 6939$ d or 6940 d (depending on leap years).

Also, $255N$ is also very close to 19 years:

$255N = 255 \times 27.212\,221 = 6939.1164$ d.

Thus solar and lunar eclipses also repeat on a 19-year "Metonic" cycle. Since $255N$ is less than $235S$, the Moon does not reach the same phase (new or full for an eclipse) until it has moved eastward relative to the node by

$(235S - 255N) \times 24h \times 0.55°/h = 7.5°$.

Thus a Metonic eclipse series will have only

eclipse season width on the ecliptic $(36°) \div 7.5° \approx 4$ or 5 eclipses;

and the geographic latitude of successive solar eclipses in a series will change substantially (north or south, depending upon whether the Moon is at its ascending node or descending node, respectively).

What about the Moon's position in its orbit relative to its perigee? Using the anomalistic month P (the Moon returns to perigee on average every 27.554 550 d),

$235S \div P = 251.85$, which is *not* near an integer.

Thus in a Metonic series the Moon's distance is not the same from one eclipse to another. Hence the type of solar eclipse (total or annular) will vary within the series.

With only about four eclipses in a series, a mix of eclipse types, and scattered geographic occurrence, a Metonic eclipse series is not as elegant or useful as a Saros series. The main feature of a Metonic eclipse series is that, like lunar phases, the successive eclipses occur on (almost) the *same day* of the year.

Examples of the Metonic cycle for a lunar phase, lunar eclipses, and two recent Western Hemisphere total solar eclipses are given below. The numbers in parentheses are Saros numbers.

Full Moon	Lunar Eclipses	Solar Eclipses
1945 Sep. 21	1965 May 15 (no eclipse)	1960 Feb. 26 (no eclipse)
1964 Sep. 21	1984 May 15 Penum. (111)	**1979** Feb. 26 Total (120)
1983 Sep. 22	**2003** May 16 Total (121)	**1998** Feb. 26 Total (130)
2002 Sep. 21	2022 May 16 Total (131)	2017 Feb. 26 Annular (140)
2021 Sep. 20	2041 May 16 Partial (141)	2036 Feb. 27 Partial (150)
2040 Sep. 20	2060 May 16 (no eclipse)	2055 Feb. 27 (no eclipse)

ECLIPSES DURING 2002
BY FRED ESPENAK

Two solar and three lunar eclipses occur in 2002 as follows:

2002 May 26	Penumbral lunar eclipse
2002 Jun. 10	Annular solar eclipse
2002 Jun. 24	Penumbral lunar eclipse
2002 Nov. 20	Penumbral lunar eclipse
2002 Dec. 4	Total solar eclipse

Predictions for the eclipses are summarized in Figures 1 to 7. World maps show the regions of visibility for each eclipse. The lunar southeastern eclipse diagrams also include the path of the Moon through Earth's shadows. Contact times for each principal phase are tabulated along with the magnitudes and geocentric coordinates of the Sun and Moon at greatest eclipse.

Penumbral Lunar Eclipse of May 26

The first eclipse of the year is a deep penumbral lunar eclipse visible from parts of the Western Hemisphere. First and last penumbral contacts occur at 10:13 UT and 13:54 UT, respectively. The Moon's path through Earth's penumbra as well as a map showing worldwide visibility of the event are shown in Figure 1 (p. 138).

Greatest eclipse occurs at 12:03 UT with a maximum penumbral eclipse magnitude of 0.7145. Observers will note subtle yet distinct shading across the southern portions of the Moon. The Moon's southern limb actually lies 9.1 arc-min north of the umbra at its closest approach.

Annular Solar Eclipse of June 10

The first solar eclipse of 2002 is annular with a path that stretches the breadth of the Pacific Ocean. The partial phases are visible from eastern Asia and most of North America, except for the northeast (Figure 2, p. 139).

The Moon's antumbral shadow first touches down on Earth at 20:53 UT along the north coast of Sulawesi. Racing across the Celebes Sea, the antumbra engulfs the Indonesian islands of Pulau Sangihe and Kepulauan Talaud. The annular phase lasts just over one minute with the early morning Sun 6° above the horizon.

Leaving Indonesia, the shadow's trajectory takes it over a long track across the Pacific. As it does so, the curvature of Earth's surface causes the path width and central duration to gradually decrease. The antumbra reaches the southern end of the Northern Mariana Islands chain at 22:10 UT (Figure 3, p. 140). Guam lies just 40 km south of the 47-km-wide path and will experience a deep partial eclipse of magnitude 0.975. About 180 km northeast of Guam, the islands Saipan and Tinian span the northern limit of the annular track. Tinian's southern tip extends a dozen kilometres into the path but still falls 10 km short of the centreline. Nevertheless, most of the 53-s-long annular phase of magnitude 0.988 will be seen from this location with the Sun 32° above the horizon.

From this point on, the antumbra encounters no other populated islands across the Pacific. Greatest eclipse[1] occurs at 23:48:15 UT about 2600 km northwest of the Hawaiian Islands. The duration of the annular phase lasts a scant 23 s, but the event takes place in open ocean with no landfall in sight.

---

[1]The instant of greatest eclipse occurs when the distance between the Moon's shadow axis and Earth's geocentre reaches a minimum. Although greatest eclipse differs slightly from the instants of greatest magnitude and greatest duration (for total eclipses), the differences are quite small.

As the track swings to the southeast, its width and central duration begin to increase, but no other islands lie in its path. Just before reaching its terminus, the antumbra passes 50 km south of the southern tip of Baja, Mexico, at 01:32 UT (Figure 4, p. 141). In the final seconds of its earthbound trajectory, the shadow reaches the Pacific coast of Mexico, 30 km south of Puerto Vallarta. Under favourable weather conditions, observers on the centreline will witness a spectacular ring of fire on the horizon as the Sun sets just after annularity. The central duration is 1 min 7 s, and the magnitude is 0.981. Atmospheric refraction will actually displace the end of the path to the southeast so that the entire annular phase will occur before sunset for observers on or near the coast.

The antumbral shadow leaves Earth's surface at 01:35 UT. Over the course of 3 h and 47 min, the Moon's antumbra travels along a path approximately 14 700 km long and covering 0.2% of Earth's surface area. Path coordinates and centreline circumstances are presented in Table 1 (p. 133).

Partial phases of the eclipse are visible from much of North America, the Pacific, and eastern Asia. Local circumstances for a number of cities are listed in Table 2 (pp. 134–135). Times are given in Universal Time. The Sun's altitude and azimuth and eclipse magnitude[2] and obscuration[3] are all given at the instant of maximum eclipse. Additional information is also available at the 2002 annular solar eclipse website:

sunearth.gsfc.nasa.gov/eclipse/ASE2002/ASE2002.html

Penumbral Lunar Eclipse of June 24

The year's second lunar eclipse follows two weeks after the annular solar eclipse. Unfortunately, the event is a very shallow penumbral eclipse, nominally visible from the Eastern Hemisphere. First and last penumbral contacts occur at 20:19 UT and 22:36 UT, respectively.

Greatest eclipse takes place at 21:27 UT, with a maximum penumbral eclipse magnitude of only 0.2347. At that time, the Moon's northern limb will dip a meagre 7.4 arc-min into the pale, penumbral shadow. Such a minor eclipse will be all but invisible, even for the sharpest-eyed observers. Given the insignificant nature of this event, no figure is included with this report. Interested readers can find a diagram for the eclipse on the NASA website:

sunearth.gsfc.nasa.gov/eclipse/OH/OH2002.html

Penumbral Lunar Eclipse of November 20

The last penumbral lunar eclipse of 2002 is also the deepest lunar eclipse of the year. The event will be observable from the Americas, Europe, Africa, and central Asia. First and last penumbral contacts occur at 23:32 UT (Nov. 19) and 04:01 UT (Nov. 20), respectively. The Moon's path through Earth's penumbra and a map depicting worldwide visibility are shown in Figure 5 (p. 142).

At greatest eclipse (01:47 UT), the penumbral magnitude reaches its maximum value of 0.8862 as the Moon's northern limb passes just 6.6 arc-min from the edge of the umbra. Observers should be able to see a subtle yet distinct shading across the northern portion of the Moon's disk. Alas, the striking colours present during total eclipses will be absent from this event. We must wait until 2003 when two total lunar eclipses take place.

---

[2]Eclipse magnitude is defined as the fraction of the Sun's *diameter* occulted by the Moon.
[3]Eclipse obscuration is defined as the fraction of the Sun's *surface area* occulted by the Moon.

Total Solar Eclipse of December 4

The final event of the year is a total solar eclipse visible from a narrow corridor that traverses the Southern Hemisphere. The path of the Moon's umbral shadow begins in the South Atlantic, crosses southern Africa and the Indian Ocean, and ends at sunset in southern Australia. A partial eclipse will be seen within the much broader path of the Moon's penumbral shadow, which includes most of Africa, western Australia, and Antarctica (Figure 6, p. 143).

The eclipse begins in the South Atlantic where the Moon's umbral shadow first touches down on Earth at 05:50 UT (Figure 7, p. 144). Along the sunrise terminator the duration is only 26 s as seen from the centre of the 31-km-wide path. Seven minutes later, the umbra reaches the Atlantic coast of Angola (05:57 UT). Quite coincidentally, the first track of Angolan land to experience totality was also within the path of the total solar eclipse of 2001 June 21. The local residents are indeed fortunate to witness a total eclipse twice within the span of 18 months.

The early morning eclipse lasts 51 s from the centreline with the Sun 19° above the horizon. The umbra carves out a 50-km-wide path as it sweeps across Angola in a southeasterly direction. Briefly straddling the Angola/Zambia border, the shadow crosses eastern Namibia before entering northern Botswana (06:09 UT). Here, the path width will have grown to 60 km, and totality will last 1 min 11 s. Following the political boundary between Zimbabwe and Botswana, the umbra travels with a ground speed of 1.2 km/s. Bulawayo, Zimbabwe, lies just north of the track, and its residents witness a deep partial eclipse of magnitude 0.987 at 06:14 UT.

The umbra crosses completely into Zimbabwe before entering northern South Africa at 06:19 UT. One minute later, the northern third of Kruger National Park is plunged into totality, which lasts 1 min 25 s as the hidden Sun stands 42° above the horizon. Quickly crossing southern Mozambique, the shadow leaves the continent at 06:28 UT and begins its long trek across the Indian Ocean.

The instant of greatest eclipse occurs at 07:31:11 UT when the axis of the Moon's shadow passes closest to the centre of Earth (gamma[4] = –0.302). The length of totality reaches its maximum duration of 2 min 4 s, the Sun's altitude is 72°, the path width is 87 km, and the umbra's velocity is 0.670 km/s. Unfortunately, the umbra is far out to sea, ~2000 km southeast of Madagascar.

During the next hour and a half, no land is encountered as the eclipse track curves to the northeast and begins to narrow. In the final 90 s of its terrestrial trajectory, the umbra traverses South Australia. The coastal town of Ceduna lies at the centre of the 35-km-wide path. Totality lasts 33 s while the Sun stands 9° above the western horizon. The accelerating ground speed of the umbra already exceeds 5 km/s. In the remaining seconds, the increasingly elliptical shadow sweeps across 900 km of the Australian Outback.

The umbra leaves Earth's surface at the sunset terminator at 09:12 UT. Over the course of 3 h and 21 min, the Moon's umbra travels along a path approximately 12 000 km long and covering 0.14% of Earth's surface area. Path coordinates and centreline circumstances are presented in Table 3 (p. 136).

Local circumstances for cities throughout the path are given in Table 4 (p. 137). All times are given in Universal Time. The Sun's altitude and azimuth and the eclipse magnitude and obscuration are all given at the instant of maximum eclipse.

A detailed report on this eclipse is available from NASA's Technical Publication series (see NASA Solar Eclipse Bulletins). Additional information is also available at

---

[4]Minimum distance of the Moon's shadow axis from Earth's centre in units of equatorial Earth radii.

the 2002 total solar eclipse website:

sunearth.gsfc.nasa.gov/eclipse/TSE2002/TSE2002.html

Solar Eclipse Figures

For each solar eclipse, an orthographic projection map of Earth shows the path of penumbral (partial) and umbral (total or annular) eclipse. North is to the top in all cases, and the daylight terminator is plotted for the instant of greatest eclipse. An asterisk (*) indicates the subsolar point[5] on Earth.

The limits of the Moon's penumbral shadow delineate the region of visibility of the partial solar eclipse. This irregular or saddle-shaped region often covers more than half of the daylight hemisphere of Earth and consists of several distinct zones or limits. At the northern and/or southern boundaries lie the limits of the penumbra's path. Partial eclipses have only one of these limits, as do central eclipses when the Moon's shadow axis falls no closer than about 0.45 radii from Earth's centre. Great loops at the western and eastern extremes of the penumbra's path identify the areas where the eclipse begins/ends at sunrise and sunset, respectively. If the penumbra has both a northern and southern limit, the rising and setting curves form two separate, closed loops. Otherwise, the curves are connected in a distorted figure 8. Bisecting the "eclipse begins/ends at sunrise and sunset" loops is the curve of maximum eclipse at sunrise (western loop) and sunset (eastern loop). The points P1 and P4 mark the coordinates where the penumbral shadow first contacts (partial eclipse begins) and last contacts (partial eclipse ends) Earth's surface. If the penumbral path has both a northern and southern limit, then points P2 and P3 are also plotted. These correspond to the coordinates where the penumbral shadow cone becomes internally tangent to Earth's disk.

A curve of maximum eclipse is the locus of all points where the eclipse is at maximum at a given time. Curves of maximum eclipse are plotted at each half hour Universal Time. They generally run between the penumbral limits in the north/south direction or from the "maximum eclipse at sunrise and sunset" curves to one of the limits. If the eclipse is central (i.e. total or annular), the curves of maximum eclipse run through the outlines of the umbral shadow, which are plotted at 10-min intervals. The curves of constant eclipse magnitude delineate the locus of all points where the magnitude at maximum eclipse is constant. These curves run exclusively between the curves of maximum eclipse at sunrise and sunset. Furthermore, they are parallel to the northern/southern penumbral limits and the umbral paths of central eclipses. In fact, the northern and southern limits of the penumbra can be thought of as curves of constant magnitude 0.0. The adjacent curves are for magnitudes 0.2, 0.4, 0.6, and 0.8 (i.e. 20%, 40%, 60%, and 80%). For total eclipses, the northern and southern limits of the umbra are curves of constant magnitude 1.0. Umbral path limits for annular eclipses are curves of maximum eclipse magnitude.

Greatest eclipse is defined as the instant when the axis of the Moon's shadow passes closest to Earth's centre. Although greatest eclipse differs slightly from the instants of greatest magnitude and greatest duration (for total eclipses), the differences are usually negligible. The point on Earth's surface intersected by the axis at greatest eclipse is marked by an asterisk. For partial eclipses, the shadow axis misses Earth entirely, so the point of greatest eclipse lies on the day/night terminator and the Sun appears in the horizon.

Data pertinent to the eclipse appear with each map. At the top are listed the instant of conjunction of the Sun and Moon in right ascension and the instant of greatest

---

[5]The subsolar point is the geographic location where the Sun appears directly overhead (zenith).

eclipse, expressed in Universal Times and Julian Dates. The eclipse magnitude is defined as the fraction of the Sun's diameter obscured by the Moon at greatest eclipse. For central eclipses (total or annular), the magnitude is replaced by the geocentric ratio of diameters of the Moon and the Sun. Gamma is the minimum distance of the Moon's shadow axis from Earth's centre in Earth radii at greatest eclipse. The Saros series of the eclipse is listed, followed by the member position. The first member number identifies the sequence position of the eclipse in the Saros, while the second is the total number of eclipses in the series.

In the upper left and right corners are the geocentric coordinates of the Sun and the Moon, respectively, at the instant of greatest eclipse. They are:

RA   Right ascension
Dec   Declination
S.D. Apparent semi-diameter
H.P. Horizontal parallax

To the lower left are exterior/interior contact times of the Moon's penumbral shadow with Earth, which are defined as follows:

P1   Instant of first exterior tangency of penumbra with Earth's limb.
      (partial eclipse begins)
P2   Instant of first interior tangency of penumbra with Earth's limb.
P3   Instant of last interior tangency of penumbra with Earth's limb.
P4   Instant of last exterior tangency of penumbra with Earth's limb.
      (partial eclipse ends)

Not all eclipses have P2 and P3 penumbral contacts. They are only present in cases where the penumbral shadow falls completely within Earth's disk. For central eclipses, the lower right corner lists exterior/interior contact times of the Moon's umbral shadow with Earth's limb which are defined as follows:

U1   Instant of first exterior tangency of umbra with Earth's limb.
      (umbral [total/annular] eclipse begins)
U2   Instant of first interior tangency of umbra with Earth's limb.
U3   Instant of last interior tangency of umbra with Earth's limb.
U4   Instant of last exterior tangency of umbra with Earth's limb.
      (umbral [total/annular] eclipse ends)

At bottom centre are the geographic coordinates of the position of greatest eclipse along with the local circumstances at that location (i.e. Sun altitude, Sun azimuth, path width, and duration of totality/annularity). At bottom left is a list of parameters used in the eclipse predictions, while bottom right gives the Moon's geocentric libration (optical + physical) at greatest eclipse.

Lunar Eclipse Figures

Each lunar eclipse has two diagrams associated with it along with data pertinent to the eclipse. The top figure shows the path of the Moon through Earth's penumbral and umbral shadows. Above this figure are listed the instant of conjunction in right ascension of the Moon with Earth's shadow axis and the instant of greatest eclipse, expressed in Universal Times and Julian Dates. The penumbral and umbral magnitudes are defined as the fraction of the Moon's diameter immersed in the two shadows at greatest eclipse. The radii of the penumbral and umbral shadows, P. Radius and U. Radius, respectively, are also listed. Gamma is the minimum distance, in Earth radii, of the Moon's centre from Earth's shadow axis at greatest eclipse, and Axis is the same parameter expressed in degrees. The Saros series of the eclipse is listed, followed by a pair of numbers. The first number identifies the sequence position of the eclipse in the Saros, while the second is the total number of eclipses in the series.

In the upper left and right corners are the geocentric coordinates of the Sun and the Moon, respectively, at the instant of greatest eclipse. They are:

RA   Right ascension
Dec. Declination
S.D. Apparent semi-diameter
H.P. Horizontal parallax

To the lower left are the semi or half durations of the penumbral, umbral (partial), and total eclipses. Below them are the Sun/Moon ephemerides used in the predictions, followed by the extrapolated value of ΔT (the difference between Terrestrial Time and Universal Time). To the lower right are the contact times of the Moon with Earth's penumbral and umbral shadows, defined as follows:

P1   Instant of first exterior tangency of Moon with penumbra.
      (penumbral eclipse begins)
P4   Instant of last exterior tangency of Moon with penumbra.
      (penumbral eclipse ends)

The bottom figure is a cylindrical equidistant projection map of Earth that shows regions of visibility for each stage of the eclipse. In particular, the moonrise/moonset terminator is plotted for each contact and is labelled accordingly. The Moon appears directly overhead (zenith) during greatest eclipse at the position indicated by an asterisk. The region that is completely unshaded will observe the entire eclipse, while the darkly shaded area will witness none of the event. The remaining lightly shaded areas will experience moonrise or moonset while the eclipse is in progress. The shaded zones east of the asterisk will witness moonset before the eclipse ends, while the shaded zones west will witness moonrise after the eclipse has begun.

Eclipse Altitudes and Azimuths

The altitude a and azimuth A of the Sun or Moon during an eclipse depend on the time and the observer's geographic coordinates. They are calculated as follows:

$$h = 15\,(GST + UT - \alpha) + \lambda$$
$$a = \arcsin\,[\sin \delta \sin \phi + \cos \delta \cos h \cos \phi]$$
$$A = \arctan\,[-(\cos \delta \sin h)/(\sin \delta \cos \phi - \cos \delta \cos h \sin \phi)]$$

where

h = hour angle of Sun or Moon
a = altitude
A = azimuth
GST = Greenwich Sidereal Time at 0:00 UT
UT = Universal Time
α = right ascension of Sun or Moon
δ = declination of Sun or Moon
λ = observer's longitude (east +, west −)
ϕ = observer's latitude (north +, south −)

During the eclipses of 2002, the values for GST and the geocentric right ascension and declination of the Sun or the Moon (at greatest eclipse) are as follows:

Eclipse	Date	GST	α	δ
Penumbral lunar	2002 May 26	16.259	16.231	–20.027
Annular solar	2002 Jun. 10	17.277	5.268	23.055
Penumbral lunar	2002 Jun. 24	18.191	18.224	–24.785
Penumbral lunar	2002 Nov. 20	3.928	3.708	18.654
Total solar	2002 Dec. 04	4.863	16.697	–22.225

Eclipses During 2003

Next year, there will be two central solar and two total lunar eclipses:

2003 May 16	Total lunar eclipse
2003 May 31	Annular solar eclipse
2003 Nov. 9	Total lunar eclipse
2003 Nov. 23	Total solar eclipse

A full report on eclipses during 2003 will be published next year in the *Observer's Handbook 2003*.

NASA Solar Eclipse Bulletins

Special bulletins containing detailed predictions and meteorological data for future solar eclipses of interest are prepared by F. Espenak and J. Anderson and are published through NASA's Publication series. The bulletins are provided as a public service to both the professional and lay communities, including educators and the media. A list of currently available bulletins and an order form can be found at:

sunearth.gsfc.nasa.gov/eclipse/SEpubs/RPrequest.html

Single copies of the eclipse bulletins are available at no cost by sending a 9 × 12–in. self-addressed envelope stamped with postage for 11 oz. (310 g). Please print the eclipse year on the envelope's lower left corner. Use stamps only because cash and cheques cannot be accepted. Requests from outside the United States and Canada should include 10 international postal coupons. Mail requests to: Fred Espenak, NASA/Goddard Space Flight Center, Code 693, Greenbelt, Maryland 20771 U.S.A.

The NASA eclipse bulletins are also available over the Internet, including out-of-print bulletins. Using a web browser, they can be read or downloaded via the World Wide Web from the GSFC/SDAC (Solar Data Analysis Center) eclipse page:

umbra.nascom.nasa.gov/eclipse/index.html

The original Microsoft Word text files and PICT figures (Macintosh format) are also available via anonymous ftp. They are stored as BinHex-encoded, StuffIt-compressed Mac folders with .hqx suffixes. For PCs, the text is available in a zip-compressed format in files with the .zip suffix. There are three sub-directories for figures (GIF format), maps (JPEG format), and tables.

Eclipse Websites

A special solar and lunar eclipse website is available at:

sunearth.gsfc.nasa.gov/eclipse/eclipse.html

The site features predictions and maps for all solar and lunar eclipses well into the 21st century. Special emphasis is placed on eclipses occurring during the next two years with detailed path maps, tables, graphs, and meteorological data. Additional catalogues list every solar and lunar eclipse over a 5000-year period.

Detailed information on solar and lunar eclipse photography and tips on eclipse observing and eye safety may be found at:

www.MrEclipse.com

Acknowledgments

All eclipse predictions were generated on a Power Macintosh 8500/150 using algorithms developed from the *Explanatory Supplement* (1974) with additional algorithms from Meeus, Grosjean, and Vanderleen (1966). The solar and lunar ephemerides were generated from Newcomb and the *Improved Lunar Ephemeris*. A correction of –0.6″ was added to the Moon's ecliptic latitude to account for the difference between the Moon's centre of mass and centre of figure. For partial solar eclipses, the value used for the Moon's radius is $k = 0.272\,488\,0$. For lunar eclipses, the diameter of the umbral shadow was enlarged by 2% to compensate for Earth's atmosphere, and corrections for the effects of oblateness have been included. Text and table composition was done on a Macintosh using Microsoft Word. Additional figure annotation was performed with Claris MacDraw Pro.

All calculations, diagrams, tables and opinions presented in this paper are those of the author and he assumes full responsibility for their accuracy.

This publication is available electronically via the Internet along with additional information and updates at:

sunearth.gsfc.nasa.gov/eclipse/OH/OH2002.html

References

Espenak, F., 1988, *Fifty Year Canon of Solar Eclipses: 1986–2035*, Sky Publishing Corp., Cambridge, MA.

Espenak, F., 1989, *Fifty Year Canon of Lunar Eclipses: 1986–2035*, Sky Publishing Corp., Cambridge, MA.

Espenak, F., & Anderson, J. 2001, *Total Solar Eclipse of 2002 Dec 04*, NASA, Washington, DC.

Explanatory Supplement to the Astronomical Ephemeris and the American Ephemeris and Nautical Almanac, 1974, Her Majesty's Nautical Almanac Office, London.

Improved Lunar Ephemeris 1952–1959, 1954, U.S. Naval Observatory, Washington, DC.

Littmann, M., Willcox, K. & Espenak, F., 1999, *Totality—Eclipses of the Sun*, Oxford University Press, New York.

Meeus, J., Grosjean, C.C. & Vanderleen, W., 1966, *Canon of Solar Eclipses*, Pergamon Press, New York.

Meeus, J., & Mucke, H., 1979, *Canon of Lunar Eclipses: –2002 to +2526*, Astronomisches Buro, Wien.

Newcomb, S., 1895, "Tables of the Motion of the Earth on its Axis Around the Sun," *Astron. Papers Amer. Eph.*, Vol. 6, Part I.

TABLE 1—PATH OF THE ANTUMBRAL SHADOW
ANNULAR SOLAR ECLIPSE OF 2002 JUNE 10

Time UT	Northern Limit Lat.	Long.	Southern Limit Lat.	Long.	Centre Line Lat.	Long.	Sun Alt °	Path Width km	Central Durat.
Limits	1°38' N	120°28' E	1°02' N	120°51' E	01°20' N	120°40' E	0	78	1m13s
21:55	3°07' N	123°51' E	3°38' N	126°30' E	03°26' N	125°21' E	5	73	1m10s
22:00	8°48' N	135°10' E	8°38' N	135°58' E	08°43' N	135°35' E	18	60	1m02s
22:05	11°49' N	140°23' E	11°37' N	140°57' E	11°43' N	140°40' E	25	52	0m58s
22:10	14°11' N	144°14' E	13°58' N	144°41' E	14°05' N	144°27' E	30	47	0m54s
22:15	16°13' N	147°23' E	16°00' N	147°46' E	16°06' N	147°34' E	35	42	0m51s
22:20	18°00' N	150°07' E	17°48' N	150°26' E	17°54' N	150°16' E	39	38	0m48s
22:25	19°37' N	152°33' E	19°26' N	152°50' E	19°31' N	152°42' E	43	35	0m45s
22:30	21°07' N	154°47' E	20°55' N	155°03' E	21°01' N	154°55' E	46	32	0m43s
22:35	22°29' N	156°53' E	22°19' N	157°06' E	22°24' N	156°59' E	49	29	0m40s
22:40	23°46' N	158°51' E	23°36' N	159°03' E	23°41' N	158°57' E	53	27	0m38s
22:45	24°58' N	160°44' E	24°49' N	160°55' E	24°53' N	160°50' E	56	25	0m36s
22:50	26°06' N	162°34' E	25°57' N	162°43' E	26°01' N	162°39' E	58	23	0m34s
22:55	27°10' N	164°20' E	27°01' N	164°29' E	27°05' N	164°25' E	61	21	0m32s
23:00	28°09' N	166°05' E	28°01' N	166°12' E	28°05' N	166°09' E	64	20	0m31s
23:05	29°06' N	167°48' E	28°58' N	167°55' E	29°02' N	167°51' E	66	19	0m29s
23:10	29°59' N	169°30' E	29°51' N	169°36' E	29°55' N	169°33' E	69	17	0m28s
23:15	30°48' N	171°12' E	30°41' N	171°17' E	30°44' N	171°14' E	71	16	0m27s
23:20	31°35' N	172°53' E	31°27' N	172°58' E	31°31' N	172°56' E	73	16	0m26s
23:25	32°18' N	174°36' E	32°11' N	174°40' E	32°15' N	174°38' E	75	15	0m25s
23:30	32°58' N	176°19' E	32°51' N	176°23' E	32°55' N	176°21' E	76	14	0m24s
23:35	33°36' N	178°03' E	33°29' N	178°06' E	33°32' N	178°05' E	77	14	0m23s
23:40	34°10' N	179°48' E	34°03' N	179°52' E	34°06' N	179°50' E	78	14	0m23s
23:45	34°41' N	178°24' W	34°34' N	178°22' W	34°37' N	178°23' W	78	13	0m23s
23:50	35°09' N	176°35' W	35°02' N	176°33' W	35°05' N	176°34' W	78	13	0m23s
23:55	35°34' N	174°44' W	35°26' N	174°42' W	35°30' N	174°43' W	77	13	0m23s
00:00	35°55' N	172°51' W	35°48' N	172°49' W	35°51' N	172°50' W	76	14	0m23s
00:05	36°13' N	170°55' W	36°05' N	170°54' W	36°09' N	170°54' W	74	14	0m24s
00:10	36°27' N	168°56' W	36°20' N	168°55' W	36°24' N	168°55' W	72	14	0m24s
00:15	36°38' N	166°54' W	36°30' N	166°53' W	36°34' N	166°54' W	70	15	0m25s
00:20	36°45' N	164°48' W	36°37' N	164°48' W	36°41' N	164°48' W	68	16	0m26s
00:25	36°48' N	162°39' W	36°39' N	162°40' W	36°44' N	162°39' W	65	17	0m27s
00:30	36°47' N	160°26' W	36°38' N	160°27' W	36°42' N	160°26' W	63	18	0m28s
00:35	36°41' N	158°08' W	36°31' N	158°10' W	36°36' N	158°09' W	60	19	0m30s
00:40	36°31' N	155°44' W	36°20' N	155°48' W	36°25' N	155°46' W	58	20	0m31s
00:45	36°15' N	153°15' W	36°03' N	153°20' W	36°09' N	153°18' W	55	22	0m33s
00:50	35°53' N	150°40' W	35°41' N	150°45' W	35°47' N	150°42' W	52	24	0m35s
00:55	35°25' N	147°56' W	35°12' N	148°03' W	35°18' N	147°59' W	49	26	0m37s
01:00	34°49' N	145°02' W	34°35' N	145°12' W	34°42' N	145°07' W	45	28	0m39s
01:05	34°05' N	141°57' W	33°51' N	142°08' W	33°58' N	142°03' W	42	31	0m41s
01:10	33°11' N	138°36' W	32°55' N	138°50' W	33°03' N	138°43' W	38	34	0m44s
01:15	32°03' N	134°54' W	31°47' N	135°12' W	31°55' N	135°03' W	33	38	0m47s
01:20	30°38' N	130°41' W	30°22' N	131°04' W	30°30' N	130°52' W	29	42	0m50s
01:25	28°47' N	125°35' W	28°31' N	126°07' W	28°39' N	125°51' W	23	48	0m54s
01:30	26°01' N	118°38' W	25°49' N	119°29' W	25°55' N	119°04' W	15	56	0m59s
Limits	20°05' N	104°38' W	19°32' N	105°01' W	19°49' N	104°50' W	0	72	1m07s

TABLE 2—LOCAL CIRCUMSTANCES FOR
SOLAR ECLIPSE OF 2002 JUNE 10

Geographic Location	Eclipse Begins h:m	Maximum Eclipse h:m	Eclipse Ends h:m	Sun Alt °	Sun Az °	Ecl. Mag.	Ecl. Obs.
CAMBODIA							
Phnum Pénh	— r	22:37 r	22:59	0	66	0.325	0.210
CANADA							
Calgary, AB	0:11	1:01	1:49	23	279	0.343	0.227
Edmonton, AB	0:11	0:58	1:43	24	277	0.287	0.175
Hamilton, ON	0:31	1:02 s	— s	0	304	0.210	0.111
Montréal, QC	0:33	0:45 s	— s	0	305	0.081	0.027
North York, ON	0:31	1:00 s	— s	0	304	0.195	0.099
Ottawa, ON	0:33	0:54 s	— s	0	306	0.130	0.055
Regina, SK	0:19	1:03	1:45	17	286	0.283	0.172
Toronto, ON	0:31	1:01 s	— s	0	304	0.199	0.103
Vancouver, BC	0:01	1:01	1:57	29	273	0.449	0.335
Victoria, BC	0:01	1:02	1:59	29	273	0.471	0.358
Winnipeg, MB	0:24	1:03	1:41	12	292	0.234	0.130
CHINA							
Beijing (Peking)	22:10	22:39	23:09	19	76	0.118	0.048
Chongqing (Chungking)	21:52	22:26	23:01	6	67	0.199	0.103
Guangzhou (Canton)	— r	22:16	23:05	7	68	0.390	0.273
Nanjing (Nanking)	21:46	22:27	23:12	17	73	0.274	0.164
Shanghai	21:42	22:26	23:15	18	74	0.318	0.204
Wuhan	21:46	22:26	23:07	12	70	0.254	0.147
GUAM							
Agana	21:01	22:09	23:29	30	71	0.975	0.962
HONG KONG							
Victoria (Xianggang)	— r	22:15	23:05	7	68	0.416	0.300
INDONESIA							
Banyuwangi	— r	22:34 r	22:50	0	67	0.257	0.149
Genteng	— r	22:35 r	22:50	0	67	0.238	0.134
Surabaya	— r	22:38 r	22:51	0	67	0.200	0.104
JAPAN							
Nagoya	21:42	22:38	23:40	34	84	0.429	0.314
Osaka	21:41	22:36	23:37	33	83	0.421	0.305
Tokyo	21:42	22:41	23:46	37	86	0.455	0.341
KOREA, SOUTH							
Soul (Seoul)	21:53	22:37	23:25	26	80	0.267	0.158
MEXICO							
Guadalajara	0:32	1:33	— s	0	295	0.951	0.930
Monterrey	0:29	1:29	— s	0	296	0.790	0.730
Puebla	0:33	1:11 s	— s	0	295	0.612	0.515
PHILIPPINES							
Manila	— r	22:06	23:06	8	68	0.662	0.575
SAIPAN							
Susupe	21:03	22:12	23:33	32	72	0.988	0.976

TABLE 2—LOCAL CIRCUMSTANCES FOR
SOLAR ECLIPSE OF 2002 JUNE 10 (continued)

Geographic Location	Eclipse Begins h:m	Maximum Eclipse h:m	Eclipse Ends h:m	Sun Alt °	Sun Az °	Ecl. Mag.	Ecl. Obs.
UNITED STATES							
Austin, TX	0:28	1:24	— s	1	296	0.652	0.562
Baton Rouge, LA	0:29	1:08 s	— s	0	298	0.515	0.405
Birmingham, AL	0:29	1:00 s	— s	0	299	0.388	0.271
Boise, ID	0:10	1:11	2:07	22	282	0.524	0.416
Chicago, IL	0:28	1:10	— s	2	300	0.305	0.192
Cleveland, OH	0:30	1:04 s	— s	0	303	0.257	0.150
Columbia, SC	0:29	0:37 s	— s	0	299	0.110	0.043
Columbus, OH	0:29	1:04 s	— s	0	302	0.294	0.182
Dallas, TX	0:27	1:22	— s	2	297	0.584	0.483
Denver, CO	0:21	1:16	2:08	11	291	0.508	0.398
Des Moines, IA	0:26	1:12	— s	5	297	0.363	0.247
Detroit, MI	0:30	1:07	— s	0	303	0.255	0.148
Honolulu, HI	23:04	0:42	2:06	60	280	0.519	0.411
Houston, TX	0:29	1:23 s	— s	0	298	0.639	0.547
Jackson, MS	0:29	1:09 s	— s	0	299	0.496	0.384
Kansas City, MO	0:26	1:15	— s	4	297	0.424	0.308
Little Rock, AR	0:28	1:18	— s	0	299	0.495	0.383
Los Angeles, CA	0:13	1:22	2:23	19	286	0.774	0.711
Louisville, KY	0:29	1:09 s	— s	0	301	0.356	0.240
Milwaukee, WI	0:28	1:08	— s	3	300	0.284	0.173
Minneapolis, MN	0:26	1:08	1:48	7	296	0.294	0.182
Montgomery, AL	0:29	0:54 s	— s	0	299	0.333	0.218
Nashville, TN	0:29	1:07 s	— s	0	300	0.397	0.280
New Orleans, LA	0:29	1:02 s	— s	0	298	0.453	0.338
Oklahoma City, OK	0:26	1:19	— s	4	296	0.530	0.422
Omaha, NE	0:25	1:13	1:58	6	295	0.392	0.275
Phoenix, AZ	0:19	1:24	2:21	13	289	0.726	0.652
Pittsburgh, PA	0:30	0:54 s	— s	0	302	0.223	0.121
Portland, OR	0:03	1:06	2:05	27	276	0.534	0.427
Rochester, NY	0:31	0:53 s	— s	0	304	0.171	0.082
Sacramento, CA	0:07	1:16	2:17	24	282	0.693	0.612
St. Louis, MO	0:28	1:14	— s	1	299	0.393	0.276
Salem, OR	0:02	1:07	2:06	27	276	0.551	0.446
Salt Lake City, UT	0:15	1:15	2:10	17	286	0.551	0.446
San Antonio, TX	0:28	1:25	— s	1	296	0.68	0.596
San Diego, CA	0:15	1:24	2:24	17	287	0.797	0.739
San Francisco, CA	0:06	1:16	2:19	24	281	0.721	0.647
San Jose, CA	0:07	1:17	2:19	23	282	0.727	0.654
Seattle, WA	0:02	1:04	2:00	28	275	0.482	0.370
Tallahassee, FL	0:29	0:41 s	— s	0	298	0.169	0.081
VIETNAM							
Ho Chi Minh City	— r	22:31 r	22:59	0	66	0.404	0.287

All times are Universal Time.
'r' indicates eclipse in progress at sunrise. 's' indicates eclipse in progress at sunset.

TABLE 3—PATH OF THE UMBRAL SHADOW
TOTAL SOLAR ECLIPSE OF 2002 DECEMBER 4

Time UT	Northern Limit Lat.	Long.	Southern Limit Lat.	Long.	Centre Line Lat.	Long.	Sun Alt °	Path Width km	Central Durat.
Limits	3°49′ S	1°40′ W	4°03′ S	01°49′ W	3°56′ S	1°45′ W	0	31	0m26s
05:55	10°34′ S	12°30′ E	10°38′ S	11°42′ E	10°36′ S	12°07′ E	16	51	0m46s
06:00	13°51′ S	18°10′ E	14°02′ S	17°27′ E	13°57′ S	17°49′ E	24	59	0m57s
06:05	16°26′ S	22°15′ E	16°41′ S	21°33′ E	16°34′ S	21°54′ E	29	65	1m05s
06:10	18°39′ S	25°35′ E	18°57′ S	24°53′ E	18°48′ S	25°14′ E	34	69	1m12s
06:15	20°38′ S	28°27′ E	20°59′ S	27°46′ E	20°48′ S	28°06′ E	39	73	1m19s
06:20	22°26′ S	31°01′ E	22°49′ S	30°20′ E	22°38′ S	30°41′ E	42	76	1m25s
06:25	24°07′ S	33°23′ E	24°31′ S	32°42′ E	24°19′ S	33°02′ E	46	78	1m30s
06:30	25°40′ S	35°35′ E	26°07′ S	34°55′ E	25°54′ S	35°15′ E	49	80	1m35s
06:35	27°08′ S	37°41′ E	27°37′ S	37°01′ E	27°22′ S	37°21′ E	52	82	1m39s
06:40	28°31′ S	39°42′ E	29°01′ S	39°03′ E	28°46′ S	39°23′ E	55	83	1m43s
06:45	29°50′ S	41°40′ E	30°22′ S	41°02′ E	30°06′ S	41°21′ E	58	84	1m47s
06:50	31°04′ S	43°36′ E	31°38′ S	42°58′ E	31°21′ S	43°17′ E	60	85	1m50s
06:55	32°15′ S	45°31′ E	32°50′ S	44°54′ E	32°33′ S	45°12′ E	63	86	1m53s
07:00	33°22′ S	47°25′ E	33°59′ S	46°49′ E	33°41′ S	47°07′ E	65	86	1m56s
07:05	34°26′ S	49°19′ E	35°04′ S	48°45′ E	34°45′ S	49°02′ E	67	87	1m58s
07:10	35°27′ S	51°15′ E	36°05′ S	50°42′ E	35°46′ S	50°58′ E	69	87	2m00s
07:15	36°24′ S	53°11′ E	37°04′ S	52°40′ E	36°44′ S	52°56′ E	70	87	2m02s
07:20	37°18′ S	55°10′ E	37°59′ S	54°40′ E	37°38′ S	54°55′ E	71	87	2m03s
07:25	38°08′ S	57°11′ E	38°50′ S	56°44′ E	38°29′ S	56°57′ E	72	87	2m03s
07:30	38°55′ S	59°15′ E	39°38′ S	58°50′ E	39°17′ S	59°02′ E	72	87	2m04s
07:35	39°39′ S	61°22′ E	40°23′ S	61°00′ E	40°01′ S	61°11′ E	72	87	2m04s
07:40	40°20′ S	63°33′ E	41°04′ S	63°13′ E	40°42′ S	63°23′ E	72	86	2m03s
07:45	40°56′ S	65°48′ E	41°41′ S	65°31′ E	41°18′ S	65°40′ E	71	86	2m02s
07:50	41°29′ S	68°07′ E	42°14′ S	67°54′ E	41°51′ S	68°01′ E	69	85	2m01s
07:55	41°58′ S	70°32′ E	42°43′ S	70°22′ E	42°20′ S	70°27′ E	68	84	1m59s
08:00	42°22′ S	73°01′ E	43°07′ S	72°55′ E	42°45′ S	72°58′ E	66	83	1m57s
08:05	42°42′ S	75°36′ E	43°27′ S	75°34′ E	43°04′ S	75°35′ E	64	82	1m55s
08:10	42°57′ S	78°18′ E	43°41′ S	78°20′ E	43°19′ S	78°19′ E	61	81	1m52s
08:15	43°07′ S	81°06′ E	43°51′ S	81°12′ E	43°29′ S	81°09′ E	59	80	1m49s
08:20	43°11′ S	84°02′ E	43°54′ S	84°12′ E	43°33′ S	84°07′ E	56	79	1m45s
08:25	43°09′ S	87°06′ E	43°50′ S	87°20′ E	43°30′ S	87°13′ E	54	77	1m41s
08:30	43°00′ S	90°19′ E	43°40′ S	90°37′ E	43°20′ S	90°28′ E	51	75	1m36s
08:35	42°44′ S	93°43′ E	43°21′ S	94°04′ E	43°03′ S	93°53′ E	47	73	1m31s
08:40	42°18′ S	97°19′ E	42°54′ S	97°44′ E	42°36′ S	97°31′ E	44	70	1m26s
08:45	41°43′ S	101°10′ E	42°15′ S	101°39′ E	41°59′ S	101°24′ E	40	68	1m20s
08:50	40°54′ S	105°21′ E	41°23′ S	105°54′ E	41°09′ S	105°37′ E	36	64	1m13s
08:55	39°50′ S	109°59′ E	40°15′ S	110°35′ E	40°03′ S	110°17′ E	32	60	1m06s
09:00	38°23′ S	115°17′ E	38°43′ S	115°56′ E	38°33′ S	115°36′ E	27	56	0m58s
09:05	36°19′ S	121°48′ E	36°33′ S	122°32′ E	36°26′ S	122°09′ E	20	49	0m48s
09:10	32°44′ S	131°37′ E	32°44′ S	132°37′ E	32°44′ S	132°06′ E	10	38	0m35s
Limits	28°25′ S	142°20′ E	28°37′ S	142°30′ E	28°31′ S	142°25′ E	0	27	0m22s

TABLE 4—LOCAL CIRCUMSTANCES FOR SOLAR ECLIPSE OF 2002 DECEMBER 4

Geographic Location	Eclipse Begins h:m	Maximum Eclipse h:m	Eclipse Ends h:m	Sun Alt °	Sun Az °	Ecl. Mag.	Ecl. Obs.
ANGOLA							
Luanda	4:56	5:53	6:57	16	111	0.946	0.935
AUSTRALIA							
Adelaide, AS	8:10	9:08	— s	7	247	0.882	0.853
Brisbane, QL	8:16	8:31 s	— s	0	244	0.285	0.175
Canberra, SW	8:11	9:04	— s	0	242	0.765	0.705
Melbourne, VC	8:09	9:04	— s	4	244	0.748	0.684
Newcastle, SW	8:13	8:48 s	— s	0	243	0.618	0.527
Perth, AW	7:58	9:07	10:08	24	258	0.824	0.780
Sydney, SW	8:12	8:54 s	— s	0	242	0.694	0.617
Wollongong, SW	8:12	8:55 s	— s	0	242	0.712	0.640
CAMEROON							
Yaoundé	— r	5:43	6:40	8	113	0.633	0.545
CONGO							
Brazzaville	4:53	5:49	6:52	16	112	0.801	0.751
DEMOCRATIC REPUBLIC OF THE CONGO							
Kinshasa	4:53	5:49	6:52	16	112	0.802	0.752
IVORY COAST							
Abidjan	— r	6:12 r	6:39	0	112	0.468	0.357
KENYA							
Nairobi	5:03	5:56	6:56	36	117	0.374	0.260
MADAGASCAR							
Antananarivo	5:22	6:35	7:59	61	102	0.631	0.544
MOZAMBIQUE							
Maputo	5:18	6:27	7:46	46	96	0.965	0.961
NIGERIA							
Lagos	— r	5:45 r	6:37	0	112	0.659	0.576
SOUTH AFRICA							
Cape Town	5:32	6:29	7:33	35	95	0.587	0.492
Durban	5:25	6:32	7:48	46	92	0.851	0.817
Johannesburg	5:18	6:24	7:38	41	97	0.886	0.860
Pretoria	5:17	6:23	7:38	41	98	0.899	0.877
TANZANIA							
Dar-es-Salaam	5:05	6:05	7:14	42	114	0.472	0.363
UGANDA							
Kampala	4:58	5:51	6:51	30	116	0.410	0.296
ZAMBIA							
Lusaka	5:03	6:07	7:21	36	107	0.880	0.852
ZIMBABWE							
Harare	5:06	6:13	7:29	40	104	0.892	0.868

All times are Universal Time.
'r' indicates eclipse in progress at sunrise. 's' indicates eclipse in progress at sunset.

FIGURE 1—PENUMBRAL LUNAR ECLIPSE OF 2002 MAY 26

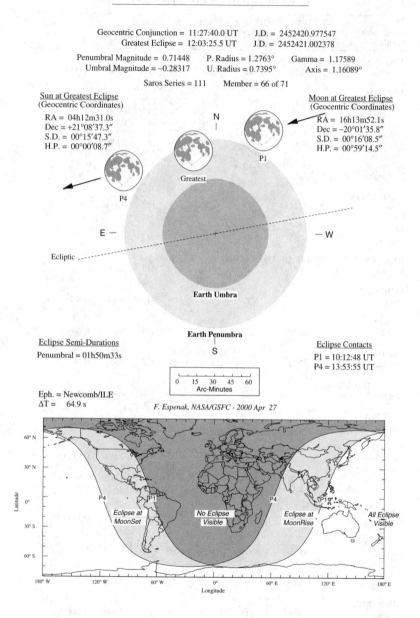

Geocentric Conjunction = 11:27:40.0 UT   J.D. = 2452420.977547
Greatest Eclipse = 12:03:25.5 UT   J.D. = 2452421.002378

Penumbral Magnitude = 0.71448   P. Radius = 1.2763°   Gamma = 1.17589
Umbral Magnitude = −0.28317   U. Radius = 0.7395°   Axis = 1.16089°

Saros Series = 111   Member = 66 of 71

Sun at Greatest Eclipse
(Geocentric Coordinates)

RA = 04h12m31.0s
Dec = +21°08'37.3"
S.D. = 00°15'47.3"
H.P. = 00°00'08.7"

N

Moon at Greatest Eclipse
(Geocentric Coordinates)

RA = 16h13m52.1s
Dec = −20°01'35.8"
S.D. = 00°16'08.5"
H.P. = 00°59'14.5"

P1

Greatest

P4

E —   — W

Ecliptic

Earth Umbra

Earth Penumbra

S

Eclipse Semi-Durations
Penumbral = 01h50m33s

Eclipse Contacts
P1 = 10:12:48 UT
P4 = 13:53:55 UT

0   15   30   45   60
Arc-Minutes

Eph. = Newcomb/ILE
ΔT =   64.9 s

F. Espenak, NASA/GSFC - 2000 Apr 27

FIGURE 2—ANNULAR SOLAR ECLIPSE OF 2002 JUNE 10

Geocentric Conjunction = 23:48:14.5 UT   J.D. = 2452436.491834
Greatest Eclipse = 23:44:17.6 UT   J.D. = 2452436.489093

Eclipse Magnitude = 0.99622   Gamma = 0.19933

Saros Series = 137   Member = 35 of 70

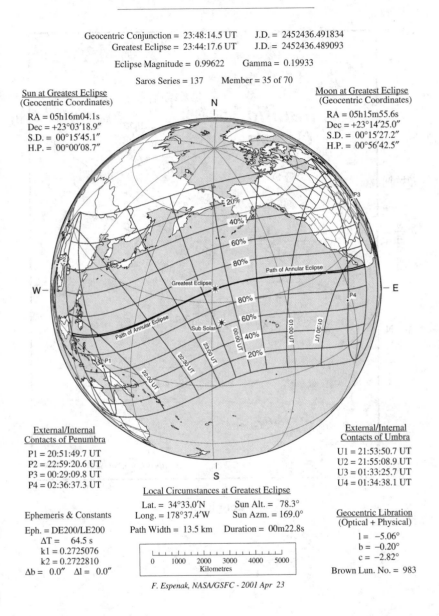

Sun at Greatest Eclipse
(Geocentric Coordinates)

RA = 05h16m04.1s
Dec = +23°03′18.9″
S.D. = 00°15′45.1″
H.P. = 00°00′08.7″

Moon at Greatest Eclipse
(Geocentric Coordinates)

RA = 05h15m55.6s
Dec = +23°14′25.0″
S.D. = 00°15′27.2″
H.P. = 00°56′42.5″

External/Internal
Contacts of Penumbra

P1 = 20:51:49.7 UT
P2 = 22:59:20.6 UT
P3 = 00:29:09.8 UT
P4 = 02:36:37.3 UT

Ephemeris & Constants

Eph. = DE200/LE200
ΔT =   64.5 s
k1 = 0.2725076
k2 = 0.2722810
Δb =   0.0″   Δl =   0.0″

Local Circumstances at Greatest Eclipse

Lat. = 34°33.0′N   Sun Alt. = 78.3°
Long. = 178°37.4′W   Sun Azm. = 169.0°
Path Width = 13.5 km   Duration = 00m22.8s

```
 |  |  |  |  |  |  |  |  |  |  |  |
 0   1000  2000  3000  4000  5000
              Kilometres
```

External/Internal
Contacts of Umbra

U1 = 21:53:50.7 UT
U2 = 21:55:08.9 UT
U3 = 01:33:25.7 UT
U4 = 01:34:38.1 UT

Geocentric Libration
(Optical + Physical)

l = −5.06°
b = −0.20°
c = −2.82°
Brown Lun. No. = 983

F. Espenak, NASA/GSFC - 2001 Apr 23

FIGURE 3—ANNULAR SOLAR ECLIPSE OF 2002 JUNE 10

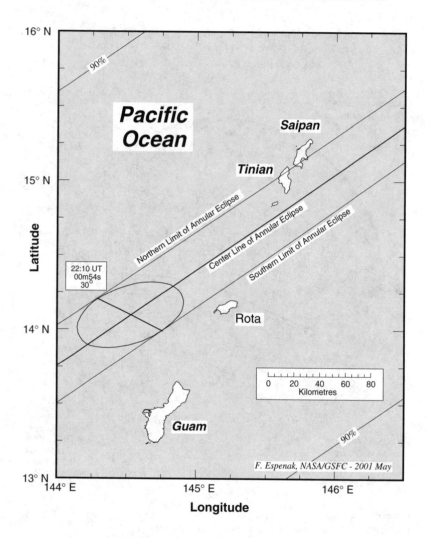

FIGURE 4—ANNULAR SOLAR ECLIPSE OF 2002 JUNE 10

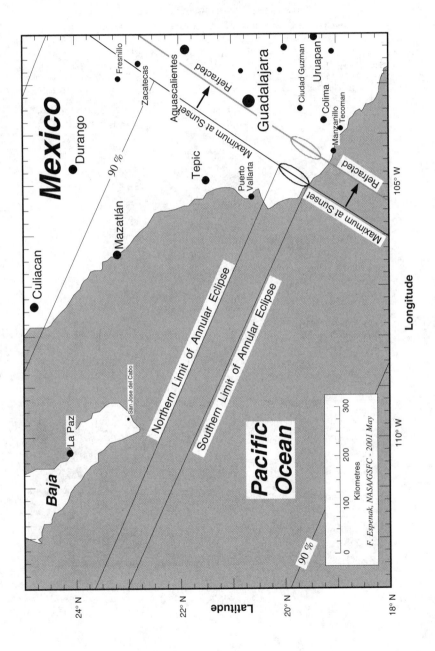

FIGURE 5—PENUMBRAL LUNAR ECLIPSE OF 2002 NOVEMBER 20

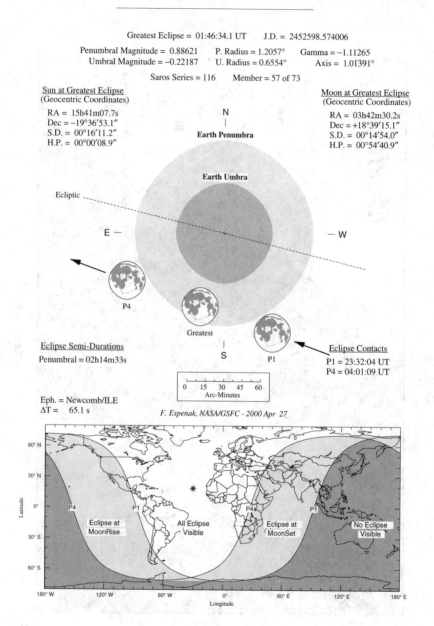

Greatest Eclipse = 01:46:34.1 UT   J.D. = 2452598.574006

Penumbral Magnitude = 0.88621   P. Radius = 1.2057°   Gamma = −1.11265
Umbral Magnitude = −0.22187   U. Radius = 0.6554°   Axis = 1.01391°

Saros Series = 116   Member = 57 of 73

Sun at Greatest Eclipse
(Geocentric Coordinates)

RA = 15h41m07.7s
Dec = −19°36′53.1″
S.D. = 00°16′11.2″
H.P. = 00°00′08.9″

N

Earth Penumbra

Earth Umbra

Moon at Greatest Eclipse
(Geocentric Coordinates)

RA = 03h42m30.2s
Dec = +18°39′15.1″
S.D. = 00°14′54.0″
H.P. = 00°54′40.9″

Ecliptic

E —

— W

P4

Greatest

S   P1

Eclipse Semi-Durations

Penumbral = 02h14m33s

Eclipse Contacts

P1 = 23:32:04 UT
P4 = 04:01:09 UT

0   15   30   45   60
Arc-Minutes

Eph. = Newcomb/ILE
ΔT =   65.1 s

F. Espenak, NASA/GSFC - 2000 Apr 27

Eclipse at
MoonRise

All Eclipse
Visible

Eclipse at
MoonSet

No Eclipse
Visible

FIGURE 6—TOTAL SOLAR ECLIPSE OF 2002 DECEMBER 4

Geocentric Conjunction = 07:38:44.0 UT   J.D. = 2452612.818565
Greatest Eclipse = 07:31:11.0 UT   J.D. = 2452612.813321

Eclipse Magnitude = 1.02437   Gamma = −0.30204

Saros Series = 142   Member = 22 of 72

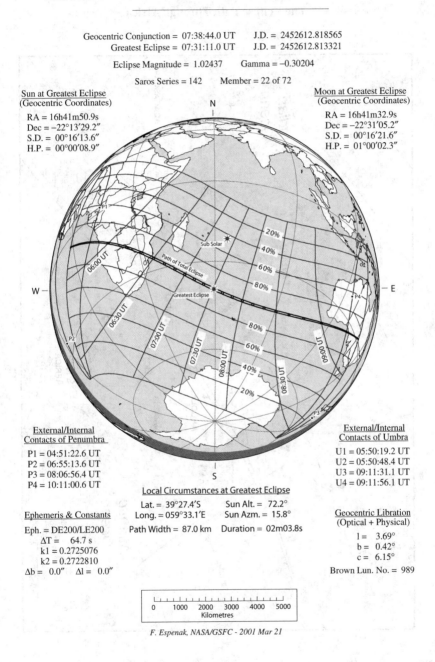

Sun at Greatest Eclipse
(Geocentric Coordinates)

RA = 16h41m50.9s
Dec = −22°13′29.2″
S.D. = 00°16′13.6″
H.P. = 00°00′08.9″

Moon at Greatest Eclipse
(Geocentric Coordinates)

RA = 16h41m32.9s
Dec = −22°31′05.2″
S.D. = 00°16′21.6″
H.P. = 01°00′02.3″

**External/Internal
Contacts of Penumbra**

P1 = 04:51:22.6 UT
P2 = 06:55:13.6 UT
P3 = 08:06:56.4 UT
P4 = 10:11:00.6 UT

Ephemeris & Constants

Eph. = DE200/LE200
ΔT =   64.7 s
k1 = 0.2725076
k2 = 0.2722810
Δb = 0.0″   Δl = 0.0″

Local Circumstances at Greatest Eclipse

Lat. = 39°27.4′S   Sun Alt. = 72.2°
Long. = 059°33.1′E   Sun Azm. = 15.8°
Path Width = 87.0 km   Duration = 02m03.8s

**External/Internal
Contacts of Umbra**

U1 = 05:50:19.2 UT
U2 = 05:50:48.4 UT
U3 = 09:11:31.1 UT
U4 = 09:11:56.1 UT

Geocentric Libration
(Optical + Physical)

l =   3.69°
b =   0.42°
c =   6.15°

Brown Lun. No. = 989

```
|  |  |  |  |  |  |  |  |  |  |  |
0    1000   2000   3000   4000   5000
            Kilometres
```

F. Espenak, NASA/GSFC - 2001 Mar 21

FIGURE 7—TOTAL SOLAR ECLIPSE OF 2002 DECEMBER 4
The Eclipse Path Through Africa

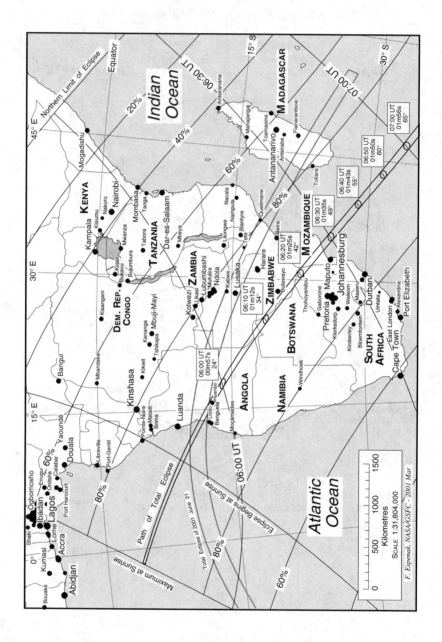

F. Espenak, NASA/GSFC · 2001 Mar

FIGURE 8—TOTAL SOLAR ECLIPSE OF 2002 DECEMBER 4
The Eclipse Path Through Australia

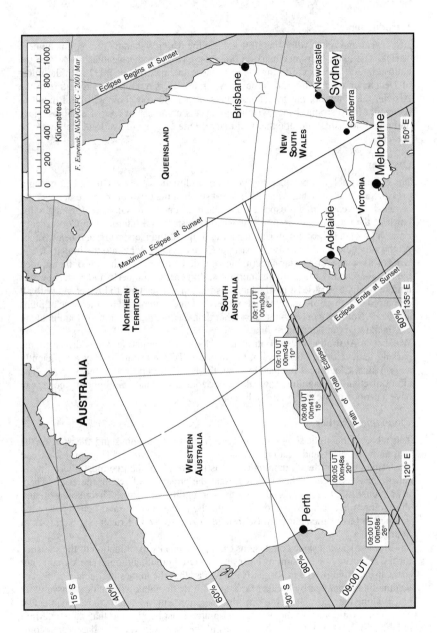

WEATHER FOR THE 2002 TOTAL SOLAR ECLIPSE
BY JAY ANDERSON

Introduction

Just a year and a half after the 2001 eclipse the Moon's shadow returns to southern Africa. The extra half-year marks a dramatic change in the weather, for where the eclipse in 2001 occurred during the dry season in June, that of 2002 is in the midst of December's wet. This time around, Australia offers a tempting alternative to the African rainy season, but the choices presented to the observer will be difficult to reconcile. In Australia, better weather prospects come at the cost of a short eclipse and a very low solar altitude that will magnify the effects of any cloud that might be present.

Overview

The eclipse track lies between two competing climatic systems. One, a belt of high-pressure anticyclones that typically lies just south of the tip of the continent, generally brings drier weather and prospects for a generous amount of sunshine. Lurking to the north of the track is a more ominous weather system, the Intertropical Convergence Zone (ITCZ), a belt of equatorial moisture, frequent thunderstorms, and heavy rains. As the anticyclones drift eastward past the Cape of Good Hope into the Indian Ocean, winds follow a semi-regular pattern, blowing first from the south and southeast, then the east, and finally the north and northwest. In general, southerly and easterly winds tend to be dry and at least partly sunny, while northerlies tend to be wet. As with all climatologies, there are many variations on the wind pattern and the presence of highs and lows. Nothing can be counted on other than the fact that it is much cloudier along the track in December than in June.

Weather in Australia is also controlled by the same alternating winds driven by the passing anticyclones, but does not tap into the ITCZ moisture supply as efficiently as in Africa. Cloudiness is much less, but the low Sun imposes a heavy penalty: The effect of cloud is magnified toward the horizon. Even relatively light sky cover can have a serious impact for a 10° high eclipse.

Cloud and Weather

The table at the right shows the percent of possible sunshine and the sum of the frequency of clear and scattered cloudiness for a selection of sites in Africa and Australia. Of all of the climatological statistics, these are the two most interesting to eclipse chasers because they best represent the prospects of seeing the event. There is precious little to recommend one site over another in Africa. The amount of sunshine ranges between 52% and 62%, with the higher values (and better prospects) inclined to favour the area from Beitbridge in Zimbabwe to Kruger National Park in South Africa.

More or less the same conclusions can be reached by examination of the statistics for the frequency of the sum of clear and scattered cloud, although the signal is not so clear-cut. Shingwedzi in Kruger National Park has the highest frequency of light or no cloudiness, but nearby Punda Maria shows little distinction from locations at other places along the track. However, sunshine measurements are a little more reliable than cloud cover estimates, so the balance of opinion must be given to that statistic. More reliably, 13 years of satellite observations of the mean cloud cover, based on a completely objective algorithm (although not without biases), shows quite distinctly that the cloud cover is lightest along the 32nd meridian, a location that corresponds to the

South Africa–Mozambique border and nearby Kruger Park. Any position between 29° and 33° east (eastern Zimbabwe, South Africa and western Mozambique) will capture the best weather that climatology can offer. The lowest value is a modest 43.8% mean cloud cover—unexceptional as eclipses go, but the best that Africa can offer.

Location	Percent of possible sunshine	Mean cloud cover	Pcpn amount (mm)	Mean days with rain	Tmax (°C)	Tmin (°C)	% Clear and scattered
Angola							
Huambo	35	0.75	233.0	17.0	25.6	14.4	—
Namibia							
Rundu	—	—	84.7	5.0	34.4	24.4	40.3
Botswana							
Francistown	—	—	89.7	6.0	33.8	22.5	47.7
Zambia							
Livingstone	37	0.75	169.1	12.0	30.4	18.9	—
Zimbabwe							
Bulawayo	52	0.63	128.0	10.0	27.0	16.0	31.9
Beitbridge	59	0.58	58.7	5.0	33.0	21.0	—
South Africa							
Messina	62	0.58	57.0		32.9	20.4	—
Shingwedzi, KNP		0.51	88.3	6.5	—	—	53.0
Punda Maria, KNP	—	0.66	92.5	7.6	—	—	40.2
Mozambique							
Maputo	52	0.88	103.0	8.0	29.0	21.0	35.6
Australia							
Ceduna AMO	67	0.45	20.5	5.2	27.2	13.9	58.2
Leigh Creek Aero		0.36	21.5	3.0	33.3	18.7	66.6
Minnipa	64		19.7	3.9	29.3	13.9	—
Woomera	74	0.39	13.7	3.3	32.2	17.5	61.8

Precipitation is both generous and frequent in December in Africa, with 6 to 12 days of the month recording a measurable amount. Temperatures tend to rise into the low 30s during the day and fall back to about the 20°C mark at night. The wet season brings mosquitoes, and the whole of the track crosses latitudes where malaria is endemic.

For Australia, the statistics look dramatically better, especially inland, away from the cloudy coastal waters. Ceduna, the first community to see the eclipse as it comes ashore from the Great Australian Bight, records 67% of possible sunshine and a 58% frequency of clear and scattered cloud, both better than any location in Africa. This improves to 74% and 62%, respectively, at Woomera, about 300 km inland. The best conditions can be found at Leigh Creek (close to Lyndhurst), where a 67% frequency of clear skies or scattered cloud can be found. Satellite measurements show a mean cloudiness of 28% over much of inland Australia.

Rainfall averages about 15 to 22 mm along the Australian section of the track. Rain falls about three days of the month inland and five on the coast at Ceduna. Temperatures demand special caution: While average daily highs are similar to those in Africa, in the low to mid-30s, the eclipse will be viewed in the outback where the mercury rises above the 40°C mark two to five times each month. These temperatures are comparable to those experienced in southern Turkey in 1999—special precautions must be taken to prevent sunstroke. Australia, because of its drier climate, is also dustier than Africa, with brisk winds, especially along the coast.

The biggest question for any eclipse chaser is, Where? Do the higher Sun and longer eclipse in Africa outweigh the disadvantage of a higher cloudiness frequency? The climatological record, even with adjustments for a low Sun angle, clearly gives the nod to inland Australia, but the penalty is very severe. Never a long eclipse to begin with, the duration at the end of the track in Australia is measured in tens of seconds, while that in Africa has the decency to at least linger for a minute and a half. The choice of an eclipse site might depend more on nonastronomical factors: cost, tourist attractions, language, and adventure.

Eclipse Viewing on the Water

Ships and boats offer an opportunity for considerable mobility when seeking those few minutes of sunshine during the critical moments of an eclipse and can often overcome the limitations of a climatologically challenged land-based site. Satellite observations show that sites off both continents are cloudier than on the land. Mean cloud cover in the Indian Ocean off Africa rises slowly, but that in the Great Australian Bight is much greater than inland Australia. While ships off either coast would offer the benefits of mobility, a water-based location in the bight can also bring the advantages that come with a much higher solar altitude.

The Great Australian Bight is a cloudy place in December, although the closer one moves toward landfall on the eclipse track, the better the weather prospects become. The tradeoff is steep, with the Sun declining rapidly in the sky as better weather prospects are approached near the coast. On the centreline south of Perth the solar elevation will be about 24°, while offshore from Ceduna the eclipse will hang just 8° above the horizon. Shipboard expeditions will require detailed weather information in order to find a break in the cloudiness off Africa and Australia, and a serious attempt cannot be made without access to satellite imagery and a detailed forecast. Examination of satellite imagery for 1999 and 2000 suggests that the shipboard chances for a view of the Sun on the bight are slightly lower than or equal to that at an inland site in Australia.

Wave heights off Africa average 1.5 to 2 m and 2 to 2.5 m off Australia. The values in waters near Africa are similar to those in the Caribbean in 1998. Wave heights are more variable in the Great Australian Bight, reflecting the stormier nature of weather systems in the region.

Acknowledgments

Preparation of this work was greatly helped by information provided by Peter Anderson of the Astronomical Association of Queensland and Nick Zambatis and Peter Tiedt for information about cloud and weather in Kruger National Park.

VIEWING A SOLAR ECLIPSE—A WARNING

Solar eclipses are among the most widely publicized and observed celestial events. It is essential to be aware of the visual danger associated with a solar eclipse. The safety rule is simple but not widely appreciated: **Never look at the surface of the Sun, either directly with the unaided eyes or through binoculars or a telescope.** To do so one risks permanent partial blindness, and this can occur almost instantly in the case of telescopic viewing. Viewing our Sun is just as dangerous on any clear day, but at the time of an eclipse people have a reason to want to look at it—and often resort to dangerous methods.

A direct view of the Sun is safe only if a suitable filter is used in a proper manner. In the case of binoculars or a telescope, the filter must be one that attaches *securely* to the *front* end of the instrument, never one that attaches to the eyepiece end (the heat developed near the eyepiece can shatter such a filter).

Filters specifically designed for solar viewing include aluminized Mylar and glass filters plated with a slightly transparent, metallic film. Such filters may be purchased at telescope supply stores. Shade #14 (no other shade) rectangular welder's glass may be used; however, since these filters are of low optical quality, they are useful only for views not involving binoculars or a telescope. All of these are commercial items and cannot be replaced with ordinary household items. For example, layers of photographic colour film, coloured glass, stacked sunglasses, crossed polarizers, smoked glass, or photographic neutral-density filters must never be used. Although one may devise a combination that dims the *visible* sunlight to a comfortable level, the makeshift filter may be quite transparent in the infrared part of the solar spectrum, and this invisible radiation will damage the retina of the observer's eye. For the same reason, one must never rely on clouds or heavy atmospheric haze to dim the solar image when using a telescope. Two layers of fully exposed and developed, silver-based, black and white photographic film provides adequate protection, but many modern films, including all colour films, are based on dyes that do not provide protection in the infrared. Thus it is best to avoid using filters made of photographic film.

One of the simplest, safest, and least known ways to observe the partial phases of a solar eclipse is *pinhole mirror projection*. Take a small pocket mirror and, with masking tape, cover all but a small section of the mirror's surface. The shape and size of the small opening are not critical, but a square about 6 mm on a side works well. Prop the mirror up on a sunny windowsill and orient the mirror so the reflected sunlight shines on the ceiling or a wall of the room—but not directly into anyone's eyes! The spot of light on the viewing surface will be a *pinhole image* of the solar disk. The mirror has a great advantage over the usual "pinhole-in-a-box arrangement" in that the image can be aimed across a substantial distance to a convenient viewing screen. The greater the projection distance, the larger, but dimmer, the Sun's image. The size of the mirror aperture should be adjusted for the best compromise between image brightness and image sharpness. With this simple device the progress of a solar eclipse can be viewed in complete safety by a group of children in a darkened room.

A sharper and brighter image of the solar disk may be projected onto a white viewing screen placed 30 or 40 cm behind the eyepiece of binoculars or a small telescope (the telescope aperture should be stopped down to about 50 mm in order to limit the intensity of sunlight passing through the instrument, and the viewing screen should be shielded from direct sunlight). However, one must *not* look through the instrument when aiming it, and, especially if children are present, a physical barrier should be used to prevent anyone from attempting to look into the eyepiece. If the telescope has a finderscope, it should be either covered or removed.

OCCULTATIONS BY THE MOON
By David W. Dunham

The Moon often passes between Earth and a star, an event called an *occultation*. During an occultation, a star suddenly disappears as the east limb of the Moon crosses the line between the star and the observer. The star reappears from behind the west limb some time later. Because the Moon moves through an angle about equal to its own diameter every hour, the longest time for an occultation is about an hour. The time is shorter if the occultation is not central. Solar eclipses are actually occultations: the star being occulted by the Moon is the Sun.

Since observing occultations is rather easy, amateur astronomers should try this activity. The slow, majestic drift of the Moon in its orbit is an interesting part of such observations, and the disappearance or reappearance of a star at the Moon's limb is a remarkable sight, particularly when it occurs as a *graze* near the Moon's northern or southern limb. During a graze, a star may disappear and reappear several times in succession as mountains and valleys in the Moon's polar regions drift by it. On rarer occasions the Moon occults a planet. (See THE SKY MONTH BY MONTH on pp. 68–91 for occultations of planets this year.)

Lunar occultation and graze observations refine our knowledge of the shape of the lunar profile and the fundamental star coordinate system. These observations complement those made by other techniques, such as Clementine laser ranging and photographs. Improved knowledge of the lunar profile is useful in determinations of the Sun's diameter from solar eclipse records. Occultation observations are also useful for detecting double stars and measuring their separations. Binaries with separations as small as 0.02″ have been discovered visually during grazes. Doubles with separations in this range are useful for filling the gap between doubles that can be directly resolved and those whose duplicity has been discovered spectroscopically.

Observations

The **International Lunar Occultation Centre (ILOC)** analyzes lunar occultation observations and is the world clearinghouse for such observations. Anyone interested in pursuing a systematic program of lunar occultation observations should write to the ILOC, Geodesy and Geophysics Division, Hydrographic Department, Tsukiji 5-3-1, Chuo-ku, Tokyo, 104-0045 Japan, for their booklet *Guide to Lunar Occultation Observations*. ILOC's web address is **www.jhd.go.jp/cue/KOHO/iloc/obsrep**.

Observers in North America should also contact the **International Occultation Timing Association (IOTA)**, 5403 Bluebird Trail, Stillwater, OK 74074, U.S.A.; email: **business@occultations.org**. IOTA provides predictions and coordination services for occultation observers. Detailed predictions for any grazing occultation are available ($1.50 U.S. each; free by email); instructions explaining the use of predictions are also available ($5.00 U.S.). Annual membership in IOTA is $30 U.S. in North America, $35 U.S. overseas. Less expensive online rates are available. Membership includes free graze predictions, descriptive materials, and a subscription to *Occultation Newsletter* (available separately for $20 U.S. in North America, $25 overseas). IOTA's administrative web address is **www.occultations.org** and its site for predictions, updates, observations, and other technical information is **www.lunar-occultations.com/iota**.

For observers in the southwestern Pacific (New Zealand, Australia, Papua New Guinea, and nearby areas), The Royal Astronomical Society of New Zealand (RASNZ) provides occultation data (total lunar, lunar grazing, planetary, and Jupiter's satellites), plus comprehensive instructions for new observers. See the RASNZ web site: occsec.wellington.net.nz.

The main information required in a lunar occultation observation is the time of the event and the observer's location. Supplementary data include the seeing conditions, telescope size, timing method, estimate of the observer's reaction time and the accuracy of the timing, and whether or not the reaction time correction has been applied. The timing should be accurate to 0.5 s or better (a shortwave radio time signal and tape recorder provide a simple, permanent time record, but a video record provides higher accuracy). The observer's longitude, latitude, and altitude should be reported to the nearest tenth of a second of arc and 10 m, respectively, and should be accurate to at least 0.5″ or 16 m. These can be determined from either GPS measurements (10 min of position averaging and an unobstructed view of the sky above 15° altitude are needed) or a suitable topographical map. For Canada, the maps are available from the Canada Map Office, Natural Resources Canada, 130 Bentley Ave., Nepean, ON K2E 6T9. In the United States (except Alaska), write to U.S. Geological Survey, Map Sales, Box 25286, Denver, CO 80225, asking for an index to topographical maps in your state, or call (800) USA-MAPS. For Alaska, write to U.S. Geological Survey, Map Sales, 101-12th Ave., #12, Fairbanks, AK 99701. Parts of USGS maps can be viewed and printed at www.topozone.com.

Observers are encouraged to develop a video capability for recording occultations in order to obtain reliable and accurate timings. Inexpensive yet sensitive video cameras are now available. Visual timings must be accurate to ±0.2 s to be good enough for further improvement of the lunar profile and other parameters, except for grazes, where ±0.5 s is adequate. For asteroidal occultations, especially the shorter duration events of 10 s or less, video or photoelectric observations are much preferred.

Pages 150–158 give tables of occultation predictions and a table and maps of northern or southern limits for grazing occultations.

1. TOTAL OCCULTATION PREDICTIONS

PREDICTIONS BY THE INTERNATIONAL LUNAR OCCULTATION CENTRE, JAPAN

The total occultation predictions, as given in the tables on pp. 156–158, are for the 18 standard stations identified on the map below; the longitudes and latitudes of these stations are given in the table headings.

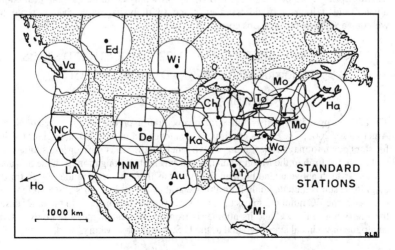

The predictions are limited to stars of magnitude 5.0 and brighter. The first five columns give for each occultation the date, the Zodiacal Catalogue (ZC) number of the star, its magnitude, the phenomenon (DD or DB = disappearance at dark limb or bright limb, respectively; RD or RB = reappearance at dark limb or bright limb, respectively), and the elongation of the Moon from the Sun in degrees (see the middle of p. 66). Under each station are given the Universal Time of the event, factors A and B (see below), and the position angle P (from the north point, eastward around the Moon's limb to the point of occurrence of the phenomenon). In several places, predictions have been replaced by the cryptic notations GBG (after moonset), GSM (before moonrise), NB2 (Sun's altitude greater than $-6°$), NSG (after sunrise), and NBM (before sunset). If A and B give an unrealistic representation, as in the case of near grazes, they are omitted.

The terms A and B are for determining corrections to the times of the events for stations within 500 km of the standard stations. If Lo* and La* represent the longitude and latitude of the standard station, and Lo and La those of the observer, then for the observer,

UT of event =
UT of event at the standard station $+ A(\text{Lo} - \text{Lo*}) + B(\text{La} - \text{La*})$,

where Lo, etc., are expressed in degrees, and A and B are in minutes of time per degree. Longitude measured *west* of Greenwich is assumed to be *positive* (which is opposite to the IAU convention and that used by IOTA's *Occult* software). Due regard must be paid to the algebraic signs of the terms. To convert UT to the standard time of the observer, see the section STANDARD TIME ZONES on pp. 40–41.

As an example, consider the occultation of ZC 5 (33 Psc) on 2002 January 19 as seen from Calgary. For Calgary, Lo = 114.08° and La = 51.08°. The nearest standard station is Edmonton, for which Lo* = 113.40° and La* = 53.60°. Therefore, the UT of the disappearance at the dark limb (DD) is $0{:}56.1 - 1.1 \times (114.08° - 113.40°)$ min $+ 0.4 \times (51.08° - 53.60°)$ min $= 0{:}54.3$. The elongation of the Moon is 61°, which corresponds to the waxing crescent phase (between new moon and first quarter). The position angle of disappearance is approximately 51°.

The number of events observable from any location increases *rapidly* as predictions are extended to fainter stars. Observers who wish to pursue such work can obtain software or more extensive lists from Walter Robinson, 515 W. Kump, Bonner Springs, KS 66012–1439, U.S.A., by providing accurate geographical coordinates and a long, self-addressed envelope (with postage); or, better, write to webmaster@lunar-occultations.com.

2. GRAZE PREDICTIONS AND DATA ON OCCULTED STARS
By Eberhard Riedel and David W. Dunham

(A) GRAZE PREDICTIONS

The table on pp. 159–160 lists lunar grazing occultation predictions for much of North America for 2002. The events are limited to stars of magnitude 7.0 or brighter (paths for stars down to magnitude 7.5 are shown when the Moon is 40% or less sunlit) that will graze the limb of the Moon when it is at a favourable elongation from the Sun and at least as high above a land horizon in degrees as the star's magnitude (e.g., a third-magnitude star is included only if its altitude is at least 3°). The star's USNO reference number is the ZC number, unless the number is prefixed with an X. In the latter case, the star is not in the ZC and its number is from the XZ catalogue, a more extensive catalogue of zodiacal stars prepared at the U.S. Naval Observatory.

The maps on pp. 161–164 show the predicted graze tracks. The maps are "false" projections, since the latitude and longitude scales are both linear. This makes it much easier for measuring coordinates or plotting locations with known coordinates than is possible with any other type of projection. The longitude scale is compressed by a factor of cos 50°. The maps are not detailed enough for locating oneself in the 2- or 3-km-wide zone where multiple disappearances of the star may occur. To obtain detailed predictions of any graze for plotting on larger-scale maps of your region, write to (or email) IOTA (see p. 150).

Each track is keyed to the sequential number in the table. The computer-drawn number appears at the east and west ends of the track and is aligned parallel to it. Some overlapping numbers have been omitted for legibility; in these cases, check the other end of the track for the number. Conditions are represented by three different types of lines:

solid line = dark limb, night
dashed line = bright limb, night
dotted line = dark or bright limb, day

Thicker lines are drawn for first-magnitude stars and planets. Many tracks begin and/or end with the letter A, B, or S: A denotes that the Moon is at a low altitude, B that the bright limb interferes, and S that sunlight or twilight interferes. The tick marks along the tracks indicate multiples of 10 min of every hour. For example, if the time for the west end of the track is $3^:16.2$, the tick marks proceeding eastward correspond to $3^:20$, $3^:30$, etc. Time always increases from west to east along the path. *The time ticks, track numbers, and the A, B, and S letters are on the side of the limit with an occultation*, that is north of southern limits and south of northern limits. The locations for the North American standard stations for lunar total occultation predictions are indicated by asterisks on the graze maps (see the map on p. 151). For grazes of planets, a *partial occultation* of the object will occur at the northern or southern limit. The line plotted is the centre of the partial occultation zone, typically several kilometres wide.

(B) NAMES OF OCCULTED STARS

The stars that are occulted by the Moon are stars that lie along the zodiac; hence they are known by their number in the ZC compiled by James Robertson and published in the *Astronomical Papers Prepared for the Use of the American Ephemeris and Nautical Almanac*, vol. 10, pt. 2 (U.S. Government Printing Office, Washington, 1940). Robertson's ZC has been out of print for several years. In 1986, Isao Sato, a member of the Lunar Occultation Observers Group in Japan, republished the ZC. This new edition is based on the epoch J2000 and includes much new data, particularly on double stars. Since stars are not usually recognized by their ZC numbers, the equivalent Bayer designations or Flamsteed numbers of the stars occulted during the year are given in the table on the next page. The last four stars are not in the ZC, so their XZ numbers are given. The ZC and XZ catalogues are available through IOTA's website.

ZC	Name	ZC	Name	ZC/XZ	Name
5	33 Psc	936	5 Gem	2159	ν Lib (Zuben Hakrabi)
150	26 Cet	954	8 Gem	2211	33 Lib
165	29 Cet	960	10 Gem	2233	41 Lib
178	35 Cet	962	11 Gem	2275	47 Lib
192	89 Psc	1030	ε Gem (Mebsuta)	2302	β¹ Sco (Acrab)
249	ν Psc	1055	37 Gem	2303	β² Sco
308	WZ Psc	1070	ω Gem	2307	ω¹ Sco (Kow Kin)
327	ξ¹ Cet	1092	48 Gem	2376	ω Oph
354	ξ Ari	1099	52 Gem	2407	15 Oph
360	VW Ari	1117	57 Gem	2434	24 Oph
362	25 (Ari)/Cet	1170	κ Gem	2490	o Oph
404	38 Ari	1221	9 Cnc	2500	θ Oph
614	43 Tau	1308	γ Cnc (Asellus Bor.)	2523	51 Oph
628	ω Tau	1484	η Leo	2672	λ Sgr (Kaus Bor.)
633	53 Tau	1514	42 Leo	2678	V4031 Sgr
700	HU Tau	1544	46 Leo	2721	φ Sgr
752	ι Tau	1689	ω Vir	2750	σ Sgr (Nunki)
766	105 Tau	1702	ν Vir	2809	ψ Sgr
792	109 Tau	1773	16 Vir	2864	52 Sgr
839	121 Tau	1941	74 Vir	3130	33 Cap
865	V731 Tau	2020	94 Vir	3141	35 Cap
882	132 Tau	2022	95 Vir	3158	37 Cap
916	1 Gem	2032	97 Vir	3343	τ¹ Aqr
923	2 Gem	2033	κ Vir	3349	τ² Aqr
929	3 Gem	2114	μ Lib	3536	30 Psc

(C) OCCULTED STARS KNOWN TO BE DOUBLE

In the table at the right are data on double stars for which graze predictions are given. This information is from DSFILE, a comprehensive file of zodiacal double star data compiled by Don Stockbauer, Henk Bulder, Mitsuru Sôma, and David Dunham; most of the data for the ZC stars are in the Sato ZC catalogue. The successive columns give the USNO reference number of the star, the number of the graze track, the double star code (**d**), the magnitudes of the brighter (**A**) and dimmer (**B**) components, the separation in seconds of arc, and the position angle of B from A measured eastward from north. If the star is triple, the third component's magnitude is given under **C**, and its separation and position angle from A are given in the last columns.

The parameters are given for the epoch of the occultation, computed from orbital elements when available or from extrapolations from a long series of observations. If there is little change in the available observations, the last-observed separation and P.A. are used. Components fainter than magnitude 11.5 are not listed, and some very close doubles whose parameters are not known, generally with separations less than 0.2″, are also not listed. The latter include spectroscopic binaries (code J, U, or sometimes V) and visual occultation doubles (most codes K and X, and many Vs). Some close pairs have rapid orbital motion so the current position angle is unknown.

The codes have the following meanings:

A, C, or G .. visual double
B or V .... close double, usually discovered by occultation
D .... primary of wide pair; secondary has separate catalogue entry
E................ secondary star of wide pair
F................ prediction is for the following component of a visual double
H................ triple, with close occultation pair and third visual component; prediction uses a mean position

I .... data for B component computed from orbital elements, but the B component is itself a close double, with data for the C component referred to B rather than A

K .... possible double from elements

Q .... = O, but A component may be close double (if triple, C-component data are computed from orbital elements)

R .... triple; close pair = O and C component also has orbit relative to centre of close pair

W .... = A or C, but A component is a spectroscopic binary

X .... probable double from occultation

Y .... triple, K or X (B component) and A or C (C component)

Z .... triple, O (B component) and V (C component)

USNO	Graze #	d	A	B	Sep. "	P.A. °	C	Sep. "	P.A. °
150	57, 100, 143	A	6.2	8.6	16.0	253			
303	38	X	7.2	7.4	0.4	115			
360	145	D	6.8	8.3	73.8	31	11.3	62.3	155
527	41	A	6.3	11.8	35.0	154			
646	174	M	6.2	8.4	1.9	169			
651	175	X	6.7	6.7	0.15	55			
761	177, 194	M	7.0	8.4	0.4	153			
916	24	Q	4.9	6.9	0.3	183	5.1	0.2	
929	25	M	5.9	8.5	0.6	346			
1015	103	M	6.5	10.4	0.5	226			
1170	89, 225	A	3.7	8.2	7.4	240			
1221	70	V	5.9	10.0	0.4	110			
1484	28, 72, 124, 181, 248, 249	C	4.1	4.6	0.1	93			
1773	4	V	5.8	5.8	0.6	76			
1856	29	M	7.5	7.6	1.0	99			
1994	31	O	6.5	7.7	3.5	98			
2064	52	M	6.6	8.0	1.2	276			
2114	74	M	5.6	6.7	1.9	2			
2233	165	M	5.6	8.8	0.3	127			
2264	32	V	7.4	7.9	0.3	80			
2275	75	M	6.1	8.1	0.6	121			
2302	9, 76, 139	H	3.2	4.2	0.001		6.0	0.5	116
2303	8	B	5.2	7.6	0.13	257			
2434	78, 156	M	6.2	6.5	1.0	302			
2490	96, 141	A	5.4	6.9	10.3	355			
2673	235	M	6.4	9.3	0.3	172			
2721	211	X	4.1	4.1	0.13	27			
2750	157, 213	Y	2.9	2.9	0.1?	90?	9.5	9.0	244
2809	55	Q	6.2	6.2	0.2	112	5.7	0.1	?
2864	130	A	4.7	9.2	2.5	174			
3343	189	A	5.8	9.0	20.2	123	10.0	63.4	34
X 4565	136	K	7.0	10.5	0.04	13			
X 5541	59	O	7.7	8.1	0.5	3			
X 7281	101	A	7.5	10.0	79.1	176			
X 9743	86	A	7.2	10.1	15.5	261			
X 9881	198	V	7.7	8.4	0.3	69			
X10425	66	A	7.3	10.3	13.7	50			
X10792	122	A	7.1	9.8	13.8	310			
X11911	152	M	7.9	8.6	0.18	173			
X12068	180	M	7.4	11.0	1.3	170			
X18067	232	V	7.9	12.8	0.03	64			

TABLE OF TOTAL LUNAR OCCULTATIONS

DATE	ZC	MAG	PH	ELG °	HALIFAX 63.6°W, 44.6°N				MONTREAL 73.6°W, 45.5°N				TORONTO 79.4°W, 43.7°N			
					TIME (UT)	A m	B m	P °	TIME (UT)	A m	B m	P °	TIME (UT)	A m	B m	P °
Jan. 9	2302	2.9	DB	314	16:13.8	—	—	169	15:57.4	—	—	167	15:55.5	—	—	175
9	2302	2.9	RD	314	16:43.5	—	—	218	16:34.8	—	—	225	16:25.9	—	—	220
15	3175	4.8	DD	27	GBG				22:15.8	-0.9	-0.9	76	NBM			
18	3536	4.7	DD	60	23:39.9	-1.3	-1.5	90	23:25.3	-1.4	-0.6	74	23:17.3	-1.6	-0.2	71
19	5	4.7	DD	61	—				1:54.0	—	—	127	1:56.0	—	—	134
25	752	4.7	DD	132	—				8:13.5	—	—	20	8:08.6	-0.5	0.2	39
26	916	4.3	DD	145	8:42.1	0.1	-0.8	72	8:41.4	-0.1	-1.1	80	8:43.1	-0.1	-1.3	91
Feb. 7	2523	4.9	RD	305	10:30.8	-2.0	1.6	247	10:12.6	-2.1	2.7	231	—			
21	SAT	0.1	DD	96	0:48.2	-1.5	1.4	40	0:34.5	-1.5	2.2	32	0:21.8	-1.5	2.2	36
21	SAT	0.1	RB	97	1:50.2	-1.1	-2.4	294	1:35.0	-1.5	-2.5	296	1:29.2	-1.8	-1.9	290
Apr.21	1308	4.7	DD	97	1:42.0	-0.7	-2.3	135	1:32.8	-0.7	-2.7	147	1:35.2	-0.4	-3.9	163
30	2513	4.3	RD	222	—				—				7:10.0	—	—	353
Jun. 7	327	4.5	RD	317	7:35.7	—	—	312	GSM				GSM			
12	MARS	1.7	DD	18	10:26.9	—	—	157	GSM				GSM			
12	MARS	1.7	RB	18	10:41.2	—	—	188	GSM				GSM			
Jul. 17	1941	4.8	DD	89	GBG				3:34.4	-0.4	-2.1	143	3:35.5	-0.5	-2.2	147
31	249	4.7	RD	258	7:37.9	-1.2	1.9	228	7:27.6	-1.2	1.8	243	7:17.8	-1.1	1.8	247
Sep.27	628	4.8	RD	242	6:40.7	-2.2	0.2	282	6:16.7	—	—	307	6:00.9	—	—	318
Oct. 3	1484	3.6	RD	317	NB2				NB2				10:23.8	—	—	347
17	3349	4.2	DD	135	5:25.1	-1.0	-1.8	95	5:13.7	-1.1	-1.0	78	5:08.4	-1.3	-0.7	75
27	1030	3.2	RD	246	5:28.3	-0.4	3.4	216	5:27.1	-0.4	2.4	233	5:21.1	-0.2	2.3	235
28	1170	3.7	RD	259	7:02.0	—	—	201	7:01.5	-0.5	3.6	221	6:52.9	-0.2	3.5	220
Nov.15	3536	4.7	DD	126	—				2:14.4	-3.1	-1.7	109	1:59.1	-2.9	-0.7	100
Dec.18	628	4.8	DD	160	0:39.4	-1.5	1.3	81	0:29.1	-0.9	1.9	65	0:21.1	-0.6	2.0	61
24	1484	3.6	RD	236	8:43.3	-0.9	-2.4	331	8:30.3	-1.3	-1.7	320	8:24.7	-1.5	-1.1	308
26	1702	4.2	RD	259	4:51.2	-0.5	1.7	264	4:49.6	-0.2	1.5	268	GSM			
28	1941	4.8	RD	287	6:48.2	-0.9	2.8	247	GSM				GSM			

DATE	ZC	MAG	PH	ELG °	WINNIPEG 97.2°W, 49.9°N				EDMONTON 113.4°W, 53.6°N				VANCOUVER 123.1°W, 49.2°N			
					TIME (UT)	A m	B m	P °	TIME (UT)	A m	B m	P °	TIME (UT)	A m	B m	P °
Jan. 1	1308	4.7	RD	207	—				—				10:50.1	—	—	347
9	2302	2.9	DB	314	15:29.1	—	—	186	—				—			
9	2302	2.9	RD	314	15:49.3	—	—	216	—				—			
19	5	4.7	DD	61	1:16.3	-1.3	-0.9	79	0:56.1	-1.1	0.4	51	NSG			
21	249	4.7	DD	85	—				—				7:24.0	—	—	352
25	752	4.7	DD	132	7:57.2	-0.9	0.3	37	7:42.2	-1.1	0.7	36	7:28.7	-1.3	0.2	57
26	916	4.3	DD	145	8:28.9	-0.5	-1.5	93	8:11.8	-0.9	-1.4	95	8:08.8	-1.1	-1.9	114
Feb.25	1308	4.7	DD	151	—				—				8:05.6	—	—	27
28	1702	4.2	RD	195	—				—				9:32.6	-0.6	-2.1	343
Mar. 7	2672	2.9	DB	289	GBG				17:03.4	-1.4	-1.3	118	16:53.1	-1.8	-1.0	117
7	2672	2.9	RD	290	GBG				GBG				18:02.5	-1.0	-0.6	239
8	2809	4.9	RD	299	NB2				NB2				13:25.5	-1.3	1.6	252
20	2033	4.3	RD	205	GBG				NB2				13:06.6	-0.5	-2.5	355
Apr.16	SAT	0.2	DD	45	19:03.9	—	—	134	18:42.6	-0.8	1.4	98	18:30.0	-0.5	1.5	94
16	SAT	0.2	RB	45	19:35.7	—	—	184	19:43.1	-0.5	2.4	222	19:29.1	-0.3	2.3	225
24	1702	4.2	DD	140	—				6:43.0	—	—	50	6:20.9	-1.8	-0.1	85
30	2513	4.3	RD	222	6:58.6	-0.2	-0.4	336	GSM				GSM			
May18	1308	4.7	DD	71	GBG				7:22.4	0.2	-1.4	90	7:30.5	0.2	-1.5	102
24	2033	4.3	DD	151	GBG				—				9:01.5	—	—	55
Jul. 17	1941	4.8	DD	89	3:11.4	-0.7	-1.9	149	NSG				NSG			
27	3349	4.2	RD	215	NB2				9:56.1	-2.4	-0.7	297	9:32.4	—	—	307
31	249	4.7	RD	258	7:12.9	-0.7	1.7	272	7:11.6	-0.2	1.6	285	GSM			
Aug.16	2307	4.1	DD	101	GBG				GBG				6:04.7	-0.9	-1.2	80
19	2750	2.1	DD	137	4:36.4	—	—	167	4:00.5	—	—	152	3:56.8	—	—	172
19	2750	2.1	RB	137	4:47.8	—	—	184	4:37.1	—	—	207	4:10.4	—	—	192
25	3536	4.7	DD	207	7:49.0	-1.0	1.5	211	7:36.7	-1.1	1.5	235	7:18.6	-1.1	1.8	239
25	5	4.7	RD	208	—				9:35.8	0.1	2.5	178	9:24.3	-0.4	2.3	187
28	327	4.5	RD	239	—				7:27.8	—	—	172	7:19.4	—	—	180
Oct. 11	2500	3.4	DD	64	GBG				GBG				2:50.2	-1.1	-0.9	76
17	3349	4.2	DD	135	4:49.1	-0.9	0.7	35	4:45.1	0.0	2.0	360	4:37.5	—	—	346
24	628	4.8	RD	216	NB2				NB2				13:58.8	-1.1	0.0	231
27	1030	3.2	RD	246	5:28.2	-0.2	1.5	270	5:30.8	-0.1	1.1	293	5:26.6	0.1	0.9	295
28	1170	3.7	RD	259	7:01.4	-0.3	1.7	260	7:03.0	-0.2	1.3	283	6:57.3	0.1	1.1	284
Nov.15	3536	4.7	DD	125	1:27.8	-1.4	1.4	61	1:16.4	-0.8	1.9	42	1:00.0	-0.7	2.1	39
15	5	4.7	DD	126	—				3:38.0	-1.8	0.3	89	3:17.6	-1.8	1.0	82
23	1030	3.2	RD	220	12:58.5	-1.4	0.1	227	12:35.1	-1.7	1.3	220	—			
24	1170	3.7	RD	232	NB2				14:27.7	-1.0	-1.1	258	14:16.2	-1.9	0.6	232
Dec.18	628	4.8	DD	160	0:31.8	0.2	2.6	25	—				—			
24	1484	3.6	RD	235	7:55.9	-1.1	-0.7	317	7:38.3	-0.8	-0.7	330	7:32.5	-0.7	0.0	315

TABLE OF TOTAL LUNAR OCCULTATIONS (continued)

DATE	ZC	MAG	PH	ELG°	MASSACHUSETTS 72.5°W, 42.5°N TIME (UT)	A m	B m	P°	WASHINGTON, D.C. 77.0°W, 38.9°N TIME (UT)	A m	B m	P°	CHICAGO 87.7°W, 41.9°N TIME (UT)	A m	B m	P°
Jan. 9	2302	2.9	DB	314	16:08.2	—	—	175	—				—			
9	2302	2.9	RD	314	16:35.0	—	—	216	—				—			
15	3175	4.8	DD	27	22:20.1	-1.1	-1.2	86	NBM				NBM			
18	3536	4.7	DD	60	23:29.3	-1.7	-1.0	85	23:24.5	-2.1	-1.0	89	23:03.3	-1.7	0.4	62
19	5	4.7	DD	61	—				—				1:49.7	—	—	130
25	752	4.7	DD	132	8:11.5	-0.5	0.5	33	8:09.4	-0.3	-0.1	53	8:04.4	-0.5	-0.3	56
26	916	4.3	DD	145	8:44.7	0.0	-1.1	86	8:49.3	0.1	-1.3	100	8:44.6	-0.2	-1.6	104
Feb. 7	2523	4.9	RD	305	10:05.5	—	—	221	—				—			
21	SAT	0.1	DD	96	0:30.8	-1.7	1.5	45	0:17.8	-1.9	1.2	56	0:05.4	-1.4	2.6	34
21	SAT	0.1	RB	97	1:43.0	-1.5	-1.8	284	1:40.4	-1.8	-1.0	270	1:15.2	-2.2	-1.4	286
Apr.21	1308	4.7	DD	97	1:42.3	-0.5	-3.2	155	1:59.6	—	—	187	—			
30	2513	4.3	RD	223	—				7:21.3	-0.9	-1.9	341	7:08.4	-0.8	-0.9	332
Jun. 4	5	4.7	RD	285	NB2				NB2				9:31.2	—	—	309
Jul. 17	1941	4.8	RD	89	3:41.2	-0.4	-2.2	148	3:47.5	-0.5	-2.4	155	3:34.7	-0.6	-2.3	153
31	249	4.7	RD	258	7:23.3	-1.2	1.9	237	7:11.2	-1.0	2.0	237	7:06.5	-0.9	1.8	254
Aug.25	3536	4.7	RD	207	—				—				7:36.1	—	—	172
Sep.27	628	4.8	RD	242	6:20.4	-2.3	0.1	293	6:09.6	-2.1	0.3	291	—			
Oct. 3	1484	3.6	RD	317	NB2				10:33.4	-1.0	-0.9	322	10:19.5	-0.9	-1.9	342
17	3349	4.2	DD	135	5:18.5	-1.3	-1.4	90	5:17.1	-1.7	-1.5	95	4:57.9	-1.5	-0.2	67
27	1030	3.2	RD	246	5:19.5	-0.2	2.9	222	5:08.9	0.1	3.0	216	5:16.1	-0.1	2.0	241
28	1170	3.7	RD	258	6:47.8	—	—	200	—				6:46.0	0.0	3.0	224
Nov.15	3536	4.7	DD	126	2:30.5	—	—	134	—				1:37.0	-2.4	0.5	87
15	3536	4.7	DD	126	2:43.0	—	—	151	—				RB			
Dec.18	628	4.8	DD	160	0:24.8	-1.1	1.7	73	0:14.3	-0.9	1.7	73	0:13.6	-0.3	2.1	53
24	1484	3.6	RD	236	8:36.7	-1.5	-1.5	312	8:33.4	-1.9	-0.8	295	8:12.6	-1.7	-0.3	294
26	1702	4.2	RD	259	4:44.5	-0.1	2.0	255	GSM				GSM			

DATE	ZC	MAG	PH	ELG°	MIAMI 80.3°W, 25.8°N TIME (UT)	A m	B m	P°	ATLANTA 84.3°W, 33.8°N TIME (UT)	A m	B m	P°	AUSTIN 97.8°W, 30.2°N TIME (UT)	A m	B m	P°
Jan. 1	1308	4.7	RD	208	NB2				RB				11:59.7	-0.4	-2.3	320
18	3536	4.7	RD	60	—				23:11.3	-2.8	-0.8	91	NBM			
25	752	4.7	DD	132	8:16.6	0.1	-1.0	97	8:09.9	-0.2	-0.7	77	8:09.7	-0.4	-1.4	103
26	916	4.3	DD	145	9:13.2	0.9	-2.6	146	8:58.3	0.2	-1.9	123	9:16.3	—	—	167
Feb.20	SAT	0.1	DD	96	24:04.4	-3.2	-0.7	99	23:56.5	-2.2	1.2	66	23:23.8	-1.7	1.9	57
21	SAT	0.1	RB	97	1:28.2	-2.2	2.1	222	1:27.5	-2.2	0.2	254	0:53.2	-2.5	0.9	253
25	1308	4.7	DD	151	—				—				8:41.1	-1.7	0.2	62
28	1702	4.2	RD	196	10:46.0	0.4	-3.6	1	—				10:32.5	-0.4	-2.6	341
Apr. 1	2302	2.9	DB	232	13:16.0	-0.2	1.1	44	—				—			
24	1702	4.2	DD	140	7:44.7	-0.9	-0.2	70	7:43.3	—	—	42	7:20.3	-1.6	-0.8	85
30	2513	4.3	RD	223	7:33.0	-2.1	-0.8	303	7:19.0	-1.4	-0.9	317	7:00.4	-1.5	0.2	288
May 1	2672	2.9	DB	235	7:28.4	-3.1	2.2	54	7:40.8	—	—	26	6:55.0	-1.7	1.6	70
1	2672	2.9	RD	236	8:33.5	-2.1	-2.0	323	8:05.8	—	—	352	8:00.7	-1.1	-0.6	314
6	3349	4.2	RD	293	8:23.7	-0.6	0.5	285	GSM				GSM			
24	2033	4.3	DD	152	GBG				GBG				9:40.3	-0.4	-0.9	87
Jun. 4	5	4.7	RD	285	9:32.4	-1.8	1.3	260	9:33.7	-1.8	0.8	283	9:13.0	-0.9	0.8	284
25	2672	2.9	DB	183	1:36.5	-1.2	1.3	77	1:45.1	-1.5	2.3	57	GSM			
25	2672	2.9	RB	309	2:41.9	-0.9	-0.5	309	2:34.1	-0.2	-0.9	327	2:29.7	-0.4	0.3	294
Jul. 15	1702	4.2	DD	62	2:38.9	-0.6	-0.6	78	2:32.9	—	—	58	2:18.4	-1.3	-1.0	89
17	1941	4.8	DD	90	—				3:57.4	-0.5	-3.0	169	DB			
19	2302	2.9	DD	125	21:46.7	-1.2	0.9	90	21:53.5	-1.5	2.3	66	GSM			
19	2302	2.9	RB	126	22:47.8	-0.5	-1.2	327	22:35.5	0.3	-1.9	348	22:37.2	-0.3	-0.3	309
27	3349	4.2	RD	215	—				NB2				10:25.1	-1.2	1.4	217
31	249	4.7	RD	257	6:39.9	-0.6	2.4	218	6:54.2	-0.8	2.0	238	6:39.7	-0.4	1.7	243
Sep.27	628	4.8	RD	242	5:52.7	-1.3	1.2	261	5:53.2	-1.8	0.3	291	5:29.0	—	—	315
Oct. 3	1484	3.6	RD	317	10:30.0	-1.0	0.7	274	10:28.7	-0.9	-0.1	304	10:20.2	-0.4	0.0	300
17	3349	4.2	DD	135	—				5:09.9	-2.4	-1.5	98	4:38.6	-2.5	0.1	78
27	1030	3.2	RD	246	—				4:56.4	0.6	2.9	211	4:55.2	0.6	2.1	224
Nov. 9	2750	2.1	DD	56	GBG				GBG				1:25.6	-0.9	0.0	58
9	2750	2.1	RB	57	GBG				GBG				2:31.1	-1.0	-1.2	279
15	3536	4.7	DD	125	—				1:54.4	—	—	124	1:02.0	-2.7	0.8	92
Dec.17	628	4.8	DD	159	23:54.8	-1.4	0.6	99	24:00.2	-0.6	1.6	73	23:50.2	0.0	1.6	62
24	1484	3.6	RD	236	8:17.5	—	—	237	8:18.6	-2.4	0.6	269	7:41.1	-2.0	3.2	239

See pp. 151–152 for an explanation of this table.

TABLE OF TOTAL LUNAR OCCULTATION PREDICTIONS (continued)

DATE	ZC	MAG	PH	ELG °	KANSAS CITY 94.5°W, 39.0°N TIME (UT)	A m	B m	P °	DENVER 105.0°W, 39.8°N TIME (UT)	A m	B m	P °	NEW MEX., ARIZ. 109.0°W, 34.0°N TIME (UT)	A m	B m	P °
Jan. 1	1308	4.7	RD	207	11:30.4	—	—	3	11:31.3	-0.2	-3.2	338	11:44.1	-0.9	-2.1	312
19	5	4.7	DD	61	1:50.0	—	—	139	1:14.8	-2.5	-1.7	101	1:16.2	—	—	118
19	5	4.7	RD	61	2:01.0	—	—	156	RB				RB			
25	752	4.7	DD	132	8:02.2	-0.6	-0.7	72	7:53.9	-0.9	-0.9	79	7:57.2	-0.9	-1.5	101
26	916	4.3	DD	145	8:48.7	-0.1	-2.0	120	8:44.6	-0.3	-2.6	131	9:13.4	—	—	181
Feb. 20	SAT	0.1	DD	96	23:48.7	-1.2	2.7	35	23:43.1	-0.2	4.1	13	23:20.8	-0.5	3.2	26
20	SAT	0.1	RB	96	1:02.2	-2.5	-0.8	281	0:32.6	-3.1	-1.6	300	0:25.5	-2.8	-0.2	283
25	1308	4.7	DD	151	—				8:34.8	—	—	34	8:20.5	-1.9	-0.2	73
28	1702	4.2	RD	196	RB				10:03.7	-0.2	-2.9	352	10:16.0	-0.9	-2.2	329
Apr. 24	1702	4.2	DD	140	7:24.8	—	—	48	7:00.8	-2.1	-0.4	74	6:57.2	-1.8	-1.0	96
30	2513	4.3	RD	222	7:04.0	-1.0	-0.3	314	6:54.6	-0.8	0.3	301	6:48.0	-1.1	0.7	280
May 1	2672	2.9	DB	235	7:26.1	—	—	28	7:03.0	-1.7	2.6	52	GSM			
1	2672	2.9	RD	235	7:50.0	—	—	352	7:49.4	-0.2	-0.8	330	7:49.5	-0.7	0.0	307
24	2033	4.3	DD	152	GBG				9:28.3	-0.7	-0.7	64	9:29.4	-0.9	-0.8	78
Jun. 4	5	4.7	RD	285	9:20.5	—	—	307	9:10.9	—	—	316	9:19.0	-0.4	0.9	284
Jul. 15	1702	4.2	DD	62	2:17.5	—	—	60	NSG				NSG			
17	1941	4.8	DD	89	3:37.3	-0.6	-2.6	163	3:29.3	-0.4	-2.9	174				
19	2302	2.9	RB	125	22:30.5	0.5	-1.6	347	GSM				GSM			
27	3349	4.2	RD	216	10:36.9	-1.3	0.4	233	10:19.7	-2.0	0.1	253	10:09.0	-2.2	0.6	247
31	249	4.7	RD	257	6:56.4	-0.6	1.7	256	6:52.7	-0.3	1.5	264	6:43.2	-0.1	1.5	256
Aug. 25	3536	4.7	RD	207	7:27.3	-0.2	3.1	183	7:21.8	-1.1	2.3	206	7:03.1	-1.0	2.7	201
Oct. 3	1484	3.6	RD	317	10:18.2	-0.7	-1.1	333	10:08.5	—	—	353	GSM			
11	2500	3.4	DD	64	GBG				GBG				3:24.5	-1.2	-1.7	113
17	3349	4.2	DD	135	4:47.2	-1.7	0.2	62	4:31.3	-1.4	1.1	43	4:17.5	-1.8	1.4	47
27	1030	3.2	RD	246	5:10.8	0.1	1.8	243	5:13.6	0.2	1.4	258	5:06.8	0.4	1.4	250
28	1170	3.7	RD	258	6:38.3	0.2	2.8	223	6:42.2	0.2	1.9	241	6:31.9	0.5	2.1	229
Nov. 9	2750	2.1	DD	56	1:28.8	-0.3	0.3	39	1:29.0	—	—	14	1:19.0	-0.6	1.3	28
9	2750	2.1	RB	57	GBG				1:58.3	—	—	327	2:06.7	-2.3	-2.6	311
15	3536	4.7	DD	125	1:18.7	-2.2	1.1	80	1:00.5	-1.5	1.7	64	0:44.3	-1.5	1.7	69
Dec. 18	628	4.8	DD	159	0:06.5	0.0	2.0	49	0:09.8	0.3	2.2	34	NSG			

DATE	ZC	MAG	PH	ELG °	LOS ANGELES 118.3°W, 34.1°N TIME (UT)	A m	B m	P °	N. CALIFORNIA 122.0°W, 38.0°N TIME (UT)	A m	B m	P °	HONOLULU 157.9°W, 21.3°N TIME (UT)	A m	B m	P °
Jan. 1	1308	4.7	RD	207	11:32.7	-1.5	-1.6	298	11:20.5	-1.4	-1.8	305	9:40.7	—	—	204
21	249	4.7	DD	85	7:11.5	-0.2	-0.3	64	7:10.1	-0.3	0.1	50	6:34.9	-2.6	-0.8	91
25	752	4.7	DD	132	7:47.2	-1.3	-1.8	108	7:36.2	-1.5	-1.2	95	—			
Feb. 20	SAT	0.1	DD	96	23:22.1	—	—	1	—							
20	SAT	0.1	RB	96	23:57.2	—	—	307	—							
25	1308	4.7	DD	151	8:02.7	-1.9	-0.6	89	7:53.6	-2.1	-0.2	82	—			
28	1702	4.2	DD	196	10:05.4	-1.4	-1.7	313	9:54.0	-1.3	-1.6	315	—			
Mar. 7	2672	2.9	DB	290	17:38.7	—	—	163	17:12.2	-2.6	-2.3	139	—			
7	2672	2.9	RD	290	17:55.4	—	—	186	18:04.0	-0.8	0.9	214	—			
8	2809	4.9	RD	299	13:03.7	-2.5	2.9	223	13:05.9	-2.0	2.5	230	—			
30	2033	4.3	RD	205	NB2				NB2				13:01.6	-3.4	0.3	259
Apr. 1	2302	2.9	DB	231	—				—				10:36.3	-0.4	-1.2	144
1	2302	2.9	RD	231	—				—				11:42.7	-2.1	0.4	274
7	3164	4.7	RD	302	12:49.7	-1.1	0.1	301	12:46.7	-0.7	-0.1	310	GSM			
16	SAT	0.2	DD	45	—				18:19.2	-1.1	0.4	120	GSM			
16	SAT	0.2	RB	45	—				18:58.8	0.5	3.3	196	GSM			
24	1702	4.2	DD	140	6:40.2	-1.8	-1.2	113	6:29.3	-1.8	-1.0	111	—			
29	2376	4.6	RD	210	—				—				8:28.8	-1.0	0.7	270
30	2513	4.3	RD	222	6:39.0	-0.9	1.2	266	GSM				—			
May 1	2672	2.9	RD	235	7:43.6	-0.6	0.4	293	GSM				—			
2	2864	4.7	RD	250	—				—				12:27.6	-0.4	-2.5	330
18	1308	4.7	DD	71	GBG				7:46.2	0.4	-1.4	118	—			
24	2033	4.3	DD	151	9:18.6	-1.4	-0.9	82	9:09.9	-1.6	-0.7	76	8:32.1	-0.6	-3.0	170
26	2302	2.9	DD	177	—				—				6:56.4	-1.0	0.0	109
26	2302	2.9	RB	178	—				—				8:06.7	-1.2	-0.8	310
Jun. 6	249	4.7	RD	309	NB2				NB2				14:23.7	-0.7	0.9	269
Jul. 21	2513	4.3	DD	144	GBG				GBG				10:04.8	-2.0	1.1	52
22	2672	2.9	DD	157	GBG				GBG				11:40.8	-1.2	0.9	50
22	2672	2.9	RB	158	GBG				GBG				12:46.7	-1.7	-1.6	294
27	3349	4.2	RD	215	9:46.0	-2.7	0.5	264	9:37.3	-2.8	0.2	279	8:18.9	-0.8	1.1	261
Aug. 16	2307	4.1	DD	101	6:29.2	-1.0	-1.5	107	6:19.8	-1.1	-1.3	97	5:37.1	-2.0	-2.1	142
16	2310	4.6	DD	101	GBG				6:48.8	-1.1	-2.2	135	—			
25	3536	4.7	RD	207	6:53.3	-1.1	2.4	214	6:58.0	-1.1	2.2	224	GSM			
Sep. 2	1030	3.2	RD	299	NB2				NB2				14:30.0	-1.0	0.9	263
3	1170	3.7	RD	312	NB2				NB2				14:38.7	-0.5	0.8	267
18	3164	4.7	DD	145	GBG				GBG				10:57.2	-1.6	0.2	68
Oct. 11	2500	3.4	DD	64	3:12.4	-1.4	-1.3	103	3:02.4	-1.4	-1.1	93	NSG			
17	3349	4.2	DD	135	4:02.3	-1.5	2.1	31	4:06.5	-1.0	2.5	17	NSG			
28	1170	3.7	RD	258	6:36.9	0.5	1.6	243	6:44.0	0.4	1.3	258	GSM			
Nov. 8	2750	2.1	DD	64	25:17.9	—	—	4	—				23:06.4	-1.9	1.2	75
9	2750	2.1	RB	57	1:35.7	—	—	339	—				0:22.6	-1.9	-0.6	301
15	5	4.7	DD	126	—				3:12.0	-3.2	0.1	105	NSG			
Dec. 24	1484	3.6	RD	235	7:24.9	-0.7	1.6	260	7:27.4	-0.6	1.0	276	GSM			

TABLE OF GRAZING LUNAR OCCULTATION PREDICTIONS

The table below and on the next page lists lunar grazing occultation predictions for much of North America for 2002. The eight maps following the table show the graze tracks (see the descriptive text on pp. 152–153).

For each graze is given:

No. .... a chronological sequential number used on the maps
Date .... the date
USNO d ... the star's USNO (U.S. Naval Observatory) reference number (see the bottom of p. 152) and its duplicity code (in the "**d**" column—see section (C) on pp. 154–155 concerning double stars)
m .... its visual magnitude
%sl .... the percent of the Moon sunlit (+ for waxing, – for waning)
L .... whether the track is a northern (N) or southern (S) limit
W.U.T. ..... the Universal Time at the west end of the track
Lo., La. .... the longitude and latitude of the west end of the track

No.	Date	USNO d	m	%sl	L	W.U.T.	Lo.	La.	No.	Date	USNO d	m	%sl	L	W.U.T.	Lo.	La.
1	Jan. 3	1544	5.4	81–	S	5:15.6	–114	21	52	Mar. 3	2064 M	6.3	79–	S	7:03.2	–62	55
2	3	1544	5.4	81–	N	5:36.8	–130	53	53	4	2211	6.7	67–	S	11:17.6	–130	48
3	4	1659	6.7	72–	S	5:14.1	–91	43	54	6	2510	6.2	45–	S	13:42.8	–120	55
4	5	1773 V	5.0	60–	N	5:35.4	–91	51	55	8	2809 Q	4.9	26–	S	12:30.7	–130	35
5	7	2020 K	6.5	37–	S	7:35.8	–83	43	56	11	3202	6.2	6–	S	13:26.0	–114	31
6	7	2032	7.2	36–	S	11:20.1	–94	55	57	16	150 A	6.1	3+	S	0:01.1	–86	36
7	9	X22023	7.5	16–	S	15:01.9	–130	51	58	16	165	6.4	3+	S	2:28.4	–123	27
8	9	2303 B	4.8	16–	S	15:24.8	–107	55	59	20	X5541 O	7.2	30+	N	3:60.0	–80	52
9	9	2302 H	2.6	16–	S	15:26.0	–106	55	60	21	X6530	7.1	39+	N	2:25.9	–84	40
10	11	2562 K	7.0	4–	S	11:45.7	–86	31	61	21	792	5.0	42+	S	7:45.0	–109	55
11	18	3536	4.4	24+	S	23:27.3	–88	24	62	22	923 K	6.7	50+	S	3:02.3	–129	50
12	19	5 L	4.6	25+	S	1:14.7	–116	27	63	22	936 V	5.8	51+	N	5:57.3	–130	35
13	19	18 K	5.8	26+	N	4:37.1	–130	46	64	22	954 K	6.1	52+	N	7:51.9	–95	55
14	20	208	7.0	41+	S	20:59.7	–60	48	65	23	1070	5.2	60+	S	1:26.9	–107	33
15	21	249	4.5	45+	N	7:30.3	–130	50	66	23	X10425 A	6.9	61+	N	3:32.6	–113	24
16	22	X3248	6.9	54+	S	5:44.2	–130	33	67	23	1080	6.7	61+	N	4:33.4	–65	55
17	22	362	6.5	55+	N	7:41.7	–106	55	68	23	1092	5.8	62+	N	6:36.3	–97	55
18	23	454	5.6	62+	S	1:12.3	–125	48	69	24	1200	6.9	70+	S	0:02.6	–85	33
19	23	577	6.0	71+	S	23:20.9	–85	24	70	24	1221 V	6.0	71+	S	2:49.3	–125	54
20	24	593 V	5.9	73+	S	4:39.7	–102	20	71	24	1239	6.6	73+	N	6:33.4	–130	35
21	24	593 V	5.9	73+	N	4:40.2	–101	53	72	26	1484 C	3.5	89+	N	1:59.4	–130	25
22	25	752 K	4.6	83+	N	8:12.2	–94	55	73	26	1479	6.4	89+	S	2:46.8	–91	55
23	25	766 K	5.8	84+	N	10:13.0	–99	55	74	31	2114 M	5.3	92–	S	3:21.9	–63	55
24	26	916 Q	4.3	91+	S	8:41.6	–130	40	75	Apr. 1	2275 M	6.0	83–	S	6:46.9	–117	42
25	26	929 M	5.8	91+	S	11:14.8	–130	49	76	1	2302 H	2.6	82–	N	11:50.4	–130	34
26	27	1050	5.7	95+	S	1:06.9	–114	33	77	1	2307	3.9	81–	S	13:17.4	–122	55
27	27	1070	5.2	96+	N	6:42.8	–110	41	78	2	2434 M	5.6	73–	S	8:47.2	–124	44
28	30	1484 C	3.5	98–	S	4:01.1	–102	20	79	7	3158	5.7	24–	S	11:06.7	–105	39
29	Feb. 2	1856 M	6.8	75–	S	5:02.7	–97	21	80	8	3276	7.3	17–	S	9:48.6	–72	44
30	3	1985	6.9	64–	S	7:13.5	–63	55	81	16	605	7.5	10+	N	4:42.8	–111	55
31	3	1994 O	6.6	64–	S	8:35.6	–123	54	82	16	SAT	0.3	14+	S	18:20.3	–130	27
32	5	2264 V	7.3	39–	S	14:35.5	–130	50	83	17	725	7.0	15+	S	0:00.4	–74	45
33	7	2523	4.8	22–	S	9:47.5	–79	44	84	17	X6332	7.3	17+	S	3:15.4	–120	52
34	8	2678	6.6	14–	S	11:10.6	–76	48	85	18	1030	3.1	33+	N	23:45.6	–130	25
35	17	X1976	7.4	20+	S	5:12.9	–130	50	86	19	X9743 A	7.0	34+	N	1:36.4	–94	53
36	18	298 K	7.1	26+	S	1:42.0	–85	20	87	19	1058	6.8	37+	N	7:02.0	–130	40
37	18	X2865	7.2	27+	S	2:55.0	–99	20	88	19	1157	6.2	43+	N	23:22.6	–65	47
38	18	303 X	6.4	27+	S	2:16.9	–128	41	89	20	1170 A	3.6	44+	N	1:21.1	–104	30
39	18	308	6.3	27+	S	3:37.1	–130	22	90	20	1195	6.8	47+	N	6:54.8	–130	46
40	19	X3701	7.5	35+	S	0:27.7	–93	23	91	21	1308 V	4.7	55+	S	1:24.9	–98	46
41	20	527 A	6.2	45+	S	2:10.7	–124	35	92	23	1569	6.9	78+	N	5:03.5	–97	55
42	20	SAT	0.2	55+	N	23:17.9	–130	29	93	23	1578 K	6.8	80+	S	8:27.8	–88	39
43	21	700 U	5.8	57+	N	6:29.4	–130	54	94	24	1689	5.2	87+	N	2:05.1	–113	27
44	21	792	5.0	64+	S	22:47.1	–77	43	95	24	1702	4.0	88+	N	6:53.0	–112	55
45	22	828	6.3	66+	S	4:11.8	–130	50	96	30	2490 A	5.2	88–	S	3:18.7	–59	49
46	22	865	6.2	70+	N	10:40.0	–130	47	97	30	2510	6.2	87–	S	5:42.0	–110	30
47	22	960	6.6	75+	S	23:08.4	–79	42	98	May 1	2672	2.8	79–	N	7:32.5	–108	48
48	22	962	6.9	75+	S	23:23.1	–85	51	99	3	2985 K	6.8	59–	S	11:17.7	–130	42
49	23	JUP	–2.0	75+	S	1:23.3	–130	54	100	9	150 A	6.1	9–	N	9:48.8	–80	20
50	24	1161	5.9	87+	S	8:42.9	–130	52	101	15	X7281 A	7.5	7+	S	4:06.2	–129	43
51	25	1308 V	4.7	94+	N	8:00.0	–130	52	102	15	865	6.2	8+	S	5:32.4	–129	55

TABLE OF GRAZING LUNAR OCCULTATION PREDICTIONS (continued)

No.	Date	USNO d	m	%sl	L	W.U.T.	Lo.	La.	No.	Date	USNO d	m	%sl	L	W.U.T.	Lo.	La.
103	May 16	1015 M	6.5	14+	N	4:08.0	−110	55	178	28	789	6.8	64−	N	9:25.1	−117	20
104	16	1023 V	6.4	14+	N	4:59.0	−123	55	179	30	1068	7.0	44−	N	5:41.8	−82	21
105	17	1157	6.2	23+	N	5:38.8	−130	40	180	Oct. 1	X12068 M	7.4	33−	N	6:29.6	−94	47
106	19	1393	6.5	40+	N	0:35.1	−78	40	181	3	1484 C	3.5	13−	N	9:59.1	−111	39
107	20	1535	6.8	54+	N	4:35.6	−74	55	182	3	1499	7.1	13−	N	13:7.3	−130	46
108	20	1544	5.4	55+	N	5:50.4	−119	55	183	4	1598 K	6.5	7−	N	8:19.9	−69	52
109	21	1647	6.7	65+	N	3:59.1	−73	55	184	4	X16870	7.5	6−	N	14:0.8	−130	45
110	21	1659	6.7	66+	N	6:05.1	−94	55	185	9	2327	6.7	17+	N	23:56.0	−94	37
111	22	1755	6.9	74+	N	1:25.5	−88	42	186	10	2348	6.8	18+	N	2:53.8	−130	38
112	24	2022	5.5	93+	N	5:15.0	−130	51	187	11	2500 J	3.3	28+	S	4:05.5	−111	20
113	24	2033	4.2	94+	N	9:14.0	−117	55	188	16	3227	6.3	77+	S	5:15.1	−91	20
114	Jun. 1	3202	6.2	65−	N	10:44.6	−126	30	189	17	3343 A	5.7	84+	S	2:54.2	−104	20
115	4	5 L	4.6	37−	N	9:03.1	−107	42	190	17	3349	4.0	85+	S	5:12.2	−95	20
116	5	106	6.6	28−	N	10:08.2	−78	20	191	17	3349	4.0	85+	N	4:33.2	−130	45
117	7	327 K	4.4	13−	N	7:28.8	−69	47	192	18	18 K	5.8	95+	S	23:16.2	−67	41
118	12	MARS	1.9	3+	N	10:31.8	−68	41	193	24	628 K	4.9	91−	S	13:24.4	−128	40
119	13	1092	5.8	4+	S	1:08.9	−84	38	194	25	761 M	6.7	86−	S	12:4.4	−88	43
120	13	1097	6.9	5+	N	1:50.8	−98	33	195	26	880	6.8	79−	N	4:37.4	−117	34
121	13	1099	5.8	5+	N	2:02.3	−107	23	196	26	882 V	5.0	79−	N	5:24.6	−130	50
122	13	X10792 A	7.3	5+	N	2:39.6	−102	42	197	27	1030	3.1	71−	N	4:23.9	−98	21
123	14	1239	6.6	10+	N	1:26.4	−81	45	198	27	X9881 V	6.8	70−	N	7:15.0	−130	38
124	15	1484 C	3.5	27+	N	23:0.5	−127	46	199	27	1046	7.0	70−	N	7:34.0	−128	20
125	16	1514	6.2	31+	N	6:59.4	−130	53	200	27	1049	6.8	70−	N	8:07.1	−130	29
126	20	1985	6.9	75+	N	6:01.4	−128	55	201	27	1055	5.7	69−	S	10:42.5	−101	31
127	21	2088	6.2	82+	N	2:00.4	−99	35	202	29	1334	7.0	47−	N	13:39.5	−130	51
128	23	2376	4.5	96+	N	3:04.2	−116	37	203	30	1435	6.5	38−	N	8:53.4	−122	34
129	25	2672	2.8	100−	N	2:14.5	−89	43	204	30	1436	6.8	37−	N	9:34.0	−130	39
130	26	2864 A	4.6	98−	N	6:15.8	−130	20	205	31	1569	6.9	26−	S	12:42.9	−112	46
131	30	3374	6.1	73−	S	4:43.0	−83	23	206	Nov. 1	1689	5.2	17−	N	10:40.2	−116	27
132	Jul. 2	60	6.9	54−	N	6:32.7	−91	39	207	3	X19361	7.4	3−	N	10:09.5	−68	9
133	4	298 K	7.1	35−	N	9:22.2	−120	27	208	3	1933	7.1	3−	S	12:25.3	−102	44
134	4	X2865	7.2	34−	N	10:35.1	−130	29	209	3	1941	4.7	3−	S	13:37.9	−124	42
135	5	404	5.2	26−	N	8:03.4	−87	20	210	6	2407 V	7.0	6+	N	23:12.2	−87	26
136	6	X4565 K	7.0	17−	N	8:14.5	−88	32	211	8	2721 X	3.2	20+	S	20:45.0	−87	51
137	15	1702	4.0	26+	N	2:17.2	−98	47	212	8	2735	7.2	21+	S	23:29.5	−91	27
138	17	1941	4.7	49+	S	4:21.5	−90	28	213	9	2750 Y	2.0	22+	N	0:59.7	−130	30
139	19	2302 H	2.6	79+	N	22:16.8	−82	37	214	9	2740	6.3	21+	S	0:27.5	−96	20
140	20	2337	6.6	81+	S	5:59.1	−86	24	215	10	3032	7.5	40+	S	22:58.5	−87	35
141	21	2490 A	5.2	89+	S	7:24.0	−102	20	216	12	X29964	7.0	51+	S	1:29.1	−79	20
142	27	3349	4.0	92−	N	9:04.3	−130	49	217	12	3178 U	6.2	51+	S	2:27.7	−83	20
143	30	150 A	6.1	69−	N	10:15.4	−130	47	218	15	3536	4.4	79+	S	1:15.7	−98	20
144	Aug. 1	354 K	5.5	52−	N	5:51.8	−78	20	219	15	5 L	4.6	79+	S	2:59.4	−130	24
145	1	360 D	6.7	51−	N	7:09.3	−112	40	220	16	106	6.6	87+	S	4:18.7	−130	24
146	1	376	7.0	50−	N	11:40.5	−130	34	221	22	882 V	5.0	95−	S	12:52.6	−130	44
147	3	605	7.5	31−	N	9:19.8	−130	43	222	23	1030	3.1	89−	S	11:49.3	−130	52
148	3	614	5.5	31−	N	10:8.7	−130	20	223	24	1117 K	5.0	84−	N	3:19.3	−116	50
149	5	898	6.0	14−	N	9:28.5	−106	32	224	24	1155	6.4	83−	S	11:27.2	−70	55
150	5	X7950	7.2	14−	N	9:42.9	−79	20	225	24	1170 A	3.6	81−	S	13:46.4	−130	47
151	6	1058	6.8	7−	N	9:57.4	−108	46	226	26	1393	6.5	65−	S	7:26.0	−73	44
152	7	X11911 M	7.4	3−	N	9:11.4	−83	49	227	27	1514	6.2	54−	S	9:23.6	−62	55
153	7	1195	6.8	3−	N	9:20.4	−90	53	228	27	1535	6.8	52−	S	12:25.7	−112	55
154	11	1659	6.7	7+	N	1:34.1	−101	27	229	27	1544	5.4	51−	S	14:02.1	−130	46
155	15	2159	5.2	47+	S	4:47.5	−117	31	230	28	1647	6.7	41−	S	11:48.9	−130	43
156	17	2434 M	5.6	68+	N	2:34.9	−116	32	231	29	X18000	7.1	32−	N	6:45.0	−74	42
157	19	2750 Y	2.0	86+	S	3:56.2	−130	52	232	29	X18067 V	7.5	31−	N	8:17.4	−96	44
158	Sep. 1	X7145	6.8	37−	N	9:26.9	−97	20	233	29	1755	6.9	30−	N	10:9.4	−123	43
159	1	839	5.4	37−	N	9:22.7	−130	23	234	Dec. 2	X20674	7.2	5−	S	10:10.9	−62	50
160	1	853	7.1	37−	N	11:38.4	−130	34	235	6	2673 M	6.3	4+	S	1:28.9	−128	35
161	1	X7314	7.1	37−	N	11:57.3	−130	20	236	8	2984 X	7.1	16+	S	1:48.0	−102	20
162	2	1030	3.1	26−	N	14:59.4	−130	49	237	8	3102 K	7.0	23+	S	20:28.5	−61	48
163	3	1155	6.4	18−	N	12:13.3	−130	53	238	9	3130	5.4	25+	S	2:32.4	−86	20
164	9	1969	7.1	11+	N	23:49.9	−81	34	239	9	X29678	7.2	25+	S	2:40.5	−130	21
165	12	2233 M	5.5	31+	S	1:14.3	−90	40	240	9	3141	5.8	25+	S	3:01.2	−130	46
166	12	X21647	7.5	32+	N	3:46.2	−130	27	241	10	3276	7.3	35+	S	4:22.3	−130	20
167	17	2985 K	6.8	81+	S	2:22.3	−79	20	242	10	3374	6.1	43+	S	23:28.5	−94	28
168	18	3130	5.4	89+	N	4:01.1	−90	20	243	13	60	6.9	62+	S	0:04.9	−104	31
169	23	192	5.1	97−	N	8:15.3	−130	34	244	13	178	6.5	71+	S	23:58.0	−98	22
170	26	517	6.1	81−	N	8:48.2	−120	20	245	14	192	5.1	73+	S	5:12.6	−103	20
171	27	628 K	4.9	74−	N	5:09.7	−114	23	246	18	628 K	4.9	97+	S	0:16.9	−76	20
172	27	633 V	5.5	74−	N	7:01.3	−79	20	247	21	1117 K	5.0	97−	S	10:51.9	−130	34
173	27	642 K	6.8	73−	N	7:18.4	−118	20	248	24	1484 C	3.5	79−	S	6:44.5	−130	22
174	27	646 M	6.1	73−	N	8:02.5	−130	43	249	24	1484 C	3.5	79−	N	7:59.8	−66	55
175	27	651 X	6.0	73−	N	8:36.1	−130	39	250	25	1598 K	6.5	69−	S	6:42.8	−106	31
176	27	665 U	5.7	72−	N	11:28.9	−130	29	251	29	2092	7.0	22−	S	14:00.9	−130	45
177	28	761 M	6.7	65−	N	3:45.8	−85	32									

GRAZING OCCULTATION MAPS

JANUARY 1 – FEBRUARY 15

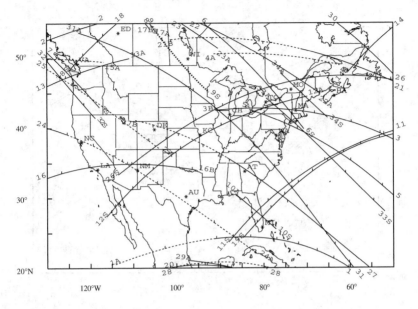

FEBRUARY 16 – MARCH 31

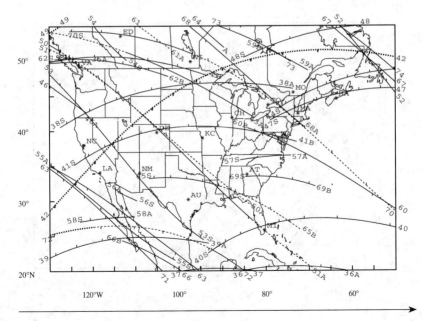

GRAZING OCCULTATION MAPS (continued)

APRIL 1 – MAY 15

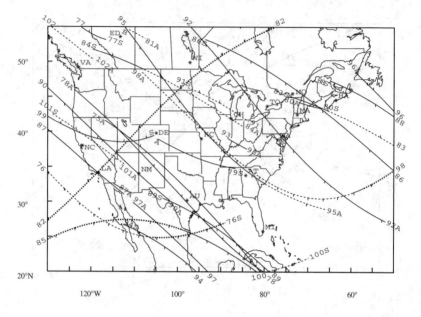

MAY 16 – JUNE 30

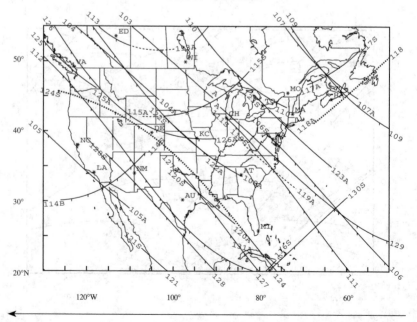

GRAZING OCCULTATION MAPS (continued)

JULY 1 – AUGUST 15

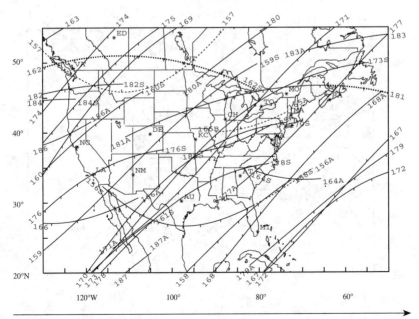

AUGUST 16 – OCTOBER 15

GRAZING OCCULTATION MAPS (continued)

OCTOBER 16 – NOVEMBER 15

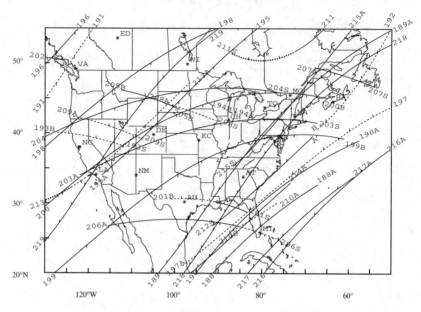

NOVEMBER 16 – DECEMBER 31

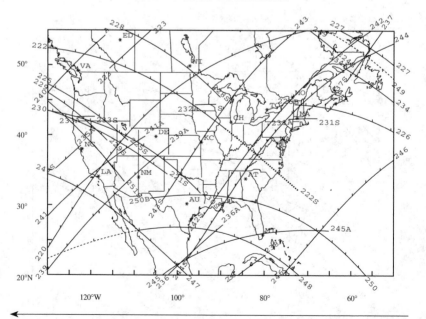

TIDES AND THE EARTH–MOON SYSTEM
BY ROY BISHOP

The tidal aspect of gravitation produces some of the most interesting phenomena in the universe, from the structure of interacting galaxies, such as M51, to the volcanoes of Io, the fragmentation of Comet Shoemaker-Levy 9 by Jupiter in 1992, the synchronous rotation of our Moon, and the pulse of the seas on our planet. Perhaps because they occur at our feet, the tides of the oceans are often overlooked when considering the heavens. These tides were known to the ancients, but an understanding of their origin came only three centuries ago with the publication of Newton's *Principia*.

In the Newtonian context, tides originate in the fact that the force of gravity decreases with distance from a massive body. The Moon exerts a force on Earth, and Earth responds by accelerating toward the Moon; however, the waters on the hemisphere facing the Moon, being closer to the Moon, accelerate more and fall ahead of Earth. Similarly, Earth itself accelerates more than the waters on the other hemisphere and falls ahead of these waters. Thus two aqueous bulges are produced, one on the side of Earth facing the Moon and one on the side facing away from the Moon:

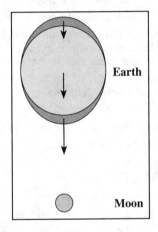

In order of decreasing length, the arrows indicate the force per unit mass (acceleration) produced by the Moon's gravity on the near side, centre, and far side of Earth. It is the resulting horizontal flow of the water toward the two points nearest and farthest from the Moon that forms the two tidal bulges (indicated by heavy shading).

As Earth rotates on its axis, the orientation of these two bulges in relation to the Moon remains fixed. Hence the rise and fall of the oceans on Earth. If Earth had no rigidity, the entire planet would flex freely in the same fashion, and there would be virtually no water tides. The very existence of the tides indicates that on a time scale of several hours our planet displays considerable rigidity.

Because of the Moon's orbital motion, it transits on the average 50.47 min later each day. Thus on successive days, high tides recur about 50 min later (or for the many regions experiencing two high tides daily, these tides recur at intervals of 12 h 25 min).

The Sun exerts a gravitational force 180 times as strong as does the Moon on Earth; however, because the Moon is so much closer, the *variation* in the Moon's force across Earth's diameter is about 2.2 times larger than the variation in the Sun's force. As described above, it is this variation that produces tides; thus the pair of bulges raised by the Moon are considerably larger than the pair raised by the Sun. As the Moon goes through its monthly cycle of phases, these two pairs of tidal bulges get in and out of step, combining in step to produce *spring tides* (no connection with the season) when the Moon is new or full and out of step to produce *neap tides* when the Moon is at first or last quarter.

Another factor having a substantial influence on tidal ranges is the elliptical shape of the Moon's orbit. Although the Moon is only 9% to 14% closer at perigee than at apogee, because the *variation* in its gravitational force varies inversely as the cube of its distance (the force itself varies inversely as the square of the distance), the Moon's tidal influence is 30% to 48% greater at perigee than at apogee. Because the Sun tidally influences the shape of the Moon's orbit, exceptionally close perigees coincide with full or new Moon, and the resulting extreme tides are known as *perigean spring tides*. In some areas, such as the Bay of Fundy in eastern Canada, the perigee–apogee influence is greater than the spring–neap influence. Although the variation of the Moon's distance is not readily apparent to observers viewing the Moon directly, to observers on the shores near the head of the Bay of Fundy, the 3 m to 6 m *increase* in the vertical tidal range makes it obvious when the Moon is near perigee, clear skies or cloudy!

There are many astronomical factors influencing the tides. These can be sorted out according to the periods they produce. The periods of the more important factors are:

(1) semidiurnal, 12 h 00 min (two solar-induced tidal bulges, as described above);

(2) semidiurnal, 12 h 25 min (two lunar-induced tidal bulges, as described above);

(3) diurnal, 24 h 50 min (the changing declinations of Moon and Sun shift the pairs of tidal bulges out of Earth's equatorial plane, resulting in a tidal component with a one-day period—this is the dominant tide in some areas, such as parts of the southern coast of Canada's Gulf of St. Lawrence);

(4) semimonthly, 13.66 days (variation in the Moon's declination);

(5) semimonthly, 14.77 days (spring–neap cycle, described above);

(6) monthly, 27.55 days (perigee–apogee cycle, described above);

(7) semiannual, 182.6 days (variation in the Sun's declination);

(8) annual, 365.26 days (perihelion–aphelion variation in the Sun's tidal influence);

(9) 8.8 years (rotation period of the Moon's perigee); and

(10) 18.6 years (rotation period of the nodes of the Moon's orbit).

In addition to astronomical factors, the tides on Earth are strongly influenced by the sizes, boundaries, and depths of ocean basins and inlets and by Earth's rotation, winds, and barometric pressure fluctuations. Tides typically have ranges (vertical high-to-low) of a metre or two, but there are regions in the oceans where the various influences conspire to produce virtually no tides at all, and others where the tides are greatly amplified. Among the latter regions are the Sea of Okhotsk, the northern coast of Australia, the English channel, and in Canada—Ungava Bay in northern Quebec and the Bay of Fundy between New Brunswick and Nova Scotia. The tidal ranges in these regions are of the order of 10 m.

The highest ocean tides on Earth occur in Minas Basin, the eastern extremity of the Bay of Fundy, where the mean tide range is 12 m and can reach 16 m when the various factors affecting the tides are in phase (although the highest tides occur typically a day or two after the astronomical influences reach their peak). The most dramatic view of this vertical range is at the Minas Basin Pulp & Power Company wharf in the town of Hantsport, Nova Scotia. Remarkably, this site is practically unknown; it is not advertised, and no special provisions have been made to accommodate spectators.

The primary cause of the immense tides of Fundy is a resonance of the Bay of Fundy–Gulf of Maine system. The system is effectively bounded at its outer end by the edge of the continental shelf with its approximately 40:1 increase in depth. The system has a natural period of approximately 12.7 hours, a Q-value of about 5, and is driven near resonance by the dominant semidiurnal tides of the Atlantic Ocean. Like a father pushing his daughter on a swing, the gentle Atlantic tidal pulse pushes the waters of the Bay of Fundy–Gulf of Maine basin at nearly the optimum frequency to cause a large oscillation.

Perhaps the most awesome display of the tides on our planet occurs at Cape Split, Nova Scotia, on the southern side of the entrance to Minas Basin (Cape Split may be reached by a pleasant two-hour walk along a popular hiking trail from the village of Scots Bay). Here, at the time of the midpoint of an incoming tide, for a considerable distance the forest on the towering cliffs is filled with a hollow roar produced by the turbulence of the waters surging over the submarine ridges below. The currents exceed 8 knots (4 m/s), and the flow in the deep, 5-km-wide channel on the north side of Cape Split equals the combined flow of all the streams and rivers of Earth (≈ 4 km^3/h). Three hours later the spectacle pauses and then begins flowing in the opposite direction.

Through friction, the tides convert Earth's rotational kinetic energy into heat at a rate of about 4 TW, comparable to humankind's total rate of energy use. Approximately 1% of this occurs in the Bay of Fundy and, since 1984, a tiny portion of this (20 MW peak) is being turned into commercial electric power at the Annapolis Basin tidal power plant in Nova Scotia. The only other large-scale tidal power installation is in France on the Rance estuary (240 MW peak).

Tidal friction also transfers angular momentum from Earth to the Moon, lengthening the day and increasing the size of the orbit of the Moon. The day is lengthening by about 1 second every 40 000 years—imperceptible on a human time scale, but of profound significance to Earth's rotation over a few billion years. (For example, 900 million years ago, when Earth was already 80% of its present age, there were about 480 18-hour days in a year.) The Moon is receding about 3.8 cm per year, with the result that within 600 million years total solar eclipses will cease. Presently we are well into the transitional phase: annular eclipses already outnumber total solar eclipses. New moons occur, on average, almost one day earlier each successive month; however, because of the increasing size of the lunar orbit, in about 300 million years the lunar (synodic) month will have lengthened to equal the average calendar month (although the average month will then contain only about twenty-eight 26-hour days).

If the Sun does not first incinerate our planet, there will come a day that is as long as the lunar month (each then equal to about 40 present days), and a more distant Moon will stand stationary in the sky, as does Earth now in the lunar sky. But this situation will not endure, for solar tides will still be present and will reduce the angular momentum of the Earth–Moon system, causing the Moon to approach Earth once more.

For more information, see the superb introduction *The Tides* by E.P. Clancy, Anchor Books, Doubleday and Co., 1969 (now, unfortunately, out of print). An excellent article dealing specifically with the tides of Fundy and tidal power installations has been written by Christopher Garrett (1984, *Endeavour* 8, #2, 58–64). The major astronomical factors influencing the tides (the phases, perigees and apogees of the Moon) are tabulated in THE SKY MONTH BY MONTH section (pp. 68–91) of this Handbook. These may be scanned to determine days favourable for large tides. Detailed predictions for tides in Canadian waters are published in *Canadian Tide and Current Tables*, the six volumes of which are individually available from Canadian Government bookstores or by mail from Hydrographic Chart Distribution Office, Fisheries and Oceans Canada, 1675 Russell Road, P.O. Box 8080, Ottawa, ON, Canada K1G 3H6. See also www.lau.chs-shc.dfo-mpo.gc.ca/marees/produits/accueil.htm.

PLANETS AND SATELLITES

GENERAL INTRODUCTION

PLANETARY HELIOCENTRIC LONGITUDES, 2002

The heliocentric longitude of a planet is the angle between the vernal equinox and the planet, as seen from the Sun. It is measured in the ecliptic plane, in the direction of the orbital motion of the planet (counterclockwise as viewed from the north side of the ecliptic plane). Knowing these heliocentric longitudes and the distances of the planets from the Sun (see p. 21), one can construct a diagram or model showing the relative orientations of the Sun and planets on any date.

UT	Me °	V °	E °	Ma °	J °	S °	U °	N °	P °
Jan. 1.0	338	273	100	26	101	73	324	308	255
Feb. 1.0	150	322	132	44	103	74	325	308	255
Mar. 1.0	248	6	160	60	106	75	325	309	256
Apr. 1.0	347	56	191	76	108	76	325	309	256
May 1.0	155	104	220	91	111	77	326	309	256
Jun. 1.0	259	155	250	106	113	78	326	309	256
Jul. 1.0	1	203	279	120	116	79	326	309	256
Aug. 1.0	173	253	309	134	118	80	327	310	257
Sep. 1.0	270	302	338	147	121	82	327	310	257
Oct. 1.0	21	349	8	160	123	83	327	310	257
Nov. 1.0	189	39	38	174	126	84	328	310	257
Dec. 1.0	278	87	69	187	128	85	328	310	257
Jan. 1.0	44	137	100	202	131	86	328	310	258

MAGNITUDES OF NAKED–EYE PLANETS IN 2002

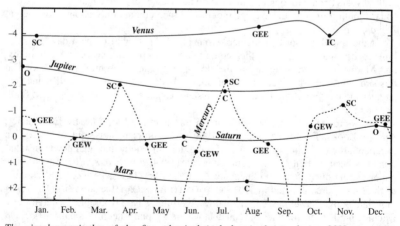

The visual magnitudes of the five, classical (naked-eye) planets during 2002 are given. Oppositions (O), conjunctions (C), inferior and superior conjunctions (IC, SC), and greatest elongations east and west (GEE, GEW) are indicated. See the diagram explaining these terms at the right.

PRONUNCIATION OF PLANET NAMES

Mercury	mûr′kū-rē
Venus	vē′nŭs
Earth	ûrth
Mars	màrz
Jupiter	joō′pĭ-tēr
Saturn	sàt′ûrn
Uranus	yoor′à-nŭs
Neptune	nĕp′tyoon
Pluto	ploō′tō

à àsk;   ē wē; ĕ mĕt; ē makēr;   ĭ bĭt;
ō gō; oo book; oō moōn;   ū ūnite; ŭ ŭp; û ûrn

SOLAR SYSTEM GEOMETRY

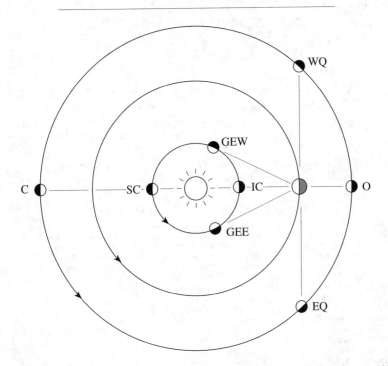

The diagram is a simplified view of our solar system, from the north side. Earth is shown (middle orbit) together with an inferior planet (i.e. Mercury or Venus) and a superior planet (e.g. Mars). Four special geometrical configurations of the inferior planet relative to Earth are shown; in counterclockwise chronological sequence they are inferior conjunction (IC), greatest elongation west (GEW), superior conjunction (SC), and greatest elongation east (GEE). Four special configurations of the superior planet relative to Earth are also shown; in clockwise chronological sequence they are opposition (O), eastern quadrature (EQ), conjunction (C), and western quadrature (WQ).

TELESCOPIC APPEARANCE OF THE PLANETS

Mercury

Venus

Mars

Jupiter

Saturn

Uranus

Neptune

```
0   10   20   30   40   50
      Seconds of arc
```

The apparent maximum and minimum observable size of seven planets is illustrated along with charateristic telescopic appearance.

PRONUNCIATION OF SATELLITE NAMES

Adrastea	à-drăs′tē-à	Galatea	gàl′à-tē′à	Pasiphae	pà-sīf′à-ē′
Amalthea	ăm″l-thē′à	Ganymede	găn′ĕ-mēd′	Phobos	fō′bŏs
Ananke	à′năn-kē	Helene	hà-lēn′	Phoebe	fē′bē
Ariel	âr′ē-ĕl	Himalia	hĭm′à-lī-à	Portia	pôr′shà
Atlas	ăt′lăs	Hyperion	hĭ-pēr′ĭ-ŏn	Prometheus	prŏ-mē′thē-ŭs
Belinda	bà-lĭn′dà	Iapetus	ī-ăp′ĕ-tŭs	Prospero	prŏs′pĕr-ō
Bianca	bē-āng′kà	Io	ī′ō	Proteus	prō′tē-ŭs
Caliban	kăl′ĭ-băn	Janus	jā′nŭs	Puck	pŭk
Callisto	kà-lĭs′tō	Juliet	jōō′lē-ĕt	Rhea	rē′à
Calypso	kà-lĭp′sō	Larissa	là-rĭs′à	Rosalind	rŏz′à-lĭnd
Carme	kàr′mē	Leda	lē′dà	Setebos	sĕt′ĕ-bŏs
Charon	kâr′ĕn	Lysithea	lĭs′ĭ-thē′à	Sinope	sĭ-nō′pē
Cordelia	kôr-dĕl′yà	Metis	mē′tĭs	Stephano	stĕf′ă-nō
Cressida	krĕs′ĭ-dà	Mimas	mī′măs	Sycorax	sīk′ō-răks
Deimos	dī′mŏs	Miranda	mĭ-răn′dà	Telesto	tà-lĕs′tō
Desdemona	dĕz′dà-mō′nà	Moon	mōon	Tethys	tē′thĭs
Despina	dĭs-pīn′à	Naiad	nī′ăd	Thalassa	thà-làs′à
Dione	dī-ō′nē	Nereid	nēr′ē-ĭd	Thebe	thē′be
Elara	ē′lâr-à	Oberon	ō′bà-rŏn	Titan	tī′t′n
Enceladus	ĕn-sĕl′à-dŭs	Ophelia	ō-fēl′yà	Titania	tĭ′tă′nē-à
Epimetheus	ĕp′à-mē′thē-ŭs	Pan	păn	Triton	trī′t′n
Europa	yoo-rō′pà	Pandora	păn-dôr′à	Umbriel	ŭm′brē-ĕl′

ā dāte; ă tăp; â câre; à àsk; ē wē; ĕ mĕt; ī īce; ĭ bĭt; ō gō; ŏ hŏt; ô ôrb; oo book; ōō mōon; ŭ ŭp

RIGHT ASCENSIONS OF THE SUN AND PLANETS IN 2002

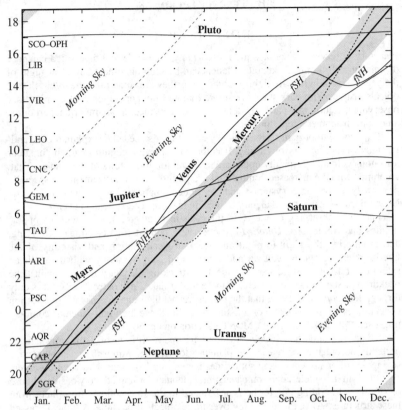

This diagram shows the variation during the year in the right ascension (vertical axis) of the Sun and the planets. The slightly curved, heavy diagonal line represents the Sun; the shaded regions approximately indicate parts of the night sky affected by twilight. The two dashed diagonal lines at the upper left and bottom right represent the boundary between the evening sky and the morning sky.

*The diagram may be used as a quick reference to determine in what part of the sky a planet may be found (including in which constellation—note the names along the vertical axis), when a superior planet is in conjunction with the Sun or at opposition (opposition is approximately where its curve intersects the dashed diagonal lines, and note that, due to retrograde motion, this point is also where the planet's curve has its maximum negative slope), when Mercury and Venus have their various greatest elongations and conjunctions, and when there are conjunctions of planets. For example, the January 1 opposition of Jupiter can be read from the extreme left of the diagram. Also note the rare grouping of **all five naked-eye planets** in the evening sky from mid-April to mid-May.*

For observers in midlatitudes, at certain times of the year the ecliptic stands steeply to the horizon in the western evening sky or the eastern morning sky, making apparitions of planets in these parts of the sky favourable from the Northern Hemisphere ("fNH" on the diagram) or favourable from the Southern Hemisphere ("fSH").

For more information on all these events, see THE SKY MONTH BY MONTH *(pp. 66–91) and* THE PLANETS FOR 2002 *(immediately following).*

THE PLANETS FOR 2002
By Terence Dickinson

INTRODUCTION

Planetary observing is perhaps the most widely accessible and diversified category of amateur astronomical pursuits. Planets can be seen on almost any clear night of the year. Indeed, in heavily light-polluted cities they are sometimes the *only* celestial objects visible. With dark skies ever more remote from population centres, planetary observing is returning—partly by default—to take its place as an important part of the amateur astronomer's repertoire.

But a more important factor than sky conditions is needed to explain the expanding interest in planetary observing. It is the widespread recognition among amateur astronomers that high-quality optics are essential for good views of the planets. That, combined with the increased commercial availability of such instruments—especially previously unavailable systems such as apochromatic refractors and Maksutov-Newtonians—means that planetary observing is more accessible than ever.

Planetary observing divides into three distinct categories, each with its opportunities and limitations. *Unaided-eye* observing consists of detecting, identifying, and monitoring the night-to-night and week-to-week motion and visibility of the five brighter planets. *Binoculars* add Uranus and Neptune along with the Galilean satellites of Jupiter. Binoculars are ideal for tracking planetary motion against the backdrop of stars, many of which are too faint for naked-eye detection. But it is only through *telescopic* observing that the planets reveal their uniqueness, and this section concentrates on that aspect. For a listing of unaided-eye highlights such as conjunctions, see THE SKY MONTH BY MONTH section on pp. 66–91.

Urban and suburban locales unsuited for many aspects of astronomy can be perfectly acceptable for telescopic planetary observing. Atmospheric turbulence—seeing—is often no worse, and sometimes better, in urban areas. However, observers should avoid using telescopes on pavement, balconies, or immediately beside a house or substantial building due to the heat radiated to the surrounding atmosphere from these structures. Also, avoid looking over these objects if possible. A typical grassed backyard is fine in most instances. For optimum performance all telescopes (except small refractors) require from 10 min to an hour to cool to outside temperature when taken outdoors. Hazy but otherwise cloudless nights are usually just as good as, and sometimes better than, clear skies for steady telescopic images of planets.

More than any other class of telescopic observing, planetary observing is most affected by seeing. Many nights are rendered useless for planet watching by ever-present ripples and undulations in Earth's atmosphere. Planets within 15° of the horizon are virtually always afflicted (as many observers of Mars noted last summer from Canadian latitudes). Minimum altitude for expectations of reasonable seeing is 25°. A further problem with low-altitude planetary targets is dispersion associated with atmospheric refraction. Refraction causes celestial objects to appear displaced to higher altitudes. Since the effect is wavelength dependent (being less for longer wavelengths), for planets at low altitudes this produces a red fringe on the lower side of the planet and a green (or blue) fringe on the upper; the effect also introduces chromatic smearing to the whole image.

Regardless of the type of telescope used for planetary observing, optical quality is far more critical than aperture. In no other type of observing are the effects of less-than-perfect optics more apparent. Other factors that can significantly degrade a telescope's planetary performance include a large *central obstruction* in the optical system (all Schmidt-Cassegrains, Maksutov-Cassegrains, and Newtonians with secondary mirror diameters exceeding 20% of their apertures), *secondary mirror supports* (most Newtonians), *chromatic aberration* (most achromatic refractors over 90 mm), *internal air currents* (all types, refractors least), optical component *cool-down time* (mostly aperture dependent, telescopes over 200 mm can take hours), *improperly light-baffled optics*, and *dirty optics*.

In the remarks below, when a planetary phenomenon is stated as being visible in a certain minimum aperture, good seeing and a moderate level of observer experience are assumed. When a specific minimum aperture is cited, an unobstructed optical system (i.e. a refractor) is assumed. Somewhat larger apertures are often required if centrally obstructed systems are used or the observer is inexperienced.

Editor's Note: The tables and figures that appear in this section were prepared by the editor or other contributors; the editor assumes full responsibility for their accuracy.

MERCURY

Of the five planets visible to the unaided eye, Mercury is by far the most difficult to observe and is seldom conveniently located for either unaided eye or telescopic observation. The problem for observers is Mercury's tight orbit, which constrains the planet to a small zone on either side of the Sun as viewed from Earth. When Mercury is east of the Sun we may see it as an evening "star" low in the west just after sunset. When it is west of the Sun we might view Mercury as a morning "star" in the east before sunrise. But due to celestial geometry involving the tilt of Earth's axis and Mercury's orbit, we get much better views of Mercury at certain times of the year.

MERCURY—MOST FAVOURABLE EVENING VIEW IN 2002 FROM NORTHERN LATITUDES

Date 0h UT	Mag.	Angular Diameter "	Percent Illuminated	Elongation from Sun °	Apparent RA (2002) h m	Dec ° '
Apr. 16	−1.5	5.4	92	10	2 11	+13 51
21	−1.1	5.8	79	15	2 49	+17 48
26	−0.6	6.5	63	18	3 24	+20 51
May 1	0.0	7.3	47	21	3 53	+22 52
6	+0.6	8.3	32	21	4 14	+23 52
11	+1.4	9.5	20	19	4 28	+23 57

From midlatitudes, the best time to see the planet in the *evening* sky is within a month or two of the spring equinox and in the *morning* sky within a month or two of the autumn equinox (this applies to both northern and southern latitudes, although the respective seasons are six months out of phase). Binoculars are of great assistance in searching for the planet about 40 min to an hour after sunset or before sunrise during the periods when it is visible. The planet's brightness, which varies by more than two magnitudes, is a more important factor influencing its visibility than its angular distance from the Sun during any particular elongation. Mercury's true colour is almost pure white, but absorption from Earth's atmosphere within 15° of the horizon, where Mercury is most easily seen, usually imparts a yellow or ochre hue to the planet.

Telescopic observers will find the rapidly changing phases of Mercury of interest. The planet appears to zip from gibbous to crescent phase in about three weeks during each of its evening elongations. The phases are accessible to users of 75-mm or larger telescopes; the 30% phase can be detected at 50×. Large apertures (over 200 mm) rarely offer an advantage due to the crippling effects of poor seeing at lower altitudes, especially following sunset when the planet is most frequently observed. Experienced planetary observers often report their most satisfying telescopic observations of Mercury in the morning sky. Near favourable western elongations, the planet may be easily located at least an hour before sunrise, then followed to higher altitudes into the daytime sky. Seeing often remains steady more than an hour after sunrise by which time the planet may be 30° above the horizon. Under such conditions the phase is sharply defined, and the small disk takes on a unique appearance, paler than Venus, with a vaguely textured surface. Surface details, though suspected in moments of fine seeing, are always elusive. Contrasts among the planet's surface features are lower than on the lunar surface, although in other respects the two bodies are similar.

VENUS

Venus is the only world in the solar system that closely resembles Earth in size and mass. It also comes nearer to Earth than any other planet, at times approaching as close as 0.27 AU. Despite the fundamental similarity, surface conditions on Earth and Venus differ greatly. The clouds and haze that cloak the planet are highly reflective, making Venus the brightest natural celestial object in the nighttime sky apart from our Moon. Whenever it is visible, it is readily recognized. Because its orbit is within that of Earth's, Venus is never separated from the Sun by an angle greater than 47°. However, this is more than sufficient for the dazzling object to dominate the morning or evening sky.

Like Mercury, Venus exhibits phases, although they are much more easily detected in small telescopes because of Venus's greater size. When it is far from us near the other side of its orbit, we see the planet nearly fully illuminated, but because of its distance it appears small—about 10″ in diameter. As Venus moves closer to Earth, the phase decreases (we see less of the illuminated portion of the planet), but the diameter increases until it is a thin slice nearly a minute of arc in diameter. It takes Venus several months to move from one of these extremes to the other, compared to just a few weeks for Mercury.

As 2002 opens, Venus is near superior conjunction (Jan. 14) and lost in the Sun's glare. In mid-March it emerges into the evening sky for northern observers, low in the west at dusk. For southerners, the brilliant planet's arrival takes a few weeks longer. After that, the scene quickly improves for observers worldwide. *For a full month, from Apr. 18 to May 18, Venus is the lead participant in a glorious one-month grouping of all five naked-eye planets in the western evening sky at dusk.* Typically a once-a-decade occurrence, this is the first time since May 1990 that the naked-eye planets have put on this type of multiweek group display in the evening sky. After the planets disperse in June, Venus continues its dominance of the evening sky until mid-August when unfavourable ecliptic geometry carries the planet very low to the southwest horizon for northern observers (although it is still well up through early October for southerners).

Venus is at inferior conjunction on Oct. 31 when it will be 6° south of the Sun, distant enough that it can be followed by telescope in the daytime sky by experienced observers—using extreme caution to avoid an accidental unprotected solar-viewing encounter. The planet will appear as a 1% illuminated crescent at this time, one minute in diameter. Following inferior conjunction, the overall observing conditions reverse compared to the months before conjunction, with northern observers gaining a fine morning sky viewing apparition while southern sky watchers will find Venus hugging the morning sky eastern horizon into 2003.

For telescopic observers, the following information will be useful: on Mar. 1 Venus is 98% illuminated and 10″ in apparent diameter; May1, 89%, 11″; Jul. 1, 72%, 15″; Sep. 1, 43%, 28″; Oct. 1, 22%, 43″.

When Venus is about a 20% crescent, even rigidly held, good-quality binoculars can be used to distinguish that the planet is not spherical or a point source. The new generation of image-stabilized binoculars beautifully display the crescent Venus. A 60-mm refractor should be capable of revealing the shape of all but the gibbous and full phases. Experienced observers prefer to observe Venus during the daytime, and indeed the planet is bright enough to be seen with the unaided eye if one knows where to look.

Because of Venus's high surface brightness (about 40 times greater than Jupiter's), Venus can accommodate the highest magnifications a telescope can deliver. The author has used magnifications over 4× per millimetre of aperture on occasion and regularly employs 1.5× to 3× per millimetre on the planet, particularly in bright twilight when the sky is moderately dark but Venus is still high enough to avoid low-altitude seeing degradation. Venus's cloud-shrouded surface appears to most observers to be featureless no matter what type of telescope is used or what the planet's phase. Broad streaks and splotches in the clouds, revealed in blue-filtered and ultraviolet images of Venus, may be vaguely detected telescopically using a violet filter (#38A or #47), although sketches of these features seldom match among different observers.

MARS

In many ways Mars is the most interesting planet to observe with the unaided eye. It moves rapidly among the stars—its motion can often be detected after an interval of less than a week—and it varies in brightness over a far greater range than any other planet. Mars may be distinguished by its pale orange-red colour, a hue that originates with rust-coloured dust that covers much of the planet. As 2002 opens, Mars is a first-magnitude evening-sky object in Aquarius. It spends February in Pisces, March in Aries, and in April and May joins the impressive five-planet array mentioned in the Venus section. From June to September Mars is buried in the Sun's glare. It emerges into the morning sky, low in the east, in late October where it remains relatively inconspicuous for the remainder of the year.

Telescopically Mars is usually a disappointingly small featureless ochre disk except within a few months of opposition when its distance from Earth is near minimum. If Mars at perihelion at these times, the separation can be as little as 56 million kilometres. Such close approaches occur at intervals of 15 to 17 years; the most recent was in 1988; the next will be in 2003. At a perihelion opposition the telescopic disk of Mars is 25″ in diameter and much detail on the planet can be distinguished with telescopes of 100-mm aperture or greater. Since this very favourable observing condition occurs in 2003, this section will be significantly expanded next year to supply extensive information for telescopic observers. This year, Mars remains less than 6″ in diameter, much too small for surface features of interest to be accessible to amateur equipment.

OPPOSITIONS OF MARS, 1997–2010

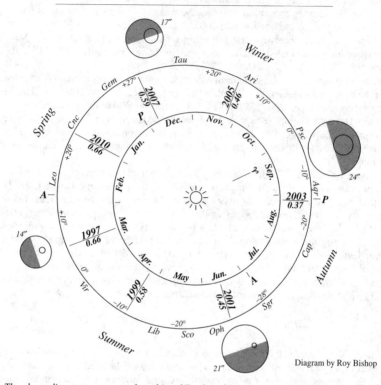

Diagram by Roy Bishop

The above diagram represents the orbits of Earth and Mars as viewed from the north ecliptic pole. Straight lines link simultaneous positions of the two planets for seven successive oppositions of Mars, beginning with that of the year 1997. The separation of the two planets (in astronomical units) at the various oppositions is indicated beside each of the connecting lines. The months inside of Earth's orbit indicate the position of Earth during the year (both planets orbit counterclockwise). For each orbit, two tick marks labelled A and P indicate the aphelion point and the perihelion point, respectively. The direction of the vernal equinox is shown (toward the late September position of Earth). Around the orbit of Mars is indicated its declination (ranges between +27° and –28°) and the constellation in which Mars resides when at opposition.

Four views of Mars are shown—at its two equinoxes and two solstices. These views show the portion of Mars illuminated by the Sun, the location and approximate size of its north polar cap, and the apparent size of Mars (labelled in arc-seconds) for oppositions occurring at these points in its orbit. The seasons of the Martian northern hemisphere are indicated around the outer margin of the diagram, and are very nearly one season ahead of those on Earth at the same orbital position. (For the southern hemisphere of Mars, the season and the configuration of the south polar cap are the same as those of the diametrically opposite view.) Note that the maximum angular diameter Mars can attain (25″) occurs near its perihelion, at a late-August opposition.

As an example of the information that can be read from this diagram: the 2003 opposition of Mars occurs in late-August with Mars 0.37 AU from Earth. Mars will be close to its maximum angular diameter, over 24″, and located near declination –15°, close to the Capricornus-Aquarius border. It will be late autumn in the northern hemisphere on Mars, with a large but hidden north polar cap and a small, observable south polar cap.

JUPITER

Jupiter, the solar system's largest planet, is a colossal ball of hydrogen and helium without any solid surface comparable to land masses on Earth. Jupiter likely has a small rocky core encased in a thick mantle of metallic hydrogen which is enveloped by a massive atmospheric cloak topped by a quilt of multicoloured clouds. These clouds are the visible surface of Jupiter—a realm of constant change characterized by alternating dark belts and brighter zones. The zones are ammonia ice-crystal clouds, the belts mainly ammonium hydrosulphide clouds. Frequently the belts intrude on the zones with dark rifts or loops called festoons.

The equatorial region of Jupiter's clouds rotates 5 min faster than the rest of the planet: 9 h 50 min compared to 9 h 55 min. This means constant interaction as one region slips by the other at about 400 km/h. It also means that there are basically two rotational systems from the viewpoint of week-to-week telescopic observation (see Jupiter—Daily Central Meridians on pp. 178–180 for daily longitudes of Jupiter's regions System I and System II). Jupiter's rapid rotation also makes the great globe markedly bulged at the equator.

Two dark belts, the North Equatorial Belt and the South Equatorial Belt, are obvious in the smallest telescopes. Larger instruments reveal several more narrow dark belts along with the famous Great Red Spot, a salmon-coloured oval vortex observed for centuries on the south edge of the South Equatorial Belt. Historically, the Red Spot has varied from being blatantly obvious to nearly invisible. For example, in 1997 it was detectable with a 100-mm aperture but could hardly be described as prominent because it closely matched its surroundings in hue and contrast. In 2002 observers should find the Red Spot near longitude 76° in System II (see Great Red Spot—Time of Transit on p. 180 for instructions on determing when the Great Red Spot crosses Jupiter's central meridian).

The smallest of telescopes will reveal Jupiter's four large satellites, each of which is equal to or larger than Earth's satellite. They provide a never-ending fascination for amateur astronomers. (For the configurations of these four Galilean satellites see the right side of the pages in the THE SKY MONTH BY MONTH section.) Sometimes the satellites are paired on either side of the belted planet; frequently one is missing—either behind Jupiter, in the planet's shadow, or in front of Jupiter. In the latter case the satellite usually blends in against Jupiter's bright clouds and is difficult to see (more on this below). Even more interesting are the occasions when one of the satellites casts its shadow on the disk of the planet (see PHENOMENA OF THE GALILEAN SATELLITES on pp. 186–192). The tiny black shadow can be particularly evident if it is cast on one of the bright zones of Jupiter. This phenomenon sometimes is evident in a 60-mm refractor under good seeing conditions. On rarer occasions, *two* shadows are cast upon the face of Jupiter. These "double shadow transits" are included on the right-hand pages of THE SKY MONTH BY MONTH section.

The satellite umbral shadows vary significantly in size from one to another. Mean opposition angular diameters are Io 0.9″, Europa 0.6″, Ganymede 1.1″, and Callisto 0.5″. The enormous contrast between the dark shadows and the bright Jovian clouds makes these tiny features visible even though they are smaller than the nominal resolution limit of a small telescope. Furthermore, the satellites' penumbral shadows are quite large, especially Callisto's, which adds a few tenths of an arc-second to their effective visual diameters. The satellites themselves have the following mean opposition apparent diameters: Io 1.2″, Europa 1.0″, Ganymede 1.7″, and Callisto 1.6″. A 150-mm telescope reveals the size differences as well as colour variations among the satellites.

When the Galilean satellites transit the disk of Jupiter, they are seldom visible in telescopes under 100 mm and are best seen near the planet's limb when entering or leaving the disk. Tracking a satellite transit completely across Jupiter is a challenging observation. Each satellite has a characteristic appearance when superimposed on the Jovian cloudscape. Europa is bright white, similar to the brightest Jovian clouds. When traversing a white cloud zone in the central sector of Jupiter, Europa is usually invisible. However, it stands out well when near the limb or against a dark belt. Callisto, the darkest satellite, is best seen in the reverse circumstances. When seen against a pale zone this greyish satellite can be mistaken for a satellite shadow, but it is often lost against a dark belt. Ganymede is intermediate in surface brightness, but because of its great size, it is the easiest of the four to track completely across Jupiter's face. Io, innermost of the Galilean satellites, is also the most frequently seen in transit. It is close to Europa in brightness but is generally easier to follow over typical cloud features, probably due to its slightly greater diameter. Near opposition, a transiting satellite often appears adjacent to its own shadow. These events are especially worth a look. Jupiter's other satellites are photographic objects for large instruments.

As 2002 opens, Jupiter is in opposition in Gemini in the southeastern evening sky after dusk. For southern observers it is in the northeast. By mid-June Jupiter becomes lost in the solar glare, conjunction with the Sun occurring on Jul. 20. By late-August, Jupiter peeks above the eastern horizon in dawn twilight for both northern and southern observers. By September it is a prominent early-morning luminary in Cancer, in which constellation it remains for the rest of the year. During the first half of this year, Jupiter is at declination +23°, close to its maximum possible altitude for northern observers.

(text continued on p. 181)

Jupiter—2002

Date UT	Mag.	Equat. Diam. "
Jan. 1.0	−2.7	47.1
Feb. 1.0	−2.6	45.4
Mar. 1.0	−2.4	42.5
Apr. 1.0	−2.2	38.1
May 1.0	−2.0	35.0
Jun. 1.0	−1.9	32.8
Jul. 1.0	−1.8	31.7
Aug. 1.0	−1.8	31.6
Sep. 1.0	−1.8	32.4
Oct. 1.0	−1.9	34.2
Nov. 1.0	−2.1	37.0
Dec. 1.0	−2.3	40.5
Jan. 1.0	−2.5	44.0

JUPITER—DAILY CENTRAL MERIDIANS

The table at the right can be used to calculate the longitude of the central meridian of the observed disk of Jupiter during the months January–May and September–December (when Jupiter is well placed for observation). System I is the most rapidly rotating region between the middle of the North Equatorial Belt and the middle of the South Equatorial Belt. System II applies to the rest of the planet. The rotation rate of System I is 36.577±0.008 °/h and that of System II is 36.258±0.008 °/h. These figures, together with the closest tabular value, can be used to determine the longitude of a system's central meridian for any given date and time (UT) of observation. **Example:** At 22:30 PST Jan. 4 = 6:30 UT Jan. 5 the longitude of the central meridian of System II is 314.3 + (36.258 × 6.5)) = 550.0°; putting this angle in the range 0°–360° by subtracting 360° leaves a longitude of 190.0°, accurate to about 0.1°.

JUPITER—TABLE OF DAILY CENTRAL MERIDIANS, 2002

Date 0h UT	System I	System II	Date 0h UT	System I	System II	Date 0h UT	System I	System II	Date 0h UT	System I	System II
JANUARY			20	248.0	29.2	11	216.8	336.5	*JUNE TO AUGUST*		
0	112.0	282.3	21	45.9	179.4	12	14.5	126.5	*SUPPRESSED*		
1	270.0	72.7	22	203.8	329.7	13	172.2	276.6			
2	68.1	223.1	23	1.6	119.9	14	329.8	66.7	**SEPTEMBER**		
3	226.1	13.5	24	159.5	270.1	15	127.5	216.7	1	84.3	192.9
4	24.1	163.9	25	317.3	60.3	16	285.2	6.8	2	242.0	343.0
5	182.2	314.3	26	115.1	210.5	17	82.9	156.9	3	39.8	133.2
6	340.2	104.7	27	273.0	0.8	18	240.6	306.9	4	197.5	283.3
7	138.2	255.1	28	70.8	151.0	19	38.3	97.0	5	355.2	73.4
8	296.2	45.5				20	196.0	247.0	6	153.0	223.5
9	94.3	195.9	**MARCH**			21	353.7	37.1	7	310.7	13.6
10	252.3	346.3	1	228.6	301.2	22	151.4	187.1	8	108.5	163.7
11	50.3	136.7	2	26.5	91.4	23	309.0	337.2	9	266.2	313.9
12	208.3	287.0	3	184.3	241.5	24	106.7	127.2	10	64.0	104.0
13	6.3	77.4	4	342.1	31.7	25	264.4	277.3	11	221.7	254.1
14	164.3	227.8	5	139.9	181.9	26	62.1	67.3	12	19.5	44.2
15	322.3	18.2	6	297.7	332.1	27	219.8	217.4	13	177.3	194.4
16	120.3	168.5	7	95.5	122.3	28	17.4	7.4	14	335.0	344.5
17	278.3	318.9	8	253.3	272.5	29	175.1	157.5	15	132.8	134.6
18	76.3	109.3	9	51.1	62.6	30	332.8	307.5	16	290.6	284.7
19	234.3	259.6	10	208.9	212.8				17	88.3	74.9
20	32.3	50.0	11	6.7	3.0	**MAY**			18	246.1	225.0
21	190.3	200.3	12	164.5	153.1	1	130.4	97.6	19	43.9	15.2
22	348.3	350.7	13	322.3	303.3	2	288.1	247.6	20	201.6	165.3
23	146.2	141.0	14	120.1	93.4	3	85.8	37.6	21	359.4	315.5
24	304.2	291.4	15	277.9	243.6	4	243.4	187.7	22	157.2	105.6
25	102.2	81.7	16	75.6	33.7	5	41.1	337.7	23	315.0	255.7
26	260.1	232.1	17	233.4	183.9	6	198.8	127.7	24	112.7	45.9
27	58.1	22.4	18	31.2	334.0	7	356.4	277.8	25	270.5	196.1
28	216.1	172.7	19	188.9	124.1	8	154.1	67.8	26	68.3	346.2
29	14.0	323.1	20	346.7	274.3	9	311.8	217.8	27	226.1	136.4
30	172.0	113.4	21	144.5	64.4	10	109.4	7.9	28	23.9	286.5
31	329.9	263.7	22	302.2	214.5	11	267.1	157.9	29	181.7	76.7
			23	100.0	4.6	12	64.7	307.9	30	339.5	226.9
FEBRUARY			24	257.7	154.8	13	222.4	98.0			
1	127.9	54.0	25	55.5	304.9	14	20.1	248.0	**OCTOBER**		
2	285.8	204.3	26	213.2	95.0	15	177.7	38.0	1	137.3	17.0
3	83.7	354.6	27	11.0	245.1	16	335.4	188.0	2	295.1	167.2
4	241.7	144.9	28	168.7	35.2	17	133.0	338.1	3	92.9	317.4
5	39.6	295.2	29	326.4	185.3	18	290.7	128.1	4	250.7	107.5
6	197.5	85.5	30	124.2	335.4	19	88.3	278.1	5	48.5	257.7
7	355.5	235.8	31	281.9	125.5	20	246.0	68.1	6	206.3	47.9
8	153.4	26.1				21	43.6	218.2	7	4.1	198.1
9	311.3	176.4	**APRIL**			22	201.3	8.2	8	161.9	348.3
10	109.2	326.7	1	79.6	275.6	23	358.9	158.2	9	319.7	138.4
11	267.1	116.9	2	237.3	65.7	24	156.6	308.2	10	117.6	288.6
12	65.0	267.2	3	35.1	215.8	25	314.2	98.3	11	275.4	78.8
13	222.9	57.5	4	192.8	5.9	26	111.9	248.3	12	73.2	229.0
14	20.8	207.7	5	350.5	156.0	27	269.6	38.3	13	231.0	19.2
15	178.7	358.0	6	148.2	306.1	28	67.2	188.3	14	28.9	169.4
16	336.5	148.2	7	305.9	96.2	29	224.9	338.4	15	186.7	319.6
17	134.4	298.5	8	103.6	246.2	30	22.5	128.4	16	344.5	109.8
18	292.3	88.7	9	261.3	36.3	31	180.2	278.4	17	142.4	260.0
19	90.2	239.0	10	59.0	186.4				18	300.2	50.2

JUPITER—TABLE OF CENTRAL MERIDIANS, 2002 (continued)

Date 0h UT	System I	System II	Date 0h UT	System I	System II	Date 0h UT	System I	System II	Date 0h UT	System I	System II
OCTOBER (ct'd)			9	173.3	115.5	**DECEMBER**			24	81.7	40.4
19	98.0	200.4	10	331.2	265.8	1	47.8	182.1	25	239.7	190.8
20	255.9	350.6	11	129.1	56.0	2	205.8	332.4	26	37.7	341.2
21	53.7	140.9	12	287.1	206.3	3	3.8	122.8	27	195.7	131.6
22	211.6	291.1	13	85.0	356.6	4	161.7	273.1	28	353.8	282.0
23	9.4	81.3	14	242.9	146.9	5	319.7	63.5	29	151.8	72.4
24	167.3	231.5	15	40.8	297.2	6	117.7	213.8	30	309.8	222.8
25	325.2	21.8	16	198.7	87.4	7	275.7	4.2	31	107.9	13.2
26	123.0	172.0	17	356.6	237.7	8	73.6	154.5	32	265.9	163.6
27	280.9	322.2	18	154.6	28.0	9	231.6	304.9			
28	78.7	112.5	19	312.5	178.3	10	29.6	95.2			
29	236.6	262.7	20	110.4	328.6	11	187.6	245.6			
30	34.5	52.9	21	268.4	118.9	12	345.6	35.9			
31	192.4	203.2	22	66.3	269.2	13	143.6	186.3			
NOVEMBER			23	224.2	59.5	14	301.6	336.7			
			24	22.2	209.9	15	99.6	127.0			
1	350.2	353.4	25	180.1	360.2	16	257.6	277.4			
2	148.1	143.7	26	338.1	150.5	17	55.6	67.8			
3	306.0	293.9	27	136.0	300.8	18	213.6	218.1			
4	103.9	84.2	28	294.0	91.1	19	11.6	8.5			
5	261.8	234.4	29	91.9	241.4	20	169.6	158.9			
6	59.7	24.7	30	249.9	31.8	21	327.6	309.3			
7	217.5	175.0				22	125.6	99.7			
8	15.4	325.2				23	283.7	250.1			

GREAT RED SPOT—TIME OF TRANSIT

The table above may be used to determine when the Great Red Spot (GRS) (near longitude 76° in System II) will cross the central meridian of the disk of Jupiter.

Example: Suppose an observer in Ontario, Canada (time zone: Eastern Standard, −5 h) is viewing Jupiter on the evening of Dec. 15. At 0h UT Dec. 16 (19h EST December 15) the table gives approximately 277° for the longitude of the central meridian in System II. A further rotation of

$$(360° − 277°) + 76° = 159°$$

will bring the GRS to the central meridian, which will require

$$159° ÷ 36.258°/h = 4.38 \text{ h} = 4 \text{ h } 23 \text{ min.}$$

Thus the GRS will transit at

$$4:23 \text{ UT Dec. } 16 = 23:23 \text{ EST Dec. } 15.$$

Note that the GRS slowly drifts in longitude, so the 76° figure is only a guide. By timing a transit of the GRS and using the table, you can update its longitude.

SATURN

Saturn is the telescopic showpiece of the night sky. The chilling beauty of the small pale orb floating in a field of velvet is something no photographs or descriptions can adequately duplicate. Any telescope magnifying more than 30× will show the rings. The view is exquisite in 100- to 200-mm instruments. The rings consist of billions of particles—largely water ice—that range in size from microscopic specks to flying mountains kilometres across. The reason "rings" is plural is that gaps and brightness differences define hundreds of distinct rings. However, from Earth only the three most prominent components—known simply as rings A, B, and C—can be distinguished visually. (See the diagram Saturn—Main Ring Features Visible From Earth on the next page.)

Cassini's division, a gap between rings A and B discovered in 1675, is visible in small telescopes when the ring system is well inclined to our view. Cassini's division is a region less densely populated with ring particles than adjacent rings. Ring B, the brightest, overpowers ring C to such an extent that ring C, also known as the *crepe ring*, is seen only with difficulty in small telescopes. A Saturn phenomenon easily seen with backyard telescopes is the shadow of the planet on the rings. From one to four months before or after opposition the shadow falling on the rings is very apparent, often giving the scene a powerful three-dimensional aura.

In addition to the rings, Saturn has a family of at least 30 satellites. Titan, the largest, is easily seen in any telescope as an 8th-magnitude object orbiting Saturn in about 16 days. At east and west elongation Titan appears about five ring diameters from the planet. Telescopes over 60 mm in aperture should reveal Rhea at 10th magnitude less than two ring diameters from Saturn. The satellite Iapetus has the peculiar property of being five times brighter at western elongation (magnitude 10.1) than at eastern elongation (11.9). One side of the satellite has the reflectivity of snow while the other resembles dark rock. When brightest, Iapetus is located about 12 ring diameters west of the parent planet. Of the remaining satellites Tethys and Dione may be glimpsed in a 150-mm telescope, but the others require larger apertures. (See CONFIGURATIONS OF SATURN'S BRIGHTEST SATELLITES on pp. 193–196.)

The disk of Saturn appears about one-sixth the area of Jupiter through the same telescope with the same magnification. In telescopes less than 75-mm aperture, probably no features will ever be seen on the cloud deck of the planet other than the shadow cast by the rings. As the size of the telescope is increased, the pale equatorial region, a dusky equatorial band, and the darker polar regions become evident. Saturn has a belt system like Jupiter's but it is much less active and the contrast is reduced. Seldom in telescopes less than 100-mm aperture do more than one or two belts come into view. Saturn is approaching its 2003 perihelion, and its angular diameter in 2002 exceeds that of any opposition in more than a quarter of a century.

Saturn begins the year in the evening sky in Taurus, near Jupiter, but becomes lost in the solar glare by early May. It is in conjunction with the Sun on May 25 and is

Saturn—2002			
Date UT	Mag.	Equat. Diam. "	Ring Incl. °
Jan. 1.0	−0.3	20.2	−25.8
Feb. 1.0	−0.1	19.4	−25.8
Mar. 1.0	0.0	18.4	−25.9
Apr. 1.0	0.1	17.5	−26.2
May 1.0	0.1	16.8	−26.5
Jun. 1.0	0.0	16.5	−26.8
Jul. 1.0	0.1	16.6	−26.8
Aug. 1.0	0.1	17.1	−26.7
Sep. 1.0	0.1	17.8	−26.5
Oct. 1.0	0.0	18.8	−26.4
Nov. 1.0	−0.2	19.8	−26.4
Dec. 1.0	−0.4	20.5	−26.5
Jan. 1.0	−0.4	20.6	−26.7

SATURN—MAIN RING FEATURES VISIBLE FROM EARTH

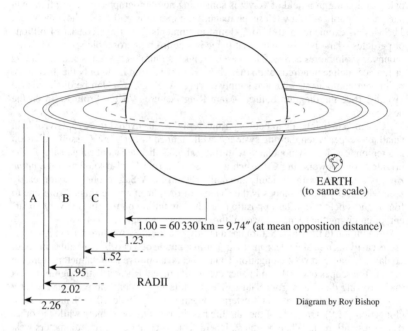

EARTH
(to same scale)

A   B   C

1.00 = 60 330 km = 9.74″ (at mean opposition distance)
1.23
1.52
1.95
2.02   RADII
2.26

Diagram by Roy Bishop

SATURN'S RING SYSTEM—MAIN STRUCTURAL REGIONS

Ring	Radius**	Discoverer
D	1.11 – 1.23	*Voyager 1* (1980)
C*	1.23 – 1.52	W.C. & G.P. Bond, W.R. Dawes (1850)
B*	1.52 – 1.95 }	{ Galileo (1610), C. Huygens (1659),
A*	2.02 – 2.26 }	{ G.D. Cassini (1675)
F	2.33	*Pioneer 11* (1979)
G	2.8	*Voyager 1* (1980)
E	3. – 8.	W.A. Feibelman (1966)

*Visible from Earth. Also, the E ring can be detected when Saturn's ring system
appears edge-on.
**In units of Saturn's equatorial radius (60 330 km).

not well placed for telescopic observing until August in the morning sky. Saturn is at opposition in Taurus on Dec. 17 when it is 8.05 AU or 67 light-min from Earth, 20.6″ in diameter, and the rings are 46.6″ across.

After having been edge-on to Earth in 1995 and 1996, Saturn's rings are now open to nearly their maximum possible extent with their south side facing Earth. During January the ring tilt is 25.8° as seen from Earth. By June, the rings have opened to 26.8°. The tilt remains above 26.3° for the rest of the year and reaches a maximum of 27.0° in March and April of 2003. This makes 2002 an excellent year for examining the divisions and structural subtleties of the rings.

URANUS

At magnitude 5.7 Uranus can be seen with the unaided eye under a clear, dark sky. However, it is much more easily located with binoculars. A 75-mm telescope will reveal its small, greenish, featureless disk.

Unlike the three other giant planets, the axis of Uranus is tipped almost parallel to the plane of the solar system. This means that we view Uranus nearly pole-on at certain points in its 84-year orbit. The southern (and counterclockwise turning) hemisphere of Uranus is now angled slightly toward Earth. Its south pole appeared nearest to (and slightly south of) the centre of its disk in 1985. Uranus has at least 21 satellites, all smaller than Earth's Moon, none of which can be detected in small or moderate-sized telescopes.

Uranus is at opposition in Capricornus on Aug. 20, when it is 18.99 AU or 2.6 light-h from Earth. It is then magnitude 5.7 and 3.7″ in apparent diameter. Use the chart below to locate this distant planet.

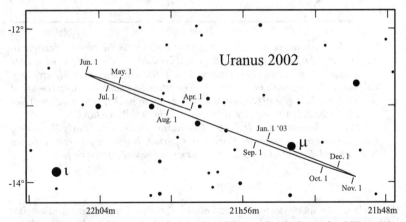

The finder chart above, provided by David Lane, shows the path of Uranus in Capricornus and Aquarius during the nine-month period 2002 April–December. Coordinates are for epoch 2000.0, and the magnitude limit is 8.0. Tick marks are drawn along the path at the beginning of each month. The 4th-magnitude star at the bottom left of the chart is ι Aqr; it is the star in south-central Aquarius just above the "S" of "AQUARIUS" in the SEPTEMBER ALL-SKY MAP *on p. 281.*

Along the five-month retrograde portion of its track, from Jun. 3 to Nov. 5 and centred at the Aug. 20 opposition, Uranus remains brighter than magnitude 5.8 and is well placed for observation. It is comparable in magnitude to the bright star in the top right corner of this chart.

NEPTUNE

Neptune is an 8th-magnitude binocular object—an easy target in 7 × 50 or larger glasses—but seeing the planet as a disk rather than a point of light is a different matter. Magnifications over 200× are usually necessary, and even then Neptune is just a tiny bluish dot with no hard edge due to limb darkening. Neptune's large satellite, Triton, can be seen by an experienced observer using a 300-mm telescope. Triton varies from 8″ to 17″ from Neptune.

In 2002 Neptune is in Capricornus and may be easily identified using the chart below. At opposition on Aug. 2, Neptune is magnitude 7.8, 29.07 AU or 4.04 light-h from Earth and 2.3″ in diameter.

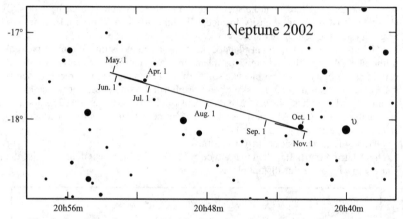

The finder chart above, provided by David Lane, shows the path of Neptune in Capricornus during the eight-month period 2002 April–November. Coordinates are in epoch 2000.0, and the magnitude limit is 8.0. Tick marks are drawn along the path at the beginning of each month. The 5th-magnitude star υ Cap is marked on the chart. In the SEPTEMBER ALL-SKY MAP on p. 281, υ (not marked) lies just above the ecliptic, directly above the "C" in "CAPRICORNUS."

Neptune lingers within 0.5° of υ Cap during October and early November, two months after opposition. During this period, it will be possible to frame Neptune and this naked-eye star in the same low-power telescopic field.

PLUTO

Besides being the solar system's smallest planet, Pluto is different from the other eight in almost every respect. Its unique characteristics include its orbit, which is so elliptical that the planet was closer to the Sun than was Neptune from 1980 through 1999.

Opposition is on Jun. 7 when the planet will be at magnitude 13.8 and 29.52 AU or 4.12 light-h from Earth. It can be identified using the chart at the right and a 200-mm or larger telescope. Pluto was near perihelion throughout the 1980s and 1990s and as bright as it ever gets. A few observers (with good optics, transparent skies, steady seeing, and high magnifications) succeeded in sighting Pluto with telescopes as small as 100-mm refractors.

FINDER CHART FOR PLUTO, 2002
BY IAN CAMERON

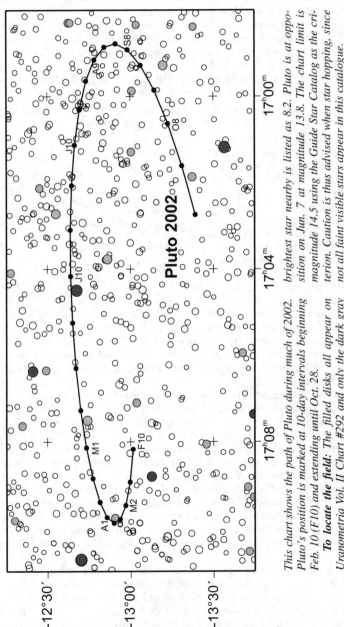

This chart shows the path of Pluto during much of 2002. Pluto's position is marked at 10-day intervals beginning Feb. 10 (F10) and extending until Oct. 28.

To locate the field: The filled disks all appear on *Uranometria Vol. II Chart #292* and only the dark gray ones appear in Tirion's *Sky Atlas 2000.0* (1st edition Chart #15). The star at the Jun. 10 position is listed in the Hubble Guide Star Catalog as magnitude 6.9 and the brightest star nearby is listed as 8.2. Pluto is at opposition on Jun. 7 at magnitude 13.8. The chart limit is magnitude 14.5 using the Guide Star Catalog as the criterion. Caution is thus advised when star hopping, since not all faint visible stars appear in this catalogue.

The chart is generated mainly using the free public-domain *Generic Mapping Tools* program.

PHENOMENA OF THE GALILEAN SATELLITES

The tables on the next six pages give the various transits, occultations, and eclipses of the four great satellites of Jupiter during January–May and September–December. Jupiter is not well-placed for observations during the other three months since it is in conjunction with the Sun on Jul. 20. Since the satellite phenomena are not instantaneous but take up to several minutes, the predicted times are for the middle of each event. The predictions were generated by the Institut de Mécanique Céleste et de Calcul des Ephémérides in Paris.

Satellites are denoted using the standard designations: I = Io; II = Europa; III = Ganymede; IV = Callisto. Events are denoted using the following abbreviations:

Ec = eclipse; **Oc** = occultation; **Tr** = transit of satellite; **Sh** = transit of shadow;
I = ingress; **E** = egress; **D** = disappearance; **R** = reappearance

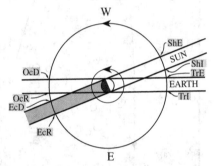

The general motion of the satellites and the successive phenomena are shown in the diagram at right, which is a view of Jupiter and the orbit of one of its satellites looking down from the north side. Satellites move from east to west across the face of the planet and from west to east behind it ("east" and "west" are here used in the sense of the observer's sky, not in the Jovian sense). Before opposition shadows fall to the west and after opposition to the east (as in the diagram).

The sequence of phenomena for the outer satellite shown in the diagram, counterclockwise beginning at the lower right, is transit ingress (TrI), transit egress (TrE), shadow ingress (ShI), shadow egress (ShE), occultation disappearance (OcD), occultation reappearance (OcR), eclipse disappearance (EcD), and eclipse reappearance (EcR). The actual sequence will depend on the actual Sun–Jupiter–Earth angle and the size of the satellite's orbit.

Approximately three-quarters of the phenomena listed will not be visible from any one locality because they occur when Jupiter is near or below the horizon or when daylight interferes. In practice, an observer usually knows when Jupiter will be conveniently placed in the night sky or, if not, can check in THE SKY MONTH BY MONTH section of this Handbook (pp. 66–91) for this information. The table can then be scanned to select those events that will occur during the intended observing period. For example, an observer near Victoria, B.C., on the evening of Jan. 3 would know that Jupiter is well-placed in the late-evening sky. If planning to observe from 10 p.m. to 1:00 a.m. PST (8 h behind UT), he or she could scan the table for events in the interval Jan. 4, 6:00 to 9:00 UT. There are two events, at 22:42 and 22:47 PST, both involving Io. The configuration of the four Galilean satellites during that evening is given in the diagram on the right-hand side of p. 69 in the THE SKY MONTH BY MONTH section.

Callisto is the only Galilean satellite that is not eclipsed during each of its revolutions. This year, however, all 22 revolutions of this outlying satellite result in eclipses, transits, and shadow transits. Callisto is involved in 3 of the 17 double shadow transits this year, on Apr. 7, Nov. 11, and Dec. 15. A total of 383 revolutions of Jupiter's Galilean satellites and 2398 events are recorded in the following tables, an average rate of one event every 2 h 45 min.

SATELLITES OF JUPITER, UT OF 2002 GEOCENTRIC PHENOMENA

JANUARY

Day	Time	Sat	Phen
0	15:35	I	ShI
	15:36	I	TrI
	17:50	I	ShE
	17:51	I	TrE
	21:27	II	EcD
1	0:15	II	OcR
	10:16	III	TrI
	10:17	III	ShI
	12:54	I	OcD
	13:18	III	TrE
	13:20	III	ShE
	15:10	I	EcR
2	10:02	I	TrI
	10:04	I	ShI
	12:16	I	TrE
	12:18	I	ShE
	16:25	II	TrI
	16:30	II	ShI
	19:13	II	TrE
	19:18	II	ShE
3	7:20	I	OcD
	9:39	I	EcR
4	4:28	I	TrI
	4:32	I	ShI
	6:42	I	TrE
	6:47	I	ShE
	10:35	II	OcD
	13:32	II	EcR
	23:55	III	OcD
5	1:46	I	OcD
	3:23	III	EcR
	4:07	I	EcR
	17:07	IV	OcD
	20:57	IV	EcR
	22:53	I	TrI
	23:01	I	ShI
6	1:08	I	TrE
	1:16	I	ShE
	5:33	II	TrI
	5:48	II	ShI
	8:21	II	TrE
	8:37	II	ShE
	20:12	I	OcD
	22:36	I	EcR
7	17:19	I	TrI
	17:29	I	ShI
	19:34	I	TrE
	19:44	I	ShE
	23:41	II	OcD
8	2:50	II	EcR
	13:32	III	TrI
	14:17	III	ShI
	14:38	I	OcD
	16:34	III	TrE
	17:05	I	EcR
	17:21	III	ShE
9	11:45	I	TrI
	11:58	I	ShI
	14:00	I	TrE
	14:13	I	ShE
	18:40	II	TrI
	19:06	II	ShI
	21:28	II	TrE
	21:55	II	ShE
10	9:04	I	OcD
	11:33	I	EcR
11	6:11	I	TrI
	6:26	I	ShI
	8:26	I	TrE
	8:41	I	ShE
	12:48	II	OcD
	16:07	II	EcR
12	3:10	III	OcD
	3:30	I	OcD
	6:02	I	EcR
	7:23	III	EcR
13	0:37	I	TrI
	0:55	I	ShI
	2:52	I	TrE
	3:10	I	ShE
	7:48	II	TrI
	8:25	II	ShI
	10:35	II	TrE
	11:14	II	ShE
	21:56	I	OcD
14	0:31	I	EcR
	1:58	IV	TrI
	4:38	IV	TrE
	4:59	IV	ShI
	7:50	IV	ShE
	19:03	I	TrI
	19:24	I	ShI
	21:18	I	TrE
	21:39	I	ShE
15	1:55	II	OcD
	5:25	II	EcR
	16:22	I	OcD
	16:48	III	TrI
	18:17	III	ShI
	18:59	I	EcR
	19:50	III	TrE
	21:21	III	ShE
16	13:29	I	TrI
	13:52	I	ShI
	15:44	I	TrE
	16:07	I	ShE
	20:55	II	TrI
	21:43	II	ShI
	23:43	II	TrE
17	0:32	II	ShE
	10:48	I	OcD
	13:28	I	EcR
18	7:55	I	TrI
	8:21	I	ShI
	10:10	I	TrE
	10:36	I	ShE
	15:03	II	OcD
	18:43	II	EcR
19	5:14	I	OcD
	6:28	III	OcD
	7:57	I	EcR
	11:24	III	EcR
20	2:21	I	TrI
	2:50	I	ShI
	4:36	I	TrE
	5:05	I	ShE
	10:04	II	TrI
	11:02	II	ShI
	12:51	II	TrE
	13:50	II	ShE
	23:40	I	OcD
21	2:26	I	EcR
	20:48	I	TrI
	21:18	I	ShI
	23:02	I	TrE
	23:33	I	ShE
22	4:10	II	OcD
	7:19	IV	OcD
	8:01	II	EcR
	10:01	IV	OcR
	12:12	IV	EcD
	15:10	IV	EcR
	18:06	I	OcD
	20:07	III	TrI
	20:54	I	EcR
	22:16	III	ShI
	23:09	III	TrE
23	1:21	III	ShE
	15:14	I	TrI
	15:47	I	ShI
	17:29	I	TrE
	18:02	I	ShE
	23:12	II	TrI
24	0:20	II	ShI
	2:00	II	TrE
	3:08	II	ShE
	12:33	I	OcD
	15:23	I	EcR
25	9:40	I	TrI
	10:16	I	ShI
	11:55	I	TrE
	12:31	I	ShE
	17:19	II	OcD
	21:19	II	EcR
26	6:59	I	OcD
	9:48	III	OcD
	9:52	I	EcR
	15:25	III	EcR
27	4:07	I	TrI
	4:44	I	ShI
	6:21	I	TrE
	6:59	I	ShE
	12:21	II	TrI
	13:39	II	ShI
	15:09	II	TrE
	16:27	II	ShE
28	1:26	I	OcD
	4:21	I	EcR
	22:33	I	TrI
	23:13	I	ShI
29	0:48	I	TrE
	1:28	I	ShE
	6:27	II	OcD
	10:37	II	EcR
	19:52	I	OcD
	22:49	I	EcR
	23:28	III	TrI
30	2:15	III	ShI
	2:30	III	TrE
	5:21	III	ShE
	16:28	IV	TrI
	17:00	I	TrI
	17:42	I	ShI
	19:08	IV	TrE
	19:14	I	TrE
	19:57	I	ShE
	23:00	IV	ShI
31	1:30	II	TrI
	2:02	IV	ShE
	2:57	II	ShI
	4:18	II	TrE
	5:45	II	ShE
	14:19	I	OcD
	17:18	I	EcR

FEBRUARY

Day	Time	Sat	Phen
1	11:26	I	TrI
	12:10	I	ShI
	13:41	I	TrE
	14:25	I	ShE
	19:36	II	OcD
	23:55	II	EcR
2	8:45	I	OcD
	11:47	I	EcR
	13:13	III	OcD
	16:16	III	OcR
	16:18	III	EcD
	19:26	III	EcR
3	5:53	I	TrI
	6:39	I	ShI
	8:07	I	TrE
	8:54	I	ShE
	14:40	II	TrI
	16:15	II	ShI
	17:28	II	TrE
	19:03	II	ShE
4	3:12	I	OcD
	6:16	I	EcR
5	0:19	I	TrI
	1:08	I	ShI
	2:34	I	TrE
	3:23	I	ShE
	8:46	II	OcD
	13:13	II	EcR
	21:39	I	OcD
6	0:44	I	EcR
	2:54	III	TrI
	5:56	III	TrE
	6:14	III	ShI
	9:21	III	ShE
	18:46	I	TrI
	19:37	I	ShI
	21:01	I	TrE
	21:52	I	ShE
7	3:51	II	TrI
	5:33	II	ShI
	6:38	II	TrE
	8:21	II	ShE
	16:06	I	OcD
	19:13	I	EcR
	22:08	IV	OcD
8	0:52	IV	OcR
	6:14	IV	EcD
	9:23	IV	EcR
	13:13	I	TrI
	14:05	I	ShI
	15:27	I	TrE
	16:20	I	ShE
	21:56	II	OcD
9	2:31	II	EcR
	10:32	I	OcD
	13:42	I	EcR
	16:40	III	OcD
	19:44	III	OcR
	20:18	III	EcD
	23:27	III	EcR
10	7:40	I	TrI
	8:34	I	ShI
	9:54	I	TrE
	10:49	I	ShE
	17:02	II	TrI
	18:52	II	ShI
	19:49	II	TrE
	21:40	II	ShE
11	4:59	I	OcD
	8:11	I	EcR
12	2:07	I	TrI
	3:03	I	ShI
	4:21	I	TrE
	5:18	I	ShE
	11:07	II	OcD
	15:50	II	EcR
	23:26	I	OcD
13	2:40	I	EcR
	6:24	III	TrI
	9:26	III	TrE
	10:15	III	ShI
	13:22	III	ShE
	20:34	I	TrI
	21:32	I	ShI
	22:48	I	TrE
	23:47	I	ShE
14	6:13	II	TrI
	8:10	II	ShI
	9:00	II	TrE
	10:58	II	ShE
	17:53	I	OcD
	21:08	I	EcR
15	15:01	I	TrI
	16:00	I	ShI
	17:16	I	TrE
	18:15	I	ShE

SATELLITES OF JUPITER, UT OF 2002 GEOCENTRIC PHENOMENA (ct'd)

FEBRUARY (ct'd)

16	0:18	II	OcD
	5:08	II	EcR
	7:44	IV	TrI
	10:27	IV	TrE
	12:21	I	OcD
	15:37	I	EcR
	17:02	IV	ShI
	20:12	III	OcD
	20:13	IV	ShE
	23:16	III	OcR
17	0:18	III	EcD
	3:28	III	EcR
	9:29	I	TrI
	10:29	I	ShI
	11:43	I	TrE
	12:44	I	ShE
	19:25	II	TrI
	21:28	II	ShI
	22:12	II	TrE
18	0:16	II	ShE
	6:48	I	OcD
	10:06	I	EcR
19	3:56	I	TrI
	4:58	I	ShI
	6:10	I	TrE
	7:13	I	ShE
	13:30	II	OcD
	18:26	II	EcR
20	1:15	I	OcD
	4:35	I	EcR
	9:59	III	TrI
	13:01	III	TrE
	14:15	III	ShI
	17:23	III	ShE
	22:23	I	TrI
	23:27	I	ShI
21	0:37	I	TrE
	1:42	I	ShE
	8:38	II	TrI
	10:46	II	ShI
	11:24	II	TrE
	13:34	II	ShE
	19:43	I	OcD
	23:04	I	EcR
22	16:51	I	TrI
	17:55	I	ShI
	19:05	I	TrE
	20:10	I	ShE
23	2:43	II	OcD
	7:45	II	EcR
	14:10	I	OcD
	17:32	I	EcR
	23:48	III	OcD
24	2:53	III	OcR
	4:17	III	EcD
	7:28	III	EcR
	11:18	I	TrI
	12:24	I	ShI
	13:32	I	TrE
	13:52	IV	OcD
	14:39	I	ShE
	16:40	IV	OcR
	21:51	II	TrI

25	0:05	II	ShI
	0:17	IV	EcD
	0:37	II	TrE
	2:52	II	ShE
	3:36	IV	EcR
	8:38	I	OcD
	12:01	I	EcR
26	5:46	I	TrI
	6:53	I	ShI
	8:00	I	TrE
	9:08	I	ShE
	15:56	II	OcD
	21:03	II	EcR
27	3:05	I	OcD
	6:30	I	EcR
	13:39	III	TrI
	16:42	III	TrE
	18:15	III	ShI
	21:24	III	ShE
28	0:13	I	TrI
	1:22	I	ShI
	2:28	I	TrE
	3:37	I	ShE
	11:04	II	TrI
	13:23	II	ShI
	13:51	II	TrE
	16:10	II	ShE
	21:33	I	OcD

MARCH

1	0:59	I	EcR
	18:41	I	TrI
	19:51	I	ShI
	20:55	I	TrE
	22:06	I	ShE
2	5:10	II	OcD
	10:22	II	EcR
	16:01	I	OcD
	19:28	I	EcR
3	3:30	III	OcD
	6:35	III	OcR
	8:17	III	EcD
	11:29	III	EcR
	13:09	I	TrI
	14:20	I	ShI
	15:23	I	TrE
	16:34	I	ShE
4	0:19	II	TrI
	2:41	II	ShI
	3:05	II	TrE
	5:29	II	ShE
	10:29	I	OcD
	13:56	I	EcR
	23:57	IV	TrI
5	2:45	IV	TrE
	7:37	I	TrI
	8:48	I	ShI
	9:51	I	TrE
	11:03	I	ShE
	11:03	IV	ShI
	14:24	IV	ShE
	18:24	II	OcD
	23:41	II	EcR

6	4:57	I	OcD
	8:25	I	EcR
	17:24	III	TrI
	20:26	III	TrE
	22:15	III	ShI
7	1:25	III	ShE
	2:05	I	TrI
	3:17	I	ShI
	4:19	I	TrE
	5:32	I	ShE
	13:34	II	TrI
	15:59	II	ShI
	16:20	II	TrE
	18:47	II	ShE
	23:25	I	OcD
8	2:54	I	EcR
	20:33	I	TrI
	21:46	I	ShI
	22:47	I	TrE
9	0:01	I	ShE
	7:40	II	OcD
	13:00	II	EcR
	17:53	I	OcD
	21:23	I	EcR
10	7:17	III	OcD
	10:23	III	OcR
	12:18	III	EcD
	15:01	I	TrI
	15:30	III	EcR
	16:15	I	ShI
	17:15	I	TrE
	18:30	I	ShE
11	2:49	II	TrI
	5:17	II	ShI
	5:35	II	TrE
	8:05	II	ShE
	12:21	I	OcD
	15:52	I	EcR
12	9:29	I	TrI
	10:44	I	ShI
	11:44	I	TrE
	12:59	I	ShE
	20:55	II	OcD
13	2:18	II	EcR
	6:35	IV	OcD
	6:49	I	OcD
	9:29	IV	OcR
	10:20	I	EcR
	18:20	IV	EcD
	21:12	III	TrI
	21:48	IV	EcR
14	0:16	III	TrE
	2:15	III	ShI
	3:58	I	TrI
	5:13	I	ShI
	5:25	III	ShE
	6:12	I	TrE
	7:28	I	ShE
	16:05	II	TrI
	18:35	II	ShI
	18:51	II	TrE
	21:23	II	ShE

15	1:17	I	OcD
	4:49	I	EcR
	22:26	I	TrI
	23:41	I	ShI
16	0:40	I	TrE
	1:56	I	ShE
	10:12	II	OcD
	15:37	II	EcR
	19:46	I	OcD
	23:18	I	EcR
17	11:08	III	OcD
	14:15	III	OcR
	16:18	III	EcD
	16:55	I	TrI
	18:10	I	ShI
	19:09	I	TrE
	19:31	III	EcR
	20:25	I	ShE
18	5:22	II	TrI
	7:54	II	ShI
	8:08	II	TrE
	10:41	II	ShE
	14:14	I	OcD
	17:47	I	EcR
19	11:23	I	TrI
	12:39	I	ShI
	13:37	I	TrE
	14:54	I	ShE
	23:29	II	OcD
20	4:56	II	EcR
	8:43	I	OcD
	12:16	I	EcR
21	1:06	III	TrI
	4:10	III	TrE
	5:52	I	TrI
	6:15	III	ShI
	7:08	I	ShI
	8:06	I	TrE
	9:23	I	ShE
	9:26	III	ShE
	17:11	IV	TrI
	18:38	II	TrI
	20:06	IV	TrE
	21:12	II	ShI
	21:25	II	TrE
	23:59	II	ShE
22	3:11	I	OcD
	5:06	IV	ShI
	6:44	I	EcR
	8:35	IV	ShE
23	0:20	I	TrI
	1:37	I	ShI
	2:34	I	TrE
	3:52	I	ShE
	12:47	II	OcD
	18:15	II	EcR
	21:40	I	OcD
24	1:13	I	EcR
	15:05	III	OcD
	18:12	III	OcR
	18:49	I	TrI
	20:06	I	ShI
	20:19	III	EcD
	21:03	I	TrE
	22:21	I	ShE
	23:33	III	EcR

25	7:56	II	TrI
	10:30	II	ShI
	10:42	II	TrE
	13:17	II	ShE
	16:08	I	OcD
	19:42	I	EcR
26	13:18	I	TrI
	14:35	I	ShI
	15:32	I	TrE
	16:50	I	ShE
27	2:05	II	OcD
	7:33	II	EcR
	10:37	I	OcD
	14:11	I	EcR
28	5:03	III	TrI
	7:46	I	TrI
	8:08	III	TrE
	9:04	I	ShI
	10:01	I	TrE
	10:14	III	ShI
	11:19	I	ShE
	13:26	III	ShE
	21:14	II	TrI
	23:47	II	ShI
29	0:00	II	TrE
	2:35	II	ShE
	5:06	I	OcD
	8:40	I	EcR
30	0:16	IV	OcD
	2:15	I	TrI
	3:19	IV	OcR
	3:32	I	ShI
	4:30	I	TrE
	5:47	I	ShE
	12:23	IV	EcD
	15:23	II	OcD
	16:00	IV	EcR
	20:52	II	EcR
	23:35	I	OcD
31	3:08	I	EcR
	19:05	III	OcD
	20:44	I	TrI
	22:01	I	ShI
	22:13	III	OcR
	22:59	I	TrE

SATELLITES OF JUPITER, UT OF 2002 GEOCENTRIC PHENOMENA (ct'd)

APRIL																			
1	0:16	I	ShE	10	7:22	II	OcD	20	8:06	I	TrI	29	4:34	I	TrI	8	1:04	I	TrI
	0:18	III	EcD		12:49	II	EcR		9:19	I	ShI		5:43	I	ShI		2:07	I	ShI
	3:34	III	EcR		14:29	I	OcD		10:21	I	TrE		6:50	I	TrE		3:19	I	TrE
	10:32	II	TrI		18:01	I	EcR		11:34	I	ShE		7:59	I	ShE		4:23	I	ShE
	13:05	II	ShI	11	11:39	I	TrI		23:26	II	OcD		11:40	III	OcD		18:19	II	OcD
	13:18	II	TrE		12:54	I	ShI	21	4:46	II	EcR		14:51	III	OcR		22:22	I	OcD
	15:53	II	ShE		13:11	III	TrI		5:25	I	OcD		16:18	III	EcD		23:21	II	EcR
	18:04	I	OcD		13:54	I	TrE		8:54	I	EcR		19:36	III	EcR	9	1:41	I	EcR
	21:37	I	EcR		15:10	I	ShE	22	2:36	I	TrI		21:13	II	TrI		19:34	I	TrI
2	15:13	I	TrI		16:18	III	TrE		3:48	I	ShI		23:27	II	ShI		20:36	I	ShI
	16:30	I	ShI		18:15	III	ShI		4:51	I	TrE		23:59	II	TrE		21:49	I	TrE
	17:28	I	TrE		21:29	III	ShE		6:03	I	ShE	30	1:53	I	OcD		22:52	I	ShE
	18:45	I	ShE	12	2:30	II	TrI		7:26	III	OcD		2:15	II	ShE	10	6:05	III	TrI
3	4:42	II	OcD		4:59	II	ShI		10:36	III	OcR		5:17	I	EcR		9:16	III	TrE
	10:11	II	EcR		5:16	II	TrE		12:17	III	EcD		23:04	I	TrI		10:15	III	ShI
	12:33	I	OcD		7:46	II	ShE		15:35	III	EcR						13:18	II	TrI
	16:06	I	EcR		8:58	I	OcD		18:31	II	TrI	**MAY**					13:33	III	ShE
4	9:06	III	TrI		12:30	I	EcR		20:52	II	ShI	1	0:12	I	ShI		15:20	II	ShI
	9:42	I	TrI	13	6:08	I	TrI		21:17	II	TrE		1:20	I	TrE		16:05	II	TrE
	10:59	I	ShI		7:23	I	ShI		23:40	II	ShE		2:28	I	ShE		16:51	I	OcD
	11:57	I	TrE		8:23	I	TrE		23:55	I	OcD		15:33	II	OcD		18:08	II	ShE
	12:11	III	TrE		9:39	I	ShE	23	3:22	I	EcR		20:23	I	OcD		20:10	I	EcR
	13:14	I	ShE		20:43	II	OcD		21:05	I	TrI		20:43	II	EcR	11	1:40	IV	TrI
	14:15	III	ShI	14	2:08	II	EcR		22:17	I	ShI		23:46	I	EcR		5:06	IV	TrE
	17:28	III	ShE		3:28	I	OcD		23:20	I	TrE	2	14:02	IV	OcD		11:14	IV	ShI
	23:51	II	TrI		6:59	I	EcR	24	0:32	I	ShE		17:25	IV	OcR		14:04	I	TrI
5	2:23	II	ShI	15	0:38	I	TrI		6:11	IV	TrI		17:34	I	TrI		15:05	IV	ShE
	2:37	II	TrE		1:52	I	ShI		9:26	IV	TrE		18:41	I	ShI		15:05	I	ShI
	5:11	II	ShE		2:53	I	TrE		12:48	II	OcD		19:49	I	TrE		16:19	I	TrE
	7:02	I	OcD		3:15	III	OcD		17:11	IV	ShI		20:57	I	ShE		17:21	I	ShE
	10:35	I	EcR		4:08	I	ShE		18:05	II	EcR	3	0:30	IV	EcD	12	7:43	II	OcD
6	4:11	I	TrI		6:25	III	OcR		18:24	I	OcD		1:48	III	TrI		11:21	I	OcD
	5:28	I	ShI		8:18	III	EcD		20:55	IV	ShE		4:23	IV	EcR		12:41	II	EcR
	6:26	I	TrE		11:34	III	EcR		21:51	I	EcR		4:58	III	TrE		14:38	I	EcR
	7:43	I	ShE		15:50	II	TrI	25	15:35	I	TrI		6:16	III	ShI	13	8:34	I	TrI
	18:02	II	OcD		18:17	II	ShI		16:45	I	ShI		9:32	III	ShE		9:34	I	ShI
	23:30	II	EcR		18:36	II	TrE		17:50	I	TrE		10:34	II	TrI		10:49	I	TrE
7	1:31	I	OcD		18:48	IV	OcD		19:01	I	ShE		12:45	II	ShI		11:50	I	ShE
	5:03	I	EcR		21:04	II	ShE		21:33	III	TrI		13:21	II	TrE		20:15	III	OcD
	11:18	IV	TrI		21:57	I	OcD	26	0:42	III	TrE		14:52	I	OcD		23:29	III	OcR
	14:22	IV	TrE		22:01	IV	OcR		2:16	III	ShI		15:33	II	ShE	14	0:18	III	EcD
	22:41	I	TrI	16	1:27	I	EcR		5:31	III	ShE		18:15	I	EcR		2:40	II	TrI
	23:08	III	OcD		6:27	IV	EcD		7:51	II	TrI	4	12:04	I	TrI		3:38	III	EcR
	23:09	IV	ShI		10:12	IV	EcR		10:10	II	ShI		13:10	I	ShI		4:38	II	ShI
	23:57	I	ShI		19:07	I	TrI		10:38	II	TrE		14:19	I	TrE		5:27	II	TrE
8	0:55	I	TrE		20:21	I	ShI		12:54	I	OcD		15:26	I	ShE		5:51	I	OcD
	2:12	I	ShE		21:22	I	TrE		12:57	II	ShE	5	4:56	II	OcD		7:26	II	ShE
	2:17	III	OcR		22:37	I	ShE		16:20	I	EcR		9:22	I	OcD		9:07	I	EcR
	2:46	IV	ShE	17	10:04	II	OcD	27	10:05	I	TrI		10:03	II	EcR	15	3:04	I	TrI
	4:18	III	EcD		15:27	II	EcR		11:14	I	ShI		12:43	I	EcR		4:03	I	ShI
	7:34	III	EcR		16:26	I	OcD		12:20	I	TrE	6	6:34	I	TrI		5:19	I	TrE
	13:10	II	TrI		19:56	I	EcR		13:30	I	ShE		7:39	I	ShI		6:19	I	ShE
	15:41	II	ShI	18	13:37	I	TrI	28	2:10	II	OcD		8:49	I	TrE		21:07	II	OcD
	15:56	II	TrE		14:50	I	ShI		7:23	I	OcD		9:55	I	ShE				
	18:28	II	ShE		15:52	I	TrE		7:25	II	EcR		15:56	III	OcD				
	20:00	I	OcD		17:05	I	ShE		10:48	I	EcR		19:09	III	OcR				
	23:32	I	EcR		17:21	III	TrI						20:17	III	EcD				
9	17:10	I	TrI		20:29	III	TrE						23:37	III	EcR				
	18:26	I	ShI		22:16	III	ShI						23:56	II	TrI				
	19:24	I	TrE	19	1:31	III	ShE					7	2:03	II	ShI				
	20:41	I	ShE		5:10	II	TrI						2:43	II	TrE				
					7:35	II	ShI						3:52	I	OcD				
					7:56	II	TrE						4:51	II	ShE				
					10:22	II	ShE						7:12	I	EcR				
					10:56	I	OcD												
					14:25	I	EcR												

SATELLITES OF JUPITER, UT OF 2002 GEOCENTRIC PHENOMENA (ct'd)

MAY (ct'd)

Day	Time	Sat	Phen
16	0:21	I	OcD
	1:59	II	EcR
	3:36	I	EcR
	21:34	I	TrI
	22:32	I	ShI
	23:50	I	TrE
17	0:48	I	ShE
	10:24	III	TrI
	13:37	III	TrE
	14:15	III	ShI
	16:02	II	TrI
	17:33	III	ShE
	17:55	II	ShI
	18:50	II	TrE
	18:51	I	OcD
	20:43	II	ShE
	22:04	I	EcR
18	16:04	I	TrI
	17:00	I	ShI
	18:20	I	TrE
	19:17	I	ShE
19	9:48	IV	OcD
	10:31	II	OcD
	13:21	I	OcD
	13:23	IV	OcR
	15:19	II	EcR
	16:33	I	EcR
	18:34	IV	EcD
	22:33	IV	EcR
20	10:34	I	TrI
	11:29	I	ShI
	12:50	I	TrE
	13:46	I	ShE
21	0:36	III	OcD
	3:51	III	OcR
	4:17	III	EcD
	5:25	II	TrI
	7:13	II	ShI
	7:38	III	EcR
	7:51	I	OcD
	8:13	II	TrE
	10:01	II	ShE
	11:02	I	EcR
22	5:04	I	TrI
	5:58	I	ShI
	7:20	I	TrE
	8:15	I	ShE
	23:55	II	OcD
23	2:21	I	OcD
	4:37	II	EcR
	5:30	I	EcR
	23:34	I	TrI
24	0:27	I	ShI
	1:50	I	TrE
	2:44	I	ShE
	14:46	III	TrI
	18:00	III	TrE
	18:15	III	ShI
	18:48	II	TrI
	20:30	II	ShI
	20:51	I	OcD
	21:35	III	ShE
	21:36	II	TrE
24	23:19	II	ShE
	23:59	I	EcR
25	18:04	I	TrI
	18:56	I	ShI
	20:21	I	TrE
	21:12	I	ShE
26	13:20	II	OcD
	15:21	I	OcD
	17:57	II	EcR
	18:28	I	EcR
27	12:35	I	TrI
	13:25	I	ShI
	14:51	I	TrE
	15:41	I	ShE
	21:37	IV	TrI
28	1:15	IV	TrE
	4:57	III	OcD
	5:15	IV	ShI
	8:11	II	TrI
	8:14	III	OcR
	8:16	III	EcD
	9:14	IV	ShE
	9:48	II	ShI
	9:51	I	OcD
	10:59	II	TrE
	11:38	III	EcR
	12:36	II	ShE
	12:56	I	EcR
29	7:05	I	TrI
	7:53	I	ShI
	9:21	I	TrE
	10:10	I	ShE
30	2:45	II	OcD
	4:21	I	OcD
	7:16	II	EcR
	7:25	I	EcR
31	1:35	I	TrI
	2:22	I	ShI
	3:51	I	TrE
	4:39	I	ShE
	19:09	III	TrI
	21:34	II	TrI
	22:15	III	ShI
	22:25	III	TrE
	22:51	I	OcD
	23:05	II	ShI

JUN. TO AUG. SUPPRESSED

SEPTEMBER

Day	Time	Sat	Phen
1	0:20	I	EcD
	3:19	I	OcR
	8:34	II	ShI
	9:56	II	TrI
	11:25	II	ShE
	12:48	II	TrE
	21:41	I	ShI
	22:23	I	TrI
	23:58	I	ShE
2	0:40	I	TrE
	2:04	III	ShI
	4:53	III	TrI
	5:33	III	ShE
	8:24	III	TrE
	18:49	I	EcD
	21:49	I	OcR
3	3:41	II	EcD
	8:01	II	OcR
	16:10	I	ShI
	16:53	I	TrI
	18:27	I	ShE
	19:10	I	TrE
4	13:17	I	EcD
	16:19	I	OcR
	21:51	II	ShI
	23:19	II	TrI
5	0:42	II	ShE
	2:11	II	TrE
	10:38	I	ShI
	11:23	I	TrI
	12:55	I	ShE
	13:40	I	TrE
	16:01	III	EcD
	17:19	IV	ShI
	21:47	IV	ShE
	22:37	III	OcR
6	0:21	IV	TrI
	4:57	IV	TrE
	7:45	I	EcD
	10:49	I	OcR
	16:59	II	EcD
	21:25	II	OcR
7	5:07	I	ShI
	5:53	I	TrI
	7:24	I	ShE
	8:10	I	TrE
8	2:14	I	EcD
	5:19	I	OcR
	11:08	II	ShI
	12:43	II	TrI
	14:00	II	ShE
	15:35	II	TrE
	23:35	I	ShI
9	0:22	I	TrI
	1:52	I	ShE
	2:40	I	TrE
	6:03	III	ShI
	9:16	III	TrI
	9:32	III	ShE
	12:48	III	TrE
	20:42	I	EcD
	23:49	I	OcR
10	6:17	II	EcD
	10:48	II	OcR
	18:04	I	ShI
	18:52	I	TrI
	20:20	I	ShE
	21:09	I	TrE
11	15:11	I	EcD
	18:18	I	OcR
12	0:26	II	ShI
	2:06	II	TrI
	3:17	II	ShE
	4:58	II	TrE
	12:32	I	ShI
	13:22	I	TrI
	14:49	I	ShE
	15:39	I	TrE
	19:59	III	EcD
13	3:00	III	OcD
	9:39	I	EcD
	12:48	I	OcR
	19:34	II	EcD
14	0:11	II	OcR
	0:46	IV	EcR
	5:21	IV	EcR
	7:01	I	ShI
	7:52	I	TrI
	9:01	IV	OcD
	9:17	I	ShE
	10:09	I	TrE
	13:45	IV	OcR
15	4:07	I	EcD
	7:18	I	OcR
	13:43	II	ShI
	15:29	II	TrI
	16:35	II	ShE
	18:21	II	TrE
16	1:29	I	ShI
	2:22	I	TrI
	3:46	I	ShE
	4:39	I	TrE
	10:02	III	ShI
	13:31	III	ShE
	13:37	III	TrI
	17:10	III	TrE
	22:36	I	EcD
17	1:48	I	OcR
	8:52	II	EcD
	13:34	II	OcR
	19:57	I	ShI
	20:52	I	TrI
	22:14	I	ShE
	23:08	I	TrE
18	17:04	I	EcD
	20:18	I	OcR
19	3:01	II	ShI
	4:51	II	TrI
	5:52	II	ShE
	7:44	II	TrE
	14:26	I	ShI
	15:21	I	TrI
	16:43	I	ShE
	17:38	I	TrE
	23:57	III	EcD
20	3:29	III	EcR
	3:45	III	OcD
	7:20	III	OcR
	11:33	I	EcD
	14:47	I	OcR
	22:09	II	EcD
21	2:57	II	OcR
	8:54	I	ShI
	9:51	I	TrI
	11:11	I	ShE
	12:08	I	TrE
22	6:01	I	EcD
	9:17	I	OcR
	11:18	IV	ShI
	15:49	IV	ShE
	16:18	II	ShI
	18:14	II	TrI
	19:10	II	ShE
	20:20	IV	TrI
	21:07	II	TrE
23	1:01	IV	TrE
	3:23	I	ShI
	4:20	I	TrI
	5:39	I	ShE
	6:37	I	TrE
	14:00	III	ShI
	17:30	III	ShE
	17:56	III	TrI
	21:29	III	TrE
24	0:29	I	EcD
	3:47	I	OcR
	11:27	II	EcD
	16:19	II	OcR
	21:51	I	ShI
	22:50	I	TrI
25	0:08	I	ShE
	1:07	I	TrE
	18:58	I	EcD
	22:16	I	OcR
26	5:35	II	ShI
	7:36	II	TrI
	8:27	II	ShE
	10:29	II	TrE
	16:20	I	ShI
	17:20	I	TrI
	18:36	I	ShE
	19:36	I	TrE
27	3:56	III	EcD
	7:28	III	EcR
	8:04	III	OcD
	11:40	III	OcR
	13:26	I	EcD
	16:46	I	OcR
28	0:44	II	EcD
	5:41	II	OcR
	10:48	I	ShI
	11:49	I	TrI
	13:05	I	ShE
	14:06	I	TrE
29	7:55	I	EcD
	11:15	I	OcR
	18:53	II	ShI
	20:59	II	TrI
	21:45	II	ShE
	23:51	II	TrE
30	5:16	I	ShI
	6:19	I	TrI
	7:33	I	ShE
	8:35	I	TrE
	17:58	III	ShI
	18:46	IV	EcD
	21:28	III	ShE
	22:12	III	TrI
	23:24	IV	EcR

SATELLITES OF JUPITER, UT OF 2002 GEOCENTRIC PHENOMENA (ct'd)

OCTOBER

1	1:46	III	TrE
	2:23	I	EcD
	4:52	IV	OcD
	5:45	I	OcR
	9:41	IV	OcR
	14:01	II	EcD
	19:03	II	OcR
	23:45	I	ShI
2	0:48	I	TrI
	2:01	I	ShE
	3:05	I	TrE
	20:51	I	EcD
3	0:14	I	OcR
	8:10	II	ShI
	10:20	II	TrI
	11:02	II	ShE
	13:13	II	TrE
	18:13	I	ShI
	19:17	I	TrI
	20:30	I	ShE
	21:34	I	TrE
4	7:54	III	EcD
	11:27	III	EcR
	12:20	III	OcD
	15:20	I	EcD
	15:56	III	OcR
	18:44	I	OcR
5	3:18	II	EcD
	8:24	II	OcR
	12:42	I	ShI
	13:47	I	TrI
	14:58	I	ShE
	16:03	I	TrE
6	9:48	I	EcD
	13:13	I	OcR
	21:28	II	ShI
	23:42	II	TrI
7	0:20	II	ShE
	2:35	II	TrE
	7:10	I	ShI
	8:16	I	TrI
	9:26	I	ShE
	10:33	I	TrE
	21:56	III	ShI
8	1:26	III	ShE
	2:26	III	TrI
	4:17	I	EcD
	6:00	III	TrE
	7:42	I	OcR
	16:36	II	EcD
	21:45	II	OcR
9	1:38	I	ShI
	2:45	I	TrI
	3:55	I	ShE
	5:02	I	TrE
	5:17	IV	ShI
	9:51	IV	ShE
	15:53	IV	TrI
	20:36	IV	TrE
	22:45	I	EcD
10	2:12	I	OcR
	10:45	II	ShI
	13:03	II	TrI
	13:37	II	ShE
	15:56	II	TrE
	20:07	I	ShI
	21:14	I	TrI
	22:23	I	ShE
	23:31	I	TrE
11	11:53	III	EcD
	15:26	III	EcR
	16:33	III	OcD
	17:13	I	EcD
	20:11	III	OcR
	20:41	I	OcR
12	5:53	II	EcD
	11:05	II	OcR
	14:35	I	ShI
	15:44	I	TrI
	16:51	I	ShE
	18:00	I	TrE
13	11:42	I	EcD
	15:10	I	OcR
14	0:03	II	ShI
	2:24	II	TrI
	2:55	II	ShE
	5:17	II	TrE
	9:03	I	ShI
	10:13	I	TrI
	11:20	I	ShE
	12:29	I	TrE
15	1:54	III	ShI
	5:24	III	ShE
	6:10	I	EcD
	6:37	III	TrI
	9:39	I	OcR
	10:12	III	TrE
	19:10	II	EcD
16	0:25	II	OcR
	3:32	I	ShI
	4:42	I	TrI
	5:48	I	ShE
	6:58	I	TrE
17	0:38	I	EcD
	4:09	I	OcR
	12:46	IV	EcD
	13:21	II	ShI
	15:45	II	TrI
	16:13	II	ShE
	17:27	IV	EcR
	18:37	II	TrE
	22:00	I	ShI
	23:11	I	TrI
18	0:11	IV	OcD
	0:16	I	ShE
	1:27	I	TrE
	5:03	IV	OcR
	15:51	III	EcD
	19:07	I	EcD
	19:24	III	EcR
	20:43	III	OcD
	22:38	I	OcR
19	0:21	III	OcR
	8:27	II	EcD
	13:45	II	OcR
	16:28	I	ShI
	17:40	I	TrI
	18:45	I	ShE
	19:56	I	TrE
20	13:35	I	EcD
	17:07	I	OcR
21	2:39	II	ShI
	5:05	II	TrI
	5:31	II	ShE
	7:58	II	TrE
	10:57	I	ShI
	12:09	I	TrI
	13:13	I	ShE
	14:25	I	TrE
22	5:52	III	ShI
	8:04	I	EcD
	9:23	III	ShE
	10:46	III	TrI
	11:36	I	OcR
	14:21	III	TrE
	21:44	II	EcD
23	3:04	II	OcR
	5:25	I	ShI
	6:37	I	TrI
	7:41	I	ShE
	8:54	I	TrE
24	2:32	I	EcD
	6:05	I	OcR
	15:56	II	ShI
	18:25	II	TrI
	18:48	II	ShE
	21:18	II	TrE
	23:53	I	ShI
25	1:06	I	TrI
	2:10	I	ShE
	3:23	I	TrE
	19:48	III	EcD
	21:00	I	EcD
	23:15	IV	ShI
	23:22	III	EcR
26	0:33	I	OcR
	0:50	III	OcD
	3:52	IV	ShE
	4:28	III	OcR
	10:49	IV	TrI
	11:01	II	EcD
	15:35	IV	TrE
	16:23	II	OcR
	18:22	I	ShI
	19:35	I	TrI
	20:38	I	ShE
	21:51	I	TrE
27	15:29	I	EcD
	19:02	I	OcR
28	5:14	II	ShI
	7:45	II	TrI
	8:06	II	ShE
	10:37	II	TrE
	12:50	I	ShI
	14:04	I	TrI
	15:06	I	ShE
	16:20	I	TrE
29	9:50	III	ShI
	9:57	I	EcD
	13:21	III	ShE
	13:31	I	OcR
	14:51	III	TrI
	18:26	III	TrE
30	0:18	II	EcD
	5:41	II	OcR
	7:18	I	ShI
	8:32	I	TrI
	9:34	I	ShE
	10:49	I	TrE
31	4:25	I	EcD
	8:00	I	OcR
	18:31	II	ShI
	21:03	II	TrI
	21:23	II	ShE
	23:56	II	TrE

NOVEMBER

1	1:47	I	ShI
	3:01	I	TrI
	4:03	I	ShE
	5:17	I	TrE
	22:54	I	EcD
	23:46	III	EcD
2	2:28	I	OcR
	3:21	III	EcR
	4:53	III	OcD
	8:32	III	OcR
	13:35	II	EcD
	18:59	II	OcR
	20:15	I	ShI
	21:29	I	TrI
	22:31	I	ShE
	23:46	I	TrE
3	6:45	IV	EcD
	11:30	IV	EcR
	17:22	I	EcD
	18:50	IV	OcD
	20:57	I	OcR
	23:43	IV	OcR
4	7:49	II	ShI
	10:22	II	TrI
	10:41	II	ShE
	13:15	II	TrE
	14:43	I	ShI
	15:58	I	TrI
	16:59	I	ShE
	18:14	I	TrE
5	11:51	I	EcD
	13:49	III	ShI
	15:26	I	OcR
	17:20	III	ShE
	18:53	III	TrI
	22:28	III	TrE
6	2:52	II	EcD
	8:16	II	OcR
	9:12	I	ShI
	10:26	I	TrI
	11:28	I	ShE
	12:42	I	TrE
7	6:19	I	EcD
	9:54	I	OcR
	21:07	II	ShI
	23:40	II	TrI
	23:59	II	ShE
8	2:33	II	TrE
	3:40	I	ShI
	4:54	I	TrI
	5:56	I	ShE
	7:11	I	TrE
9	0:47	I	EcD
	3:44	III	EcD
	4:22	I	OcR
	7:19	III	EcR
	8:53	III	OcD
	12:31	III	OcR
	16:09	II	EcD
	21:32	II	OcR
	22:08	I	ShI
	23:23	I	TrI
10	0:24	I	ShE
	1:39	I	TrE
	19:16	I	EcD
	22:51	I	OcR
11	10:25	II	ShI
	12:58	II	TrI
	13:17	II	ShE
	15:51	II	TrE
	16:36	I	ShI
	17:13	IV	ShI
	17:51	I	TrI
	18:52	I	ShE
	20:07	I	TrE
	21:52	IV	ShE
12	5:01	IV	TrI
	9:47	IV	TrE
	13:44	I	EcD
	17:19	I	OcR
	17:46	III	ShI
	22:18	III	ShE
	22:50	III	TrI
13	2:25	III	TrE
	5:25	II	EcD
	10:49	II	OcR
	11:05	I	ShI
	12:19	I	TrI
	13:21	I	ShE
	14:35	I	TrE
14	8:12	I	EcD
	11:47	I	OcR
	23:42	II	ShI
15	2:15	II	TrI
	2:35	II	ShE
	5:08	II	TrE
	5:33	I	ShI
	6:47	I	TrI
	7:49	I	ShE
	9:03	I	TrE

SATELLITES OF JUPITER, UT OF 2002 GEOCENTRIC PHENOMENA (ct'd)

NOVEMBER (ct'd)

```
16   2:41  I   EcD
     6:15  I   OcR
     7:43  III EcD
    11:18  III EcR
    12:49  III OcD
    16:28  III OcR
    18:42  II  EcD
17   0:01  I   ShI
     0:04  II  OcR
     1:15  I   TrI
     2:17  I   ShE
     3:31  I   TrE
    21:09  I   EcD
18   0:44  I   OcR
    13:00  II  ShI
    15:32  II  TrI
    15:53  II  ShE
    18:25  II  TrE
    18:29  I   ShI
    19:43  I   TrI
    20:46  I   ShE
    21:59  I   TrE
19  15:38  I   EcD
    19:12  I   OcR
    21:43  III ShI
20   0:45  IV  EcD
     1:16  III ShE
     2:42  III TrI
     5:31  IV  EcR
     6:18  III TrE
     7:59  II  EcD
    12:38  IV  OcD
    12:58  I   ShI
    13:19  II  OcR
    14:11  I   TrI
    15:14  I   ShE
    16:27  I   TrE
    17:31  IV  OcR
21  10:06  I   EcD
    13:40  I   OcR
22   2:18  II  ShI
     4:48  II  TrI
     5:10  II  ShE
     7:26  I   ShI
     7:41  II  TrE
     8:39  I   TrI
     9:42  I   ShE
    10:55  I   TrE
23   4:34  I   EcD
     8:07  I   OcR
    11:41  III EcD
    15:17  III EcR
    16:40  III OcD
    20:19  III OcR
    21:15  II  EcD
24   1:54  I   ShI
     2:34  II  OcR
     3:06  I   TrI
     4:10  I   ShE
     5:23  I   TrE
    23:03  I   EcD

25   2:35  I   OcR
    15:36  II  ShI
    18:04  II  TrI
    18:29  II  ShE
    20:23  I   ShI
    20:57  II  TrE
    21:34  I   TrI
    22:39  I   ShE
    23:50  I   TrE
26  17:31  I   EcD
    21:03  I   OcR
27   1:41  III ShI
     5:13  III ShE
     6:31  III TrI
    10:06  III TrE
    10:32  II  EcD
    14:51  I   ShI
    15:48  II  OcR
    16:02  I   TrI
    17:07  I   ShE
    18:18  I   TrE
28  11:11  IV  ShI
    12:00  I   EcD
    15:31  I   OcR
    15:52  IV  ShE
    22:21  IV  TrI
29   3:06  IV  TrE
     4:53  II  ShI
     7:18  II  TrI
     7:46  II  ShE
     9:19  I   ShI
    10:12  II  TrE
    10:29  I   TrI
    11:35  I   ShE
    12:45  I   TrE
30   6:28  I   EcD
     9:58  I   OcR
    15:40  III EcD
    19:16  III EcR
    20:27  III OcD
    23:49  II  EcD
```

DECEMBER

```
 1   0:06  III OcR
     3:47  I   ShI
     4:57  I   TrI
     5:01  II  OcR
     6:03  I   ShE
     7:13  I   TrE
 2   0:56  I   EcD
     4:26  I   OcR
    18:11  II  ShI
    20:33  II  TrI
    21:05  II  ShE
    22:16  I   ShI
    23:24  I   TrI
    23:26  II  TrE
 3   0:32  I   ShE
     1:40  I   TrE
    19:25  I   EcD
    22:53  I   OcR

 4   5:38  III ShI
     9:11  III ShE
    10:14  III TrI
    13:05  II  EcD
    13:50  III TrE
    16:44  I   ShI
    17:51  I   TrI
    18:14  II  OcR
    19:00  I   ShE
    20:08  I   TrE
 5  13:53  I   EcD
    17:21  I   OcR
 6   7:29  II  ShI
     9:46  II  TrI
    10:22  II  ShE
    11:12  I   ShI
    12:18  I   TrI
    12:40  II  TrE
    13:28  I   ShE
    14:35  I   TrE
    18:44  IV  EcD
    23:33  IV  EcR
 7   5:29  IV  OcD
     8:22  I   EcD
    10:21  IV  OcR
    11:48  I   OcR
    19:37  III EcD
    23:14  III EcR
 8   0:09  III OcD
     2:22  II  EcD
     3:48  III OcR
     5:40  I   ShI
     6:46  I   TrI
     7:27  II  OcR
     7:57  I   ShE
     9:02  I   TrE
 9   2:50  I   EcD
     6:15  I   OcR
    20:47  II  ShI
    23:00  II  TrI
    23:41  II  ShE
10   0:09  I   ShI
     1:13  I   TrI
     1:54  II  TrE
     2:25  I   ShE
     3:29  I   TrE
    21:19  I   EcD
11   0:43  I   OcR
     9:36  III ShI
    13:10  III ShE
    13:54  III TrI
    15:39  II  EcD
    17:30  III TrE
    18:37  I   ShI
    19:40  I   TrI
    20:38  II  OcR
    20:53  I   ShE
    21:56  I   TrE
12  15:47  I   EcD
    19:10  I   OcR
13  10:05  II  ShI
    12:12  II  TrI
    12:58  II  ShE
    13:05  I   ShI
    14:07  I   TrI
    15:06  II  TrE

13  15:21  I   ShE
    16:23  I   TrE
14  10:15  I   EcD
    13:37  I   OcR
    23:35  III EcD
15   3:12  III EcR
     3:45  III OcD
     4:55  II  EcD
     5:08  IV  ShI
     7:24  III OcR
     7:33  I   ShI
     8:34  I   TrI
     9:49  II  OcR
     9:50  I   ShE
     9:52  IV  ShE
    10:50  I   TrE
    14:40  IV  TrI
    19:26  IV  TrE
16   4:44  I   EcD
     8:04  I   OcR
    23:23  II  ShI
17   1:25  II  TrI
     2:02  I   ShI
     2:17  II  ShE
     3:00  I   TrI
     4:18  I   ShE
     4:19  II  TrE
     5:17  I   TrE
    23:12  I   EcD
18   2:31  I   OcR
    13:34  III ShI
    17:08  III ShE
    17:29  III TrI
    18:12  II  EcD
    20:30  I   ShI
    21:05  III TrE
    21:27  I   TrI
    22:46  I   ShE
    23:00  II  OcR
    23:44  I   TrE
19  17:41  I   EcD
    20:58  I   OcR
20  12:40  II  ShI
    14:36  II  TrI
    14:58  I   ShI
    15:34  II  ShE
    15:54  I   TrI
    17:15  I   ShE
    17:30  I   TrE
    18:10  I   TrE
21  12:09  I   EcD
    15:24  I   OcR
22   3:33  III EcD
     7:10  III EcR
     7:17  III OcD
     7:29  II  EcD
     9:26  I   ShI
    10:21  I   TrI
    10:57  III OcR
    11:43  I   ShE
    12:10  II  OcR
    12:37  I   TrE

23   6:38  I   EcD
     9:51  I   OcR
    12:44  IV  EcD
    17:35  IV  EcR
    21:18  IV  OcD
24   1:59  II  ShI
     2:10  IV  OcR
     3:48  II  TrI
     3:55  I   ShI
     4:47  I   TrI
     4:53  II  ShE
     6:11  I   ShE
     6:42  II  TrE
     7:04  I   TrE
25   1:06  I   EcD
     4:18  I   OcR
    17:32  III ShI
    20:45  II  EcD
    20:59  III TrI
    21:07  III ShE
    22:23  I   ShI
    23:14  I   TrI
26   0:36  III TrE
     0:40  I   ShE
     1:19  II  OcR
     1:30  I   TrE
    19:35  I   EcD
    22:44  I   OcR
27  15:17  II  ShI
    16:51  I   ShI
    16:58  II  TrI
    17:40  I   TrI
    18:11  II  ShE
    19:08  I   ShE
    19:52  II  TrE
    19:57  I   TrE
28  14:03  I   EcD
    17:11  I   OcR
29   7:31  III EcD
    10:02  II  EcD
    11:20  I   ShI
    12:06  I   TrI
    13:36  I   ShE
    14:23  I   TrE
    14:24  III OcR
    14:28  II  OcR
30   8:32  I   EcD
    11:37  I   OcR
31   4:35  II  ShI
     5:48  I   ShI
     6:08  II  TrI
     6:33  I   TrI
     7:29  II  ShE
     8:05  I   ShE
     8:50  I   TrE
     9:02  II  TrE
    23:06  IV  ShI
32   3:00  I   EcD
     3:51  IV  ShE
     6:02  IV  TrI
     6:04  I   OcR
    10:48  IV  TrE
    21:30  III ShI
    23:19  II  EcD
```

CONFIGURATIONS OF SATURN'S BRIGHTEST SATELLITES
By Larry D. Bogan

The diagrams on the next three pages give the relative locations of the five brightest satellites of Saturn for January through April and August through December 2002. The names and magnitudes of these satellites, in order of increasing distance from Saturn, are Enceladus 11.8, Tethys 10.3, Dione 10.4, Rhea 9.7, and Titan 8.4.

The curves in the diagrams show the elongations of the satellites from Saturn for day 0.0 UT to day 32.0 UT for each month. The dashed curves represent Enceladus and Dione, the first and third out from Saturn. The narrow, central, vertical band represents the disk of Saturn, and the wider band the outer edge of Saturn's "A" ring.

At the top of each monthly diagram is a scale drawing of Saturn, its rings, and the orbits of four of the five brightest satellites as seen through an inverting telescope (in the Northern Hemisphere). South is up. Because of the small size of the scale drawing, no orbit is shown for the innermost satellite, Enceladus. Due to its faintness and proximity to the bright rings, Enceladus is best seen when near a maximum elongation, but even then good seeing, good optics, and an aperture of at least 250 mm are required.

During 2002, we see Saturn and its satellites from south of the ring plane. The tilt for 2002 only varies between 25.8° and 26.8° during the year. The direction of motion of the satellites is clockwise as viewed with a telescope having an even number (0, 2, 4,...) of reflections in its optics.

A particular configuration of the satellites may be determined by drawing a horizontal line across the monthly curves at the time (UT) of interest. The intersection of this line with the curves gives the relative elongations of the satellites. Project these elongations onto the drawing of the orbits at the top of the diagram. The east side of the "A" ring vertical band has been extended up to the drawing to facilitate transfer of each elongation. A millimetre scale, pair of dividers, or a strip of paper on which to mark enables one to do this quickly and accurately.

The direction of the orbital motion of a satellite determines on which side of its orbit (north or south) a satellite is located. A satellite *moving right* (east) will be *above* (south of) Saturn in the scale drawing, and a satellite *moving left* (west) will be *below* (north of) Saturn in the drawing. The March diagram shows an example configuration for March 2 at 9:00 p.m. EST (March 3 at 2h UT).

Greatest Elongations and Conjunctions for Iapetus

Iapetus has a magnitude comparable to the five plotted satellites, but varies from magnitude 10.1 (western elongation) to 11.9 (eastern elongation). Its orbit is about 2.9 times the size of Titan's and is tilted 15° to Saturn's ring plane; its period is 79 days. Iapetus is easiest to find near conjunctions when it is just north or south of Saturn. The table below lists times (UT) of greatest elongations and conjunctions during 2002.

Eastern Elong.			Inferior Conj.			Western Elong.			Superior Conj.		
—			—			Jan.	11	17.2h	Jan.	30	10.9h
Feb.	19	12.6h	Mar.	12	13.3h	Apr.	1	10.5h	Apr.	20	17.6h
May	11	10.5h	June	1	20.5h	June	21	19.9h	July	11	7.2h
Aug.	1	3.8h	Aug.	22	07.6h	Sep.	10	21.1h	Sep.	30	0.8h
Oct.	20	10.7h	Nov.	9	22.9h	Nov.	28	23.1h	Dec.	17	15.1h

Note: Two freeware computer programs that display the configurations of Saturn's satellites are *SATSAT2* and *Meridian*. *SATSAT2*, by Dan Bruton, is a DOS program and is available at www.physics.sfasu.edu/astro/dansoftware.html. *Meridian,* by Claude Duplessis, is a Windows program and is available at page.infinit.net/merid/index.html.

CONFIGURATIONS OF SATURN'S SATELLITES
2002 JANUARY–MARCH

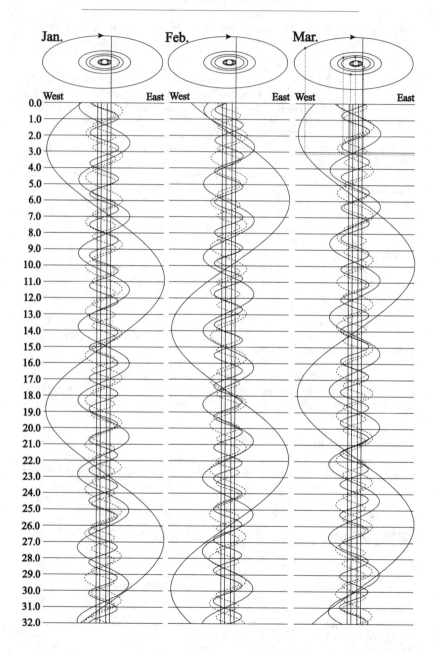

CONFIGURATIONS OF SATURN'S SATELLITES
2002 APRIL, AUGUST, SEPTEMBER

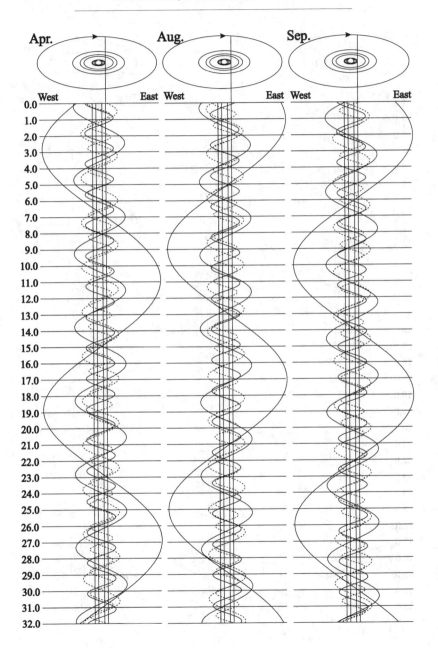

CONFIGURATIONS OF SATURN'S SATELLITES
2002 OCTOBER–DECEMBER

ASTEROIDS

THE BRIGHTEST ASTEROIDS

On the next two pages are ephemerides for asteroids (identified by number and name) that will be brighter than or equal to visual magnitude 10.0 and more than 90° from the Sun during 2002. The positions are based on TT, although the equivalent but older designation "ET" appears on the tables. TT differs by about one minute from UT (see TIME AND TIME SCALES on pp. 34–38). "Mag" is visual magnitude. These data were derived from current osculating elements.

Using the ephemerides provided and an appropriate star atlas, charts displaying the motion of each asteroid can be produced. For example, the chart below, provided by David Lane, shows the path of Ceres as it moves through its retrograde loop in Cetus from June to December. Like most asteroids, Ceres has a large orbital inclination (10.6°) and so it wanders away from the zodiacal constellations, spending this year in Aquarius's southern neighbour.

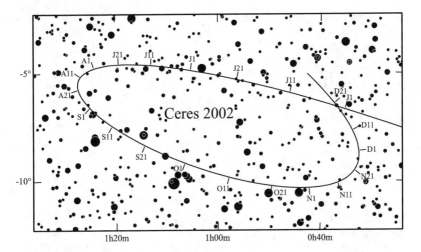

The coordinates in the chart are for epoch 2000.0 and the chart magnitude limit is 9.0. Tick marks along Ceres' path locate its position at ten-day intervals, beginning with Jun. 1 (J1) and ending with Dec. 21. The brightest star in the chart is η Cet.

Ceres brightens to visual magnitude 7.6 when at opposition on Oct. 4. Although Vesta is brighter, starting the year at magnitude 7.1, it does not reach opposition in 2002 and circumstances for Vesta are poor this year. Ceres, with a diameter of 1003 km and opposition distance of 1.96 AU, will have an angular diameter of 0.63″, and should be resolvable with large telescopes under steady skies.

Ceres was the first asteroid discovered (on the first day of the 19th century), hence its designation (1) Ceres. Pallas, Juno, and Vesta were discovered in the following few years. For most of the century Vesta was thought to be larger than Ceres because of its brightness; however Ceres is in fact the largest asteroid, almost twice the diameter of third-place Vesta.

For a listing of the orbital elements of selected asteroids see p. 21.

EPHEMERIDES FOR THE BRIGHTEST ASTEROIDS IN 2002
BY BRIAN G. MARSDEN

Date 0h ET	RA (2000) h m	Dec ° '	Mag.	Date 0h ET	RA (2000) h m	Dec ° '	Mag.
(1) Ceres				**(6) Hebe**			
Jul. 15	1 15.6	−4 40	8.9	May 6	19 04.5	−6 34	10.0
25	1 21.3	−4 42	8.7	16	19 05.7	−6 03	9.8
Aug. 4	1 25.2	−4 56	8.6	26	19 04.2	−5 43	9.6
14	1 27.1	−5 23	8.4	Jun. 5	18 59.9	−5 36	9.3
24	1 26.8	−6 01	8.3	15	18 53.2	−5 48	9.1
Sep. . 3	1 24.2	−6 49	8.1	25	18 44.4	−6 20	8.9
13	1 19.4	−7 42	7.9	Jul. 5	18 34.6	−7 12	8.8
23	1 12.6	−8 36	7.7	15	18 24.9	−8 23	8.9
Oct. 3	1 04.6	−9 24	7.6	25	18 16.5	−9 46	9.0
13	0 56.1	−10 00	7.6	Aug. 4	18 10.3	−11 18	9.2
23	0 48.0	−10 20	7.8	14	18 07.0	−12 52	9.3
Nov. 2	0 41.0	−10 22	8.0	24	18 06.9	−14 25	9.5
12	0 35.9	−10 04	8.2	Sep. . 3	18 10.1	−15 52	9.6
22	0 33.0	−9 28	8.3	13	18 16.3	−17 12	9.8
Dec. 2	0 32.4	−8 38	8.5	23	18 25.2	−18 23	9.9
12	0 34.0	−7 34	8.6				
22	0 37.7	−6 20	8.8	**(7) Iris**			
				Jun. 5	22 16.7	−5 19	9.9
(2) Pallas				15	22 24.4	−3 58	9.7
Jun. 15	21 24.0	+15 47	10.0	25	22 30.2	−2 44	9.5
25	21 21.9	+16 12	9.9	Jul. 5	22 33.8	−1 39	9.2
Jul. 5	21 18.0	+16 18	9.8	15	22 34.7	−0 47	9.0
15	21 12.4	+16 04	9.6	25	22 32.9	−0 11	8.7
25	21 05.6	+15 25	9.5	Aug. 4	22 28.2	+0 07	8.4
Aug. 4	20 58.0	+14 22	9.4	14	22 21.0	+0 03	8.1
14	20 50.2	+12 56	9.4	24	22 12.0	−0 21	7.8
24	20 43.0	+11 11	9.4	Sep. . 3	22 02.5	−1 01	7.8
Sep. . 3	20 37.0	+9 13	9.5	13	21 53.9	−1 51	8.0
13	20 32.6	+7 10	9.6	23	21 47.6	−2 43	8.2
23	20 30.2	+5 07	9.7	Oct. 3	21 44.3	−3 28	8.4
Oct. 3	20 29.8	+3 10	9.9	13	21 44.7	−4 02	8.6
13	20 31.4	+1 24	10.0	23	21 48.6	−4 20	8.7
				Nov. 2	21 55.7	−4 21	8.9
(3) Juno				12	22 05.7	−4 05	9.1
Jan. 6	9 49.3	+0 02	8.8	22	22 18.2	−3 31	9.2
16	9 44.7	+0 43	8.6				
26	9 37.8	+1 49	8.5	**(8) Flora**			
Feb. 5	9 29.5	+3 16	8.4	Jan. 16	11 06.3	+11 09	9.9
15	9 21.0	+4 58	8.4	26	11 03.1	+12 12	9.7
25	9 13.4	+6 43	8.6	Feb. 5	10 56.9	+13 30	9.5
Mar. 7	9 07.8	+8 22	8.9	15	10 48.2	+14 57	9.3
17	9 04.6	+9 49	9.1	25	10 38.1	+16 22	9.2
27	9 04.2	+11 00	9.4	Mar. 7	10 28.0	+17 34	9.4
Apr. 6	9 06.4	+11 54	9.6	17	10 19.2	+18 26	9.7
16	9 11.0	+12 30	9.8	27	10 12.8	+18 56	10.0
26	9 17.6	+12 50	10.0				
				(9) Metis			
(4) Vesta				Jan. 6	7 49.1	+27 57	8.7
Jan. 6	3 47.8	+14 49	7.2	16	7 38.0	+28 49	8.6
16	3 46.1	+15 22	7.4	26	7 27.4	+29 27	8.9
26	3 47.4	+16 01	7.6	Feb. 5	7 19.0	+29 46	9.2
Feb. 5	3 51.3	+16 47	7.8	15	7 13.9	+29 50	9.5
15	3 57.7	+17 36	7.9	25	7 12.5	+29 41	9.7
				Mar. 7	7 14.9	+29 23	10.0

EPHEMERIDES FOR THE BRIGHTEST ASTEROIDS IN 2002 (cont.)

Date 0h ET	RA (2000) h m	Dec ° ′	Mag.	Date 0h ET	RA (2000) h m	Dec ° ′	Mag.
(15) Eunomia				**(27) Euterpe**			
Jun. 15	23 10.1	+2 09	9.8	Feb. 15	11 49.5	+3 55	9.9
25	23 18.0	+4 06	9.6	25	11 42.2	+4 51	9.7
Jul. 5	23 24.0	+5 58	9.4	Mar. 7	11 33.2	+5 55	9.4
15	23 28.0	+7 45	9.2	17	11 23.6	+6 58	9.5
25	23 29.5	+9 22	9.0	27	11 14.9	+7 50	9.9
Aug. 4	23 28.4	+10 47	8.8				
14	23 24.4	+11 56	8.6	**(29) Amphitrite**			
24	23 18.0	+12 43	8.3	Jun. 25	20 36.5	−27 14	9.8
Sep. .3	23 09.5	+13 05	8.1	Jul. 5	20 29.4	−27 45	9.6
13	23 00.1	+13 02	8.0	15	20 20.2	−28 14	9.4
23	22 51.0	+12 36	8.1	25	20 09.9	−28 35	9.3
Oct. 3	22 43.6	+11 55	8.2	Aug. 4	19 59.7	−28 44	9.5
13	22 38.8	+11 07	8.4	14	19 50.8	−28 40	9.7
23	22 37.2	+10 22	8.6	24	19 44.1	−28 25	9.9
Nov. 2	22 38.9	+9 46	8.8				
12	22 43.7	+9 23	8.9				
22	22 51.3	+9 15	9.1	**(44) Nysa**			
Dec. 2	23 01.2	+9 24	9.3	Oct. 23	4 01.3	+14 20	9.9
12	23 13.3	+9 48	9.4	Nov. 2	3 54.9	+13 46	9.7
				12	3 46.0	+13 12	9.4
(18) Melpomene				22	3 36.0	+12 40	9.4
Jul. 5	23 59.8	+0 24	9.9	Dec. 2	3 26.2	+12 17	9.5
15	0 13.1	+0 46	9.6	12	3 18.2	+12 07	9.7
25	0 24.9	+0 45	9.4	22	3 12.9	+12 12	9.9
Aug. 4	0 34.6	+0 19	9.1				
14	0 41.8	−0 37	8.9				
24	0 46.1	−2 04	8.6	**(349) Dembowska**			
Sep. .3	0 47.2	−4 00	8.3	Nov. 2	4 53.3	+28 43	10.0
13	0 45.2	−6 17	8.0	12	4 46.3	+29 10	9.9
23	0 40.7	−8 41	7.8	22	4 37.1	+29 27	9.7
Oct. 3	0 34.7	−10 54	7.8	Dec. 2	4 26.9	+29 34	9.6
13	0 28.7	−12 38	8.0	12	4 16.9	+29 30	9.7
23	0 24.4	−13 42	8.3	22	4 08.2	+29 19	9.9
Nov. 2	0 22.7	−14 02	8.6				
12	0 24.2	−13 41	8.8				
22	0 28.8	−12 46	9.1	**(511) Davida**			
Dec. 2	0 36.4	−11 24	9.3	Dec. 12	7 04.2	+17 22	10.0
12	0 46.4	−9 41	9.5	22	6 56.8	+18 31	9.8
22	0 58.6	−7 44	9.7				
(20) Massalia				**(654) Zelinda**			
Oct. 13	5 28.3	+22 43	10.0	Jan. 6	7 30.0	+14 45	9.8
23	5 32.8	+22 41	9.8	16	7 16.8	+12 05	9.8
Nov. 2	5 33.9	+22 35	9.5				
12	5 31.2	+22 28	9.3				
22	5 25.0	+22 17	9.0				
Dec. 2	5 16.0	+22 04	8.7				
12	5 05.4	+21 48	8.5				
22	4 55.2	+21 31	8.8				
(25) Phocaea							
Jun. 15	18 12.6	+13 18	10.0				
25	18 04.7	+15 31	10.0				
Jul. 5	17 56.7	+16 50	10.0				

PLANETARY APPULSES AND OCCULTATIONS
By David W. Dunham and James Stamm

Planets, satellites, asteroids, and comets, as they move across the sky, will on occasion pass near an observer's line of sight to a distant star. Such close passes are called appulses. More rarely, the moving object's trajectory will carry it directly between the observer and the star, thereby producing an occultation. Astronomers have learned much about various solar system bodies by carefully monitoring the changing apparent brightness of stars during the immersion and emersion phases of occultations. If the occulting body does not have an atmosphere, the occultation is virtually instantaneous; an atmosphere causes the star's disappearance and reappearance to occur gradually. The rate of disappearance/reappearance is related to the temperature and composition of the atmosphere. If a planet has rings or other debris in its environs, the extent and degree of transparency of this material can be precisely mapped. The rings of Uranus, the ring arcs of Neptune, and the atmosphere of Pluto were all discovered by occultation observations. In addition, if an occultation can be observed at several appropriately distributed sites, it is often possible to determine the size and shape of the occulting body more accurately than by other Earth-based techniques.

Amateur astronomers can sometimes make important contributions to occultation observing campaigns. This is particularly true for asteroid occultations, where the strip across Earth from which an event is observable is often very narrow and uncertain in location (due to uncertainties in both the star's position and the ephemeris of the asteroid). By recording the times of the star's disappearance and reappearance as seen from several sites (i.e. by noting the edges of the asteroid's shadow as it sweeps across Earth), the asteroid's profile can be directly determined. Often timings of adequate accuracy can be made by visual observers using modest telescopes.

When observing an occultation, it is important that an observer know his or her location to within a fraction of a kilometre. Geographic longitude, latitude, and altitude of an observing site can be determined from a high-quality topographic map. If observations are to be of maximum value, the times of immersion and emersion must be determined as accurately as possible—certainly to better than 0.5 s, and better than 0.2 s for the shortest events (those less than about 10 s in duration). **Photoelectric equipment** with high-speed digital recording systems is well suited for this work. Attaching a low-light-level **video camera,** especially one with an image intensifier, to a telescope is another good method for accurately timing these events. **Visual observers** equipped with tape recorders and shortwave time signal receivers are also valuable contributors. Even simple measurements of the duration of an occultation made with an ordinary stopwatch can be of value. **CCD observers** should be aware that most of these systems are incapable of timing accuracies better than about 2 s; hence visual observation may be better. A trick that some CCD observers have used is to turn off the telescope clock drive shortly before the predicted time and let the images trail. The occultation will appear as a break in the trail that can be measured to a few tenths of a second, depending on seeing conditions and whether the moment the drive is turned off is accurately timed.

Occultation observations are coordinated in North America by the International Occultation Timing Association (IOTA). Whether you are a member of IOTA or not, this organization wants to inform you and others in your area who can locate 9th- and 10th-magnitude stars of last-minute prediction updates. Please send the approximate (or accurate) longitude and latitude (or location from the nearest town if in the United States) of convenient observing sites, telescope size(s), and whether mobile, by email to dunham@erols.com. IOTA publishes a newsletter and maintains a "hotline" for disseminating last-minute prediction updates: within a few days of each event, improved predictions may be obtained from recorded telephone messages at (301) 474-4945 (Greenbelt, MD) or from the asteroidal occultation section of IOTA's website, www.lunar-occultations.com/iota. Individuals interested in joining IOTA should refer to p. 150 in the section OCCULTATIONS BY THE MOON in this Handbook.

Other sources of occultation information include the *Solar System Photometry Handbook* (published by Willmann-Bell, Inc., 1983), *Sky & Telescope* (particularly each year's February issue), and occasional papers in the *Astronomical Journal, Icarus,* and other scientific journals.

Observations of this type of occultation, *including* negative observations, should be sent to Jan Manek, Stefanik Observatory, Petrin 205, 118 46 Praha (Prague) 1, Czech Republic (email: jmanek@mbox.vol.cz) for publication by IOTA. When reporting timings, include your geographic longitude, latitude, and altitude (to the nearest second of arc and 30 m, respectively), and telescope size; describe your timing method and give an estimate of the observer's reaction time (if applicable) and the accuracy of the timing and state whether the reaction time correction has been applied.

The following two-page table of predictions of asteroidal and planetary occultations visible from North America for 2002 is based on predictions by Edwin Goffin in Belgium.

The successive columns in the table list: (1) the date and time of the event; (2) the name of the occulting body; (3) the apparent magnitude of the asteroid or planet; (4) the catalogue number of the occulted star; (5) the apparent visual magnitude of the star; (6) the right ascension and (7) declination of the star; (8) the expected magnitude change from the combined brightness; (9) the predicted maximum duration of the occultation in seconds; and (10) the approximate region from which the occultation is predicted to be visible. Due to uncertainties in the catalogue positions of the stars and the ephemerides of the asteroids from which these predictions are derived, the exact region of visibility of an occultation cannot be derived until CCD observations link the star and asteroid to the new HIPPARCOS reference frame, usually about a week prior to the event.

For North American observers, finder charts and further details on these and other occultations can be found in the *2002 Planetary Occultation Supplement to Occultation Newsletter* available from IOTA. (See p. 150 in this Handbook for information on IOTA and on The Royal Astronomical Society of New Zealand. The latter organization provides information on occultations visible from the southwestern Pacific region.)

Notes regarding some of the events in the table:

(1) Oct. 16: The star is ζ Arietis = ZC 472 = FK6 1089 = HR 972. A gradual occultation of the star was reported by Henk Bril in the Netherlands on 1992 March 9, indicating possible duplicity.

(2) Nov. 3: The star is ZC 593 = FK6 2288 = HR 1238. It is a spectroscopic binary and a member of the Hyades.

(3) Nov. 10: The star is π Arietis = ZC 416 = HIP 13165 = HR 836, a short-period spectroscopic binary with a third star, mag. 8.4, 3.2″ away in position angle 120°.

(4) Dec. 9, (77) Frigga: The star, HIP 23814, is a spectroscopic binary.

IOTA SELECTED LIST OF NORTH AMERICAN OCCULTATIONS BY SOLAR SYSTEM OBJECTS FOR THE YEAR 2002

Date	UT	Occulting Body	(Mag.)	Star	(Mag.)	RA (2000) h m s	Dec ° ' "	ΔMag.	Dur. s	Nominal Path
Jan. 12	2:46	74 Galatea	13.2	HIP 1512	10.4	0 18 51.22	+1 03 46.6	2.9	4.2	Southern California to New York City
14	0:13	516 Amherstia	12.3	SAO 60107	7.6	7 28 44.09	+34 26 12.9	4.7	5.3	Northern Florida
16	11:43	754 Malabar	14.2	SAO 138364	8.2	11 42 48.70	-9 20 30.4	6.0	24.9	Honduras to eastern Cuba
18	6:28	134 Sophrosyne	11.7	TYC 2480-01151-1	9.9	7 57 00.51	+36 26 24.6	2.0	10.2	Northern Florida to Baja California Sur
24	1:58	667 Denise	12.9	TYC 4806-01589-1	10.3	6 31 00.70	-5 08 16.9	2.7	6.3	South Carolina to N British Columbia
27	14:22	8 Flora	9.7	PPM 127926	9.5	11 02 20.11	+12 23 14.0	0.9	18.8	Western Utah to Northwest Territories
30	1:53	88 Thisbe	12.0	TYC 1327-01656-1	11.2	6 16 52.27	+22 25 39.0	1.3	25.3	Southern Florida to central Mexico
31	1:32	361 Bononia	13.0	TYC 2495-00265-1	11.5	9 00 12.12	+34 45 36.8	1.7	11.9	E Newfoundland to Baja California Sur
Feb. 21	6:30	535 Montague	13.3	PPM 98443	10.9	8 11 24.15	+27 49 07.1	2.5	11.2	Georgia to Oregon
21	11:54	28 Bellona	9.9	TAC +12° 02875	10.5	10 23 43.81	+12 33 43.4	0.5	12.1	West of Baja California Sur to Alaska
28	10:10	804 Hispania	13.2	SAO 207513	10.1	16 17 19.74	-35 56 56.1	3.2	7.4	Colorado through Central America
Mar. 4	4:44	194 Prokne	12.4	TYC 0319-00151-1	12.0	14 07 21.79	+2 50 31.0	1.0	17.3	Eastern West Indies to Minnesota
5	7:23	784 Pickeringia	13.4	TYC 6180-00053-1	11.0	15 01 47.79	-20 58 30.0	2.5	9.9	Montana to western West Indies
10	9:07	9 Metis	10.0	SAO 79232	9.2	7 16 31.89	+29 14 27.9	1.3	31.8	Eastern Alaska to Baja California Sur
18	3:01	194 Prokne	12.1	PPM 160308	10.1	14 04 04.67	+5 13 13.8	2.2	14.1	Georgia to eastern Texas
19	6:17	88 Thisbe	12.8	TYC 1327-01000-1	11.3	6 17 45.94	+21 51 45.1	1.8	20.2	Southern Alaska to Georgia
27	2:24	654 Zelinda	11.6	TYC 0168-02620-1	10.0	7 17 14.62	+3 10 50.7	1.9	10.9	Southern Idaho to North Carolina
Apr. 16	2:51	1309 Hyperborea	15.4	SAO 117121	7.3	8 47 15.25	+7 36 33.6	8.2	5.5	Idaho to Newfoundland
20	7:50	139 Juewa	10.8	PPM 731421	10.3	13 54 10.47	-21 53 06.1	1.0	16.2	Eastern Quebec to northern California
20	8:13	87 Sylvia	12.3	TYC 0310-00106-1	11.1	13 32 28.99	+2 41 04.0	1.5	18.5	Southern Central America to Hawaii
May 5	5:17	28 Bellona	11.7	TYC 1419-00791-1	10.3	10 14 04.72	+16 50 36.6	1.6	11.6	Southeastern Yukon to S New Jersey
6	5:01	3540 Protesilaos	16.0	TAC +03° 06200	9.6	12 33 44.95	+3 17 24.8	6.4	4.2	North Carolina to Baja California Norte
10	7:45	638 Moira	12.6	TYC 5614-00026-1	11.2	15 54 10.22	-9 44 49.6	1.7	8.4	Virginia to central California
25	3:43	359 Georgia	12.7	SAO 183428	8.8	15 23 35.89	-27 15 38.2	3.9	4.0	Southern West Indies to N California
25	9:20	596 Scheila	12.0	SAO 184638	9.9	16 47 23.47	-21 46 35.6	2.2	11.2	W New York to Baja California Sur
28	5:25	147 Protogeneia	12.8	SAO 159377	10.2	15 36 36.09	-19 49 02.7	2.7	11.0	West Indies to northern California
Jun. 19	9:59	466 Tisiphone	13.4	SAO 188204	8.3	19 30 12.80	-25 26 14.8	5.2	9.2	Southern Florida to Baja California Sur

IOTA SELECTED LIST OF NORTH AMERICAN OCCULTATIONS BY SOLAR SYSTEM OBJECTS FOR THE YEAR 2002 (continued)

Date	UT	Occulting Body	(Mag.)	Star	RA (2000) h m s	Dec ° ' "	ΔMag.	Dur. s	Nominal Path
Jul. 9	6:51	145 Adeona	12.4	TYC 7408-00274-1	11.8	18 47 28.79	−31 07 10.4	1.1	11.3	Northern Ontario to north of Hawaii
13	6:58	268 Adorea	12.8	TYC 6336-01340-1	11.5	20 16 41.16	−19 34 00.0	1.6	11.3	S Nunavut to SW British Columbia
19	1:44	754 Malabar	15.1	SAO 119170	8.0	12 01 27.66	+63 0 21.9	7.0	3.0	Southern Mexico to Nicaragua
Sep. 5	1:48	759 Vinifera	12.9	TYC 0558-00652-1	10.6	22 03 01.52	+1 48 23.4	2.4	5.2	New York City to eastern Montana
18	8:51	51 Nemausa	12.3	TYC 0728-01505-1	11.4	5 56 50.96	+13 33 19.0	1.3	7.7	Baja California Sur to central Florida
18	9:50	201 Penelope	11.3	SAO 109751	9.6	1 14 40.28	+2 17 58.2	1.9	9.8	Eastern West Indies to Nicaragua
28	4:45	302 Clarissa	13.5	PPM 144222	9.4	1 03 51.83	+7 14 49.0	4.2	4.8	S New Jersey to Baja California Norte
Oct. 8	8:57	1542 Schalen	15.8	SAO 78915	7.7	6 57 46.01	+20 27 59.1	8.1	3.4	N Queen Charlotte Islands to N Quebec
15	5:23	161 Athor	12.8	SAO 76241	9.3	3 49 42.42	+26 37 37.1	3.6	6.6	Georgia to Baja California Norte
16	4:25	3171 Wangshouguan	15.0	SAO 75810	4.9	3 14 54.09	+21 02 39.8	10.2	5.3	Southern Nova Scotia to N California
27	8:34	738 Alagasta	15.6	SAO 97305	9.1	7 51 06.83	+18 40 11.9	6.5	5.2	Southern California to Virginia
Nov. 3	1:43	431 Nephele	13.2	SAO 93721	5.9	4 00 48.79	+18 11 38.3	7.3	8.7	Northern Florida
10	6:35	828 Lindemannia	14.8	SAO 93127	5.2	2 49 17.56	+17 27 51.5	9.5	4.1	Central Florida to central Mexico
14	7:46	350 Ornamenta	12.3	PPM 148516	9.9	5 08 52.29	+7 10 12.0	2.5	11.3	West Indies to central California
15	1:47	279 Thule	15.6	SAO 164844	7.5	22 04 27.88	−14 26 48.9	8.1	11.9	Southeastern Yukon to eastern Yukon
16	5:56	Jupiter	−2.2	SAO 98512	9.1	9 20 39.61	+16 09 06.1	0.0	16 K	Eastern North America
Dec. 7	7:12	671 Carnegia	15.2	SAO 80909	6.4	9 33 59.13	+23 27 13.9	8.8	10.1	Guatemala to central West Indies
7	3:11	29 Amphitrite	11.1	SAO 164073	9.3	22 01 58.14	−19 14 43.7	2.0	6.5	Northern California to Montana
9	6:09	120 Lachesis	12.6	TYC 2439-00673-1	11.9	6 40 59.96	+32 18 25.3	1.2	15.0	Central Florida to Baja California Sur
9	6:50	77 Frigga	11.2	SAO 76965	7.8	5 07 05.15	+26 59 45.3	3.5	7.5	West Indies to central Mexico
18	0:53	424 Gratia	12.9	TYC 1291-01293-1	11.5	5 17 06.46	+19 00 40.0	1.7	8.4	Nova Scotia to southern Nevada
20	23:06	176 Iduna	12.4	HIP 16456	10.6	3 32 00.48	−3 42 26.8	2.0	22.3	Southern Nova Scotia to Iowa
24	10:00	334 Chicago	13.6	SAO 97327	8.5	7 52 45.59	+18 49 37.4	5.1	12.9	Southern New Jersey to SW Alaska
28	7:34	1691 Oort	15.0	SAO 76696	9.2	4 40 09.62	+20 32 53.7	5.8	5.0	Delaware to Oregon
30	6:58	356 Liguria	12.2	TYC 1428-00488-1	11.3	10 48 40.50	+15 17 51.2	1.3	65.2	Southern California to North Carolina

METEORS, COMETS, AND DUST

METEORS

By Robert L. Hawkes

The term "meteor" applies to the streak of light (and related phenomena such as ionization) produced when an interplanetary particle (a *meteoroid*) enters Earth's upper atmosphere and the meteoroid material ablates (evaporates). Heights of ablation for typical meteors are 65 to 135 km above Earth's surface (higher-speed meteors ablate at greater heights). Evaporated meteoroid atoms undergo high-speed collisions with atmospheric constituents, and it is the decay of these excited states that produces the meteor luminosity. Most meteoroids are very small—a bright visual meteor is typically produced by a grain smaller than a pea. Very bright meteors are termed "fireballs" (see the section FIREBALLS on p. 208). If a solid object reaches the ground, it is termed a "meteorite."

The meteoroid complex can be conveniently divided into two parts: a *stream* component, made up of particles in highly correlated orbits, and a more or less random *sporadic* component. About 5 to 10 sporadic meteors per hour are visible (by a single observer with dark-adapted eyes) from a dark-sky location on any given night. When Earth's orbit intersects a meteor stream, an enhancement of the meteor rate—a meteor *shower*—is observed. Perspective causes the parallel paths of shower meteors to appear to radiate from a point when plotted on a star map. The constellation in which this point of divergence, or *radiant*, seems to lie is used in naming the shower. When two or more showers have radiants in the same constellation, a nearby bright star is used in the designation (e.g. the η-Aquarids). The radiant of the Quadrantid shower, named after the obsolete constellation Quadrans Muralis, is in Boötes.

The sporadic meteor component is derived from the stream component by dispersion due to collisions with smaller meteoroids, radiative effects, and differential gravitational perturbations. The division between shower and sporadic meteors is not precise, and there continues to be debate regarding the validity of some minor meteor showers. A detailed list of showers, including the minor ones, is available in the annual meteor shower calendar published by the International Meteor Organization (IMO) (see **www.amsmeteors.org/imo-mirror**).

The activity of a meteor shower is usually specified by the *zenithal hourly rate* (ZHR). The ZHR is the number of meteors a single perfect observer would see per hour from a shower with a radiant directly overhead in a dark-sky location under exceptional conditions, where +6.5 magnitude stars are visible. Even from dark sky locations an observer will observe fainter meteors effectively over a much smaller field of view. Thus the ZHR figures are *not* expected visual meteor rates, which will always be significantly less than the ZHR. They do, however, provide a widely accepted standardized method to report meteor rates.

Several research groups have produced independent models of the Leonid stream that predict strong activity again in 2002 (for the last time in the current series of Leonid outbursts). In 2002, Earth will pass close to the dust ejected from P/Comet Tempel-Tuttle on three different perihelion passages, with the two most significant peaks shown in the table. The times of maxima are believed to be well determined, but the strengths at maximum are much less certain. This Handbook goes to press prior to the 2001 Leonid shower, and it is expected that the predictions will be refined based on the 2001 results, so other references should be consulted. Extensive information on the Leonid shower is available at **leonid.arc.nasa.gov**.

In a number of cases orbital similarity permits a link between a meteor shower and a parent object. For example, the η-Aquarids and Orionids are derived from P/Comet Halley, the Leonids from P/Comet Tempel-Tuttle, the Perseids from P/Comet Swift-Tuttle, the Taurid complex from P/Comet Encke, and the Geminids from Asteroid Phaethon.

Dedicated amateur meteor astronomers contribute the majority of visual observations. For visual observations it is critical to choose a dark sky location free from obstructions and to allow at least 20 min for dark adaptation. In general, one should not observe near the horizon (at least 40° elevation) and should look roughly 40° away from the radiant of the shower. Carefully estimate your limiting magnitude to the nearest tenth of a magnitude (see the LIMITING MAGNITUDES section on pp. 56–57), and record it, the UT of the observing session, and observing direction (centre of field of view). The simplest observation method involves making an instantaneous decision regarding whether each individual meteor belongs to a shower (from the radiant and apparent speed). The shower association, brightness, and time for each meteor can be recorded orally on a tape recorder for uninterrupted observing periods. Visual observations of this type (after application of correction factors) are valuable for determining rate profiles and population indices of showers. Extensive information on observing meteors by visual and other methods is available from the IMO, the North American Meteor Network (www.namnmeteors.org), and the American Meteor Society (www.amsmeteors.org). These organizations also collect and analyze visual observations from amateurs.

Telescopic observations of meteors (usually employing binoculars) allow the plotting of trails with more precision and emphasize those showers rich in faint meteors (although generally at faint magnitudes the meteor population is dominated by sporadic meteors). Photographic observations can be made with normal or wide-angle lenses, typically using exposures of 5 to 30 min. A rotating shutter permits determination of apparent angular velocity. Increasingly amateurs are using video equipment for meteor observations. A standard home camcorder is limited to about magnitude +2 and will lead to very low rates (a meteor every several hours) except during a strong meteor shower. Image intensifiers (now available as reasonably priced second-hand units) coupled to video cameras (one can simply use the macro lens of the camcorder to image the output phosphor of the image intensifier) can extend the sensitivity to magnitude +9, with sporadic meteor rates of 15/hour. Intermediate sensitivity can be achieved using specialized unintensified, low light level monochrome CCD cameras.

Any of these techniques can be extended to simultaneous observations from two stations, and triangulation will yield the precise trajectory and orbital information. Baselines of 20 to 150 km are appropriate, with intersection heights at about 90 km. Addition of a diffraction grating (preferably a blazed grating, which concentrates visible light in the first order spectrum) in front of the objective lens can be used to make meteor spectra with the photographic or video observation techniques. Typically gratings with 200 to 800 lines per millimetre are used for this work. A meteor produces an ionization trail in the atmosphere, which can be used to reflect electromagnetic waves from distant television or radio transmitters. Meteors will be detected using this forward scatter radio technique as brief (usually a few tenths of a second) reception of the signal from the distant station, which is normally blocked by the curvature of Earth. See RADIO DETECTION OF METEORS on p. 207 for more details.

In addition to the URLs listed above, *The Handbook for Visual Meteor Observers* is available from the International Meteor Organization, and Neil Bone's book *Meteors* (Sky Publishing, 1993) provides an excellent introduction to visual, telescopic, and photographic meteor observation.

TABLE OF METEOR SHOWERS 2002

The more prominent nighttime showers visible from the Northern Hemisphere are included in the following table, with the most visually impressive ones given in **bold** type. Explanations of the entries in the various columns are given following the table.

Shower	Max (UT)		λ (2000)	D (d)	ZHR	R	Moon (%)	r	RA h m	Dec (°)	v (km/s)
Quadrantid	Jan. 3	18h	283.16	0.8	90	√	56	2.1	15 30	+50	42
Lyrid	Apr. 22	11h	32.1	6	15	√	3	2.9	18 16	+34	48
η–Aquarid	May 5	4h	44.5	8	20	>03	92	2.7	22 27	00	65
S δ–Aquarid	Jul. 29	0h	125.7	12	20	>23	65	3.2	22 38	−16	41
Perseid	Aug. 12	22h	140.0	5	100	√	49	2.2	3 06	+58	60
Orionid	Oct. 22	8h	208.7	8	20	>23	30	2.8	6 22	+16	66
S Taurid	Nov. 3	8h	220.7	30	10	√	96	2.3	3 24	+14	28
N Taurid	Nov. 13	7h	230.7	30	15	√	7	2.3	3 55	+23	29
Leonid a	Nov. 19	4h	236.60	0.2	3000?	>00	11	2.7?	10 18	+22	71
Leonid b	Nov. 19	11h	236.88	0.2	6000?	>00	11	2.8?	10 18	+22	71
Geminid	Dec. 14	9h	262.2	3	95	√	1	2.6	7 30	+33	35
Ursid	Dec. 22	18h	270.7	2	20	√	47	3.0	14 28	+75	34

The column labelled **Max** lists the date and hour (Universal Time) of the 2002 intersection of Earth with the densest region of the stream. These maxima are based on the solar longitude values (λ) for each shower given in the third column (epoch 2000). Many streams have a complex rate profile; for example, the Orionid shower has an earlier peak for faint meteors (λ = 207.5) than for bright meteors (λ = 209.8). Most showers show activity over a number of days, as shown in the next column, D (defined as the duration in days of 1/4 peak activity or more). Some showers (e.g. the Quadrantids) are highly concentrated with strong displays lasting only a few hours, while others are spread over weeks (e.g. the Taurid complex). Concentrated showers are more likely to be of recent formation. There are no records of the Quadrantid shower before the 19th century, while several showers have been observed for hundreds or thousands of years (e.g. the Perseids). Some showers (such as the Leonids) have meteoroids concentrated in a small region of the orbit and hence have much higher peak rates in certain years.

The column labelled **ZHR** gives the predicted zenithal hourly rate.

The higher the radiant is in the sky, the more direct the projection of the stream cross section on the sky area above the observer, and the apparent activity will be higher. The column labelled R indicates when the radiant is above the horizon for an observer at 43°N latitude; for example, >23 means that the shower can be observed after 11 p.m. local time. A √ means that the radiant is above the horizon throughout night hours. The number of meteors observed varies strongly with limiting magnitude; therefore, effective meteor observations must be made in the absence of significant moonlight. In the column labelled **Moon** the percentage of illumination of the Moon at the date of shower maximum is given. The rise and set times of the Moon must also be taken into account, however.

The relative number of bright and faint meteors is given by the *population index, r*, which is defined as the ratio of the number of meteors of magnitude $M + 1$ to the number of magnitude M. The number of meteors that can be observed is a strong function of limiting sensitivity. For example, for a limiting magnitude of +3.5, a shower with a ZHR of 60 and a population index $r = 2.8$ would have the number of observable meteors per hour reduced by a factor of $(2.8)^3$ to a rate of only 2.7 meteors per hour.

The next two columns give the right ascension (**RA**) and declination (**Dec**) of the shower radiant. A typical meteor shower is active over several days, and the apparent radiant moves somewhat during this period. The tables published by the IMO give the daily motion of the radiant, which must be taken into account if one is observing meteor showers on dates significantly removed from the maximum of the shower. Meteors can only be observed when the radiant is above the local horizon (or nearly so). Finally, the geocentric speed v of the meteors in each shower is given in kilometres per second in the final column.

RADIO DETECTION OF METEORS
By Philip Gebhardt

The term "meteor" applies not only to the streak of light produced by a meteoroid, but also to the column of ionized atoms and molecules along the path behind the meteoroid. These meteor trails are capable of scattering radio signals from terrestrial stations. Unlike visual observation, radio detection of sporadic meteors or shower meteors can be undertaken in daylight and during inclement weather. Similarly, a night sky illuminated by the full Moon has no adverse effect on radio detection. Radio detection rates tend to be higher than visual observation rates because particles down to 10^{-5} kg can be detected visually, while particles down to 10^{-10} kg can be detected by radio. Assuming a density of 1 t/m^3, these mass limits correspond to diameters of about 3 mm and 0.06 mm, respectively.

Two types of meteor trails exist, *underdense* and *overdense*; they are determined by the density of free electrons. Reradiated signals from underdense trails (fewer than 2×10^{14} electrons per metre) rise above the receiver noise almost instantaneously and then decay exponentially. The duration of many meteor bursts is about a second or less. Reflected signals from overdense trails may have higher amplitude and longer duration, but destructive interference due to reflection from different parts of the trail can produce fluctuations in the signal. Note that other means of signal propagation may be heard on the FM band, but only meteor signals have their characteristic fast rise-time and short duration.

Data for selected meteor showers appear in the table at the left. These data are for visual observations and should be considered as guidelines only for radio purposes. The sporadic meteor rate (visual and radio) peaks about 6 a.m. local time (i.e. on the advancing side of Earth in its orbit) and is minimum near 6 p.m. The rate will vary from a few per hour for off-peak times for sporadic meteors to several hundred per hour during a very active shower. Frequencies between 20 and 150 MHz are typically used for meteor detection. Both amplitude and duration of meteor bursts are frequency-dependent—they decrease with increasing frequency. At the lower frequencies, however, galactic as well as human-made noise (particularly in urban areas) become limiting factors. Also, as the wavelength becomes comparable to the width of the meteor trail, the echo strength decreases.

The commercial FM broadcast band (88 to 108 MHz) provides the best introductory opportunity for meteor detection. The abundance of over-the-horizon stations transmitting 24 hours a day ensures that a meteor burst can be heard from a suitably positioned meteor regardless of the time of day.

The technique involves listening on a frequency not used by a local FM station. A receiver with a digital frequency readout is therefore an asset. Frequencies throughout North America are assigned at 200-kHz intervals between 88.1 and 107.9 MHz. In the absence of a clear frequency, it is possible to use a frequency occupied by a station with a very weak signal although weak meteor bursts will be masked. Alternatively, a TV set (channels 2 through 6) can be used, provided the set is connected to an antenna rather than through cable TV. For either the FM band or the TV channels, an outdoor antenna is preferable. It is also possible to listen using the FM radio in your car.

Further information can be found on the following websites:

www.odxa.on.ca/meteor.html
www.amsmeteors.org/imo-mirror/calendar/ca102.html
www.spaceweather.com/glossary/nasameteorradar.html
www.ionosonde.iap-kborn.de/sky_main.htm

Also see *Sky & Telescope*, **94**, no. 6 (December 1997), p. 108.

FIREBALLS
By Jeremy Tatum and Damien Lemay

Exceptionally bright meteors that are spectacular enough to attract the attention of the public and light up the countryside over a wide area are generally referred to as fireballs. With camera networks and satellite-based detections now providing statistical information on the entry of fireballs into Earth's atmosphere, the main reasons to collect fireball reports are to assist with meteorite recovery and to provide orbital information for recovered meteorites. Rapid recovery of meteorites is vital for the study of short-lived radioactive isotopes produced by cosmic ray bombardment of the meteorite while in interplanetary space. Small but potentially recoverable meteorites can be produced by fireballs that are no brighter than magnitude −6 A very slow fireball with no indication of terminal breakup is a good candidate for meteorite survival. The presence of delayed sound indicates penetration into the lower atmosphere and probable meteorite fall. The value of a meteorite is significantly greater when we know something of its atmospheric trajectory and orbit. Visual data can, under favourable circumstances, be used to obtain an approximate atmospheric trajectory. The Meteorites and Impacts Advisory Committee, MIAC (Comité consultatif sur les météorites et les impacts, CCMI), of the Canadian Space Agency maintains a website with images and information on fireballs, meteorites, and impact craters at miac.uqac.uquebec.ca/. If you want information on recent Canadian fireball or meteorite events, check the MIAC/CCMI bulletin board at:

miac.uqac.uquebec.ca/MIAC/wwwboard/wwwboard.html

The preferred method for submitting fireball reports is to complete an electronic fireball reporting form at one of the following locations:

Canada (only): miac.uqac.uquebec.ca/MIAC/fireball.htm
United States (AMS): www.amsmeteors.org/
Global (IMO): www.amsmeteors.org/imo-mirror/fireball/report.html
North American Meteor Network (NAMN):
  visual: www.namnmeteors.org/fireball_form.html
  photographic: www.namnmeteors.org/photo_form.html

If you do not have access to the web, write a brief report with the following information:

(1) The name, telephone number, and address of the observer(s).
(2) The time of occurrence (and uncertainty in this time).
(3) The location of the observer at the time the fireball was seen (preferably in precise longitude and latitude).
(4) The beginning and ending points of the fireball, in terms of either right ascension and declination or azimuth and elevation. If possible, indicate the uncertainty in these angles. Indicate whether the true beginning was observed and whether the ending point was blocked by horizon objects.
(5) A direct apparent magnitude estimate if possible; if not, note whether the fireball was brighter than, approximately equal to, or fainter than the full Moon.
(6) The duration of the fireball and the persistent train (if any).
(7) A qualitative description of the event (colour, flares, fragmentation, and sound). Report the absence as well as the presence of features such as sound and fragmentation. In the case of sound, report the delay between the fireball appearance and the sound.
(8) The existence of any video or photographic records.

Within Canada, email your report to fireball@mta.ca (MIAC/CCMI); outside Canada use fidac@imo.net or lunro.imo.usa@home.com (IMO).

METEORITE IDENTIFICATION
BY RICHARD K. HERD

Meteorites are rocks that have fallen to Earth from space. Some have lain on Earth for many thousands of years; others are recent arrivals. Those observed to traverse Earth's atmosphere, and recovered based on those observations, are called meteorite *falls*. Those with no record of arrival are meteorite *finds* when recognized. Meteorites are named for where they are found. Over 25 000 meteorites are known worldwide: 18 000 are from Antarctica and a few thousand from deserts in Africa and Asia. The best general reference on meteorites is *Rocks from Space* by O. Richard Norton, 2nd ed., Mountain Press, 1998.

Often there is confusion over when and where meteorites have fallen or have been preserved, and also over what they are and look like. All are significantly different than Earth rocks. Samples sent to experts for identification, even by other scientists, are usually "meteorwrongs"—terrestrial rocks or minerals, human-made slag, metals, alloys, or concrete—that rarely resemble meteorites. Less than 60 identified meteorites are known in Canada. There have been three falls since 1994: Tagish Lake, B.C., January 18, 2000; Kitchener, Ontario, July 12, 1998; and St-Robert, Quebec, June 14, 1994.

Meteorites probably begin as streams of fragments *(meteoroids)* that are debris from collisions between larger objects. The calculated orbits of several falls intersect the Asteroid Belt; their ultimate origin in space and time may be elsewhere. About 20 meteorites have come from the Moon. The petrological and isotopic evidence is compelling that a similar number are from Mars, blasted off the surface by impacts. Based on the meteorites' reflectance spectra or density, links have been suggested between other types or groups of meteorites and specific asteroids or asteroid types or comets, but the provenance of most is uncertain. Yet they are an unparalleled source of information about our solar system, from its primitive beginnings to the present. Some even contain extrasolar mineral grains and primordial compounds made in other stars, yielding information about the origin of the universe. In the absence of extensive space exploration, and to prepare for it, they are scientifically invaluable.

Popular ideas about when and where meteorites fall are connected with the observation of *meteors*, the brief streaks of light produced when high-speed, interplanetary particles enter Earth's upper atmosphere. Sporadic meteors and *meteor showers* do not result in meteorites; their fragile cometary debris fragments are reduced to dust high in the atmosphere. Earth collects over 100 tonnes of cosmic dust debris per day. In contrast, stronger, larger space rocks can survive a fiery passage through the atmosphere and result in meteorites. These first appear as bright *fireballs,* are slowed to terminal speeds by atmospheric friction, and cease to show a bright trail long before they reach Earth's surface. Fireballs, which may seem very close, are usually quite high in the atmosphere, 50 km or further from the observer. Even if an extraterrestrial object does reach the surface, it is likely to plunge into the 70% that is water or be lost among forests, jungles, or mountainous regions. In only uncommonly recorded cases have meteorites struck or landed within a few metres of humans (see "Possible Hazards of Meteorite Falls" by C.E. Spratt, *JRASC, 85,* p. 263, October 1991). Rare meteoroids of masses exceeding 100 tonnes are not slowed appreciably by Earth's atmosphere and produce impact craters. The larger impacts may have dramatically altered the history of life on our planet, but they do not result in meteorites—the kinetic energy is sufficiently high to vaporize the impacting body completely and to deform and melt the target area in a fraction of a second. Crater diameters are typically 10 times the diameter of the impacting body. Glassy *tektites* found scattered over several continents may be evidence of such impacts, but they do not have meteorite compositions or characteristics. Information about meteorites, tektites, and impacts is now widely available on the Internet.

Meteorites are divided into three groups that vary widely both in appearance and properties: *stones* or *stony meteorites (aerolites), stony-irons (siderolites)*, and *irons* or *iron meteorites (siderites)*. All usually contain metallic nickel-iron compounds (with traces of other metals) and are mildly to strongly magnetic. Those that have lain on Earth's surface for long periods may be rusted almost beyond recognition. Some require laboratory tests to confirm their identity. Specimens generally have a quite soft, dull black to brown fusion crust; more prevalent on stones and stony-irons, it may have partially flaked off. Meteorites never contain bubble-like cavities, nor are they ever almost perfectly spherical and smooth. During atmospheric entry, only their surface is affected. Surfaces of irons and stony-irons are dimpled rather than bulbous. They rust easily so there may be no bright metal showing. Stony meteorites do not show protuberances; weathered varieties are rusty, even on broken surfaces. Fresh stony meteorites may have a whitish rock interior, with bright metal specks. Their crusts are black or smoky grey, varying from quite glassy to dull; telltale lines and bubbled patches orient their flight through the air. More metallic samples may also be oriented.

Stones are the most abundant; they resemble some terrestrial rocks but are denser. Most (called *chondrites*) consist of spheres of silicate minerals (called *chondrules*) visible on broken, cut, or polished surfaces and scattered grains of metal. Chondrites are the oldest, most primitive, least altered meteorites. Rare stony meteorites without chondrules are called *achondrites*; these are thought to be melt products from chondrites, samples of younger volcanic planetary surfaces. In August 1996, NASA scientists announced the discovery of fossil and chemical evidence of bacterial life in an ancient achondrite from Mars, but other scientists disagree. This controversy has resulted in renewed interest in missions to Mars and in finding water and life on Mars and elsewhere, even in extreme conditions on Earth. Irons and stony-irons are dense, with up to equal amounts of silicates and iron, and are often irregular in shape. They are thought to be core/mantle material of planets formed by melting chondrites.

Rare *carbonaceous chondrites* are grey to black, some resembling charcoal with silicate inclusions. The dark colour is from iron oxides and sulphides. They contain a few percent carbon in very fine-grained carbonates, carbides, graphite, diamonds, and primitive organic molecules, detectable mainly by isotopic analyses. They may have had biologically significant roles in providing seeds for the origin of life. They probably come from comet nucleii or similar ice-rich asteroids. Their organic molecules originate in interstellar space as coatings on dust. The study of interplanetary or interstellar dust particles has become important in deciphering the origins of meteorites and, therefore, of our solar system and everything in it. We are all composed of recycled stardust.

The Geological Survey of Canada (GSC) maintains the National Meteorite Collection of about 2000 specimens, identifies meteorites, and supports research on them. It also offers to pay the owner a minimum of $500 for the first specimen of any new Canadian meteorite. Should you find a suspected meteorite, you may forward it to **Geological Survey of Canada, Natural Resources Canada, 601 Booth St., Ottawa, ON K1A 0E8, Attention: Meteorite Identification** (telephone: (613) 992-4042; fax: (613) 943-1286; email: herd@nrcan.gc.ca). The specimen will be examined and reported on free of charge. If it is too large for mailing, a description of its appearance, or a photograph, and its exact location should be sent. The GSC also makes available a free brochure on meteorites, with pictures of meteorites and comparative nonmeteorites. Write to the GSC's Publication Office at the above address. Meteorites of Canadian origin are subject to the provisions of the Cultural Property Export and Import Act and may not be exported from Canada without a permit.

METEORITE IMPACT CRATERS OF NORTH AMERICA
BY RICHARD A.F. GRIEVE

The first recognition of meteorite impact craters on Earth, and the basis of their scientific investigation, occurred in North America. Daniel Barringer, an American engineer and entrepreneur, first argued in 1905 that an approximately 1-km-diameter hole in the Arizona desert was the result of the impact of a large iron meteorite. Barringer had hoped to exploit the several million tonnes of iron meteorite that he believed lay buried beneath the crater floor. Unfortunately, virtually all of the impacting body had been destroyed as a consequence of the extreme pressures and temperatures generated by the impact. Barringer's ideas were controversial, and it was not until 1960, when Ed Chao and Gene Shoemaker discovered coesite, the high-pressure form of the mineral quartz, that what is now known as Barringer or Meteor Crater (#3 in the accompanying table and map) was unequivocally proven to be of impact origin. It was 30 years after Barringer's proposal for an impact origin for Meteor Crater that American scientists John Boon and Claude Albritton Jr. suggested that several other puzzling, generally circular features in the American midwest were, in fact, further evidence of meteorite impact on Earth. These structures—Decatureville, Flynn Creek, Jeptha Knob, Kentland, Serpent Mound, Sierra Madera, Upheaval Dome, Wells Creek—had been postulated earlier as being due to explosive volcanism. The lack of a crater rim and meteorite fragments at any of these sites led to the realization that these were no longer prerequisite evidence for defining an ancient meteorite impact crater.

As in the United States, crater investigations in Canada also stemmed from an interest in their economic potential. Discovery of the New Quebec Crater in the 1940s on military air photographs prompted Fred Chubb, a prospector, to seek support for a visit to this remote, circular landmark. He hoped to confirm that it was a large kimberlite "pipe," similar to the diamond-bearing ones of South Africa. Vic Meen of the Royal Ontario Museum led two expeditions to the site in 1950 and 1951 and concluded, based on its morphology and lack of volcanic evidence, that meteorite impact was the most likely cause of the crater. On the strength of Meen's discovery, Carlyle Beals, who was the Dominion Astronomer for Canada, instituted a crater research program at the Dominion Observatory, which included a systematic search of aerial photographs and led to confirmation of the Holleford crater. As the Observatory program became known, other scientists and laymen reported unusual, circular topographic features in Canada (e.g. Brent, Clearwater).

Research programs at government laboratories and universities in Canada, the United States, Germany, Austria, South Africa, and Russia, in particular, have confirmed over 160 impact sites on Earth. Only about 10% retain meteorite fragments. In craters larger than approximately 1 km in diameter, the extreme shock pressures and temperatures vaporize and melt the impacting body. The bulk of these impact sites are identified by characteristic deformation features in the target rocks—features uniquely produced in nature only by hypervelocity impact and known as shock metamorphic features.

Approximately five confirmed meteorite craters are added to the world list each year. Many of the recent additions have been identified through the discovery of shock features, which in turn led to recognition of a degraded and sometimes partially buried circular structure. In a few cases, such as Beaverhead, where shatter cones are simply found within an intensely disturbed oval zone, no circular morphologic feature is yet apparent. In the following table, therefore, values for crater diameter may represent a defined outer margin, whether an upraised rim or a peripheral fault, or the diameter may be a reconstruction from geologic and geophysical data with no obvious, morphological counterpart.

For more information and images of many craters, visit gdcinfo.agg.nrcan.gc.ca.

TABLE OF METEORITE IMPACT CRATERS OF NORTH AMERICA

#	Name, Location	Lat. (N)	Long. (W)	Diam. km	Age* Ma	Surface Expression	Visible Geologic Features
1	Ames, Oklahoma, U.S.A.	36° 15'	98° 12'	16.	470. (30)	buried 3 km	none
2	Avak, Alaska, U.S.A.	71 15	156 38	12.	100. (5)	buried 30 m	none
3	Barringer (Meteor) Crater, Arizona, U.S.A.	35 02	111 01	1.2	0.049 (0.003)	rimmed polygonal crater	fragments of meteorite, highly shocked sandstone
4	Beaverhead, Montana, U.S.A.	44 36	113 00	60.	≈600.	oval area of crushed sandstone, and shatter cones	shatter cones
5	Brent, Ontario	46 05	78 29	3.8	450. (30)	sediment-filled shallow depression	fracturing
6	Calvin, Michigan, U.S.A.	41 50	85 57	8.5	450. (10)	buried 400 m	none
7	Carswell, Saskatchewan	58 27	109 30	39.	115. (10)	discontinuous circular ridge	shatter cones, breccia, impact melt
8	Charlevoix, Quebec	47 32	70 18	54.	357. (15)	semicircular trough, central peak	breccia, shatter cones, impact melt
9	Chesapeake Bay, Virginia, U.S.A.	37 17	76 01	85	35.5 (0.6)	buried 400–500 m, ring structure	none
10	Chicxulub, Mexico	21 20	89 30	180.	64.98 (0.05)	buried 1 km, ring of sink holes	none (related to the K/T mass extinction event)
11	Clearwater East, Quebec	56 05	74 07	26.	290. (20)	circular lake	sedimentary float
12	Clearwater West, Quebec	56 13	74 30	36.	290. (20)	island ring in circular lake	impact melt, breccias
13	Couture, Quebec	60 08	75 20	8.	430. (25)	circular lake	breccia float
14	Crooked Creek, Missouri, U.S.A.	37 50	91 23	7.	320. (80)	oval area of disturbed rocks, shallow marginal depression	breccia, shatter cones
15	Decaturville, Missouri, U.S.A.	37 54	92 43	6.	<300.	slight oval depression	breccia, shatter cones
16	Deep Bay, Saskatchewan	56 24	102 59	13.	100. (50)	circular bay	sedimentary float
17	Des Plaines, Illinois, U.S.A.	42 03	87 52	8.	<280.	buried, 15–100 m	none
18	Eagle Butte, Alberta	49 42	110 30	10.	<65.	minor structural disturbance	shatter cones
19	Elbow, Saskatchewan	50 59	106 43	8.	395. (25)	buried, small mound	none
20	Flynn Creek, Tennessee, U.S.A.	36 17	85 40	3.8	360. (20)	sediment-filled shallow depression with small central peak	breccia, shatter cones
21	Glasford, Illinois, U.S.A.	40 36	89 47	4.	<430.	buried 350 m	none
22	Glover Bluff, Wisconsin, U.S.A.	43 58	89 32	8.	<500.	disturbed dolomite exposed	shatter cones
23	Gow, Saskatchewan	56 27	104 29	5.	<250.	lake and central island	breccia, impact melt
24	Haughton, N.W.T.	75 22	89 41	24.	23.4 (1.0)	shallow circular depression	shatter cones, breccia
25	Haviland, Kansas, U.S.A.	37 35	99 10	0.015	<0.001	excavated depression	fragments of meteorite
26	Holleford, Ontario	44 28	76 38	2.4	550. (100)	sediment-filled shallow depression	sedimentary fill
27	Ile Rouleau, Quebec	50 41	73 53	4.	<300.	island is central peak of submerged structure	shatter cones, breccia dykes

* Numbers in parentheses are possible errors.

TABLE OF METEORITE IMPACT CRATERS OF NORTH AMERICA (ct'd)

#	Name, Location	Lat. (N)	Long. (W)	Diam. km	Age* Ma	Surface Expression	Visible Geologic Features
28	Kentland, Indiana, U.S.A.	40 45	87 24	13.	<97.	central peak exposed in quarries, rest buried	breccia, shatter cones, disturbed rocks
29	La Moinerie, Quebec	57 26	66 37	8.	400. (50)	lake-filled, depression	breccia float
30	Manicouagan, Quebec	51 23	68 42	100.	214. (1)	circumferential lake, central peak	impact melt, breccia
31	Manson, Iowa, U.S.A.	42 35	94 33	35.	73.8 (0.3)	none, central elevation buried 30 m	none
32	Maple Creek, Saskatchewan	49 48	109 06	6.	<75.	buried, small mound	disturbed rocks
33	Marquez, Texas, U.S.A.	31 17	96 18	12.7	58. (2)	circular area of disturbed rock	shatter cones
34	Middlesboro, Kentucky, U.S.A.	36 37	83 44	6.	<300.	circular depression	disturbed rocks
35	Mistastin, Labrador	55 53	63 18	28.	38. (4)	elliptical lake and central island	breccia, impact melt
36	Montagnais, Nova Scotia	42 53	64 13	45.	50.5 (0.8)	none, under water (115 m) and sediment	none
37	New Quebec, Quebec	61 17	73 40	3.4	1.4 (0.1)	rimmed, circular lake	raised rim, impact melt
38	Newporte, North Dakota, U.S.A.	48 58	101 58	3.	<500.	none, buried 3 km	none
39	Nicholson, N.W.T.	62 40	102 41	12.5	<400.	irregular lake with islands	breccia
40	Odessa, Texas, U.S.A.	31 45	102 29	0.17	<0.05	sediment-filled depression with very slight rim, 4 others buried & smaller	fragments of meteorite
41	Pilot, N.W.T.	60 17	111 01	6.	445. (2)	circular lake	fracturing, breccia float
42	Presqu'ile, Quebec	49 43	74 48	24.	<500.	none, heavily eroded	shatter cones
43	Red Wing, North Dakota, U.S.A.	47 36	103 33	9.	200. (25)	none, buried 1.5 km	none
44	St. Martin, Manitoba	51 47	98 32	40.	220. (32)	none, partially buried	impact melt
45	Serpent Mound, Ohio, U.S.A.	39 02	83 24	8.	<320.	circular area of disturbed rock, slight central peak	breccia, shatter cones
46	Sierra Madera, Texas, U.S.A.	30 36	102 55	13.	<100.	central hills, annular depression, outer ring of hills	breccia, shatter cones
47	Slate Islands, Ontario	48 40	87 00	30.	≈450.	islands are central peak of submerged structure	shatter cones, breccia dykes
48	Steen River, Alberta	59 30	117 38	25.	95. (7)	none, buried 200 m	none
49	Sudbury, Ontario	46 36	81 11	250.	1850. (3)	deformed elliptical basin	breccia, impact melt, shatter cones, breccia dykes
50	Upheaval Dome, Utah, U.S.A.	38 26	109 54	10.	<65.	circular area of disturbed rock buried 1 km	breccia dykes
51	Viewfield, Saskatchewan	49 35	103 34	25.	190. (20)	none, buried 1 km	none
52	Wanapitei, Ontario	46 45	80 45	7.5	37. (2)	lake-filled, depression	breccia float
53	Wells Creek, Tennessee, U.S.A.	36 23	87 40	12.	200. (100)	basin with central hill, inner and outer annular valleys, ridges	breccia, shatter cones
54	West Hawk Lake, Manitoba	49 46	95 11	2.4	100. (50)	circular lake	none

* Numbers in parentheses are possible errors.

MAP OF NORTH AMERICAN METEORITE IMPACT STRUCTURES

Of the 160 plus impact structures identified on Earth, 54 are located in North America (29 in Canada, 24 in the United States, and 1 in Mexico). These are identified on the above map; the numbers correspond to the listing in the table on the preceding two pages. Although the oceans cover 70% of Earth, only two impact structures have been identified on the seafloor (#36 and Mjølnir in the Barents Sea). Also, with the exception of structure #49, all of those shown occurred within approximately the last 10% of Earth's history. Evidence of many earlier craters has been erased by geologic processes. It is possible, however, to calculate a terrestrial cratering rate by focusing only on geologically stable areas of Earth (known as cratons), with low erosion and sedimentation rate. One such area is the North American craton. These rate calculations indicate that Earth has received at least 10 000 impacts sufficient to result in craters greater than 20 km in diameter over the last 3.5 billion years. Very early in Earth history, the cratering rate was even higher, perhaps reaching 100 times the current rate. Doubtless some of these impacts have had profound influence upon the evolution of life on this planet. For example, Chicxulub (#10), the very large structure in Mexico, is linked to a major extinction event 65 million years ago. Some impact craters are the source of considerable economic resources: in North America, hydrocarbons are extracted from #1, 2, 6, 32, 33, 38, 43, 46, 48, 49; #7 produces uranium and #51 is the site of a world class nickel and copper mining camp.

COMETS IN 2002
By Brian G. Marsden

Listed below are the periodic comets expected at perihelion in 2002. The orbital elements are given with sufficient precision to allow an ephemeris computation good to about one arcminute (1'). The angular elements are referred to the ecliptic and mean equinox J2000.0.

Comet	Perihelion Date T TT	Dist. q AU	Eccen. e	Rev. Per. P a	Arg. Peri. ω °	Asc. Node Ω °	Incl. i °
96P	Jan. 8.63	0.1241	0.9588	5.2	14.58	94.61	60.19
31P	18.52	3.4086	0.1953	8.7	18.40	114.19	4.55
125P	28.05	1.5286	0.5115	5.5	87.30	153.24	9.98
6P	Feb. 3.59	1.3528	0.6128	6.5	178.11	138.94	19.50
15P	7.17	1.0341	0.7105	6.8	323.64	41.96	3.67
89P	Mar. 22.91	2.2901	0.3979	7.4	249.22	42.48	12.03
7P	May 15.72	1.2581	0.6341	6.4	172.29	93.45	22.28
90P	Jun. 23.02	2.9655	0.5089	14.8	28.20	13.53	9.62
124P	Jul. 27.03	1.4671	0.5426	5.7	181.24	1.39	31.35
57P	31.16	1.7295	0.4991	6.4	115.24	188.93	2.84
54P	Aug. 7.45	2.1461	0.4306	7.3	2.14	358.93	6.09
67P	18.31	1.2923	0.6315	6.6	11.45	50.97	7.12
46P	26.97	1.0588	0.6579	5.4	356.40	82.17	11.74
77P	Sep. 4.72	2.3095	0.3582	6.8	196.45	14.98	24.40
92P	23.06	1.8074	0.6634	12.4	163.05	182.35	18.76
26P	Nov. 29.72	1.1179	0.6327	5.3	1.62	211.74	22.35
22P	Dec. 12.08	1.5836	0.5433	6.5	162.75	120.93	4.72
P/1986 A1	15.02	1.8137	0.7268	17.1	14.94	97.27	6.39
39P	21.72	5.4707	0.2446	19.5	56.37	331.58	1.94
P/1993 K2	22.45	3.1101	0.3077	9.5	163.69	92.02	9.87
115P	23.87	2.0417	0.5208	8.8	119.88	176.76	11.68
30P	24.40	1.8775	0.5021	7.3	13.29	119.76	8.13
28P	27.38	1.5521	0.7756	18.2	346.92	347.03	14.19

For an explanation of these elements see p. 20; the elements are for an epoch within 20 days of perihelion.

The returns of 7P/Pons–Winnecke, 57P/du Toit–Neujmin–Delporte, 92P/Sanguin and P/1986 A1 (Shoemaker) are favourable, as are those of 31P/Schwassmann–Wachmann, 39P/Oterma, and 54P/de Vico–Swift, considering that perturbations have significantly increased the perihelion distances since their previous perihelion passages. The returns of 22P/Kopff, 28P/Neujmin, 30P/Reinmuth, 67P/Churyumov–Gerasimenko, 77P/Longmore, 89P/Russell, 90P/Gehrels, 115P/Maury, 124P/Mrkos, 125P/Spacewatch, and P/1993 K2 (Helin–Lawrence) are fair. The returns of 6P/d'Arrest, 15P/Finlay and 96P/Machholz are poor, while those of 26P/Grigg–Skjellerup and 46P/Wirtanen are very poor.

OBSERVING COMETS
By David H. Levy

Comets are interesting and fun to observe because each has its own unique, changing appearance. Observationally, comets are very much like deep-sky objects. Even in large telescopes an observer can confuse a comet with a galaxy or a diffuse planetary nebula. Comets near a telescope's limit are virtually impossible to spot without an accurate position extracted from a detailed atlas like *Uranometria* or *Millennium*. It is difficult to define a telescope's limiting magnitude for comets because the more diffuse a comet, the more difficult it is to find. Typically, under a dark sky a 150-mm telescope will catch a 9th magnitude comet, a 200-mm telescope will see 10th, and a 400-mm should have no trouble with a 13th magnitude comet.

If you are sure you have discovered a comet, follow the procedure given in this Handbook (see REPORTING OF ASTRONOMICAL DISCOVERIES on p. 9). For more information on comet observing and hunting, read *Observing Comets, Asteroids, Meteors, and the Zodiacal Light,* by Stephen J. Edberg and David H. Levy (Cambridge University Press, 1994).

Magnitude Estimates

The brightness of the coma can be estimated using a variety of methods, the most common of which is the "In-Out" method:

(1) Study the coma until you become familiar with its "average" brightness, an easy process if the coma is of uniform brightness but rather difficult if there is a strong central condensation.

(2) Using a variable star chart or some source in which star magnitudes are listed, find a comparison star at approximately the same altitude as the comet.

(3) Defocus the star to the size of the in-focus coma.

(4) Compare the star's out-of-focus brightness with that of the coma.

Repeat the last three steps with a second star, or more if needed, until an interpolation can be made.

Physical Characteristics

A comet magnitude estimate becomes more useful if an estimate of the coma diameter is made at the same time. An observer seeing a 3' (3 minutes of arc) coma, for example, will estimate much brighter than another observer who sees only a 1' coma at the same time. The simplest way of estimating coma size is to draw the coma with the embedded and surrounding field stars and then compare the drawing to an atlas, using its scale to determine the size.

A nightly measurement of a comet's degree of condensation is a good way of studying its changing behaviour. A comet undergoing an outburst of dust from its nucleus might begin its display by showing almost overnight the development of an increased condensation. Use an integer scale from 0 to 9, where 0 means a diffuse coma with absolutely uniform brightness, 3 means a diffuse coma with gradually increasing brightness toward the centre, 6 involves a definite central condensation, and 9 refers to an almost stellar image.

Because of the changing Earth–Sun–comet geometry and the changing activity in a comet, the length and position angle of a tail should be measured. A rough way to measure the length of a tail is to sketch it and compare with a detailed atlas, as with the coma. Observers can also measure the position angle using an atlas and a protractor.

Visual Comet Hunting

The key ingredient to a successful comet search is perseverance. Although there are stories of people finding comets very quickly (Mark Whitaker discovered Comet Whitaker-Thomas 1968 V after three nights of comet hunting), these are the exception. Don Machholz searched for some 1700 hours for each of his first two comets, and I spent more than 917 hours before my first discovery. In contrast, neither Alan Hale nor Tom Bopp was comet hunting when they independently discovered what later became the Great Comet of 1997.

It is important to know the sky well before beginning a comet search program, but it is more important to know the difference between the fuzzy appearances of comets compared to galaxies, nebulae, and clusters. Observing all the objects in Messier's Catalogue (see pp. 258–261) provides an excellent education in what these distant objects look like, and observing as many known comets as possible is good preparation for recognizing an interloper. Generally, comets lack the bilateral symmetry of spiral galaxies and the mottled appearance of globular clusters. More important, they usually have unsharp edges, fading off into space so that it is often difficult to tell where the comet ends and the sky begins.

Although most comet hunters still use traditional star atlases to check their suspects, some are moving into a new mode of comet hunting. These hunters have attached encoders to their telescopes that allow an instant reading of the suspect's position in right ascension and declination. If the telescope has been properly set up, this approach allows faster checking of suspicious objects. However, a sense of the nature of the fuzzy object in the field of view is still important since thousands of nonstellar objects dot the sky.

Comets may appear at any time, but they are usually found within 90° of the Sun. Good areas to search are in the evening western sky during the week after full Moon and in the morning eastern sky before dawn around new Moon.

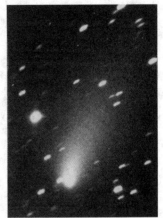

Comet C/1988 F1 (Levy) *was discovered visually on 1988 March 19. Not long afterwards, Gene and Carolyn Shoemaker and Henry Holt discovered C/1988 J1 (Shoemaker-Holt). Conrad Bardwell, then of the Minor Planet Center (MPC), subsequently noted that the new comet followed Comet Levy in a similar orbit and that Comet Levy arrived at perihelion about 70 days earlier. MPC Director Dr. Brian Marsden deduced that the two comets had separated some 12 000 years ago. CCD image by the author with the 61-inch Kuiper Telescope and International Halley Watch CCD system with a Cousins red-band filter.*

Although comet hunters differ in their approaches to searching, one way is to use an altazimuth mount and make horizontal sweeps. In the western sky, begin near the end of twilight at the horizon, sweep across, then return to the point of origin, move upward about half a field of view and sweep again, etc. In the morning reverse the process.

Photographic and Electronic Comet Hunting

It is now possible to discover comets photographically and by using CCDs. With film and a wide-angle camera like a Schmidt camera, take photographs of selected areas of sky, then repeat these exposures after at least 45 minutes. Using a stereomicroscope or a blink microscope, it is then possible to spot moving objects. Through a stereomicroscope, the comet will appear to "float" above or "sink" below the stellar background, an elegant way to discover comets. If a blink microscope is used, the comet will appear to jump back and forth.

Using a CCD, take at least three images of each field, then examine either visually or by a moving-object detection program. Visual inspection is like blinking, so moving objects appear to move steadily through the three pictures, then jump back and begin moving again.

Finally, it is possible to discover comets over the Internet. Since images from the SOHO spacecraft are made available soon after they are taken, amateur astronomers can scan these images for Sun-grazing comets. RASC member Michael Boschat won the 2001 Ken Chilton Prize for his discoveries of several SOHO comets in this way.

Designation of Comets

At the International Astronomical Union's 22nd General Assembly in The Hague in 1994, Commission 20 of the IAU approved a resolution that changes the way comets are designated. Under the old system, a comet was designated according to its order of discovery or recovery in a given year (e.g. 1982i, Comet Halley, was the ninth comet to appear in 1982). After cometary information was complete for a given year, each comet also received a Roman numeral designation based on the order of perihelion passage (e.g. Halley at its last return was also known as 1986 III).

Under the new system, which went into effect in January 1995 but which is retroactive to every comet for which a reasonable orbit is available, a comet is assigned only one designation which is similar to, although not identical to, the provisional designation system for asteroids. With this system the year is divided into periods called "half-months" beginning with A (the first half of January) and concluding with Y (the last half of December), omitting the letter I. In addition, there is a letter indicating the comet's status: C for a long period comet, P for a "periodic comet" (defined as having a period of less than 200 years), X for a comet for which a reasonable orbit cannot be computed, and D for a disappeared comet. Once the orbit of a periodic comet is well known, that comet receives a permanent number according to the order in which the comet's periodicity was recognized. Thus Comet Hale-Bopp, as the first comet to be found in the O part of 1995, is labelled C/1995 O1. Comet Shoemaker-Levy 9 was 1993e; its new designation as the second comet to be found in the F part of 1993 is D/1993 F2. The new designation for Comet Halley is 1P/Halley.

When a comet becomes well known, the vast majority of scientists, press, and public ignore the official designation, preferring instead to use more easily remembered names. Our experience with comets Hale-Bopp and C/1996 B2 (Hyakutake) showed clearly that people were more comfortable with proper names. However, with 2 comets named Hyakutake, more than 200 named SOHO, and more than 50 named LINEAR, we need to become familiar with the official designation in order to separate one comet from the others.

A handful of comets are named not for their discoverers but for their orbit computors. The most famous of these is P/Halley, which has been well observed since at least 240 BC. It was finally identified as a comet appearing every 76 years or so by Edmond Halley in 1705. Two others are 2P/Encke and 27P/Crommelin.

Editor's Note: David Levy is the discoverer of 21 comets: 8 by visual searches (comets Levy-Rudenko 1984t, Levy 1987a, Levy 1987y, Levy 1988e, Okazaki-Levy-Rudenko 1989r, Levy 1990c, P/Levy 1991q, and Takamizawa-Levy 1994f) and 13 comets discovered photographically at Palomar under the combined name Shoemaker-Levy. One of these, Shoemaker-Levy 9 (D/1993 F2), collided with Jupiter in July 1994. Brief descriptions of the first 12 to be discovered are given in *JRASC*, *85*, 384, 1991. In 1990, David Levy and H.E. Holt discovered the first Martian Trojan asteroid: 1990MB.

INTERPLANETARY DUST
By Roy Bishop

Outside of the astronomical community it is not generally realized that the inner solar system contains a vast cloud of dust. The particles in this cloud are concentrated near the plane of the ecliptic and toward the Sun, their spatial particle density in the ecliptic falling off somewhat more rapidly than the reciprocal of their distance from the Sun. Measurements from spacecraft indicate that the cloud extends well beyond the orbit of Mars but is negligible in the vicinity of Jupiter's orbit and beyond.

The particles composing the cloud have a continuum of sizes, from pebble-sized clumps down to specks with diameters comparable to the wavelength of visible light and smaller. The smaller particles are the more numerous, although the mass distribution appears to peak near 10^{-8} kg, corresponding to a particle diameter of a few tenths of a millimetre. The total mass of the cloud is small, amounting to perhaps 10^{-14} of the mass of the solar system. It is as if the satellites of Mars had been pulverized and spread throughout the inner solar system.

Like the planetary system, the interplanetary dust cloud is not static. Its particles generally move in orbits about the Sun. In addition, the particles undergo continual fragmentation due to collisions, sputtering associated with bombardment by the solar wind, electrostatic bursting, and sublimation. This progression toward smaller and smaller sizes is of crucial significance for the cloud, since particles with diameters appreciably less than a tenth of a millimetre have a sufficiently large surface-to-volume ratio that the radiation pressure of sunlight has a significant effect upon their motion—aberration of sunlight results in a small backward force which slows the dust particles (the Poynting–Robertson Effect), and they slowly spiral inward toward the Sun. During a total solar eclipse in 1983, instruments carried by a balloon detected a ring-like concentration of dust only a couple of solar diameters from the Sun. Its inner edge apparently marks the point at which solar heat vaporizes the infalling particles. The resulting tiny gas molecules, like the smallest particles of dust, are blown out of the solar system by the dominant radiation pressure and interactions with the solar wind.

Because of the above-mentioned influences on the sizes and motions of the dust particles, the estimated mean life of a cloud particle is about 10^4 years. Since this is much less than the age of the solar system, it is obvious that the cloud must be in a dynamic equilibrium—that is, it must be gaining new material as it loses the old. Part of the tail of a bright comet is the result of significant quantities of dust ejected from its nucleus, and it is generally assumed that comets provide a sizeable fraction of the supply of new dust to the cloud. Since comet nuclei are believed to consist of the undifferentiated matter that the solar system formed out of, much of the dust of the interplanetary cloud is most likely composed of this same low-density, fragile, primitive material. IRAS (Infrared Astronomical Satellite) data indicate that collisions of asteroids are also a significant source of dust, but it is not yet known whether comets or asteroids provide the greater input of dust to the cloud.

To an observer on Earth, the most noticeable aspect of the dust cloud is meteors—larger particles of the cloud that encounter Earth at high speeds and vaporize in the upper atmosphere. In addition, sunlight scattered by the dust cloud appears as a faint (fortunately!) glow in the vicinity of the ecliptic. This glow is brightest toward the Sun, is due primarily to particles with diameters between a few micrometres and a millimetre, and is referred to as the *zodiacal light*. A slight brightening in the sky opposite the Sun, called the *Gegenschein* (German for "counterglow"), is due to a phase effect (analogous to full moon) and also, possibly, to a concentration of dust at the L3 Lagrangian Point of the Earth–Sun system. As astronomical objects, the zodiacal light and the Gegenschein are unusual in that they can be seen only with the unaided eye. Both are invisible in binoculars or a telescope.

The Zodiacal Light

Poetic references to the zodiacal light go back several centuries (e.g. see *The Observatory*, *108*, 181, 1988). The 19th-century poet Edward FitzGerald is noted for his translation of the famous poem "Rubaiyat" by the Persian Omar Khayyam. In one of the stanzas, Khayyam's reference to the morning was altered by FitzGerald into haunting references to the zodiacal light: "Dreaming when Dawn's Left Hand was in the Sky" (in midnorthern latitudes, the zodiacal light and the first glow of the early autumn dawn combine to produce a large, glowing, ghostly figure having an upraised left arm); and "Before the phantom of False morning died" (the zodiacal light soon vanishes in the glow of the true dawn).

When conditions are favourable, the zodiacal light is indeed a mysterious and beautiful sight. Because the zodiacal light is brightest nearest the Sun, it is best seen after the end of evening twilight and before the beginning of morning twilight (for times of twilight, see the index) and when the ecliptic is at a steep angle relative to the horizon. In the tropics the ecliptic is always at a steep angle to the horizon, and the short duration of twilight is an added advantage. In midnorthern latitudes the optimum geometry occurs in the evening western sky in February and March, and in the morning eastern sky in September and October. The zodiacal light appears as a huge, softly radiant pyramid of white light with its base near the horizon and its axis centred on the zodiac. In its brightest parts it exceeds the luminance of the central Milky Way.

Despite its brightness, most people have not seen the zodiacal light. As mentioned above, certain times of night and year are more favourable than others. In addition, moonlight, haze, or light pollution rule out any chance of seeing this phenomenon. Even with a dark, transparent sky the inexperienced observer may confuse the zodiacal light with twilight and thus ignore it, or may not notice it because he or she is expecting a much smaller object.

The Gegenschein

The zodiacal light extends all around the zodiac with a shallow minimum in brightness some 120° to 150° from the Sun; nevertheless, this "zodiacal band" or "light bridge" is exceedingly faint and hence seldom visible. However, the slight brightening in the vicinity of the antisolar point can be seen under the right conditions.

The Gegenschein is very faint. Haze, moonlight, bright nearby stars, planets, or light pollution will hide it completely. Most observers, including experienced ones, have not seen it. The Gegenschein is sufficiently faint that, except from high-altitude sites with very dark skies, a person will not see it without making a special effort to *look* for it. It is a ghostly apparition best seen near midnight, and in midnorthern latitudes, in the autumn or winter when the antisolar point is nearest the zenith. To avoid interference from bright stars or the Milky Way, the periods late September to early November and late January to early February are best. At these times, the Gegenschein is in Pisces and Cancer, respectively. It appears as a faint yet distinct, somewhat elliptical glow perhaps 10° in diameter. The luminance of the Gegenschein is about 10^{-4} cd/m^2, some 10 orders of magnitude dimmer than the brightest light the human eye can tolerate.

Don't determine the antisolar point before you look—imagination is too powerful. Find the antisolar point by locating the Gegenschein, and *then* check your star charts!

STARS

CONSTELLATIONS—NAMES AND ABBREVIATIONS

Nominative & Pronunciation	Genitive & Pronunciation	Abbr.	Meaning
Andromeda, ăn-drŏm'ē-dà	Andromedae, ăn-drŏm'ē-dē'	And	Daughter of Cassiopeia
Antlia, ănt'lĭ-à	Antliae, ănt'lē-ē'	Ant	The Air Pump
Apus, ā'pŭs	Apodis, ăp'ă-dĭs	Aps	Bird of Paradise
Aquarius, à-kwâr'ē-ŭs	Aquarii, à-kwâr'ē-ī'	Aqr	The Water-bearer
Aquila, à-kwĭl'à	Aquilae, à-kwĭl'ē	Aql	The Eagle
Ara, ā'rà	Arae, ā'rē	Ara	The Altar
Aries, âr'ēz	Arietis, à-rī'ē-tĭs	Ari	The Ram
Auriga, ô-rī'gà	Aurigae, ô-rī'jē	Aur	The Charioteer
Bootes, bō-ō'tēz	Bootis, bō-ō'tĭs	Boo	The Herdsman
Caelum, sē'lŭm	Caeli, sē'lī	Cae	The Chisel
Camelopardalis kà-mĕl'ō-pàr'dà-lĭs	Camelopardalis kà-mĕl'ō-pàr'dà-lĭs	Cam	The Giraffe
Cancer, kăn'sēr	Cancri, kăn'krē	Cnc	The Crab
Canes Venatici kā'nēz vē-năt'ĭ-sī	Canum Venaticorum kā'nŭm vē-năt'ĭ-kôr'ŭm	CVn	The Hunting Dogs
Canis Major, kā'nĭs mā'jēr	Canis Majoris, kā'nĭs mà-jôr'ĭs	CMa	The Big Dog
Canis Minor, kā'nĭs mī'nēr	Canis Minoris, kā'nĭs mī-ñôr'ĭs	CMi	The Little Dog
Capricornus, kăp'rĭ-kôr-nŭs	Capricorni, kăp'rĭ-kôr-nī	Cap	The Goat
Carina, kà-rī'-nà	Carinae, kà-rī'-nē	Car	The Keel
Cassiopeia, kăs'ĭ-ō-pē'yà	Cassiopeiae, kăs'ĭ-ō-pē'yē	Cas	The Queen
Centaurus, sĕn-tôr'ŭs	Centauri, sĕn-tôr'ī	Cen	The Centaur
Cepheus, sē'fē-ŭs	Cephei, sē'fē-ī'	Cep	The King
Cetus, sē'tŭs	Ceti, sē'tī	Cet	The Whale
Chamaeleon, kà-mē'lē-ŭn	Chamaeleontis, kà-mē'lē-ŏn'tĭs	Cha	The Chameleon
Circinus, sûr'sĭ-nŭs	Circini, sûr'sĭ-nī	Cir	The Compasses
Columba, kŏ-lŭm'bà	Columbae, kŏ-lŭm'bē	Col	The Dove
Coma Berenices kō'mà bĕr'ē-nī'sēz	Comae Berenices kō'mē bĕr'ē-nī'sēz	Com	Berenice's Hair
Corona Australis kō-rō'nà ôs-trā'lĭs	Coronae Australis kō-rō'nē ôs-trā'lĭs	CrA	The Southern Crown
Corona Borealis kō-rō'nà bôr'ē-ăl'ĭs	Coronae Borealis kō-rō'nē bôr'ē-ăl'ĭs	CrB	The Northern Crown
Corvus, kôr'vŭs	Corvi, kôr'vī	Crv	The Crow
Crater, krā'tēr	Crateris, krā-tēr'ĭs	Crt	The Cup
Crux, krŭks	Crucis, krōō'sĭs	Cru	The Cross
Cygnus, sĭg'nŭs	Cygni, sĭg'nī	Cyg	The Swan
Delphinus, dĕl-fī'nŭs	Delphini, dĕl-fī'nī	Del	The Dolphin
Dorado, dō-rà'dō	Doradus, dō-rà'dŭs	Dor	The Swordfish
Draco, drā'kō	Draconis, drā'kō'nĭs	Dra	The Dragon
Equuleus, ē-kwōō'lē-ŭs	Equulei, ē-kwōō'lē-ī'	Equ	The Little Horse
Eridanus, ē-rĭd'à-nŭs	Eridani, ē-rĭd'à-nī'	Eri	The River
Fornax, fôr'năks	Fornacis, fôr-nās'ĭs	For	The Furnace
Gemini, jĕm'ĭ-nī	Geminorum, jĕm'ĭ-nôr'ŭm	Gem	The Twins
Grus, grŭs	Gruis, grōō'ĭs	Gru	The Crane (bird)
Hercules, hûr'kū-lēz	Herculis, hûr'kū-lĭs	Her	The Son of Zeus
Horologium, hŏr'ō-lō'jĭ-ŭm	Horologii, hŏr'ō-lō'jĭ-ī	Hor	The Clock
Hydra, hī'drà	Hydrae, hī'drē	Hya	The Water Snake (♀)
Hydrus, hī'drŭs	Hydri, hī'drī	Hyi	The Water Snake (♂)
Indus, ĭn'dŭs	Indi, ĭn'dī	Ind	The Indian
Lacerta, là-sûr'tà	Lacertae, là-sûr'tē	Lac	The Lizard

CONSTELLATIONS—NAMES AND PRONUNCIATIONS (continued)

Nominative & Pronunciation	Genitive & Pronunciation	Abbr.	Meaning
Leo, lē'ō	Leonis, lē'ō'nĭs	Leo	The Lion
Leo Minor, lē'ō mī'nēr	Leonis Minoris	LMi	The Little Lion
	lē'ō'nĭs mī-nôr'ĭs		
Lepus, lē'pŭs	Leporis, lĕp'ôr-ĭs	Lep	The Hare
Libra, lē'brȧ	Librae, lē'brē	Lib	The Balance
Lupus, loo'pŭs	Lupi, loo'pī	Lup	The Wolf
Lynx, lĭnks	Lyncis, lĭn'sĭs	Lyn	The Lynx
Lyra, lī'rȧ	Lyrae, lī'rē	Lyr	The Lyre
Mensa, mĕn'sȧ	Mensae, mĕn'sē	Men	The Table
Microscopium	Microscopii	Mic	The Microscope
mī'krō-skō'pē-ŭm	mī'krō-skō'pē-ī'		
Monoceros, mō-nŏs'ēr-ŏs	Monocerotis, mō-nŏs'ēr-ō'tĭs	Mon	The Unicorn
Musca, mŭs'kȧ	Muscae, mŭs'ē	Mus	The Fly
Norma, nôr'mȧ	Normae, nôr'mē	Nor	The Square
Octans, ŏk'tănz	Octantis, ŏk'tăn'tĭs	Oct	The Octant
Ophiuchus, ō'fē-ū'kŭs	Ophiuchi, ō'fē-ū'kī	Oph	The Serpent-bearer
Orion, ō-rī'ŏn	Orionis, ôr'ē-ō'nĭs	Ori	The Hunter
Pavo, pā'vō	Pavonis, pȧ-vō'nĭs	Pav	The Peacock
Pegasus, pĕg'ȧ-sŭs	Pegasi, pĕg'ȧ-sī	Peg	The Winged Horse
Perseus, pûr'sē-ŭs	Persei, pûr'sē-ī'	Per	Rescuer of
			Andromeda
Phoenix, fē'nĭks	Phoenicis, fē-nī'cĭs	Phe	The Phoenix
Pictor, pĭk'tēr	Pictonis, pĭk-tor'ĭs	Pic	The Painter
Pisces, pī'sēz	Piscium, pĭsh'ē-ŭm	Psc	The Fishes
Piscis Austrinus,	Piscis Austrini,	PsA	The Southern Fish
pī'sĭs ôs-trī'nŭs	pī'sĭs ôs-trī'nī		
Puppis, pŭp'ĭs	Puppis, pŭp'ĭs	Pup	The Stern
Pyxis, pĭk'sĭs	Pyxidis, pĭk'sĭ-dĭs	Pyx	The Compass
Reticulum, rē-tĭk'-ū-lŭm	Reticuli, rē-tĭk'-ū-lī	Ret	The Reticle
Sagitta, sȧ-jĭt'ȧ	Sagittae, sȧ-jĭt'ē	Sge	The Arrow
Sagittarius, săj'ĭ-târ'ē-ŭs	Sagittarii, săj'ĭ-târ'ē-ī'	Sgr	The Archer
Scorpius, skôr'pē-ŭs	Scorpii, skôr'pē-ī	Sco	The Scorpion
Sculptor, skŭlp'tēr	Sculptoris, skŭlp'tôr'ĭs	Scl	The Sculptor
Scutum, skū'tŭm	Scuti, skoo'tī	Sct	The Shield
Serpens, sûr'pĕnz	Serpentis, sûr-pĕn'tĭs	Ser	The Serpent
Sextans, sĕks'tănz	Sextantis, sĕks-tăn'tĭs	Sex	The Sextant
Taurus, tôr'ŭs	Tauri, tôr'ī	Tau	The Bull
Telescopium tĕl'ȧ-skō'pē-ŭm	Telescopii, tĕl'ȧ-skō'pē-ī	Tel	The Telescope
Triangulum, trī-ăng'gū-lŭm	Trianguli, trī-ăng'gū-lī'	Tri	The Triangle
Triangulum Australe	Trianguli Australis	TrA	The Southern
trī-ăng'gū-lŭm ôs-trā'lē	trī-ăng'gū-lī' ôs-trā'lĭs		Triangle
Tucana, too-kăn'ȧ	Tucanae, too-kăn'ē	Tuc	The Toucan
Ursa Major, ûr'sȧ mā'jēr	Ursae Majoris, ûr'sē mȧ-jôr'ĭs	UMa	The Great Bear
Ursa Minor, ûr'sȧ mī'nēr	Ursae Minoris, ûr'sē mī-nôr'ĭs	UMi	The Little Bear
Vela, vē'lȧ	Velorum, vē-lôr'ŭm	Vel	The Sails
Virgo, vûr'gō	Virginis, vûr'jĭn-ĭs	Vir	The Maiden
Volans, vō'lănz	Volantis, vō-lăn'tĭs	Vol	The Flying Fish
Vulpecula, vŭl-pĕk'ū-lȧ	Vulpeculae, vŭl-pĕk'ū-lē'	Vul	The Fox

ā dāte; ă tăp; â câre; ȧ ȧsk; ē wē; ĕ mĕt; ē makēr; ī īce; ĭ bĭt; ō gō; ŏ hŏt; ô ôrb; oo moon; ū ūnite; ŭ ŭp; û ûrn

In terms of area (based on the official IAU boundaries), of the 88 constellations the 3 largest are Hydra (1303 square degrees), Virgo (1294), and Ursa Major (1280); the 3 smallest: Sagitta (80), Equuleus (72), and Crux (68). A complete list of the areas of the constellations appears in the 1972 edition of *The Handbook of the British Astronomical Association*, and was reproduced in the June 1976 issue of *Sky and Telescope* (p. 408).

FINDING LIST OF SOME NAMED STARS

Name & Pronunciation	Con.	RA	Name & Pronunciation	Con.	RA
Acamar, ā′kà-màr	θ Eri	2	Gienah, jē′nà	γ Crv	12
Achernar, ā′kĕr-nàr	α Eri	1	Hadar, hăd′ar	β Cen	14
Acrux, ā′krŭks	α Cru	12	Hamal, hăm′al	α Ari	2
Adara, à-dā′rà	ε CMa	6	Kaus Australis,	ε Sgr	18
Al Na′ir, ăl-nâr′	α Gru	22	kôs ôs-trā′lĭs		
Albireo, ăl-bĭr′ē-ō	β Cyg	19	Kochab, kō′kăb	β UMi	14
Alcor, ăl-kôr′	80 UMa	13	Markab, màr′kăb	α Peg	23
Alcyone, ăl-sī′ō-nē	η Tau	3	Megrez, me′grĕz	δ UMa	12
Aldebaran,	α Tau	4	Menkar, mĕn′kàr	α Cet	3
ăl-dĕb′à-ràn			Menkent, mĕn′kĕnt	τ Cen	14
Alderamin,	α Cep	21	Merak, mē′răk	β UMa	11
ăl-dĕr′à-mĭn			Merope, mĕr′ō-pē	23 Tau	3
Algeiba, ăl-jē′bà	γ Leo	10	Miaplacidus,	β Car	9
Algenib, ăl-jē′nĭb	γ Peg	0	mī′à-plăs′ĭ-dŭs		
Algol, ăl′gŏl	β Per	3	Mintaka, mĭn-tà′kà	δ Ori	5
Alioth, ăl′ĭ-ŏth	ε UMa	12	Mira, mī′rà	o Cet	2
Alkaid, ăl-kād′	η UMa	13	Mirach, mī′răk	β And	1
Almach, ăl′măk	γ And	2	Mirfak, mir′făk	α Per	3
Alnilam, ăl-nī′lăm	ε Ori	5	Mizar, mi′zàr	ζ UMa	13
Alphard, ăl′fàrd	α Hya	9	Nunki, nŭn′kē	σ Sgr	18
Alphecca, ăl-fĕk′à	α CrB	15	Peacock, pē′kŏk	α Pav	20
Alpheratz, ăl-fē′răts	α And	0	Phecda, fĕk′dà	γ UMa	11
Altair, ăl-târ′	α Aqi	19	Polaris, pō-lâr′ĭs	α UMi	2
Ankaa, ăn′kà	α Phe	0	Pollux, pŏl′ŭks	β Gem	7
Antares, ăn-tā′rēs	α Sco	16	Procyon, prō′sĭ-ŏn	α CMi	7
Arcturus, ark-tū′rŭs	α Boo	14	Pulcherrima,	ε Boo	14
Atria, ā′trĭ-a	α TrA	16	pŭl-kĕr′ĭ-mà		
Avior, ă-vĭ-ôr′	ε Car	8	Ras-Algethi,	α Her	17
Bellatrix, bĕ-lā′trĭks	γ Ori	5	ràs′ăl-jē′thē		
Betelgeuse, bĕt′ĕl-jūz	α Ori	5	Rasalhague, ràs′ăl-hā′gwē	α Oph	17
Canopus, kà-nō′pŭs	α Car	6	Regulus, rĕg′ū-lŭs	α Leo	10
Capella, kàp-pĕl′à	α Aur	5	Rigel, rī′gĕl	β Ori	5
Caph, kăf	β Cas	0	Rigil Kentaurus,	α Cen	14
Castor, kàs′tĕr	α Gem	7	rī′jĭl kĕn-tô′rŭs		
Cor Caroli, kôr kăr′ō-lī	α CVn	12	Sabik, sā′bĭk	η Oph	17
Deneb, dĕn′ĕb	α Cyg	20	Scheat, shē′ăt	β Peg	23
Denebola, dĕn-nĕb′ō-la	β Leo	11	Schedar, shĕd′àr	α Cas	0
Diphda, dĭf′dà	β Cet	0	Shaula, shô′là	λ Sco	17
Dubhe, dŭb′ē	α UMa	11	Sirius, sĭr′ĭ-ŭs	α CMa	6
Elnath, ĕl′năth	β Tau	5	Spica, spī′kà	α Vir	13
Eltanin, ĕl-tā′nĭn	γ Dra	17	Suhail, sŭ-hāl′	λ Vel	9
Enif, ĕn′ĭf	ε Peg	21	Thuban, thoo′ban	α Dra	14
Fomalhaut, fō′măl-ôt	α PsA	22	Vega, ve′gà	α Lyr	18
Gacrux, gà′krŭks	γ Cru	12	Zubenelgenubi,	α Lib	14
Gemma, jĕm′à	α CrB	15	zoo-bĕn′ĕl-jĕ-nū′bē		

Key to pronunciation on previous page.

THE BRIGHTEST STARS
BY ROBERT F. GARRISON AND TOOMAS KARMO

In the following tables the 314 stars brighter than apparent magnitude 3.55 are listed.

Star Name: For stars that are visual doubles the data are for the brighter component (A). The brightness and separation of the second component (B) are given in the last column. Sometimes the double is too close to be conveniently resolved; in these cases the data refer to the combined light (AB). In interpreting such data the magnitudes of the two components must be considered. The given positions are for 2002.5.

Apparent Visual Magnitude (*V*): These magnitudes are based on photoelectric observations compiled for the HIPPARCOS catalogue. The *V* filter is yellow and corresponds roughly to the response of the eye. The photometric system is that of H.L. Johnson and W.W. Morgan in *Ap. J., 117*, p. 313, 1953. It is as likely as not that the true magnitude is within 0.03 of the quoted figure, on the average. Variability, range, and period of variable stars are given in the Remarks column.

Colour Index (*B–V*): The blue magnitude *B* is the brightness of a star as observed photoelectrically through a blue filter. The difference *B–V* is therefore a measure of the colour of a star. There is a close relation between *B–V* and the spectral type, but some of the stars are reddened by interstellar dust. The probable error of a value of *B–V* is about 0.02 at most. The *B–V* values are from the HIPPARCOS catalogue.

Spectral Classification (**MK Type**): A "temperature" type (O, B, A, F, G, K, M) is given first, followed by a finer subtype (0–9) and a "luminosity" class (Roman numerals I–V, with an "a" or "b" added occasionally to indicate slightly brighter or fainter). The sequences are as follows: the O stars are hottest, M stars are coolest, Ia stars are the most luminous supergiants, III stars are giants, and V stars are the most numerous; the V stars are known as dwarfs or main-sequence stars. Other symbols used in the column are "p" for peculiar, "e" for hydrogen emission, "m" for strong metallic lines, "f" for broad, nonhydrogen emission in hot stars, and "n" or "nn" for unusually broad lines (= rotation). The table contains the best types available, either from the literature or from Garrison's own plates.

Parallax (**π**): Parallaxes are shown in milliarcseconds (mas) and have been taken from the HIPPARCOS catalogue.

Absolute Visual Magnitude (*M_V*) and *Distance in Light-Years* (*D*): The absolute magnitudes and distances are newly derived from the parallaxes. The exceptions are marked by a colon following the absolute magnitude and are determined from a calibration of the spectral classification. The effect of the absorption of light was corrected by comparing the spectral classification and the *B–V* using an intrinsic-colour calibration by Garrison (unpublished).

Proper Motion (**μ**) and *Position Angle* (**PA**): From *The Bright Star Catalogue,* by D. Hoffleit and C. Jaschek, Yale University Press, 1982. Proper motions given are the absolute value of the vector resultant from the individual-coordinate proper motions given in *The Bright Star Catalogue*. The position angle indicates the direction of the proper motion with an angle measured in degrees from the north through the east.

Radial Velocity (**RV**): From *The Bright Star Catalogue* referenced above. The symbol "V" indicates a variable velocity; an orbit is usually not known. On the other hand, "SB" indicates a spectroscopic binary, which is an unresolved system whose duplicity is revealed by periodic oscillations of the lines in its spectrum and for which an orbit is generally known. If the lines of both stars are detectable, the symbol "SB2" is used; "+" indicates motion away from, "–" toward, the observer.

Remarks: This column contains data on companions and variability as well as notes on the spectra. Traditional names have been selected from *The Bright Star Catalogue*. The navigation stars are in **bold type.**

TABLE OF BRIGHTEST STARS

Star Name	RA (2002.5) h m	Dec ° ′	V	B–V	MK Type	π mas	Mv	D ly	μ ″/yr	PA °	RV km/s	Remarks	
Sun	—	—	-26.75	0.63	G2 V	—	4.8	8 lm	—	—	varies		Sun
α And	0 08.5	+29 06	2.07	-0.04	B9p IV: (HgMn)	34	-0.5	97	0.209	139	-12 SB	var.: 2.25–2.31, 0.10 d	Alpheratz
β Cas	0 09.3	+59 10	2.28	0.38	F2 III	60	1.2	54	0.555	109	+11 SB		Caph
γ Peg	0 13.4	+15 12	2.83	-0.19	B2 IV	10	-2.4	333	0.008	176	+4 SB	var.: 2.80–2.87, 0.15 d	Algenib
β Hyi	0 25.7	-77 15	2.82	0.62	G2 IV	134	3.4	24	2.255	82	23		
α Phe	0 26.5	-42 18	2.40	1.08	K0 IIIb	42	-0.3	77	0.442	152	+75 SB		Ankaa
δ And A	0 39.5	+30 52	3.27	1.27	K3 III	32	0.9	101	0.161	122	-7 SB		
α Cas	0 40.7	+56 33	2.24	1.17	K0 IIIa	14	-2.5	228	0.058	117	-4 V?		Schedar
β Cet	0 43.8	-17 59	2.04	1.02	K0 III	34	-1.0	96	0.234	81	13		Diphda
η Cas A	0 49.3	+57 50	3.46	0.59	G0 V	168	4.6	19	1.218	115	+9 SB	B: 7.51, K4 Ve, 12″	
γ Cas	0 56.9	+60 44	2.15	-0.05	B0 IVnpe (shell)	5	-5.0	613	0.026	90	-7 SB	var.: 1.6–3.0; B: 8.8, 2″	
β Phe AB	1 06.1	-46 42	3.32	0.89	G8 III	16	0.3:	147	0.030	279	-1	AB similar in light, spectrum, 1″	
η Cet	1 08.8	-10 10	3.46	1.16	K1.5 III CN1	28	-0.1	118	0.250	122	12		
β And	1 09.9	+35 38	2.07	1.58	M0 IIIa	16	-1.9	199	0.210	121	+3 V		Mirach
δ Cas	1 26.0	+60 15	2.66	0.16	A5 IV	33	0.2	99	0.303	99	+7 SB	ecl.? 2.68–2.76, 759 d	Ruchbah
γ Phe	1 28.5	-43 18	3.41	1.54	K7 IIIa	14	-1.6	234	0.204	184	+26 SB	var.: 3.39–3.49	
α Eri	1 37.7	-57 13	0.45	-0.16	B3 Vnp (shell)	23	-2.9	144	0.108	105	+16 V		Achernar
τ Cet	1 44.3	-15 56	3.49	0.73	G8 V	274	5.7	12	1.921	296	-16		
α Tri	1 53.3	+29 36	3.42	0.49	F6 IV	51	1.8	64	0.230	177	-13 SB		Metallah
ε Cas	1 54.6	+63 41	3.35	-0.15	B3 IV:p (shell)	7	-2.5	442	0.036	114	-8 V		Segin
β Ari	1 54.9	+20 49	2.64	0.17	A4 V	55	1.3	60	0.145	138	-2 SB		Sharatan
α Hyi	1 58.9	-61 34	2.86	0.29	F0 III–IVn	46	1.1	71	0.271	83	+1 V		
γ And A	2 04.1	+42 20	2.10	1.87	K3 IIb	9	-3.0	355	0.066	136	-12 SB	B: 5.4, B9 V, 10″; C: 6.2, A0 V; BC: 1″	Almaak
α Ari	2 07.4	+23 28	2.01	1.15	K2 IIab	49	0.5	66	0.238	127	-14 SB	calcium weak?	Hamal
β Tri	2 09.7	+34 59	3.01	1.04	A5 IV	26	0.1	124	0.153	104	+10 SB2		
ο Cet A	2 19.5	-2 59	6.47	0.97	M5–10 IIIe	8	3.0	418	0.232	183	+64 V	LPV, 2–10; B: VZ Cet, 9.5v, Bpe, 1″	Mira
α UMi A	2 34.5	+89 16	1.97	0.64	F5–8 Ib	8	-4.1	431	0.046	95	-17 SB	low amp. Cep., 4 d; B: 8.2, F3 V, 18″	Polaris
γ Cet AB	2 43.5	+3 15	3.56	0.11	A2 Va	40	1.3	82	0.203	224	-5 V	A: 3.57; B: 6.23, 3″	Kaffaljidhma
θ Eri A	2 58.4	-40 18	3.28	0.17	A5 IV	20	-0.3	161	0.065	294	+12 SB2	B: 4.35, A1 Va, 8″	Acamar
α Cet	3 02.4	+4 06	2.54	1.63	M2 III	15	-1.7	220	0.075	189	-26		Menkar
γ Per	3 05.0	+53 31	2.91	0.72	G8 III + A2 V	13	-0.8:	196	0.002	180	+3 SB	composite spectrum	
ρ Per	3 05.4	+38 51	3.32	1.53	M4 II	10	-1.3	325	0.165	128	28	semiregular var.: 3.3–4.0	
β Per	3 08.4	+40 58	2.09	0.00	B8 V + F:	35	-0.5	93	0.004	124	+4 SB	ecl.: 2.12–3.4,2.87 d; composite	Algol
α Per	3 24.6	+49 52	1.79	0.48	F5 Ib	6	-4.9	592	0.033	131	-2 V	in cluster	Mirphak
δ Per	3 43.2	+47 47	3.01	-0.13	B5 IIIn	6	-3.1	528	0.042	139	+4 SB		
ο Eri	3 43.4	-9 46	3.52	0.92	K0 IV	111	3.4	29	0.752	352	-6		

TABLE OF BRIGHTEST STARS (continued)

Star Name	RA (2002.5) h m	Dec ° ′	V	B–V	MK Type	π mas	Mv	D ly	μ ″/yr	PA °	RV km/s	Remarks	Name
γ Hyi	3 47.2	−74 14	3.26	1.59	M2 III	15	−1.0	214	0.128	24	16		
η Tau	3 47.7	+24 06	2.85	−0.09	B7 IIIn	9	−1.6:	212	0.048	157	+10 V?	in Pleiades	Alcyone
ζ Per A	3 54.4	+31 53	2.84	0.27	B1 Ib	3	−6.0	982	0.011	146	+20 SB	B: 9.16, B8 V, 13″	
ε Per A	3 58.0	+40 01	2.90	−0.20	B0.5 IV	6	−3.4	538	0.029	145	+1 SB2	B: 7.39, B9.5 V, 9″	
γ Eri	3 58.2	−13 30	2.97	1.59	M1 IIIb	15	−1.6	221	0.124	153	62	calcium, chromium weak	Zaurak
λ Tau A	4 00.9	+12 30	3.41	−0.10	B3 V	9	−2.3	370	0.011	218	+18 SB2	ecl.: 3.3–3.8, 3.95 d; B: A4 IV	
α Ret A	4 14.5	−62 28	3.33	0.92	G8 II-III	20	−0.5	163	0.068	43	+36 SB?		
θ² Tau	4 28.8	+15 53	3.40	0.18	A7 III	22	0.2	149	0.105	103	+40 SB	in Hyades	
ε Tau	4 28.9	+19 11	3.53	1.01	K0 III	21	0.1	155	0.114	108	39	in Hyades	Ain
α Dor AB	4 34.1	−55 03	3.62	−0.08	A0p V: (Si)	19	0.2	176	0.051	89	26	A: 3.8; B: 4.3, B9 IV, 0.2″	
α Tau A	4 36.1	+16 30	0.87	1.54	K5 III	50	−0.8	65	0.200	161	+54 SB	var: 0.75–0.95	Aldebaran
π³ Ori	4 50.0	+06 58	3.19	0.48	F6 V	125	3.7	26	0.463	88	+24 SB2		
ι Aur	4 57.2	+33 10	2.69	1.49	K3 II	6	−3.6	512	0.018	167	18	var.?	Hassaleh
ε Aur A	5 02.2	+43 50	3.03	0.54	A9 Iae + B		−8.0:	7824	0.004	166	−3 SB	ecl.: 2.94–3.83, 9892 d	Al Anz
ε Lep	5 05.5	−22 22	3.19	1.46	K4 III	14	−2.0	227	0.073	166	1		
η Aur	5 06.7	+41 14	3.18	−0.15	B3 V	15	−1.2	219	0.073	157	+7 V?		Hoedus II
β Eri	5 08.0	−05 05	2.78	0.16	A3 IVn	37	0.4	89	0.128	231	−9		Kursa
μ Lep	5 13.0	−16 12	3.29	−0.11	B9p IV: (HgMn)	18	−0.4	184	0.043	129	28	var: 2.97–3.36, 2 d	
β Ori A	5 14.7	−08 12	0.18	−0.03	B8 Ia	4	−6.6	773	0.004	236	+21 SB	B: 7.6, B5 V, 9″; C: 7.6; BC: 0.1″	Rigel
α Aur AB	5 16.9	+45 60	0.08	0.80	G6:III + G2:III	77	−0.8	42	0.430	169	+30 SB	composite; A: 0.6; B: 1.1, 0.04″	Capella
η Ori AB	5 24.6	−02 23	3.35	−0.24	B0.5 V + B	4	−3.9	901	0.003	288	+20 SB2	ecl.: 3.14–3.35.8 d; A: 3.6; B: 5.0, 1.6″	
γ Ori	5 25.3	+06 21	1.64	−0.22	B2 III	13	−2.8	243	0.018	221	+18 SB?		Bellatrix
β Tau	5 26.6	+28 37	1.65	−0.13	B7 III	25	−1.3	131	0.178	172	+9 V		Alnath
β Lep A	5 28.4	−20 45	2.81	0.81	G5 II	20	−0.7	159	0.090	185	−14	B: 7.4, 2.6″	
δ Ori A	5 32.2	−0 18	2.25	−0.18	O9.5 II	4	−5.4	916	0.002	252	+16 SB	ecl.: 1.94–2.13, 5.7 d	Mintaka
α Lep	5 32.9	−17 50	2.58	0.21	F0 Ib	3	−5.5	1283	0.006	279	24		Arneb
β Dor	5 33.6	−62 30	3.76	0.64	F7-G2 Ib	3	−4.2	1038	0.007	8	+7 V	Cepheid: 3.43–4.06, 9.8 d	
λ Ori A	5 35.4	+09 56	3.39	−0.16	O8 III	3	−4.6	1055	0.006	191	34	B: 5.61, B0 V, 4″	Meissa
ι Ori A	5 35.6	−05 55	2.75	−0.21	O9 III	2	−5.6	1325	0.005	284	+22 SB2	B: 7.3, B7 IIIp(He wk), 11″	Nair al Saif
ε Ori	5 36.4	−01 12	1.69	−0.18	B0 Ia	2	−6.6	1342	0.004	236	+26 SB		Alnilam
ζ Tau	5 37.8	+21 08	2.97	−0.15	B2 IIIpe (shell)	8	−2.8	417	0.023	177	+20 SB	var: 2.90–3.03; B: 5.0, 0.007″	
α Col A	5 39.7	−34 05	2.65	−0.12	B7 IV	12	−1.9	268	0.026	178	+35 V?		Phaet
ζ Ori A	5 40.9	−01 57	1.74	−0.20	O9.5 Ib	4	−5.5	817	0.002	207	+18 SB		Alnitak
κ Lep	5 47.1	−14 50	3.55	0.10	A2 Vann	46	1.7	70	0.023	263	+20 SB?		
κ Ori	5 48.0	−09 40	2.07	−0.17	B0.5 Ia	5	−5.0:	815	0.006	211	+21 V?	B: 4.2, B0 III, 2.4″	Saiph
β Col	5 51.0	−35 46	3.12	1.15	K1.5 III	38	0.2	86	0.405	7	+89 V		Wezn

TABLE OF BRIGHTEST STARS (continued)

Star Name	RA (2002.5) h m	Dec ° '	V	B–V	MK Type	π mas	Mv	D ly	μ "/yr	PA °	RV km/s	Remarks	
α Ori	5 55.3	+7 24	0.45	1.50	M2 Iab	8	−5.0:	522	0.028	68	+21 SB	var: 0.4–1.3	**Betelgeuse**
β Aur	5 59.8	+44 57	1.90	0.08	A1 IV	40	−0.2	82	0.055	269	−18 SB2	ecl.: 1.93–2.02, 4 d (= mags.)	**Menkalinan**
θ Aur AB	5 59.9	+37 13	2.65	−0.08	A0p II: (Si)	19	−1.0	173	0.097	149	+30 SB	B: 7.2, G2 V, 4″	
η Gem	6 15.0	+22 31	3.31	1.60	M3 III	9	−1.8	349	0.068	259	+19 SB	var: 3.3–3.9; B: 8.8, 1.6″	Propus
ζ CMa	6 20.4	−30 03	3.02	−0.16	B2.5 V	10	−2.2	336	0.006	59	+32 SB		Phurud
β CMa	6 22.8	−17 57	1.98	−0.24	B1 II–III	7	−4.0	499	0.014	253	+34 SB	var: 1.93–2.00, 0.25 d	Murzim
μ Gem	6 23.1	+22 31	2.87	1.62	M3 IIIab	14	−1.5	232	0.125	154	55		Tejat Posterior
α Car	6 24.0	−52 41	−0.62	0.16	A9 Ib	10	−5.4	313	0.034	50	21	var: 2.76–3.02	**Canopus**
ν Pup	6 37.8	−43 12	3.17	−0.10	B8 IIIn	8	−2.4	423	0.010	234	+28 SB		
γ Gem	6 37.9	+16 24	1.93	0.00	A1 IVs	31	−0.6	105	0.061	136	−13 SB		Alhena
ε Gem	6 44.1	+25 08	3.06	1.38	G8 Ib	4	−5.0	903	0.016	195	+10 SB		Mebsuta
α CMa A	6 45.3	−16 43	−1.44	0.01	A0mA1 Va	379	1.5	9	1.324	204	−8 SB	B: 8.5, WDA, 50 y, 10″ (1980)	**Sirius**
ξ Gem	6 45.5	+12 53	3.35	0.44	F5 IV	57	2.2	57	0.224	211	+25 V?		Alzirr
α Pic	6 48.2	−61 57	3.24	0.23	A6 Vn	33	0.7	99	0.275	345	21		
τ Pup	6 50.0	−50 37	2.94	1.21	K1 III	18	−1.9	183	0.079	157	+36 SB		
ε CMa A	6 58.7	−28 58	1.50	−0.21	B2 II	8	−4.1	431	0.002	27	27		**Adara**
σ CMa	7 01.8	−27 56	3.49	1.73	K7 Ib	3	−4.7	1216	0.008	284	22	var: 3.43–3.49	
o² CMa	7 03.2	−23 50	3.02	−0.08	B3 Ia	1	−6.6	2567	0.007	262	+48 SB		
δ CMa	7 08.5	−26 24	1.83	0.67	F8 Ia	2	−7.2	1791	0.008	291	+34 SB		Wezen
L₂ Pup	7 13.6	−44 38	4.42	1.33	M5 IIIe	16	1.5	198	0.346	18	+53 V?	long-period var.: 2.6–6.2	HR2748
π Pup	7 17.2	−37 06	2.86	1.62	K3 Ib	3	−5.1	1094	0.012	284	16		
δ Gem AB	7 20.3	+21 59	3.50	0.37	F0 IV	55	2.2	59	0.029	241	+4 SB	B: 8.2, K3 V, 0.2″	Wasat
η CMa	7 24.2	−29 18	2.45	−0.08	B5 Ia	1	−7.5	3196	0.008	284	+41 V		Aludra
β CMi	7 27.4	+8 18	2.89	−0.10	B8 V	19	−0.8	170	0.065	233	+22 SB		Gomeisa
σ Pup A	7 29.3	−43 19	3.25	1.51	K5 III	18	−1.6	184	0.195	342	+88 SB	B: 8.6, G5: V, 22″	
α Gem A	7 34.8	+31 53	1.58	0.03	A1mA2 Va	63	0.6	52	0.199	241	+6 SB	AB: 3″ separation	Castor
α Gem B	7 34.9	+31 53	1.93	0.03	A2mA5 V:	63	1.0	52	0.199	239	−1 SB	BA: 3″ separation	Castor
α CMi A	7 39.5	+5 13	0.41	0.43	F5 IV–V	286	2.8	11	1.248	214	−3 SB	B: 10.3, 4″	**Procyon**
β Gem	7 45.5	+28 01	1.16	0.99	K0 IIIb	97	1.1	34	0.629	265	+3 V		**Pollux**
ξ Pup	7 49.5	−24 52	3.34	1.22	G6 Ia	2	−7.5:	3260	0.033	240	+3 SB		
χ Car	7 56.8	−52 59	3.46	−0.18	B3 IVp (note)	8	−2.0	387	0.042	306	+19 V	Si II strong	
ζ Pup	8 03.6	−40 00	2.21	−0.27	O5 Iafn	2	−6.1	1399	0.033	290	−24 V?		Naos
ρ Pup	8 07.7	−24 18	2.83	0.46	F2mF5 II: (var)	52	1.4	63	0.100	290	+46 SB2	delta Del spec.; var.: 2.68–2.78, 0.14 d	
γ² Vel	8 09.6	−47 20	1.75	−0.15	WC8 + O9 I:	4	−5.8	840	0.007	304	+35 SB2	var: 1.6–1.8, 154 s	Suhail al Muhlif
β Cnc	8 16.7	+9 11	3.59	1.48	K4 III	11	−1.2	290	0.068	220	22		Altarf
ε Car	8 22.5	−59 31	2.17	1.20	K3:III + B2:V	5	−4.8	632	0.030	301	2	ecl.? 3.1–3.4p, 785 d	Avior

TABLE OF BRIGHTEST STARS (continued)

Star Name	RA (2002.5) h m	Dec ° '	V	B–V	MK Type	π mas	Mv	D ly	μ "/yr	PA °	RV km/s	Remarks
ο UMa A	8 30.5	+60 43	3.35	0.86	G5 III	18	−0.3	184	0.171	230	20	var: 3.3–3.8, 358 d — Talitha
δ Vel AB	8 44.7	−54 43	1.99	0.04	A1 Va	41	0.0	80	0.082	164	+2 V?	B: 5.0, 2" — Suhail
ε Hya ABC	8 46.9	+6 24	3.38	0.69	G5:III + A:	24	0.0	135	0.198	254	+36 SB	composite A: 3.8; B: 4.7, 0.2"; C: 7.8,3"
ζ Hya	8 55.5	+5 56	3.11	0.98	G9 II-III	22	−0.2	151	0.101	277	23	
λ UMa A	8 59.4	+48 02	3.12	0.22	A7 IVn	68	2.2	48	0.501	242	+9 SB	BC: 10.8. M1 V, 4"
ι Vel	9 08.0	−43 26	2.23	1.67	K4 Ib–IIa	6	−4.8	573	0.026	299	18	var: 2.14–2.22
a Car	9 11.0	−58 58	3.43	−0.19	B2 IV–V	8	−2.2	418	0.028	283	+23 SB2	ecl.: 3.2–3.6, 6.7 d — HR3659
β Car	9 13.2	−69 43	1.67	0.07	A1 III	29	−1.1	111	0.183	304	−5 V?	Miaplacidus
ι Car	9 17.1	−59 17	2.21	0.19	A7 Ib	5	−4.4	694	0.019	285	13	Turais
α Lyn	9 21.2	+34 23	3.14	1.55	K7 IIIab	15	−1.3	222	0.223	273	38	
κ Vel	9 22.2	−55 01	2.47	−0.14	B2 IV–V	6	−3.9	539	0.012	315	+22 SB	
α Hya	9 27.8	−8 40	1.99	1.44	K3 II-III	18	−2.1	177	0.034	327	−4 V?	Alphard
N Vel	9 31.2	−57 02	3.16	1.54	K5 III	14	−1.3	238	0.034	268	−14	HR3803
θ UMa	9 33.1	+51 41	3.17	0.48	F6 IV	74	2.6	44	1.094	252	+15 SB	
ο Leo AB	9 41.3	+9 53	3.52	0.52	F5 II + A5?	24	0.1	135	0.149	254	+27 SB	A: occ. bin. (= mags.) — Subra
l Car	9 45.3	−62 31	3.69	1.01	F9–G5 Ib	2	−5.8	1509	0.016	281	+4 V	Cepheid var: 3.39–4.12, 35.5 d — HR3884
ε Leo	9 46.1	+23 46	2.97	0.81	G2 II	13	−1.6	251	0.048	252	+4 V?	Ras Elased Australis
υ Car AB	9 47.1	−65 04	3.10	0.29	A6 II	2	−2.5:	326	0.012	305	14	B: 6.26, B7 III, 5"
φ Vel	9 56.9	−54 34	3.52	−0.07	B5 Ib	2	−5.5	1929	0.013	293	14	
η Leo	10 07.6	+16 45	3.48	−0.03	A0 Ib	2	−5.5	2131	0.006	189	+3 V	B: 4.5, 0.1"
α Leo A	10 08.5	+11 57	1.36	−0.09	B7 Vn	42	−0.6	77	0.248	271	+6 SB	**Regulus**
ω Car	10 13.8	−70 03	3.29	−0.07	B8 IIIn	9	−2.1	370	0.032	275	+7 V	
ζ Leo	10 16.9	+23 24	3.43	0.31	F0 IIIa	13	−1.1	260	0.023	124	−16 SB	Adhafera
q Car	10 17.1	−61 21	3.39	1.54	K3 IIa	4	−4.2	736	0.027	276	8	var: 3.36–3.42 — HR4050
λ UMa	10 17.3	+42 54	3.45	0.03	A1 IV	24	0.4	134	0.170	255	+18 V	Tania Borealis
γ Leo A	10 20.2	+19 50	2.61	1.13	K1 IIIb Fe-0.5	26	−0.7	126	0.342	116	−37 SB	AB: 5" separation — Algieba
γ Leo B	10 20.2	+19 50	3.16	1.42	G7 III Fe-1	26	−1.9	126	0.358	119	−36 SB	BA: 5" separation
μ UMa	10 22.5	+41 29	3.06	1.60	M0 IIIp	13	−1.5	249	0.088	290	−21 SB	Ca II emission — Tania Australis
p Car	10 32.0	−61 42	3.30	−0.09	B4 Vne	7	−2.0:	326	0.021	287	26	var: 3.27–3.37 — HR4140
θ Car	10 43.0	−64 24	2.74	−0.22	B0.5 Vp	28	−3.1	439	0.022	291	+24 SB	nitrogen enhanced
μ Vel AB	10 46.9	−49 26	2.90	1.07	G5 III + F8:V	28	−0.9	116	0.085	125	+6 SB	B: 6.4, 2"
ν Hya	10 49.8	−16 12	3.11	1.20	K2 III	24	−0.3	138	0.215	24	−1	
β UMa	11 02.0	+56 22	2.34	0.03	A0mA1 IV–V	41	0.4	79	0.087	70	−12 SB	Merak
α UMa AB	11 03.9	+61 44	1.81	1.06	K0 IIIa	26	−1.3	124	0.138	239	−9 SB	A: 1.86, B: 4.8. A8 V, <1" — Dubhe
ψ UMa	11 09.9	+44 29	3.00	1.14	K1 III	22	−0.5	147	0.075	245	−4	
δ Leo	11 14.3	+20 31	2.56	0.13	A4 IV	57	1.3	58	0.197	133	−20 V	Zosma

TABLE OF BRIGHTEST STARS (continued)

Star Name	RA (2002.5) h m	Dec ° ′	V	B–V	MK Type	π mas	Mv	D ly	μ ″/yr	PA °	RV km/s	Remarks	
θ Leo	11 14.3	+15 25	3.33	0.00	A2 IV (K var.)	18	-0.2	178	0.104	216	+8 V		Chort
ν UMa	11 18.6	+33 05	3.49	1.40	K3 III Ba0.3	8	-3.2	421	0.036	309	-9 SB	B: 9.5, 7″	Alula Borealis
ξ Hya	11 33.2	-31 52	3.54	0.95	G7 III	25	0.0	129	0.211	259	-5 V		
λ Cen	11 36.0	-63 02	3.11	-0.04	B9.5 IIn	8	-2.5	410	0.039	258	-1 V		
β Leo	11 49.2	+14 34	2.14	0.09	A3 Va	90	1.9	36	0.511	257	0 V		Denebola
γ UMa	11 54.0	+53 41	2.41	0.04	A0 Van	39	0.2	84	0.094	86	-13 SB		Phad
δ Cen	12 08.5	-50 44	2.58	-0.13	B2 IVne	8	-3.1	395	0.034	249	+11 V	var: 2.51-2.65	
ε Crv	12 10.3	-22 38	3.02	1.33	K2 III	11	-2.3	303	0.073	278	5		Minkar
δ Cru	12 15.3	-58 45	2.79	-0.19	B2 IV	9	-2.6	364	0.039	255	+22 V?	var: 2.25-2.31p, 3.7 h	
δ UMa	12 15.6	+57 01	3.32	0.08	A2 Van	40	1.4	81	0.102	88	-13 V		Megrez
γ Crv	12 16.0	-17 33	2.58	-0.11	B8 III	20	-0.9	165	0.163	276	-4 SB	sp. var.?	Gienah Ghurab
α Cru A	12 26.8	-63 06	1.25	-0.20	B0.5 IV	10	-4.0	321	0.030	236	-11 SB	AB: 5″	Acrux
α Cru B	12 26.8	-63 06	1.64	-0.18	B1 Vn	10	-3.6	321	0.031	248	-1	BA: 5″	
δ Crv A	12 30.0	-16 31	2.94	-0.01	B9.5 IVn	37	-2.0	88	0.255	236	+9 V	B: 8.26, K2 V, 24″	Algorab
γ Cru A	12 31.4	-57 07	1.59	1.60	M3.5 III	37	-0.7	88	0.269	174	21	var: 1.6-1.9	Gacrux
β Crv	12 34.5	-23 24	2.65	0.89	G5 II	23	-0.5	140	0.059	179	-8		Kraz
α Mus	12 37.3	-69 09	2.69	-0.18	B2 IV–V	11	-2.3	306	0.043	248	+13 V	var: 2.17-2.24p, 2 h	
γ Cen A	12 41.7	-48 58	2.95	-0.02	A1 V	25	-0.1	130	0.190	268	-6 SB	AB: 5″	
γ Cen B	12 41.7	-48 58	2.85	-0.02	A0 IV	25	-0.1	130	0.190	268	-6 SB	BA: 5″	
γ Vir AB	12 41.8	-1 28	2.74	0.37	F1 V + F0mF2 V	85	2.2	39	0.567	271	-20 SB	BA: 5″	Porrima
β Mus AB	12 46.4	-68 07	3.51	-0.18	B2 V + B2.5 V	10	-2.2	424	0.041	233	+42 V	A: 3.48, B: 3.50, 4″	
β Cru	12 47.9	-59 42	1.25	-0.24	B0.5 III	9	-4.0	352	0.042	246	+16 SB	A: 3.58, B: 4.10, 1″	Becrux
ε UMa	12 54.2	+55 57	1.76	-0.02	A0p IV: (CrEu)	40	-0.2	81	0.109	95	-9 SB?	var: 1.23-1.31, 0.7 d?	Alioth
δ Vir	12 55.7	+3 23	3.39	1.57	M3 III	16	-0.5	202	0.474	263	-18 V?	var: 1.76-1.79, 5.1 d	Auva
α² CVn A	12 56.2	+38 18	2.85	-0.06	A0p (SiEu)	30	0.4	110	0.242	282	-3 V	B: 5.6, F0 V, 20″	Cor Caroli
ε Vir	13 02.4	+10 57	2.85	0.93	G9 IIIab	32	0.4	102	0.274	274	-14		Vindemiatrix
γ Hya	13 19.1	-23 11	2.99	0.92	G8 IIIa	25	-0.6	132	0.081	127	-5 V?		
ι Cen	13 20.8	-36 43	2.75	0.07	A2 Va	56	1.4	59	0.351	255	0		
ζ UMa A	13 24.0	+54 56	2.23	0.06	A1 Va	42	0.3	78	0.122	102	-6 SB2	B: 3.94, A1mA7 IV-V, 14″	Mizar
α Vir	13 25.3	-11 10	0.98	-0.24	B1 V	12	-3.6	262	0.054	232	+1 SB2	var: 0.97-1.04; mult. 3.1, 4.5, 7.5	Spica
ζ Vir	13 34.9	0 37	3.38	0.11	A2 IV	45	1.6	73	0.287	277	-13		Heze
ε Cen	13 40.1	-53 29	2.29	-0.17	B1 III	9	-3.3	376	0.028	232	3		
η UMa	13 47.6	+49 18	1.85	0.19	B3 V	32	-1.8	101	0.127	264	-11 SB?		Alkaid
ν Cen	13 49.7	-41 42	3.41	-0.23	B2 IV	7	-2.4	475	0.035	227	+9 SB		
μ Cen	13 49.8	-42 29	3.47	-0.17	B2 IV–V pne	6	-2.8	527	0.034	220	+9 SB	variable shell: 2.92-3.43	
η Boo	13 54.9	+18 23	2.68	0.58	G0 IV	88	2.4	37	0.370	190	0 SB		Mufrid

TABLE OF BRIGHTEST STARS (continued)

Star Name	RA (2002.5) h m	Dec ° '	V	B-V	MK Type	π mas	M_v	D ly	μ "/yr	PA °	RV km/s	Remarks	
ζ Cen	13 55.8	-47 18	2.55	-0.18	B2.5 IV	8	-2.9	384	0.072	232	+7 SB2		
β Cen AB	14 04.1	-60 22	0.58	-0.23	B1 III	6	-5.5	526	0.030	221	+6 SB	var: 0.61–0.68; B: 3.9, 1"	**Hadar**
π Hya	14 06.6	-26 41	3.25	1.09	K2 IIIb	32	0.2	101	0.049	163	27		
θ Cen	14 06.9	-36 22	2.06	1.01	K0 IIIb	54	0.1	61	0.738	225	1		Menkent
α Boo	14 15.9	+19 11	-0.05	1.24	K1.5 III Fe-0.5	89	-0.6	37	2.281	209	-5 V?	high space velocity	Arcturus
ι Lup	14 19.6	-46 04	3.55	-0.18	B2.5 IVn	9	-1.7	352	0.014	266	22		
γ Boo	14 32.2	+38 18	3.04	0.19	A7 IV+	38	1.0	85	0.189	322	-37 V		Seginus
η Cen	14 35.7	-42 10	2.33	-0.16	B1.5 IV pne	11	-2.8	308	0.049	226	0 SB	variable shell	
α Cen A	14 39.9	-60 50	0.14	0.71	G2 V	742	4.2	4	3.678	281	-25 SB	AB: 21"	**Rigil Kentaurus**
α Cen B	14 39.9	-60 51	1.24	0.90	K1 V	742	6.2	4	3.678	281	-21 V?	BA: 21"; C: Proxima, 12.4, M5e, 2°	
α Lup	14 42.1	-47 24	2.30	-0.15	B1.5 III	6	-4.1	548	0.026	220	+5 SB	var.: 2.28–2.31, 0.26 d	
α Cir	14 42.7	-64 59	3.18	0.26	A7p (Sr)	61	1.9	53	0.302	218	+7 SB?	B: 8.6, K5 V, 16"	
ε Boo AB	14 45.0	+27 04	2.65	1.34	K0 II-III+A0 V	16	-2.6	210	0.054	289	-17 V	A: 2.70; B: 5.12, 3"	Izar
β UMi	14 50.7	+74 09	2.07	1.97	K4 III	26	-1.1	126	0.036	286	+17 V		Kocab
α Lib A	14 51.1	-16 03	2.75	0.15	A3 III-IV	42	0.7	77	0.130	237	-23 SB		Zubenelgenubi
β Lup	14 58.7	-43 09	2.68	-0.18	B2 IV	6	-3.5	523	0.057	221	0 SB		
κ Cen	14 59.4	-42 07	3.34	-0.21	B2 V	6	-2.8	539	0.033	215	+8 SB		
β Boo	15 02.0	+40 23	3.49	0.96	G8 IIIa (note)	15	-0.7	219	0.056	235	-20	Ba 0.4. Fe -0.5	Nekkar
σ Lib	15 04.1	-25 17	3.25	1.67	M2.5 III	11	-1.9	292	0.087	237	-4	var.: 3.20–3.36	Brachium
ζ Lup	15 12.5	-52 07	3.41	0.92	G8 III	28	0.1	116	0.128	237	-10		
δ Boo	15 15.6	+33 18	3.46	0.96	G8 III Fe-1	28	0.6	117	0.143	144	-12 SB		
β Lib	15 17.1	-9 24	2.61	-0.07	B8 IIIn	20	-1.0	160	0.101	275	-35 SB		Zubenelschemali
γ TrA	15 19.1	-68 41	2.87	0.01	A1 IIIn	18	-0.8	183	0.067	243	-3 V		
γ UMi	15 20.7	+71 49	3.01	0.06	A3 III	7	-0.1:	147	0.031	308	-4 V		Pherkad
δ Lup	15 21.6	-40 40	3.22	-0.23	B1.5 IVn	6	-2.8	510	0.036	207	0 V?		
ε Lup AB	15 22.9	-44 42	3.56	-0.19	B2 IV-V	6	-2.5	504	0.024	232	+8 SB2	A: 3.5; B: 5.0, <1"	
ι Dra	15 25.0	+58 57	3.29	1.17	K2 III	32	0.8	102	0.020	311	-11		Ed Asich
α CrB	15 34.8	+26 43	2.22	0.03	A0 IV (composite)	44	0.3	75	0.151	127	+2 SB	ecl.: 2.21–2.32, 17.4 d	Alphekka
γ Lup AB	15 35.3	-41 10	3.40	-0.22	B2 IVn	6	-2.8	567	0.035	207	+2 V	A: 3.5; B: 3.6, <1"; similar spectra	
α Ser	15 44.4	+6 25	2.63	1.17	K2 IIIb CN1	45	0.9	73	0.143	72	+3 V?	var.?	Unukalhai
μ Ser	15 49.8	-3 26	3.54	-0.04	A0 III	21	0.3	156	0.094	253	-9 SB		
β TrA	15 55.4	-63 26	2.83	0.32	F0 IV	81	2.3	40	0.438	205	0		
π Sco A	15 59.1	-26 07	2.89	-0.18	B1 V + B2 V	7	-3.0	459	0.028	198	-3 SB2	A: occ. bin.: 3.4 + 4.5, 0.0003" sep.	
T CrB	15 59.5	+25 55	10.08	1.34	gM3: + Bep	0	-9.3	...	0.013	327	-29 SB	recurrent nova 1866, 1946; now V = 11	
η Lup A	16 00.3	-38 24	3.42	-0.21	B2.5 IVn	7	-2.5	493	0.040	213	+8 V	A: 3.47, B: 7.70, 15"	
δ Sco AB	16 00.5	-22 38	2.29	-0.12	B0.3 IV	8	-4.4:	522	0.027	202	-7 SB	AB: sep. < 1"; C: 4.9, B2 IV–V, 8"	Dschubba

TABLE OF BRIGHTEST STARS (continued)

Star Name	RA (2002.5) h m	Dec ° ′	V	B–V	MK Type	π mas	Mv	D ly	μ ″/yr	PA °	RV km/s	Remarks
β Sco AB	16 05.6	−19 49	2.56	−0.07	B0.5 V	6	−4.2	530	0.022	196	−1 SB	A: 2.78; B: 5.04, 1″; C: 4.93, 14″ Graffias
δ Oph	16 14.5	−3 42	2.73	1.58	M1 III	19	−0.8	170	0.153	198	−20 V	Yed Prior
ε Oph	16 18.5	−4 42	3.23	0.97	G9.5 IIIb	30	0.8	107	0.089	64	−10 V	Yed Posterior
σ Sco A	16 21.3	−25 36	2.91	0.13	B1 III	4	−4.8:	522	0.025	201	+3 SB	var.: 2.94–3.06, 0.25 d; B: 8.3, B9 V, 20″
η Dra A	16 24.0	+61 30	2.73	0.91	G8 IIIab	37	0.7	88	0.064	338	−14 SB?	B: 8.7, 6″
α Sco A	16 29.6	−26 27	1.06	1.87	M1.5 Iab	5	−5.8	604	0.024	197	−3 SB	B: 5.37, B2.5 V, 3″ Antares
β Her	16 30.4	+21 29	2.78	0.95	G7 IIIa	22	−0.5	148	0.100	260	−26 SB	Kornephoros
τ Sco	16 36.0	−28 13	2.82	−0.21	B0 V	8	−3.1	430	0.026	198	+2 V	
ζ Oph	16 37.4	−10 34	2.54	0.04	O9.5 Vn	7	−4.3	458	0.026	28	−15 V	
ζ Her AB	16 41.4	+31 36	2.81	0.65	G1 IV	93	2.5	35	0.614	310	−70 SB	A: 2.90; B: 5.53, G7 V, 1.1″
η Her	16 42.9	+38 56	3.48	0.92	G7.5 IIIb Fe−1	29	0.1	112	0.089	158	+8 V?	
α TrA	16 48.9	−69 02	1.91	1.45	K2 IIb–IIIa	8	−5.0	415	0.044	141	−3	Atria
ε Sco	16 50.4	−34 17	2.29	1.14	K2 III	50	0.1	65	0.661	247	−3	
μ¹ Sco	16 52.1	−38 03	3.00	−0.20	B1.5 IVn	4	−4.1	821	0.031	202	−25 SB2	ecl.: 2.80–3.08, 1.4 d
κ Oph	16 57.9	+9 22	3.19	1.16	K2 III	38	1.1	86	0.293	268	−56	
ζ Ara	16 58.8	−55 59	3.12	1.55	K4 III	6	−4.5	574	0.037	200	−6	
ζ Dra	17 08.8	+65 43	3.17	−0.12	B6 III	10	−2.0	340	0.033	310	−17 V	Aldhibah
η Oph AB	17 10.6	−15 44	2.43	0.06	A2.5 Va	39	0.8	84	0.102	22	−1 SB	A: 3.0; B: 3.5, A3 V, 1″ Sabik
η Sco	17 12.4	−43 15	3.30	0.44	F2p (Cr)	46	1.4	72	0.286	175	−27	
α Her AB	17 14.8	+14 23	2.78	1.16	M5 Ib–II	9	−3.5:	1369	0.035	348	−33 V	var.: 3.0–4.0; B: 5.4, 5″ Ras Algethi
π Her	17 15.1	+36 48	3.16	1.44	K3 IIab	9	−2.2	367	0.029	276	−26	
δ Her	17 15.2	+24 50	3.12	0.08	A1 Vann	42	1.2	78	0.159	188	−40 SB	B: 8.8, 9″ Sarin
θ Oph	17 22.2	−24 60	3.27	−0.19	B2 IV	6	−3.1	563	0.021	188	−2 SB	occ. bin.: 3.4, 5.4; var.: 3.25–3.29, 0.14 d
β Ara	17 25.5	−55 32	2.84	1.48	K3 Ib–IIa	5	−4.1	603	0.024	182	0	
γ Ara A	17 25.6	−56 23	3.31	−0.15	B1 Ib	3	−5.7:	652	0.011	170	−3 V	broad lines for Ib: B: 10.0, 18″
β Dra A	17 30.5	+52 18	2.79	0.95	G2 Ib–IIa	9	−2.9	361	0.026	301	−20 V	B: 11.5, 4″ Restaban
υ Sco	17 31.0	−37 18	2.70	−0.18	B2 IV	6	−3.5	518	0.032	182	8 SB	
α Ara	17 32.0	−49 52	2.84	−0.14	B2 Vne	13	−1.8	242	0.075	199	0 SB	
λ Sco	17 33.8	−37 06	1.62	−0.23	B1.5 IV	5	−3.6:	359	0.029	178	−3 SB2	var.: 1.59–1.65, 0.21 d Shaula
α Oph	17 35.2	+12 34	2.08	0.16	A5 Vnn	70	1.3	47	0.255	157	+13 SB?	Rasalhague
θ Sco	17 37.6	−43 00	1.97	0.41	F1 III	12	−3.0	272	0.016	90	1	Sargas
ξ Ser	17 37.8	−15 24	3.54	0.26	F0 IIIb	31	0.9	105	0.076	216	−43 SB	
κ Sco	17 42.7	−39 02	2.39	−0.17	B1.5 III	7	−3.6	464	0.030	194	−14 SB	
β Oph	17 43.6	+4 34	2.76	1.17	K2 III	40	0.7	82	0.164	345	−12 V	Cebalrai
μ Her A	17 46.5	+27 44	3.42	0.75	G5 IV	119	3.6	27	0.808	202	−16 V	BC: 9.78, 33″
ι¹ Sco	17 47.8	−40 07	2.99	0.51	F2 Ia	2	−8.0:	3619	0.006	171	−28 SB	

TABLE OF BRIGHTEST STARS (continued)

Star Name	RA (2002.5) h m	Dec ° '	V	B–V	MK Type	π mas	Mv	D ly	μ "/yr	PA °	RV km/s	Remarks
G Sco	17 50.0	−37 02	3.19	1.19	K2 III	26	−0.6	127	0.064	58	25	HR6630
γ Dra	17 56.7	+51 29	2.24	1.52	K5 III	22	−1.1	148	0.025	213	−28	Etamin
ν Oph	17 59.2	−9 46	3.32	0.99	G9.5 IIIa	21	0.0	153	0.118	184	13	
γ² Sgr	18 06.0	−30 25	2.98	0.98	K0 III	34	0.1	96	0.192	196	+22 SB	Nash
η Sgr A	18 17.8	−36 46	3.10	1.50	M3.5 IIIab	22	−0.1	149	0.210	218	+1 V?	var.: 3.08–3.12; B: 8.33, G8: IV:, 4"
δ Sgr	18 21.2	−29 50	2.72	1.38	K2.5 IIIa	11	−3.3	306	0.050	127	−20	Kaus Meridionalis
η Ser	18 21.5	−2 54	3.23	0.94	K0 III–IV	53	1.4	62	0.890	218	+9 V?	
ε Sgr	18 24.4	−34 23	1.79	−0.03	A0 II:n (shell?)	23	−1.4	145	0.129	194	−15	Kaus Australis
α Tel	18 27.2	−45 58	3.49	−0.18	B3 IV	13	−1.0	249	0.048	198	0 V?	
λ Sgr	18 28.1	−25 26	2.82	1.03	K1 IIIb	42	0.4	77	0.190	193	−43	Kaus Borealis
α Lyr	18 37.0	+38 47	0.03	0.00	A0 Va	129	0.6	25	0.348	35	−14 V	**Vega**
φ Sgr	18 45.8	−26 59	3.17	−0.11	B8 III	14	−1.0	231	0.052	89	+22 SB	
β Lyr	18 50.1	+33 22	3.52	0.00	B7 Vpe (shell)	4	−4.1	881	0.002	180	−19 SB	Sheliak, ecl.: 3.34–4.34, 12.9 d
σ Sgr	18 55.4	−26 18	2.05	−0.13	B3 IV	15	−2.4	224	0.056	166	−11 V	Nunki
ζ² Sgr	18 57.9	−21 06	3.52	1.15	K1 III	3	0.1	913	0.035	111	−20	
γ Lyr	18 58.9	+32 41	3.25	−0.05	B9 II	5	−3.3	634	0.007	288	−21 V	Sulaphat
ζ Sgr AB	19 02.8	−29 53	3.27	0.06	A2 IV–V + A4:V:	37	1.1	89	0.014	266	+22 SB	Ascella, A: 3.2; B: 3.5, <1"
ζ Aql A	19 05.6	+13 52	2.99	0.01	A0 Vann	39	0.9	83	0.095	184	−25 SB	
λ Aql	19 06.4	−4 53	3.43	−0.10	B9 Vnp (kB7HeA0)	26	0.6	125	0.090	193	−12 V	
τ Sgr	19 07.1	−27 40	3.32	1.17	K1.5 IIIb	27	−0.4	120	0.255	192	+45 SB	
π Sgr ABC	19 09.9	−21 01	2.88	0.38	F2 II–III	7	−3.1	440	0.035	180	−10	Albaldah, A: 3.7; B: 3.8; C: 6.0, <1"
δ Dra	19 12.6	+67 40	3.07	0.99	G9 III	33	0.6	100	0.130	44	25	Nodus Secundus
δ Aql	19 25.7	+3 07	3.36	0.32	F2 IV	65	2.6	50	0.267	72	−30 SB	
β Cyg A	19 30.8	+27 58	3.36	1.09	K3 II + B9.5 V	8	−2.3	385	0.002	153	−24 V	Albireo, B: 5.11, 35"; C: Δm = 1.5, 0.4"
δ Cyg AB	19 45.0	+45 08	2.86	0.00	B9.5 III	19	−0.7	171	0.069	45	−20 SB	B: 6.4, F1 V, 2"
γ Aql	19 46.4	+10 37	2.72	1.51	K3 II	7	−2.6:	326	0.016	83	−2 V	Tarazed
α Aql	19 51.0	+8 52	0.76	0.22	A7 Vnn	194	2.1	17	0.662	54	−26	**Altair**
η Aql	19 52.6	+1 01	3.87	0.63	F6–G1 Ib	3	−4.3	1173	0.009	131	−15 SB	Cepheid var.: 3.53–4.33, 7.2 d
γ Sge	19 58.9	+19 30	3.51	1.57	M0 III	12	−0.9	274	0.070	69	−33	
θ Aql	20 11.5	+0 49	3.24	−0.07	B9.5 III	11	−1.4	287	0.037	79	−27 SB2	
β Cap A	20 21.2	−14 47	3.05	0.79	K0: II: + A5: V:n	9	−1.4	344	0.039	86	−19 SB	Dabih, A: mult.: 4.0 + 4.3 + 4.8 + 6.7, <1"
γ Cyg	20 22.2	+40 15	2.23	0.67	F8 Ib	2	−4.1:	522	0.001	27	−8	Sadr
α Pav	20 25.8	−56 44	1.94	−0.12	B2.5 V	18	−2.1	183	0.087	169	+2 SB	Peacock
α Ind	20 37.7	−47 17	3.11	1.00	K0 III CN−1	32	0.1	101	0.090	39	−1	
α Cyg	20 41.5	+45 18	1.25	0.09	A2 Ia	1	−7.5:	1467	0.005	11	−5 V	**Deneb**
β Pav	20 45.2	−66 11	3.42	0.16	A6 IV	23	0.6	141	0.041	295	10	

TABLE OF BRIGHTEST STARS (continued)

Star Name	RA (2002.5) h m	Dec ° ′	V	B–V	MK Type	π mas	Mv	D ly	μ ″/yr	PA °	RV km/s	Remarks
η Cep	20 45.3	+61 51	3.41	0.91	K0 IV	70	2.7	47	0.827	6	–87	
ε Cyg	20 46.3	+33 59	2.48	1.02	K0 III	45	0.7	72	0.484	47	–11 SB	
ζ Cyg	21 13.1	+30 14	3.21	0.99	G8 IIIa Ba 0.6	22	0.2	151	0.052	181	+17 SB	
α Cep	21 18.6	+62 35	2.45	0.26	A7 Van	67	1.4	49	0.159	71	–10 V	Alderamin
β Cep	21 28.7	+70 34	3.23	–0.20	B1 III	5	–4.0:	815	0.016	38	–8 SB	Alphirk var.: 3.16–3.27, 0.2 d; B: 7.8, 13″
β Aqr	21 31.7	–5 34	2.91	0.83	G0 Ib	5	–3.5	612	0.020	105	7	Sadalsuud
ε Peg	21 44.3	+9 52	2.38	1.52	K2 Ib	5	–5.2	672	0.030	81	+5 V	Enif var.: 0.7–3.5 (flare in 1972)
δ Cap	21 47.3	–16 08	2.85	0.18	A3mF2 IV:	85	2.2	39	0.394	138	–6 SB	var.: 2.83–3.05, 1 d; occ. bin.: 3.2 + 5.2
γ Gru	21 54.1	–37 22	3.00	–0.08	B8 IV–Vs	16	–1.1	203	0.104	99	–2 V?	
α Aqr	22 05.9	0 18	2.95	0.97	G2 Ib	4	–4.3	756	0.016	104	+8 V?	Sadalmelik
α Gru	22 08.3	–46 57	1.73	–0.07	B7 Vn	32	–0.9	101	0.198	139	12	Al Nair
θ Peg	22 10.4	+6 13	3.52	0.09	A2mA1 IV–V	34	1.0	97	0.277	83	–6 SB2	Baham
ζ Cep	22 10.9	+58 13	3.39	1.56	K1.5 Ib	4	–4.2	726	0.015	58	–18 SB	
α Tuc	22 18.7	–60 15	2.87	1.39	K3 III	16	–2.2	199	0.071	237	+42 SB	
δ Cep A	22 29.2	+58 26	4.07	0.78	F5–G2 Ib	3	–4.4	950	0.012	67	–16 SB	Cepheid variable: 3.55–4.41, 5.4 d
ζ Peg	22 41.6	+10 51	3.41	–0.09	B8.5 III	16	–0.7	208	0.080	96	+7 V?	Homam
β Gru	22 42.8	–46 52	2.07	1.60	M5 III	19	–1.4	170	0.138	92	2	var.: 2.0–2.3
η Peg	22 43.2	+30 14	2.93	0.85	G8 II + F0 V	3	–1.2	1113	0.025	148	+4 SB	Matar
ε Gru	22 48.7	–51 18	3.49	0.08	A2 Va	25	0.4	130	0.126	120	0 V	
ι Cep	22 49.7	+66 13	3.51	1.05	K0 III	28	0.6	115	0.137	209	–12	
μ Peg	22 50.2	+24 37	3.51	0.93	G8 III	28	0.8	117	0.152	104	14	
δ Aqr	22 54.9	–15 49	3.27	0.07	A3p (weak 4481)	20	–0.1	159	0.047	242	+18 V	Skat
α PsA	22 57.9	–29 37	1.17	0.15	A3 Va	130	1.6	25	0.373	116	7	Fomalhaut
β Peg	23 04.0	+28 06	2.44	1.66	M2 II–III	16	–1.7	199	0.236	53	+9 V	Scheat var.: 2.31–2.74
α Peg	23 04.9	+15 13	2.49	0.00	A0 III–IV	23	–0.9	140	0.073	121	–4 SB	Markab
γ Cep	23 39.5	+77 38	3.21	1.03	K1 III–IV	72	2.1	45	0.168	337	–42	Alrai

THE NEAREST STARS
By Alan H. Batten

The *annual parallax* of a star is the difference between its direction as seen from Earth and the Sun. Astronomers began to look for stellar parallax as soon as they began to take seriously the idea that the Sun, and not Earth, is the centre of the planetary system. The great distances of the other stars ensured, however, that determination of parallax would be beyond the powers of early telescopes. James Bradley (1693–1762) came close to succeeding and correctly deduced that even the largest parallaxes must be less than 2″, but about another century was to elapse before success was achieved. Then, between 1838 and 1840, Bessel, Struve, and Henderson all published trust-worthy parallaxes for three different stars. Two of those star systems, α Centauri (Henderson) and 61 Cygni (Bessel), are indeed so close to us that they appear in this table. Struve measured the parallax of Vega, which, although a relatively close neighbour of the Sun, lies some distance beyond the limit adopted here. Progress in measuring other parallaxes remained rather slow until it became possible, toward the end of the 19th century, to apply photography to the problem.

A table like the one presented here looks rather static but, if we think on a long enough time scale, the stars within the sphere of approximately 17 ly radius, centred on the Sun, are changing all the time—moving in and out of the sphere. Proxima Centauri has not always been our nearest neighbour nor will it always be, even though it is at present coming closer to us. Calculations by R.A.J. Matthews some time ago indicated that 32 000 years ago L726-8 was closer to us and that in another 33 000 years Ross 248 will be closer. More recent calculations by García-Sanchez and others, based on HIPPARCOS measurements, extend the picture over some tens of millions of years. Seven million years ago, Algol would have featured in this table and would have been appreciably brighter in the sky than Sirius now is. In 1.4 million years, Gliese 710 (now over 60 ly away from us) will be only 1.3 ly away and a moderately bright naked-eye star. All such calculations are approximate, of course, because there are still uncertainties in our knowledge of the distances and motions of the stars.

The table emphasizes the relative rarity of massive hot stars. Ignoring the white dwarfs, which are not massive, only Sirius, Procyon, and Altair are hotter and more massive than the Sun, and only α Centauri equals the Sun in these respects. Most of the objects in the table are very faint, cool stars. On the other hand, there is only one example of a "brown dwarf": LP944-20 (at 16.22 ly in the table). These objects are not massive enough to shine by the light of thermonuclear reactions, and they derive their energy from their gravitational contraction. They are necessarily difficult to detect, and there may be others still to be found within the region covered by this table, including some of the suspected unseen companions to some of the stars. The recently resolved component G208-44B is described as "in the transition region between stars and brown dwarfs." Another known brown dwarf, Gliese 229B, lies just beyond the limit of this table.

The HIPPARCOS-based Table

The table has been thoroughly revised to include recent results from HIPPARCOS, the satellite launched to obtain high-precision parallaxes and proper motions for a large number of stars down to an approximate limiting magnitude $V = 12.5$. The results largely confirm earlier ground-based work, at least for nearby stars. Parallaxes are now more precisely known, so the order of stars in the list has been changed—but mostly not by very much, and not at all until ε Eridani. According to HIPPARCOS, however, the next star in this list, CD–36°15693, is a whole light-year nearer than we thought; the last star in the old table, AC+79°3888, now lies beyond the arbitrary adopted limit of 17 ly. HIPPARCOS has added four new stars to the table and recent ground-based observations a fifth (L372-58 or LHS 1565). Two stars, HIP 82725 and 85605, which were added on the strength of the initial HIPPARCOS list, have been deleted because a new analysis throws considerable doubt on the originally measured parallaxes of about 203 mas. We still rely on ground-based observations for stars fainter than $V = 12.5$ and for BD+20°2465, close in the sky to the much brighter (but much more distant) γ Leonis. Most data for stars not observed by HIPPARCOS are from the *Yale Catalogue of Trigonometrical Parallaxes*.

We can either incorporate the HIPPARCOS data in weighted means with the ground-based data or assume that the new values are definitive. Although the latter course is somewhat unfair to the earlier work, I have adopted it, to make immediately clear what HIPPARCOS has achieved. There are few significant differences between the results of the two treatments. The satellite's results have been published in 16 volumes, also available on CD-ROM. Table 3.6.1 of Volume 1 lists the 150 stars closest to the Sun measured by HIPPARCOS and contains all the information presented here, except the radial velocities. I have taken all the stars from that table, out to and including Altair, and interspersed stars from the Yale Catalogue that have parallaxes within the same limit, and L372-58. Our new table contains 37 single stars, 11 pairs (including common-proper-motion pairs), and 4 triples (α Centauri A and B, with Proxima, L789-6, a pair whose brighter component is a spectroscopic binary, G208-45 with G208-44 A and B, which have recently been resolved, and o² Eridani A, B and C), 71 objects in all, not counting the planetary companions mentioned below.

HIPPARCOS parallaxes are quoted in milliarcseconds (mas, 0″.001) rather than the arcseconds formerly used. I have adopted the new units since the elimination of the zero and decimal point before the significant figures makes room for more information, as described below. I have given HIPPARCOS parallaxes to the nearest tenth of a milliarcsecond. They are not that precise, even though the HIPPARCOS catalogue quotes them to five significant figures. The best determined values have uncertainties of several tenths of a milliarcsecond; most are uncertain by one or two milliarcseconds—better than ground-based observations, but not outstandingly so. A few are considerably less certain than good ground-based determinations. Most Yale Catalogue parallaxes are given to the nearest tenth of a milliarcsecond, but I have always rounded them off. Readers, therefore, may tell at once, by the appearance of a figure after the decimal point, whether a given parallax was determined from HIPPARCOS. The order in which stars appear, however, is decided by that fourth significant figure, even if it is suppressed. That is why the star LP731-58 appears, at first sight, to be out of order in the table.

Recently we have learned more about LP944-20, the least luminous object known near the Sun and, as mentioned above, a brown dwarf. The spectral type of such a cool object is necessarily uncertain and M9V is the earliest this can be. There are no good photometric measurements of the visual magnitude of the star, but from measurements in the red and infrared its absolute bolometric magnitude is found to be 14.32. Again, the bolometric correction for so cool an object is uncertain, but I have tried to give an approximate estimate of the likely absolute visual magnitude (17.*). The star BD+20°2465 is very close in the sky to a 10.2 magnitude star with almost the same proper motion and a parallax of 183 mas. The two may well form a common-proper-motion pair, but the fainter one at a distance of 17.8 ly falls outside the scope of the present table. A possible addition to this table, at a distance of just under 14 ly, is a dM9e star, DENIS1048-39. No trigonometric parallax has yet been determined for this star, however, and, if the star proves to be a binary, it could lie beyond the limit of this table. We shall await confirmation before adding it.

Many years ago we used to list in this table stars believed to have unseen companions. The existence of these companions was inferred from astrometric observations, mainly those made by Peter van de Kamp and his colleagues. The most famous example was Barnard's star, which van de Kamp believed to have one, or even two, planetary companions. Later, doubts arose about the interpretation of many of these observations and the companions were no longer indicated. Radial-velocity measurements can now be made with sufficient precision to detect the effect of planets at least as large as Jupiter. Two stars in this table, BD+36°2147 (also known as Lalande 21185 and one of the stars that van de Kamp listed) and BD−15°6290 (Gleise 876), do have planetary companions. In addition, 61 Cygni B and ε Eridani may have such companions. On the other hand, there is still no firm evidence for companions of Barnard's star, and the object near Proxima Centauri that was thought to have been photographed has not been confirmed by either astrometric or spectroscopic observation.

Subject to these comments, the table is arranged as previously. Successive columns give the name or designation of the star, the right ascension (**RA**) and declination (**Dec**) for the equinox 2000, the parallax (π) in milliarcseconds, the distance (**D**) in light-years (if you prefer the scientific unit of parsecs, just take the reciprocal of the parallax; one parsec is approximately 3.26 ly). Subsequent columns give the spectral type (**Sp.**, on the MK system whenever possible), the total proper motion (μ) in milliarcseconds/year, the position angle of the proper motion (θ) measured in degrees from north through east, the total space motion (**W**) in kilometres per second for those stars with known radial velocities, and the apparent and absolute visual magnitudes (**V** and M_V, respectively). Distances of HIPPARCOS stars are given to 0.01 ly and of the others to 0.1 ly. Again, I stress that we rarely know distances that precisely. Except for stars new to the list, I have usually retained the spectral types previously used. The K and M stars were classified by R.F. Wing some years ago. Recent reclassification resulted in few significant changes. Many M-type stars are flare stars, variable in both magnitude and spectral type. The space motion is given the same sign as the radial velocity (+ for recession). This is a little misleading for the two components of BD+59°1915, whose radial velocities are small, and which are travelling together, despite the difference in sign of their space motions. Only the radial velocity of o² Eridani C is given, but B and C are a known orbital pair. Several of the radial velocities are based on only one or two observations and are the least reliable data in the table. The velocities of the centres of mass of the binaries α Centauri, Sirius, Procyon, and 70 Ophiuchi are, however, reasonably well known. I have taken magnitudes from HIPPARCOS whenever possible, except for 70 Ophiuchi, for which the HIPPARCOS value appears to refer to the total light of the system. Magnitudes quoted to only one decimal are not photoelectrically determined.

HIPPARCOS has determined parallaxes and proper motions separately for each component of some binary systems. The components of α Centauri have the same parallax, but those of 61 Cygni are different; the components of Procyon are between them in distance, and BD+59°1915B turns out to be closer than its brighter companion. The two components of the common-proper-motion pair CD−25°10553, included in earlier versions of this table, have been removed because further analysis makes it doubtful that they are as close as previously thought. I have suppressed parallax and proper-motion entries for those components of binaries for which separate determinations were *not* made, sometimes condensing the entry to a single line. Only the B components of two BD stars are in the table: they form optical pairs with their respective brighter and more distant components.

Unfortunately, there is no uniform nomenclature for these predominantly faint stars; for some, names exist in several different systems. Preferred designations are as follows: proper names and Bayer Greek letters, Bonn or Cordoba *Durchmusterungen* numbers and a miscellany of designations for fainter stars; usually I chose the one I thought most familiar.

With so much new data, some errors are likely to have made their way into the table. Either I or the editor will be pleased to have them pointed out. The preparation of this table was greatly assisted by access to the HIPPARCOS and SIMBAD catalogues provided by the Canadian Astronomy Data Centre.

Editor's Note: For more information see "Our Changing Views of the Solar Neighbourhood," A.H. Batten, *JRASC*, 92, 1998, 231–237.

TABLE OF NEAREST STARS

Name	RA (2000) h m	Dec ° '	π mas	D ly	Sp.	μ mas/y	θ °	W km/s	V	Mv
Sun					G2V				−26.72	4.85
Proxima	14 30	−62 41	772.3	4.22	M5.5Ve	3 853	281	−29	11.01	15.45
α Cen A	14 40	−60 50	742.1	4.40	G2V	3 709	277	−32	−0.01	4.34
B					K1V	3 724	285	−32	1.35	5.70
Barnard's	17 58	+4 41	549.0	5.94	M5V	10 358	356	−139	9.54	13.24
Wolf 359	10 56	+7 01	419	7.79	M6.5Ve	4 702	235	+55	13.46	16.57
BD+36°2147	11 03	+35 58	392.4	8.31	M2+V	4 802	187	−104	7.49	10.46
Sirius A	6 45	−16 43	379.2	8.60	A1Vm	1 339	204	−18	−1.44	1.45
B					DA2				8.44	11.33
L726-8 A	1 39	−17 57	373	8.7	M5.5Ve	3 360	80	+52	12.56	15.42
B					M5.5Ve			+53	12.96	15.82
Ross 154	18 50	−23 50	336.5	9.69	M3.6Ve	6 660	107	−10	10.37	13.00
Ross 248	23 42	+44 09	316	10.3	M5.5Ve	1 588	176	−84	12.27	14.77
ε Eri	3 33	−9 27	310.8	10.50	K2V	977	271	+22	3.72	6.18
CD−36°15693	23 06	−35 51	303.9	10.73	M2V	6 896	79	+108	7.35	9.76
Ross 128	11 48	+0 48	299.6	10.89	M4+V	1 361	154	−26	11.12	13.50
L789-6 ABC	22 39	−15 17	290	11.2	M5+Ve	3 256	47	−80	12.32	14.63
61 Cyg A	21 07	+38 45	287.1	11.36	K5V	5 281	52	−108	5.20	7.49
Procyon A	7 39	+5 13	285.9	11.41	F5IV–V	1 259	215	−21	0.40	2.68
B					DF				10.7	13.0
61 Cyg B	21 07	+38 45	285.4	11.43	K7V	5 172	53	−107	6.05	8.33
BD+59°1915 B	18 43	+59 38	284.5	11.47	M4V	2 312	323	+39	9.70	11.97
A			280.3	11.64	M3.5V	2 238	324	−38	8.94	11.18
BD+43°44 A	0 18	+44 01	280.3	11.64	M2V	2 918	82	+51	8.09	10.33
B					M4V			+54	11.10	13.34
G51-15	8 30	+26 48	276	11.8	M6.5Ve	1 270	242		14.81	17.01
ε Ind	22 03	−56 47	275.8	11.83	K4Ve	4 704	123	−90	4.69	6.89
τ Cet	1 44	−15 56	274.2	11.90	G8V	1 922	296	−37	3.49	5.68
L372-58	3 36	−44 30	273	11.9	M4.5V	831	119		13.03	15.21
L725-32	1 12	−17 00	269.1	12.12	M5.5Ve	1 372	62	+37	12.10	14.25
BD+5°1668	7 27	+5 14	263.3	12.39	M4V	3 738	171	+72	9.84	11.94
Kapteyn's	5 12	−45 01	255.3	12.78	M1VIp	8 671	131	+294	8.86	10.89
CD−39°14192	21 17	−38 52	253.4	12.87	M0Ve	3 455	251	+69	6.69	8.71
Krüger 60 A	22 28	+57 42	249.5	13.07	M3.5V	990	242	−30	9.59	11.58
B					M4Ve			−37	11.3	13.3
Ross 614 A	6 29	−2 49	242.9	13.43	M4.0Ve	930	132	+30	11.1	13.0
B					M5.5V				14.4	16.3
BD−12°4523	16 30	−12 40	234.5	13.91	M4V	1 189	185	−27	10.10	11.95
CD−37°15492	0 05	−37 21	229.3	14.23	M2V	6 100	113	+128	8.56	10.36
Wolf 424 A	12 33	+09 03	228	14.3	M5+Ve	1 811	277	−38	13.10	14.89
B									13.4	15.2
BD−13°637 B	3 22	−13 16	227.5	14.34		320	201		12.16	13.94

TABLE OF NEAREST STARS (continued)

Name	RA (2000) h m	Dec ° '	π mas	D ly	Sp.	μ mas/y	θ °	W km/s	V	M_V
van Maanen's	0 49	+5 23	227.0	14.37	DG	2978	156	+82	12.37	14.15
L1159-16	2 00	+13 01	224	14.6	M4.5Ve	2096	148		12.26	14.01
L143-23	10 45	−61 10	222	14.7	M4	1657	348		13.87	15.60
BD+68°946	17 36	+68 20	220.9	14.77	M3.5V	1310	194	−36	9.15	10.87
LP731-58	10 48	−11 21	221	14.8	M6.5V	1645	158		15.60	17.32
CD−46°11540	17 29	−46 53	220.4	14.80	M3V	1050	147		9.38	11.10
G208-45	19 54	+44 24	220	14.8	M6Ve	616	139		14.01	15.72
44 A					M6Ve	681	142		13.47	15.18
44 B									16.76	18.47
BD−15°6346 B	23 07	−14 52	216.5	15.07		140	53		12.24	13.92
L145-141	11 46	−64 50	216.4	15.07	DC:	2688	97		11.50	13.18
G158-27	0 07	−7 34	213	15.3	M5−5.5V	2028	204		13.74	15.38
BD−15°6290	22 53	−14 16	212.7	15.34	M5V	1174	125	+28	10.16	11.80
BD+44°2051 A	11 05	+43 32	206.9	15.77	M1V	4511	282	+122	8.82	10.40
B					M5de				14.40	15.93
BD+50°1725	10 11	+49 27	205.2	15.90	K7V	1452	250	−42	6.60	8.16
BD+20°2465	10 20	+19 52	205	15.9	M3.5Ve	491	264	+16	9.43	10.99
CD−49°13515	21 34	−49 00	202.5	16.11	M2V	819	183	+22	8.66	10.19
LP944-20	3 40	−35 26	201	16.22	≥M9V	439	176	+14		17.*
CD−44°11909	17 37	−44 18	198.3	16.43	M4V	1176	217	−66	10.94	12.43
o² Eri A	4 15	−7 39	198.2	16.46	K1V	4088	213	−106	4.43	5.92
B					DA	4070	212	−100	9.52	11.01
C					M4.5Ve			(−45)	11.17	12.66
BD+43°4305 A	22 47	+44 20	198.1	16.47	M4−Ve	841	237	−20	10.29	11.77
70 Oph A	18 05	+2 30	196.6	16.59	K0V	971	173	−24	4.20	5.67
B					K4V				5.99	7.46
Altair	19 51	+8 52	194.4	16.78	A7V	661	54	−31	0.76	2.20

DOUBLE AND MULTIPLE STARS
BY BRIAN D. MASON

Approximately 85% of stars are found in double or multiple systems. While the first detection of these double systems dates back to the early 17th century, it was not until systematic work with large-aperture telescopes was done (notably by William Herschel) that the physical rather than optical nature of these systems was ascertained. The larger the aperture of the telescope, the closer the stars that can be separated under good conditions. The resolving power in arcseconds can be estimated as $120/D$, where D is the diameter of the telescope objective in millimetres. Astronomers using long-baseline optical interferometry have measured double-star separations that are less than a milliarcsecond (0.001″).

The double stars in the table (two pages ahead) were selected to cover a wide variety of interests. While wide or slowly moving pairs are good for evaluating optical performance or estimating seeing, with the preponderance of inexpensive, large-aperture telescopes and the availability of interferometry for the amateur (in *Sky & Telescope* see the article by A. Maurer, p. 91, March 1997, and the article by H.A. McAlister, p. 34, November 1996), closer systems have been added to the list. Of the 36 listed systems, 9 have separations less than one arcsecond, and 9 more between one and two arcseconds. A pair of binaries with white dwarf secondaries (α CMa and α CMi) is included to demonstrate the detection difficulty imposed by a large magnitude difference. Also, one-quarter of the list consists of stars south of the equator. Since many of the stars selected exhibit significant motion, the predicted position angles and separations are given for both 2002.0 and 2003.0. P.A. (Position Angle) is the angular direction of the fainter star (B) from the brighter (A), measured counterclockwise from north (*clockwise* in an optical system having an *odd* number of reflections). Note that data for 2002.0 have been changed for some systems due to improvements in orbit calculations or more recent measurements. Also included are notes on selected systems.

Other double stars appear in THE NEAREST STARS (pp. 234–238) and THE BRIGHTEST STARS (pp. 224–233) sections in this Handbook. For more information about observing double stars, see the following articles in *Sky & Telescope:* A. Adler (Jan. 2001, 131); S. Haas (May 2000, 112); L. Argüelles (Feb. 2000, 111); R. Tanguay (Feb. 1999, 116); J. Mullaney (Mar. 1993, 112); J. Ashbrook (Nov. 1980, 379); J. Meeus (Jan. and Feb. 1971, 21, 88); and C.E. Worley (Aug., Sep., and Nov. 1961, 73, 140, 261).

Notes on some double and multiple stars in the table:

85 Peg: This system, discovered by Burnham, has been seen over four complete orbital cycles and thus has a very accurately determined period. The fainter C and D components are probably optical.

γ And: The AB system is striking in colour, the brighter star golden and the secondary blue. The B component is itself a triple system consisting of a close (2.7-day) spectroscopic binary and the wider BC pair also listed in the table. (In the NOVEMBER ALL-SKY MAP on p. 282, γ And is the bright star immediately west of the word "Algol.")

α CMa: The companion to Sirius is a difficult target, usually observable only during periods of exceptional seeing when you can use the highest magnification and move the primary off the field of view. The white dwarf secondary, predicted by Bessel and first observed by Alvan Clark, remains a challenging target for visual observers.

α CMi: Like Sirius, Procyon has a white dwarf companion. It was first detected in 1840 by the variation in the proper motion of the star but not resolved until 1896 by Shaeberle with the 36-in. refractor of Lick Observatory.

ζ Cnc: A gorgeous and easily seen triple system, the wide C component is quite bright and is well separated (6°). While its period is very uncertain, preliminary orbital analysis yields a period of about 1150 years. A new, close component to C has been found by infrared adaptive optics and lunar occultation; it has been confirmed with reprocessing of the HIPPARCOS data. An astrometric solution by Wulff Heintz yields a period of 17 years for the new close companion to C. For an excellent history of this system, see Roger Griffin's article in the February 2000 *Observatory*.

σ² UMa: Previous observers claimed a marked colour difference and that the secondary was variable; both are uncertain. The motion of this system is quite slow and the binary period is very uncertain.

ξ UMa: Many "firsts" are associated with this system. It was one of the first discovered systems (Herschel), one of the first systems whose motion led to the discovery of the physical (rather than optical) nature of double stars (Struve), and was the first star to have an orbit calculated for it (Savary). Always relatively wide and with an obvious mean motion of 6° per year, this is a system that will never fail to please, observing season to observing season. For an excellent history of this system, see Roger Griffin's article in the October 1998 *Observatory*. (In the MAY ALL-SKY MAP on p. 279, ξ UMa is the star nearest to the letter "S" in the word "BERENICES.")

ζ UMa: This is the well-known bright binary Mizar and a new entry in the Double and Multiple Stars list for this year. The intermediate separation pair is listed in the table. The wider pairing with Alcor is at a separation of 708″. Mizar is also the first known spectroscopic binary and was first resolved by Francis Pease using the 20-ft beam interferometer mounted on the front end of the 100-in. at Mt. Wilson (see **www.mtwilson.edu/Tour/100inch/20ftl**). It has subsequently been resolved using the Navy Prototype Optical Interferometer (NPOI). See **ad.usno.navy.mil/npoi/science/mizarArev.gif** for a movie of the orbital motion showing recent resolutions of the NPOI. For a list of nearby doubles, see the article by Sissy Haas listed above.

α Cen: Our closest neighbour is a quick-moving double star. The brighter component is a near twin of the Sun, while the B component is cooler. The C component, Proxima, which is slightly closer to the Sun, is an extremely faint red dwarf, 2.2° away.

α Sco: Antares is a double consisting of a cool supergiant and a hot dwarf star. A significant colour difference may be seen in a telescope if you can overcome the large Δm.

α Her: A slowly moving, easy-to-separate system, this binary has a significant colour difference between the two companions, A being reddish and B appearing green. The period is very uncertain. See also the *Variable Star of the Year* in the 1998 *Observer's Handbook*. (In the JULY ALL-SKY MAP on p. 280, α Her is the star in the stick pattern of HERCULES closest to OPHIUCHUS.)

β Cyg: Also known as Albireo. If a neophyte doubts the colour of stars, this jewel of the summer sky should change his or her view. Appearing as brilliant yellow and a deep blue, this wide double has shown no apparent motion. The A component also has a close interferometric companion at a separation of about 0.4″. (In the JULY ALL-SKY MAP on p. 280, β Cyg lies at the south end of the stick pattern for CYGNUS.)

16 Cyg: The fainter component of this double star system, 16 Cyg B (which is the same type as the Sun) has one of the recently discovered extra-solar planets orbiting it. See the March 1998 *Sky & Telescope* (p. 30) article by Marcy and Butler. (In the SEPTEMBER ALL-SKY MAP on p. 281, note the line of three stars just north of the letter "S" in the word "CYGNUS"; 16 Cyg lies 1° ENE of the eastern star of this trio.)

δ Cep: Also new to the list for this year, this is the prototype of the Cepheid variables and was the *Variable Star of the Year* in the 1994 *Observer's Handbook*. The component listed here (designated C) is also variable and a spectroscopic binary. The B component is much fainter.

TABLE OF DOUBLE AND MULTIPLE STARS

Star	RA (2000) Dec			Magnitudes comb. A B			2002.0 P.A. Sep.		2003.0 P.A. Sep.		Period
	h m	°	′	comb.	A	B	°	″	°	″	years
85 Peg*	0 02.2	+27	05	5.7	5.8	8.8	204	0.8	214	0.8	26
γ Ari	1 53.5	+19	18	3.8	3.9	3.9	0	7.7			
α Psc	2 02.0	+02	46	3.9	4.3	5.2	270	1.8	269	1.8	930
γ And AB*	2 03.9	+42	20	2.0	2.1	4.8	64	9.8			
γ And BC*	2 03.9	+42	20	4.5	4.8	6.0	104	0.4	104	0.4	64
γ Per	3 04.8	+53	30	2.9	3.2	4.4	64	0.2	64	0.2	15
33 Ori	5 31.2	+03	18	5.5	5.8	6.9	28	1.9			
α CMa*	6 45.1	−16	43	−1.5	−1.5	8.5	131	5.4	123	5.8	50
α Gem	7 34.6	+31	53	1.6	2.0	2.9	63	4.0	62	4.1	445
α Cmi*	7 39.3	+5	14	0.4	0.4	10.8	84	4.0	92	3.7	41
ζ Cnc AB*	8 12.2	+17	39	5.0	5.6	6.0	71	0.9	66	0.9	60
ι Cnc	8 46.7	+28	46	3.9	4.0	6.6	307	30.8			
10 UMa	9 00.6	+41	47	3.9	4.1	6.1	25	0.7	16	0.7	22
σ² Uma*	9 10.4	+67	08	4.8	4.9	7.9	353	3.9	352	3.9	1100
ψ Vel	9 30.7	−40	28	3.6	4.0	4.8	281	0.5	294	0.5	34
γ Leo	10 20.0	+19	50	2.3	2.6	3.8	125	4.4	125	4.4	620
ξ Uma*	11 18.2	+31	32	3.8	4.3	4.8	263	1.8	257	1.8	60
α Cru	12 26.6	−63	06	0.2	0.8	1.2	114	4.0			
γ Vir	12 41.7	−1	27	2.7	3.4	3.5	248	1.1	236	0.9	170
ζ Uma*	13 23.9	+54	56	2.0	2.2	3.9	153	14.6			
α Cen*	14 39.6	−60	50	−0.3	0.0	1.3	225	12.8	226	12.0	80
ε Boo	14 45.0	+27	04	2.0	2.3	4.5	341	2.6			
η CrB	15 23.2	+30	17	5.1	5.6	6.1	79	0.6	88	0.6	42
α Sco*	16 29.4	−26	26	1.0	1.0	5.4	274	2.6	274	2.6	880
λ Oph	16 30.9	+01	59	3.6	4.0	5.0	31	1.4	32	1.4	130
ζ Her	16 41.3	+31	36	3.0	3.0	6.5	296	0.5	261	0.6	34
α Her*	17 14.6	+14	23	3.3	3.5	5.4	104	4.7	104	4.6	3600
τ Oph	18 03.1	−8	11	4.8	5.3	5.8	282	1.7	282	1.7	260
70 Oph	18 05.5	+02	30	3.8	4.0	6.0	144	4.2	142	4.5	88
ε Lyr AB	18 44.3	+39	40	4.7	5.0	6.1	350	2.6	350	2.6	1200
ε Lyr CD	18 44.3	+39	40	4.6	5.2	5.5	82	2.3	81	2.3	720
β Cyg*	19 30.7	+27	58	2.9	3.1	5.1	52	34.3			
16 Cyg*	19 41.8	+50	32	5.3	6.0	6.2	133	39.5			
δ Cyg	19 45.0	+45	08	2.9	2.9	7.9	224	2.6	223	2.6	780
π Aql	19 48.7	+11	49	5.7	6.1	6.9	105	1.4			
β Cap	20 21.0	−14	47	2.9	3.0	6.1	267	205.			
τ Cyg	21 14.8	+38	03	3.7	3.8	6.3	291	0.8	284	0.8	50
μ Cyg	21 44.1	+28	45	4.4	4.7	6.1	310	1.8	311	1.8	790
ζ Aqr	22 28.8	−0	01	3.7	4.4	4.6	182	2.0	181	2.0	760
δ Cep*	22 29.4	+58	25	4.0	4.1	6.3	191	40.9			

*See the preceding note.

VARIABLE STARS
By Janet A. Mattei

Variable stars provide information about many stellar properties. Depending upon their type, variables can reveal the mass, radius, temperature, luminosity, internal and external structure, composition, and evolution history of stars. The systematic observation of variable stars is an area in which amateur astronomers can make a valuable contribution to astronomy.

For beginning observers, charts of the fields of four different types of bright variable stars are shown below. On each chart the magnitudes (with decimal point omitted) of several suitable comparison stars are shown. A brightness estimate of the variable is made using two comparison stars, one brighter, one fainter than the variable. The magnitude, date, and time of each observation are recorded. When a number of observations have been made, a graph of magnitude versus date can be plotted. The shape of this "light curve" depends on the type of variable. Further information about variable star observing may be obtained from the American Association of Variable Star Observers (AAVSO), 25 Birch St., Cambridge MA 02138-1205, U.S.A. (email: aavso@aavso.org; website: www.aavso.org).

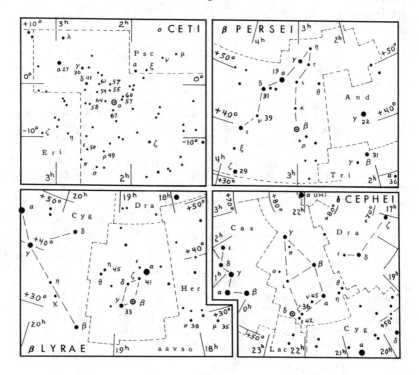

Table 1 is a list of long-period variables, brighter than magnitude 8.0 at maximum and north of −20°. The first column (the Harvard designation of the star) gives the position for the year 1900: the first four characters give the hours and minutes of right ascension, the next three the declination in degrees. The column headed **"Max."** gives the mean maximum magnitude. The period **(Per.)** is in days. **"Epoch"** gives the predicted date of the earliest maximum occurring this year; by adding multiples of the period to this epoch, the dates of subsequent maxima may be found. These variables may reach maximum two or three weeks before or after the epoch and may remain at maximum for several weeks. This table is prepared using the observations of the AAVSO.

Table 2 (on the following page) lists stars that are representative of some other types of variables. The data for the preparation of the predicted epoch of maximum or minimum are taken from the *General Catalogue of Variable Stars*, Vols. I and II, 4th ed., and the data for eclipsing binaries and RR Lyrae variables are from *Rocznik Astronomiczny Obserwatorium Krakowskiego 2001, International Supplement*.

TABLE 1—LONG-PERIOD VARIABLE STARS NORTH OF −20°

Variable		Max. m_v	Per. d	Epoch 2002	Variable		Max m_v	Per. d	Epoch 2002
0017+55	T Cas	7.8	445	Sep. 22	1425+39	V Boo	7.9	258	Feb. 9??
0018+38	R And	7.0	409	Nov. 8	1432+27	R Boo	7.2	223	Mar. 21
0211+43A	W And	7.0	397	Nov. 26	1517+31	S CrB	7.3	361	Oct. 23
0214−03	o Cet	3.4	332	Aug. 3	1546+39	V CrB	7.5	358	Apr. 20
0228−13	U Cet	7.5	235	Jul. 11	1546+15	R Ser	6.9	357	Dec. 17
0231+33	R Tri	6.2	266	May 24	1606+25	RU Her	8.0	484	—
0430+65	T Cam	8.0	374	May 17	1621+19	U Her	7.5	406	Sep. 14
0455−14	R Lep	6.8	432	Sep. 24	1621−12	V Oph	7.5	298	Feb. 17
0509+53	R Aur	7.7	459	—	1632+66	R Dra	7.6	245	May 11
0549+20A	U Ori	6.3	372	Dec. 12	1647+15	S Her	7.6	307	May 30
0617−02	V Mon	7.0	335	Feb. 4	1702−15	R Oph	7.9	302	Aug. 10
0653+55	R Lyn	7.9	379	Apr. 2	1717+23	RS Her	7.9	219	May 3
0701+22	R Gem	7.1	370	Nov. 13	1805+31	T Her	8.0	165	Apr. 15
0703+10	R CMi	8.0	338	Jun. 11	1811+36	W Lyr	7.9	196	Apr. 19
0727+08	S CMi	7.5	332	Sep. 8	1833+08	X Oph	6.8	334	Jun. 15
0811+12	R Cnc	6.8	362	Oct. 25	1901+08A	R Aql	6.1	270	Mar. 26
0816+17	V Cnc	7.9	272	Aug. 14	1910−17	T Sgr	8.0	392	—
0848+03	S Hya	7.8	257	Jan. 21	1910−19	R Sgr	7.3	269	Aug. 8
0850−08	T Hya	7.8	288	Mar. 11	1934+49	R Cyg	7.5	426	—
0939+34	R LMi	7.1	372	Oct. 26	1940+48	RT Cyg	7.3	190	Apr. 14
0942+11	R Leo	5.8	313	Jan. 14	1946+32	χ Cyg	5.2	407	Mar. 5
1037+69	R UMa	7.5	302	Aug. 18	2016+47	U Cyg	7.2	465	Jun. 3
1214−18	R Crv	7.5	317	Feb. 4	2044−05	T Aqr	7.7	202	May 25
1220+01	SS Vir	6.8	355	Sep. 12	2108+68	T Cep	6.0	390	Sep. 4
1231+60	T UMa	7.7	257	Jan. 16	2137+53	RU Cyg	8.0	234	Jul. 12??
1233+07	R Vir	6.9	146	Jan. 10	2301+10	R Peg	7.8	378	Nov. 7
1239+61	S UMa	7.8	226	Jan. 15	2307+59	V Cas	7.9	228	Apr. 1
1315+46	V CVn	6.8	192	May 10?	2315+08	S Peg	8.0	319	Feb. 20
1327+06	S Vir	7.0	378	Dec. 31	2338−15	R Aqr	6.5	387	Aug. 7
1344+40	R CVn	7.7	328	Jun. 6	2353+50	R Cas	7.0	431	—
1425+84	R Cam	7.9	270	Mar. 3	2357−15	W Cet	7.6	351	Oct. 11

TABLE 2—OTHER TYPES OF VARIABLE STARS

Variable		Max. m_v	Min. m_v	Type	Sp. Cl.	Period d	Epoch 2002 UT
0053+81	U Cep	6.7	9.8	Ecl.	B8 + gG2	2.493 085 6‡	Jan. 3.14*
0258+38	ρ Per	3.3	4.0	Semi R	M4	33–55, 1100	—
0301+40	β Per	2.1	3.3	Ecl.	B8 + G	2.867 315	†
0355+12	λ Tau	3.5	4.0	Ecl.	B3	3.952 952	Jan. 2.16*
0608+22	η Gem	3.1	3.9	Semi R	M3	233.4	—
0619+07	T Mon	5.6	6.6	Cep	F7–K1	27.024 649	Jan. 22.88
0658+20	ζ Gem	3.6	4.2	Cep	F7–G3	10.150 73	Jan. 7.29
1544+28	R CrB	5.8	14.8	R CrB	cFpep	—	—
1710+14	α Her	3.0	4.0	Semi R	M5	50–130, 6 y	—
1842–05	R Sct	5.0	7.0	RV Tau	G0e–K0p	144	—
1846+33	β Lyr	3.4	4.3	Ecl.	B8	12.940 047‡	Jan. 2.72*
1922+42	RR Lyr	6.9	8.0	RR Lyr	A2–F1	0.566 807 9‡	Jan. 1.11
1947+00	η Aql	3.5	4.3	Cep	F6–G4	7.176 641	Jan. 7.83
2225+57	δ Cep	3.5	4.4	Cep	F5–G2	5.366 341	Jan. 1.93

‡Changing period (period revised for 2002).
*Minimum.
†Predictions for all minima in 2002 are given in THE SKY MONTH BY MONTH section.

DESCRIPTION OF VARIABLE STAR TYPES

Variable stars are divided into four main classes: (1) pulsating and (2) eruptive variables, where variability is intrinsic due to physical changes in the star or stellar system; (3) eclipsing binary and (4) rotating stars, where variability is extrinsic due to an eclipse of one star by another or the effect of stellar rotation. A brief and general description of the major types in each class is given below.

(1) Pulsating Variables

Cepheids are variables that pulsate with periods of 1 to 70 days. They have high luminosity, and the amplitude of light variation ranges from 0.1 to 2 magnitudes. The prototypes of the group are located in open clusters and obey the well-known period–luminosity relation. They are of F spectral class at maximum and G to K at minimum. The later (cooler) the spectral class of a Cepheid, the longer its period. Typical representative: δ Cephei.

RR Lyrae types are pulsating, giant variables with periods ranging from 0.05 to 1.2 days with amplitude of light variation between 1 and 2 magnitudes. They are usually of A spectral class. Typical representative: RR Lyrae.

RV Tauri types are supergiant variables with a characteristic light curve of alternating deep and shallow minima. The periods, defined as the interval between two deep minima, range from 30 to 150 days. The amplitude of light variation may be as much as 3 magnitudes. Many show long-term cyclic variation of 500 to 9000 days. Generally the spectral classes range from G to K. Typical representative: R Scuti.

Long-period—Mira Ceti variables are giant variables that vary with amplitudes from 2.5 to 5 magnitudes or more. They have well-defined periodicity, ranging from 80 to 1000 days. They show characteristic emission spectra of late spectral classes M, C, and S. Typical representative: o Ceti (Mira).

Semiregular variables are giants or supergiants showing appreciable periodicity accompanied by intervals of irregularities of light variation. The periods range from

30 to 1000 days with amplitudes not more than 1 to 2 magnitudes in general. Typical representative: R Ursae Minoris.

Irregular variables are stars that at times show only a trace of periodicity or none at all. Typical representative: RX Leporis.

(2) Eruptive Variables

Novae are close binary systems consisting of a normal star and a white dwarf that increase 7 to 16 magnitudes in brightness in one to several hundred days. After the outburst the star fades slowly until the initial brightness is reached in several years or decades. Near maximum brightness the spectrum is generally similar to A or F giants. Typical representative: CP Puppis (Nova 1942).

Supernovae increase in brightness by 20 or more magnitudes due to a gigantic stellar explosion. The general appearance of the light curve is similar to novae. Typical representative: CM Tauri (Supernova of 1054 AD and the central star of the Crab Nebula).

U Geminorum types are dwarf novae that have long intervals of quiescence at minimum with sudden rises to maximum. Depending upon the star, the amplitude of eruptions ranges from 2 to 6 magnitudes, and the duration between outbursts tens to thousands of days. Most of these stars are spectroscopic binaries with periods of a few hours. Typical representative: SS Cygni.

Z Camelopardalis types are variables similar to U Gem stars in their physical and spectroscopic properties. They show cyclic variations interrupted by intervals of constant brightness ("stillstands") lasting for several cycles, approximately one-third of the way from maximum to minimum. Typical representative: Z Camelopardalis.

SU Ursae Majoris types are dwarf novae similar to U Gem and Z Cam stars in their physical and spectroscopic properties. They have frequent, faint, and narrow eruptions that last from one to a few days, along with infrequent, bright, and long eruptions, "superoutbursts," that last 10 to 20 days. During superoutbursts there are small amplitude, periodic variations, "superhumps," 2% to 3% longer than the orbital period of the system. Typical representative: SU Ursae Majoris.

R Coronae Borealis types are highly luminous variables that have nonperiodic drops in brightness from 1 to 9 magnitudes due to the formation of "carbon soot" in the stars' atmosphere. The duration of minima varies from a few months to years. Members of this group have F to K and R spectral class. Typical representative: R Coronae Borealis.

(3) Eclipsing Binaries

These are binary stars with the orbital plane lying near the line of sight of the observer. The components periodically eclipse each other, causing a decrease in the apparent brightness of the system. The period of the eclipses coincides with the period of the orbital motion. Typical representative: β Persei (Algol).

(4) Rotating Variables

These are rapidly rotating stars, usually close binary systems that undergo small amplitude changes in light that may be due to dark or bright spots on their surface. Eclipses may also be present in such systems. Typical representative: RS Canum Venaticorum.

SU UMA AND THE AAVSO CCD PHOTOMETRY PROGRAM
JOHN R. PERCY, JANET A. MATTEI, AND KERRIANN H. MALATESTA

Thousands of amateur astronomers have access to CCD (charge-coupled device) cameras, which are digital, linear, and sensitive. Mostly these are used for imaging, which they do very well. A few dozen amateur astronomers, however, are using CCD cameras for research, an activity that is both challenging and satisfying. Precision brightness measurement of variable stars is one example. The AAVSO supports this activity through its CCD Program and Committee, chaired by Gary Walker. See the AAVSO website **www.aavso.org/committees/ccd.stm** for more information. The two main CCD observing programs deal with faint long-period variable stars and with cataclysmic variables. Faint CCD observations of these stars complement the visual observations and make their light curves more complete.

Every year we highlight a variable star and invite amateur astronomers, using CCD photometry and/or visual observations, to help us solve its mysteries. This year it's SU Ursae Majoris, a *cataclysmic variable*. SU UMa (R.A. (2000) 8h 12m 28.2s, Dec. (2000) +62°36′23″) belongs to the dwarf nova class of cataclysmic variables—a close binary system, consisting of a solar-type "normal" star and a white dwarf in close mutual orbit; the period of SU UMa is only 1 h 50 min, and the whole system would fit inside our Sun. The dense white dwarf, with its strong gravitational potential, pulls streams of gas from its companion star. The transferred gas collects in a disk, called an accretion disk, around the white dwarf. Every few weeks the system brightens by several magnitudes, then returns to quiescence a few days later. This explosive phenomenon is how this type of variable star earned its ominous name.

But SU UMa does more than this. It is the prototype of a subclass of dwarf novae that have frequent, faint, and narrow dwarf nova outbursts along with infrequent, long, and bright "superoutbursts." The narrow outbursts occur every 11 to 17 days and typically last 1 to 3 days; the superoutbursts occur every 153 to 260 days (although the interval can be as long as three years, much to the consternation of observers). Superoutbursts can be a magnitude brighter than normal and last for 10 to 18 days. **Figure 1** shows a section of the AAVSO SU UMa light curve, including both narrow outbursts and a superoutburst. During superoutburst, the system varies in brightness by several tenths of a magnitude with a period that is 2% to 3% longer than the orbital period of the system, which is less than two hours! These fluctuations are called "superhumps."

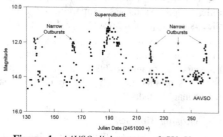

Figure 1: *AAVSO light curve of SU Ursae Majoris showing the narrow and superoutbursts from November 1998 to April 1999. The points are individual visual observations in the AAVSO international database.*

Why does all this happen? Although the cause of dwarf nova outbursts in general is still not fully understood, it is generally thought that when the density of the accretion disk reaches a critical value, thermal instabilities cause the disk to collapse and the material to be accreted onto the white dwarf, releasing gravitational energy and causing the outburst. The cause of superoutbursts is even less certain, but it may be that, in addition to the thermal instability, there is an instability due to tides in the disk as well. The disk expands until it reaches a critical size at which a resonance is achieved, just as well-timed pushes on a playground swing can cause the swing to go higher and higher. The tidal instabilities then produce the superoutburst, bringing the disk back to normal size. In this theory the superhumps are a result of precession of an elliptical accretion disk.

You can help to unravel the mystery. Variable-star observers have a long history of supporting research on cataclysmic variables (CVs) by monitoring them from the ground and watching for outbursts; their reports can trigger X-ray and ultraviolet observations of the outbursts with spacecraft such as Hubble Space Telescope and Chandra X-ray Observatory. You can participate in these projects by observing SU UMa and contributing your measurements to the AAVSO international database.

SU UMa, located near the tip of the nose of the Great Bear, can be observed year-round in the Northern Hemisphere with a moderate-sized telescope (150 mm or larger) with a CCD camera. It is normally about magnitude 15 but can reach magnitude 11 or brighter at maximum. CCD photometry is almost essential for studying superhumps, although they can be observed visually, with care. Observations, every few minutes for several hours, will cover several orbits of the star. Things happen fast in a CV! For more information about SU UMa, see the AAVSO's online "Variable Star of the Month" feature for February 2000 by Kerri Malatesta at www.aavso.org/vstar/vsotm/0200.stm.

The AAVSO has a wealth of support material for CCD photometrists. Start with www.aavso.org/committees/ccd.stm, which lists the information and services that the AAVSO can provide. Sign up for the electronic edition of CCD Views, which contains lists of new targets, new observing program ideas, and news of the activity of program stars. **Figure 2** shows a chart for SU UMa, showing stars down to magnitude 14.6 and covering half a degree in the sky. Charts that cover larger areas can be downloaded from the AAVSO charts website charts.aavso.org or ordered from the AAVSO (see the contact information on p. 242).

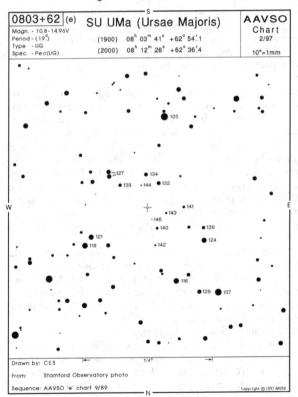

Figure 2: *AAVSO finding chart of SU UMa and some nearby comparison stars. The numbers beside the stars are their visual magnitudes, with the decimal point removed. North is down and east is to the right. SU UMa is indicated with a cross hair in the centre of the chart.*

STAR CLUSTERS

By Anthony Moffat and Peter Jedicke

The study of star clusters is crucial to the understanding of stellar structure and evolution. For most purposes, it can be assumed that the stars seen in a given cluster formed nearly simultaneously from the same parent cloud of gas and dust; thus the basic factor that distinguishes one star from another is the quantity of matter each contains. Comparing one cluster with another, it is essentially only the age and the chemical composition of their stars that differ. But what makes one cluster *appear* different from another in the sky is mainly the degree of concentration and regularity, the spread in magnitude and colour of the member stars, all of which vary mainly with age, and the total number of stars. Extremely young clusters are often irregular in shape with clumps of newly formed stars, pervaded by lanes of obscuring dust and bright nebulosity (e.g. the Orion Nebula around the Trapezium Cluster), while the oldest clusters, if they were fortunate enough not to have already dissipated or been torn apart by external forces, tend to be symmetric in shape, with only the slower-burning, low-mass stars remaining visible; the massive stars will have spent their nuclear fuel and passed to the degenerate graveyard of white dwarfs, neutron stars, or black holes, depending on their original mass.

The star clusters in the following lists were selected as the most conspicuous. Two types can be recognized: *open* and *globular.* Open clusters often appear as irregular aggregates of tens to thousands of stars, sometimes barely distinguishable from random fluctuations of the general field; they are concentrated toward the disk of the Milky Way and generally contain stars of chemical abundance like the Sun. They range in age from very young to very old.

Sometimes we observe loose, extended groups of very young stars. When precise methods of photometry, spectroscopy, and kinematics are applied, we see that these stars often have a common, but not necessarily strictly coeval, origin. Such loose concentrations of stars are referred to as *associations.* Dynamically, they are generally unbound over time scales of the order of ten million years, being subject to the strong tidal forces of passing clouds and the background Milky Way Galaxy. Often, they contain subconcentrations of young open clusters (e.g. the double cluster h and χ Persei of slightly different ages despite their proximity, in the association Per OB1, which stretches over some 6° on the sky) with a strong gradient in age as the star formation process rips through them from one edge to another. In view of their sparse nature, we do not consider it appropriate here to list any of the over 100-odd catalogued Milky Way associations.

For the larger and brighter globular clusters, which are generally those closer to the solar system, the observer's goal is to see them well enough to distinguish a generous sprinkling of individual stars against a diffuse glowing background. A globular cluster is "resolved" to the extent that these individual stars are seen. Large telescope apertures and good skies will help resolve globular clusters. Higher powers are helpful for identification of smaller, more distant globular clusters.

The table at the right includes all well-defined open clusters in the Milky Way Galaxy with diameters greater than 40′ and/or integrated magnitudes brighter than 5.0, as well as the richest clusters and some of special interest. The apparent integrated photographic magnitude (m_{pg}) is from Collinder, the angular diameter (**Diam.**) is generally from Trumpler, and the photographic magnitude of the fifth-brightest star (m_5) is from Shapley, except where in italics, which are new data. The distance (**Dist.**) is mainly from Becker and Fenkart (*Astr. Astrophys. Suppl. 4,* 241, 1971). The earliest spectral type of cluster stars (**Sp**) is a measure of the age as follows: expressed in millions of years, O5 = 2, B0 = 8, B5 = 70, A0 = 400, A5 = 1000, F0 = 3000, and F5 = 10 000.

OPEN CLUSTERS

NGC/ other†	RA (2000) Dec		Mag. m_{pg}	Diam. ′	m_5	Dist. 10^3 ly	Sp	Remarks
	h m	° ′						
188	0 44.0	+85 21	9.3	14	14.6	5.0	F2	Oldest known
752	1 57.8	+37 41	6.6	45	9.6	1.2	A5	
869	2 19.0	+57 10	4.3	30	9.5	7.0	B1	h Per
884	2 22.4	+57 07	4.4	30	9.5	8.1	B0	χ Per, M supergiants
Perseus	3 22	+48 36	2.3	240	5	0.6	B1	Moving cl.; α Per
Pleiades	3 47.1	+24 08	1.6	120	4.2	0.41	B6	M45, best known
Hyades	4 20	+15 38	0.8	400	3.9	0.15	A2	Moving cl. **, in Taurus
1912	5 28.6	+35 50	7.0	18	9.7	4.6	B5	M38
1976/80	5 35.4	−5 23	2.5	50	5.5	1.3	O5	Trapezium, very young
2099	5 52.4	+32 32	6.2	24	9.7	4.2	B8	M37
2168	6 08.8	+24 21	5.6	29	9.0	2.8	B5	M35
2232	6 26.5	−4 45	4.1	20	7	1.6	B1	
2244	6 32.4	+4 52	5.2	27	8.0	5.3	O5	Rosette, very young
2264	6 41.0	+9 53	4.1	30	8.0	2.4	O8	S Mon
2287	6 47.1	−20 44	5.0	32	8.8	2.2	B4	M41
2362	7 18.8	−24 56	3.8	7	9.4	5.4	O9	τ CMa
2422	7 35.6	−14 30	4.3	30	9.8	1.6	B3	
2437	7 41.8	−14 49	6.6	27	10.8	5.4	B8	M46
2451	7 45.4	−37 58	3.7	37	6	1.0	B5	
2516	7 58.3	−60 54	3.3	50	10.1	1.2	B8	
2546	8 12.5	−37 39	5.0	45	7	2.7	B0	
2632	8 40.1	+20 00	3.9	90	7.5	0.59	A0	Praesepe, M44
IC2391	8 40.3	−53 03	2.6	45	3.5	0.5	B4	
IC2395	8 41.0	−48 11	4.6	20	10.1	2.9	B2	
2682	8 50.4	+11 50	7.4	18	10.8	2.7	F2	M67, very old
3114	10 02.6	−60 07	4.5	37	7	2.8	B5	
IC2602	10 43.3	−64 23	1.6	65	6	0.5	B1	θ Car
Tr16	10 45.2	−59 42	6.7	10	10	9.6	O3	η Car and Nebula
3532	11 06.4	−58 39	3.4	55	8.1	1.4	B8	
3766	11 36.1	−61 37	4.4	12	8.1	5.8	B1	
Coma	12 25.1	+26 06	2.9	300	5.5	0.3	A1	Very sparse
4755	12 53.6	−60 20	5.2	12	7	6.8	B3	κ Cru, "Jewel Box"
6067	16 13.3	−54 13	6.5	16	10.9	4.7	B3	G, K supergiants
6231	16 54.0	−41 48	3.5	16	7.5	5.8	O9	O supergiants, WR stars
Tr 24	16 57.0	−40 40	3.5	60	7.3	5.2	O5	
6405	17 40.1	−32 13	4.6	26	8.3	1.5	B4	M6
IC4665	17 46.7	+5 44	5.4	50	7	1.1	B8	
6475	17 53.9	−34 48	3.3	50	7.4	0.8	B5	M7
6494	17 56.9	−19 01	5.9	27	10.2	1.4	B8	M23
6523	18 03.1	−24 23	5.2	45	7	5.1	O5	M8, Lagoon Nebula
6611	18 18.9	−13 47	6.6	8	10.6	5.5	O7	M16, nebula
IC4725	18 31.7	−19 15	6.2	35	9.3	2.0	B3	M25, Cepheid U Sgr
IC4756	18 39.3	+5 27	5.4	50	8.5	1.4	A3	
6705	18 51.1	−6 17	6.8	12.5	12	5.6	B8	M11, very rich
Mel 227	20 11.2	−79 19	5.2	60	9	0.8	B9	
IC1396	21 38.9	+57 30	5.1	60	8.5	2.3	O6	Tr 37
7790	23 58.4	+61 13	7.1	4.5	11.7	10.3	B1	Cepheids CEa, CEb and CF Cas

†IC = Index Catalogue; Tr = Trumpler; Mel = Melotte; **Basic for distance determination

The table below includes all the globular clusters in the Messier list and most of the globular clusters with a total apparent visual magnitude brighter than about 8.0. The data are taken from a compilation by Arp (*Galactic Structure*, ed. Blaauw and Schmidt, U. Chicago, 1965), supplemented by H.S. Hogg's Bibliography (*Publ. David Dunlap Obs. 2*, No. 12, 1963) and by the table of Milky Way globular cluster data as published on the website of W.E. Harris of McMaster University (see physun.mcmaster.ca/~harris/WEHarris.html). The apparent diameter (**Diam.**) given contains 90% of the stars, except values in italics, which are from miscellaneous sources. The concentration class (**Conc.**) is such that I is the most compact, XII the least. The integrated spectral type (**Int. Sp. T.**) varies mainly with the abundances.

GLOBULAR CLUSTERS

NGC	M/ other	RA (2000) h m	Dec ° '	Mag. m_v	Diam. '	Conc.	Int. Sp.T.	Dist. 10^3 ly
104†	47 Tuc	0 24.0	−72 04	3.95	*44*	III	G4	15
362		1 03.2	−70 50	6.4	*17.7*	III	F9	28
1851*		5 14.0	−40 02	7.14	*11.5*	II	F7	46
1904	79	5 24.1	−24 31	7.73	*7.8*	V	F5	42
2808		9 11.9	−64 51	6.2	*18.8*	I	F7	30
3201		10 17.6	−46 24	6.75	*29.3*	X	F6	17
4590	68	12 39.5	−26 44	7.84	6.4	X	F2	33
4833		12 59.5	−70 52	6.91	*12.7*	VIII	F3	20
5024	53	13 12.9	+18 10	7.61	8.3	V	F6	60
5139†	ω Cen	13 26.8	−47 28	3.68	*65.4*	VIII	F5	17
5272†	3	13 42.2	+28 22	6.19	9.3	VI	F6	35
5904	5	15 18.5	+2 04	5.65	10.7	V	F7	26
6093	80	16 17.0	−22 58	7.33	8.6	II	F6	33
6121	4	16 23.6	−26 31	5.63	22.6	IX	F8	14
6171	107	16 32.5	−13 03	7.93	12.8	X	G0	21
6205	13	16 41.7	+36 27	5.78	12.9	V	F6	21
6218	12	16 47.1	−1 56	6.7	21.5	IX	F8	24
6254	10	16 57.1	−4 05	6.6	16.2	VII	F3	20
6266	62	17 01.2	−30 06	6.45	8.8	IV	F9	22
6273	19	17 02.6	−26 16	6.77	9.3	VIII	F7	28
6333	9	17 19.2	−18 30	7.72	7.9	VIII	F5	27
6341	92	17 17.1	+43 08	6.44	12.3	IV	F2	26
6388		17 36.3	−44 44	6.72	*6.8*	III	G2	37
6397		17 40.7	−53 40	5.73	*19*	IX	F4	9
6402	14	17 37.6	−3 14	7.59	10.8	VIII	F4	29
6541†		18 08.0	−43 42	6.3	23.2	III	F6	13
6626	28	18 24.5	−24 52	6.79	9.1	IV	F8	19
6637	69	18 31.4	−32 20	7.64	6.8	V	G2	28
6656†	22	18 36.3	−23 54	5.1	26.2	VII	F5	10
6681	70	18 43.2	−32 17	7.87	5.1	V	F5	29
6715	54	18 55.0	−30 28	7.6	4.8	III	F7	89
6752		19 10.9	−59 58	5.4	*41.9*	VI	F4	17
6779	56	19 16.6	+30 11	8.27	10.1	X	F5	33
6809	55	19 40.1	−30 57	6.32	21.1	XI	F4	20
6838	71	19 53.8	+18 46	8.19	10.2	‡	G1	13
6864	75	20 06.0	−21 55	8.52	4.9	I	F9	61
6981	72	20 53.5	−12 32	9.27	6.4	IX	F7	55
7078*	15	21 30.1	+12 10	6.2	9.4	IV	F3	34
7089	2	21 33.5	−0 50	6.47	6.8	II	F4	40
7099	30	21 40.4	−23 10	7.19	6.8	V	F3	26

†These clusters contain dim X-ray sources.
*Bright, compact X-ray sources were discovered in these clusters in 1975.
‡Originally thought to be an open cluster; never assigned a concentration class.

AN EXAMPLE: THE HYADES
THE CLOSEST CLUSTER AND THE FUNDAMENT FOR DISTANCES
IN THE UNIVERSE

The Hyades cluster provides the foundation for essentially all distances, both local in our own galaxy and extragalactic, beyond about 300 ly from Earth. Once the distance of the Hyades is determined, the intrinsic brightnesses of its members can be found, leading to a calibration of its Main Sequence (MS) in the Colour–Magnitude diagram. Comparison of this MS with those of other clusters allows one to determine the distances of those clusters. By various methods of "boot-strapping," one obtains distances of globular clusters, Cepheid variable stars, and a host of other objects, eventually leading to the calibration of distances to the far corners of the universe.

At 147 ly, the distance to the centre of the Hyades cluster can now be readily found with very high accuracy using the so-called method of secular parallaxes. This is thanks to the high precision of the astrometric satellite HIPPARCOS proper motions and trigonometric parallaxes, which allow one to fix the distances to individual stars in the Hyades to within an error of about 2%. This in turn leads to a colour–absolute-magnitude diagram that displays an incredibly narrow MS: see the figure below (which is Fig.1 from de Bruijne, Hoogerwerf, and de Zeeuw, *Astrophys. J., 544*, L65, 2000). For the first time, one sees various gaps in the Hyades MS, some of which are intimately related to surface convective properties in the atmospheres of the stars. This in turn provides strong constraints on the stellar models.

Future astrometric satellites, such as NASA's FAME and ESA's GAIA, will improve the accuracy of such distances by several orders of magnitude, allowing one to study star clusters at much greater distances. This will then allow one to carry out revolutionary tests of the theory of stellar evolution with unprecedented accuracy.

The Hyades can be viewed with the unaided eye from both hemispheres as a loose clump of stars extending over some dozen Moon diameters near the head of Taurus the Bull. It is most conveniently seen, only some 15° from the well-known but more distant Pleiades cluster, in the evening hours of January–March. Although the bright giant star Aldebaran is seen in the same direction as the Hyades, it is not a member, being a mere superposition along the line of sight at a different distance.

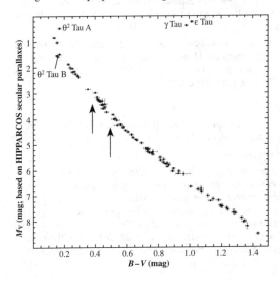

Colour–absolute-visual-magnitude diagram for 92 single-star members of the Hyades open cluster with high-precision HIPPARCOS secular parallaxes. Four bright member stars are identified, two of which are red giants. The two arrows indicate gaps caused by sudden changes in the properties of the convective atmospheres of the stars there.

AMATEUR SUPERNOVA HUNTING
By Rev. Robert Evans

The first discovery of a supernova by an amateur astronomer was photographic, by G. Romano of Italy (SN 1957B in NGC 4564); the first visual discovery was by J. Bennett of South Africa (SN 1968L in M83). In Australia in 1980, the author began systematic visual searching using a simple 250-mm backyard telescope and made two discoveries the following year. K. Okazaki of Japan, who discovered two supernovae, one each in 1983 and 1984, was the first amateur to perform a systematic photographic search.

By the late 1980s, most of the supernovae brighter than 15th magnitude were being found visually by amateurs. In the early 1990s, professional astronomers started using supernova studies to address major problems in cosmology; at that time, they were very dependent upon amateur searches to provide them with the best and brightest supernovae in nearby galaxies. These nearby supernovae provided much of the benchmark information needed for studying supernovae at remote distances, which led to independent estimates for the expansion, age, and fate of the universe.

CCD Supernova Hunting

In the last few years, the cost of charge-coupled devices (CCDs) has fallen to the point where many amateurs can afford to use them on computer-controlled telescopes. Some of these amateurs are hunting supernovae with resounding success. There are a number of advantages to using telescopes with CCDs and computer control:

(1) You can observe in locations with some light pollution or in the presence of fairly strong moonlight.

(2) With a computer to direct the telescope to individual galaxies, it is no longer necessary to know the sky well.

(3) With appropriate computer control of the telescope, you can sit in a warm room facing the computer screen.

(4) If your equipment is good enough, it will find supernovae without your presence.

(5) Stars as faint as 18th or 19th magnitude become accessible, which includes most supernovae in nearby galaxies plus the brighter supernovae in many distant galaxies, out to about 300 million light-years.

Using a CCD brings so many thousands of galaxies within range that you will never have enough time to observe them all! However, you will need reference materials for all the galaxies on your observing list—even if you make the reference images yourself—so that you can tell when a new object appears near a galaxy.

Visual Supernova Hunting

Visual supernova hunting has special requirements, but it has a number of advantages over using a CCD. The requirements are as follows:

(1) A reasonably dark observing site is needed.

(2) Your telescope needs to be easily manageable so that you can locate objects quickly, and the aperture needs to be big enough so that you can see down to about 15th magnitude. You can then observe all the nearby galaxies (out to, say, 100 million light-years). You will then be able to see most supernovae in galaxies out to about 25 million light-years and the brighter supernovae out to 100 million light-years or more. But, naturally, your chances of success decrease with the distance of the galaxy. Fainter supernovae in any given galaxy may be more numerous than the brighter ones, although the latter are the most interesting, scientifically.

(3) As in CCD searches, charts or suitable photographs of all your target galaxies are needed, so that you can tell when a new object appears.

The advantages of visual searching are the following:

(1) The equipment is less expensive than that needed for CCD work.

(2) An experienced visual observer usually knows the location and the normal appearance of many target galaxies and can thus work through observations of galaxies at 10 times the speed of anyone using a CCD on an amateur telescope. Professional-standard CCDs are quicker but are still much more expensive than those used by amateurs.

(3) You become very familiar with the night sky. (Personally, I think this is a great benefit of visual searching.)

(4) Amateurs who rely on computers to find galaxies are deceived by technology into being ignorant of the sky. Thus, when the technology fails (as it does from time to time), the search halts since the observer does not know where to locate target galaxies. A visual observer who knows the sky is immune to this problem.

Verification and Reporting

Verification of any suspected new discovery is vitally important. The first step is to check any suspect against all available photographs, CCD images, or charts of that galaxy. Measure carefully the offset of the new star from the nucleus of the galaxy. Watch the object for any possible movement against nearby stars. Note the time of your discovery (UT). It is necessary to have a team of other observers who can make independent observations of the new object, and who will do so immediately, if asked. These other observers must also have enough galaxy resources so that they can eliminate anything that is not a supernova, and they should be spread out over a number of locations in case bad weather puts any one observer out of action.

The Central Bureau for Astronomical Telegrams has issued instructions describing how much verification is needed about any possible new supernova, and these should be consulted. CCD observers need at least five observations covering 24 hours. A visual observer should have independent observations by people who know what they are doing. And even after the Central Bureau has been notified, spectra will probably need to be obtained through one of the main observatories before the Bureau will finally announce a discovery.

When notifying the Central Bureau, provide full details of all observations of the new object: the name and location of the person making the report, the discoverer's name and location, details of the reference materials consulted, details concerning the equipment used, universal time of all observations, name and position of the galaxy, offset and brightness of the supernova, and similar details about each verifying observation. Observers who are not already known at the Bureau should be especially thorough in detailing and supporting their report. All discoveries can be emailed to the Central Bureau at cbat@cfa.harvard.edu.

Much helpful advice is available in the *AAVSO Supernova Search Manual*, which is available from the AAVSO, 25 Birch Street, Cambridge, MA 02138, U.S.A., for the cost of postage only. It can also be downloaded through the Internet at www.aavso.org/supernovatwo.stm (see also www.aavso.org/supernovaone.stm).

Editor's Note: Robert Evans, who made his first supernova discovery in 1981, holds the record for visual discoveries of supernovae: 33. Ten of these were found using a 250-mm telescope, 2 using a 310-mm telescope, 18 with a 410-mm instrument (these telescopes were "backyard" variety newtonians), and 3 using the 1.02-m telescope at Siding Spring Observatory (Australian National University). In addition, he has discovered 4 supernovae (plus a comet) on U.K. Schmidt films specially exposed by Anglo Australian Observatory staff in a Pro-Am project which Evans shared with Dr. Brian Schmidt of Mount Stromlo Observatory and Robert McNaught.

EXPIRED STARS
By Roy Bishop

Stars are where the action is, and the action is fuelled by gravitation and thermo-nuclear fusion. Gravitation, the midwife and undertaker, forms a star, heats it to the temperatures necessary to ignite successive stages of fusion reactions, and when nuclear fuel runs out, crushes the ashes of the star into one of three final states: white dwarf, neutron star, or black hole. Thermonuclear fusion merely delays the onset of further collapse and higher temperatures. In the case of our Sun, the first and by far the longest delay, the "hang-up" provided by hydrogen-to-helium fusion, is already half over.

White Dwarfs

Stars comparable to our Sun have insufficient gravity to reach the temperatures neces-sary to form nuclei heavier than carbon or oxygen. When the thermal support pressure generated by fusion wanes, gravity gradually crushes the central portion of the star. If the mass of this core is less than 1.4 solar masses (a limit discovered by a leading astrophysicist of the 20th century, Subramanyan Chandrasekhar), the collapse halts at a very hot, Earth-sized remnant known as a white dwarf. At this point, the squeeze of gravity is offset by *electron degeneracy pressure*, an intrinsic aspect of the wave–particle nature of matter and the same pressure responsible for the stability and size of an atom. However, in the case of a white dwarf, the pressure is such that the electrons are not tied to individual atomic nuclei but occupy the whole star. In this sense, the star has become a giant atom. In physics jargon: electrons are fermions (i.e. they obey Fermi–Dirac quantum statistics) and, hence, abide by the Pauli Exclusion Principle, which dictates that no two electrons can occupy the same quantum state. This results in an immense pressure, sufficient to prevent further collapse, provided the mass is less than the Chandrasekhar limit. White dwarf diameters are about 1% that of our Sun, which has a nearly water-like average density (1 g/cm^3). Thus a cubic centimetre of white dwarf material has a mass near 100^3 g or one tonne (like a Honda Civic crushed into a sugar cube).

Because of their immense thermal energy and small surface area, white dwarfs cool extremely slowly. Also, they are intrinsically very faint and thus only those close to the solar system can be seen.

Only one white dwarf is easily observable with a small telescope: **Omicron 2 Eridani B** (also designated 40 Eridani B), located 16.5 light-years from Earth. Omicron 2 Eridani A, the bright (mag. 4.4) companion to the dim (mag. 9.5) white dwarf, is shown on the JANUARY ALL-SKY CHART on p. 277: o^2 Eri A is the eastern (left-hand) member of the close pair of stars located due west of the word "Rigel." Omicron 2 Eridani B, the white dwarf, is located only 83″ east-southeast of o^2 Eri A (position angle ≈110°). Remarkably, stars A and B are accompanied by a third star, a faint (mag. 11.2) red dwarf star, o^2 Eri C, which resides only 9″ north of B. (There is a brighter and closer white dwarf, the companion of Sirius, α CMa B, but it is usu-ally lost in the glare of Sirius. See THE NEAREST STARS (pp. 234–238) and DOUBLE AND MULTIPLE STARS (pp. 239–241) for more information on both of these stellar systems.)

For the observer with a small telescope, o^2 Eri B is the only Earth-sized object visible in the depths of interstellar space, the only visible object with a mass density far exceeding that of ordinary matter, the only accessible star no longer powered by nuclear reactions, and the only star that has expired and can still be seen.

Neutron Stars

For a large star of about eight or more solar masses, energy-releasing reactions end in its centre with the fusion of silicon nuclei into iron. Iron has the most tightly bound nucleus (per nuclear particle) and, hence, is no good as a fuel for further fusion. Electron degeneracy pressure supports the inert iron core until silicon fusion in a surrounding shell supplies enough additional iron to push the inert core over the Chandrasekhar limit. Gravity then overwhelms electron degeneracy pressure and the core collapses in less than a second. Gravitation-induced temperatures rise past 10^{10} K, sufficient to disassemble heavy nuclei synthesized over the life of the star. This absorbs energy, accelerating the collapse. Also, electrons attain sufficient energy to combine with protons to form neutrons and neutrinos, another energy-absorbing reaction that also removes electrons, further hastening the collapse.

Provided the infalling mass is less than about three solar masses, like a hammer striking an anvil, when the core reaches a diameter of about 20 km the infall is violently arrested by a combination of *neutron* degeneracy pressure and the short-range repulsive nature of the strong nuclear force, the same agents that govern the size and structure of the nuclei of atoms of ordinary matter. With a diameter 500 times smaller than that of a white dwarf, the density at this stage is 500^3 larger, 100 million tonnes per cubic centimetre (like an aircraft carrier crushed to the size of the ball of a ballpoint pen). This is the density of ordinary atomic nuclei. The star's core has effectively become a gigantic nucleus, composed primarily of neutrons.

The abrupt rebound of the nearly rigid central core reverses the infall of the outer layers, turning the implosion into a spectacular explosion, a Type II supernova. The subsequent steps are complex and not yet well understood, but appear to involve interactions with the immense numbers of neutrinos generated in the neutron production. The gravitational energy released in the sudden collapse of the couple of solar masses now locked in the central neutron star is about 10^{46} J. This is far more energy than our Sun will produce in its entire 10-billion-year lifetime.

Over the next several thousand years, the remnants of the outer layers of the star form an expanding, glowing cloud of gas and dust, seeding interstellar space with the heavy chemical elements (oxygen, silicon, iron, uranium, etc.) synthesized in its outer layers both before and during the supernova explosion. The potassium ions moving in the neurons of your brain as you read these words emerged from such a conflagration some 5 billion years ago.

No neutron stars are visible in a small telescope, although one is *indirectly* visible in the **Crab Nebula**, M1. The Crab supernova was a bright, naked-eye star in the skies of Earth in the year 1054 AD, although it had taken 6000 years for the light of the explosion to reach our planet. The nebula we see today is the expanding debris cloud as it was nearly 1000 years after the initial explosion.

The Crab Nebula glows across the electromagnetic spectrum, from radio waves to gamma rays, powered by the energy contained in the gravitational field and the rapid but decreasing spin of the neutron star at its centre. The glow of the debris cloud is like the glow of a red-hot disk brake slowing the spin of a wheel. The visible light from the cloud is *synchrotron radiation* emitted by electrons as they spiral in the tangled magnetic field of the neutron star. Nowhere else in the heavens is such an exotic light visible in a small telescope, polarized light with the brilliance of a thousand suns, emitted not by atoms but by free electrons being flung about by a spinning neutron star. The neutron star itself is known as a *pulsar* because it flashes 30 times per second, in step with its spin. However, even if the Crab pulsar were bright enough to be visible in a small telescope, the flashing would not be apparent because, as in a motion picture or cathode-ray tube monitor, the flicker is too rapid for the eye to follow.

Colour photographs of the Crab Nebula reveal a celestial gift: a package of bluish synchrotron radiation wrapped in the loops of a tattered red ribbon—fragments of the shattered star, fluorescing in hydrogen-alpha light. Unfortunately, the luminance of the fluorescence is below the threshold for retinal cone vision, and rod vision is blind to H-alpha light. Thus all we can see is the ghostly cloud of synchrotron radiation.

The Crab Nebula is located 1° northwest of the star at the tip of the east horn of the constellation Taurus, ζ Tau. In the JANUARY ALL-SKY CHART on p. 277, the nebula is the tiny circle of dots 5 mm to the right of the cross marking the summer solstice (SS). In a telescope the nebula appears merely as a small glowing cloud, but to the knowledgeable observer, this synchrotron radiation brake of a spinning neutron star is an object for profound contemplation.

Black Holes

Stars whose masses are greater than about 20 suns likely retain more than 3 solar masses in their imploding cores. This is sufficient that gravitation will overwhelm not only the degeneracy pressure of electrons, but also the highly incompressible nature of nuclear matter. Within seconds, space-time itself closes around the imploding stellar core, removing all but the core's gravitational field from the observable universe. The star has become a black hole.

The earliest and best candidate for a stellar black hole is **Cygnus X-1**, one of the strongest galactic X-ray sources in the sky. Cygnus X-1 is the invisible companion of a star that can be seen in a small telescope: HDE 226868, an O9.7Iab star, a very luminous, very hot supergiant located several thousand light-years from the Sun. It orbits its nearby, unseen companion with a 5.6-day period. The mass of the companion is between 10 and 16 solar masses, far too large for it to be a white dwarf or neutron star. X-rays are generated as material from the supergiant falls toward the invisible companion. The X-rays extend to energies of 100 keV and vary on time scales as short as milliseconds, indicative of a very compact companion.

At 9th magnitude, the supergiant HDE 226868 is visible in any small telescope. It is less than half a degree from the 4th magnitude star Eta Cygni. Eta Cygni is the

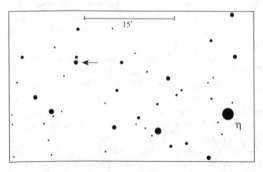

star in the neck of the swan, next to the "C" in CYGNUS on the SEPTEMBER ALL-SKY CHART on p. 281. Any low magnification will more than encompass the field shown in the **finder chart** at the left. North is upward, Eta Cygni is at the lower right, and HDE 226868 is indicated by the small arrow. The chart magnitude limit is about 13. Although HDE 226868 is a blue supergiant, in telescopes of sufficient aperture this star appears orange because of interstellar dust between us and the star.

All that is to be seen is the hot supergiant, but the view will be worth the search if you know that at this same location in the field of your telescope lurks one of the most likely candidates for a black hole, a knot in the fabric of space-time where a giant star has vanished. No painting, computer simulation, or Hollywood movie can match this observation.

NEBULAE AND GALAXIES

GALACTIC NEBULAE

BY WILLIAM HERBST

The following objects were selected from the brightest and largest of the various classes to illustrate the different types of interactions between stars and interstellar matter in our galaxy. *Emission regions* (HII) are excited by the strong ultraviolet flux of young, hot stars and are characterized by the lines of hydrogen in their spectra. *Reflection nebulae* (Ref) result from the diffusion of starlight by clouds of interstellar dust. At certain stages of their evolution stars become unstable and explode, shedding their outer layers into what becomes a *planetary nebula* (Pl) or a *supernova remnant* (SN). *Protostellar nebulae* (PrS) are objects still poorly understood; they are somewhat similar to the reflection nebulae, but their associated stars, often variable, are very luminous infrared stars that may be in the earliest stages of stellar evolution. Also included in the selection are three *extended complexes* (Comp) of special interest for their rich population of dark and bright nebulosities of various types. In the table S is the optical surface brightness in magnitude per square second of arc of representative regions of the nebula, and $m*$ is the magnitude of the associated star.

NGC	M	Con	RA (2000) h m	Dec ° '	Type	Size '	S mag/sq"	m*	Dist. 10^3 ly	Remarks
1435		Tau	3 47.5	+24 05	Ref	15	20	4	0.4	Merope nebula
1535		Eri	4 14.2	−12 45	Pl	0.5	17	12		
1952	1	Tau	5 34.5	+22 01	SN	5	19	16v	4	"Crab" + pulsar
1976	42	Ori	5 35.3	−5 24	HII	30	18	4	1.5	Orion Nebula
2070		Dor	5 38.6	−69 05	HII	20	—	13	200	Tarantula Nebula
ζ Ori		Ori	5 40.8	−1 56	Comp	2°			1.5	Incl. "Horsehead"
2068	78	Ori	5 46.8	+0 02	Ref	5	20		1.5	
1C443		Gem	6 17.6	+22 36	SN	40			2	
2244		Mon	6 32.4	+4 52	HII	50	21	7	3	Rosette Nebula
2261		Mon	6 39.1	+8 43	PrS	2		12v	4	Hubble's Variable Neb.
2392		Gem	7 29.2	+20 54	Pl	0.3	18	10	10	Clown Face Nebula
2626		Vel	8 35.6	−40 38	Ref	2	—	10	3	
3132		Vel	10 07.0	−40 25	Pl	1	17	10	—	Eight-Burst
3324		Car	10 37.5	−58 38	HII	15	—	8	9	
3372		Car	10 45.1	−59 41	HII	80	—	6v	9	Carina Nebula
3503		Car	11 01.3	−60 43	Ref	3	—	11	9	
3587	97	UMa	11 14.8	+55 01	Pl	3	21	13	12	Owl Nebula
—		Cru	12 51	−63	Dark	6°	—	—	0.5	Coal Sack
5189		Mus	13 33.8	−66 00	HII	150	—	10	—	
ρ Oph		Oph	16 25.6	−23 27	Comp	4°			0.5	Bright + dark nebula
6514	20	Sgr	18 02.4	−23 02	HII	15	19		3.5	Trifid Nebula
6523	8	Sgr	18 03.6	−24 23	HII	40	18		4.5	Lagoon Nebula
6543		Dra	17 58.6	+66 37	Pl	0.4	15	11	3.5	
6618	17	Sgr	18 20.9	−16 11	HII	20	19		3.5	Horseshoe Nebula
6720	57	Lyr	18 53.6	+33 03	Pl	1.2	18	15	5	Ring Nebula
6726		CrA	19 01.7	−36 54	PrS	5	—	7	0.5	
6853	27	Vul	19 59.5	+22 43	Pl	7	19	13	3.5	Dumbbell Nebula
6888		Cyg	20 12.3	+38 25	HII	15				
γ Cyg		Cyg	20 22.2	+40 16	Comp	6°				HII + dark nebula
6960/95		Cyg	20 45.6	+30 42	SN	150			2.5	Cygnus loop
7000		Cyg	20 58.9	+44 19	HII	100	22		3.5	North America Nebula
7009		Aqr	21 04.1	−11 23	Pl	0.5	16	12	3	Saturn Nebula
7027		Cyg	21 07.1	+42 14	Pl	0.2	15	13		
7129		Cep	21 43.0	+65 06	Ref	3	21	10	2.5	Small cluster
7293		Aqr	22 29.6	−20 48	Pl	13	22	13		Helix Nebula

THE MESSIER CATALOGUE
By Alan Dyer

Charles Messier's Catalogue provides a selection of the best and brightest deep-sky wonders for Northern Hemisphere viewers. Messier compiled his list in the late 1700s to aid prospective comet hunters. Some of these objects he discovered himself, some were first seen by other astronomers of the day, while a few (the Pleiades and the Beehive) were known since antiquity. The Messier numbers do not follow an ordered sequence across the sky. Rather, they are numbered in the order he discovered and catalogued them. Although he intended to, Messier never did publish a list with entries renumbered in order of right ascension.

In our version of the Messier Catalogue, we've listed the objects by season *for the evening observer*, grouping the objects within their respective constellations. The constellations are then listed roughly in order of increasing right ascension, that is constellations farther to the east and which rise later in the night are farther down the list. This is to help plan the sequence of an evening's Messier hunt.

The identity of some Messier objects is controversial. There is evidence that M91 and M102 are mistaken observations of M58 and M101, respectively. M104 and M109 were found by a colleague, Pierre Mechain, and reported to Messier for inclusion in his Catalogue. NGC 205, one of the companion galaxies to M31, the Andromeda Galaxy, was apparently found by Messier but never included in his Catalogue. Modern-day observers have dubbed this object M110. In our list, we have included 110 entries, including two objects that some have suggested as alternative candidates for M91 and M102.

Modern-day Messier hunters often wonder what telescopes Messier used. The largest were 190-mm and 200-mm reflectors. However, their speculum metal mirrors would have had the equivalent light gathering power of a modern 80-mm to 100-mm reflector. He also used a number of 90-mm refractors. Today, a dark site and a good 80-mm refractor or 100-mm reflector should be sufficient for completing the entire list. Objects M6 and M7 are the most southerly, while M74 and M76 are often considered the faintest and most difficult. M83's low altitude and diffuse appearance make it a challenge for Canadian observers north of 50° latitude

The columns contain the Messier number, the object's NGC (New General Catalogue) number, the constellation, the type of object, its epoch 2000 coordinates, visual magnitude m_v, and angular size in minutes of arc (planetary nebula sizes are given in seconds of arc "). Entries marked "!!" are showpiece objects. OC = open cluster; GC = globular cluster; PN = planetary nebula; EN = emission nebula; RN = reflection nebula; E/RN = combination of emission and reflection nebula; SNR = supernova remnant; G = galaxy (E = elliptical, I = irregular, SA = normal spiral, SB = barred spiral, S0 = lenticular). Data are taken from *The Deep Sky Field Guide to Uranometria 2000.0* (published by Willmann-Bell, Inc., 1993), compiled by Murray Cragin, James Lucyk, and Barry Rappaport from a variety of contemporary catalogues. Some sizes have been rounded to two significant figures. Also recommended as an excellent guide is *The Messier Objects*, by Stephen James O'Meara (Cambridge University Press, 1998).

The RASC offers observing certificates for members who observe the 110 objects in the Messier list or the 110 objects in the Finest NGC list (see pp. 262–264). For beginners or observers using binoculars the Society also offers the "Explore the Universe" Certificate. Contact your local Centre or the RASC National Office (see pp. 8–9) for details.

NUMERICAL LISTING OF MESSIER OBJECTS

M#	Sky	Con	M#	Sky	Con	M#	Sky	Con	M#	Sky	Con	M#	Sky	Con
1	Win	Tau	23	Sum	Sgr	45	Win	Tau	67	Spr	Cnc	89	Spr	Vir
2	Aut	Aqr	24	Sum	Sgr	46	Win	Pup	68	Spr	Hya	90	Spr	Vir
3	Spr	CVn	25	Sum	Sgr	47	Win	Pup	69	Sum	Sgr	91	Spr	Com
4	Sum	Sco	26	Sum	Sct	48	Win	Hya	70	Sum	Sgr	92	Sum	Her
5	Spr	Ser	27	Sum	Vul	49	Spr	Vir	71	Sum	Sge	93	Win	Pup
6	Sum	Sco	28	Sum	Sgr	50	Win	Mon	72	Aut	Aqr	94	Spr	CVn
7	Sum	Sco	29	Sum	Cyg	51	Spr	CVn	73	Aut	Aqr	95	Spr	Leo
8	Sum	Sgr	30	Aut	Cap	52	Aut	Cas	74	Aut	Psc	96	Spr	Leo
9	Sum	Oph	31	Aut	And	53	Spr	Com	75	Sum	Sgr	97	Spr	UMa
10	Sum	Oph	32	Aut	And	54	Sum	Sgr	76	Aut	Per	98	Spr	Com
11	Sum	Sct	33	Aut	Tri	55	Sum	Sgr	77	Aut	Cet	99	Spr	Com
12	Sum	Oph	34	Aut	Per	56	Sum	Lyr	78	Win	Ori	100	Spr	Com
13	Sum	Her	35	Win	Gem	57	Sum	Lyr	79	Win	Lep	101	Spr	UMa
14	Sum	Oph	36	Win	Aur	58	Spr	Vir	80	Sum	Sco	102	Spr	Dra?
15	Aut	Peg	37	Win	Aur	59	Spr	Vir	81	Spr	UMa	103	Aut	Cas
16	Sum	Ser	38	Win	Aur	60	Spr	Vir	82	Spr	UMa	104	Spr	Vir
17	Sum	Sgr	39	Sum	Cyg	61	Spr	Vir	83	Spr	Hya	105	Spr	Leo
18	Sum	Sgr	40	Spr	UMa	62	Sum	Oph	84	Spr	Vir	106	Spr	CVn
19	Sum	Oph	41	Win	CMa	63	Spr	CVn	85	Spr	Com	107	Sum	Oph
20	Sum	Sgr	42	Win	Ori	64	Spr	Com	86	Spr	Vir	108	Spr	UM
21	Sum	Sgr	43	Win	Ori	65	Spr	Leo	87	Spr	Vir	109	Spr	UMa
22	Sum	Sgr	44	Spr	Cnc	66	Spr	Leo	88	Spr	Com	110	Aut	And

SEASONAL LISTING OF MESSIER OBJECTS

M#	NGC	Con	Type	RA (2000) h m	Dec ° '	m_v	Size '	Remarks
The Winter Sky								
1	1952	Tau	SNR	5 34.5	+22 01	8.4	6 × 4	!! famous Crab Neb. supernova remnant
45	—	Tau	OC	3 47.0	+24 07	1.2	110	!! Pleiades; look for subtle nebulosity
36	1960	Aur	OC	5 36.1	+34 08	6.0	12	bright but scattered group; use low pow.
37	2099	Aur	OC	5 52.4	+32 33	5.6	20	!! finest of 3 Auriga clusters; very rich
38	1912	Aur	OC	5 28.7	+35 50	6.4	21	look for small cluster NGC 1907 1/2° S
42	1976	Ori	E/RN	5 35.4	−5 27	—	65 × 60	!! Orion Nebula; finest in northern sky
43	1982	Ori	E/RN	5 35.6	−5 16	—	20 × 15	detached part of Orion Nebula
78	2068	Ori	RN	5 46.7	+0 03	—	8 × 6	bright featureless reflection nebula
79	1904	Lep	GC	5 24.5	−24 33	7.8	8.7	200-mm telescope needed to resolve
35	2168	Gem	OC	6 08.9	+24 20	5.1	28	!! look for sm. cluster NGC 2158 1/4° S
41	2287	CMa	OC	6 47.0	−20 44	4.5	38	4° south of Sirius; bright but coarse
50	2323	Mon	OC	7 03.2	−8 20	5.9	16	between Sirius & Procyon; use low mag.
46	2437	Pup	OC	7 41.8	−14 49	6.1	27	!! contains planetary nebula NGC 2438
47	2422	Pup	OC	7 36.6	−14 30	4.4	29	coarse cluster 1.5° west of M46
93	2447	Pup	OC	7 44.6	−23 52	≈6.2	22	compact, bright cluster; fairly rich
48	2548	Hya	OC	8 13.8	−5 48	5.8	54	former "lost" Messier; large, sparse cl.

SEASONAL LISTING OF MESSIER OBJECTS (continued)

M#	NGC	Con	Type	RA (2000) h m	Dec ° '	m_v	Size '	Remarks
The Spring Sky								
44	2632	Cnc	OC	8 40.1	+19 59	3.1	95	!! Beehive or Praesepe; use low power
67	2682	Cnc	OC	8 50.4	+11 49	6.9	29	one of the oldest star clusters known
40	—	UMa	2 stars	12 22.4	+58 05	8.0	—	double star Winnecke 4; separation 50″
81	3031	UMa	G-SAab	9 55.6	+69 04	6.9	24 × 13	!! bright spiral visible in binoculars
82	3034	UMa	G-I0	9 55.8	+69 41	8.4	12 × 6	!! the "exploding" galaxy; M81 1/2° S
97	3587	UMa	PN	11 14.8	+55 01	9.9	194″	!! Owl Nebula; distinct grey oval
101	5457	UMa	G-SABcd	14 03.2	+54 21	7.9	26 × 26	!! Pinwheel Gal.; diffuse face-on spiral
108	3556	UMa	G-SBcd	11 11.5	+55 40	10.0	8.1 × 2.1	nearly edge-on; paired with M97 3/4° SE
109	3992	UMa	G-SBbc	11 57.6	+53 23	9.8	7.6 × 4.3	barred spiral near γ UMa
65	3623	Leo	G-SABa	11 18.9	+13 05	9.3	8.7 × 2.2	!! bright elongated spiral
66	3627	Leo	G-SABb	11 20.2	+12 59	8.9	8.2 × 3.9	!! M65 and NGC 3628 in same field
95	3351	Leo	G-SBb	10 44.0	+11 42	9.7	7.8 × 4.6	bright barred spiral
96	3368	Leo	G-SABab	10 46.8	+11 49	9.2	6.9 × 4.6	M95 in same field
105	3379	Leo	G-E1	10 47.8	+12 35	9.3	3.9 × 3.9	bright elliptical near M95 and M96
53	5024	Com	GC	13 12.9	+18 10	7.5	12.6	150-mm telescope needed to resolve
64	4826	Com	G-SAab	12 56.7	+21 41	8.5	9.2 × 4.6	!! Black Eye Gal.; eye needs big scope
85	4382	Com	G-SA0+	12 25.4	+18 11	9.1	7.5 × 5.7	bright elliptical shape
88	4501	Com	G-SAb	12 32.0	+14 25	9.6	6.1 × 2.8	bright multiple-arm spiral
91	4548	Com	G-SBb	12 35.4	+14 30	10.2	5.0 × 4.1	some lists say M91 = M58, not NGC4548
98	4192	Com	G-SABab	12 13.8	+14 54	10.1	9.1 × 2.1	nearly edge-on spiral near star 6 Com. B.
99	4254	Com	G-SAc	12 18.8	+14 25	9.9	4.6 × 4.3	nearly face-on spiral near M98
100	4321	Com	G-SABbc	12 22.9	+15 49	9.3	6.2 × 5.3	face-on spiral with starlike nucleus
49	4472	Vir	G-E2	12 29.8	+8 00	8.4	8.1 × 7.1	very bright elliptical
58	4579	Vir	G-SABb	12 37.7	+11 49	9.7	5.5 × 4.6	bright barred spiral; M59 and M60 1° E
59	4621	Vir	G-E5	12 42.0	+11 39	9.6	4.6 × 3.6	bright elliptical paired with M60
60	4649	Vir	G-E2	12 43.7	+11 33	8.8	7.1 × 6.1	bright elliptical with M59 and NGC 4647
61	4303	Vir	G-SABbc	12 21.9	+4 28	9.7	6.0 × 5.9	face-on two-armed spiral
84	4374	Vir	G-E1	12 25.1	+12 53	9.1	5.1 × 4.1	!! w/ M86 in Markarian's Chain
86	4406	Vir	G-E3	12 26.2	+12 57	8.9	12 × 9	!! w/ many NGC galaxies in Chain
87	4486	Vir	G-E0-1	12 30.8	+12 24	8.6	7.1 × 7.1	the one with famous jet and black hole
89	4552	Vir	G-E	12 35.7	+12 33	9.8	3.4 × 3.4	elliptical; resembles M87 but smaller
90	4569	Vir	G-SABab	12 36.8	+13 10	9.5	10 × 4	bright barred spiral near M89
104	4594	Vir	G-SA	12 40.0	−11 37	8.0	7.1 × 4.4	!! Sombrero Galaxy; look for dust lane
3	5272	CVn	GC	13 42.2	+28 23	5.9	16.2	!! contains many variable stars
51	5194/5	CVn	G-SAbc	13 29.9	+47 12	8.4	8 × 7	!! Whirlpool Galaxy; superb in big scope
63	5055	CVn	G-SAbc	13 15.8	+42 02	8.6	14 × 8	!! Sunflower Galaxy; bright, elongated
94	4736	CVn	G-SAab	12 50.9	+41 07	8.2	13 × 11	very bright and comet-like
106	4258	CVn	G-SABbc	12 19.0	+47 18	8.4	20 × 8	!! superb large, bright spiral
68	4590	Hya	GC	12 39.5	−26 45	7.7	12	150-mm telescope needed to resolve
83	5236	Hya	G-SABc	13 37.0	−29 52	7.6	16 × 13	large and diffuse; superb from far south
102	5866?	Dra	G-SA0+	15 06.5	+55 46	9.9	6.6 × 3.2	or is M102 = M101? (look for 5907)
5	5904	Ser	GC	15 18.6	+2 05	5.7	17.4	!! one of the sky's finest globulars
The Summer Sky								
13	6205	Her	GC	16 41.7	+36 28	5.7	16.6	!! Hercules Cluster; NGC 6207 1/2° NE
92	6341	Her	GC	17 17.1	+43 08	6.4	11.2	9° NE of M13; fine but often overlooked
9	6333	Oph	GC	17 19.2	−18 31	7.6	9.3	smallest of Ophiuchus globulars
10	6254	Oph	GC	16 57.1	−4 06	6.6	15.1	rich globular cluster; M12 is 3° NW
12	6218	Oph	GC	16 47.2	−1 57	6.8	14.5	loose globular cluster near M10
14	6402	Oph	GC	17 37.6	−3 15	7.6	11.7	200-mm telescope needed to resolve
19	6273	Oph	GC	17 02.6	−26 16	6.7	13.5	oblate globular; M62 4° south
62	6266	Oph	GC	17 01.2	−30 07	6.7	14.1	asymmetrical; in rich field

SEASONAL LISTING OF MESSIER OBJECTS (continued)

M#	NGC	Con	Type	RA (2000) Dec		m_v	Size	Remarks
				h m	° ′		′	
Summer Sky continued…								
107	6171	Oph	GC	16 32.5	−13 03	8.1	10.0	small, faint globular
4	6121	Sco	GC	16 23.6	−26 32	5.8	26.3	bright globular near Antares
6	6405	Sco	OC	17 40.1	−32 13	4.2	33	!! Butterfly Cluster; best at low power
7	6475	Sco	OC	17 53.9	−34 49	3.3	80	!! excellent in binocs or rich-field scope
80	6093	Sco	GC	16 17.0	−22 59	7.3	8.9	very compressed globular
16	6611	Ser	EN + OC	18 18.6	−13 58	—	35 × 28	Eagle Neb. w/ open cl.; use neb. filter
8	6523	Sgr	EN	18 03.8	−24 23	—	45 × 30	!! Lagoon Nebula w/ open cl. NGC 6530
17	6618	Sgr	EN	18 20.8	−16 11	—	20 × 15	!! Swan or Omega Nebula; use neb. filter
18	6613	Sgr	OC	18 19.9	−17 08	6.9	10	sparse cluster; 1° south of M17
20	6514	Sgr	E/RN	18 02.3	−23 02	—	20 × 20	!! Trifid Nebula; look for dark lanes
21	6531	Sgr	OC	18 04.6	−22 30	5.9	13	0.7° NE of M20; sparse cluster
22	6656	Sgr	GC	18 36.4	−23 54	5.1	24	spectacular from southern latitude
23	6494	Sgr	OC	17 56.8	−19 01	5.5	27	bright, loose open cluster
24	—	Sgr	starcloud	18 16.5	−18 50	4.6	95 × 35	rich star cloud; best in big binoculars
25	IC4725	Sgr	OC	18 31.6	−19 15	4.6	32	bright but sparse open cluster
28	6626	Sgr	GC	18 24.5	−24 52	6.8	11.2	compact globular near M22
54	6715	Sgr	GC	18 55.1	−30 29	7.6	9.1	not easily resolved
55	6809	Sgr	GC	19 40.0	−30 58	6.4	19.0	bright, loose globular cluster
69	6637	Sgr	GC	18 31.4	−32 21	7.6	7.1	small, poor globular cluster
70	6681	Sgr	GC	18 43.2	−32 18	8.0	7.8	small globular 2° east of M69
75	6864	Sgr	GC	20 06.1	−21 55	8.5	6	small and distant; 59 000 ly away
11	6705	Sct	OC	18 51.1	−6 16	5.8	13	!! Wild Duck Cl.; the best open cluster?
26	6694	Sct	OC	18 45.2	−9 24	8.0	14	bright, coarse cluster
56	6779	Lyr	GC	19 16.6	+30 11	8.3	7.1	within a rich starfield
57	6720	Lyr	PN	18 53.6	+33 02	8.8	>71″	!! Ring Nebula; an amazing smoke ring
71	6838	Sge	GC	19 53.8	+18 47	8.0	7.2	loose globular; looks like an open cluster
27	6853	Vul	PN	19 59.6	+22 43	7.3	>348″	!! Dumbbell Nebula; a superb object
29	6913	Cyg	OC	20 23.9	+38 32	6.6	6	small, poor open cluster 2° S of γ Cygni
39	7092	Cyg	OC	21 32.2	+48 26	4.6	31	very sparse cluster; use low power
The Autumn Sky								
2	7089	Aqr	GC	21 33.5	−0 49	6.4	12.9	200-mm telescope needed to resolve
72	6981	Aqr	GC	20 53.5	−12 32	9.3	5.9	near the Saturn Nebula, NGC 7009
73	6994	Aqr	OC	20 59.0	−12 38	8.9p	2.8	group of 4 stars only; an "asterism"
15	7078	Peg	GC	21 30.0	+12 10	6.0	12.3	rich, compact globular
30	7099	Cap	GC	21 40.4	−23 11	7.3	11	toughest in 1-night Messier marathon
52	7654	Cas	OC	23 24.2	+61 35	6.9	12	young, rich cl.; faint Bubble Neb. nearby
103	581	Cas	OC	1 33.2	+60 42	7.4	6	three NGC open clusters nearby
31	224	And	G-SAb	0 42.7	+41 16	3.4	185 × 75	!! Andromeda Gal.; look for dust lanes
32	221	And	G-E5 pec	0 42.7	+40 52	8.1	11 × 7	closest companion to M31
110	205	And	G-E3 pec	0 40.4	+41 41	8.1	20 × 12	more distant companion to M31
33	598	Tri	G-SAcd	1 33.9	+30 39	5.7	67 × 42	large, diffuse spiral; requires dark sky
74	628	Psc	G-SAc	1 36.7	+15 47	9.4	11 × 11	faint, elusive spiral; tough in small scope
77	1068	Cet	G-SABab	2 42.7	−0 01	8.9	8.2 × 7.3	a Seyfert galaxy; with starlike nucleus
34	1039	Per	OC	2 42.0	+42 47	5.2	35	best at low power
76	650/51	Per	PN	1 42.4	+51 34	10.1	>65″	Little Dumbbell; faint but distinct

THE FINEST NGC OBJECTS
By Alan Dyer

Those looking for an observing project beyond the Messier Catalogue turn to the New General Catalogue (NGC). The NGC contains 7840 entries and forms the core database of today's computerized backyard telescopes. To match the Messier Catalogue, this list contains 110 of the finest NGC objects visible from midnorthern latitudes. The seasonal order is similar to that used in the Messier list, and there is no overlap. While the brightness of the best NGCs rivals many Messier targets, at least a 200-mm telescope is required to see all 110 objects on this list. Most are easy; a few are challenging.

The NGC was originally published by J.L.E. Dreyer in 1888, a work that expanded upon John Herschel's 1864 "General Catalogue." Supplementary "Index Catalogues" were published by Dreyer in 1895 and 1908. The first IC extends the NGC with another 1529 objects discovered visually between 1888 and 1894. Most are faint, elusive targets. (To provide a flavour of this extension to the NGC, one entry from the first IC is included on this list, IC 289.) The Second Index Catalogue contains 3857 entries, most discovered photographically between 1895 and 1907.

The *Sky Atlas 2000.0*, the sets of index card charts called *AstroCards*, *The Night Sky Observer's Guide Vol. 1 and 2* by Kepple and Sanner, and the *Uranometria 2000.0* star atlas (the latter two published by Willmann-Bell, Inc.) are recommended finder aids. Most planetarium and deep-sky charting computer programs, as well as computerized telescopes, include all the objects on this list and many more.

Notation below is as in the Messier list. Magnitudes (m_v) are visual, with the exception of those marked "p," which are photographic, or blue, magnitudes. Most galaxies appear smaller than the sizes listed. For open clusters, the number of stars (*) is also given. Data are taken from *The Deep Sky Field Guide to Uranometria 2000.0* (see the introduction to the Messier list), with some sizes rounded to two significant figures.

SEASONAL LISTING OF FINEST NGC OBJECTS

#	NGC	Con	Type	RA (2000) h m	Dec ° ′	m_v	Size ′	Remarks
The Autumn Sky								
1	7009	Aqr	PN	21 04.2	−11 22	8.3p	>25″	!! Saturn Nebula; small bright oval
2	7293	Aqr	PN	22 29.6	−20 48	7.3	>769″	!! Helix Nebula; large, diffuse; use filter
3	7331	Peg	G-SAb	22 37.1	+34 25	9.5	10 × 4	!! large, bright spiral galaxy
4	7635	Cas	EN	23 20.7	+61 12	—	15 × 8	Bubble Neb.; very faint; 1/2° SW of M52
5	7789	Cas	OC	23 57.0	+56 44	6.7	15	!! 300*; faint but very rich cluster
6	185	Cas	G-E3	0 39.0	+48 20	9.2	14 × 12	companion to M31; small and faint
7	281	Cas	EN	0 52.8	+56 37	—	35 × 30	!! large faint nebulosity near η Cas
8	457	Cas	OC	1 19.1	+58 20	6.4	13	80*; rich; one of the best Cas. clusters
9	663	Cas	OC	1 46.0	+61 15	7.1	16	80*; look for NGCs 654 and 659 nearby
10	IC 289	Cas	PN	3 10.3	+61 19	13.3	>34″	dim oval smudge; use nebula filter!
11	7662	And	PN	23 25.9	+42 33	8.3	>12″	!! Blue Snowball; annular at high power
12	891	And	G-SAb	2 22.6	+42 21	9.9	13 × 3	!! faint, classic edge-on with dust lane
13	253	Scl	G-SABc	0 47.6	−25 17	7.6	30 × 7	!! very large and bright but at low altitude
14	772	Ari	G-SAb	1 59.3	+19 01	10.3	7.3 × 4.6	diffuse spiral galaxy
15	246	Cet	PN	0 47.0	−11 53	10.9	225″	large and faint with mottled structure
16	936	Cet	G-SB	2 27.6	−1 09	10.2	5.7 × 4.6	near M77; NGC 941 in the same field

SEASONAL LISTING OF FINEST NGC OBJECTS (continued)

#	NGC	Con	Type	RA (2000) h m	Dec ° '	m_v	Size '	Remarks
\			Autumn Sky continued...					
17	869/884	Per	OC	2 21.0	+57 08	≈5	30/30	!! Double Cluster; 315*; use low power
18	1023	Per	G-SB0-	2 40.4	+39 04	9.3	8.6 × 4.2	bright lens-shaped galaxy near M34
19	1491	Per	EN	4 03.4	+51 19	—	25 × 25	visually small and faint emission nebula
20	1501	Cam	PN	4 07.0	+60 55	11.5	52"	faint; dark centre; look for NGC 1502
21	1232	Eri	G-SABc	3 09.8	−20 35	10.0	6.8 × 5.6	face-on spiral; look for NGC 1300 nearby
22	1535	Eri	PN	4 14.2	−12 44	9.6p	>18"	bright planetary with blue-grey disk

The Winter Sky

#	NGC	Con	Type	RA (2000) h m	Dec ° '	m_v	Size '	Remarks
23	1514	Tau	PN	4 09.2	+30 47	10.9	>114"	faint glow around 9.4^m central star
24	1931	Aur	E/RN	5 31.4	+34 15	—	4 × 4	haze surrounding four close stars
25	1788	Ori	RN	5 06.9	−3 21	—	5 × 3	fairly bright but diffuse reflection nebula
26	1973+	Ori	E/RN	5 35.1	−4 44	—	≈20 × 10	NGC 1973-5-7 just N. of M42 and M43
27	2022	Ori	PN	5 42.1	+9 05	11.9	>18"	small, faint & distinct with annular form
28	2024	Ori	EN	5 41.9	−1 51	—	30 × 30	bright but masked by glow from ζ Ori
29	2194	Ori	OC	6 13.8	+12 48	8.5	8	80*, fairly rich; look for 2169 nearby
30	2371/2	Gem	PN	7 25.6	+29 29	11.3	>55"	faint double-lobed planetary; use filter
31	2392	Gem	PN	7 29.2	+20 55	9.2	>15"	!! Clown Face or Eskimo Nebula
32	2237+	Mon	EN	6 32.3	+5 03	—	80 × 60	!! Rosette Neb.; very large; use filter
33	2261	Mon	E/RN	6 39.2	+8 44	var	3.5 × 1.5	Hubble's Variable Neb.; comet-shaped
34	2359	CMa	EN	7 18.6	−13 12	—	9 × 6	bright; look for 2360 & 2362 nearby
35	2440	Pup	PN	7 41.9	−18 13	9.4	>14"	almost starlike; irregular at high power
36	2539	Pup	OC	8 10.7	−12 50	6.5	21	50*; rich cluster; near M46 and M47
37	2403	Cam	G-SABc	7 36.9	+65 36	8.5	26 × 13	!! very large & bright; visible in binocs.
38	2655	Cam	G-SAB0	8 55.6	+78 13	10.1	6.0 × 5.3	bright ellipse with starlike nucleus

The Spring Sky

#	NGC	Con	Type	RA (2000) h m	Dec ° '	m_v	Size '	Remarks
39	2683	Lyn	G-SAb	8 52.7	+33 25	9.8	8.4 × 2.4	nearly edge-on spiral; very bright
40	2841	UMa	G-SAb	9 22.0	+50 58	9.2	6.8 × 3.3	!! classic elongated spiral; very bright
41	3079	UMa	G-SBc	10 02.2	+55 41	10.9	8.0 × 1.5	edge-on spiral; NGC 2950 nearby
42	3184	UMa	G-SABc	10 18.3	+41 25	9.8	7.8 × 7.2	large, diffuse face-on spiral
43	3877	UMa	G-SAc	11 46.1	+47 30	11.0	5.1 × 1.1	edge-on; same field as χ UMa
44	3941	UMa	G-SB0°	11 52.9	+36 59	10.3	3.7 × 2.6	small, bright and elliptical
45	4026	UMa	G-S0	11 59.4	+50 58	10.8	4.6 × 1.2	lens-shaped edge-on near γ UMa
46	4088	UMa	G-SABbc	12 05.6	+50 33	10.6	5.4 × 2.1	nearly edge-on; NGC 4085 in same field
47	4157	UMa	G-SABb	12 11.1	+50 29	11.3	7.1 × 1.2	a thin sliver; NGC 4026 and 4088 nearby
48	4605	UMa	G-SBcp	12 40.0	+61 37	10.3	6.4 × 2.3	bright, distinct edge-on spiral
49	3115	Sex	G-S0-	10 05.2	−7 43	8.9	8.1 × 2.8	Spindle Galaxy; bright and elongated
50	3242	Hya	PN	10 24.8	−18 38	7.8	>16"	!! Ghost of Jupiter; small but bright
51	3003	LMi	G-Sbc?	9 48.6	+33 25	11.9	5.2 × 1.6	faint elongated streak
52	3344	LMi	G-SABbc	10 43.5	+24 55	9.9	6.9 × 6.4	diffuse face-on barred spiral
53	3432	LMi	G-SBm	10 52.5	+36 37	11.2	6.9 × 1.9	nearly edge-on; faint flat streak
54	2903	Leo	G-SABbc	09 32.2	+21 30	9.0	12 × 6	!! very large, bright elongated spiral
55	3384	Leo	G-SB0-	10 48.3	+12 38	9.9	5.5 × 2.9	same field as M105 and NGC 3389
56	3521	Leo	G-SAb	11 05.8	−0 02	9.0	12 × 6	very large, bright spiral
57	3607	Leo	G-SA0°	11 16.9	+18 03	9.9	4.6 × 4.1	NGC 3605 & 3608 in same field
58	3628	Leo	G-Sb pec	11 20.3	+13 36	9.5	14 × 4	large edge-on; same field as M65 & M66
59	4111	CVn	G-SA0+	12 07.1	+43 04	10.7	4.4 × 0.9	bright lens-shaped edge-on spiral
60	4214	CVn	G-I AB	12 15.6	+36 20	9.8	10 × 8	large irregular galaxy
61	4244	CVn	G-SAcd	12 17.5	+37 49	10.4	17 × 2	!! large distinct edge-on spiral

SEASONAL LISTING OF FINEST NGC OBJECTS (continued)

#	NGC	Con	Type	RA (2000) Dec		m_v	Size	Remarks
				h m	° ′		′	
Spring Sky continued ...								
62	4449	CVn	G-I Bm	12 28.2	+44 06	9.6	5.5 × 4.1	bright with odd rectangular shape
63	4490	CVn	G-SBd p	12 30.6	+41 38	9.8	6.4 × 3.3	Cocoon Gal.; bright spiral; 4485 in field
64	4631	CVn	G-SBd	12 42.1	+32 32	9.2	16 × 3	!! large edge-on; with companion 4627
65	4656/7	CVn	G-SBm p	12 44.0	+32 10	10.5	20 × 3	!! in field with 4631; NE end curves up
66	5005	CVn	G-SABbc	13 10.9	+37 03	9.8	5.8 × 2.8	bright elongated spiral near α CVn
67	5033	CVn	G-SAc	13 13.4	+36 36	10.2	10 × 5	large bright spiral near NGC 5005
68	4274	Com	G-SBab	2 19.8	+29 37	10.4	6.7 × 2.5	NGCs 4278/83/86 in same field
69	4414	Com	G-SAc	12 26.4	+31 13	10.1	4.4 × 3.0	bright spiral with starlike nucleus
70	4494	Com	G-E1-2	12 31.4	+25 47	9.8	4.6 × 4.4	small bright elliptical
71	4559	Com	G-SABc	12 36.0	+27 58	10.0	12 × 5	large spiral with coarse structure
72	4565	Com	G-SAb	12 36.3	+25 59	9.6	14 × 2	!! superb edge-on spiral with dust lane
73	4725	Com	G-SABab	12 50.4	+25 30	9.4	10 × 8	very bright, large spiral
74	4038/9	Crv	G-SB/IB	12 01.9	−18 52	≈10.4	≈5 × 3 ea.	"Antennae" interacting galaxies
75	4361	Crv	PN	12 24.5	−18 48	10.9	>45″	small and bright; with 13^m central star
76	4216	Vir	G-SABb	12 15.9	+13 09	10.0	7.8 × 1.6	nearly edge-on; with NGC 4206 and 4222
77	4388	Vir	G-SAb	12 25.8	+12 40	11.0	5.7 × 1.6	with M84 and M86 in Markarian's Chain
78	4438	Vir	G-SA0/a	12 27.8	+13 01	10.2	8.9 × 3.6	paired w/ NGC 4435 to form the "Eyes"
79	4517	Vir	G-Scd	12 32.8	+0 07	10.4	9.9 × 1.4	faint edge-on spiral
80	4526	Vir	G-SAB0°	12 34.0	+7 42	9.7	7.1 × 2.9	between two 7th mag. stars
81	4535	Vir	G-SABc	12 34.3	+8 12	10.0	7.1 × 6.4	near M49 and 3/4° N of NGC 4526
82	4567/8	Vir	G-SAbc	12 36.5	+11 15	≈11	≈3 × 2 ea.	"Siamese Twins" interacting galaxies
83	4699	Vir	G-Sab	12 49.0	−8 40	9.5	4.4 × 3.2	small & bright; look for NGC 4697 3° N
84	4762	Vir	G-SB0°?	12 52.9	+11 14	10.3	9.1 × 2.2	flattest galaxy known; 4754 in same field
85	5746	Vir	G-SA?b	14 44.9	+1 57	10.3	6.8 × 1.0	fine edge-on near 109 Virginis
86	5466	Boo	GC	14 05.5	+28 32	9.0	11	loose class XII; like rich open cl.; faint
87	5907	Dra	G-SAc	15 15.9	+56 20	10.3	12 × 2	!! fine edge-on with dust lane; near 5866
88	6503	Dra	G-SAcd	17 49.4	+70 09	10.2	7.3 × 2.4	bright elongated spiral
89	6543	Dra	PN	17 58.6	+66 38	8.1	>18″	Cat's Eye Nebula; with 10.9^m central star

The Summer Sky

#	NGC	Con	Type	RA (2000) Dec		m_v	Size	Remarks
90	6210	Her	PN	16 44.5	+23 49	8.8	>14″	blue starlike planetary
91	6369	Oph	PN	17 29.3	−23 46	11.4	>30″	"Little Ghost"; look for 6309 nearby
92	6572	Oph	PN	18 12.1	+6 51	8.1	8″	tiny bright blue oval
93	6633	Oph	OC	18 27.7	+6 34	4.6	27	sparse wide field cluster; IC 4756 nearby
94	6712	Sct	GC	18 53.1	−8 42	8.2	7.2	small globular; look for IC 1295 in field
95	6781	Aql	PN	19 18.4	+6 33	11.4	>109″	pale version of the Owl Nebula, M97
96	6819	Cyg	OC	19 41.3	+40 11	7.3	9.5	150*; faint but rich cluster in Milky Way
97	6826	Cyg	PN	19 44.8	+50 31	8.8	>25″	!! Blinking Planetary; 10.6^m central star
98	6888	Cyg	EN	20 12.0	+38 21	—	18 × 13	Crescent Nebula; faint; use nebula filter
99a	6960	Cyg	SNR	20 45.7	+30 43	—	70 × 6	!! Veil Nebula west half; use filter!
99b	6992/5	Cyg	SNR	20 56.4	+31 43	—	72 × 8	!! Veil Nebula east half; use filter!
100	7000	Cyg	EN	20 58.8	+44 20	—	120 × 100	!! North America; use filter & low power
101	7027	Cyg	PN	21 07.1	+42 14	8.5	15″	unusual protoplanetary nebula
102	6445	Sgr	PN	17 49.2	−20 01	11.2	>34″	small, bright and annular; near M23
103	6520	Sgr	OC	18 03.4	−27 54	7.6p	6	60*; small; dark nebula B86 in same field
104	6818	Sgr	PN	19 44.0	−14 09	9.3	>17″	"Little Gem"; annular; NGC 6822 0.75° S
105	6802	Vul	OC	19 30.6	+20 16	8.8	3.2	50*, at east end of Brocchi's Cluster
106	6940	Vul	OC	20 34.6	+28 18	6.3	31	60*; fairly rich cluster in Milky Way
107	6939	Cep	OC	20 31.4	+60 38	7.8	7	80*; very rich; NGC 6946 in same field
108	6946	Cep	G-SABcd	20 34.8	+60 09	8.8	13 × 13	faint, diffuse face-on spiral near 6939
109	7129	Cep	RN	21 42.8	+66 06	—	7 × 7	faint reflection neb. around sparse cluster
110	40	Cep	PN	0 13.0	+72 32	12.4	>37″	unusual red planetary; 11.6^m central star

DEEP-SKY CHALLENGE OBJECTS
BY ALAN DYER AND ALISTER LING

For those who wish to get a taste of the unusual, here is a selection of 45 "challenge" targets. Most require a 250- to 450-mm telescope. However, for detecting challenge objects, the quality of sky, quality of the optics, use of an appropriate filter, and the observer's experience are often more important than sheer aperture. Don't be afraid to tackle some of these with a smaller telescope.

Objects are listed in order of right ascension. Abbreviations are the same as in the Messier and NGC lists. Two columns have been added: one lists the page where you'll find that object in the *Uranometria 2000.0*; the last column suggests the minimum aperture in mm needed to see that object. Most data are taken from *Sky Catalogue 2000.0 Vol. 2*. Some visual magnitudes are from other sources.

#	Object	Con	Type	RA (2000) Dec h m ° ′	m_v	Size ′	pg	Min Aperture
1	NGC 7822	Cep	E/RN	0 03.6 +68 37	—	60 × 30	15	300
	large, faint emission neb.; rated "eeF"; also look for E/R nebula Ced 214 (assoc'd with star cluster Berkeley 59) 1° S							
2	IC 59	Cas	E/RN	0 56.7 +61 04	—	10 × 5	36	200–250
	faint emission/reflection nebula paired with IC 63 very close to γ Cas.; requires clean optics; rated as "pF"							
3	NGC 609	Cas	OC	1 37.2 +64 33	11.0	3.0	16	250–300
	faint patch at low power; high power needed to resolve this rich cluster (also look for Trumpler 1 cluster 3° S)							
4	IC 1795	Cas	EN	2 24.7 +61 54	—	27 × 13	17	200
	brightest part of a complex of nebulosity that includes IC 1805 and IC 1848; use a nebula filter							
5	Maffei I	Cas	G-E3	2 36.3 +59 39	≈14	5 × 3	38	300
	heavily reddened galaxy; very faint; requires large aperture and black skies; nearby Maffei II for extremists							
6	NGC 1049	For	GC	2 39.7 −34 29	11.0	0.6	354	250–300
	Class V globular in dwarf "Fornax System" Local Group galaxy 630 000 ly away; galaxy itself invisible?							
7	Abell 426	Per	Gs	3 19.8 +41 31	12–16	≈30′	63	200–400
	Perseus galaxy cluster 300 million ly away; mag. 11.6 NGC 1275 Perseus A at centre; see Webb Vol. 5							
8	NGC 1432/35	Tau	RN	3 46.1 +23 47	—	30 × 30	132	100–150
	Pleiades nebulosity (also includes IC 349); brightest around Merope; requires transparent skies and clean optics							
9	IC 342	Cam	G-SBc	3 46.8 +68 06	≈12	17 × 17	18	200–300
	large and diffuse face–on spiral; member of UMa–Cam cloud (Kemble's Cascade of stars also on this chart)							
10	NGC 1499	Per	EN	4 00.7 +36 37	—	145 × 40	95	80–125 RFT
	California Nebula; very large and faint; use a wide–field telescope or big binoculars plus H–Beta filter							
11	NGC 1554/5	Tau	RN	4 21.8 +19 32	—	var.	133	200?
	Hind's Variable Neb.; small reflect. neb. around 9ᵐ–13ᵐ var. star T Tau; use high power; difficulty varies							
12	IC 405	Aur	E/RN	5 16.2 +34 16	—	30 × 19	97	200
	Flaming Star Neb. assoc'd with runaway star AE Aurigae; see Burnham's Handbook p. 285 (also look for IC 410)							
13	IC 434 / B 33	Ori	E/DN	5 40.9 −2 28	—	60 × 10	224	100–150 in dark sky!
	B33 is the Horsehead Nebula, a dark neb. superimposed on a very faint emission neb. IC 434; use H–Beta filter							
14	Sh 2-276	Ori	EN	5 48 +1 —	—	600 × 30!	226	100–150 RFT
	Barnard's Loop; SNR or interstellar bubble?; difficult to detect due to size; use filter and sweep with wide field							
15	Abell 12	Ori	PN	6 02.4 +9 39	≈13	37″	181	250–300
	also called PK 198 −6.1; faint; not plotted on Uranometria but is on NW edge of μ Orionis; OIII filter required							
16	IC 443	Gem	SNR	6 16.9 +22 47	—	50 × 40	137	250–300
	faint supernova remnant very close to η Gem.; use filter (also look for NGC 2174 and Sh 2–247 on this chart)							
17	J 900	Gem	PN	6 25.9 +17 47	12.2	8″	137	200
	Jonckheere 900; bright starlike planetary; plotted as PK 194 +2.1 in Uranometria; use OIII filter & high power							
18	IC 2177	Mon	E/RN	7 05.1 −10 42	—	120 × 40	273	200–300
	Seagull Nebula; large, faint; contains bright patches Gum 1 (−10°28′), NGC 2327 (−11°18′) & Ced 90 (−12°20′)							
19	PK 205 +14.1	Gem	PN	7 29.0 +13 15	≈13	≈700″	184	200–250
	Medusa Nebula or Abell 21; much larger than plotted in Uranometria; impressive in large aperture w/ OIII filter							
20	PK 164 +31.1	Lyn	PN	7 57.8 +53 25	≈14	400″	43	250
	extremely faint with two small components; use OIII filter; sometimes confused with nearby NGC 2474–75							

DEEP-SKY CHALLENGE OBJECTS (continued)

#	Object	Con	Type	RA (2000) h m	Dec ° '	m_v	Size '	pg	Min Aperture
21	**Leo I**	Leo	G–E3	10 08.4	+12 18	9.8	10.7 × 8.3	189	300

dwarf elliptical; satellite of Milky Way; very low surface brightness; 0.3° N of Regulus!; requires clean optics

| 22 | **Abell 1367** | Leo | Gs | 11 44.0 | +19 57 | 13–16 | ≈60 | 147 | 300–400 |

cluster of some 30 or more galaxies within a 1 degree field near 93 Leonis; see Webb Handbook Vol. 5, p. 139

| 23 | **NGC 3172** | UMi | G-? | 11 50.2 | +89 07 | 13.6 | 0.7 × 0.7 | 2 | 250 |

"Polarissima Borealis"—closest galaxy to the North Celestial Pole; small, faint and otherwise unremarkable

| 24 | **NGC 4236** | Dra | G-SBb | 12 16.7 | +69 28 | 9.6 | 18.6 × 6.9 | 25 | 200–250 |

very large, dim barred spiral; a diffuse glow (NGC 4395 on Chart #108 a similar large diffuse face-on)

| 25 | **Mrk 205** | Dra | Quasar | 12 21.6 | +75 18 | 14.5 | stellar | 9 | 300 |

Markarian 205; a faint star on SW edge of NGC 4319; plotted as a radio source; centre of red-shift controversy

| 26 | **3C 273** | Vir | Quasar | 12 29.1 | +2 03 | 12≈13 | stellar | 238 | 250–300 |

at 2 to 3 billon ly away one of the most distant objects visible in amateur telescopes; magnitude variable

| 27 | **NGC 4676** | Com | Gs | 12 46.2 | +30 44 | 14.lp | 2 × 1 | 108 | 250 |

"The Mice" or VV 224—two classic interacting galaxies; very faint double nature detectable at high power

| 28 | **Abell 1656** | Com | Gs | 13 00.1 | +27 58 | 12–16 | ≈60 | 149 | 250–300 |

Coma Berenices gal. cl.; very rich; 400 million ly away; brightest member NGC 4889; see Webb Vol. 5

| 29 | **NGC 5053** | Com | GC | 13 16.4 | +17 42 | 9.8 | 10.5 | 150 | 100–200 |

faint and very loose globular 1° SE of M53; requires large aperture to resolve; difficult in hazy skies; Class XI

| 30 | **NGC 5897** | Lib | GC | 15 17.4 | –21 01 | 8.6 | 12.6 | 334 | 150–200 |

large, faint and loose globular; mag. 10.9 in Atlas Coeli Catalogue; requires large aperture to resolve; Class XI

| 31 | **Abel 2065** | CrB | Gs | 15 22.7 | –27 43 | ≈16 | ≈30 | 154 | 500 in superb sky! |

Corona Borealis gal. cluster; perhaps the most difficult object for amateur telescopes; 1.5 billion ly away

| 32 | **NGC 6027** | Ser | Gs | 15 59.2 | +20 45 | ≈15 | 2 × 1 | 155 | 400 |

Seyfert's Sextet (6027 A–F); compact group of 6 small and very faint galaxies; see Burnham's Handbook p. 1793

| 33 | **B 72** | Oph | DN | 17 23.5 | –23 38 | — | 30 | 338 | 80–125 RFT |

Barnard's dark S-Nebula or "The Snake"; opacity of 6/6; 1.5° NNE of θ Ophiuchi; area rich in dark nebulas

| 34 | **NGC 6791** | Lyr | OC | 19 20.7 | +37 51 | 9.5 | 16 | 118 | 200–250 |

large, faint but very rich open cluster with 300 stars; a faint smear in smaller instruments; Type II 3 r

| 35 | **PK 64 +5.1** | Cyg | PN | 19 34.8 | +30 31 | 9.6 | 8″ | 118 | 200 |

Campbell's Hydrogen Star; very bright but very starlike; also catalogued as star BD +30°3639

| 36 | **M 1-92** | Cyg | RN | 19 36.3 | +29 33 | 11.0 | 12″ × 6″ | 118 | 250–300 |

Minkowski 1-92 or Footprint Nebula; bright, starlike reflection neb.; double at high mag.; assoc'd star invisible

| 37 | **NGC 6822** | Sgr | G-Irr | 19 44.9 | –14 48 | ≈11 | 10.2 × 9.5 | 297 | 100–150 |

Barnard's Galaxy; member of the Local Group; large but very low surface brightness; requires transparent skies

| 38 | **Palomar 11** | Aql | GC | 19 45.2 | –8 00 | 9.8 | 3.2′ | 297 | 200–300 |

Brightest of 15 heavily reddened GCs found on Sky Survey; magnitude is misleading; 11 Terzan GCs more challenging

| 39 | **IC 4997** | Sge | PN | 20 20.2 | +16 45 | 10.9 | 2″ | 163 | 200 |

bright but starlike planetary; the challenge is to see the disk!; blink the field with and without a nebula filter

| 40 | **IC 1318** | Cyg | EN | 20 26.2 | +40 30 | — | large | 84 | 80–150 RFT |

complex of nebulosity around γ Cygni; multitude of patches in rich starfield; use a very wide field plus filter

| 41 | **PK 80 –6.1** | Cyg | PN? | 21 02.3 | +36 42 | 13.5 | 16″ | 121 | 250 |

the "Egg Nebula"; a very small proto-planetary nebula; can owners of large telescopes detect polarization?

| 42 | **IC 1396** | Cep | EN | 21 39.1 | +57 30 | — | 170 × 140 | 57 | 100–125 RFT |

extremely large and diffuse area of emission nebulosity; use nebula filter and very wide field optics in dark sky

| 43 | **IC 5146** | Cyg | E/RN | 21 53.5 | +47 16 | — | 12 × 12 | 86 | 200–250 |

Cocoon Nebula; faint and diffuse; use H-Beta filter; at the end of the long filamentary dark nebula Barnard 168

| 44 | **NGC 7317–20** | Peg | Gs | 22 36.1 | +33 57 | 13–14 | ≈1′ ea. | 123 | 250–300 |

Stephan's Quintet; 0.5° SSW of NGC 7331; easy to pick out 3 or 4 (also look for "companions" to 7331)

| 45 | **Jones 1** | Peg | PN | 23 35.9 | +30 28 | 12.1 | 332″ | 124 | 250–300 |

plotted as PK 104 –29.1 (from Perek & Kohoutek catalogue) in Uranometria; large dim glow; OIII filter required

GALAXIES: BRIGHTEST AND NEAREST
By Barry F. Madore

External galaxies are generally of such low surface brightness that they often prove disappointing objects for the amateur observer. However, it must be remembered that many of these galaxies were discovered with very small telescopes and that the enjoyment of their discovery can be recaptured. In addition, the central concentration of light varies from galaxy to galaxy, making a visual classification of the types possible at the telescope. Indeed, the type of galaxy as listed in **Table 1** is in part based on the fraction of light coming from the central bulge of the galaxy as compared to the contribution from a disk component. Disk galaxies with dominant bulges are classified as Sa; as the nuclear contribution declines, types of Sb, Sc, and Sd are assigned until the nucleus is absent at type Sm. Often the disks of these galaxies show spiral symmetry, the coherence and strength of which is denoted by Roman numerals I through V, smaller numbers indicating well-formed global spiral patterns. Those spirals with central bars are designated SB, while those with only a hint of a disk embedded in the bulge are called SO. A separate class of galaxies that possess no disk component are called ellipticals and can only be further classified numerically by their apparent flattening, E0 being apparently round and E7 being the most flattened.

Environment appears to play an important role in determining the types of galaxies we see at the present epoch. Rich clusters of galaxies, such as the system in Coma, are dominated by ellipticals and gas-free SO galaxies. The less dense clusters and groups tend to be dominated by the spiral, disk galaxies. Remarkably, pairs of galaxies are much more frequently of the same Hubble type than random selection would predict. Encounters between disk galaxies may in some cases result in the instabilities necessary to form the spiral structure we often see. M51 (the Whirlpool) and its companion NGC 5195 are an often-cited example of this type of interaction. In the past, when the universe was much more densely packed, interactions and collisions may have been sufficiently frequent that entire galaxies merged to form a single large new system; it has been suggested that some elliptical galaxies formed in this way.

Table 1 lists the 40 brightest galaxies taken from the Revised Shapley-Ames Catalog. As well as their designations, positions, and types, the table also lists the total blue magnitudes, major and minor axis lengths (to the nearest minute of arc), one modern estimate of their distances in kiloparsecs, and their radial velocities corrected for the motion of our Sun about the galactic centre. Although the universe as a whole is in expansion, there are parts that are still bound together (or at very least, held back in their expansion) by gravity. These groups and clusters are, in essence, representative of the largest material structures in the universe. Recently, large-scale flows of material have been reported, far in excess of the velocities expected due to the perturbing presence of other galaxies and clusters of galaxies. Either there are exceedingly large concentrations of matter yet to be discovered just beyond our limited view of the world, or the universe has had a much more interesting history than our present theories indicate. The brightest and nearest galaxies in Table 1 may be moving not only as a result of the universal expansion but also through very complex interactions with distant parts as yet only postulated but not seen.

TABLE 1—THE 40 OPTICALLY BRIGHTEST SHAPLEY-AMES GALAXIES

NGC/IC	Other	RA (2000) Dec h m s ° ′	Type	Mag. B_T	Size ′	Distance kpc	Rad. Vel. km/s
55		0 15 08 −39 13.2	Sc	8.22	25 × 3	3 100	+115
205	M110	0 40 23 +41 41.3	S0/E5pec	8.83	8 × 3	730	+49
221	M32	0 42 41 +40 51.9	E2	9.01	3 × 3	730	+86
224	M31	0 42 45 +41 16.5	Sb I–II	4.38	160 × 40	730	−10
247		0 47 10 −20 45.6	Sc III–IV	9.51	18 × 5	3 100	+604
253		0 47 36 −25 17.4	Sc	8.13	22 × 6	4 200	+504
SMC		0 52 38 −72 48.0	Im IV–V	2.79	216 × 216	60	+359
300		0 54 53 −37 41.2	Sc III	8.70	20 × 10	2 400	+625
598	M33	1 33 53 +30 39.2	Sc II–III	6.26	60 × 40	670	+506
628	M74	1 36 42 +15 47.2	Sc I	9.77	8 × 8	17 000	+507
1068	M77	2 42 41 −0 00.9	Sb II	9.55	3 × 2	25 000	+510
1291		3 17 19 −41 06.5	SBa	9.42	5 × 2	15 000	+512
1313		3 18 16 −66 29.9	SBc III–IV	9.37	5 × 3	5 200	+261
1316	Fornax A	3 22 42 −37 12.5	Sa (pec)	9.60	4 × 3	30 000	+1713
LMC		5 23 36 −69 45.4	SBm III	0.63	432 × 432	50	+34
2403		7 36 54 +65 35.9	Sc III	8.89	16 × 10	3 600	+299
2903		9 32 10 +21 29.9	Sc I–III	9.50	11 × 5	9 400	+472
3031	M81	9 55 34 +69 04.1	SbI–II	7.86	16 × 10	3 600	+124
3034	M82	9 55 54 +69 40.7	Amorphous	9.28	7 × 2	3 600	+409
3521		11 05 49 −0 02.0	Sb II–III	9.64	7 × 2	13 000	+627
3627	M66	11 20 15 +12 59.1	Sb II	9.74	8 × 3	12 000	+593
4258	M106	12 18 57 +47 18.4	Sb II	8.95	20 × 6	10 000	+520
4449		12 28 12 +44 05.8	Sm IV	9.85	5 × 3	5 000	+250
4472	M49	12 29 47 +7 59.8	E1/S0	9.32	5 × 4	22 000	+822
4486	M87	12 30 50 +12 23.6	E0	9.62	3 × 3	22 000	+1136
4594	M104	12 40 00 −11 37.4	Sa/b	9.28	7 × 2	17 000	+873
4631		12 42 05 +32 32.4	Sc	9.84	12 × 1	12 000	+606
4649	M60	12 43 40 +11 33.1	S0	9.83	4 × 3	22 000	+1142
4736	M94	12 50 54 +41 07.1	Sab	8.92	5 × 4	6 900	+345
4826	M64	12 56 45 +21 41.0	Sab II	9.37	8 × 4	7 000	+350
4945		13 05 26 −49 28.0	Sc	9.60	12 × 2	7 000	+275
5055	M63	13 15 50 +42 01.7	Sbc II–III	9.33	8 × 3	11 000	+550
5128	Cen A	13 25 29 −43 01.0	S0 (pec)	7.89	10 × 3	6 900	+251
5194	M51	13 29 53 +47 11.9	Sbc I–II	8.57	12 × 6	11 000	+541
5236	M83	13 37 00 −29 52.0	SBc II	8.51	10 × 8	6 900	+275
5457	M101	14 03 13 +54 21.0	Sc I	8.18	22 × 22	7 600	+372
6744		19 09 46 −63 51.3	Sbc II	9.24	9 × 9	13 000	+663
6822		19 44 57 −14 47.7	Im IV–V	9.35	20 × 10	680	+15
6946		20 34 51 +60 09.4	Sc II	9.68	13 × 9	6 700	+336
7793		23 57 49 −32 35.4	Sd IV	9.65	6 × 4	4 200	+241

The nearest galaxies, listed in **Table 2,** form what is known as the Local Group of Galaxies. Many of the distances are still quite uncertain. However, in the present Hubble Space Telescope era these galaxies are prime targets for a generation of astronomers intent on accurately determining each of their distances to the best possible precision.

TABLE 2—THE NEAREST GALAXIES—OUR LOCAL GROUP

Name	RA (2000.0) Dec h m ° '		Mag. B_T	Type	Distance kpc
M31 = NGC 224	0 42.7	+41 16	4.38	Sb I–II	730
Milky Way Galaxy	—	—	—	Sb/c	—
M33 = NGC 598	1 33.9	+30 39	6.26	Sc II–III	670
LMC	5 23.7	–69 45	0.63	SBm III	50
SMC	0 52.7	–72 49	2.79	Im IV–V	60
NGC 6822	19 45.0	–14 48	9.35	Im IV–V	520
IC 1613	1 04.8	+02 07	10.00	Im V	740
M110 = NGC 205	0 40.4	+41 41	8.83	S0/E5 pec	730
M32 = NGC 221	0 42.7	+40 52	9.01	E2	730
NGC 185	0 38.9	+48 20	10.13	dE3 pec	730
NGC 147	0 33.2	+48 30	10.36	dE5	610
Fornax	2 39.9	–34 32	9.1	dE	130
Sculptor	1 00.2	–33 42	10.5	dE	85
Leo I	10 08.5	+12 19	11.27	dE	230
Leo II	11 13.5	+22 09	12.85	dE	230
Draco	17 20.1	+57 55	—	dE	80
Ursa Minor	15 08.8	+67 12	—	dE	75
Carina	6 41.6	–50 58	—	dE	170
And I	0 45.7	+38 01	13.5	dE	790
And II	1 16.5	+33 26	13.5	dE	730
And III	0 35.3	+36 31	13.5	dE	730
LGS 3	1 03.8	+21 53	—	?	730
Sextans	10 13.0	–1 36	—	dE	85
Antlia	10 04.0	–27 20	—	dE	1200
IC 10	0 20.4	+59 17	11.8	IBm	800

Editor's Notes:

(i) Aside from those famous companions of the Milky Way Galaxy, the Large Magellanic Cloud (LMC) and the Small Magellanic Cloud (SMC), there is only one galaxy beyond our own that is easily visible to unaided human eyes: M31, the Andromeda Galaxy (730 kpc or 2.4 Mly distant). M33, the Triangulum Galaxy, can also be seen, but this is a difficult observation. To locate M31, see the NOVEMBER ALL-SKY MAP on p. 282, where the tiny cluster of six dots above the first "A" of "ANDROMEDA" indicates its location. With modest optical aid (e.g. binoculars) a dozen or more of the galaxies listed in Table 1 can be seen by experienced observers under dark skies. With a 200-mm telescope, the quasar 3C273 at one thousand times the distance of M31 can elicit a noticeable signal in the visual cortex (see the section VARIABLE GALAXIES on p. 275).

(ii) An interesting article by G. Lake entitled "Cosmology of the Local Group" appears in *Sky & Telescope*, December 1992, p. 613.

(iii) The *National Aeronautics and Space Administration/Infrared Processing and Analysis Center* (NASA/IPAC) Extragalactic Database (NED) is a comprehensive compilation of extragalactic data for over 3.7 million distinct extragalactic objects. The database includes most major catalogues and offers references to and abstracts of articles of extragalactic interest that have appeared in most major journals. Also online are over 3.4 million photometric measurements and hundreds of thousands of images. It is possible to search the main NED database for objects selected by catalogue prefix, position, type, or redshift. The database is available at:

> nedwww.ipac.caltech.edu

A knowledgebase of review articles and basic information is available at:

> nedwww.ipac.caltech.edu/level5

GALAXIES WITH PROPER NAMES

BY BARRY F. MADORE

Below are the catalogue designations and positions of galaxies known to have proper names which usually honour the discoverer (e.g. McLeish's Object), identify the constellation in which the galaxy is found (e.g. Andromeda Galaxy), or describe the galaxy in some easily remembered way (e.g. Whirlpool Galaxy).

Galaxy Name	Other Names / Remarks	RA (2000) h m	Dec ° ′
Ambartsumian's Knot	NGC 3561, UGC 06224, ARP 105	11 11.2	+28 42
Andromeda Galaxy	M31, NGC 224, UGC 00454	0 42.7	+41 16
Andromeda I		0 45.7	+38 01
Andromeda II		1 16.5	+33 26
Andromeda III		0 35.3	+36 31
Antennae Galaxy	Ring Tail, NGC 4038/39, ARP 244	12 01.9	−18 52
Antlia Dwarf	AM 1001-270	10 04.0	−27 20
Aquarius Dwarf	DDO 210	20 46.9	−12 51
Arp's Galaxy		11 19.6	+51 30
Atoms For Peace	NGC 7252, ARP 226	22 20.8	−24 41
Baade's Galaxies A & B	MCG+07-02-018/19	0 49.9	+42 35
Barbon's Galaxy	Markarian 328, ZWG 497.042	23 37.7	+30 08
Barnard's Galaxy	NGC 6822, IC 4895, DDO 209	19 44.9	−14 48
Bear's Paw (Claw)	NGC 2537, UGC 04274, ARP 6	8 13.2	+46 00
BL Lacertae		22 02.7	+42 17
Black Eye Galaxy	M64, NGC 4826, UGC 08062	12 56.7	+21 41
Bode's Galaxies	M81/82, NGC 3031/4, UGC 05318/22	9 55.7	+69 23
Burbidge Chain	MCG-04-03-010 to 13	0 47.5	−20 26
BW Tauri	UGC 03087, MCG+01-12-009	4 33.2	+5 21
Carafe Galaxy	Cannon's Carafe, near NGC 1595/98	4 28.0	−47 54
Carina Dwarf		6 41.6	−50 58
Cartwheel Galaxy	Zwicky's Cartwheel, MCG-06-02-022a	0 37.4	−33 44
Centaurus A	NGC 5128, ARP 153	13 25.5	−43 01
Circinus Galaxy		14 13.2	−65 20
Coddington's Nebula	IC 2574, UGC 05666, DDO 81	10 28.4	+68 25
Copeland Septet	MCG+04-28-004/05/07 to 11, UGC 06597, UGC 06602, ARP 320, NGC 3745/46/48/50/51/53/54†	11 37.8	+21 59
Cygnus A	MCG+07-41-003	19 59.4	+40 43
Draco Dwarf	UGC 10822, DDO 208	17 20.2	+57 55
Exclamation Mark Galaxy		0 39.3	−43 06
The Eyes	NGC 4435/8, UGC 07574/5, ARP 120a,b	12 27.7	+13 03
Fath 703	NGC 5892	15 13.7	−15 29
Fornax A	NGC 1316, ARP 154	3 22.7	−37 12
Fornax Dwarf	MCG-06-07-001	2 39.9	−34 32
Fourcade-Figueroa	MCG-07-28-004	13 34.8	−45 33
The Garland	S of NGC 3077 = UGC 05398	10 04.2	+68 40
Grus Quartet	NGC 7552/82/90/99	23 17.8	−42 26
GR 8 (Gibson Reaves)	UGC 08091, DDO 155	12 58.7	+14 13
Hardcastle's Galaxy	MCG-05-31-039	13 13.0	−32 41
Helix Galaxy	NGC 2685, UGC 04666, ARP 336	8 55.6	+58 44
Hercules A	MCG+01-43-006	16 51.2	+4 59
Hoag's Object		15 17.2	+21 35

†Position errors caused these to be historically marked as nonexistent in the NGC and RNGC.

GALAXIES WITH PROPER NAMES (continued)

Galaxy Name	Other Names / Remarks	RA (2000) h m	Dec ° '
Holmberg I	UGC 05139, DDO 63	9 40.5	+71 11
Holmberg II	UGC 04305, DDO 50, ARP 268	8 19.3	+70 43
Holmberg III	UGC 04841	9 14.6	+74 14
Holmberg IV	UGC 08837, DDO 185	13 54.7	+53 54
Holmberg V	UGC 08658	13 40.6	+54 20
Holmberg VI	NGC 1325a	3 24.9	−21 20
Holmberg VII	UGC 07739, DDO 137	12 34.7	+06 17
Holmberg VIII	UGC 08303, DDO 166	13 13.3	+36 12
Holmberg IX	UGC 05336, DDO 66	9 57.6	+69 03
Horologium Dwarf	Schuster's Spiral	3 59.2	−45 52
Hydra A	MCG-02-24-007	9 18.1	−12 06
Integral Sign Galaxy	UGC 03697, MCG+12-07-028	7 11.4	+71 50
Keenan's System	NGC 5216/16a/18, UGC 08528/9, ARP 104	13 32.2	+62 43
Kowal's Object		19 29.9	−17 41
Large Magellanic Cloud	Nubecula Major	5 23.6	−69 45
Leo I	Regulus Dwarf, UGC 05470, DDO 74, Harrington-Wilson #1	10 08.5	+12 18
Leo II	Leo B, UGC 06253, DDO 93, Harrington-Wilson #2	11 13.4	+22 10
Leo III	Leo A, UGC 05364, DDO 69	9 59.3	+30 45
Lindsay-Shapley Ring	Graham A	6 42.8	−74 15
Lost Galaxy	NGC 4535, UGC 07727	12 34.3	+8 11
McLeish's Object		20 09.7	−66 13
Maffei I	UGCA 34	2 36.3	+59 39
Maffei II	UGCA 39	2 42.0	+59 37
Malin 1		12 37.0	+14 20
Mayall's Object	MCG+07-23-019, ARP 148	11 03.9	+40 50
Mice	NGC 4676a/b, UGC 07938/9, IC 819/20, ARP 242	12 46.1	+30 44
Miniature Spiral	NGC 3928, UGC 06834	11 51.8	+48 41
Minkowski's Object	ARP 133 (NE of NGC 541)	1 25.8	−01 21
Pancake	NGC 2685, UGC 04666, ARP 336	8 55.6	+58 44
Papillon	IC 708, UGC 06549	11 33.9	+49 03
Pegasus Dwarf	UGC 12613, DDO 216	23 28.5	+14 44
Perseus A	NGC 1275/6, UGC 02669	3 19.8	+41 31
Phoenix Dwarf Irr.		1 51.1	−44 26
Pinwheel Galaxy	see also Triangulum Galaxy	1 33.9	+30 39
Pinwheel Galaxy	M99, NGC 4254, UGC 07345	12 18.8	+14 25
Pinwheel Galaxy	M101, NGC 5457, UGC 08981, ARP 26	14 03.3	+54 22
Pisces Cloud	NGC 379/80/82-85, UGC 00682/3/6-9, ARP 331	1 07.5	+32 25
Pisces Dwarf	LGS 3	0 03.8	+21 54
Polarissima Australis	NGC 2573	1 42.0‡	−89 20
Polarissima Borealis	NGC 3172, ZWG 370.002	11 50.3‡	+89 07
Reinmuth 80	NGC 4517a, UGC 07685	12 32.5	+0 23
Reticulum Dwarf	Sersic 040.03	4 36.2	−58 50
Sagittarius Dwarf		19 30.0	−17 41
Sculptor Dwarf	MCG-06-03-015	1 00.2	−33 42
Sculptor Dwarf Irr.		0 08.1	−34 34

‡The high declination of these objects makes the RA particularly uncertain.

GALAXIES WITH PROPER NAMES (continued)

Galaxy Name	Other Names / Remarks	RA (2000) Dec h m	° '
Seashell Galaxy	Companion to NGC 5291	13 47.4	−30 23
Sextans A	UGCA 205, MCG-01-26-030, DDO 75	10 11.0	−4 41
Sextans B	UGC 05373, DDO 70	10 00.0	+5 19
Sextans C	UGC 05439	10 05.6	+00 04
Sextans Dwarf		10 13.1	−1 37
Seyfert's Sextet	Serpens Sextet, NGC 6027/6027a-e, UGC 10116	15 59.2	+20 46
Shapley-Ames 1		1 05.1	−6 13
Shapley-Ames 2	NGC 4507	12 35.1	−39 55
Shapley-Ames 3	MCG-02-33-015	12 49.4	−10 07
Shapley-Ames 4	UGC 08041	12 55.2	+0 07
Shapley-Ames 5	MCG-07-42-001	20 24.0	−44 00
Shapley-Ames 6		21 23.2	45 46
Siamese Twins	NGC 4567/4568	12 36.5	+11 15
Silver Coin	Sculptor Galaxy, NGC 253, UGCA 13	0 47.6	−25 18
Small Magellanic Cloud	Nubecula Minor	0 52.7	−72 50
Sombrero Galaxy	M104, NGC 4594	12 39.9	−11 37
Spider	UGC 05829, DDO 84	10 42.6	+34 27
Spindle Galaxy	NGC 3115	10 05.2	−7 42
Stephan's Quintet	NGC 7317-20, UGC 12099-102, ARP 319	22 36.0	+33 58
Sunflower Galaxy	M63, NGC 5055, UGC 08334	13 15.8	+42 02
Triangulum Galaxy	Pinwheel, M33, NGC 598, UGC 01117	1 33.9	+30 39
Ursa Minor Dwarf	UGC 09749, DDO 199	15 08.8	+67 12
Virgo A	M87, NGC 4486, UGC 07654, ARP 152	12 30.8	+12 23
Whirlpool Galaxy	Rosse's Galaxy, Question Mark Galaxy, M51, NGC 5194/5, UGC 08493/4, ARP 85	13 29.9	+47 12
Wild's Triplet	MCG-01-30-032 to 34, ARP 248	11 46.8	−3 49
Wolf-Lundmark-Melotte	MCG-03-01-015, DDO 221	0 02.0	−15 28
Zwicky #2	UGC 06955, DDO 105	11 58.4	+38 03
Zwicky's Triplet	UGC 10586, ARP 103	16 49.5	+45 30

Catalogues:

AM *Catalogue of Southern Peculiar Galaxies and Associations*, by H.C. Arp and B.F. Madore, Cambridge University Press (1987).

ARP *Atlas of Peculiar Galaxies*, H. Arp, *Ap. J. Suppl. 14*, 1 (1966).

DDO *David Dunlap Observatory Publ.*, S. van den Bergh, II, No. 5, 147 (1959).

IC *Index Catalogue*, J.L.E. Dreyer, *Mem. R.A.S.* (1895–1910).

MCG *Morphological Catalogue of Galaxies*, B.A. Vorontsov-Velyaminov et al., Moscow State University, Moscow (1961–1974).

NGC *New General Catalogue of Nebulae and Clusters of Stars*, J.L.E. Dreyer, *Mem. R.A.S.* (1888).

RNGC *The Revised New General Catalogue of Nonstellar Astronomical Objects*, J.W. Sulentic and W.G. Tifft, University of Arizona Press (1973).

UGC *Uppsala General Catalogue of Galaxies*, P. Nilson, *Nova Acta Regiae Societatis Scientiarum Upsaliensis*, Ser. V: A, Vol. 1, Uppsala, Sweden (1973).

UGCA *Catalogue of Selected Non-UGC Galaxies*, P. Nilson, Uppsala Astronomical Observatory (1974).

ZWG *Catalogue of Galaxies and Clusters of Galaxies*, F. Zwicky et al., Vol. 1–6, California Institute of Technology (1961–1968).

RADIO SOURCES
BY KEN TAPPING

There are many types of cosmic radio sources, driven by a wide variety of processes. Some are thermal, that is, producing radio emissions through their temperature. Others involve the interaction of high-energy electrons with magnetic fields or complicated interactions of waves with plasmas. There are radio spectral lines from some atoms (such as the 21-cm emission from cosmic hydrogen) and an ever-increasing number of discovered molecular lines originating in cold, dense parts of the interstellar medium.

The list below is not complete; nor does it include only the strongest sources. It is intended to be a representative sampling of the types of sources that have been discovered. Some sources within reach of small (amateur-built) radio telescopes are included. Where possible, the flux densities at 100, 500, and 1000 MHz are given. The unit of flux density used is the jansky (Jy), where $1 \text{ Jy} = 10^{-26} \text{ W·m}^{-2}\text{Hz}^{-1}$. In the Remarks column, m denotes visual magnitude, z redshift, and P period.

For information on radio astronomy, see *Radio Astronomy*, by J.D. Kraus (Cygnus-Quasar Books, Powell, Ohio, 1986). Some maps of the radio sky can be found in *Sky & Telescope*, *63*, 230 (1982). Information for amateur radio astronomers can be found in *Astronomy*, *5* (12), 50 (1977), in a series of articles in *JRASC*, *72*, L5, L22, L38,… (1978), and in *Sky & Telescope, 55*, 385 and 475, and *56*, 28 and 114 (1978). A number of small, simple radio telescopes and some projects to try are described in *Radio Astronomy Projects*, by William Lonc, Radio-Sky Publishing, 1997.

TABLE OF RADIO SOURCES

Source	RA (2000) Dec h m ° ′	Flux Density (Jy) 100, 500, 1000 MHz Remarks
3C10	0 25.3 +64 08	180, 85, 56 Remnant of Tycho's Supernova (1572)
W3	2 25.4 +62 06	—, 80, 150 IC1795; multiple HII region; OH source
Algol	3 07.9 +40 56	* Eclipsing binary star
3C84	3 19.8 +41 32	70, 25, 17 NGC1725; Seyfert gal.; $m = 12.7$, $z = 0.018$
Fornax A	3 20.4 −37 22	900, 160, 110 NGC 1316; galaxy; $m = 10.1$; $z = 0.006$
Pictor A	5 19.9 −45 47	440, 140, 100 Galaxy; $m = 15.8$, $z = 0.034$
V371 Orionis	5 33.7 +1 55	* Red dwarf (flare) star
Taurus A	5 34.5 +22 01	1450, 1250, 1000 Crab Nebula; remnant of 1054 Supernova
NP0532	5 34.5 +22 01	15, 0.5, 1 Crab Pulsar; $P = 0.0331$ s
Orion A	5 35.3 −5 25	90, 200, 360 Orion Nebula; HII region. OH, IR source
3C157	6 17.6 +22 42	360, 195, 180 IC443; supernova remnant
VY CMa	7 23.1 −20 44	* Optical variable start; OH, IR source
Puppis A	8 20.3 −42 48	650, 300, 100 Supernova remnant

TABLE OF RADIO SOURCES (continued)

Source	RA (2000) Dec h m ° ′	Flux Density (Jy) 100, 500, 1000 MHz Remarks
Hydra A	9 18.1 −12 05	390, 110, 65 Galaxy; $m = 14.8$, $z = 0.052$
3C273	12 29.1 +2 03	150, 57, 49 Strongest quasar; $m = 13.0$, $z = 0.158$
Virgo A	12 30.8 +12 23	1950, 450, 300 M87; elliptical galaxy with jet
Centaurus A	13 25.4 −43 02	8500, 2500, 1400 NGC 5128; galaxy; $m = 7.5$, $z = 0.002$
3C295	14 11.4 +52 12	95, 60, 28 Galaxy; $m = 20.5$, $z = 0.461$
OQ172	14 45.3 +9 59	10, 4, 2 Quasar; $m = 18.4$, $z = 3.53$
Scorpius X1	16 19.9 −15 38	* X-ray, radio, and optical variable star
Hercules A	16 51.2 +5 01	800, 120, 65 Galaxy; $m = 18.5$, $z = 0.154$
Galactic Centre	17 42.0 −28 50	4400, 2900, 1800 Strong, diffuse emission
Sagittarius A	17 42.5 −28 55	100, 250, 200 Associated with galactic centre
Sagittarius B2	17 47.3 −28 24	—, 10, 70 Contains many different molecules
SS433	19 11.9 +4 58	* Compact object with high-velocity jets
CP1919	19 21.6 +21 52	0.08, 0.03, 0.005(?) First pulsar discovered; $P = 1.3375$ s
PSR 1937+21	19 39.6 +21 35	5, 0.2(?), 0.04(?) Millisecond pulsar; $P = 0.001\,558$ s
Cygnus A	19 59.5 +40 44	15 500, 4000, 2100 Strong radio galaxy
Cygnus X	20 22.6 +40 23	400, 150, 30 Complex region
BL Lacertae	22 02.7 +42 17	—, 5, 4 Radio galaxy; $m = 14.0$, $z = 0.07$
Cassiopeia A	23 23.4 +58 49	25 000, 4500, 2800 Supernova remnant
Jupiter		Bursts at metre wavelengths
Moon		Thermal source ($\approx$225 K)
Sun		20 000, 300 000, 900 000 Also intense bursts and strong, varying emissions

*Important source, although emission is weak and/or sporadic. Mean flux density less than one jansky.

VARIABLE GALAXIES

Some peculiar galaxies (Seyfert galaxies, BL Lacertae objects, and quasars) have bright, star-like nuclei that vary in brightness by up to several magnitudes on a time scale of months to years. These variations can be studied by amateurs and students, especially using photographic or electronic techniques. The table below lists the brightest variable galaxies. For more information, see *Sky & Telescope, 55*, p. 372 (1978), which gives finder charts and comparison stars for the four brightest Seyfert galaxies (indicated with asterisks in the table).

3C 273, the brightest quasar, was also the first quasar to be identified (in 1963). Charts for finding 3C 273 are at the bottom of this page. Start with the right-hand chart, which shows a "binocular-sized" field of view down to nearly 10th magnitude. The stars η Vir (magnitude 3.9), 16 Vir (5.0), and 17 Vir (6.5) are labelled; η Vir is the star immediately east of the autumnal equinox on the MARCH ALL-SKY MAP on p. 278. The two brightest stars to the west and southwest of the small rectangle are each magnitude 7.6. The area covered by the small rectangle is shown enlarged on the left-hand chart, on which several stars have their visual magnitudes indicated to the nearest tenth of a magnitude (with the decimal point omitted). The position of 3C 273 is indicated by a small cross. With a redshift $z = 0.158$, 3C 273 is receding from us at 44 000 km/s and is probably 2 or 3 billion ly from Earth, making it, by far, the intrinsically brightest (output $\approx 10^{39}$ W), most distant object that can be seen in a small telescope.

Name	Type	RA (2000) h m	Dec ° ′	Magnitude
NGC 1275*	Seyfert?	3 19.8	+41 31	11–13
3C 120	Seyfert	4 33.2	+5 21	14–16
OJ 287	BL Lac	8 54.9	+20 07	12–16
NGC 4151*	Seyfert	12 10.5	+39 24	10–12
3C 273	Quasar	12 29.2	+2 03	12–13
3C 345	Quasar	16 43.0	+39 48	14–17
Mkn. 509*	Seyfert	20 44.2	−10 43	12–13
BL Lac	BL Lac	22 02.8	+42 17	14–17
NGC 7469*	Seyfert	23 03.2	+8 52	12–13

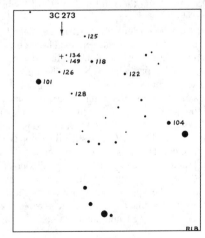

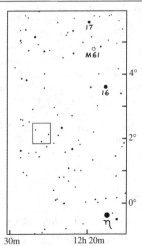

MAPS OF THE NIGHT SKY
By Roy Bishop

The maps on the next seven pages cover the entire sky. Stars are shown down to a magnitude of 4.5 or 5, that is, those that are readily apparent to the unaided eye on a reasonably dark night.

The first six maps are drawn for latitude 45°N but are useful for latitudes several degrees north or south of this. They show the hemisphere of sky visible at various times of year. Because the aspect of the night sky changes continuously with both longitude and time, while time zones change discontinuously with both longitude and time of year, it is not possible to state simply when a particular observer will find that his or her sky fits exactly one of the six maps. The month indicated above each map is the time of year when the map will match the "late evening" sky. On any particular night, successive maps will represent the sky as it appears every four hours later. For example, at 2 a.m. or 3 a.m. on a March night, the May map should be used. Just after dinner on a January night, the November map will be appropriate. The centre of each map is the *zenith,* the point directly overhead; the circumference is the horizon. To identify the stars, hold the map in front of you so that the part of the horizon you are facing (west, for instance) is downward. (The four letters around the periphery of each map indicate compass directions.)

The southern sky map is centred on the south celestial pole and extends to 20°S declination at its periphery. Thus there is considerable overlap with the southern areas of the other maps. Note that the orientation of the various names is generally inverted compared to that on the first six maps. This is in recognition that most users of this Handbook will be residents of the Northern Hemisphere and will make use of the southern sky map when they make trips to the tropics. Thus in "normal" use this map will be read in an area above its centre, unlike the first six maps which are normally read below their centres. The months indicated around the edge of the map may be used to orient it to each of the preceding six maps and have the same "late evening" significance as explained above. Tick marks around the edge of the map indicate hours of right ascension, with hours 0, 3, 6, etc., labelled. Starting at the centre of the map, the series of small crosses along 0h right ascension indicates southern declinations 90°, 80°, 70°,..., 20°. With the aid of a drawing compass, an observer in the Northern Hemisphere can quickly locate a circle, centred on the south celestial pole, which represents the southern limit of his or her sky.

On all seven maps, stars forming the usual constellation patterns are linked by straight lines, constellation names being given in uppercase letters. Three constellations (Horologium, Mensa, and Microscopium) consist of faint stars; hence no patterns are indicated and the names are placed in parentheses. Small clusters of dots indicate the positions of bright star clusters, nebulae, or galaxies. The pair of wavy dotted lines indicates roughly the borders of the Milky Way. Small asterisks locate the directions of the galactic centre (GC), the north galactic pole (NGP), and the south galactic pole (SGP). LMC, SMC, and CS signify, respectively, the Large Magellanic Cloud, the Small Magellanic Cloud, and the Coal Sack. Two dashed lines appear on each of the first six maps. The one with more dashes is the celestial equator. Tick marks along this indicate hours of right ascension, the odd hours being labelled. The line with fewer dashes is the ecliptic, the apparent annual path of the Sun across the heavens. Letters along this line indicate the approximate position of the Sun at the beginning of each month. Also located along the ecliptic are the Northern Hemisphere vernal equinox (VE), summer solstice (SS), autumnal equinox (AE), and winter solstice (WS).

JANUARY ALL-SKY MAP

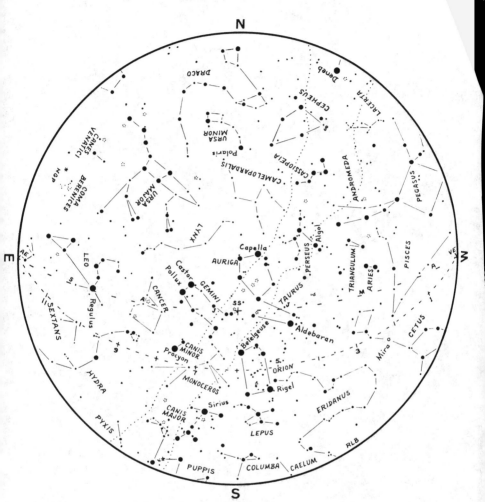

Notes:

MARCH ALL-SKY MAP

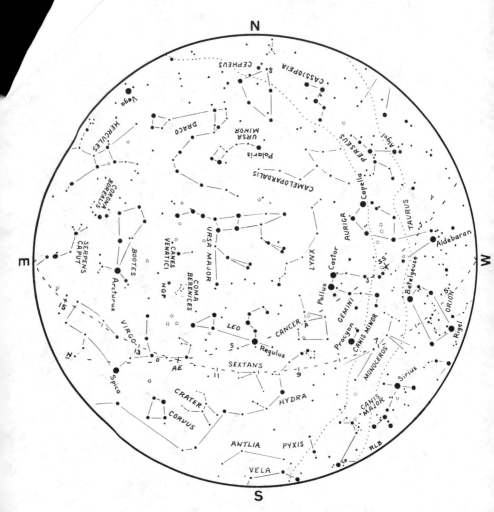

Notes:

MAY ALL-SKY MAP

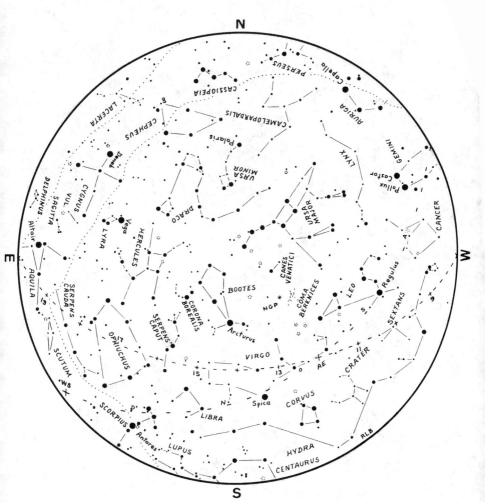

Notes:

JULY ALL-SKY MAP

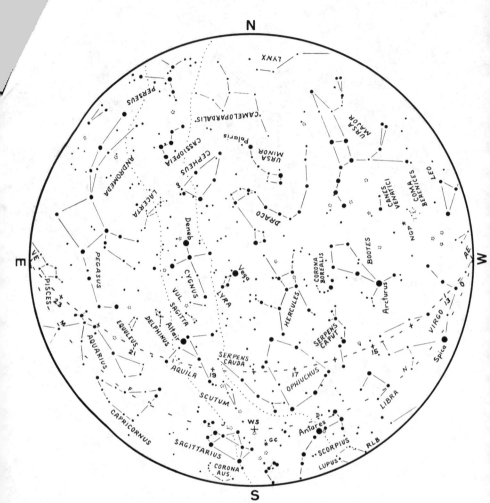

Notes:

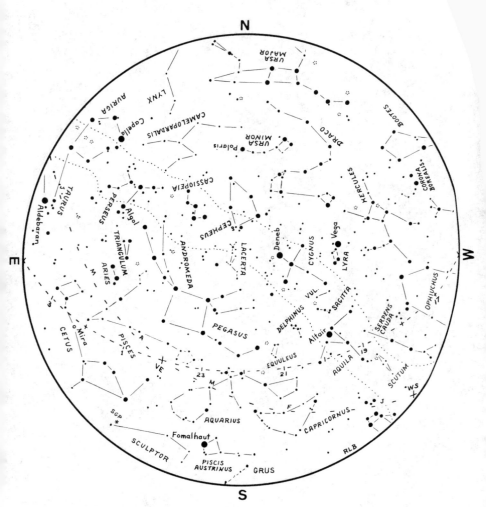

SEPTEMBER ALL-SKY MAP

Notes:

NOVEMBER ALL-SKY MAP

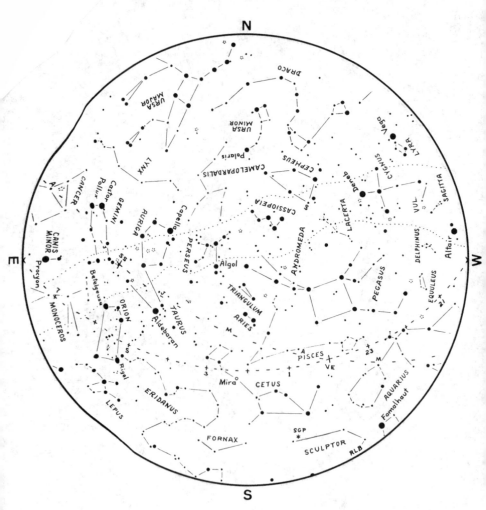

Notes:

THE SOUTHERN SKY

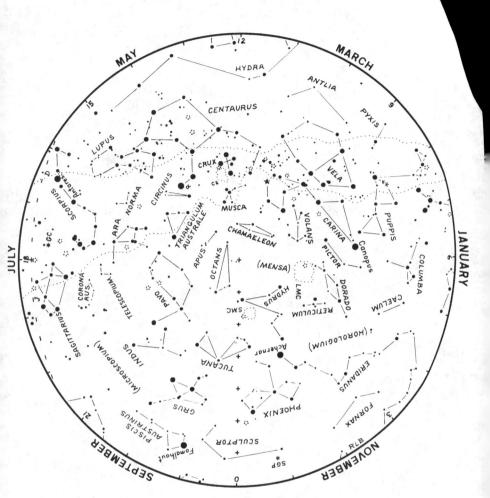

Notes:

This page intentionally left blank.

OBSERVER'S HANDBOOK 2003
ORDER FORM

(The *Observer's Handbook* for the year 2003 will be
available in September 2002.)

Price per copy
Includes shipping and handling

# copies*	Canada†	United States	Elsewhere‡
1–4	$26.70	$24.95 U.S.	$28.95 U.S.

*bulk-order pricing available upon request
†includes GST; GST registration number 119126282
‡shipped via airmail

Please send .... copies of the 2003 *Observer's Handbook*

Name   ....

Address   ....

....

....

Payment Enclosed $ ....   [ ] Cheque   [ ] Money Order

    [ ] VISA   [ ] Mastercard   [ ] Amex

    Number ....

    Name   ....

    Expiry .... Signature..

    Telephone (.........)..

    Email   ....

Order on the Internet using your credit card at **www.store.rasc.ca**

or send this order form to:

    The Royal Astronomical Society of Canada
    136 Dupont Street
    Toronto ON M5R 1V2
    Canada

    Phone: (416) 924-7973; fax: (416) 924-2911; email: orders@rasc.ca

To order any of the other publications of the RASC, including the award-winning
Observer's Calendar, please contact the Society or visit **www.store.rasc.ca**.

This page intentionally left blank.

INDEX

E HOLIDAYS AND SPECIAL DATES, 2002

ar's Day... Tue.   Jan.   1
.n Luther King Jr.'s Birthday (U.S.A.) ..... Mon.   Jan.   21

Winter Star Party, Florida .... Mon.   Feb.   11 – Sat.   Feb.   16
Chinese New Year .... Tue.   Feb.   12
Valentine's Day .... Thu.   Feb.   14

Islamic New Year .... Thu.   Mar.   14
First Day of Passover (Pesach) .... Thu.   Mar.   28
Good Friday .... Fri.   Mar.   29
Easter Sunday.. Sun.   Mar.   31

International Astronomy Day.......................... Sat.   Apr.   20

Texas Star Party .... Sun.   May   5 – Sun. May 12
Mother's Day .... Sun.   May   12
RASC General Assembly (Montreal QC)........ Fri.   May   17 – Sun. May 19
Victoria Day (Canada) .... Mon.   May   20
Riverside Telescope Makers Conference .... Fri.   May   24 – Sun. May 26
Memorial Day (U.S.A.) .... Mon.   May   27

Father's Day.. Sun.   Jun.   16
St.-Jean-Baptiste Day (Québec)....................... Mon.   Jun.   24

Canada Day... Mon.   Jul.   1
Independence Day (U.S.A.)............................. Thu.   Jul.   4

Mount Kobau Star Party, BC .... Sat.   Aug.   3 – Sun. Aug. 11
Civic Holiday (Canada) .... Mon.   Aug.   5
Starfest, Mount Forest ON .... Thu.   Aug.   8 – Sun. Aug. 11
Nova East, Smiley's Provincial Park NS .... Fri.   Aug.   9 – Sun. Aug. 11
Saskatchewan Star Party, Cypress Hills SK..... Fri.   Aug.   9 – Sun. Aug. 11
Stellafane Convention, Springfield VT .... Fri.   Aug.   9 – Sat. Aug. 10

Labour Day .... Mon.   Sep.   2
Rosh Hashanah.. Sat.   Sep.   7
Yom Kippur... Mon.   Sep.   16

Thanksgiving Day (Canada) .... Mon.   Oct.   14
Halloween .... Thu.   Oct.   31

First day of Ramadân .... Wed.   Nov.   6
Remembrance Day (Canada) .... Mon.   Nov.   11
Veteran's Day (U.S.A.) .... Mon.   Nov.   11
Thanksgiving Day (U.S.A.) .... Thu.   Nov.   28

Christmas Day.. Wed.   Dec.   25